Radi Doncheva

# Data Mining:
# Concepts and Techniques

# The Morgan Kaufmann Series in Data Management Systems

*Series Editor:* Jim Gray, Microsoft Research

*Data Mining: Concepts and Techniques*
Jiawei Han and Micheline Kamber

*Information Visualization in Data Mining and Knowledge Discovery*
Edited by Usama Fayyad, Georges Girnstein, and Andreas Wierse

*Component Database Systems*
Klaus R. Dittrich and Andreas Geppert

*Managing Reference Data in Enterprise Databases: Binding Corporate Data to the Wider World*
Malcolm Chisholm

*Understanding SQL and Java Together: A Guide to SQLJ, JDBC, and Related Technologies*
Jim Melton and Andrew Eisenberg

*Database: Principles, Programming, and Performance, Second Edition*
Patrick and Elizabeth O'Neil

*The Object Data Standard: ODMG 3.0*
Edited by R. G. G. Cattell and Douglas K. Barry

*Data on the Web: From Relations to Semistructured Data and XML*
Serge Abiteboul, Peter Buneman, Dan Suciu

*Data Mining: Practical Machine Learning Tools and Techniques with Java Implementations*
Ian Witten, Eibe Frank

*Joe Celko's SQL for Smarties: Advanced SQL Programming, Second Edition*
Joe Celko

*Joe Celko's Data and Databases: Concepts in Practice*
Joe Celko

*Developing Time-Oriented Database Applications in SQL*
Richard T. Snodgrass

*Web Farming for the Data Warehouse*
Richard D. Hackathorn

*Database Modeling & Design, Third Edition*
Toby J. Teorey

*Management of Heterogeneous and Autonomous Database Systems*
Edited by Ahmed Elmagarmid, Marek Rusinkiewicz, and Amit Sheth

*Object-Relational DBMSs: Tracking the Next Great Wave, Second Edition*
Michael Stonebraker and Paul Brown with Dorothy Moore

*A Complete Guide to DB2 Universal Database*
Don Chamberlin

*Universal Database Management: A Guide to Object/Relational Technology*
Cynthia Maro Saracco

*Readings in Database Systems, Third Edition*
Edited by Michael Stonebraker and Joseph M. Hellerstein

*Understanding SQL's Stored Procedures: A Complete Guide to SQL/PSM*
Jim Melton

*Principles of Multimedia Database Systems*
V. S. Subrahmanian

*Principles of Database Query Processing for Advanced Applications*
Clement T. Yu and Weiyi Meng

*Advanced Database Systems*
Carlo Zaniolo, Stefano Ceri, Christos Faloutsos, Richard T. Snodgrass, V. S. Subrahmanian, and Roberto Zicari

*Principles of Transaction Processing*
Philip A. Bernstein and Eric Newcomer

*Using the New DB2: IBM's Object-Relational Database System*
Don Chamberlin

*Distributed Algorithms*
Nancy A. Lynch

*Active Database Systems: Triggers and Rules For Advanced Database Processing*
Edited by Jennifer Widom and Stefano Ceri

*Migrating Legacy Systems: Gateways, Interfaces, & the Incremental Approach*
Michael L. Brodie and Michael Stonebraker

*Atomic Transactions*
Nancy Lynch, Michael Merritt, William Weihl, and Alan Fekete

*Query Processing for Advanced Database Systems*
Edited by Johann Christoph Freytag, David Maier, and Gottfried Vossen

*Transaction Processing: Concepts and Techniques*
Jim Gray and Andreas Reuter

*Understanding the New SQL: A Complete Guide*
Jim Melton and Alan R. Simon

*Building an Object-Oriented Database System: The Story of $O_2$*
Edited by François Bancilhon, Claude Delobel, and Paris Kanellakis

*Database Transaction Models for Advanced Applications*
Edited by Ahmed K. Elmagarmid

*A Guide to Developing Client/Server SQL Applications*
Setrag Khoshafian, Arvola Chan, Anna Wong, and Harry K. T. Wong

*The Benchmark Handbook for Database and Transaction Processing Systems, Second Edition*
Edited by Jim Gray

*Camelot and Avalon: A Distributed Transaction Facility*
Edited by Jeffrey L. Eppinger, Lily B. Mummert, and Alfred Z. Spector

*Readings in Object-Oriented Database Systems*
Edited by Stanley B. Zdonik and David Maier

# Data Mining:
# Concepts and Techniques

Jiawei Han

Micheline Kamber

*Simon Fraser University*

MORGAN KAUFMANN PUBLISHERS

AN IMPRINT OF Elsevier

SAN FRANCISCO   SAN DIEGO   NEW YORK   BOSTON
LONDON   SYDNEY   TOKYO

*Executive Editor*  Diane D. Cerra
*Production Editor*  Howard Severson
*Assistant Editor*  Belinda Breyer
*Cover Design*  Ross Carron
*Cover Image*  © Araldo de Lucu / CORBIS
*Text Design*  Rebecca Evans
*Copyeditor*  Ken DellaPenta
*Proofreader*  Carol Leyba
*Composition*  Windfall Software, using ZzTeX
*Illustration*  Dartmouth Publishing, Inc.
*Indexer*  Bill Evans
*Printer*  Courier Corporation

Designations used by companies to distinguish their products are often claimed as trademarks or registered trademarks. In all instances where Morgan Kaufmann Publishers is aware of a claim, the product names appear in initial capital or all capital letters. Readers, however, should contact the appropriate companies for more complete information regarding trademarks and registration.

ACADEMIC PRESS
An Imprint of Elsevier
525 B Street, Suite 1900, San Diego, CA 92101-4495, USA
*http://www.academicpress.com*

Academic Press
Harcourt Place, 32 Jamestown Road, London,NW1 7BY, United Kingdom
*http://www.academicpress.com/*

Morgan Kaufmann Publishers
340 Pine Street, Sixth Floor, San Francisco, CA 94104-3205, USA
*http://www.mkp.com*

**Library of Congress Cataloging-in-Publication Data**

Han, Jiawei.
    Data mining : concepts and techniques / Jiawei Han and Micheline Kamber.
      p.  cm.
    Includes bibliographical references and index.
    ISBN 1-55860-489-8
    1. Data mining.  I. Kamber, Micheline.  II. Title.
QA76.9.D343 H36 2001
006.3—dc21                                                    00-042822

This book is printed on acid-free paper.

# Foreword

by Jim Gray
*Microsoft Research*

We are deluged by data—scientific data, medical data, demographic data, financial data, and marketing data. People have no time to look at this data. Human attention has become a precious resource. So, we must find ways to automatically analyze the data, to automatically classify it, to automatically summarize it, to automatically discover and characterize trends in it, and to automatically flag anomalies. This is one of the most active and exciting areas of the database research community. Researchers in areas such as statistics, visualization, artificial intelligence, and machine learning are contributing to this field. The breadth of the field makes it difficult to grasp its extraordinary progress over the last few years.

Jiawei Han and Micheline Kamber have done a wonderful job of organizing and presenting data mining in this very readable textbook. They begin by giving quick introductions to database and data mining concepts with particular emphasis on data analysis. They review the current product offerings by presenting a general framework that covers them all. They then cover in a chapter-by-chapter tour the concepts and techniques that underlie classification, prediction, association, and clustering. These topics are presented with examples, a tour of the best algorithms for each problem class, and pragmatic rules of thumb about when to apply each technique. I found this presentation style to be very readable, and I certainly learned a lot from reading the book. Jiawei Han and Micheline Kamber have been leading contributors to data mining research. This is the text they use with their students to bring them up to speed on the field. The field is evolving very rapidly, but this book is a quick way to learn the basic ideas, and to understand where the field is today. I found it very informative and stimulating, and I expect you will too.

# Contents

**Foreword   vii**

**Preface   xix**

Chapter 1   **Introduction   1**

1.1   **What Motivated Data Mining? Why Is It Important?   1**

1.2   **So, What Is Data Mining?   5**

1.3   **Data Mining—On What Kind of Data?   10**

1.3.1   Relational Databases   10

1.3.2   Data Warehouses   12

1.3.3   Transactional Databases   15

1.3.4   Advanced Database Systems and Advanced Database Applications   16

1.4   **Data Mining Functionalities—What Kinds of Patterns Can Be Mined?   21**

1.4.1   Concept/Class Description: Characterization and Discrimination   21

1.4.2   Association Analysis   23

1.4.3   Classification and Prediction   24

1.4.4   Cluster Analysis   25

1.4.5   Outlier Analysis   25

1.4.6   Evolution Analysis   26

1.5   **Are All of the Patterns Interesting?   27**

1.6   **Classification of Data Mining Systems   28**

1.7   **Major Issues in Data Mining   30**

1.8   **Summary   33**

**Exercises   34**

**Bibliographic Notes   35**

Chapter 2   **Data Warehouse and OLAP Technology for Data Mining   39**

2.1   **What Is a Data Warehouse?   39**

2.1.1   Differences between Operational Database Systems and Data Warehouses   42

2.1.2   But, Why Have a Separate Data Warehouse?   44

2.2   **A Multidimensional Data Model   44**
   2.2.1 From Tables and Spreadsheets to Data Cubes   45
   2.2.2 Stars, Snowflakes, and Fact Constellations: Schemas for Multidimensional
       Databases   48
   2.2.3 Examples for Defining Star, Snowflake, and Fact Constellation
       Schemas   52
   2.2.4 Measures: Their Categorization and Computation   54
   2.2.5 Introducing Concept Hierarchies   56
   2.2.6 OLAP Operations in the Multidimensional Data Model   58
   2.2.7 A Starnet Query Model for Querying Multidimensional Databases   61

2.3   **Data Warehouse Architecture   62**
   2.3.1 Steps for the Design and Construction of Data Warehouses   63
   2.3.2 A Three-Tier Data Warehouse Architecture   65
   2.3.3 Types of OLAP Servers: ROLAP versus MOLAP versus HOLAP   69

2.4   **Data Warehouse Implementation   71**
   2.4.1 Efficient Computation of Data Cubes   71
   2.4.2 Indexing OLAP Data   79
   2.4.3 Efficient Processing of OLAP Queries   81
   2.4.4 Metadata Repository   83
   2.4.5 Data Warehouse Back-End Tools and Utilities   84

2.5   **Further Development of Data Cube Technology   85**
   2.5.1 Discovery-Driven Exploration of Data Cubes   85
   2.5.2 Complex Aggregation at Multiple Granularities: Multifeature Cubes   89
   2.5.3 Other Developments   92

2.6   **From Data Warehousing to Data Mining   93**
   2.6.1 Data Warehouse Usage   93
   2.6.2 From On-Line Analytical Processing to On-Line Analytical Mining   95

2.7   **Summary   98**
   **Exercises   99**
   **Bibliographic Notes   103**


Chapter 3 **Data Preprocessing   105**
3.1   **Why Preprocess the Data?   105**
3.2   **Data Cleaning   109**
   3.2.1 Missing Values   109
   3.2.2 Noisy Data   110
   3.2.3 Inconsistent Data   112

3.3   **Data Integration and Transformation   112**
   3.3.1 Data Integration   112
   3.3.2 Data Transformation   114

3.4    **Data Reduction    116**
    3.4.1  Data Cube Aggregation    117
    3.4.2  Dimensionality Reduction    119
    3.4.3  Data Compression    121
    3.4.4  Numerosity Reduction    124

3.5    **Discretization and Concept Hierarchy Generation    130**
    3.5.1  Discretization and Concept Hierarchy Generation for Numeric
           Data    132
    3.5.2  Concept Hierarchy Generation for Categorical Data    138

3.6    **Summary    140**
       **Exercises    141**
       **Bibliographic Notes    142**

Chapter 4  **Data Mining Primitives, Languages, and System
Architectures    145**

4.1    **Data Mining Primitives: What Defines a Data Mining Task?    146**
    4.1.1  Task-Relevant Data    148
    4.1.2  The Kind of Knowledge to be Mined    150
    4.1.3  Background Knowledge: Concept Hierarchies    151
    4.1.4  Interestingness Measures    155
    4.1.5  Presentation and Visualization of Discovered Patterns    157

4.2    **A Data Mining Query Language    159**
    4.2.1  Syntax for Task-Relevant Data Specification    160
    4.2.2  Syntax for Specifying the Kind of Knowledge to be Mined    162
    4.2.3  Syntax for Concept Hierarchy Specification    165
    4.2.4  Syntax for Interestingness Measure Specification    166
    4.2.5  Syntax for Pattern Presentation and Visualization Specification    167
    4.2.6  Putting It All Together—An Example of a DMQL Query    167
    4.2.7  Other Data Mining Languages and the Standardization of Data Mining
           Primitives    169

4.3    **Designing Graphical User Interfaces Based on a Data Mining
Query Language    170**

4.4    **Architectures of Data Mining Systems    171**

4.5    **Summary    174**
       **Exercises    174**
       **Bibliographic Notes    176**

Chapter 5  **Concept Description: Characterization and Comparison    179**

5.1    **What Is Concept Description?    179**

5.2    **Data Generalization and Summarization-Based
Characterization    181**

5.2.1 Attribute-Oriented Induction   182
5.2.2 Efficient Implementation of Attribute-Oriented Induction   187
5.2.3 Presentation of the Derived Generalization   190

5.3 **Analytical Characterization: Analysis of Attribute Relevance   194**
5.3.1 Why Perform Attribute Relevance Analysis?   195
5.3.2 Methods of Attribute Relevance Analysis   196
5.3.3 Analytical Characterization: An Example   198

5.4 **Mining Class Comparisons: Discriminating between Different Classes   200**
5.4.1 Class Comparison Methods and Implementations   201
5.4.2 Presentation of Class Comparison Descriptions   204
5.4.3 Class Description: Presentation of Both Characterization and Comparison   206

5.5 **Mining Descriptive Statistical Measures in Large Databases   208**
5.5.1 Measuring the Central Tendency   209
5.5.2 Measuring the Dispersion of Data   210
5.5.3 Graph Displays of Basic Statistical Class Descriptions   213

5.6 **Discussion   217**
5.6.1 Concept Description: A Comparison with Typical Machine Learning Methods   218
5.6.2 Incremental and Parallel Mining of Concept Description   220

5.7 **Summary   220**
**Exercises   222**
**Bibliographic Notes   223**

Chapter 6 **Mining Association Rules in Large Databases   225**
6.1 **Association Rule Mining   226**
6.1.1 Market Basket Analysis: A Motivating Example for Association Rule Mining   226
6.1.2 Basic Concepts   227
6.1.3 Association Rule Mining: A Road Map   229

6.2 **Mining Single-Dimensional Boolean Association Rules from Transactional Databases   230**
6.2.1 The Apriori Algorithm: Finding Frequent Itemsets Using Candidate Generation   230
6.2.2 Generating Association Rules from Frequent Itemsets   236
6.2.3 Improving the Efficiency of Apriori   236
6.2.4 Mining Frequent Itemsets without Candidate Generation   239
6.2.5 Iceberg Queries   243

6.3 **Mining Multilevel Association Rules from Transaction Databases   244**

6.3.1 Multilevel Association Rules  244
6.3.2 Approaches to Mining Multilevel Association Rules  246
6.3.3 Checking for Redundant Multilevel Association Rules  250

6.4 **Mining Multidimensional Association Rules from Relational Databases and Data Warehouses  251**

6.4.1 Multidimensional Association Rules  251
6.4.2 Mining Multidimensional Association Rules Using Static Discretization of Quantitative Attributes  253
6.4.3 Mining Quantitative Association Rules  254
6.4.4 Mining Distance-Based Association Rules  257

6.5 **From Association Mining to Correlation Analysis  259**

6.5.1 Strong Rules Are Not Necessarily Interesting: An Example  259
6.5.2 From Association Analysis to Correlation Analysis  260

6.6 **Constraint-Based Association Mining  262**

6.6.1 Metarule-Guided Mining of Association Rules  263
6.6.2 Mining Guided by Additional Rule Constraints  265

6.7 **Summary  269**

**Exercises  271**

**Bibliographic Notes  276**

Chapter 7 **Classification and Prediction  279**

7.1 **What Is Classification? What Is Prediction?  279**

7.2 **Issues Regarding Classification and Prediction  282**

7.2.1 Preparing the Data for Classification and Prediction  282
7.2.2 Comparing Classification Methods  283

7.3 **Classification by Decision Tree Induction  284**

7.3.1 Decision Tree Induction  285
7.3.2 Tree Pruning  289
7.3.3 Extracting Classification Rules from Decision Trees  290
7.3.4 Enhancements to Basic Decision Tree Induction  291
7.3.5 Scalability and Decision Tree Induction  292
7.3.6 Integrating Data Warehousing Techniques  and Decision Tree Induction  294

7.4 **Bayesian Classification  296**

7.4.1 Bayes Theorem  296
7.4.2 Naive Bayesian Classification  297
7.4.3 Bayesian Belief Networks  299
7.4.4 Training Bayesian Belief Networks  301

7.5 **Classification by Backpropagation  303**

7.5.1 A Multilayer Feed-Forward Neural Network  303
7.5.2 Defining a Network Topology  304

7.5.3 Backpropagation   305

7.5.4 Backpropagation and Interpretability   310

7.6    **Classification Based on Concepts from Association Rule Mining   311**

7.7    **Other Classification Methods   314**

7.7.1 *k*-Nearest Neighbor Classifiers   314

7.7.2 Case-Based Reasoning   315

7.7.3 Genetic Algorithms   316

7.7.4 Rough Set Approach   316

7.7.5 Fuzzy Set Approaches   317

7.8    **Prediction   319**

7.8.1 Linear and Multiple Regression   319

7.8.2 Nonlinear Regression   321

7.8.3 Other Regression Models   322

7.9    **Classifier Accuracy   322**

7.9.1 Estimating Classifier Accuracy   323

7.9.2 Increasing Classifier Accuracy   324

7.9.3 Is Accuracy Enough to Judge a Classifier?   325

7.10   **Summary   326**

       **Exercises   328**

       **Bibliographic Notes   330**

Chapter 8  **Cluster Analysis   335**

8.1    **What Is Cluster Analysis?   335**

8.2    **Types of Data in Cluster Analysis   338**

8.2.1 Interval-Scaled Variables   339

8.2.2 Binary Variables   341

8.2.3 Nominal, Ordinal, and Ratio-Scaled Variables   343

8.2.4 Variables of Mixed Types   345

8.3    **A Categorization of Major Clustering Methods   346**

8.4    **Partitioning Methods   348**

8.4.1 Classical Partitioning Methods: *k*-Means and *k*-Medoids   349

8.4.2 Partitioning Methods in Large Databases: From *k*-Medoids to CLARANS   353

8.5    **Hierarchical Methods   354**

8.5.1 Agglomerative and Divisive Hierarchical Clustering   355

8.5.2 BIRCH: Balanced Iterative Reducing and Clustering Using Hierarchies   357

8.5.3 CURE: Clustering Using REpresentatives   358

8.5.4 Chameleon: A Hierarchical Clustering Algorithm Using Dynamic Modeling   361

8.6 **Density-Based Methods 363**
8.6.1 DBSCAN: A Density-Based Clustering Method Based on Connected Regions with Sufficiently High Density 363
8.6.2 OPTICS: Ordering Points To Identify the Clustering Structure 365
8.6.3 DENCLUE: Clustering Based on Density Distribution Functions 366

8.7 **Grid-Based Methods 370**
8.7.1 STING: STatistical INformation Grid 370
8.7.2 WaveCluster: Clustering Using Wavelet Transformation 372
8.7.3 CLIQUE: Clustering High-Dimensional Space 374

8.8 **Model-Based Clustering Methods 376**
8.8.1 Statistical Approach 376
8.8.2 Neural Network Approach 379

8.9 **Outlier Analysis 381**
8.9.1 Statistical-Based Outlier Detection 382
8.9.2 Distance-Based Outlier Detection 384
8.9.3 Deviation-Based Outlier Detection 386

8.10 **Summary 388**
**Exercises 389**
**Bibliographic Notes 391**

Chapter 9 **Mining Complex Types of Data 395**
9.1 **Multidimensional Analysis and Descriptive Mining of Complex Data Objects 396**
9.1.1 Generalization of Structured Data 396
9.1.2 Aggregation and Approximation in Spatial and Multimedia Data Generalization 397
9.1.3 Generalization of Object Identifiers and Class/Subclass Hierarchies 399
9.1.4 Generalization of Class Composition Hierarchies 399
9.1.5 Construction and Mining of Object Cubes 400
9.1.6 Generalization-Based Mining of Plan Databases by Divide-and-Conquer 401

9.2 **Mining Spatial Databases 405**
9.2.1 Spatial Data Cube Construction and Spatial OLAP 405
9.2.2 Spatial Association Analysis 410
9.2.3 Spatial Clustering Methods 411
9.2.4 Spatial Classification and Spatial Trend Analysis 411
9.2.5 Mining Raster Databases 412

9.3 **Mining Multimedia Databases 412**
9.3.1 Similarity Search in Multimedia Data 412
9.3.2 Multidimensional Analysis of Multimedia Data 414
9.3.3 Classification and Prediction Analysis of Multimedia Data 416

9.3.4 Mining Associations in Multimedia Data   417

9.4 **Mining Time-Series and Sequence Data   418**

9.4.1 Trend Analysis   418
9.4.2 Similarity Search in Time-Series Analysis   421
9.4.3 Sequential Pattern Mining   424
9.4.4 Periodicity Analysis   426

9.5 **Mining Text Databases   428**

9.5.1 Text Data Analysis and Information Retrieval   428
9.5.2 Text Mining: Keyword-Based Association and Document Classification   433

9.6 **Mining the World Wide Web   435**

9.6.1 Mining the Web's Link Structures to Identify Authoritative Web Pages   437
9.6.2 Automatic Classification of Web Documents   439
9.6.3 Construction of a Multilayered Web Information Base   440
9.6.4 Web Usage Mining   441

9.7 **Summary   443**

**Exercises   444**

**Bibliographic Notes   446**


Chapter 10 **Applications and Trends in Data Mining   451**

10.1 **Data Mining Applications   451**

10.1.1 Data Mining for Biomedical and DNA Data Analysis   451
10.1.2 Data Mining for Financial Data Analysis   453
10.1.3 Data Mining for the Retail Industry   455
10.1.4 Data Mining for the Telecommunication Industry   456

10.2 **Data Mining System Products and Research Prototypes   457**

10.2.1 How to Choose a Data Mining System   458
10.2.2 Examples of Commercial Data Mining Systems   461

10.3 **Additional Themes on Data Mining   462**

10.3.1 Visual and Audio Data Mining   462
10.3.2 Scientific and Statistical Data Mining   464
10.3.3 Theoretical Foundations of Data Mining   470
10.3.4 Data Mining and Intelligent Query Answering   471

10.4 **Social Impacts of Data Mining   472**

10.4.1 Is Data Mining a Hype or a Persistent, Steadily Growing Business?   473
10.4.2 Is Data Mining Merely Managers' Business or Everyone's Business?   475
10.4.3 Is Data Mining a Threat to Privacy and Data Security?   476

10.5 **Trends in Data Mining   478**

10.6 **Summary 480**

**Exercises 481**

**Bibliographic Notes 483**

Appendix A **An Introduction to Microsoft's OLE DB for Data Mining 485**

A.1 **Creating a DMM object 486**

A.2 **Inserting Training Data into the Model and Training the Model 488**

A.3 **Using the Model 488**

Appendix B **An Introduction to DBMiner 493**

B.1 **System Architecture 494**

B.2 **Input and Output 494**

B.3 **Data Mining Tasks Supported by the System 495**

B.4 **Support for Task and Method Selection 498**

B.5 **Support of the KDD Process 499**

B.6 **Main Applications 499**

B.7 **Current Status 499**

**Bibliography 501**

**Index 533**

# Preface

Our capabilities of both generating and collecting data have been increasing rapidly in the last several decades. Contributing factors include the widespread use of bar codes for most commercial products, the computerization of many business, scientific, and government transactions, and advances in data collection tools ranging from scanned text and image platforms to satellite remote sensing systems. In addition, popular use of the World Wide Web as a global information system has flooded us with a tremendous amount of data and information. This explosive growth in stored data has generated an urgent need for new techniques and automated tools that can intelligently assist us in transforming the vast amounts of data into useful information and knowledge.

This book explores the concepts and techniques of *data mining*, a promising and flourishing frontier in database systems and new database applications. Data mining, also popularly referred to as *knowledge discovery in databases (KDD)*, is the automated or convenient extraction of patterns representing knowledge implicitly stored in large databases, data warehouses, and other massive information repositories.

Data mining is a multidisciplinary field, drawing work from areas including database technology, artificial intelligence, machine learning, neural networks, statistics, pattern recognition, knowledge-based systems, knowledge acquisition, information retrieval, high-performance computing, and data visualization. We present the material in this book from a *database perspective*. That is, we focus on issues relating to the feasibility, usefulness, efficiency, and scalability of techniques for the discovery of patterns hidden *in large databases*. As a result, this book is not intended as an introduction to database systems, machine learning, statistics, or other such areas, although we do provide the background necessary in these areas in order to facilitate the reader's comprehension of their respective roles in data mining. Rather, the book is a comprehensive introduction to data mining, presented with database issues in focus. It should be useful for computing science students, application developers, and business professionals, as well as researchers involved in any of the disciplines listed above.

Data mining emerged during the late 1980s, has made great strides during the 1990s, and is expected to continue to flourish into the new millennium. This book presents an overall picture of the field from a database researcher's point of view, introducing interesting data mining techniques and systems, and discussing applications and research directions. An important motivation for writing this book was the need to build an organized framework for the study of data mining—a challenging task owing to the extensive multidisciplinary nature of this fast developing field. We hope that this book will encourage people with different backgrounds and experiences to exchange their views regarding data mining so as to contribute toward the further promotion and shaping of this exciting and dynamic field.

## To the Teacher

This book is designed to give a broad, yet in-depth overview of the field of data mining. You will find it useful for teaching a course on data mining at an advanced undergraduate level or the first-year graduate level. In addition, individual chapters may be included as material for courses on selected topics in database systems or in artificial intelligence. We have tried to make the chapters as self-contained as possible so that you are not confined to reading each chapter in sequence. For a course taught at the undergraduate level, you might use Chapters 1 through 8 as the core course material. Remaining class material may be selected from among the more advanced topics described in Chapters 9 and 10. For a graduate-level course, you may choose to cover the entire book in one semester.

Each chapter ends with a set of exercises, suitable as assigned homework. The exercises are either short questions that test basic mastery of the material covered, or longer questions that require analytical thinking.

## To the Student

We hope that this textbook will spark your interest in the fresh, yet evolving field of data mining. We have attempted to present the material in a clear manner, with careful explanation of the topics covered. Each chapter ends with a summary describing the main points. We have included many figures and illustrations throughout the text in order to make the book more enjoyable and "reader-friendly." Although this book was designed as a textbook, we have tried to organize it so that it will also be useful to you as a reference book or handbook, should you later decide to pursue a career in data mining.

What do you need to know in order to read this book?

- You should have some knowledge of the concepts and terminology associated with database systems. However, we do try to provide enough background of the basics in database technology, so that if your memory is a bit rusty, you will not have trouble following the discussions in the book. You should have some knowledge of database querying, although knowledge of any specific query language is not required.

- You should have some programming experience. In particular, you should be able to read pseudocode, and understand simple data structures such as multidimensional arrays.

- It will be helpful to have some preliminary background in statistics, machine learning, or pattern recognition. However, we will familiarize you with the basic concepts of these areas that are relevant to data mining from a database perspective.

## To the Professional

This book was designed to cover a broad range of topics in the field of data mining. As a result, it is an excellent handbook on the subject. Because each chapter is designed to be as stand-alone as possible, you can focus on the topics that most interest you. Much of the book is suited to applications programmers or information service managers like yourself who wish to learn about the key ideas of data mining on their own.

The techniques and algorithms presented are of practical utility. Rather than selecting algorithms that perform well on small "toy" databases, the algorithms described in the book are geared for the discovery of data patterns hidden in large, real databases. In Chapter 10, we briefly discuss data mining systems in commercial use, as well as promising research prototypes. Each algorithm presented in the book is illustrated in pseudocode. The pseudocode is similar to the C programming language, yet is designed so that it should be easy to follow by programmers unfamiliar with C or C++. If you wish to implement any of the algorithms, you should find the translation of our pseudocode into the programming language of your choice to be a fairly straightforward task.

## Organization of the Book

The book is organized as follows.

Chapter 1 provides an introduction to the multidisciplinary field of data mining. It discusses the evolutionary path of database technology that has led to the need for data mining, and the importance of its application potential. The basic architecture of data mining systems is described, and a brief introduction to the concepts of database systems and data warehouses is given. A detailed classification of data mining tasks is presented, based on the different kinds of knowledge to be mined. A classification of data mining systems is presented, and major challenges in the field are discussed.

Chapter 2 is an introduction to data warehouses and OLAP (On-Line Analytical Processing). Topics include the concept of data warehouses and multidimensional databases, the construction of data cubes, the implementation of on-line analytical processing, and the relationship between data warehousing and data mining.

Chapter 3 describes techniques for preprocessing the data prior to mining. Methods of data cleaning, data integration and transformation, and data reduction are discussed, including the use of concept hierarchies for dynamic and static discretization. The automatic generation of concept hierarchies is also described.

Chapter 4 introduces the primitives of data mining that define the specification of a data mining task. It describes a data mining query language (DMQL) and provides examples of data mining queries. Other languages are also described, as well as the construction of graphical user interfaces and data mining architectures.

Chapter 5 describes techniques for concept description, including characterization and discrimination. An attribute-oriented generalization technique is introduced, as well as its different implementations including a generalized relation technique and a multidimensional data cube technique. Several forms of knowledge presentation and visualization are illustrated. Relevance analysis is discussed. Methods for class comparison at multiple abstraction levels and methods for the extraction of characteristic rules and discriminant rules with interestingness measurements are presented. In addition, statistical measures for descriptive mining are discussed.

Chapter 6 presents methods for mining association rules in transaction databases as well as relational databases and data warehouses. It includes a classification of association rules, a presentation of the basic Apriori algorithm and its variations, and techniques for mining multilevel association rules, multidimensional association rules, quantitative association rules, and correlation rules. A new technique called frequent pattern growth is introduced, which mines frequent patterns without candidate set generation. Strategies for finding interesting rules by constraint-based mining and the use of interestingness measures to focus the rule search are also described.

Chapter 7 describes methods for data classification and prediction, including decision tree induction, Bayesian classification, the neural network technique of backpropagation, $k$-nearest neighbor classifiers, case-based reasoning, genetic algorithms, rough set theory, and fuzzy set approaches. Classification based on concepts from association rule mining is presented. Methods of regression are introduced, and issues regarding classifier accuracy are discussed.

Chapter 8 describes methods of cluster analysis. It first introduces the concept of data clustering and then presents several major data clustering approaches, including partition-based clustering, hierarchical clustering, and model-based clustering. Methods for clustering continuous data, discrete data, and data in multidimensional data cubes are presented. The scalability of clustering algorithms is discussed in detail.

Chapter 9 discusses methods for data mining in advanced database systems. It includes data mining in object-oriented databases, spatial databases, multimedia databases, time-series databases, text databases, and the World Wide Web.

Finally, in Chapter 10, we summarize the concepts presented in this book and discuss applications of data mining and some challenging research issues.

Throughtout the text, italic is used to emphasize terms that are defined, while bold is used to highlight main ideas.

## Errors

It is likely that this book may contain typos, errors, or omissions. If you notice any errors, have suggestions regarding additional exercises, or have other constructive criticism, we would be very happy to hear from you. We welcome and appreciate your suggestions. You can send your comments to

Data Mining: Concepts and Techniques
Intelligent Database Systems Research Laboratory
School of Computing Science
Simon Fraser University
Burnaby, British Columbia
Canada V5A 1S6
Fax: (604) 291-3045

Alternatively, you can use electronic mail to submit bug reports, request a list of known errors, or make constructive suggestions. To receive instructions, send e-mail to *dmbook@cs.sfu.ca* with "Subject: help" in the message header. We regret that we cannot personally respond to all e-mail messages. The errata of the book and other updated information related to the book can be found by referencing the Web address *www.cs.sfu.ca/~han/DM_Book*.

## Acknowledgments

We would like to express our sincere thanks to all those who have worked or are currently working with us on data mining related research and/or the DBMiner project, or have provided us with various support in data mining. These include Rakesh Agrawal, Stella Atkins, Yvan Bedard, Binay Bhattacharya, Dora (Yandong) Cai, Nick Cercone, Surajit Chaudhuri, Sonny H. S. Chee, Jianping Chen, Ming-Syan Chen, Qing Chen, Qiming Chen, Shan Cheng, David Cheung, Shi Cong, Son Dao, Umeshwar Dayal, James Delgrande, Guozhu Dong, Carole Edwards,

Max Egenhofer, Martin Ester, Usama Fayyad, Ling Feng, Ada Fu, Yongjian Fu, Daphne Gelbart, Randy Goebel, Jim Gray, Robert Grossman, Wan Gong, Yike Guo, Eli Hagen, Howard Hamilton, Jing He, Larry Henschen, Jean Hou, Mei-Chun Hsu, Kan Hu, Haiming Huang, Yue Huang, Julia Itskevitch, Wen Jin, Tiko Kameda, Hiroyuki Kawano, Rizwan Kheraj, Eddie Kim, Won Kim, Krzysztof Koperski, Hans-Peter Kriegel, Vipin Kumar, Laks V.S. Lakshmanan, Joyce Man Lam, James Lau, Deyi Li, George (Wenmin) Li, Jin Li, Ze-Nian Li, Nancy Liao, Gang Liu, Junqiang Liu, Ling Liu, Alan (Yijun) Lu, Hongjun Lu, Tong Lu, Wei Lu, Xuebin Lu, Wo-Shun Luk, Heikki Mannila, Runying Mao, Abhay Mehta, Gabor Melli, Alberto Mendelzon, Tim Merrett, Harvey Miller, Drew Miners, Behzad Mortazavi-Asl, Richard Muntz, Raymond T. Ng, Vicent Ng, Shojiro Nishio, Beng-Chin Ooi, Tamer Ozsu, Jian Pei, Gregory Piatetsky-Shapiro, Helen Pinto, Fred Popowich, Amynmohamed Rajan, Peter Scheuermann, Shashi Shekhar, Wei-Min Shen, Avi Silberschatz, Evangelos Simoudis, Nebojsa Stefanovic, Yin Jenny Tam, Simon Tang, Zhaohui Tang, Dick Tsur, Anthony K. H. Tung, Ke Wang, Wei Wang, Zhaoxia Wang, Tony Wind, Lara Winstone, Ju Wu, Betty (Bin) Xia, Cindy M. Xin, Xiaowei Xu, Qiang Yang, Yiwen Yin, Clement Yu, Jeffrey Yu, Philip S. Yu, Osmar R. Zaiane, Carlo Zaniolo, Shuhua Zhang, Zhong Zhang, Yvonne Zheng, Xiaofang Zhou, and Hua Zhu. We are also grateful to Jean Hou, Helen Pinto, Lara Winstone, and Hua Zhu for their help with some of the original figures in this book, and to Eugene Belchev for his careful proofreading of each chapter.

We also wish to thank Diane Cerra, our Executive Editor at Morgan Kaufmann Publishers, for her enthusiasm, patience, and support during our writing of this book, as well as Howard Severson, our Production Editor, and his staff for their conscientious efforts regarding production. We are indebted to all of the reviewers for their invaluable feedback. Finally, we thank our families for their wholehearted support throughout this project.

# Introduction

**This book is an introduction** to what has come to be known as *data mining* and *knowledge discovery in databases*. The material in this book is presented from a database perspective, where emphasis is placed on basic data mining concepts and techniques for uncovering interesting data patterns hidden in *large data sets*. The implementation methods discussed are particularly oriented towards the development of *scalable* and *efficient* data mining tools. In this chapter, you will learn how data mining is part of the natural evolution of database technology, why data mining is important, and how it is defined. You will learn about the general architecture of data mining systems, as well as gain insight into the kinds of data on which mining can be performed, the types of patterns that can be found, and how to tell which patterns represent useful knowledge. In addition to studying a classification of data mining systems, you will read about challenging research issues for building data mining tools of the future.

## 1.1 What Motivated Data Mining? Why Is It Important?

Necessity is the mother of invention.

The major reason that data mining has attracted a great deal of attention in the information industry in recent years is due to the wide availability of huge amounts of data and the imminent need for turning such data into useful information and knowledge. The information and knowledge gained can be used for applications ranging from business management, production control, and market analysis, to engineering design and science exploration.

Data mining can be viewed as a result of the natural evolution of information technology. An evolutionary path has been witnessed in the database industry in the development of the following functionalities (Figure 1.1): *data collection and database creation, data management* (including data storage and retrieval, and database transaction processing), and *data analysis and understanding* (involving data warehousing and data mining). For instance, the early development of data

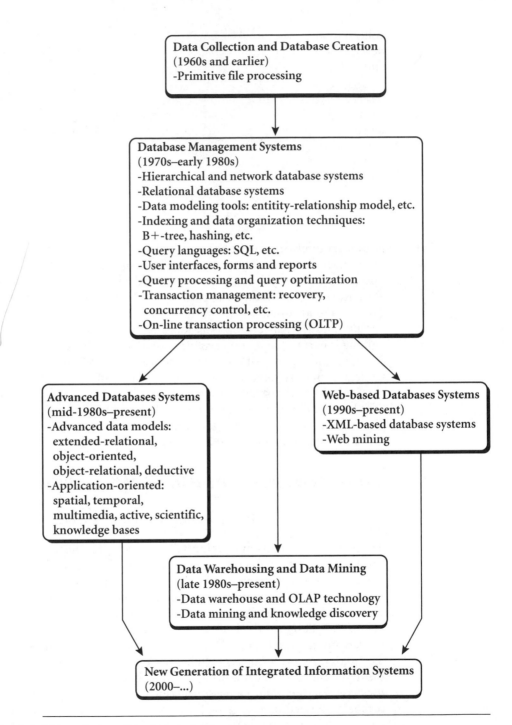

**Figure 1.1**  The evolution of database technology.

collection and database creation mechanisms served as a prerequisite for later development of effective mechanisms for data storage and retrieval, and query and transaction processing. With numerous database systems offering query and transaction processing as common practice, data analysis and understanding has naturally become the next target.

Since the 1960s, database and information technology has been evolving systematically from primitive file processing systems to sophisticated and powerful database systems. The research and development in database systems since the 1970s has progressed from early hierarchical and network database systems to the development of relational database systems (where data are stored in relational table structures; see Section 1.3.1), data modeling tools, and indexing and data organization techniques. In addition, users gained convenient and flexible data access through query languages, user interfaces, optimized query processing, and transaction management. Efficient methods for **on-line transaction processing (OLTP)**, where a query is viewed as a read-only transaction, have contributed substantially to the evolution and wide acceptance of relational technology as a major tool for efficient storage, retrieval, and management of large amounts of data.

Database technology since the mid-1980s has been characterized by the popular adoption of relational technology and an upsurge of research and development activities on new and powerful database systems. These employ advanced data models such as extended-relational, object-oriented, object-relational, and deductive models. Application-oriented database systems, including spatial, temporal, multimedia, active, and scientific databases, knowledge bases, and office information bases, have flourished. Issues related to the distribution, diversification, and sharing of data have been studied extensively. Heterogeneous database systems and Internet-based global information systems such as the World Wide Web (WWW) have also emerged and play a vital role in the information industry.

The steady and amazing progress of computer hardware technology in the past three decades has led to large supplies of powerful and affordable computers, data collection equipment, and storage media. This technology provides a great boost to the database and information industry, and makes a huge number of databases and information repositories available for transaction management, information retrieval, and data analysis.

Data can now be stored in many different types of databases. One database architecture that has recently emerged is the **data warehouse** (Section 1.3.2), a repository of multiple heterogeneous data sources, organized under a unified schema at a single site in order to facilitate management decision making. Data warehouse technology includes data cleansing, data integration, and **On-Line Analytical Processing (OLAP)**, that is, analysis techniques with functionalities such as summarization, consolidation, and aggregation, as well as the ability to view information from different angles. Although OLAP tools support multidimensional analysis and decision making, additional data analysis tools are required for

**Figure 1.2**  We are data rich, but information poor.

in-depth analysis, such as data classification, clustering, and the characterization of data changes over time.

The abundance of data, coupled with the need for powerful data analysis tools, has been described as a *data rich but information poor* situation. The fast-growing, tremendous amount of data, collected and stored in large and numerous databases, has far exceeded our human ability for comprehension without powerful tools (Figure 1.2). As a result, data collected in large databases become "data tombs"—data archives that are seldom visited. Consequently, important decisions are often made based not on the information-rich data stored in databases but rather on a decision maker's intuition, simply because the decision maker does not have the tools to extract the valuable knowledge embedded in the vast amounts of data. In addition, consider current expert system technologies, which typically rely on users or domain experts to *manually* input knowledge into knowledge bases. Unfortunately, this procedure is prone to biases and errors, and is extremely time-consuming and costly. Data mining tools perform data analysis and may uncover important data patterns, contributing greatly to business strategies, knowledge bases, and scientific and medical research. The widening gap between data and information calls for a systematic development of *data mining tools* that will turn data tombs into "golden nuggets" of knowledge.

**Figure 1.3** Data mining—searching for knowledge (interesting patterns) in your data.

## 1.2 So, What Is Data Mining?

Simply stated, **data mining** refers to *extracting or "mining" knowledge from large amounts of data*. The term is actually a misnomer. Remember that the mining of gold from rocks or sand is referred to as *gold* mining rather than rock or sand mining. Thus, data mining should have been more appropriately named "knowledge mining from data," which is unfortunately somewhat long. "Knowledge mining," a shorter term, may not reflect the emphasis on mining from large amounts of data. Nevertheless, mining is a vivid term characterizing the process that finds a small set of precious nuggets from a great deal of raw material (Figure 1.3). Thus, such a misnomer that carries both "data" and "mining" became a popular choice. There are many other terms carrying a similar or slightly different meaning to data mining, such as **knowledge mining from databases, knowledge extraction, data/pattern analysis, data archaeology**, and **data dredging**. *data searching*

Many people treat data mining as a synonym for another popularly used term, **Knowledge Discovery in Databases**, or **KDD**. Alternatively, others view data mining as simply an essential step in the process of knowledge discovery in databases. Knowledge discovery as a process is depicted in Figure 1.4 and consists of an iterative sequence of the following steps:

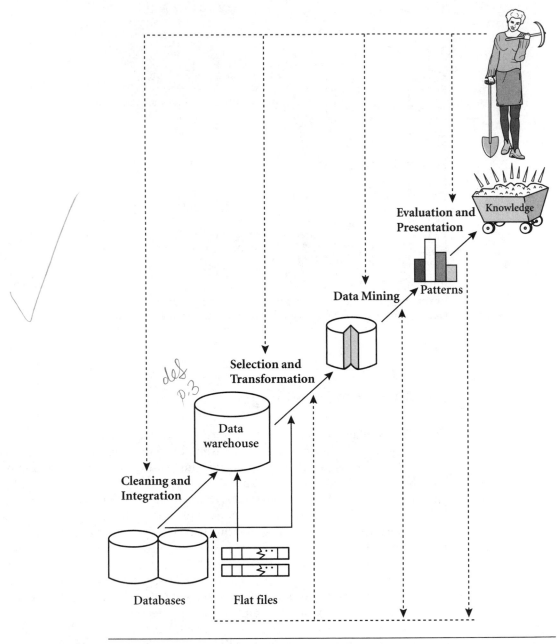

**Figure 1.4**   Data mining as a step in the process of knowledge discovery.

1. **Data cleaning** (to remove noise and inconsistent data)

2. **Data integration** (where multiple data sources may be combined)[1]

3. **Data selection** (where data relevant to the analysis task are retrieved from the database)

4. **Data transformation** (where data are transformed or consolidated into forms appropriate for mining by performing summary or aggregation operations, for instance)[2]

5. **Data mining** (an essential process where intelligent methods are applied in order to extract data patterns)

6. **Pattern evaluation** (to identify the truly interesting patterns representing knowledge based on some **interestingness measures**; Section 1.5)

7. **Knowledge presentation** (where visualization and knowledge representation techniques are used to present the mined knowledge to the user)

The data mining step may interact with the user or a knowledge base. The interesting patterns are presented to the user, and may be stored as new knowledge in the knowledge base. Note that according to this view, data mining is only one step in the entire process, albeit an essential one since it uncovers hidden patterns for evaluation.

We agree that data mining is a step in the knowledge discovery process. However, in industry, in media, and in the database research milieu, the term data mining is becoming more popular than the longer term of knowledge discovery in databases. Therefore, in this book, we choose to use the term data mining. We adopt a broad view of data mining functionality: data mining is the process of discovering interesting knowledge from large amounts of data stored either in databases, data warehouses, or other information repositories.

Based on this view, the architecture of a typical data mining system may have the following major components (Figure 1.5):

- **Database, data warehouse, or other information repository:** This is one or a set of databases, data warehouses, spreadsheets, or other kinds of information repositories. Data cleaning and data integration techniques may be performed on the data.

- **Database or data warehouse server:** The database or data warehouse server is responsible for fetching the relevant data, based on the user's data mining request.

---

[1] A popular trend in the information industry is to perform data cleaning and data integration as a preprocessing step where the resulting data are stored in a data warehouse.

[2] Sometimes data transformation and consolidation are performed before the data selection process, particularly in the case of data warehousing.

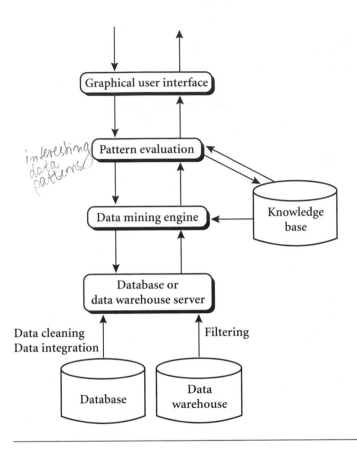

*interesting data patterns*

**Figure 1.5**   Architecture of a typical data mining system.

- **Knowledge base:** This is the domain knowledge that is used to guide the search, or evaluate the interestingness of resulting patterns. Such knowledge can include **concept hierarchies**, used to organize attributes or attribute values into different levels of abstraction. Knowledge such as user beliefs, which can be used to assess a pattern's interestingness based on its unexpectedness, may also be included. Other examples of domain knowledge are additional interestingness constraints or thresholds, and metadata (e.g., describing data from multiple heterogeneous sources).

- **Data mining engine:** This is essential to the data mining system and ideally consists of a set of functional modules for tasks such as characterization, association, classification, cluster analysis, and evolution and deviation analysis.

- **Pattern evaluation module:** This component typically employs interestingness measures (Section 1.5) and interacts with the data mining modules so as to *focus* the search towards interesting patterns. It may use interestingness thresholds to filter out discovered patterns. Alternatively, the pattern evaluation module may be integrated with the mining module, depending on the implementation of the data mining method used. For efficient data mining, it is highly recommended to push the evaluation of pattern interestingness as deep as possible into the mining process so as to confine the search to only the interesting patterns.

- **Graphical user interface:** This module communicates between users and the data mining system, allowing the user to interact with the system by specifying a data mining query or task, providing information to help focus the search, and performing exploratory data mining based on the intermediate data mining results. In addition, this component allows the user to browse database and data warehouse schemas or data structures, evaluate mined patterns, and visualize the patterns in different forms.

From a data warehouse perspective, data mining can be viewed as an advanced stage of on-line analytical processing (OLAP). However, data mining goes far beyond the narrow scope of summarization-style analytical processing of data warehouse systems by incorporating more advanced techniques for data understanding.

While there may be many "data mining systems" on the market, not all of them can perform true data mining. A data analysis system that does not handle large amounts of data should be more appropriately categorized as a machine learning system, a statistical data analysis tool, or an experimental system prototype. A system that can only perform data or information retrieval, including finding aggregate values, or that performs deductive query answering in large databases should be more appropriately categorized as a database system, an information retrieval system, or a deductive database system.

Data mining involves an integration of techniques from multiple disciplines such as database technology, statistics, machine learning, high-performance computing, pattern recognition, neural networks, data visualization, information retrieval, image and signal processing, and spatial data analysis. We adopt a database perspective in our presentation of data mining in this book. That is, emphasis is placed on *efficient* and *scalable* data mining techniques for *large* databases. For an algorithm to be **scalable**, its running time should grow linearly in proportion to the size of the database, given the available system resources such as main memory and disk space. By performing data mining, interesting knowledge, regularities, or high-level information can be extracted from databases and viewed or browsed from different angles. The discovered knowledge can be applied to decision making, process control, information management, and query processing. Therefore, data mining is considered one of the most important frontiers in database systems and one of the most promising interdisciplinary developments in the information industry.

# 1.3 Data Mining—On What Kind of Data?

In this section, we examine a number of different data stores on which mining can be performed. In principle, data mining should be applicable to any kind of information repository. This includes relational databases, data warehouses, transactional databases, advanced database systems, flat files, and the World Wide Web. Advanced database systems include object-oriented and object-relational databases, and specific application-oriented databases, such as spatial databases, time-series databases, text databases, and multimedia databases. The challenges and techniques of mining may differ for each of the repository systems.

Although this book assumes that readers have primitive knowledge of information systems, we provide a brief introduction to each of the major data repository systems listed above. In this section, we also introduce the fictitious *AllElectronics* store, which will be used to illustrate concepts throughout the text.

## 1.3.1 Relational Databases

A database system, also called a **database management system (DBMS)**, consists of a collection of interrelated data, known as a **database**, and a set of software programs to manage and access the data. The software programs involve mechanisms for the definition of database structures; for data storage; for concurrent, shared, or distributed data access; and for ensuring the consistency and security of the information stored, despite system crashes or attempts at unauthorized access.

A **relational database** is a collection of **tables**, each of which is assigned a unique name. Each table consists of a set of **attributes** (*columns* or *fields*) and usually stores a large set of **tuples** (*records* or *rows*). Each tuple in a relational table represents an object identified by a unique *key* and described by a set of attribute values. A semantic data model, such as an **entity-relationship** (ER) data model, which models the database as a set of entities and their relationships, is often constructed for relational databases.

Consider the following example.

**Example 1.1** The *AllElectronics* company is described by the following relation tables: *customer, item, employee,* and *branch*. Fragments of the tables described here are shown in Figure 1.6.

- The relation *customer* consists of a set of attributes, including a unique customer identity number (*cust_ID*), customer name, address, age, occupation, annual income, credit information, category, and so on.
- Similarly, each of the relations *item, employee,* and *branch* consists of a set of attributes, describing their properties.

**customer**

| cust_ID | name | address | age | income | credit_info | ... |
|---------|------|---------|-----|--------|-------------|-----|
| C1 | Smith, Sandy | 5463 E Hastings, Burnaby, BC V5A 4S9, Canada | 21 | $27000 | 1 | ... |
| ... | ... | ... | ... | ... | ... | ... |
| ... | ... | ... | ... | ... | ... | ... |

**item**

| item_ID | name | brand | category | type | price | place_made | supplier | cost |
|---------|------|-------|----------|------|-------|------------|----------|------|
| 13 | high-res-TV | Toshiba | high resolution | TV | $988.00 | Japan | NikoX | $600.00 |
| 18 | multidisc-CDplay | Sanyo | multidisc | CD player | $369.00 | Japan | MusicFront | $120.00 |
| ... | | ... | ... | ... | ... | ... | ... | ... |

**employee**

| empl_ID | name | category | group | salary | commission |
|---------|------|----------|-------|--------|------------|
| E55 | Jones, Jane | home entertainment | manager | $18,000 | 2% |
| ... | ... | ... | ... | ... | ... |

**branch**

| branch_ID | name | address |
|-----------|------|---------|
| B1 | City Square | 369 Cambie St., Vancouver, BC V5L 3A2, Canada |
| ... | ... | ... |

**purchases**

| trans_ID | cust_ID | empl_ID | date | time | method_paid | amount |
|----------|---------|---------|------|------|-------------|--------|
| T100 | C1 | E55 | 09/21/98 | 15:45 | Visa | $1357.00 |
| ... | ... | ... | ... | ... | ... | ... |

**items_sold**

| trans_ID | item_ID | qty |
|----------|---------|-----|
| T100 | I3 | 1 |
| T100 | I8 | 2 |
| ... | ... | ... |

**works_at**

| empl_ID | branch_ID |
|---------|-----------|
| E55 | B1 |
| ... | ... |

**Figure 1.6**   Fragments of relations from a relational database for *AllElectronics*.

- Tables can also be used to represent the relationships between or among multiple relation tables. For our example, these include *purchases* (customer purchases items, creating a sales transaction that is handled by an employee), *items_sold* (lists the items sold in a given transaction), and *works_at* (employee works at a branch of *AllElectronics*).

Relational data can be accessed by **database queries** written in a relational query language, such as SQL, or with the assistance of graphical user interfaces. In the latter, the user may employ a menu, for example, to specify attributes to be included in the query, and the constraints on these attributes. A given query is transformed into a set of relational operations, such as join, selection, and projection, and is then optimized for efficient processing. A query allows retrieval of specified subsets of the data. Suppose that your job is to analyze the

*AllElectronics* data. Through the use of relational queries, you can ask things like "Show me a list of all items that were sold in the last quarter." Relational languages also include aggregate functions such as sum, avg (average), count, max (maximum), and min (minimum). These allow you to ask things like "Show me the total sales of the last month, grouped by branch," or "How many sales transactions occurred in the month of December?" or "Which sales person had the highest amount of sales?"

When data mining is applied to relational databases, one can go further by *searching for trends or data patterns*. For example, data mining systems may analyze customer data to predict the credit risk of new customers based on their income, age, and previous credit information. Data mining systems may also detect deviations, such as items whose sales are far from those expected in comparison with the previous year. Such deviations can then be further investigated (e.g., has there been a change in packaging of such items, or a significant increase in price?).

Relational databases are one of the most popularly available and rich information repositories, and thus they are a major data form in our study of data mining.

### 1.3.2   Data Warehouses

Suppose that *AllElectronics* is a successful international company, with branches around the world. Each branch has its own set of databases. The president of *AllElectronics* has asked you to provide an analysis of the company's sales per item type per branch for the third quarter. This is a difficult task, particularly since the relevant data are spread out over several databases, physically located at numerous sites.

If *AllElectronics* had a data warehouse, this task would be easy. A **data warehouse** is a repository of information collected from multiple sources, stored under a unified schema, and which usually resides at a single site. Data warehouses are constructed via a process of data cleaning, data transformation, data integration, data loading, and periodic data refreshing. This process is discussed in Chapters 2 and 3. Figure 1.7 shows the basic architecture of a data warehouse for *AllElectronics*.

In order to facilitate decision making, the data in a data warehouse are *organized around major subjects*, such as customer, item, supplier, and activity. The data are stored to provide information from a *historical perspective* (such as from the past 5–10 years) and are typically *summarized*. For example, rather than storing the details of each sales transaction, the data warehouse may store a summary of the transactions per item type for each store or, summarized to a higher level, for each sales region.

A data warehouse is usually modeled by a multidimensional database structure, where each **dimension** corresponds to an attribute or a set of attributes in the schema, and each **cell** stores the value of some aggregate measure, such as *count* or *sales_amount*. The actual physical structure of a data warehouse may

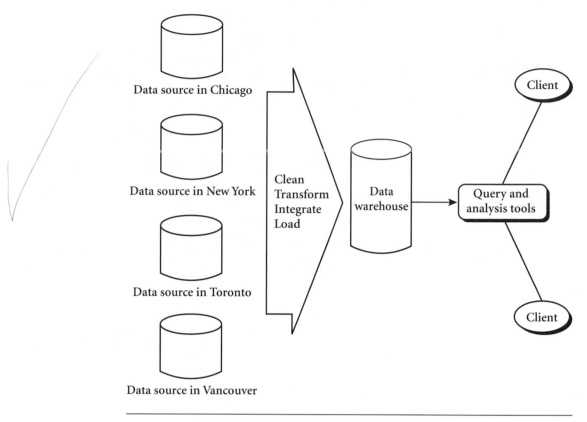

**Figure 1.7**  Typical architecture of a data warehouse for *AllElectronics*.

be a relational data store or a **multidimensional data cube**. It provides a multi-dimensional view of data and allows the precomputation and fast accessing of summarized data.

**Example 1.2**  A data cube for summarized sales data of *AllElectronics* is presented in Figure 1.8(a). The cube has three *dimensions*: address (with *city* values *Chicago, New York, Toronto, Vancouver*), time (with *quarter* values *Q1, Q2, Q3, Q4*), and item (with item *type* values *home entertainment, computer, phone, security*). The aggregate value stored in each cell of the cube is *sales_amount* (in thousands). For example, the total sales for the first quarter, *Q1*, for items relating to security systems in Vancouver is $400,000, as stored in cell ⟨*Vancouver, Q1, security*⟩. Additional cubes may be used to store aggregate sums over each dimension, corresponding to the aggregate values obtained using different SQL group-bys (e.g., the total sales amount per city and quarter, or per city and item, or per quarter and item, or per each individual dimension).  ∎

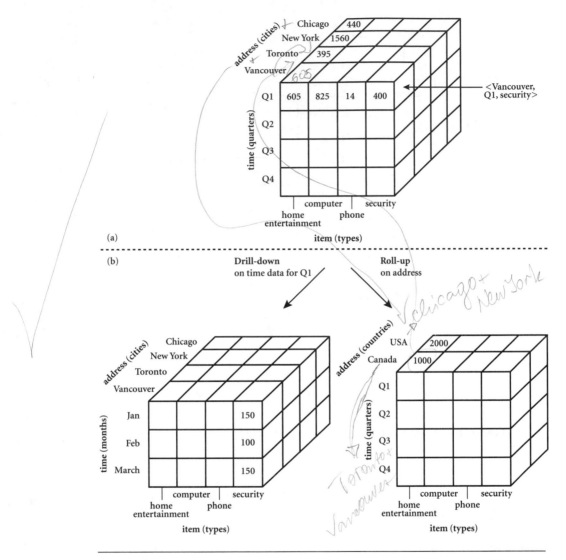

**Figure 1.8** A multidimensional data cube, commonly used for data warehousing, *(a)* showing summarized data for *AllElectronics* and *(b)* showing summarized data resulting from drill-down and roll-up operations on the cube in *(a)*. For improved readability, only some of the cube cell values are shown.

*"I have also heard about data marts. What is the difference between a data warehouse and a data mart?"* you may ask. A data warehouse collects information about subjects that span an *entire organization*, and thus its scope is *enterprise-wide*. A **data mart**, on the other hand, is a department subset of a data warehouse. It focuses on selected subjects, and thus its scope is *department-wide*.

By providing multidimensional data views and the precomputation of summarized data, data warehouse systems are well suited for **On-Line Analytical Processing**, or **OLAP**. OLAP operations make use of background knowledge regarding the domain of the data being studied in order to allow the presentation of data at *different levels of abstraction*. Such operations accommodate different user viewpoints. Examples of OLAP operations include **drill-down** and **roll-up**, which allow the user to view the data at differing degrees of summarization, as illustrated in Figure 1.8(b). For instance, one may drill down on sales data summarized by *quarter* to see the data summarized by *month*. Similarly, one may roll up on sales data summarized by *city* to view the data summarized by *country*.

Although data warehouse tools help support data analysis, additional tools for data mining are required to allow more in-depth and automated analysis. Data warehouse technology is discussed in detail in Chapter 2.

### 1.3.3  Transactional Databases

In general, a **transactional database** consists of a file where each record represents a transaction. A transaction typically includes a unique transaction identity number (*trans_ID*), and a list of the **items** making up the transaction (such as items purchased in a store). The transactional database may have additional tables associated with it, which contain other information regarding the sale, such as the date of the transaction, the customer ID number, the ID number of the sales person and of the branch at which the sale occurred, and so on.

**Example 1.3**   Transactions can be stored in a table, with one record per transaction. A fragment of a transactional database for *AllElectronics* is shown in Figure 1.9. From the relational database point of view, the *sales* table in Figure 1.9 is a nested relation because the attribute *list of item_IDs* contains a set of *items*. Since most relational database systems do not support nested relational structures, the transactional

*sales*

| trans_ID | list of item_IDs |
|----------|------------------|
| T100     | I1, I3, I8, I16  |
| ...      | ...              |

**Figure 1.9**   Fragment of a transactional database for sales at *AllElectronics*.

database is usually either stored in a flat file in a format similar to that of the table in Figure 1.9, or unfolded into a standard relation in a format similar to that of the *items_sold* table in Figure 1.6.    ∎

As an analyst of the *AllElectronics* database, you may like to ask, "Show me all the items purchased by Sandy Smith" or "How many transactions include item number I3?" Answering such queries may require a scan of the entire transactional database.

Suppose you would like to dig deeper into the data by asking, "Which items sold well together?" This kind of *market basket data analysis* would enable you to bundle groups of items together as a strategy for maximizing sales. For example, given the knowledge that printers are commonly purchased together with computers, you could offer an expensive model of printers at a discount to customers buying selected computers, in the hopes of selling more of the expensive printers. A regular data retrieval system is not able to answer queries like the one above. However, data mining systems for transactional data can do so by identifying sets of items that are frequently sold together.

## 1.3.4  Advanced Database Systems and Advanced Database Applications

Relational database systems have been widely used in business applications. With the advances of database technology, various kinds of advanced database systems have emerged and are undergoing development to address the requirements of new database applications.

The new database applications include handling spatial data (such as maps), engineering design data (such as the design of buildings, system components, or integrated circuits), hypertext and multimedia data (including text, image, video, and audio data), time-related data (such as historical records or stock exchange data), and the World Wide Web (a huge, widely distributed information repository made available by the Internet). These applications require efficient data structures and scalable methods for handling complex object structures, variable-length records, semistructured or unstructured data, text and multimedia data, and database schemas with complex structures and dynamic changes.

In response to these needs, advanced database systems and specific application-oriented database systems have been developed. These include object-oriented and object-relational database systems, spatial database systems, temporal and time-series database systems, text and multimedia database systems, heterogeneous and legacy database systems, and Web-based global information systems.

While such databases or information repositories require sophisticated facilities to efficiently store, retrieve, and update large amounts of complex data, they also provide fertile grounds and raise many challenging research and implementation issues for data mining. In this section, we describe each of the advanced database systems listed above.

### Object-Oriented Databases

**Object-oriented databases** are based on the object-oriented programming paradigm, where in general terms, each entity is considered as an **object**. Following the *AllElectronics* example, objects can be individual employees, customers, or items. Data and code relating to an object are *encapsulated* into a single unit. Each object has associated with it the following:

- A set of **variables** that describe the objects. These correspond to attributes in the entity-relationship and relational models.
- A set of **messages** that the object can use to communicate with other objects, or with the rest of the database system.
- A set of **methods**, where each method holds the code to implement a message. Upon receiving a message, the method returns a value in response. For instance, the method for the message *get_photo*(*employee*) will retrieve and return a photo of the given employee object.

Objects that share a common set of properties can be grouped into an **object class**. Each object is an **instance** of its class. Object classes can be organized into class/subclass hierarchies so that each class represents properties that are common to objects in that class. For instance, an *employee* class can contain variables like *name, address*, and *birthdate*. Suppose that the class *sales_person* is a subclass of the class *employee*. A *sales_person* object would **inherit** all of the variables pertaining to its superclass of *employee*. In addition, it has all of the variables that pertain specifically to being a sales person (e.g., *commission*). Such a class inheritance feature benefits information sharing.

### Object-Relational Databases

**Object-relational databases** are constructed based on an object-relational data model. This model extends the relational model by providing a rich data type for handling complex objects and object orientation. In addition, special constructs for relational query languages are included to manage the added data types. The object-relational model extends the basic relational data model by adding the power to handle complex data types, class hierarchies, and object inheritance as described above. Object-relational databases are becoming increasingly popular in industry and applications.

Data mining in object-oriented and object-relational systems share some similarities. In comparison with relational data mining, techniques need to be developed for handling complex object structures, complex data types, class and subclass hierarchies, property inheritance, and methods and procedures.

## Spatial Databases

**Spatial databases** contain spatial-related information. Such databases include geographic (map) databases, VLSI chip design databases, and medical and satellite image databases. Spatial data may be represented in **raster format**, consisting of *n*-dimensional bit maps or pixel maps. For example, a 2-D satellite image may be represented as raster data, where each pixel registers the rainfall in a given area. Maps can be represented in **vector format**, where roads, bridges, buildings, and lakes are represented as unions of basic geometric constructs, such as points, lines, polygons, and the partitions and networks formed by these shapes.

Geographic databases have a number of applications, ranging from forestry and ecology planning, to providing public service information regarding the location of telephone and electric cables, pipes, and sewage systems. In addition, geographic databases are used in vehicle navigation and dispatching systems. An example of such a system for taxis would store a city map with information regarding one-way streets, suggested routes for moving from region A to region B during rush hour, the location of restaurants and hospitals, as well as the current location of each driver.

*"What kind of data mining can be performed on spatial databases?"* you may ask. Data mining may uncover patterns describing the characteristics of houses located near a specified kind of location, such as a park, for instance. Other patterns may describe the climate of mountainous areas located at various altitudes, or describe the change in trend of metropolitan poverty rates based on city distances from major highways. In addition, "spatial data cubes" may be constructed to organize data into multidimensional structures and hierarchies, on which OLAP operations (such as drill-down and roll-up) can be performed.

## Temporal Databases and Time-Series Databases

Temporal databases and time-series databases both store time-related data. A **temporal database** usually stores relational data that include time-related attributes. These attributes may involve several timestamps, each having different semantics. A **time-series database** stores sequences of values that change with time, such as data collected regarding the stock exchange.

Data mining techniques can be used to find the characteristics of object evolution, or the trend of changes for objects in the database. Such information can be useful in decision making and strategy planning. For instance, the mining of banking data may aid in the scheduling of bank tellers according to the volume of customer traffic. Stock exchange data can be mined to uncover trends that could help you plan investment strategies (e.g., when is the best time to purchase *All-Electronics* stock?). Such analyses typically require defining multiple granularities of time. For example, time may be decomposed according to fiscal years, academic years, or calendar years. Years may be further decomposed into quarters or months.

## Text Databases and Multimedia Databases

**Text databases** are databases that contain word descriptions for objects. These word descriptions are usually not simple keywords but rather long sentences or paragraphs, such as product specifications, error or bug reports, warning messages, summary reports, notes, or other documents. Text databases may be highly unstructured (such as some Web pages on the World Wide Web). Some text databases may be somewhat structured, that is, *semistructured* (such as e-mail messages and many HTML/XML Web pages), while others are relatively well structured (such as library databases). Text databases with highly regular structures typically can be implemented using relational database systems.

*"What can data mining on text databases uncover?"* Ultimately, it may uncover general descriptions of object classes, as well as keyword or content associations, and the clustering behavior of text objects. To do this, standard data mining methods need to be integrated with information retrieval techniques and the construction or use of hierarchies specifically for text data (such as dictionaries and thesauruses), as well as discipline-oriented term classification systems (such as in chemistry, medicine, law, or economics).

**Multimedia databases** store image, audio, and video data. They are used in applications such as picture content-based retrieval, voice-mail systems, video-on-demand systems, the World Wide Web, and speech-based user interfaces that recognize spoken commands. Multimedia databases must support large objects, since data objects such as video can require gigabytes of storage. Specialized storage and search techniques are also required. Since video and audio data require real-time retrieval at a steady and predetermined rate in order to avoid picture or sound gaps and system buffer overflows, such data are referred to as **continuous-media** data.

For multimedia database mining, storage and search techniques need to be integrated with standard data mining methods. Promising approaches include the construction of multimedia data cubes, the extraction of multiple features from multimedia data, and similarity-based pattern matching.

## Heterogeneous Databases and Legacy Databases

A **heterogeneous database** consists of a set of interconnected, autonomous component databases. The components communicate in order to exchange information and answer queries. Objects in one component database may differ greatly from objects in other component databases, making it difficult to assimilate their semantics into the overall heterogeneous database.

Many enterprises acquire legacy databases as a result of the long history of information technology development (including the application of different hardwares and operating systems). A **legacy database** is a group of *heterogeneous databases* that combines different kinds of data systems, such as relational or object-oriented databases, hierarchical databases, network databases, spreadsheets, multimedia databases, or file systems. The heterogeneous databases in a legacy database may be connected by intra- or inter-computer networks.

Information exchange across such databases is difficult since one needs to work out precise transformation rules from one representation to another, considering diverse semantics. Consider, for example, the problem in exchanging information regarding student academic performance among different schools. Each school may have its own computer system and use its own curriculum and grading system. One university may adopt a quarter system, offer three courses on database systems, and assign grades from A+ to F, while another may adopt a semester system, offer two courses on databases, and assign grades from 1 to 10. It is very difficult to work out precise course-to-grade transformation rules between the two universities, making information exchange difficult. Data mining techniques may provide an interesting solution to the information exchange problem by transforming the given data into higher, more generalized, conceptual levels (such as *fair*, *good*, or *excellent* for student grades), from which information exchange can then more easily be performed.

## The World Wide Web

The World Wide Web and its associated distributed information services, such as America Online, Yahoo!, AltaVista, and Prodigy, provide rich, world-wide, on-line information services, where data objects are linked together to facilitate interactive access. Users seeking information of interest traverse from one object via links to another. Such systems provide ample opportunities and challenges for data mining. For example, understanding user access patterns will not only help improve system design (by providing efficient access between highly correlated objects), but also leads to better marketing decisions (e.g., by placing advertisements in frequently visited documents, or by providing better customer/user classification and behavior analysis). Capturing user access patterns in such distributed information environments is called **mining path traversal patterns.**

Although Web pages may appear fancy and informative to human readers, they can be highly unstructured and lack a predefined schema, type, or pattern. Thus it is difficult for computers to understand the semantic meaning of diverse Web pages and structure them in an organized way for systematic information retrieval and data mining. Web services that provide keyword-based searches without understanding the context behind particular Web pages can only offer limited help to users. For example, a Web search based on a single keyword may return hundreds of Web page pointers containing the keyword, but most of the pointers will be unrelated to what the user wants to find. Can data mining provide more help here than Web search services? Can data mining help us learn about the distribution of information on the Web in general, Web page characteristics, and associations among different Web pages? Can it help find authoritative Web pages on any specific topic? Can it produce a good classification of pages on the Internet? These questions pose additional challenging issues for advanced data mining.

# 1.4 Data Mining Functionalities—What Kinds of Patterns Can Be Mined?

We have observed various types of data stores and database systems on which data mining can be performed. Let us now examine the kinds of data patterns that can be mined.

Data mining functionalities are used to specify the kind of patterns to be found in data mining tasks. In general, data mining tasks can be classified into two categories: **descriptive** and **predictive**. Descriptive mining tasks characterize the general properties of the data in the database. Predictive mining tasks perform inference on the current data in order to make predictions.

In some cases, users may have no idea which kinds of patterns in their data may be interesting, and hence may like to search for several different kinds of patterns in parallel. Thus it is important to have a data mining system that can mine multiple kinds of patterns to accommodate different user expectations or applications. Furthermore, data mining systems should be able to discover patterns at various granularities (i.e., different levels of abstraction). Data mining systems should also allow users to specify hints to guide or focus the search for interesting patterns. Since some patterns may not hold for all of the data in the database, a measure of certainty or "trustworthiness" is usually associated with each discovered pattern.

Data mining functionalities, and the kinds of patterns they can discover, are described below.

## 1.4.1 Concept/Class Description: Characterization and Discrimination

Data can be associated with classes or concepts. For example, in the *AllElectronics* store, classes of items for sale include *computers* and *printers*, and concepts of customers include *bigSpenders* and *budgetSpenders*. It can be useful to describe individual classes and concepts in summarized, concise, and yet precise terms. Such descriptions of a class or a concept are called **class/concept descriptions**. These descriptions can be derived via (1) *data characterization*, by summarizing the data of the class under study (often called the **target class**) in general terms, or (2) *data discrimination*, by comparison of the target class with one or a set of comparative classes (often called the **contrasting classes**), or (3) both data characterization and discrimination.

**Data characterization** is a summarization of the general characteristics or features of a target class of data. The data corresponding to the user-specified class are typically collected by a database query. For example, to study the characteristics of software products whose sales increased by 10% in the last year, the data related to such products can be collected by executing an SQL query.

There are several methods for effective data summarization and characterization. For instance, the data cube-based OLAP roll-up operation (Section 1.3.2) can be used to perform user-controlled data summarization along a specified dimension. This process is further detailed in Chapter 2, which discusses data warehousing. An *attribute-oriented induction* technique can be used to perform data generalization and characterization without step-by-step user interaction. This technique is described in Chapter 5.

The output of data characterization can be presented in various forms. Examples include **pie charts**, **bar charts**, **curves**, **multidimensional data cubes**, and **multidimensional tables**, including crosstabs. The resulting descriptions can also be presented as **generalized relations** or in rule form (called **characteristic rules**). These different output forms and their transformations are discussed in Chapter 5.

**Example 1.4** A data mining system should be able to produce a description summarizing the characteristics of customers who spend more than $1000 a year at *AllElectronics*. The result could be a general profile of the customers, such as they are 40–50 years old, employed, and have excellent credit ratings. The system should allow users to drill down on any dimension, such as on *occupation* in order to view these customers according to their type of employment.    ∎

**Data discrimination** is a comparison of the general features of target class data objects with the general features of objects from one or a set of contrasting classes. The target and contrasting classes can be specified by the user, and the corresponding data objects retrieved through database queries. For example, the user may like to compare the general features of software products whose sales increased by 10% in the last year with those whose sales decreased by at least 30% during the same period. The methods used for data discrimination are similar to those used for data characterization.

*"How are discrimination descriptions output?"* The forms of output presentation are similar to those for characteristic descriptions, although discrimination descriptions should include comparative measures that help distinguish between the target and contrasting classes. Discrimination descriptions expressed in rule form are referred to as **discriminant rules**. The user should be able to manipulate the output for characteristic and discriminant descriptions.

**Example 1.5** A data mining system should be able to compare two groups of *AllElectronics* customers, such as those who shop for computer products regularly (more than two times a month) versus those who rarely shop for such products (i.e., less than three times a year). The resulting description could be a general comparative profile of the customers, such as 80% of the customers who frequently purchase computer products are between 20 and 40 years old and have a university education, whereas 60% of the customers who infrequently buy such products are either seniors or young, and have no university degree. Drilling down on a dimension, such as *occupation*, or adding new dimensions, such as *income_level*, may help in finding even more discriminative features between the two classes.    ∎

Concept description, including characterization and discrimination, is the topic of Chapter 5.

## 1.4.2 Association Analysis

*"What is association analysis?"* **Association analysis** is the discovery of *association rules* showing attribute-value conditions that occur frequently together in a given set of data. Association analysis is widely used for market basket or transaction data analysis.

More formally, **association rules** are of the form $X \Rightarrow Y$, that is, "$A_1 \wedge \cdots \wedge A_m \rightarrow B_1 \wedge \cdots \wedge B_n$", where $A_i$ (for $i \in \{1, \ldots, m\}$) and $B_j$ (for $j \in \{1, \ldots, n\}$) are attribute-value pairs. The association rule $X \Rightarrow Y$ is interpreted as "database tuples that satisfy the conditions in $X$ are also likely to satisfy the conditions in $Y$."

**Example 1.6** Given the *AllElectronics* relational database, a data mining system may find association rules like

$$age(X, \text{"20...29"}) \wedge income(X, \text{"20K...29K"}) \Rightarrow buys(X, \text{"CD player"})$$

$$[support = 2\%, confidence = 60\%]$$

where $X$ is a variable representing a customer. The rule indicates that of the *AllElectronics* customers under study, 2% (**support**) are 20 to 29 years of age with an income of 20K to 29K and have purchased a CD player at *AllElectronics*. There is a 60% probability (**confidence**, or certainty) that a customer in this age and income group will purchase a CD player.

Note that this is an association between more than one attribute, or predicate (i.e., *age*, *income*, and *buys*). Adopting the terminology used in multidimensional databases, where each attribute is referred to as a dimension, the above rule can be referred to as a **multidimensional association rule**.

Suppose, as a marketing manager of *AllElectronics*, you would like to determine which items are frequently purchased together within the same transactions. An example of such a rule is

$$contains(T, \text{"computer"}) \Rightarrow contains(T, \text{"software"})$$

$$[support = 1\%, confidence = 50\%]$$

meaning that if a transaction, $T$, contains *"computer"*, there is a 50% chance that it contains *"software"* as well, and 1% of all of the transactions contain both. This association rule involves a single attribute or predicate (i.e., *contains*) that repeats. Association rules that contain a single predicate are referred to as **single-dimensional association rules**. Dropping the predicate notation, the above rule can be written simply as "*computer* $\Rightarrow$ *software* $[1\%, 50\%]$". ∎

In recent years, many algorithms have been proposed for the efficient mining of association rules. Association rule mining is discussed in detail in Chapter 6.

## 1.4.3  Classification and Prediction

*[handwritten margin notes: bank loans — safe or risky, class labels, def, def, def]*

**Classification** is the process of finding a set of **models** (or functions) that describe and distinguish data classes or concepts, for the purpose of being able to use the model to predict the class of objects whose class label is unknown. The derived model is based on the analysis of a set of **training data** (i.e., data objects whose class label is known).

*"How is the derived model presented?"* The derived model may be represented in various forms, such as *classification (IF-THEN) rules*, *decision trees*, *mathematical formulae*, or *neural networks*. A **decision tree** is a flow-chart-like tree structure, where each node denotes a test on an attribute value, each branch represents an outcome of the test, and tree leaves represent classes or class distributions. Decision trees can be easily converted to classification rules. A **neural network**, when used for classification, is typically a collection of neuron-like processing units with weighted connections between the units.

Classification can be used for predicting the class label of data objects. However, in many applications, users may wish to predict some missing or unavailable *data values* rather than class labels. This is usually the case when the predicted values are numerical data and is often specifically referred to as **prediction**. Although prediction may refer to both data value prediction and class label prediction, it is usually confined to data value prediction and thus is distinct from classification. Prediction also encompasses the identification of distribution *trends* based on the available data.

Classification and prediction may need to be preceded by **relevance analysis**, which attempts to identify attributes that do not contribute to the classification or prediction process. These attributes can then be excluded.

**Example 1.7**  Suppose, as sales manager of *AllElectronics*, you would like to classify a large set of items in the store, based on three kinds of responses to a sales campaign: *good response*, *mild response*, and *no response*. You would like to derive a model for each of these three classes based on the descriptive features of the items, such as *price*, *brand*, *place_made*, *type*, and *category*. The resulting classification should maximally distinguish each class from the others, presenting an organized picture of the data set. Suppose that the resulting classification is expressed in the form of a decision tree. The decision tree, for instance, may identify *price* as being the single factor that best distinguishes the three classes. The tree may reveal that, after *price*, other features that help further distinguish objects of each class from another include *brand* and *place_made*. Such a decision tree may help you understand the impact of the given sales campaign and design a more effective campaign for the future.                                                                                          ■

Chapter 7 discusses classification and prediction in further detail.

## 1.4.4  Cluster Analysis

*"What is cluster analysis?"* Unlike classification and prediction, which analyze
class-labeled data objects, **clustering** analyzes data objects without consulting
a known class label. In general, the class labels are not present in the training
data simply because they are not known to begin with. Clustering can be used to
generate such labels. The objects are clustered or grouped based on the principle
of *maximizing the intraclass similarity and minimizing the interclass similarity*.
That is, clusters of objects are formed so that objects within a cluster have high
similarity in comparison to one another, but are very dissimilar to objects in other
clusters. Each cluster that is formed can be viewed as a class of objects, from which
rules can be derived. Clustering can also facilitate **taxonomy formation**, that is, the
organization of observations into a hierarchy of classes that group similar events
together.

**Example 1.8**  Cluster analysis can be performed on *AllElectronics* customer data in order to
identify homogeneous subpopulations of customers. These clusters may represent
individual target groups for marketing. Figure 1.10 shows a 2-D plot of customers
with respect to customer locations in a city. Three clusters of data points are
evident.                                                                              ∎

Cluster analysis forms the topic of Chapter 8.

## 1.4.5  Outlier Analysis

A database may contain data objects that do not comply with the general behavior
or model of the data. These data objects are **outliers**. Most data mining methods
discard outliers as noise or exceptions. However, in some applications such as
fraud detection, the rare events can be more interesting than the more regularly
occurring ones. The analysis of outlier data is referred to as **outlier mining**.

Outliers may be detected using statistical tests that assume a distribution or
probability model for the data, or using distance measures where objects that are
a substantial distance from any other cluster are considered outliers. Rather than
using statistical or distance measures, deviation-based methods identify outliers
by examining differences in the main characteristics of objects in a group.

**Example 1.9**  Outlier analysis may uncover fraudulent usage of credit cards by detecting purchases of extremely large amounts for a given account number in comparison to
regular charges incurred by the same account. Outlier values may also be detected
with respect to the location and type of purchase, or the purchase frequency.    ∎

Outlier analysis is also discussed in Chapter 8.

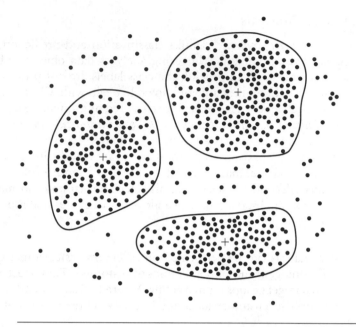

**Figure 1.10** A 2-D plot of customer data with respect to customer locations in a city, showing three data clusters. Each cluster "center" is marked with a "+".

### 1.4.6 Evolution Analysis

Data **evolution analysis** describes and models regularities or trends for objects whose behavior changes over time. Although this may include characterization, discrimination, association, classification, or clustering of *time-related* data, distinct features of such an analysis include time-series data analysis, sequence or periodicity pattern matching, and similarity-based data analysis.

**Example 1.10** Suppose that you have the major stock market (time-series) data of the last several years available from the New York Stock Exchange and you would like to invest in shares of high-tech industrial companies. A data mining study of stock exchange data may identify stock evolution regularities for overall stocks and for the stocks of particular companies. Such regularities may help predict future trends in stock market prices, contributing to your decision making regarding stock investments.

■

Data evolution analysis is discussed in Chapter 9.

# 1.5 Are All of the Patterns Interesting?

A data mining system has the potential to generate thousands or even millions of patterns, or rules.

"*So*," you may ask, "*are all of the patterns interesting?*" Typically not—only a small fraction of the patterns potentially generated would actually be of interest to any given user.

This raises some serious questions for data mining. You may wonder, "*What makes a pattern interesting? Can a data mining system generate all of the interesting patterns? Can a data mining system generate only interesting patterns?*"

To answer the first question, a pattern is **interesting** if (1) it is *easily understood* by humans, (2) *valid* on new or test data with some degree of *certainty*, (3) potentially *useful*, and (4) *novel*. A pattern is also interesting if it validates a hypothesis that the user *sought to confirm*. An interesting pattern represents **knowledge**.

Several **objective measures of pattern interestingness** exist. These are based on the structure of discovered patterns and the statistics underlying them. An objective measure for association rules of the form $X \Rightarrow Y$ is rule **support**, representing the percentage of transactions from a transaction database that the given rule satisfies. This is taken to be the probability $P(X \cup Y)$, where $X \cup Y$ indicates that a transaction contains both $X$ and $Y$, that is, the union of item sets $X$ and $Y$. Another objective measure for association rules is **confidence**, which assesses the degree of certainty of the detected association. This is taken to be the conditional probability $P(Y|X)$, that is, the probability that a transaction containing $X$ also contains $Y$. More formally, support and confidence are defined as

$$support(X \Rightarrow Y) = P(X \cup Y).$$

$$confidence(X \Rightarrow Y) = P(Y|X).$$

In general, each interestingness measure is associated with a threshold, which may be controlled by the user. For example, rules that do not satisfy a confidence threshold of, say, 50% can be considered uninteresting. Rules below the threshold likely reflect noise, exceptions, or minority cases and are probably of less value.

Although objective measures help identify interesting patterns, they are insufficient unless combined with subjective measures that reflect the needs and interests of a particular user. For example, patterns describing the characteristics of customers who shop frequently at *AllElectronics* should interest the marketing manager, but may be of little interest to analysts studying the same database for patterns on employee performance. Furthermore, many patterns that are interesting by objective standards may represent common knowledge and, therefore, are actually uninteresting. **Subjective interestingness measures** are based on user beliefs in the data. These measures find patterns interesting if they are **unexpected** (contradicting a user's belief) or offer strategic information on which the user can act. In the latter case, such patterns are referred to as **actionable**. Patterns that are **expected** can be interesting if they confirm a hypothesis that the user wished to validate, or resemble a user's hunch.

The second question—*"Can a data mining system generate* all *of the interesting patterns?"*—refers to the **completeness** of a data mining algorithm. It is often unrealistic and inefficient for data mining systems to generate all of the possible patterns. Instead, user-provided constraints and interestingness measures should be used to focus the search. For some mining tasks, such as association, this is often sufficient to ensure the completeness of the algorithm. Association rule mining is an example where the use of constraints and interestingness measures can ensure the completeness of mining. The methods involved are examined in detail in Chapter 6.

Finally, the third question—*"Can a data mining system generate* only *interesting patterns?"*—is an optimization problem in data mining. It is highly desirable for data mining systems to generate only interesting patterns. This would be much more efficient for users and data mining systems, since neither would have to search through the patterns generated in order to identify the truly interesting ones. Progress has been made in this direction. However, such optimization remains a challenging issue in data mining.

Measures of pattern interestingness are essential for the efficient discovery of patterns of value to the given user. Such measures can be used after the data mining step in order to rank the discovered patterns according to their interestingness, filtering out the uninteresting ones. More importantly, such measures can be used to guide and constrain the discovery process, improving the search efficiency by pruning away subsets of the pattern space that do not satisfy prespecified interestingness constraints.

Methods to assess pattern interestingness, and their use to improve data mining efficiency, are discussed throughout the book, with respect to each kind of pattern that can be mined.

## 1.6 Classification of Data Mining Systems

Data mining is an interdisciplinary field, the confluence of a set of disciplines (as shown in Figure 1.11), including database systems, statistics, machine learning, visualization, and information science. Moreover, depending on the data mining approach used, techniques from other disciplines may be applied, such as neural networks, fuzzy and/or rough set theory, knowledge representation, inductive logic programming, or high performance computing. Depending on the kinds of data to be mined or on the given data mining application, the data mining system may also integrate techniques from spatial data analysis, information retrieval, pattern recognition, image analysis, signal processing, computer graphics, Web technology, economics, business, bioinformatics, or psychology.

Because of the diversity of disciplines contributing to data mining, data mining research is expected to generate a large variety of data mining systems. There-

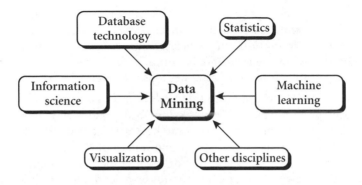

**Figure 1.11**    Data mining as a confluence of multiple disciplines.

fore, it is necessary to provide a clear classification of data mining systems. Such a classification may help potential users distinguish data mining systems and identify those that best match their needs. Data mining systems can be categorized according to various criteria, as follows.

1. **Classification according to the *kinds of databases* mined:**   A data mining system can be classified according to the kinds of databases mined. Database systems themselves can be classified according to different criteria (such as data models, or the types of data or applications involved), each of which may require its own data mining technique. Data mining systems can therefore be classified accordingly.

    For instance, if classifying according to data models, we may have a relational, transactional, object-oriented, object-relational, or data warehouse mining system. If classifying according to the special types of data handled, we may have a spatial, time-series, text, or multimedia data mining system, or a World Wide Web mining system.

2. **Classification according to the *kinds of knowledge* mined:**   Data mining systems can be categorized according to the kinds of knowledge they mine, that is, based on data mining functionalities, such as characterization, discrimination, association, classification, clustering, outlier analysis, and evolution analysis. A comprehensive data mining system usually provides multiple and/or integrated data mining functionalities.

    Moreover, data mining systems can be distinguished based on the granularity or levels of abstraction of the knowledge mined, including generalized knowledge (at a high level of abstraction), primitive-level knowledge (at a raw data level), or knowledge at multiple levels (considering several levels of abstraction). An advanced data mining system should facilitate the discovery of knowledge at multiple levels of abstraction.

Data mining systems can also be categorized as those that mine data regularities (commonly occurring patterns) versus those that mine data irregularities (such as exceptions, or outliers). In general, concept description, association analysis, classification, prediction, and clustering mine data regularities, rejecting outliers as noise. These methods may also help to detect outliers.

3) **Classification according to the *kinds of techniques* utilized:** Data mining systems can be categorized according to the underlying data mining techniques employed. These techniques can be described according to the degree of user interaction involved (e.g., autonomous systems, interactive exploratory systems, query-driven systems) or the methods of data analysis employed (e.g., database-oriented or data warehouse–oriented techniques, machine learning, statistics, visualization, pattern recognition, neural networks, and so on). A sophisticated data mining system will often adopt multiple data mining techniques or work out an effective, integrated technique that combines the merits of a few individual approaches.

4) **Classification according to the *applications adapted*:** Data mining systems can also be categorized according to the applications they adapt. For example, there could be data mining systems tailored specifically for finance, telecommunications, DNA, stock markets, e-mail, and so on. Different applications often require the integration of application-specific methods. Therefore, a generic, all-purpose data mining system may not fit domain-specific mining tasks.

Chapters 5 to 8 of this book are organized according to the various kinds of knowledge mined. In Chapter 9, we discuss the mining of complex types of data on a variety of advanced database systems. In Chapter 10, some data mining applications are discussed.

# 1.7 Major Issues in Data Mining

The scope of this book addresses major issues in data mining regarding mining methodology, user interaction, performance, and diverse data types. These issues are introduced below:

**Mining methodology and user interaction issues:** These reflect the kinds of knowledge mined, the ability to mine knowledge at multiple granularities, the use of domain knowledge, ad hoc mining, and knowledge visualization.

- *Mining different kinds of knowledge in databases:* Since different users can be interested in different kinds of knowledge, data mining should cover a wide spectrum of data analysis and knowledge discovery tasks, including data characterization, discrimination, association, classification, clustering, trend and deviation analysis, and similarity analysis. These tasks may use the same database in different ways and require the development of numerous data mining techniques.

- *Interactive mining of knowledge at multiple levels of abstraction:* Since it is difficult to know exactly what can be discovered within a database, the data mining process should be *interactive*. For databases containing a huge amount of data, appropriate sampling techniques can first be applied to facilitate interactive data exploration. Interactive mining allows users to focus the search for patterns, providing and refining data mining requests based on returned results. Specifically, knowledge should be mined by drilling down, rolling up, and pivoting through the data space and knowledge space interactively, similar to what OLAP can do on data cubes. In this way, the user can interact with the data mining system to view data and discovered patterns at multiple granularities and from different angles.

- *Incorporation of background knowledge:* Background knowledge, or information regarding the domain under study, may be used to guide the discovery process and allow discovered patterns to be expressed in concise terms and at different levels of abstraction. Domain knowledge related to databases, such as integrity constraints and deduction rules, can help focus and speed up a data mining process, or judge the interestingness of discovered patterns.

- *Data mining query languages and ad hoc data mining:* Relational query languages (such as SQL) allow users to pose ad hoc queries for data retrieval. In a similar vein, high-level **data mining query languages** need to be developed to allow users to describe ad hoc data mining tasks by facilitating the specification of the relevant sets of data for analysis, the domain knowledge, the kinds of knowledge to be mined, and the conditions and constraints to be enforced on the discovered patterns. Such a language should be integrated with a database or data warehouse query language, and optimized for efficient and flexible data mining.

- *Presentation and visualization of data mining results:* Discovered knowledge should be expressed in high-level languages, visual representations, or other expressive forms so that the knowledge can be easily understood and directly usable by humans. This is especially crucial if the data mining system is to be interactive. This requires the system to adopt expressive knowledge representation techniques, such as trees, tables, rules, graphs, charts, crosstabs, matrices, or curves.

- *Handling noisy or incomplete data:* The data stored in a database may reflect noise, exceptional cases, or incomplete data objects. When mining data regularities, these objects may confuse the process, causing the knowledge model constructed to overfit the data. As a result, the accuracy of the discovered patterns can be poor. Data cleaning methods and data analysis methods that can handle noise are required, as well as outlier mining methods for the discovery and analysis of exceptional cases.

- *Pattern evaluation—the interestingness problem:* A data mining system can uncover thousands of patterns. Many of the patterns discovered may be uninteresting to the given user, representing common knowledge or lacking novelty. Several challenges remain regarding the development of techniques to assess the interestingness of discovered patterns, particularly with regard to subjective measures that estimate the value of patterns with respect to a given user class, based on user beliefs or expectations. The use of interestingness measures to guide the discovery process and reduce the search space is another active area of research.

**Performance issues:** These include efficiency, scalability, and parallelization of data mining algorithms.

- *Efficiency and scalability of data mining algorithms:* To effectively extract information from a huge amount of data in databases, data mining algorithms must be efficient and scalable. In other words, the running time of a data mining algorithm must be predictable and acceptable in large databases. From a database perspective on knowledge discovery, efficiency and scalability are key issues in the implementation of data mining systems. Many of the issues discussed above under *mining methodology and user interaction* must also consider efficiency and scalability.

- *Parallel, distributed, and incremental mining algorithms:* The huge size of many databases, the wide distribution of data, and the computational complexity of some data mining methods are factors motivating the development of **parallel and distributed data mining algorithms**. Such algorithms divide the data into partitions, which are processed in parallel. The results from the partitions are then merged. Moreover, the high cost of some data mining processes promotes the need for **incremental** data mining algorithms that incorporate database updates without having to mine the entire data again "from scratch." Such algorithms perform knowledge modification incrementally to amend and strengthen what was previously discovered.

**Issues relating to the diversity of database types:**

- *Handling of relational and complex types of data:* Since relational databases and data warehouses are widely used, the development of efficient and effective data mining systems for such data is important. However, other databases may contain complex data objects, hypertext and multimedia data, spatial data, temporal data, or transaction data. It is unrealistic to expect one system to mine all kinds of data, given the diversity of data types and different goals of data mining. Specific data mining systems should be constructed for mining specific kinds of data. Therefore, one may expect to have different data mining systems for different kinds of data.

- *Mining information from heterogeneous databases and global information systems:* Local- and wide-area computer networks (such as the Internet) connect many sources of data, forming huge, distributed, and heterogeneous databases. The discovery of knowledge from different sources of structured, semistructured, or unstructured data with diverse data semantics poses great challenges to data mining. Data mining may help disclose high-level data regularities in multiple heterogeneous databases that are unlikely to be discovered by simple query systems and may improve information exchange and interoperability in heterogeneous databases. Web mining, which uncovers interesting knowledge about Web contents, Web usage, and Web dynamics, becomes a very challenging and highly dynamic field in data mining.

The above issues are considered major requirements and challenges for the further evolution of data mining technology. Some of the challenges have been addressed in recent data mining research and development, *to a certain extent*, and are now considered *requirements*, while others are still at the research stage. The issues, however, continue to stimulate further investigation and improvement. Additional issues relating to applications, privacy, and the social impacts of data mining are discussed in Chapter 10, the final chapter of this book.

# 1.8 Summary

- **Database technology** has evolved from primitive file processing to the development of database management systems with query and transaction processing. Further progress has led to the increasing demand for efficient and effective data analysis and data understanding tools. This need is a result of the explosive growth in data collected from applications including business and management, government administration, science and engineering, and environmental control.

- **Data mining** is the task of discovering interesting patterns from large amounts of data where the data can be stored in databases, data warehouses, or other information repositories. It is a young interdisciplinary field, drawing from areas such as database systems, data warehousing, statistics, machine learning, data visualization, information retrieval, and high-performance computing. Other contributing areas include neural networks, pattern recognition, spatial data analysis, image databases, signal processing, and many application fields, such as business, economics, and bioinformatics.

- A **knowledge discovery process** includes data cleaning, data integration, data selection, data transformation, data mining, pattern evaluation, and knowledge presentation.

- Data patterns can be mined from many different kinds of **databases**, such as relational databases, data warehouses, and transactional, object-relational, and object-oriented databases. Interesting data patterns can also be extracted from other kinds of **information repositories**, including spatial, time-related, text, multimedia, and legacy databases, and the World Wide Web.

■ A **data warehouse** is a repository for long-term storage of data from multiple sources, organized so as to facilitate management decision making. The data are stored under a unified schema and are typically summarized. Data warehouse systems provide some data analysis capabilities, collectively referred to as **OLAP** (**On-Line Analytical Processing**).

■ **Data mining functionalities** include the discovery of concept/class descriptions, association, classification, prediction, clustering, trend analysis, deviation analysis, and similarity analysis. Characterization and discrimination are forms of data summarization.

■ A pattern represents **knowledge** if it is easily understood by humans; valid on test data with some degree of certainty; and potentially useful, novel, or validates a hunch about which the user was curious. Measures of **pattern interestingness**, either *objective* or *subjective*, can be used to guide the discovery process.

■ **Data mining systems** can be **classified** according to the kinds of databases mined, the kinds of knowledge mined, the techniques used, or the applications adapted.

■ Efficient and effective data mining in large databases poses numerous requirements and great challenges to researchers and developers. The issues involved include data mining methodology, user interaction, performance and scalability, and the processing of a large variety of data types. Other issues include the exploration of data mining applications and their social impacts.

## Exercises

1.1 What is *data mining*? In your answer, address the following:

(a) Is it another hype?

(b) Is it a simple transformation of technology developed from databases, statistics, and machine learning?

(c) Explain how the evolution of database technology led to data mining.

(d) Describe the steps involved in data mining when viewed as a process of knowledge discovery.

1.2 Present an example where data mining is crucial to the success of a business. What *data mining functions* does this business need? Can they be performed alternatively by data query processing or simple statistical analysis?

1.3 Suppose your task as a software engineer at *Big-University* is to design a data mining system to examine their university course database, which contains the following information: the name, address, and status (e.g., undergraduate or graduate) of each student, the courses taken, and their cumulative grade point average (GPA). Describe the *architecture* you would choose. What is the purpose of each component of this architecture?

**1.4** How is a *data warehouse* different from a database? How are they similar?

**1.5** Briefly describe the following *advanced database systems* and applications: object-oriented databases, spatial databases, text databases, multimedia databases, the World Wide Web.

**1.6** Define each of the following *data mining functionalities*: characterization, discrimination, association, classification, prediction, clustering, and evolution analysis. Give examples of each data mining functionality, using a real-life database that you are familiar with.

**1.7** What is the difference between discrimination and classification? Between characterization and clustering? Between classification and prediction? For each of these pairs of tasks, how are they similar?

**1.8** Based on your observation, describe another possible kind of knowledge that needs to be discovered by data mining methods but has not been listed in this chapter. Does it require a mining methodology that is quite different from those outlined in this chapter?

**1.9** Describe three challenges to data mining regarding *data mining methodology* and *user interaction issues*.

**1.10** Describe two challenges to data mining regarding *performance issues*.

## Bibliographic Notes

The book *Knowledge Discovery in Databases*, edited by Piatetsky-Shapiro and Frawley [PSF91], is an early collection of research papers on knowledge discovery in databases. The book *Advances in Knowledge Discovery and Data Mining*, edited by Fayyad, Piatetsky-Shapiro, Smyth, and Uthurusamy [FPS+96], is a good collection of recent research results on knowledge discovery and data mining. Other books on data mining include *Predictive Data Mining* by Weiss and Indurkhya [WI98], *Machine Learning and Data Mining: Methods and Applications* by Michalski, Brakto, and Kubat [MBK98], *Data Mining Solutions: Methods and Tools for Solving Real-World Problems* by Westphal and Blaxton [WB98], *Mastering Data Mining: The Art and Science of Customer Relationship Management* by Berry and Linoff [BL99], *Building Data Mining Applications for CRM* by Berson, Smith, and Thearling [BST99], and *Data Mining: Building Competitive Advantage* by Groth [Gro99]. There are also books containing collections of papers on particular aspects of knowledge discovery, such as *Rough Sets, Fuzzy Sets and Knowledge Discovery*, edited by Ziarko [Zia94], as well as many tutorial notes on data mining, such as *Tutorial Notes of the 1999 International Conference on Knowledge Discovery and Data Mining (KDD'99)* published by ACM Press.

*KDD Nuggets* is a regular, free electronic newsletter containing information relevant to knowledge discovery and data mining. Contributions can be e-mailed with a descriptive subject line (and a URL) to *editor@kdnuggets.com*. Information regarding subscriptions can be found at *http://www.kdnuggets.com/news/subscribe .html*. *KDD Nuggets* has been moderated by Piatetsky-Shapiro since 1991. The Internet site *Knowledge Discovery Mine*, located at *http://www.kdnuggets.com/*, contains a good collection of KDD-related information.

The data mining community started its first international conference on knowledge discovery and data mining in 1995 [FU96]. The conference evolved from the four international workshops on knowledge discovery in databases, held from 1989 to 1994 [PS89, PS91a, FUP93, FU94]. The research community of data mining set up a new academic organization called ACM-SIGKDD, a Special Interested Group on Knowledge Discovery in Databases under ACM in 1998. In 1999, ACM-SIGKDD organized the fifth international conference on knowledge discovery and data mining (KDD'99). A dedicated journal, *Data Mining and Knowledge Discovery*, published by Kluwers Publishers, has been available since 1997. ACM-SIGKDD also publishes a quarterly newsletter, *SIGKDD Explorations*, which is available to SIGKDD members. There are a few other international or regional conferences on data mining, such as the Pacific Asian Conference on Knowledge Discovery and Data Mining (PAKDD), the European Conference on Principles and Practice of Knowledge Discovery in Databases (PKDD), and the International Conference on Data Warehousing and Knowledge Discovery (DaWaK).

Research in data mining has also been published in books, conferences, and journals on databases, statistics, machine learning, and data visualization. References to such sources are listed below.

Popular textbooks on database systems include *Principles of Database and Knowledge-Base Systems, Vol. 1,* by Ullman [Ull88], *Fundamentals of Database Systems, 2nd ed.,* by Elmasri and Navathe [EN94], *Database System Concepts, 3rd ed.,* by Silberschatz, Korth, and Sudarshan [SKS97], *A First Course in Database Systems* by Ullman and Widom [UW97], and *Database Management Systems, 2nd ed.,* by Ramakrishnan and Gehrke [RG00]. For an edited collection of seminal articles on database systems, see *Readings in Database Systems* by Stonebraker and Hellerstein [SH98]. Overviews and discussions on the achievements and research challenges in database systems can be found in Stonebraker, Agrawal, Dayal, et al. [SAD$^+$93], and Silberschatz, Stonebraker, and Ullman [SSU96].

Many books on data warehouse technology, systems, and applications have been published in the last several years, such as *The Data Warehouse Toolkit* by Kimball [Kim96], *Building the Data Warehouse* by Inmon [Inm96], and *OLAP Solutions: Building Multidimensional Information Systems* by Thomsen [Tho97]. Chaudhuri and Dayal [CD97] present a comprehensive overview of data warehouse technology.

Research results relating to data mining and data warehousing have been published in the proceedings of many international database conferences, including the *ACM-SIGMOD International Conference on Management of Data (SIGMOD)*, the *International Conference on Very Large Data Bases (VLDB)*, the *ACM SIGACT-SIGMOD-SIGART Symposium on Principles of Database Systems (PODS)*, the *International Conference on Data Engineering (ICDE)*, the *International Conference on Extending Database Technology (EDBT)*, the *International Conference on Database Theory (ICDT)*, the *International Conference on Information and Knowledge Management (CIKM)*, the *International Conference on Database and Expert Systems Applications (DEXA)*, and the *International Symposium on Database Systems for Advanced Applications (DASFAA)*. Research in data mining is also published in major database journals, such as *IEEE Transactions on Knowledge and Data Engineering (TKDE), ACM Transactions on Database Systems (TODS), Journal of ACM (JACM), Information Systems, The VLDB Journal, Data and Knowledge Engineering*, and *International Journal of Intelligent Information Systems (JIIS)*.

There are many textbooks covering different topics in statistical analysis, such as *Probability and Statistics for Engineering and the Sciences, 4th ed.*, by Devore [Dev95], *Applied Linear Statistical Models, 4th ed.*, by Neter, Kutner, Nachtsheim, and Wasserman [NKNW96], *An Introduction to Generalized Linear Models* by Dobson [Dob90], *Applied Statistical Time Series Analysis* by Shumway [Shu88], and *Applied Multivariate Statistical Analysis, 3rd ed.*, by Johnson and Wichern [JW92].

Research in statistics is published in the proceedings of several major statistical conferences, including *Joint Statistical Meetings, International Conference of the Royal Statistical Society*, and *Symposium on the Interface: Computing Science and Statistics*. Other sources of publication include the *Journal of the Royal Statistical Society, The Annals of Statistics, Journal of American Statistical Association, Technometrics*, and *Biometrika*.

Textbooks and reference books on machine learning include *Machine Learning, An Artificial Intelligence Approach*, Vols. 1–4, edited by Michalski et al. [MCM83, MCM86, KM90, MT94], *C4.5: Programs for Machine Learning* by Quinlan [Qui93], *Elements of Machine Learning* by Langley [Lan96], and *Machine Learning* by Mitchell [Mit97]. The book *Computer Systems That Learn: Classification and Prediction Methods from Statistics, Neural Nets, Machine Learning, and Expert Systems* by Weiss and Kulikowski [WK91] compares classification and prediction methods from several different fields. For an edited collection of seminal articles on machine learning, see *Readings in Machine Learning* by Shavlik and Dietterich [SD90].

Machine learning research is published in the proceedings of several large machine learning and artificial intelligence conferences, including the *International Conference on Machine Learning (ML)*, the *ACM Conference on Computational Learning Theory (COLT)*, the *International Joint Conference on Artificial Intelligence (IJCAI)*, and the *American Association of Artificial Intelligence Conference (AAAI)*. Other sources of publication include major machine learning, artificial intelligence, and knowledge system journals, some of which have been mentioned above. Others include *Machine Learning (ML), Artificial Intelligence Journal (AI)*, and *Cognitive Science*. An overview of classification from a statistical pattern recognition perspective can be found in Duda and Hart [DH73].

Pioneering work on data visualization techniques is described in *The Visual Display of Quantitative Information* [Tuf83] and *Envisioning Information* [Tuf90], both by Tufte, and *Graphics and Graphic Information Processing* by Bertin [Ber81]. *Visual Techniques for Exploring Databases* by Keim [Kei97] presents a broad tutorial on visualization for data mining. Major conferences and symposiums on visualization include *ACM Human Factors in Computing Systems (CHI)*, *Visualization*, and the *International Symposium on Information Visualization*. Research on visualization is also published in *Transactions on Visualization and Computer Graphics*, *Journal of Computational and Graphical Statistics*, and *IEEE Computer Graphics and Applications*.

# Data Warehouse and OLAP Technology for Data Mining

**The construction of data warehouses,** which involves data cleaning and data integration, can be viewed as an important preprocessing step for data mining. Moreover, data warehouses provide *on-line analytical processing (OLAP)* tools for the interactive analysis of multidimensional data of varied granularities, which facilitates effective data mining. Furthermore, many other data mining functions, such as classification, prediction, association, and clustering, can be integrated with OLAP operations to enhance interactive mining of knowledge at multiple levels of abstraction. Hence, the data warehouse has become an increasingly important platform for data analysis and on-line analytical processing and will provide an effective platform for data mining. Therefore, prior to presenting a systematic coverage of data mining technology in the remainder of this book, we devote this chapter to an overview of data warehouse technology. Such an overview is essential for understanding data mining technology.

In this chapter, you will learn the basic concepts, general architectures, and major implementation techniques employed in data warehouse and OLAP technology, as well as their relationship with data mining.

## 2.1 What Is a Data Warehouse?

Data warehousing provides architectures and tools for business executives to systematically organize, understand, and use their data to make strategic decisions. A large number of organizations have found that data warehouse systems are valuable tools in today's competitive, fast-evolving world. In the last several years, many firms have spent millions of dollars in building enterprise-wide data warehouses. Many people feel that with competition mounting in every industry, data warehousing is the latest must-have marketing weapon—a way to keep customers by learning more about their needs.

"*So,*" you may ask, full of intrigue, "*what exactly is a data warehouse?*" Data warehouses have been defined in many ways, making it difficult to formulate a rigorous definition. Loosely speaking, a data warehouse refers to a database that is maintained separately from an organization's operational databases. Data warehouse systems allow for the integration of a variety of application systems. They support information processing by providing a solid platform of consolidated historical data for analysis.

According to W. H. Inmon, a leading architect in the construction of data warehouse systems, "A data warehouse is a subject-oriented, integrated, time-variant, and nonvolatile collection of data in support of management's decision making process" [Inm96]. This short, but comprehensive definition presents the major features of a data warehouse. The four keywords, *subject-oriented, integrated, time-variant*, and *nonvolatile*, distinguish data warehouses from other data repository systems, such as relational database systems, transaction processing systems, and file systems. Let's take a closer look at each of these key features.

- **Subject-oriented**: A data warehouse is organized around major subjects, such as customer, supplier, product, and sales. Rather than concentrating on the day-to-day operations and transaction processing of an organization, a data warehouse focuses on the modeling and analysis of data for decision makers. Hence, data warehouses typically provide a simple and concise view around particular subject issues by excluding data that are not useful in the decision support process.

- **Integrated**: A data warehouse is usually constructed by integrating multiple heterogeneous sources, such as relational databases, flat files, and on-line transaction records. Data cleaning and data integration techniques are applied to ensure consistency in naming conventions, encoding structures, attribute measures, and so on.

- **Time-variant**: Data are stored to provide information from a historical perspective (e.g., the past 5–10 years). Every key structure in the data warehouse contains, either implicitly or explicitly, an element of time.

- **Nonvolatile**: A data warehouse is always a physically separate store of data transformed from the application data found in the operational environment. Due to this separation, a data warehouse does not require transaction processing, recovery, and concurrency control mechanisms. It usually requires only two operations in data accessing: *initial loading of data* and *access of data*.

In sum, a data warehouse is a semantically consistent data store that serves as a physical implementation of a decision support data model and stores the information on which an enterprise needs to make strategic decisions. A data warehouse is also often viewed as an architecture, constructed by integrating data from multiple heterogeneous sources to support structured and/or ad hoc queries, analytical reporting, and decision making.

*"OK,"* you now ask, *"what, then, is data warehousing?"* Based on the above, we view data warehousing as the *process of constructing and using data warehouses*. The construction of a data warehouse requires data integration, data cleaning, and data consolidation. The utilization of a data warehouse often necessitates a collection of *decision support* technologies. This allows "knowledge workers" (e.g., managers, analysts, and executives) to use the warehouse to quickly and conveniently obtain an overview of the data, and to make sound decisions based on information in the warehouse. Some authors use the term "data warehousing" to refer only to the process of data warehouse *construction*, while the term "warehouse DBMS" is used to refer to the *management and utilization* of data warehouses. We will not make this distinction here.

*"How are organizations using the information from data warehouses?"* Many organizations use this information to support business decision making activities, including (1) increasing customer focus, which includes the analysis of customer buying patterns (such as buying preference, buying time, budget cycles, and appetites for spending); (2) repositioning products and managing product portfolios by comparing the performance of sales by quarter, by year, and by geographic regions, in order to fine-tune production strategies; (3) analyzing operations and looking for sources of profit; and (4) managing the customer relationships, making environmental corrections, and managing the cost of corporate assets.

Data warehousing is also very useful from the point of view of *heterogeneous database integration*. Many organizations typically collect diverse kinds of data and maintain large databases from multiple, heterogeneous, autonomous, and distributed information sources. To integrate such data, and provide easy and efficient access to it, is highly desirable, yet challenging. Much effort has been spent in the database industry and research community towards achieving this goal.

The traditional database approach to heterogeneous database integration is to build **wrappers** and **integrators** (or **mediators**) on top of multiple, heterogeneous databases (examples include IBM Data Joiner and Informix DataBlade). When a query is posed to a client site, a metadata dictionary is used to translate the query into queries appropriate for the individual heterogeneous sites involved. These queries are then mapped and sent to local query processors. The results returned from the different sites are integrated into a global answer set. This **query-driven approach** requires complex information filtering and integration processes, and competes for resources with processing at local sources. It is inefficient and potentially expensive for frequent queries, especially for queries requiring aggregations.

Data warehousing provides an interesting alternative to the traditional approach of heterogeneous database integration described above. Rather than using a query-driven approach, data warehousing employs an **update-driven** approach in which information from multiple, heterogeneous sources is integrated in advance and stored in a warehouse for direct querying and analysis. Unlike online transaction processing databases, data warehouses do not contain the most current information. However, a data warehouse brings high performance to the integrated heterogeneous database system since data are copied, preprocessed, integrated, annotated, summarized, and restructured into one semantic data store. Furthermore, query processing in data warehouses does not interfere with the processing at local sources. Moreover, data warehouses can store and integrate historical information and support complex multidimensional queries. As a result, data warehousing has become very popular in industry.

### 2.1.1 Differences between Operational Database Systems and Data Warehouses

Since most people are familiar with commercial relational database systems, it is easy to understand what a data warehouse is by comparing these two kinds of systems.

The major task of on-line operational database systems is to perform on-line transaction and query processing. These systems are called **on-line transaction processing (OLTP)** systems. They cover most of the day-to-day operations of an organization, such as purchasing, inventory, manufacturing, banking, payroll, registration, and accounting. Data warehouse systems, on the other hand, serve users or knowledge workers in the role of data analysis and decision making. Such systems can organize and present data in various formats in order to accommodate the diverse needs of the different users. These systems are known as **on-line analytical processing (OLAP)** systems.

The major distinguishing features between OLTP and OLAP are summarized as follows.

- **Users and system orientation**: An OLTP system is *customer-oriented* and is used for transaction and query processing by clerks, clients, and information technology professionals. An OLAP system is *market-oriented* and is used for data analysis by knowledge workers, including managers, executives, and analysts.

- **Data contents**: An OLTP system manages current data that, typically, are too detailed to be easily used for decision making. An OLAP system manages large amounts of historical data, provides facilities for summarization and aggregation, and stores and manages information at different levels of granularity. These features make the data easier to use in informed decision making.

- **Database design**: An OLTP system usually adopts an entity-relationship (ER) data model and an application-oriented database design. An OLAP system typically adopts either a *star* or *snowflake* model (to be discussed in Section 2.2.2) and a subject-oriented database design.

- **View**: An OLTP system focuses mainly on the current data within an enterprise or department, without referring to historical data or data in different organizations. In contrast, an OLAP system often spans multiple versions of

**Table 2.1** Comparison between OLTP and OLAP systems.

| Feature | OLTP | OLAP |
|---|---|---|
| Characteristic | operational processing | informational processing |
| Orientation | transaction | analysis |
| User | clerk, DBA, database professional | knowledge worker (e.g., manager, executive, analyst) |
| Function | day-to-day operations | long-term informational requirements, decision support |
| DB design | ER based, application-oriented | star/snowflake, subject-oriented |
| Data | current; guaranteed up-to-date | historical; accuracy maintained over time |
| Summarization | primitive, highly detailed | summarized, consolidated |
| View | detailed, flat relational | summarized, multidimensional |
| Unit of work | short, simple transaction | complex query |
| Access | read/write | mostly read |
| Focus | data in | information out |
| Operations | index/hash on primary key | lots of scans |
| Number of records accessed | tens | millions |
| Number of users | thousands | hundreds |
| DB size | 100 MB to GB | 100 GB to TB |
| Priority | high performance, high availability | high flexibility, end-user autonomy |
| Metric | transaction throughput | query throughput, response time |

NOTE: Table is partially based on [CD97].

a database schema, due to the evolutionary process of an organization. OLAP systems also deal with information that originates from different organizations, integrating information from many data stores. Because of their huge volume, OLAP data are stored on multiple storage media.

- **Access patterns:** The access patterns of an OLTP system consist mainly of short, atomic transactions. Such a system requires concurrency control and recovery mechanisms. However, accesses to OLAP systems are mostly read-only operations (since most data warehouses store historical rather than up-to-date information), although many could be complex queries.

Other features that distinguish between OLTP and OLAP systems include database size, frequency of operations, and performance metrics. These are summarized in Table 2.1.

### 2.1.2 **But, Why Have a Separate Data Warehouse?**

*"Since operational databases store huge amounts of data,"* you observe, *"why not perform on-line analytical processing directly on such databases instead of spending additional time and resources to construct a separate data warehouse?"* A major reason for such a separation is to help promote the *high performance of both systems.* An operational database is designed and tuned from known tasks and workloads, such as indexing and hashing using primary keys, searching for particular records, and optimizing "canned" queries. On the other hand, data warehouse queries are often complex. They involve the computation of large groups of data at summarized levels, and may require the use of special data organization, access, and implementation methods based on multidimensional views. Processing OLAP queries in operational databases would substantially degrade the performance of operational tasks.

Moreover, an operational database supports the concurrent processing of multiple transactions. Concurrency control and recovery mechanisms, such as locking and logging, are required to ensure the consistency and robustness of transactions. An OLAP query often needs read-only access of data records for summarization and aggregation. Concurrency control and recovery mechanisms, if applied for such OLAP operations, may jeopardize the execution of concurrent transactions and thus substantially reduce the throughput of an OLTP system.

Finally, the separation of operational databases from data warehouses is based on the different structures, contents, and uses of the data in these two systems. Decision support requires historical data, whereas operational databases do not typically maintain historical data. In this context, the data in operational databases, though abundant, is usually far from complete for decision making. Decision support requires consolidation (such as aggregation and summarization) of data from heterogeneous sources, resulting in high-quality, clean, and integrated data. In contrast, operational databases contain only detailed raw data, such as transactions, which need to be consolidated before analysis. Since the two systems provide quite different functionalities and require different kinds of data, it is presently necessary to maintain separate databases. However, many vendors of operational relational database management systems are beginning to optimize such systems so as to support OLAP queries. As this trend continues, the separation between OLTP and OLAP systems is expected to decrease.

## 2.2 **A Multidimensional Data Model**

Data warehouses and OLAP tools are based on a **multidimensional data model**. This model views data in the form of a *data cube*. In this section, you will learn how data cubes model *n*-dimensional data. You will also learn about concept hierarchies and how they can be used in basic OLAP operations to allow interactive mining at multiple levels of abstraction.

### 2.2.1 From Tables and Spreadsheets to Data Cubes

*"What is a data cube?"* A **data cube** allows data to be modeled and viewed in multiple dimensions. It is defined by dimensions and facts.

In general terms, **dimensions** are the perspectives or entities with respect to which an organization wants to keep records. For example, *AllElectronics* may create a *sales* data warehouse in order to keep records of the store's sales with respect to the dimensions *time*, *item*, *branch*, and *location*. These dimensions allow the store to keep track of things like monthly sales of items, and the branches and locations at which the items were sold. Each dimension may have a table associated with it, called a **dimension table**, which further describes the dimension. For example, a dimension table for *item* may contain the attributes *item_name*, *brand*, and *type*. Dimension tables can be specified by users or experts, or automatically generated and adjusted based on data distributions.

A multidimensional data model is typically organized around a central theme, like *sales*, for instance. This theme is represented by a fact table. **Facts** are numerical measures. Think of them as the quantities by which we want to analyze relationships between dimensions. Examples of facts for a sales data warehouse include *dollars_sold* (sales amount in dollars), *units_sold* (number of units sold), and *amount_budgeted*. The **fact table** contains the names of the *facts*, or measures, as well as keys to each of the related dimension tables. You will soon get a clearer picture of how this works when we look at multidimensional schemas.

Although we usually think of cubes as 3-D geometric structures, in data warehousing the data cube is *n*-dimensional. To gain a better understanding of data cubes and the multidimensional data model, let's start by looking at a simple 2-D data cube that is, in fact, a table or spreadsheet for sales data from *AllElectronics*. In particular, we will look at the *AllElectronics* sales data for items sold per quarter in the city of Vancouver. These data are shown in Table 2.2. In this 2-D representation, the sales for Vancouver are shown with respect to the *time* dimension

**Table 2.2** A 2-D view of sales data for *AllElectronics* according to the dimensions *time* and *item*, where the sales are from branches located in the city of Vancouver. The measure displayed is *dollars_sold* (in thousands).

| | **location** = *"Vancouver"* | | | |
|---|---|---|---|---|
| | **item** (type) | | | |
| **time** (quarter) | home entertainment | computer | phone | security |
| Q1 | 605 | 825 | 14 | 400 |
| Q2 | 680 | 952 | 31 | 512 |
| Q3 | 812 | 1023 | 30 | 501 |
| Q4 | 927 | 1038 | 38 | 580 |

**Table 2.3**  A 3-D view of sales data for *AllElectronics*, according to the dimensions *time*, *item*, and *location*. The measure displayed is *dollars_sold* (in thousands).

| | location = "Chicago" item | | | | location = "New York" item | | | | location = "Toronto" item | | | | location = "Vancouver" item | | | |
|---|---|---|---|---|---|---|---|---|---|---|---|---|---|---|---|---|
| time | home ent. | comp. | phone | sec. | home ent. | comp. | phone | sec. | home ent. | comp. | phone | sec. | home ent. | comp. | phone | sec. |
| Q1 | 854 | 882 | 89 | 623 | 1087 | 968 | 38 | 872 | 818 | 746 | 43 | 591 | 605 | 825 | 14 | 400 |
| Q2 | 943 | 890 | 64 | 698 | 1130 | 1024 | 41 | 925 | 894 | 769 | 52 | 682 | 680 | 952 | 31 | 512 |
| Q3 | 1032 | 924 | 59 | 789 | 1034 | 1048 | 45 | 1002 | 940 | 795 | 58 | 728 | 812 | 1023 | 30 | 501 |
| Q4 | 1129 | 992 | 63 | 870 | 1142 | 1091 | 54 | 984 | 978 | 864 | 59 | 784 | 927 | 1038 | 38 | 580 |

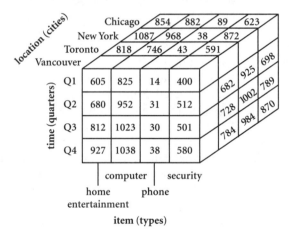

**Figure 2.1**  A 3-D data cube representation of the data in Table 2.3, according to the dimensions *time*, *item*, and *location*.  The measure displayed is *dollars_sold* (in thousands).

(organized in quarters) and the *item* dimension (organized according to the types of items sold). The fact or measure displayed is *dollars_sold* (in thousands).

Now, suppose that we would like to view the sales data with a third dimension. For instance, suppose we would like to view the data according to *time*, *item*, as well as *location* for the cities Chicago, New York, Toronto, and Vancouver. These 3-D data are shown in Table 2.3. The 3-D data of Table 2.3 are represented as a series of 2-D tables. Conceptually, we may also represent the same data in the form of a 3-D data cube, as in Figure 2.1.

Suppose that we would now like to view our sales data with an additional fourth dimension, such as *supplier*. Viewing things in 4-D becomes tricky. However, we

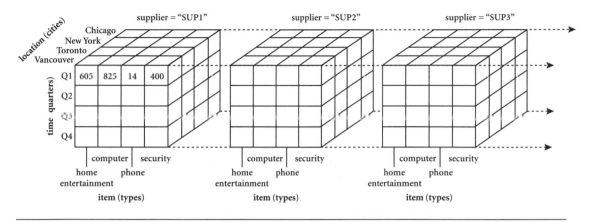

**Figure 2.2** A 4-D data cube representation of sales data, according to the dimensions *time*, *item*, *location*, and *supplier*. The measure displayed is *dollars_sold* (in thousands). For improved readability, only some of the cube values are shown.

can think of a 4-D cube as being a series of 3-D cubes, as shown in Figure 2.2. If we continue in this way, we may display any *n*-D data as a series of $(n-1)$-D "cubes." The data cube is a metaphor for multidimensional data storage. The actual physical storage of such data may differ from its logical representation. The important thing to remember is that data cubes are *n*-dimensional and do not confine data to 3-D.

The above tables show the data at different degrees of summarization. In the data warehousing research literature, a data cube such as each of the above is referred to as a **cuboid**. Given a set of dimensions, we can construct a *lattice* of cuboids, each showing the data at a different level of summarization, or **group by**[1] (i.e., summarized by a different subset of the dimensions). The lattice of cuboids is then referred to as a data cube. Figure 2.3 shows a lattice of cuboids forming a data cube for the dimensions *time*, *item*, *location*, and *supplier*.

The cuboid that holds the lowest level of summarization is called the **base cuboid**. For example, the 4-D cuboid in Figure 2.2 is the base cuboid for the given *time*, *item*, *location*, and *supplier* dimensions. Figure 2.1 is a 3-D (nonbase) cuboid for *time*, *item*, and *location*, summarized for all suppliers. The 0-D cuboid, which holds the highest level of summarization, is called the **apex cuboid**. In our example, this is the total sales, or *dollars_sold*, summarized over all four dimensions. The apex cuboid is typically denoted by **all**.

---

[1] Note that in this text, query language keywords are displayed in sans serif font.

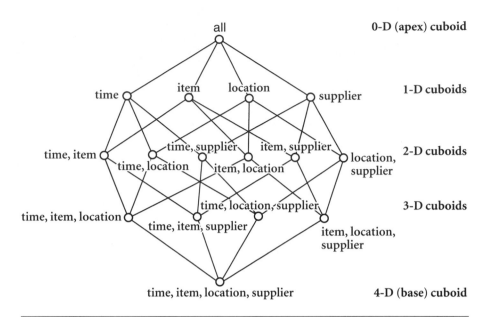

**Figure 2.3**  Lattice of cuboids, making up a 4-D data cube for the dimensions *time*, *item*, *location*, and *supplier*. Each cuboid represents a different degree of summarization.

### 2.2.2 Stars, Snowflakes, and Fact Constellations: Schemas for Multidimensional Databases

The entity-relationship data model is commonly used in the design of relational databases, where a database schema consists of a set of entities and the relationships between them. Such a data model is appropriate for on-line transaction processing. A data warehouse, however, requires a concise, subject-oriented schema that facilitates on-line data analysis.

The most popular data model for a data warehouse is a **multidimensional model**. Such a model can exist in the form of a **star schema**, a **snowflake schema**, or a **fact constellation schema**. Let's have a look at each of these schema types.

**Star schema:**   The most common modeling paradigm is the star schema, in which the data warehouse contains (1) a large central table (**fact table**) containing the bulk of the data, with no redundancy, and (2) a set of smaller attendant tables (**dimension tables**), one for each dimension. The schema graph resembles a starburst, with the dimension tables displayed in a radial pattern around the central fact table.

**Example 2.1**   An example of a star schema for *AllElectronics* sales is shown in Figure 2.4. Sales are considered along four dimensions, namely, *time, item, branch*, and *location*.

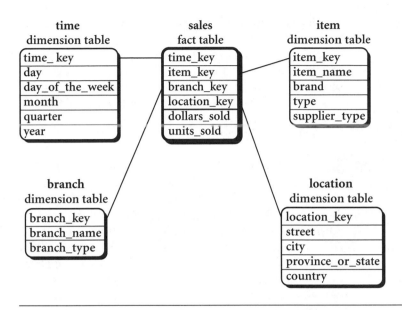

**Figure 2.4**  Star schema of a data warehouse for sales.

The schema contains a central fact table for *sales* that contains keys to each of the four dimensions, along with two measures: *dollars_sold* and *units_sold*. To minimize the size of the fact table, dimension identifiers (such as *time_key* and *item_key*) are system-generated identifiers.   ∎

Notice that in the star schema, each dimension is represented by only one table, and each table contains a set of attributes. For example, the *location* dimension table contains the attribute set {*location_key, street, city, province_or_state, country*}. This constraint may introduce some redundancy. For example, "*Vancouver*" and "*Victoria*" are both cities in the Canadian province of British Columbia. Entries for such cities in the *location* dimension table will create redundancy among the attributes *province_or_state* and *country*, that is, (..., Vancouver, British Columbia, Canada) and (..., Victoria, British Columbia, Canada). Moreover, the attributes within a dimension table may form either a hierarchy (total order) or a lattice (partial order).

**Snowflake schema:**   The snowflake schema is a variant of the star schema model, where some dimension tables are *normalized*, thereby further splitting the data into additional tables. The resulting schema graph forms a shape similar to a snowflake.

The major difference between the snowflake and star schema models is that the dimension tables of the snowflake model may be kept in normalized form to reduce redundancies. Such a table is easy to maintain and saves storage space because a large dimension table can become enormous when the dimensional structure is included as columns. However, this saving of space is negligible in comparison to the typical magnitude of the fact table. Furthermore, the snowflake structure can reduce the effectiveness of browsing since more joins will be needed to execute a query. Consequently, the system performance may be adversely impacted. Hence, the snowflake schema is not as popular as the star schema in data warehouse design.

**Example 2.2** An example of a snowflake schema for *AllElectronics* sales is given in Figure 2.5. Here, the *sales* fact table is identical to that of the star schema in Figure 2.4. The main difference between the two schemas is in the definition of dimension tables. The single dimension table for *item* in the star schema is normalized in the snowflake schema, resulting in new *item* and *supplier* tables. For example, the *item* dimension table now contains the attributes *item_key, item_name, brand, type*, and *supplier_key*, where *supplier_key* is linked to the *supplier* dimension table, containing *supplier_key* and *supplier_type* information. Similarly, the single dimension table for *location* in the star schema can be normalized into two new tables: *location* and *city*. The *city_key* in the new *location* table links to the *city* dimension. Notice that further normalization can be performed on *province_or_state* and *country* in the snowflake schema shown in Figure 2.5, when desirable. ∎

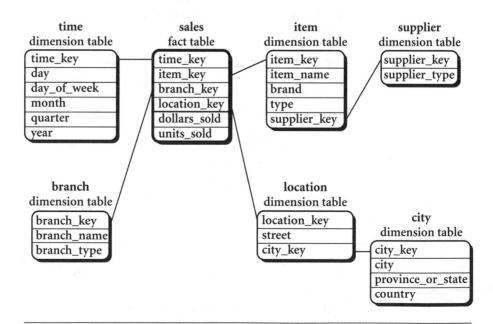

**Figure 2.5** Snowflake schema of a data warehouse for sales.

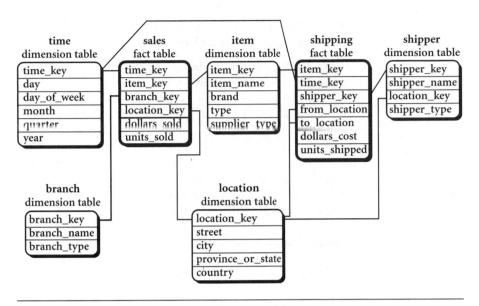

**Figure 2.6**    Fact constellation schema of a data warehouse for sales and shipping.

*too complex*

**Fact constellation:**   Sophisticated applications may require multiple fact tables to *share* dimension tables. This kind of schema can be viewed as a collection of stars, and hence is called a **galaxy schema** or a **fact constellation**.

**Example 2.3**    An example of a fact constellation schema is shown in Figure 2.6. This schema specifies two fact tables, *sales* and *shipping*. The *sales* table definition is identical to that of the star schema (Figure 2.4). The *shipping* table has five dimensions, or keys: *item_key, time_key, shipper_key, from_location*, and *to_location*, and two measures: *dollars_cost* and *units_shipped*. A fact constellation schema allows dimension tables to be shared between fact tables. For example, the dimensions tables for *time, item*, and *location* are shared between both the *sales* and *shipping* fact tables. ∎

In data warehousing, there is a distinction between a data warehouse and a data mart. A data warehouse collects information about subjects that span the *entire organization*, such as *customers, items, sales, assets*, and *personnel*, and thus its scope is *enterprise-wide*. For data warehouses, the fact constellation schema is commonly used since it can model multiple, interrelated subjects. A **data mart**, on the other hand, is a department subset of the data warehouse that focuses on selected subjects, and thus its scope is *department-wide*. For data marts, the *star* or *snowflake* schema are commonly used since both are geared towards modeling single subjects, although the star schema is more popular and efficient.

### 2.2.3 Examples for Defining Star, Snowflake, and Fact Constellation Schemas

*"How can I define a multidimensional schema for my data?"* Just as relational query languages like SQL can be used to specify relational queries, a **data mining query language** can be used to specify data mining tasks. In particular, we examine an SQL-based data mining query language called **DMQL**, which contains language primitives for defining data warehouses and data marts. Language primitives for specifying other data mining tasks, such as the mining of concept/class descriptions, associations, classifications, and so on, will be introduced in Chapter 4.

Data warehouses and data marts can be defined using two language primitives, one for *cube definition* and one for *dimension definition*. The *cube definition* statement has the following syntax.

> **define cube** ⟨ cube_name⟩ **[**⟨ dimension_list)**]** : ⟨ measure_list⟩

The *dimension definition* statement has the following syntax.

> **define dimension** ⟨ dimension_name⟩ **as (**⟨ attribute_or_subdimension_list⟩**)**

Let's look at examples of how to define the star, snowflake, and fact constellation schemas of Examples 2.1 to 2.3 using DMQL. DMQL keywords are displayed in **sans serif** font.

**Example 2.4** The star schema of Example 2.1 and Figure 2.4 is defined in DMQL as follows.

> **define cube** sales_star [time, item, branch, location]:
> dollars_sold = sum(sales_in_dollars), units_sold = count(*)
> **define dimension** time **as** (time_key, day, day_of_week, month, quarter, year)
> **define dimension** item **as** (item_key, item_name, brand, type, supplier_type)
> **define dimension** branch **as** (branch_key, branch_name, branch_type)
> **define dimension** location **as** (location_key, street, city, province_or_state, country)

The **define cube** statement defines a data cube called *sales_star*, which corresponds to the central *sales* fact table of Example 2.1. This command specifies the dimensions and the two measures, *dollars_sold* and *units_sold*. The data cube has four dimensions, namely, *time, item, branch,* and *location*. A **define dimension** statement is used to define each of the dimensions. ∎

**Example 2.5** The snowflake schema of Example 2.2 and Figure 2.5 is defined in DMQL as follows.

> **define cube** sales_snowflake [time, item, branch, location]:
> dollars_sold = sum(sales_in_dollars), units_sold = count(*)
> **define dimension** time **as** (time_key, day, day_of_week, month, quarter, year)

> **define dimension** item **as** (item_key, item_name, brand, type,
>         supplier (supplier_key, supplier_type))
> **define dimension** branch **as** (branch_key, branch_name, branch_type)
> **define dimension** location **as** (location_key, street,
>         city (city_key, city, province_or_state, country))

This definition is similar to that of *sales_star* (Example 2.4), except that, here, the *item* and *location* dimension tables are normalized. For instance, the *item* dimension of the *sales_star* data cube has been normalized in the *sales_snowflake* cube into two dimension tables, *item* and *supplier*. Note that the dimension definition for *supplier* is specified within the definition for *item*. Defining *supplier* in this way implicitly creates a *supplier_key* in the *item* dimension table definition. Similarly, the *location* dimension of the *sales_star* data cube has been normalized in the *sales_snowflake* cube into two dimension tables, *location* and *city*. The dimension definition for *city* is specified within the definition for *location*. In this way, a *city_key* is implicitly created in the *location* dimension table definition. ■

Finally, a fact constellation schema can be defined as a set of interconnected cubes. Below is an example.

**Example 2.6** The fact constellation schema of Example 2.3 and Figure 2.6 is defined in DMQL as follows.

> **define cube** sales [time, item, branch, location]:
>         dollars_sold = sum(sales_in_dollars), units_sold = count(*)
> **define dimension** time **as** (time_key, day, day_of_week, month, quarter, year)
> **define dimension** item **as** (item_key, item_name, brand, type, supplier_type)
> **define dimension** branch **as** (branch_key, branch_name, branch_type)
> **define dimension** location **as** (location_key, street, city, province_or_state, country)
> **define cube** shipping [time, item, shipper, from_location, to_location]:
>         dollars_cost = sum(cost_in_dollars), units_shipped = count(*)
> **define dimension** time **as** time **in cube** sales
> **define dimension** item **as** item **in cube** sales
> **define dimension** shipper **as** (shipper_key, shipper_name,
>         location **as** location **in cube** sales, shipper_type)
> **define dimension** from_location **as** location **in cube** sales
> **define dimension** to_location **as** location **in cube** sales

A **define cube** statement is used to define data cubes for *sales* and *shipping*, corresponding to the two fact tables of the schema of Example 2.3. Note that the *time*, *item*, and *location* dimensions of the *sales* cube are shared with the *shipping* cube. This is indicated for the *time* dimension, for example, as follows. Under the **define cube** statement for *shipping*, the statement "**define dimension** *time* **as** *time* **in cube** *sales*" is specified. ■

## 2.2.4 Measures: Their Categorization and Computation

*"How are measures computed?"* To answer this question, we will first look at how measures can be categorized. Note that a multidimensional point in the data cube space can be defined by a set of dimension-value pairs, for example, ⟨*time* = *"Q1"*, *location* = *"Vancouver"*, *item* = *"computer"*⟩. A data cube **measure** is a numerical function that can be evaluated at each point in the data cube space. A measure value is computed for a given point by aggregating the data corresponding to the respective dimension-value pairs defining the given point. We will look at concrete examples of this shortly.

Measures can be organized into three categories, based on the kind of aggregate functions used.

**Distributive:** An aggregate function is *distributive* if it can be computed in a distributed manner as follows. Suppose the data are partitioned into *n* sets. The computation of the function on each partition derives one aggregate value. If the result derived by applying the function to the *n* aggregate values is the same as that derived by applying the function on all the data without partitioning, the function can be computed in a distributed manner. For example, count() can be computed for a data cube by first partitioning the cube into a set of subcubes, computing count() for each subcube, and then summing up the counts obtained for each subcube. Hence, count() is a distributive aggregate function. For the same reason, sum(), min(), and max() are distributive aggregate functions. A measure is *distributive* if it is obtained by applying a distributive aggregate function.

**Algebraic:** An aggregate function is *algebraic* if it can be computed by an algebraic function with *M* arguments (where *M* is a bounded positive integer), each of which is obtained by applying a distributive aggregate function. For example, avg() (average) can be computed by sum()/count() where both sum() and count() are distributive aggregate functions. Similarly, it can be shown that min_N(), max_N(), and standard_deviation() are algebraic aggregate functions. A measure is *algebraic* if it is obtained by applying an algebraic aggregate function.

**Holistic:** An aggregate function is *holistic* if there is no constant bound on the storage size needed to describe a subaggregate. That is, there does not exist an algebraic function with *M* arguments (where *M* is a constant) that characterizes the computation. Common examples of holistic functions include median(), mode() (i.e., the most frequently occurring item(s)), and rank(). A measure is *holistic* if it is obtained by applying a holistic aggregate function.

Most large data cube applications require efficient computation of distributive and algebraic measures. Many efficient techniques for this exist. In contrast, it can be difficult to compute holistic measures efficiently. Efficient techniques to *approximate* the computation of some holistic measures, however, do exist. For example, instead of computing the exact median(), there are techniques that can estimate the approximate median value for a large data set with satisfactory results. In many cases, such techniques are sufficient to overcome the difficulties of efficient computation of holistic measures.

**Example 2.7** Many measures of a data cube can be computed by relational aggregation operations. In Figure 2.4, we saw a star schema for *AllElectronics* sales that contains two measures, namely, *dollars_sold* and *units_sold*. In Example 2.4, the *sales_star* data cube corresponding to the schema was defined using DMQL commands. *"But, how are these commands interpreted in order to generate the specified data cube?"*

Suppose that the relational database schema of *AllElectronics* is the following:

time(time_key, day, day_of_week, month, quarter, year)
item(item_key, item_name, brand, type, supplier_type)
branch(branch_key, branch_name, branch_type)
location(location_key, street, city, province_or_state, country)
sales(time_key, item_key, branch_key, location_key, number_of_units_sold, price)

The DMQL specification of Example 2.4 is translated into the following SQL query, which generates the required *sales_star* cube. Here, the sum aggregate function is used to compute both *dollars_sold* and *units_sold*.

```
select s.time_key, s.item_key, s.branch_key, s.location_key,
       sum(s.number_of_units_sold * s.price), sum(s.number_of_units_sold)
from time t, item i, branch b, location l, sales s,
where s.time_key = t.time_key and s.item_key = i.item_key
       and s.branch_key = b.branch_key and s.location_key = l.location_key
group by s.time_key, s.item_key, s.branch_key, s.location_key
```

The cube created in the above query is the base cuboid of the *sales_star* data cube. It contains all of the dimensions specified in the data cube definition, where the granularity of each dimension is at the **join key** level. A join key is a key that links a fact table and a dimension table. The fact table associated with a base cuboid is sometimes referred to as the **base fact table**.

By changing the **group by** clauses, we may generate other cuboids for the *sales_star* data cube. For example, instead of grouping by *s.time_key*, we can group by *t.month*, which will sum up the measures of each group by month. Also, removing "**group by** *s.branch_key*" will generate a higher-level cuboid (where sales are summed for all branches, rather than broken down per branch). Suppose we modify the above SQL query by removing *all* of the **group by** clauses. This will result in obtaining the total sum of *dollars_sold* and the total count of *units_sold* for the given data. This zero-dimensional cuboid is the apex cuboid of the *sales_star* data cube. In addition, other cuboids can be generated by applying selection and/or projection operations on the base cuboid, resulting in a lattice of cuboids as described in Section 2.2.1. Each cuboid corresponds to a different degree of summarization of the given data. ∎

Most of the current data cube technology confines the measures of multidimensional databases to *numerical data*. However, measures can also be applied to other kinds of data, such as spatial, multimedia, or text data. Techniques for this are discussed in Chapter 9.

## 2.2.5 Introducing Concept Hierarchies

*"What is a concept hierarchy?"* A **concept hierarchy** defines a sequence of mappings from a set of low-level concepts to higher-level, more general concepts. Consider a concept hierarchy for the dimension *location*. City values for *location* include Vancouver, Toronto, New York, and Chicago. Each city, however, can be mapped to the province or state to which it belongs. For example, Vancouver can be mapped to British Columbia, and Chicago to Illinois. The provinces and states can in turn be mapped to the country to which they belong, such as Canada or the USA. These mappings form a concept hierarchy for the dimension *location*, mapping a set of low-level concepts (i.e., cities) to higher-level, more general concepts (i.e., countries). The concept hierarchy described above is illustrated in Figure 2.7.

Many concept hierarchies are implicit within the database schema. For example, suppose that the dimension *location* is described by the attributes *number*,

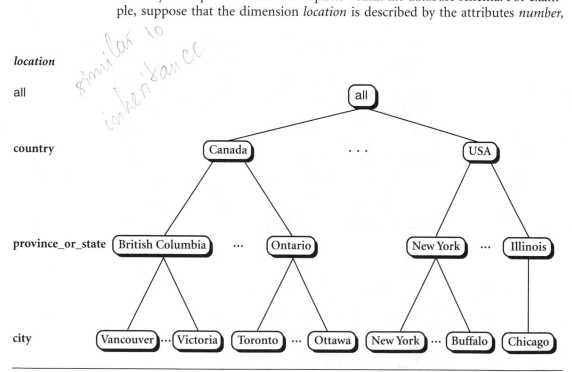

**Figure 2.7**   A concept hierarchy for the dimension *location*. Due to space limitations, not all of the nodes of the hierarchy are shown (as indicated by the use of " . . . " between nodes).

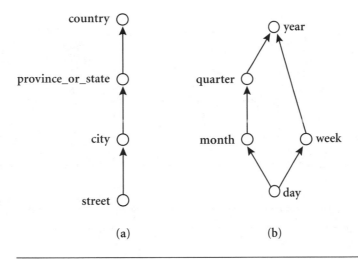

**Figure 2.8** Hierarchical and lattice structures of attributes in warehouse dimensions: (a) a hierarchy for *location*; (b) a lattice for *time*.

*street, city, province_or_state, zipcode*, and *country*. These attributes are related by a total order, forming a concept hierarchy such as "*street* < *city* < *province_or_state* < *country*". This hierarchy is shown in Figure 2.8(a). Alternatively, the attributes of a dimension may be organized in a partial order, forming a **lattice**. An example of a partial order for the *time* dimension based on the attributes *day, week, month, quarter*, and *year* is "*day* < *{month <quarter; week}* < *year*".[2] This lattice structure is shown in Figure 2.8(b). A concept hierarchy that is a total or partial order among attributes in a database schema is called a **schema hierarchy**. Concept hierarchies that are common to many applications may be predefined in the data mining system, such as the the concept hierarchy for *time*. Data mining systems should provide users with the flexibility to tailor predefined hierarchies according to their particular needs. For example, users may like to define a fiscal year starting on April 1, or an academic year starting on September 1.

Concept hierarchies may also be defined by discretizing or grouping values for a given dimension or attribute, resulting in a **set-grouping hierarchy**. A total or partial order can be defined among groups of values. An example of a set-grouping hierarchy is shown in Figure 2.9 for the dimension *price*, where an interval ($X ... $Y] denotes the range from $X (exclusive) to $Y (inclusive).

---

[2] Since a *week* often crosses the boundary of two consecutive months, it is usually not treated as a lower abstraction of *month*. Instead, it is often treated as a lower abstraction of *year*, since a year contains approximately 52 weeks.

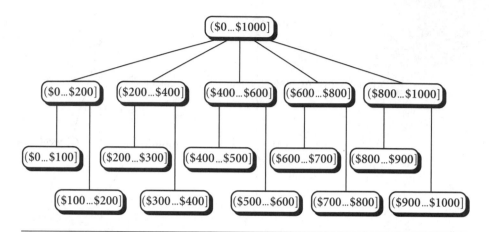

**Figure 2.9** A concept hierarchy for the attribute *price*.

There may be more than one concept hierarchy for a given attribute or dimension, based on different user viewpoints. For instance, a user may prefer to organize *price* by defining ranges for *inexpensive, moderately_priced*, and *expensive*.

Concept hierarchies may be provided manually by system users, domain experts, knowledge engineers, or automatically generated based on statistical analysis of the data distribution. The automatic generation of concept hierarchies is discussed in Chapter 3. Concept hierarchies are further discussed in Chapter 4.

Concept hierarchies allow data to be handled at varying levels of abstraction, as we shall see in the following subsection.

## 2.2.6 OLAP Operations in the Multidimensional Data Model

*"How are concept hierarchies useful in OLAP?"* In the multidimensional model, data are organized into multiple dimensions, and each dimension contains multiple levels of abstraction defined by concept hierarchies. This organization provides users with the flexibility to view data from different perspectives. A number of OLAP data cube operations exist to materialize these different views, allowing interactive querying and analysis of the data at hand. Hence, OLAP provides a user-friendly environment for interactive data analysis.

**Example 2.8**  Let's have a look at some typical OLAP operations for multidimensional data. Each of the operations described below is illustrated in Figure 2.10. At the center of the figure is a data cube for *AllElectronics* sales. The cube contains the dimensions *location, time*, and *item*, where *location* is aggregated with respect to city values, *time* is aggregated with respect to quarters, and *item* is aggregated with respect to item types. To aid in our explanation, we refer to this cube as the central cube. The

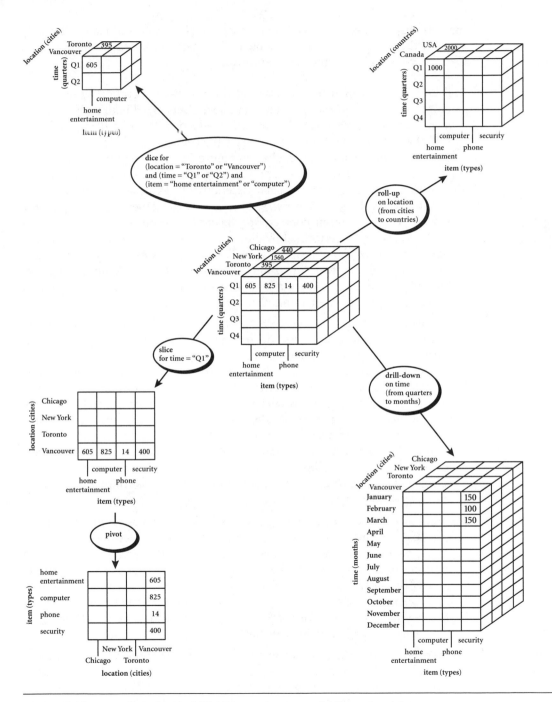

**Figure 2.10**   Examples of typical OLAP operations on multidimensional data.

measure displayed is *dollars-sold* (in thousands). (For improved readability, only some of the cubes' cell values are shown.) The data examined are for the cities Chicago, New York, Toronto, and Vancouver.

**Roll-up:** The roll-up operation (also called the *drill-up* operation by some vendors) performs aggregation on a data cube, either by *climbing up a concept hierarchy* for a dimension or by *dimension reduction*. Figure 2.10 shows the result of a roll-up operation performed on the central cube by climbing up the concept hierarchy for *location* given in Figure 2.7. This hierarchy was defined as the total order *street < city < province_or_state < country*. The roll-up operation shown aggregates the data by ascending the *location* hierarchy from the level of *city* to the level of *country*. In other words, rather than grouping the data by city, the resulting cube groups the data by country.

When roll-up is performed by dimension reduction, one or more dimensions are removed from the given cube. For example, consider a sales data cube containing only the two dimensions *location* and *time*. Roll-up may be performed by removing, say, the *time* dimension, resulting in an aggregation of the total sales by location, rather than by location and by time.

**Drill-down:** Drill-down is the reverse of roll-up. It navigates from less detailed data to more detailed data. Drill-down can be realized by either *stepping down a concept hierarchy* for a dimension or *introducing additional dimensions*. Figure 2.10 shows the result of a drill-down operation performed on the central cube by stepping down a concept hierarchy for *time* defined as *day < month < quarter < year*. Drill-down occurs by descending the *time* hierarchy from the level of *quarter* to the more detailed level of *month*. The resulting data cube details the total sales per month rather than summarized by quarter.

Since a drill-down adds more detail to the given data, it can also be performed by adding new dimensions to a cube. For example, a drill-down on the central cube of Figure 2.10 can occur by introducing an additional dimension, such as *customer_type*.

**Slice and dice:** The *slice* operation performs a selection on one dimension of the given cube, resulting in a subcube. Figure 2.10 shows a slice operation where the sales data are selected from the central cube for the dimension *time* using the criterion *time = "Q1"*. The *dice* operation defines a subcube by performing a selection on two or more dimensions. Figure 2.10 shows a dice operation on the central cube based on the following selection criteria that involve three dimensions: (*location = "Toronto"* **or** *"Vancouver"*) **and** (*time = "Q1"* **or** *"Q2"*) **and** (*item = "home entertainment"* **or** *"computer"*).

**Pivot (rotate):** *Pivot* (also called *rotate*) is a visualization operation that rotates the data axes in view in order to provide an alternative presentation of the data. Figure 2.10 shows a pivot operation where the *item* and *location* axes in a 2-D slice are rotated. Other examples include rotating the axes in a 3-D cube, or transforming a 3-D cube into a series of 2-D planes.

**Other OLAP operations:**   Some OLAP systems offer additional drilling operations. For example, **drill-across** executes queries involving (i.e., across) more
than one fact table. The **drill-through** operation makes use of relational SQL
facilities to drill through the bottom level of a data cube down to its back-end
relational tables.

Other OLAP operations may include ranking the top $N$ or bottom $N$ items
in lists, as well as computing moving averages, growth rates, interests, internal
rates of return, depreciation, currency conversions, and statistical functions.  ■

OLAP offers analytical modeling capabilities, including a calculation engine for
deriving ratios, variance, and so on, and for computing measures across multiple
dimensions. It can generate summarizations, aggregations, and hierarchies at
each granularity level and at every dimension intersection. OLAP also supports
functional models for forecasting, trend analysis, and statistical analysis. In this
context, an OLAP engine is a powerful data analysis tool.

### OLAP Systems versus Statistical Databases

Many of the characteristics of OLAP systems, such as the use of a multidimensional data model and concept hierarchies, the association of measures with dimensions, and the notions of roll-up and drill-down, also exist in earlier work
on statistical databases (SDBs). A **statistical database** is a database system that is
designed to support statistical applications. Similarities between the two types of
systems are rarely discussed, mainly due to differences in terminology and application domains.

OLAP and SDB systems, however, have distinguishing differences. While SDBs
tend to focus on socioeconomic applications, OLAP has been targeted for business
applications. Privacy issues regarding concept hierarchies are a major concern for
SDBs. For example, given summarized socioeconomic data, it is controversial to
allow users to view the corresponding low-level data. Finally, unlike SDBs, OLAP
systems are designed for handling huge amounts of data efficiently.

## 2.2.7 A Starnet Query Model for Querying Multidimensional Databases

The querying of multidimensional databases can be based on a **starnet model**. A
starnet model consists of radial lines emanating from a central point, where each
line represents a concept hierarchy for a dimension. Each abstraction level in the
hierarchy is called a **footprint**. These represent the granularities available for use
by OLAP operations such as drill-down and roll-up.

**Example 2.9** A starnet query model for the *AllElectronics* data warehouse is shown in Figure 2.11. This starnet consists of four radial lines, representing concept hierarchies
for the dimensions *location, customer, item,* and *time,* respectively. Each line consists of footprints representing abstraction levels of the dimension. For example,

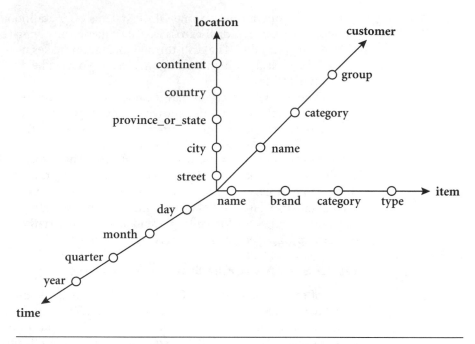

**Figure 2.11** Modeling business queries: a starnet model.

the *time* line has four footprints: "day," "month," "quarter," and "year." A concept hierarchy may involve a single attribute (like *date* for the *time* hierarchy), or several attributes (e.g., the concept hierarchy for *location* involves the attributes *street, city, province_or_state*, and *country*). In order to examine the item sales at *AllElectronics*, users can roll up along the *time* dimension from *month* to *quarter*, or, say, drill down along the *location* dimension from *country* to *city*. Concept hierarchies can be used to **generalize** data by replacing low-level values (such as "day" for the *time* dimension) by higher-level abstractions (such as "year"), or to **specialize** data by replacing higher-level abstractions with lower-level values. ∎

# 2.3 Data Warehouse Architecture

In this section, we discuss issues regarding data warehouse architecture. Section 2.3.1 gives a general account of how to design and construct a data warehouse. Section 2.3.2 describes a three-tier data warehouse architecture. Section 2.3.3 presents various types of warehouse servers for OLAP processing.

## 2.3.1 Steps for the Design and Construction of Data Warehouses

This subsection presents a business analysis framework for data warehouse design. The basic steps involved in the design process are also described.

### The Design of a Data Warehouse: A Business Analysis Framework

*"What does the data warehouse provide for business analysts?"* First, having a data warehouse may provide a *competitive advantage* by presenting relevant information from which to measure performance and make critical adjustments in order to help win over competitors. Second, a data warehouse can enhance business *productivity* since it is able to quickly and efficiently gather information that accurately describes the organization. Third, a data warehouse facilitates *customer relationship management* since it provides a consistent view of customers and items across all lines of business, all departments, and all markets. Finally, a data warehouse may bring about *cost reduction* by tracking trends, patterns, and exceptions over long periods of time in a consistent and reliable manner.

To design an effective data warehouse one needs to understand and analyze business needs and construct a *business analysis framework*. The construction of a large and complex information system can be viewed as the construction of a large and complex building, for which the owner, architect, and builder have different views. These views are combined to form a complex framework that represents the top-down, business-driven, or owner's perspective, as well as the bottom-up, builder-driven, or implementor's view of the information system.

Four different views regarding the design of a data warehouse must be considered: the *top-down view*, the *data source view*, the *data warehouse view*, and the *business query view*.

- The **top-down view** allows the selection of the relevant information necessary for the data warehouse. This information matches the current and coming business needs.

- The **data source view** exposes the information being captured, stored, and managed by operational systems. This information may be documented at various levels of detail and accuracy, from individual data source tables to integrated data source tables. Data sources are often modeled by traditional data modeling techniques, such as the entity-relationship model or CASE (computer-aided software engineering) tools.

- The **data warehouse view** includes fact tables and dimension tables. It represents the information that is stored inside the data warehouse, including precalculated totals and counts, as well as information regarding the source, date, and time of origin, added to provide historical context.

- Finally, the **business query view** is the perspective of data in the data warehouse from the viewpoint of the end user.

Building and using a data warehouse is a complex task since it requires *business skills, technology skills*, and *program management skills*. Regarding *business skills*, building a data warehouse involves understanding how such systems store and manage their data, how to build **extractors** that transfer data from the operational system to the data warehouse, and how to build **warehouse refresh software** that keeps the data warehouse reasonably up-to-date with the operational system's data. Using a data warehouse involves understanding the significance of the data it contains, as well as understanding and translating the business requirements into queries that can be satisfied by the data warehouse. Regarding *technology skills*, data analysts are required to understand how to make assessments from quantitative information and derive facts based on conclusions from historical information in the data warehouse. These skills include the ability to discover patterns and trends, to extrapolate trends based on history and look for anomalies or paradigm shifts, and to present coherent managerial recommendations based on such analysis. Finally, *program management skills* involve the need to interface with many technologies, vendors, and end users in order to deliver results in a timely and cost-effective manner.

### The Process of Data Warehouse Design

*"How can I design a data warehouse?"* A data warehouse can be built using a *top-down approach*, a *bottom-up approach*, or a *combination of both*. The **top-down approach** starts with the overall design and planning. It is useful in cases where the technology is mature and well known, and where the business problems that must be solved are clear and well understood. The **bottom-up approach** starts with experiments and prototypes. This is useful in the early stage of business modeling and technology development. It allows an organization to move forward at considerably less expense and to evaluate the benefits of the technology before making significant commitments. In the **combined approach**, an organization can exploit the planned and strategic nature of the top-down approach while retaining the rapid implementation and opportunistic application of the bottom-up approach.

From the software engineering point of view, the design and construction of a data warehouse may consist of the following steps: *planning, requirements study, problem analysis, warehouse design, data integration and testing*, and finally *deployment of the data warehouse*. Large software systems can be developed using two methodologies: the *waterfall method* or the *spiral method*. The **waterfall method** performs a structured and systematic analysis at each step before proceeding to the next, which is like a waterfall, falling from one step to the next. The **spiral method** involves the rapid generation of increasingly functional systems, with short intervals between successive releases. This is considered a good choice for data warehouse development, especially for data marts, because the turnaround time is short, modifications can be done quickly, and new designs and technologies can be adapted in a timely manner.

In general, the warehouse design process consists of the following steps:

1. Choose a *business process* to model, for example, orders, invoices, shipments, inventory, account administration, sales, and the general ledger. If the business process is organizational and involves multiple complex object collections, a data warehouse model should be followed. However, if the process is departmental and focuses on the analysis of one kind of business process, a data mart model should be chosen.

2. Choose the *grain* of the business process. The grain is the fundamental, atomic level of data to be represented in the fact table for this process, for example, individual transactions, individual daily snapshots, and so on.

3. Choose the *dimensions* that will apply to each fact table record. Typical dimensions are time, item, customer, supplier, warehouse, transaction type, and status.

4. Choose the *measures* that will populate each fact table record. Typical measures are numeric additive quantities like *dollars_sold* and *units_sold*.

Since data warehouse construction is a difficult and long-term task, its implementation scope should be clearly defined. The goals of an initial data warehouse implementation should be *specific, achievable*, and *measurable*. This involves determining the time and budget allocations, the subset of the organization that is to be modeled, the number of data sources selected, and the number and types of departments to be served.

Once a data warehouse is designed and constructed, the initial deployment of the warehouse includes initial installation, rollout planning, training, and orientation. Platform upgrades and maintenance must also be considered. Data warehouse administration includes data refreshment, data source synchronization, planning for disaster recovery, managing access control and security, managing data growth, managing database performance, and data warehouse enhancement and extension. Scope management includes controlling the number and range of queries, dimensions, and reports; limiting the size of the data warehouse; or limiting the schedule, budget, or resources.

Various kinds of data warehouse design tools are available. **Data warehouse development tools** provide functions to define and edit metadata repository contents (such as schemas, scripts, or rules), answer queries, output reports, and ship metadata to and from relational database system catalogues. **Planning and analysis tools** study the impact of schema changes and of refresh performance when changing refresh rates or time windows.

## 2.3.2 A Three-Tier Data Warehouse Architecture

*"What is data warehouse architecture like?"* Data warehouses often adopt a three-tier architecture, as presented in Figure 2.12.

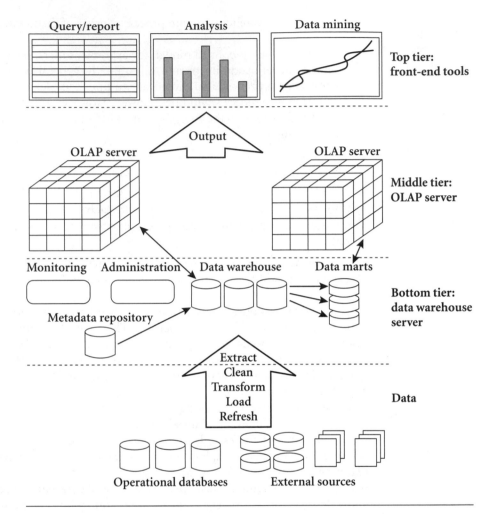

**Figure 2.12** A three-tier data warehousing architecture.

1. The bottom tier is a **warehouse database server** that is almost always a relational database system. *"How are the data extracted from this tier in order to create the data warehouse?"* Data from operational databases and external sources (such as customer profile information provided by external consultants) are extracted using application program interfaces known as **gateways**. A gateway is supported by the underlying DBMS and allows client programs to generate SQL code to be executed at a server. Examples of gateways include ODBC (Open Database Connection) and OLE-DB (Open Linking and Embedding for Databases), by Microsoft, and JDBC (Java Database Connection).

**2.** The middle tier is an **OLAP server** that is typically implemented using either (1) a **relational OLAP (ROLAP)** model, that is, an extended relational DBMS that maps operations on multidimensional data to standard relational operations; or (2) a **multidimensional OLAP (MOLAP)** model, that is, a special-purpose server that directly implements multidimensional data and operations. OLAP servers are discussed in Section 2.3.3.

**3.** The top tier is a client, which contains query and reporting tools, analysis tools, and/or data mining tools (e.g., trend analysis, prediction, and so on).

From the architecture point of view, there are three data warehouse models: the *enterprise warehouse*, the *data mart*, and the *virtual warehouse*.

**Enterprise warehouse:** An enterprise warehouse collects all of the information about subjects spanning the entire organization. It provides corporate-wide data integration, usually from one or more operational systems or external information providers, and is cross-functional in scope. It typically contains detailed data as well as summarized data, and can range in size from a few gigabytes to hundreds of gigabytes, terabytes, or beyond. An enterprise data warehouse may be implemented on traditional mainframes, UNIX superservers, or parallel architecture platforms. It requires extensive business modeling and may take years to design and build.

**Data mart:** A data mart contains a subset of corporate-wide data that is of value to a specific group of users. The scope is confined to specific selected subjects. For example, a marketing data mart may confine its subjects to customer, item, and sales. The data contained in data marts tend to be summarized.

Data marts are usually implemented on low-cost departmental servers that are UNIX- or Windows/NT-based. The implementation cycle of a data mart is more likely to be measured in weeks rather than months or years. However, it may involve complex integration in the long run if its design and planning were not enterprise-wide.

Depending on the source of data, data marts can be categorized as independent or dependent. *Independent* data marts are sourced from data captured from one or more operational systems or external information providers, or from data generated locally within a particular department or geographic area. *Dependent* data marts are sourced directly from enterprise data warehouses.

**Virtual warehouse:** A virtual warehouse is a set of views over operational databases. For efficient query processing, only some of the possible summary views may be materialized. A virtual warehouse is easy to build but requires excess capacity on operational database servers.

The top-down development of an enterprise warehouse serves as a systematic solution and minimizes integration problems. However, it is expensive, takes a long time to develop, and lacks flexibility due to the difficulty in achieving consistency and consensus for a common data model for the entire organization. The bottom-up approach to the design, development, and deployment of independent data marts provides flexibility, low cost, and rapid return of investment. It, however, can lead to problems when integrating various disparate data marts into a consistent enterprise data warehouse.

A recommended method for the development of data warehouse systems is to implement the warehouse in an incremental and evolutionary manner, as shown in Figure 2.13. First, a high-level corporate data model is defined within a reasonably short period of time (such as one or two months) that provides a corporate-wide, consistent, integrated view of data among different subjects and potential usages. This high-level model, although it will need to be refined in the further development of enterprise data warehouses and departmental data marts, will greatly reduce future integration problems. Second, independent data marts can be implemented in parallel with the enterprise warehouse based on the same corporate data model set as above. Third, distributed data marts can be constructed to integrate different data marts via hub servers. Finally, a **multitier data ware-**

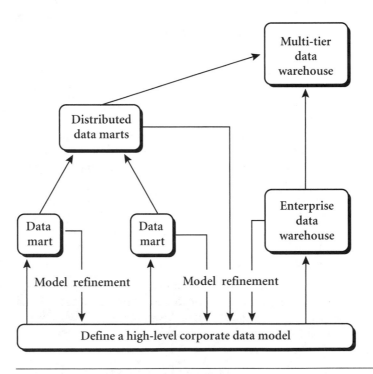

**Figure 2.13**    A recommended approach for data warehouse development.

**house** is constructed where the enterprise warehouse is the sole custodian of all warehouse data, which is then distributed to the various dependent data marts.

## 2.3.3 Types of OLAP Servers: ROLAP versus MOLAP versus HOLAP

*"What kinds of OLAP servers exist?"* Logically, OLAP servers present business users with multidimensional data from data warehouses or data marts, without concerns regarding how or where the data are stored. However, the physical architecture and implementation of OLAP servers must consider data storage issues. Implementations of a warehouse server for OLAP processing include the following:

**Relational OLAP (ROLAP) servers:** These are the intermediate servers that stand in between a relational back-end server and client front-end tools. They use a relational or extended-relational DBMS to store and manage warehouse data, and OLAP middleware to support missing pieces. ROLAP servers include optimization for each DBMS back end, implementation of aggregation navigation logic, and additional tools and services. ROLAP technology tends to have greater scalability than MOLAP technology. The DSS server of Microstrategy and Metacube of Informix, for example, adopt the ROLAP approach.[3]

**Multidimensional OLAP (MOLAP) servers:** These servers support multidimensional views of data through array-based multidimensional storage engines. They map multidimensional views directly to data cube array structures. For example, Essbase of Arbor is a MOLAP server. The advantage of using a data cube is that it allows fast indexing to precomputed summarized data. Notice that with multidimensional data stores, the storage utilization may be low if the data set is sparse. In such cases, sparse matrix compression techniques (see Section 2.4) should be explored.

Many MOLAP servers adopt a two-level storage representation to handle sparse and dense data sets: the dense subcubes are identified and stored as array structures, while the sparse subcubes employ compression technology for efficient storage utilization.

**Hybrid OLAP (HOLAP) servers:** The hybrid OLAP approach combines ROLAP and MOLAP technology, benefiting from the greater scalability of ROLAP and the faster computation of MOLAP. For example, a HOLAP server may allow large volumes of detail data to be stored in a relational database, while aggregations are kept in a separate MOLAP store. The Microsoft SQL Server 7.0 OLAP Services supports a hybrid OLAP server.

---

[3] Information on these products can be found at *www.microstrategy.com* and *www.informix.com*, respectively.

**Specialized SQL servers:** To meet the growing demand of OLAP processing in relational databases, some relational and data warehousing firms (e.g., Redbrick of Informix) implement specialized SQL servers that provide advanced query language and query processing support for SQL queries over star and snowflake schemas in a read-only environment.

*"So, how are data actually stored in ROLAP and MOLAP architectures?"* As its name implies, ROLAP uses relational tables to store data for on-line analytical processing. Recall that the fact table associated with a base cuboid is referred to as a *base fact table*. The base fact table stores data at the abstraction level indicated by the join keys in the schema for the given data cube. Aggregated data can also be stored in fact tables, referred to as **summary fact tables**. Some summary fact tables store both base fact table data and aggregated data, as in Example 2.10. Alternatively, separate summary fact tables can be used for each level of abstraction, to store only aggregated data.

**Example 2.10** Table 2.4 shows a summary fact table that contains both base fact data and aggregated data. The schema of the table is "$\langle record\_identifier\ (RID),\ item,\ \ldots,\ day,\ month,\ quarter,\ year,\ dollars\_sold$ (i.e., sales amount)$\rangle$", where *day, month, quarter*, and *year* define the date of sales. Consider the tuples with an RID of 1001 and 1002, respectively. The data of these tuples are at the base fact level, where the date of sales is October 15, 2000, and October 23, 2000, respectively. Consider the tuple with an RID of 5001. This tuple is at a more general level of abstraction than the tuples 1001 and 1002. The *day* value has been generalized to **all**, so that the corresponding *time* value is October 2000. That is, the *dollars_sold* amount shown is an aggregation representing the entire month of October 2000, rather than just October 15 or 23, 2000. The special value **all** is used to represent subtotals in summarized data.  ∎

MOLAP uses multidimensional array structures to store data for on-line analytical processing. For example, the data cube structure described and referred to throughout this chapter is such an array structure.

**Table 2.4** Single table for base and summary facts.

| RID | item | . . . | day | month | quarter | year | dollars_sold |
|-----|------|-------|-----|-------|---------|------|--------------|
| 1001 | TV | . . . | 15 | 10 | Q4 | 2000 | 250.60 |
| 1002 | TV | . . . | 23 | 10 | Q4 | 2000 | 175.00 |
| ⋮ | | | | | | | |
| 5001 | TV | . . . | **all** | 10 | Q4 | 2000 | 45,786.08 |
| ⋮ | | | | | | | |

Most data warehouse systems adopt a client-server architecture. A relational data store always resides at the data warehouse/data mart server site. A multidimensional data store can reside at either the database server site or the client site.

# 2.4 Data Warehouse Implementation

Data warehouses contain huge volumes of data. OLAP servers demand that decision support queries be answered in the order of seconds. Therefore, it is crucial for data warehouse systems to support highly efficient cube computation techniques, access methods, and query processing techniques. *"How can this be done?"* you may wonder. In this section, we examine methods for the efficient implementation of data warehouse systems.

## 2.4.1 Efficient Computation of Data Cubes

At the core of multidimensional data analysis is the efficient computation of aggregations across many sets of dimensions. In SQL terms, these aggregations are referred to as **group-by's**.

### The compute cube Operator and Its Implementation

One approach to cube computation extends SQL so as to include a **compute cube** operator. The **compute cube** operator computes aggregates over all subsets of the dimensions specified in the operation.

**Example 2.11** Suppose that you would like to create a data cube for *AllElectronics* sales that contains the following: *item, city, year*, and *sales_in_dollars*. You would like to be able to analyze the data, with queries such as the following:

- *"Compute the sum of sales, grouping by item and city."*
- *"Compute the sum of sales, grouping by item."*
- *"Compute the sum of sales, grouping by city."*

What is the total number of cuboids, or group-by's, that can be computed for this data cube? Taking the three attributes, *city, item*, and *year*, as three dimensions and *sales_in_dollars* as the measure, the total number of cuboids, or group-by's, that can be computed for this data cube is $2^3 = 8$. The possible group-by's are the following: {(*city, item, year*), (*city, item*), (*city, year*), (*item, year*), (*city*), (*item*), (*year*), ()}, where () means that the group-by is empty (i.e., the dimensions are not grouped). These group-by's form a lattice of cuboids for the data cube, as shown in Figure 2.14. The base cuboid contains all three dimensions, *city, item*, and *year*.

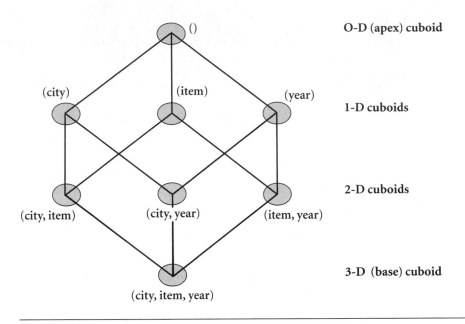

**Figure 2.14**  Lattice of cuboids, making up a 3-D data cube.  Each cuboid represents a different group-by. The base cuboid contains the three dimensions *city, item*, and *year*.

It can return the total sales for any combination of the three dimensions. The apex cuboid, or 0-D cuboid, refers to the case where the group-by is empty. It contains the total sum of all sales.  ■

An SQL query containing no group-by, such as "compute the sum of total sales," is a *zero-dimensional operation*. An SQL query containing one group-by, such as "compute the sum of sales, group by city," is a *one-dimensional operation*. A cube operator on *n* dimensions is equivalent to a collection of **group by** statements, one for each subset of the *n* dimensions. Therefore, the cube operator is the *n*-dimensional generalization of the **group by** operator. Based on the syntax of DMQL introduced in Section 2.2.3, the data cube in Example 2.11 can be defined as

**define cube** sales [item, city, year]: **sum**(sales_in_dollars)

For a cube with *n* dimensions, there are a total of $2^n$ cuboids, including the base cuboid. The statement

**compute cube** sales

explicitly instructs the system to compute the sales aggregate cuboids for all of the eight subsets of the set {*item, city, year*}, including the empty subset. A cube computation operator was first proposed and studied by Gray et al. [GCB+97].

On-line analytical processing may need to access different cuboids for different queries. Therefore, it does seem like a good idea to compute all or at least some of the cuboids in a data cube in advance. Precomputation leads to fast response time and avoids some redundant computation. Actually, most, if not all, OLAP products resort to some degree of precomputation of multidimensional aggregates.

A major challenge related to this precomputation, however, is that the required storage space may explode if all of the cuboids in a data cube are precomputed, especially when the cube has many dimensions associated with multiple level hierarchies.

"*How many cuboids are there in an* n-*dimensional data cube?*" If there were no hierarchies associated with each dimension, then the total number of cuboids for an *n*-dimensional data cube, as we have seen above, is $2^n$. However, in practice, many dimensions do have hierarchies. For example, the dimension *time* is usually not just one level, such as *year*, but rather a hierarchy or a lattice, such as *day* < *week* < *month* < *quarter* < *year*. For an *n*-dimensional data cube, the total number of cuboids that can be generated (including the cuboids generated by climbing up the hierarchies along each dimension) is

$$T = \prod_{i=1}^{n} (L_i + 1),$$

where $L_i$ is the number of levels associated with dimension $i$ (excluding the *virtual* top level **all** since generalizing to **all** is equivalent to the removal of a dimension). This formula is based on the fact that at most one abstraction level in each dimension will appear in a cuboid. For example, if the cube has 10 dimensions and each dimension has 4 levels, the total number of cuboids that can be generated will be $5^{10} \approx 9.8 \times 10^6$.

By now, you probably realize that it is unrealistic to precompute and materialize all of the cuboids that can possibly be generated for a data cube (or from a base cuboid). If there are many cuboids, and these cuboids are large in size, a more reasonable option is *partial materialization*, that is, to materialize only *some* of the possible cuboids that can be generated.

## Partial Materialization: Selected Computation of Cuboids

There are three choices for data cube materialization given a base cuboid: (1) do not precompute any of the "nonbase" cuboids (**no materialization**), (2) precompute all of the cuboids (**full materialization**), and (3) selectively compute a proper subset of the whole set of possible cuboids (**partial materialization**). The first choice leads to computing expensive multidimensional aggregates on the fly, which could be slow. The second choice may require huge amounts of memory space in order to store all of the precomputed cuboids. The third choice presents an interesting trade-off between storage space and response time.

The partial materialization of cuboids should consider three factors: (1) identify the subset of cuboids to materialize, (2) exploit the materialized cuboids during query processing, and (3) efficiently update the materialized cuboids during load and refresh.

The selection of the subset of cuboids to materialize should take into account the queries in the workload, their frequencies, and their accessing costs. In addition, it should consider workload characteristics, the cost for incremental updates, and the total storage requirements. The selection must also consider the broad context of physical database design, such as the generation and selection of indices. Several OLAP products have adopted heuristic approaches for cuboid selection. A popular approach is to materialize the set of cuboids on which other popularly referenced cuboids are based.

Once the selected cuboids have been materialized, it is important to take advantage of them during query processing. This involves determining the relevant cuboid(s) from among the candidate materialized cuboids, how to use available index structures on the materialized cuboids, and how to transform the OLAP operations onto the selected cuboid(s). These issues are discussed in Section 2.4.3.

Finally, during load and refresh, the materialized cuboids should be updated efficiently. Parallelism and incremental update techniques for this should be explored.

### Multiway Array Aggregation in the Computation of Data Cubes

In order to ensure fast on-line analytical processing, however, we may need to precompute all of the cuboids for a given data cube. Cuboids may be stored on secondary storage and accessed when necessary. Hence, it is important to explore efficient methods for computing all of the cuboids making up a data cube, that is, for full materialization. These methods must take into consideration the limited amount of main memory available for cuboid computation, as well as the time required for such computation. To simplify matters, we may exclude the cuboids generated by climbing up existing hierarchies along each dimension.

Since relational OLAP (ROLAP) uses tuples and relational tables as its basic data structures, while the basic data structure used in multidimensional OLAP (MOLAP) is the multidimensional array, one would expect that ROLAP and MOLAP each explore very different cube computation techniques.

ROLAP cube computation uses the following major optimization techniques.

- Sorting, hashing, and grouping operations are applied to the dimension attributes in order to reorder and cluster related tuples.

- Grouping is performed on some subaggregates as a "partial grouping step." These "partial groupings" may be used to speed up the computation of other subaggregates.

- Aggregates may be computed from previously computed aggregates, rather than from the base fact tables.

*"How do these optimization techniques apply to MOLAP?"* ROLAP uses value-based addressing, where dimension values are accessed by key-based addressing search strategies. In contrast, MOLAP uses direct array addressing, where dimension values are accessed via the position or index of their corresponding array locations. Hence, MOLAP cannot perform the value-based reordering of the first optimization technique listed above for ROLAP. Therefore, a different approach should be developed for the array-based cube construction of MOLAP, such as the following:

1. Partition the array into chunks. A **chunk** is a subcube that is small enough to fit into the memory available for cube computation. **Chunking** is a method for dividing an *n*-dimensional array into small *n*-dimensional chunks, where each chunk is stored as an object on disk. The chunks are compressed so as to remove wasted space resulting from empty array cells (i.e., cells that do not contain any valid data). For instance, *"chunkID + offset"* can be used as a cell addressing mechanism to **compress a sparse array structure** and when searching for cells within a chunk. Such a compression technique is powerful enough to handle sparse cubes, both on disk and in memory.

2. Compute aggregates by visiting (i.e., accessing the values at) cube cells. The order in which cells are visited can be optimized so as to *minimize the number of times that each cell must be revisited*, thereby reducing memory access and storage costs. The trick is to exploit this ordering so that partial aggregates can be computed simultaneously, and any unnecessary revisiting of cells is avoided.

   Since this chunking technique involves "overlapping" some of the aggregation computations, it is referred to as **multiway array aggregation** in data cube computation.

We explain this approach to MOLAP cube construction by looking at a concrete example.

**Example 2.12** Consider a 3-D data array containing the three dimensions $A$, $B$, and $C$.

The 3-D array is partitioned into small, memory-based chunks. In this example, the array is partitioned into 64 chunks as shown in Figure 2.15. Dimension $A$ is organized into four equal-sized partitions, $a_0, a_1, a_2$, and $a_3$. Dimensions $B$ and $C$ are similarly organized into four partitions each. Chunks 1, 2, . . . , 64 correspond to the subcubes $a_0 b_0 c_0, a_1 b_0 c_0, \ldots, a_3 b_3 c_3$, respectively. Suppose the size of the array for each dimension, $A$, $B$, and $C$, is 40, 400, and 4000, respectively. The size of each partition in $A$, $B$, and $C$ is therefore 10, 100, and 1000, respectively.

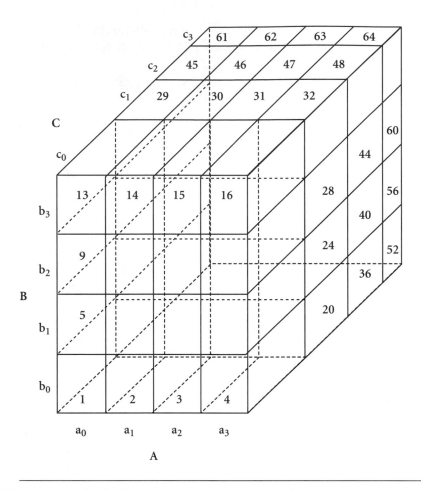

**Figure 2.15** A 3-D array for the dimensions $A$, $B$, and $C$, organized into 64 *chunks*.

Full materialization of the corresponding data cube involves the computation of all of the cuboids defining this cube. These cuboids consist of

- The base cuboid, denoted by $ABC$ (from which all of the other cuboids are directly or indirectly computed). This cube is already computed and corresponds to the given 3-D array.

- The 2-D cuboids, $AB$, $AC$, and $BC$, which respectively correspond to the group-by's $AB$, $AC$, and $BC$. These cuboids must be computed.

- The 1-D cuboids, $A$, $B$, and $C$, which respectively correspond to the group-by's $A$, $B$, and $C$. These cuboids must be computed.

■ The 0-D (apex) cuboid, denoted by **all**, which corresponds to the group-by ();
that is, there is no group-by here. This cuboid must be computed.

Let's look at how the multiway array aggregation technique is used in this
computation. There are many possible orderings with which chunks can be read
into memory for use in cube computation. Consider the ordering labeled from 1 to
64, shown in Figure 2.15. Suppose we would like to compute the $b_0c_0$ chunk of the
$BC$ cuboid. We allocate space for this chunk in *chunk memory*. By scanning chunks
1 to 4 of $ABC$, the $b_0c_0$ chunk is computed. That is, the cells for $b_0c_0$ are aggregated
over $a_0$ to $a_3$. The chunk memory can then be assigned to the next chunk, $b_1c_0$,
which completes its aggregation after the scanning of the next four chunks of $ABC$:
5 to 8. Continuing in this way, the entire $BC$ cuboid can be computed. Therefore,
only *one* chunk of $BC$ needs to be in memory, at a time, for the computation of
all of the chunks of $BC$.

In computing the $BC$ cuboid, we will have scanned each of the 64 chunks.
*"Is there a way to avoid having to rescan all of these chunks for the computa-
tion of other cuboids, such as AC and AB?"* The answer is, most definitely—
*yes*. This is where the multiway computation idea comes in. For example, when
chunk 1 (i.e., $a_0b_0c_0$) is being scanned (say, for the computation of the 2-D
chunk $b_0c_0$ of $BC$, as described above), all of the other 2-D chunks relating to
$a_0b_0c_0$ can be simultaneously computed. That is, when $a_0b_0c_0$ is being scanned,
each of the three chunks, $b_0c_0$, $a_0c_0$, and $a_0b_0$, on the three 2-D aggregation
planes, $BC$, $AC$, and $AB$, should be computed then as well. In other words, multiway computation aggregates to each of the 2-D planes while a 3-D chunk is in
memory.

Now let's look at how different orderings of chunk scanning and of cuboid
computation can affect the overall data cube computation efficiency. Recall that
the size of the dimensions $A$, $B$, and $C$ is 40, 400, and 4000, respectively. Therefore,
the largest 2-D plane is $BC$ (of size $400 \times 4000 = 1,600,000$). The second largest
2-D plane is $AC$ (of size $40 \times 4000 = 160,000$). $AB$ is the smallest 2-D plane (with
a size of $40 \times 400 = 16,000$).

Suppose that the chunks are scanned in the order shown, from chunk 1 to
64. By scanning in this order, one chunk of the largest 2-D plane, $BC$, is *fully*
computed for each row scanned. That is, $b_0c_0$ is fully aggregated after scanning
the row containing chunks 1 to 4; $b_1c_0$ is fully aggregated after scanning chunks
5 to 8, and so on. In comparison, the complete computation of one chunk of the
second largest 2-D plane, $AC$, requires scanning 13 chunks (given the ordering
from 1 to 64). For example, $a_0c_0$ is fully aggregated after the scanning of chunks 1,
5, 9, and 13. Finally, the complete computation of one chunk of the smallest 2-D
plane, $AB$, requires scanning 49 chunks. For example, $a_0b_0$ is fully aggregated after
scanning chunks 1, 17, 33, and 49. Hence, $AB$ requires the longest scan of chunks
in order to complete its computation. To avoid bringing a 3-D chunk into memory
more than once, the minimum memory requirement for holding all relevant 2-
D planes in chunk memory, according to the chunk ordering of 1 to 64, is as

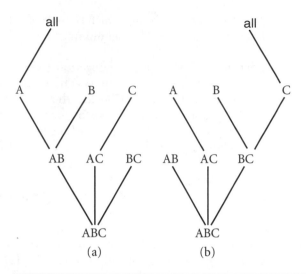

**Figure 2.16**  Two orderings of multiway array aggregation for computation of the 3-D cube of Example 2.12: (a) most efficient ordering of array aggregation (minimum memory requirements = 156,000 memory units); (b) least efficient ordering of array aggregation (minimum memory requirements = 1,641,000 memory units).

follows: $40 \times 400$ (for the whole *AB* plane) + $40 \times 1000$ (for one row of the *AC* plane) + $100 \times 1000$ (for one chunk of the *BC* plane) = $16,000 + 40,000 + 100,000$ = $156,000$.

Suppose, instead, that the chunks are scanned in the order 1, 17, 33, 49, 5, 21, 37, 53, and so on. That is, suppose the scan is in the order of first aggregating towards the *AB* plane, and then towards the *AC* plane, and lastly towards the *BC* plane. The minimum memory requirement for holding 2-D planes in chunk memory would be as follows: $400 \times 4000$ (for the whole *BC* plane) + $40 \times 1000$ (for one row of the *AC* plane) + $10 \times 100$ (for one chunk of the *AB* plane) = $1,600,000 + 40,000 + 1000 = 1,641,000$. Notice that this is *more than 10 times* the memory requirement of the scan ordering of 1 to 64.

Similarly, we can work out the minimum memory requirements for the multiway computation of the 1-D and 0-D cuboids. Figure 2.16 shows the most efficient ordering and the least efficient ordering, based on the minimum memory requirements for the data cube computation. The most efficient ordering is the chunk ordering of 1 to 64. ∎

Example 2.12 assumes that there is enough memory space for *one-pass* cube computation (i.e., to compute all of the cuboids from one scan of all of the chunks). If there is insufficient memory space, the computation will require more than one pass through the 3-D array. In such cases, however, the basic principle of ordered chunk computation remains the same.

*"Which is faster—ROLAP or MOLAP cube computation?"* With the use of appropriate sparse array compression techniques and careful ordering of the computation of cuboids, it has been shown by experiments that MOLAP cube computation is significantly faster than ROLAP (relational record-based) computation. Unlike ROLAP, the array structure of MOLAP does not require saving space to store search keys. Furthermore, MOLAP uses direct array addressing, which is faster than the key-based addressing search strategy of ROLAP. For ROLAP cube computation, instead of cubing a table directly, it can be faster to convert the table to an array, cube the array, and then convert the result back to a table. However, this observation works only for cubes with a relatively small number of dimensions since the number of cuboids to be computed is exponential to the number of dimensions. To overcome the curse of dimensionality, recent studies have proposed to compute only **iceberg cubes**. These are cubes that store only cube partitions where the aggregate value (e.g., count) for each cell in the partition is above some minimum support or occurrence threshold.

*"What if I would like to add in some new data to a precomputed cube or phase out some of the older data stored in it?"* Efficient **incremental update** methods have been developed for this purpose that allow data to be added into or phased out of a precomputed cube without having to recompute the cube from scratch. Concrete methods for such updating are left to the reader as an exercise.

## 2.4.2　Indexing OLAP Data

To facilitate efficient data accessing, most data warehouse systems support index structures and materialized views (using cuboids). Methods to select cuboids for materialization were discussed in the previous section. In this section, we examine how to index OLAP data by *bitmap indexing* and *join indexing*.

The **bitmap indexing** method is popular in OLAP products because it allows quick searching in data cubes. The bitmap index is an alternative representation of the *record_ID (RID)* list. In the bitmap index for a given attribute, there is a distinct bit vector, $Bv$, for each value $v$ in the domain of the attribute. If the domain of a given attribute consists of $n$ values, then $n$ bits are needed for each entry in the bitmap index (i.e., there are $n$ bit vectors). If the attribute has the value $v$ for a given row in the data table, then the bit representing that value is set to 1 in the corresponding row of the bitmap index. All other bits for that row are set to 0.

**Example 2.13** In the *AllElectronics* data warehouse, suppose the dimension *item* at the top level has four values (representing item types): *"home entertainment"*, *"computer"*, *"phone"*, and *"security"*. Each value (e.g., *"computer"*) is represented by a bit vector in the bitmap index table for *item*. Suppose that the cube is stored as a relation table with 100,000 rows. Since the domain of *item* consists of four values, the bitmap index table requires four bit vectors (or lists), each with 100,000 bits. Figure 2.17 shows a base (data) table containing the dimensions *item* and *city*, and its mapping to bitmap index tables for each of the dimensions. ∎

| Base table | | |
| --- | --- | --- |
| RID | item | city |
| R1 | H | V |
| R2 | C | V |
| R3 | P | V |
| R4 | S | V |
| R5 | H | T |
| R6 | C | T |
| R7 | P | T |
| R8 | S | T |

| Item bitmap index table | | | | |
| --- | --- | --- | --- | --- |
| RID | H | C | P | S |
| R1 | 1 | 0 | 0 | 0 |
| R2 | 0 | 1 | 0 | 0 |
| R3 | 0 | 0 | 1 | 0 |
| R4 | 0 | 0 | 0 | 1 |
| R5 | 1 | 0 | 0 | 0 |
| R6 | 0 | 1 | 0 | 0 |
| R7 | 0 | 0 | 1 | 0 |
| R8 | 0 | 0 | 0 | 1 |

| City bitmap index table | | |
| --- | --- | --- |
| RID | V | T |
| R1 | 1 | 0 |
| R2 | 1 | 0 |
| R3 | 1 | 0 |
| R4 | 1 | 0 |
| R5 | 0 | 1 |
| R6 | 0 | 1 |
| R7 | 0 | 1 |
| R8 | 0 | 1 |

Note: H for "home entertainment," C for "computer," P for "phone," S for "security," V for "Vancouver," T for "Toronto."

**Figure 2.17** Indexing OLAP data using bitmap indices.

Bitmap indexing is advantageous compared to hash and tree indices. It is especially useful for low-cardinality domains because comparison, join, and aggregation operations are then reduced to bit arithmetic, which substantially reduces the processing time. Bitmap indexing leads to significant reductions in space and I/O since a string of characters can be represented by a single bit. For higher-cardinality domains, the method can be adapted using compression techniques. The **join indexing** method gained popularity from its use in relational database query processing. Traditional indexing maps the value in a given column to a list of rows having that value. In contrast, join indexing registers the joinable rows of two relations from a relational database. For example, if two relations $R(RID, A)$ and $S(B, SID)$ join on the attributes $A$ and $B$, then the join index record contains the pair $(RID, SID)$, where $RID$ and $SID$ are record identifiers from the $R$ and $S$ relations, respectively. Hence, the join index records can identify joinable tuples without performing costly join operations. Join indexing is especially useful for maintaining the relationship between a foreign key[4] and its matching primary keys, from the joinable relation.

The star schema model of data warehouses makes join indexing attractive for cross table search because the linkage between a fact table and its corresponding dimension tables are the foreign key of the fact table and the primary key of the dimension table. Join indexing maintains relationships between attribute values of a dimension (e.g., within a dimension table) and the corresponding rows in the fact table. Join indices may span multiple dimensions to form **composite join indices**. We can use join indices to identify subcubes that are of interest.

---

[4] A set of attributes in a relation schema that forms a primary key for another relation schema is called a **foreign key**.

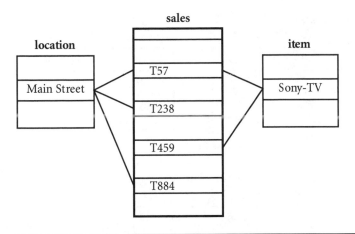

**Figure 2.18** Linkages between a *sales* fact table and dimension tables for *location* and *item*.

**Example 2.14** In Example 2.4, we defined a star schema for *AllElectronics* of the form "*sales_star* [*time, item, branch, location*]: *dollars_sold* = **sum** *(sales_in_dollars)*". An example of a join index relationship between the *sales* fact table and the dimension tables for *location* and *item* is shown in Figure 2.18. For example, the "*Main Street*" value in the *location* dimension table joins with tuples T57, T238, and T884 of the *sales* fact table. Similarly, the "*Sony-TV*" value in the *item* dimension table joins with tuples T57 and T459 of the *sales* fact table. The corresponding join index tables are shown in Figure 2.19.

Suppose that there are 360 time values, 100 items, 50 branches, 30 locations, and 10 million sales tuples in the *sales_star* data cube. If the *sales* fact table has recorded sales for only 30 items, the remaining 70 items will obviously not participate in joins. If join indices are not used, additional I/Os have to be performed to bring the joining portions of the fact table and dimension tables together.    ■

To further speed up query processing, the join indexing and bitmap indexing methods can be integrated to form **bitmapped join indices**. Microsoft SQL Server and Sybase IQ support bitmap indices. Oracle 8 uses bitmap and join indices.

## 2.4.3 Efficient Processing of OLAP Queries

The purpose of materializing cuboids and constructing OLAP index structures is to speed up query processing in data cubes. Given materialized views, query processing should proceed as follows:

**1. Determine which operations should be performed on the available cuboids:** This involves transforming any selection, projection, roll-up (group-by), and drill-down operations specified in the query into corresponding SQL and/or

Join index table for
location/sales

| location | sales_key |
|---|---|
| ... | ... |
| Main Street | T57 |
| Main Street | T238 |
| Main Street | T884 |
| ... | ... |

Join index table for
item/sales

| item | sales_key |
|---|---|
| ... | ... |
| Sony-TV | T57 |
| Sony-TV | T459 |
| ... | ... |

Join index table linking two dimensions
location/item/sales

| location | item | sales_key |
|---|---|---|
| ... | ... | ... |
| Main Street | Sony-TV | T57 |
| ... | ... | ... |

**Figure 2.19** Join index tables based on the linkages between the *sales* fact table and dimension tables for *location* and *item* shown in Figure 2.18.

OLAP operations. For example, slicing and dicing of a data cube may correspond to selection and/or projection operations on a materialized cuboid.

2. **Determine to which materialized cuboid(s) the relevant operations should be applied:** This involves identifying all of the materialized cuboids that may potentially be used to answer the query, pruning the above set using knowledge of "dominance" relationships among the cuboids, estimating the costs of using the remaining materialized cuboids, and selecting the cuboid with the least cost.

**Example 2.15** Suppose that we define a data cube for *AllElectronics* of the form "*sales* [*time, item, location*]: **sum**(*sales_in_dollars*)". The dimension hierarchies used are "*day < month < quarter < year*" for *time*, "*item_name < brand < type*" for *item*, and "*street < city < province_or_state < country*" for *location*.

Suppose that the query to be processed is on {*brand, province_or_state*}, with the selection constant "*year = 2000*". Also, suppose that there are four materialized cuboids available, as follows:

- cuboid 1: {*item_name, city, year*}
- cuboid 2: {*brand, country, year*}
- cuboid 3: {*brand, province_or_state, year*}
- cuboid 4: {*item_name, province_or_state*} where *year = 2000*

*"Which of the above four cuboids should be selected to process the query?"* Finer-granularity data cannot be generated from coarser-granularity data. Therefore, cuboid 2 cannot be used since *country* is a more general concept than *province_or_state*. Cuboids 1, 3, and 4 can be used to process the query since (1) they have the same set or a superset of the dimensions in the query, (2) the selection clause in the query can imply the selection in the cuboid, and (3) the abstraction levels for the *item* and *location* dimensions in these cuboids are at a finer level than *brand* and *province_or_state*, respectively.

*"How would the costs of each cuboid compare if used to process the query?"* It is likely that using cuboid 1 would cost the most since both *item_name* and *city* are at a lower level than the *brand* and *province_or_state* concepts specified in the query. If there are not many *year* values associated with *items* in the cube, but there are several *item_names* for each *brand*, then cuboid 3 will be smaller than cuboid 4, and thus cuboid 3 should be chosen to process the query. However, if efficient indices are available for cuboid 4, then cuboid 4 may be a better choice. Therefore, some cost-based estimation is required in order to decide which set of cuboids should be selected for query processing.   ∎

Since the storage model of a MOLAP server is an *n*-dimensional array, the front-end multidimensional queries are mapped directly to server storage structures, which provide direct addressing capabilities. The straightforward array representation of the data cube has good indexing properties, but has poor storage utilization when the data are sparse. For efficient storage and processing, sparse matrix and data compression techniques (Section 2.4.1) should therefore be applied.

The storage structures used by dense and sparse arrays may differ, making it advantageous to adopt a two-level approach to MOLAP query processing: use array structures for dense arrays, and sparse matrix structures for sparse arrays. The two-dimensional dense arrays can be indexed by B-trees.

To process a query in MOLAP, the dense one- and two-dimensional arrays must first be identified. Indices are then built to these arrays using traditional indexing structures. The two-level approach increases storage utilization without sacrificing direct addressing capabilities.

## 2.4.4 Metadata Repository

*"What are metadata?"* **Metadata** are data about data. When used in a data warehouse, metadata are the data that define warehouse objects. Metadata are created for the data names and definitions of the given warehouse. Additional metadata are created and captured for timestamping any extracted data, the source of the extracted data, and missing fields that have been added by data cleaning or integration processes.

A metadata repository should contain the following:

- A description of *the structure of the data warehouse*, which includes the warehouse schema, view, dimensions, hierarchies, and derived data definitions, as well as data mart locations and contents

- *Operational metadata*, which include data lineage (history of migrated data and the sequence of transformations applied to it), currency of data (active, archived, or purged), and monitoring information (warehouse usage statistics, error reports, and audit trails)

- *The algorithms used for summarization*, which include measure and dimension definition algorithms, data on granularity, partitions, subject areas, aggregation, summarization, and predefined queries and reports

- *The mapping from the operational environment to the data warehouse*, which includes source databases and their contents, gateway descriptions, data partitions, data extraction, cleaning, transformation rules and defaults, data refresh and purging rules, and security (user authorization and access control)

- *Data related to system performance*, which include indices and profiles that improve data access and retrieval performance, in addition to rules for the timing and scheduling of refresh, update, and replication cycles

- *Business metadata*, which include business terms and definitions, data ownership information, and charging policies

A data warehouse contains different levels of summarization, of which metadata is one type. Other types include current detailed data (which are almost always on disk), older detailed data (which are usually on tertiary storage), lightly summarized data and highly summarized data (which may or may not be physically housed).

Metadata play a very different role than other data warehouse data, and are important for many reasons. For example, metadata are used as a directory to help the decision support system analyst locate the contents of the data warehouse, as a guide to the mapping of data when the data are transformed from the operational environment to the data warehouse environment, and as a guide to the algorithms used for summarization between the current detailed data and the lightly summarized data, and between the lightly summarized data and the highly summarized data. Metadata should be stored and managed persistently (i.e., on disk).

## 2.4.5 Data Warehouse Back-End Tools and Utilities

Data warehouse systems use back-end tools and utilities to populate and refresh their data. These tools and facilities include the following functions:

- **Data extraction**, which typically gathers data from multiple, heterogeneous, and external sources

- **Data cleaning**, which detects errors in the data and rectifies them when possible

- **Data transformation**, which converts data from legacy or host format to warehouse format

- **Load**, which sorts, summarizes, consolidates, computes views, checks integrity, and builds indices and partitions

- **Refresh**, which propagates the updates from the data sources to the warehouse

Besides cleaning, loading, refreshing, and metadata definition tools, data warehouse systems usually provide a good set of data warehouse management tools.

Data cleaning and data transformation are important steps in improving the quality of the data and, subsequently, of the data mining results. They are described in Chapter 3. Since we are mostly interested in the aspects of data warehousing technology related to data mining, we will not get into the details of the remaining tools and recommend interested readers to consult books dedicated to data warehousing technology.

# 2.5 Further Development of Data Cube Technology

In this section, you will study further developments of data cube technology. Section 2.5.1 describes data mining by *discovery-driven exploration of data cubes*, where anomalies in the data are automatically detected and marked for the user with visual cues. Section 2.5.2 describes *multifeature cubes* for complex data mining queries involving multiple dependent aggregates at multiple granularities. Other developments are described in Section 2.5.3.

## 2.5.1 Discovery-Driven Exploration of Data Cubes

As we have seen in this chapter, data can be summarized and stored in a multidimensional data cube of an OLAP system. A user or analyst can search for interesting patterns in the cube by specifying a number of OLAP operations, such as drill-down, roll-up, slice, and dice. While these tools are available to help the user explore the data, the discovery process is not automated. It is the user who, following her own intuition or hypotheses, tries to recognize exceptions or anomalies in the data. This **hypothesis-driven exploration** has a number of disadvantages. The search space can be very large, making manual inspection of the data a daunting and overwhelming task. High-level aggregations may give no indication of anomalies at lower levels, making it easy to overlook interesting patterns. Even when looking at a subset of the cube, such as a slice, the user is typically faced with many data values to examine. The sheer volume of data values alone makes it easy for users to miss exceptions in the data if using hypothesis-driven exploration.

**Discovery-driven exploration** is an alternative approach in which precomputed measures indicating data exceptions are used to guide the user in the data analysis process, at all levels of aggregation. We hereafter refer to these measures as *exception indicators*. Intuitively, an **exception** is a data cube cell value that is significantly different from the value anticipated, based on a statistical model. The model considers variations and patterns in the measure value across *all of the dimensions* to which a cell belongs. For example, if the analysis of item-sales data reveals an increase in sales in December in comparison to all other months, this may seem like an exception in the time dimension. However, it is not an exception if the item dimension is considered, since there is a similar increase in sales for other items during December. The model considers exceptions hidden at all aggregated group-by's of a data cube. Visual cues such as background color are used to reflect the degree of exception of each cell, based on the precomputed exception indicators. Efficient algorithms have been proposed for cube construction, as discussed in Section 2.4.1. The computation of exception indicators can be overlapped with cube construction, so that the overall construction of data cubes for discovery-driven exploration is efficient.

Three measures are used as exception indicators to help identify data anomalies. These measures indicate the degree of surprise that the quantity in a cell holds, with respect to its expected value. The measures are computed and associated with every cell, for all levels of aggregation. They are

- **SelfExp:** This indicates the degree of surprise of the cell value, relative to other cells at the same level of aggregation.

- **InExp:** This indicates the degree of surprise somewhere beneath the cell, if we were to drill down from it.

- **PathExp:** This indicates the degree of surprise for each drill-down path from the cell.

The use of these measures for discovery-driven exploration of data cubes is illustrated in the following example.

**Example 2.16** Suppose that you would like to analyze the monthly sales at *AllElectronics* as a percentage difference from the previous month. The dimensions involved are *item*, *time*, and *region*. You begin by studying the data aggregated over all items and sales regions for each month, as shown in Figure 2.20.

| Sum of sales | Month | | | | | | | | | | | |
|---|---|---|---|---|---|---|---|---|---|---|---|---|
| | Jan | Feb | Mar | Apr | May | Jun | Jul | Aug | Sep | Oct | Nov | Dec |
| Total | | 1% | −1% | 0% | 1% | 3% | −1% | −9% | −1% | 2% | −4% | 3% |

**Figure 2.20** Change in sales over time.

| Avg. sales | Month | | | | | | | | | | | |
|---|---|---|---|---|---|---|---|---|---|---|---|---|
| *Item* | Jan | Feb | Mar | Apr | May | Jun | Jul | Aug | Sep | Oct | Nov | Dec |
| Sony b/w printer | | 9% | −8% | 2% | −5% | 14% | −4% | 0% | 41% | −13% | −15% | −11% |
| Sony color printer | | 0% | 0% | 3% | 2% | 4% | −10% | −13% | 0% | 4% | −6% | 4% |
| HP b/w printer | | −2% | 1% | 2% | 3% | 8% | 0% | −12% | −9% | 3% | −3% | 6% |
| HP color printer | | 0% | 0% | −2% | 1% | 0% | −1% | −7% | −2% | 1% | −4% | 1% |
| IBM desktop computer | | 1% | −2% | −1% | −1% | 3% | 3% | −10% | 4% | 1% | −4% | −1% |
| IBM laptop computer | | 0% | 0% | −1% | 3% | 4% | 2% | −10% | −2% | 0% | −9% | 3% |
| Toshiba desktop computer | | −2% | −5% | 1% | 1% | −1% | 1% | 5% | −3% | −5% | −1% | −1% |
| Toshiba laptop computer | | 1% | 0% | 3% | 0% | −2% | −2% | −5% | 3% | 2% | −1% | 0% |
| Logitech mouse | | 3% | −2% | −1% | 0% | 4% | 6% | −11% | 2% | 1% | −4% | 0% |
| Ergo-way mouse | | 0% | 0% | 2% | 3% | 1% | −2% | −2% | −5% | 0% | −5% | 8% |

**Figure 2.21**  Change in sales for each item-time combination.

To view the exception indicators, you would click on a button marked **highlight exceptions** on the screen. This translates the SelfExp and InExp values into visual cues, displayed with each cell. The background color of each cell is based on its SelfExp value. In addition, a box is drawn around each cell, where the thickness and color of the box are a function of its InExp value. Thick boxes indicate high InExp values. In both cases, the darker the color, the greater the degree of exception. For example, the dark, thick boxes for sales during July, August, and September signal the user to explore the lower-level aggregations of these cells by drilling down.

Drill-downs can be executed along the aggregated *item* or *region* dimensions. "*Which path has more exceptions?*" you wonder. To find this out, you select a cell of interest and trigger a **path exception** module that colors each dimension based on the PathExp value of the cell. This value reflects the degree of surprise of that path. Suppose that the path along *item* contains more exceptions.

A drill-down along *item* results in the cube slice of Figure 2.21, showing the sales over time for each item. At this point, you are presented with many different sales values to analyze. By clicking on the **highlight exceptions** button, the visual cues are displayed, bringing focus towards the exceptions. Consider the sales difference of 41% for "*Sony b/w printers*" in September. This cell has a dark background, indicating a high SelfExp value, meaning that the cell is an exception. Consider now the the sales difference of −15% for "*Sony b/w printers*" in November, and of −11% in December. The −11% value for December is marked as an exception, while the −15% value is not, even though −15% is a bigger deviation than −11%. This is because the exception indicators consider all of the dimensions

| Avg. sales | Month | | | | | | | | | | | |
|---|---|---|---|---|---|---|---|---|---|---|---|---|
| Region | Jan | Feb | Mar | Apr | May | Jun | Jul | Aug | Sep | Oct | Nov | Dec |
| North | | −1% | −3% | −1% | 0% | 3% | 4% | −7% | 1% | 0% | −3% | −3% |
| South | | −1% | 1% | −9% | 6% | −1% | −39% | 9% | −34% | 4% | 1% | 7% |
| East | | −1% | −2% | 2% | −3% | 1% | 18% | −2% | 11% | −3% | −2% | −1% |
| West | | 4% | 0% | −1% | −3% | 5% | 1% | −18% | 8% | 5% | −8% | 1% |

**Figure 2.22**  Change in sales for the item *IBM desktop computer* per region.

that a cell is in. Notice that the December sales of most of the other items have a large positive value, while the November sales do not. Therefore, by considering the position of the cell in the cube, the sales difference for *"Sony b/w printers"* in December is exceptional, while the November sales difference of this item is not.

The InExp values can be used to indicate exceptions at lower levels that are not visible at the current level. Consider the cells for *"IBM desktop computers"* in July and September. These both have a dark, thick box around them, indicating high InExp values. You may decide to further explore the sales of *"IBM desktop computers"* by drilling down along *region*. The resulting sales difference by region is shown in Figure 2.22, where the **highlight exceptions** option has been invoked. The visual cues displayed make it easy to instantly notice an exception for the sales of *"IBM desktop computers"* in the southern region, where such sales have decreased by −39% and −34% in July and September, respectively. These detailed exceptions were far from obvious when we were viewing the data as an item-time group-by, aggregated over region in Figure 2.21. Thus, the InExp value is useful for searching for exceptions at lower-level cells of the cube. Since there are no other cells in Figure 2.22 having a high InExp value, you may roll up back to the data of Figure 2.21, and choose another cell from which to drill down. In this way, the exception indicators can be used to guide the discovery of interesting anomalies in the data.                                                                                          ■

*"How are the exception values computed?"* The SelfExp, InExp, and PathExp measures are based on a statistical method for table analysis. They take into account all of the group-by's (aggregations) in which a given cell value participates. A cell value is considered an exception based on how much it differs from its expected value, where its expected value is determined with a statistical model described below. The difference between a given cell value and its expected value is called a **residual**. Intuitively, the larger the residual, the more the given cell value is an exception. The comparison of residual values requires us to scale the values based on the expected standard deviation associated with the residuals. A cell

value is therefore considered an exception if its scaled residual value exceeds a prespecified threshold. The SelfExp, InExp, and PathExp measures are based on this scaled residual.

The expected value of a given cell is a function of the higher-level group-by's of the given cell. For example, given a cube with the three dimensions $A$, $B$, and $C$, the expected value for a cell at the $i$th position in $A$, the $j$th position in $B$, and the $k$th position in $C$ is a function of $\gamma$, $\gamma_i^A$, $\gamma_j^B$, $\gamma_k^C$, $\gamma_{ij}^{AB}$, $\gamma_{ik}^{AC}$, and $\gamma_{jk}^{BC}$, which are coefficients of the statistical model used. The coefficients reflect how different the values at more detailed levels are, based on generalized impressions formed by looking at higher-level aggregations. In this way, the exception quality of a cell value is based on the exceptions of the values below it. Thus, when seeing an exception, it is natural for the user to further explore the exception by drilling down.

*"How can the data cube be efficiently constructed for discovery-driven explo-ration?"* This computation consists of three phases. The first step involves the computation of the aggregate values defining the cube, such as sum or count, over which exceptions will be found. There are several efficient techniques for cube computation, such as the multiway array aggregation technique discussed in Section 2.4.1. The second phase consists of model fitting, in which the coefficients mentioned above are determined and used to compute the standardized residuals. This phase can be overlapped with the first phase since the computations involved are similar. The third phase computes the SelfExp, InExp, and PathExp values, based on the standardized residuals. This phase is computationally similar to phase 1. Therefore, the computation of data cubes for discovery-driven exploration can be done efficiently.

## 2.5.2 Complex Aggregation at Multiple Granularities: Multifeature Cubes

Data cubes facilitate the answering of data mining queries as they allow the computation of aggregate data at multiple levels of granularity. In this section, you will learn about *multifeature cubes,* which compute complex queries involving multiple dependent aggregates at multiple granularities. These cubes are very useful in practice. Many complex data mining queries can be answered by multifeature cubes without any significant increase in computational cost, in comparison to cube computation for simple queries with standard data cubes.

All of the examples in this section are from the Purchases data of *AllElectronics*, where an *item* is purchased in a sales *region* on a business day (*year, month, day*). The shelf life in months of a given item is stored in *shelf*. The item price and sales (in dollars) at a given region are stored in *price* and *sales*, respectively. To aid in our study of multifeature cubes, let's first look at an example of a simple data cube.

**Example 2.17** *Query 1: A simple data cube query.* Find the total sales in 2000, broken down by item, region, and month, with subtotals for each dimension.

To answer Query 1, a data cube is constructed that aggregates the total sales at the following eight different levels of granularity: {(*item, region, month*), (*item, region*), (*item, month*), (*month, region*), (*item*), (*month*), (*region*), ()}, where () represents **all**. There are several techniques for computing such data cubes efficiently (Section 2.4.1).                                                                   ∎

Query 1 uses a data cube like that studied so far in this chapter. We call such a data cube a simple data cube since it does not involve any dependent aggregates.

*"What is meant by 'dependent aggregates'?"* We answer this by studying the following example of a complex query.

**Example 2.18**  *Query 2: A complex query.* Grouping by all subsets of {item, region, month}, find the maximum price in 2000 for each group, and the total sales among all maximum price tuples.

The specification of such a query using standard SQL can be long, repetitive, and difficult to optimize and maintain. Alternatively, Query 2 can be specified concisely using an extended SQL syntax as follows:

```
select      item, region, month, MAX(price), SUM(R.sales)
from        Purchases
where       year = 2000
cube by     item, region, month: R
such that   R.price = MAX(price)
```

The tuples representing purchases in 2000 are first selected. The **cube by** clause computes aggregates (or group-by's) for all possible combinations of the attributes *item, region,* and *month*. It is an *n*-dimensional generalization of the **group by** clause. The attributes specified in the **cube by** clause are the **grouping attributes**. Tuples with the same value on all grouping attributes form one group. Let the groups be $g_1, \ldots, g_r$. For each group of tuples $g_i$, the maximum price $max_{g_i}$ among the tuples forming the group is computed. The variable $R$ is a **grouping variable**, ranging over all tuples in group $g_i$ whose price is equal to $max_{g_i}$ (as specified in the **such that** clause). The sum of sales of the tuples in $g_i$ that $R$ ranges over is computed and returned with the values of the grouping attributes of $g_i$. The resulting cube is a **multifeature cube** in that it supports complex data mining queries for which multiple dependent aggregates are computed at a variety of granularities. For example, the sum of sales returned in Query 2 is dependent on the set of maximum price tuples for each group.                                                    ∎

Let's look at another example.

**Example 2.19**  *Query 3: An even more complex query.* Grouping by all subsets of *{item, region, month}*, find the maximum price in 2000 for each group. Among the maximum price tuples, find the minimum and maximum item shelf lives. Also find the

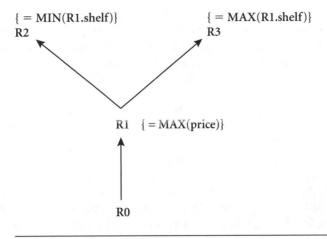

**Figure 2.23** A multifeature cube graph for Query 3.

fraction of the total sales due to tuples that have minimum shelf life within the set of all maximum price tuples, and the fraction of the total sales due to tuples that have maximum shelf life within the set of all maximum price tuples.

The **multifeature cube graph** of Figure 2.23 helps illustrate the aggregate dependencies in the query. There is one node for each grouping variable, plus an additional initial node, R0. Starting from node R0, the set of maximum price tuples in 2000 is first computed (node R1). The graph indicates that grouping variables R2 and R3 are "dependent" on R1, since a directed line is drawn from R1 to each of R2 and R3. In a multifeature cube graph, a directed line from grouping variable $R_i$ to $R_j$ means that $R_j$ always ranges over a subset of the tuples that $R_i$ ranges over. When expressing the query in extended SQL, we write "$R_j$ **in** $R_i$" as shorthand to refer to this case. For example, the minimum shelf life tuples at R2 range over the maximum price tuples at R1, that is, "**R2 in R1**". Similarly, the maximum shelf life tuples at R3 range over the maximum price tuples at R1, that is, "**R3 in R1**".

From the graph, we can express Query 3 in extended SQL as follows:

| | |
|---|---|
| **select** | item, region, month, MAX(price), MIN(R1.shelf), MAX(R1.shelf), SUM(R1.sales), SUM(R2.sales), SUM(R3.sales) |
| **from** | Purchases |
| **where** | year = 2000 |
| **cube by** | item, region, month: R1, R2, R3 |
| **such that** | R1.price = MAX(price) **and** |
| | R2 **in** R1 **and** R2.shelf = MIN(R1.shelf) **and** |
| | R3 **in** R1 **and** R3.shelf = MAX(R1.shelf) |

*"How can multifeature cubes be computed efficiently?"* The computation of a multifeature cube depends on the types of aggregate functions used in the cube. Recall in Section 2.2.4 we saw that aggregate functions can be categorized as either *distributive* (such as count(), sum(), min(), and max()), *algebraic* (such as avg(), min_N(), max_N()), or *holistic* (such as median(), mode(), and rank()). Multifeature cubes can be organized into the same categories.

The type of multifeature cube determines the approach used in its computation. There are a number of methods for the efficient computation of data cubes. The basic strategy of these algorithms is to exploit the lattice structure of the multiple granularities defining the cube, where higher-level granularities are computed from lower-level granularities. This approach suits distributive multifeature cubes. Intuitively, Query 2 is a distributive multifeature cube since we can distribute its computation by incrementally generating the output of the cube at a higher-level granularity using only the output of the cube at a lower-level granularity. The computation of MAX(price) at a higher granularity group can be done by taking the maximum of all of the MAX(price) values at the lower granularity groups. Similarly, SUM(sales) can be computed for a higher-level group by summing all of the SUM(sales) values in its lower-level groups. Some algorithms for efficient cube construction employ optimization techniques based on the estimated size of answers of groups within a data cube. Since the output size for each group in a multifeature cube is constant, the same estimation techniques can be used to estimate the size of intermediate results. Thus, the basic algorithms for efficient computation of simple data cubes can be used to compute distributive multifeature cubes for complex queries without any increase in I/O complexity. There may be a negligible increase in the CPU cost if the aggregate function of the multifeature cube is more complex than, say, a simple SUM(). Algebraic multifeature cubes must first be transformed into distributive multifeature cubes in order for these algorithms to apply. The computation of holistic multifeature cubes is sometimes significantly more expensive than the computation of distributive cubes, although the CPU cost involved is generally acceptable. Therefore, multifeature cubes can be used to answer complex queries with very little additional expense in comparison to simple data cube queries.

## 2.5.3 Other Developments

*"Are there any strategies for answering queries quickly?"* Strategies for answering queries quickly concentrate on providing *intermediate feedback* to the users. For example, in **on-line aggregation**, a data mining system can display "what it knows so far" instead of waiting until the query is fully processed. Such an approximate answer to the given data mining query is periodically refreshed and refined as the computation process continues. Confidence intervals are associated with each estimate, providing the user with additional feedback regarding the reliability of the answer so far. This promotes interactivity with the system—the user gains insight as to whether or not she is probing in the "right" direction without having

to wait until the end of the query. While on-line aggregation does not improve the total time to answer a query, the overall data mining process should be quicker due to the increased interactivity with the system.

Another approach is to employ **top N queries**. Suppose that you are interested in finding only the best-selling items among the millions of items sold at *AllElectronics*. Rather than waiting to obtain a list of all store items, sorted in decreasing order of sales, you would like to see only the top $N$. Using statistics, query processing can be optimized to return the top $N$ items, rather than the whole sorted list. This results in faster response time while helping to promote user interactivity and reduce wasted resources.

## 2.6 From Data Warehousing to Data Mining

*"How do data warehousing and OLAP relate to data mining?"* In this section, we study the usage of data warehousing for information processing, analytical processing, and data mining. We also introduce on-line analytical mining (OLAM), a powerful paradigm that integrates OLAP with data mining technology.

### 2.6.1 Data Warehouse Usage

Data warehouses and data marts are used in a wide range of applications. Business executives in almost every industry use the data collected, integrated, preprocessed, and stored in data warehouses and data marts to perform data analysis and make strategic decisions. In many firms, data warehouses are used as an integral part of a *plan-execute-assess* "closed-loop" feedback system for enterprise management. Data warehouses are used extensively in banking and financial services, consumer goods and retail distribution sectors, and controlled manufacturing, such as demand-based production.

Typically, the longer a data warehouse has been in use, the more it will have evolved. This evolution takes place throughout a number of phases. Initially, the data warehouse is mainly used for generating reports and answering predefined queries. Progressively, it is used to analyze summarized and detailed data, where the results are presented in the form of reports and charts. Later, the data warehouse is used for strategic purposes, performing multidimensional analysis and sophisticated slice-and-dice operations. Finally, the data warehouse may be employed for knowledge discovery and strategic decision making using data mining tools. In this context, the tools for data warehousing can be categorized into *access and retrieval tools*, *database reporting tools*, *data analysis tools*, and *data mining tools*.

Business users need to have the means to know what exists in the data warehouse (through metadata), how to access the contents of the data warehouse, how to examine the contents using analysis tools, and how to present the results of such analysis.

There are three kinds of data warehouse applications: *information processing,* *analytical processing*, and *data mining*:

- **Information processing** supports querying, basic statistical analysis, and reporting using crosstabs, tables, charts, or graphs. A current trend in data warehouse information processing is to construct low-cost Web-based accessing tools that are then integrated with Web browsers.

- **Analytical processing** supports basic OLAP operations, including slice-and-dice, drill-down, roll-up, and pivoting. It generally operates on historical data in both summarized and detailed forms. The major strength of on-line analytical processing over information processing is the multidimensional data analysis of data warehouse data.

- **Data mining** supports knowledge discovery by finding hidden patterns and associations, constructing analytical models, performing classification and prediction, and presenting the mining results using visualization tools.

"*How does data mining relate to information processing and on-line analytical processing?*" Information processing, based on queries, can find useful information. However, answers to such queries reflect the information directly stored in databases or computable by aggregate functions. They do not reflect sophisticated patterns or regularities buried in the database. Therefore, information processing is not data mining.

On-line analytical processing comes a step closer to data mining since it can derive information summarized at multiple granularities from user-specified subsets of a data warehouse. Such descriptions are equivalent to the class/concept descriptions discussed in Chapter 1. Since data mining systems can also mine generalized class/concept descriptions, this raises some interesting questions: "*Do OLAP systems perform data mining? Are OLAP systems actually data mining systems?*"

The functionalities of OLAP and data mining can be viewed as disjoint: OLAP is a data summarization/aggregation *tool* that helps simplify data analysis, while data mining allows the *automated discovery* of implicit patterns and interesting knowledge hidden in large amounts of data. OLAP tools are targeted toward simplifying and supporting interactive data analysis, whereas the goal of data mining tools is to automate as much of the process as possible, while still allowing users to guide the process. In this sense, data mining goes one step beyond traditional on-line analytical processing.

An alternative and broader view of data mining may be adopted in which data mining covers both data description and data modeling. Since OLAP systems can present general descriptions of data from data warehouses, OLAP functions are essentially for user-directed data summary and comparison (by drilling, pivoting, slicing, dicing, and other operations). These are, though limited, data mining functionalities. Yet according to this view, data mining covers a much broader spectrum than simple OLAP operations because it not only performs data summary and comparison, but also performs association, classification, prediction, clustering, time-series analysis, and other data analysis tasks.

Data mining is not confined to the analysis of data stored in data warehouses. It may analyze data existing at more detailed granularities than the summarized data provided in a data warehouse. It may also analyze transactional, spatial, textual, and multimedia data that are difficult to model with current multidimensional database technology. In this context, data mining covers a broader spectrum than OLAP with respect to data mining functionality and the complexity of the data handled.

Since data mining involves more automated and deeper analysis than OLAP, data mining is expected to have broader applications. Data mining can help business managers find and reach more suitable customers, as well as gain critical business insights that may help to drive market share and raise profits. In addition, data mining can help managers understand customer group characteristics and develop optimal pricing strategies accordingly, correct item bundling based not on intuition but on actual item groups derived from customer purchase patterns, reduce promotional spending, and at the same time increase the overall net effectiveness of promotions.

## 2.6.2 From On-Line Analytical Processing to On-Line Analytical Mining

In the field of data mining, substantial research has been performed for data mining at various platforms, including transaction databases, relational databases, spatial databases, text databases, time-series databases, flat files, data warehouses, and so on.

Among many different paradigms and architectures of data mining systems, **on-line analytical mining (OLAM)** (also called **OLAP mining**), which integrates on-line analytical processing (OLAP) with data mining and mining knowledge in multidimensional databases, is particularly important for the following reasons:

- **High quality of data in data warehouses:** Most data mining tools need to work on integrated, consistent, and cleaned data, which requires costly data cleaning, data transformation, and data integration as preprocessing steps. A data warehouse constructed by such preprocessing serves as a valuable source of high-quality data for OLAP as well as for data mining. Notice that data mining may also serve as a valuable tool for data cleaning and data integration as well.

- **Available information processing infrastructure surrounding data warehouses:** Comprehensive information processing and data analysis infrastructures have been or will be systematically constructed surrounding data warehouses, which include accessing, integration, consolidation, and transformation of multiple heterogeneous databases, ODBC/OLE DB connections, Web-accessing and service facilities, and reporting and OLAP analysis tools.

It is prudent to make the best use of the available infrastructures rather than constructing everything from scratch.

- **OLAP-based exploratory data analysis:** Effective data mining needs exploratory data analysis. A user will often want to traverse through a database, select portions of relevant data, analyze them at different granularities, and present knowledge/results in different forms. On-line analytical mining provides facilities for data mining on different subsets of data and at different levels of abstraction, by drilling, pivoting, filtering, dicing and slicing on a data cube and on some intermediate data mining results. This, together with data/knowledge visualization tools, will greatly enhance the power and flexibility of exploratory data mining.

- **On-line selection of data mining functions:** Often a user may not know what kinds of knowledge she would like to mine. By integrating OLAP with multiple data mining functions, on-line analytical mining provides users with the flexibility to select desired data mining functions and swap data mining tasks dynamically.

### Architecture for On-Line Analytical Mining

An OLAM server performs analytical mining in data cubes in a similar manner as an OLAP server performs on-line analytical processing. An integrated OLAM and OLAP architecture is shown in Figure 2.24, where the OLAM and OLAP servers both accept user on-line queries (or commands) via a graphical user interface API and work with the data cube in the data analysis via a cube API. A metadata directory is used to guide the access of the data cube. The data cube can be constructed by accessing and/or integrating multiple databases via an MDDB API and/or by filtering a data warehouse via a database API that may support OLE DB or ODBC connections. Since an OLAM server may perform multiple data mining tasks, such as concept description, association, classification, prediction, clustering, time-series analysis, and so on, it usually consists of multiple integrated data mining modules and is more sophisticated than an OLAP server.

The following chapters of this book are devoted to the study of data mining techniques. As we have seen, the introduction to data warehousing and OLAP technology presented in this chapter is essential to our study of data mining. This is because data warehousing provides users with large amounts of clean, organized, and summarized data, which greatly facilitates data mining. For example, rather than storing the details of each sales transaction, a data warehouse may store a summary of the transactions per item type for each branch or, summarized to a higher level, for each country. The capability of OLAP to provide multiple and dynamic views of summarized data in a data warehouse sets a solid foundation for successful data mining.

Moreover, we also believe that data mining should be a human-centered process. Rather than asking a data mining system to generate patterns and knowledge automatically, a user will often need to interact with the system to perform

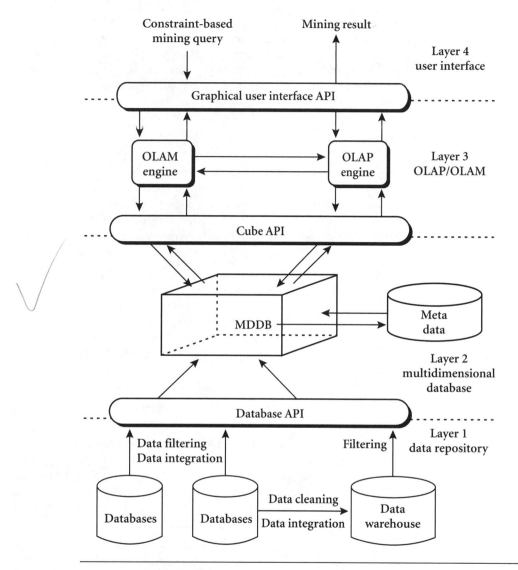

**Figure 2.24**  An integrated OLAM and OLAP architecture.

exploratory data analysis. OLAP sets a good example for interactive data analysis and provides the necessary preparations for exploratory data mining. Consider the discovery of association patterns, for example. Instead of mining associations at a primitive (i.e., low) data level among transactions, users should be allowed to specify roll-up operations along any dimension. For example, a user may like to roll up on the *item* dimension to go from viewing the data for particular TV sets that were purchased to viewing the brands of these TVs, such as SONY or

Panasonic. Users may also navigate from the transaction level to the customer level or customer-type level in the search for interesting associations. Such an OLAP-style of data mining is characteristic of OLAP mining. In our study of the principles of data mining in the following chapters, we place particular emphasis on OLAP mining, that is, on the *integration of data mining and OLAP technology*.

## 2.7 Summary

- A **data warehouse** is a *subject-oriented, integrated, time-variant*, and *nonvolatile* collection of data organized in support of management decision making. Several factors distinguish data warehouses from operational databases. Since the two systems provide quite different functionalities and require different kinds of data, it is necessary to maintain data warehouses separately from operational databases.

- A **multidimensional data model** is typically used for the design of corporate *data warehouses* and *departmental data marts*. Such a model can adopt a *star schema, snowflake schema*, or *fact constellation schema*. The core of the *multidimensional model* is the **data cube**, which consists of a large set of *facts* (or *measures*) and a number of *dimensions*. Dimensions are the entities or perspectives with respect to which an organization wants to keep records and are hierarchical in nature.

- **Concept hierarchies** organize the values of attributes or dimensions into gradual levels of abstraction. They are useful in mining at multiple levels of abstraction.

- **On-line analytical processing (OLAP)** can be performed in data warehouses/marts using the multidimensional data model. Typical OLAP operations include *roll-up, drill-(down, across, through), slice-and-dice, pivot (rotate)*, as well as statistical operations such as ranking, computing moving averages and growth rates, and so on. OLAP operations can be implemented efficiently using the data cube structure.

- Data warehouses often adopt a **three-tier architecture**. The bottom tier is a *warehouse database server*, which is typically a relational database system. The middle tier is an *OLAP server*, and the top tier is a *client*, containing query and reporting tools.

- OLAP servers may use **relational OLAP (ROLAP)**, or **multidimensional OLAP (MOLAP)**, or **hybrid OLAP (HOLAP)**. A ROLAP server uses an extended relational DBMS that maps OLAP operations on multidimensional data to standard relational operations. A MOLAP server maps multidimensional data views directly to array structures. A HOLAP server combines ROLAP and MOLAP. For example, it may use ROLAP for historical data while maintaining frequently accessed data in a separate MOLAP store.

- A data cube consists of a **lattice of cuboids**, each corresponding to a different degree of summarization of the given multidimensional data. **Partial materialization** refers to the selective computation of a subset of the cuboids in the lattice. **Full materialization** refers to the computation of all of the cuboids in the lattice. If the cubes are implemented using MOLAP, then **multiway array aggregation** can be used. This technique "overlaps" some of the aggregation computation so that full materialization can be computed efficiently.

- OLAP query processing can be made more efficient with the use of indexing techniques. In **bitmap indexing**, each attribute has its own bitmap index table. Bitmap indexing reduces join, aggregation, and comparison operations to bit arithmetic. **Join indexing** registers the joinable rows of two or more relations from a relational database, reducing the overall cost of OLAP join operations. **Bitmapped join indexing**, which combines the bitmap and join methods, can be used to further speed up OLAP query processing.

- Data warehouse **metadata** are data defining the warehouse objects. A metadata repository provides details regarding the warehouse structure, data history, the algorithms used for summarization, mappings from the source data to warehouse form, system performance, and business terms and issues.

- A data warehouse contains **back-end tools and utilities** for populating and refreshing the warehouse. These cover data extraction, data cleaning, data transformation, loading, refreshing, and warehouse management.

- **Discovery-driven exploration** of data cubes uses precomputed measures and visual cues to indicate data exceptions at all levels of aggregation, guiding the user in the data analysis process. **Multifeature cubes** compute complex queries involving multiple dependent aggregates at multiple granularities. The computation of cubes for discovery-driven exploration and of multifeature cubes can be achieved efficiently by taking advantage of efficient algorithms for standard data cube computation.

- Data warehouses are used for *information processing* (querying and reporting), *analytical processing* (which allows users to navigate through summarized and detailed data by OLAP operations), and *data mining* (which supports knowledge discovery). OLAP-based data mining is referred to as **OLAP mining**, or on-line analytical mining (**OLAM**), which emphasizes the interactive and exploratory nature of OLAP mining.

## Exercises

2.1 State why, for the integration of multiple heterogeneous information sources, many companies in industry prefer the *update-driven approach* (which constructs and uses data warehouses), rather than the *query-driven approach* (which applies wrappers and integrators). Describe situations where the query-driven approach is preferable over the update-driven approach.

2.2 Briefly compare the following concepts. You may use an example to explain your point(s).

(a) Snowflake schema, fact constellation, starnet query model
(b) Data cleaning, data transformation, refresh
(c) Discovery-driven cube, multifeature cube, virtual warehouse

2.3 Suppose that a data warehouse consists of the three dimensions *time, doctor*, and *patient*, and the two measures *count* and *charge*, where *charge* is the fee that a doctor charges a patient for a visit.

(a) Enumerate three classes of schemas that are popularly used for modeling data warehouses.
(b) Draw a schema diagram for the above data warehouse using one of the schema classes listed in (a).
(c) Starting with the base cuboid [*day, doctor, patient*], what specific *OLAP operations* should be performed in order to list the total fee collected by each doctor in 2000?
(d) To obtain the same list, write an SQL query assuming the data is stored in a relational database with the schema *fee* (*day, month, year, doctor, hospital, patient, count, charge*).

2.4 Suppose that a data warehouse for *Big-University* consists of the following four dimensions: *student, course, semester*, and *instructor*, and two measures *count* and *avg_grade*. When at the lowest conceptual level (e.g., for a given student, course, semester, and instructor combination), the *avg_grade* measure stores the actual course grade of the student. At higher conceptual levels, *avg_grade* stores the average grade for the given combination.

(a) Draw a *snowflake schema* diagram for the data warehouse.
(b) Starting with the base cuboid [*student, course, semester, instructor*], what specific *OLAP operations* (e.g., roll-up from *semester* to *year*) should one perform in order to list the average grade of *CS* courses for each *Big-University* student.
(c) If each dimension has five levels (including **all**), such as *student < major < status < university < **all***, how many cuboids will this cube contain (including the base and apex cuboids)?

2.5 Suppose that a data warehouse consists of the four dimensions *date, spectator, location*, and *game*, and the two measures *count* and *charge*, where *charge* is the fare that a spectator pays when watching a game on a given date. Spectators may be students, adults, or seniors, with each category having its own charge rate.

(a) Draw a *star schema* diagram for the data warehouse.

(b) Starting with the base cuboid [*date*, *spectator*, *location*, *game*], what specific *OLAP operations* should one perform in order to list the total charge paid by student spectators at GM_Place in 2000?

(c) *Bitmap indexing* is useful in data warehousing. Taking this cube as an example, briefly discuss advantages and problems of using a bitmap index structure.

**2.6** Design a data warehouse for a regional weather bureau. The weather bureau has about 1000 probes, which are scattered throughout various land and ocean locations in the region to collect basic weather data, including air pressure, temperature, and precipitation at each hour. All data are sent to the central station, which has collected such data for over 10 years. Your design should facilitate efficient querying and on-line analytical processing, and derive general weather patterns in multidimensional space.

**2.7** Regarding the *computation of measures* in a data cube:

(a) Enumerate three categories of measures, based on the kind of aggregate functions used in computing a data cube.

(b) For a data cube with the three dimensions *time, location*, and *product*, which category does the function *variance* belong to? Describe how to compute it if the cube is partitioned into many chunks.

   Hint: The formula for computing *variance* is $\frac{1}{n}\sum_{i=1}^{n}(x_i)^2 - \bar{x}_i^2$, where $\bar{x}_i$ is the average of $x_i$s.

(c) Suppose the function is "*top 10 sales*." Discuss how to efficiently compute this measure in a data cube.

**2.8** Suppose that one needs to record three measures in a data cube: min, average, and median. Design an efficient computation and storage method for each measure given that the cube allows data to be *deleted incrementally* (i.e., in small portions at a time) from the cube.

**2.9** A popular data warehouse implementation is to construct a multidimensional database, known as a data cube. Unfortunately, this may often generate a huge, yet very sparse multidimensional matrix.

(a) Present an example illustrating such a huge and sparse data cube.

(b) Design an implementation method that can elegantly overcome this sparse matrix problem. Note that you need to explain your data structures in detail and discuss the space needed, as well as how to retrieve data from your structures.

(c) Modify your design in (b) to handle *incremental data updates*. Give the reasoning behind your new design.

**2.10** In data warehouse technology, a multiple dimensional view can be implemented by a relational database technique (ROLAP), or by a multidimensional database technique (MOLAP), or by a hybrid database technique (HOLAP).

(a) Briefly describe each implementation technique.

(b) For each technique, explain how each of the following functions may be implemented:

    i.   The generation of a data warehouse (including aggregation)

    ii.  Roll-up

    iii. Drill-down

    iv. Incremental updating

    Which implementation techniques do you prefer, and why?

**2.11** Suppose that a data warehouse contains 20 dimensions, each with about five levels of granularity.

(a) Users are mainly interested in four particular dimensions, each having three frequently accessed levels for rolling up and drilling down. How would you design a data cube structure to support this preference efficiently?

(b) At times, a user may want to *drill through* the cube, down to the raw data for one or two particular dimensions. How would you support this feature?

**2.12** Suppose that a base cuboid has three dimensions $A, B, C$, with the following number of cells: $|A| = 1,000,000$, $|B| = 100$, and $|C| = 1000$. Suppose that each dimension is evenly partitioned into 10 portions for chunking.

(a) Assuming each dimension has only one level, draw the complete lattice of the cube.

(b) If each cube cell stores one measure with 4 bytes, what is the total size of the computed cube if the cube is *dense*?

(c) State the order for computing the chunks in the cube that requires the least amount of space, and compute the total amount of main memory space required for computing the 2-D planes.

**2.13** Consider the following *multifeature cube* query: Grouping by all subsets of {*item, region, month*}, find the minimum shelf life in 2000 for each group, and the fraction of the total sales due to tuples whose price is less than $100, and whose shelf life is between 1.25 and 1.5 of the minimum shelf life.

(a) Draw the multifeature cube graph for the query.

(b) Express the query in extended SQL.

(c) Is this a *distributive* multifeature cube? Why or why not?

**2.14** What are the differences between the three main types of data warehouse usage: *information processing*, *analytical processing*, and *data mining*? Discuss the motivation behind *OLAP mining (OLAM)*.

## Bibliographic Notes

There are a good number of introductory-level textbooks on data warehousing and OLAP technology, including Inmon [Inm96], Kimball [Kim96], Berson and Smith [BS97], and Thomsen [Tho97]. Chaudhuri and Dayal [CD97] provide a general overview of data warehousing and OLAP technology.

The history of decision support systems can be traced back to the 1960s. However, the proposal of the construction of large data warehouses for multidimensional data analysis is credited to Codd [CCS93] who coined the term *OLAP* for *on-line analytical processing*. The OLAP council was established in 1995. Widom [Wid95] identified several research problems in data warehousing. Kimball [Kim96] provides an overview of the deficiencies of SQL regarding the ability to support comparisons that are common in the business world. For an overview of OLAP systems versus statistical databases, see Shoshani [Sho97].

The DMQL data mining query language was proposed by Han et al. [HFW+96a]. Data mining query languages are further discussed in Chapter 4. Other SQL-based languages for data mining are proposed in Imielinski, Virmani, and Abdulghani [IVA96], Meo, Psaila, and Ceri [MPC96], and Baralis and Psaila [BP97].

Gray et al. [GCB+97] proposed the data cube as a relational aggregation operator generalizing group-by, crosstabs, and subtotals. Harinarayan, Rajaraman, and Ullman [HRU96] proposed a greedy algorithm for the partial materialization of cuboids in the computation of a data cube. Agarwal et al. [AAD+96] proposed several methods for the efficient computation of multidimensional aggregates for ROLAP servers. The chunk-based multiway array aggregation method described in Section 2.4.1 for data cube computation in MOLAP was proposed in Zhao, Deshpande, and Naughton [ZDN97]. Additional methods for the fast computation of data cubes can be found in Beyer and Ramakrishnan [BR99], and Ross and Srivastava [RS97]. Sarawagi and Stonebraker [SS94] developed a chunk-based computation technique for the efficient organization of large multidimensional arrays. Iceberg queries are described in Fang, Shivakumar, Garcia-Molina, et al. [FSGM+98], and Beyer and Ramakrishnan [BR99].

The use of join indices to speed up relational query processing was proposed by Valduriez [Val87]. O'Neil and Graefe [OG95] proposed a bitmapped join index method to speed up OLAP-based query processing. A discussion of the performance of bitmapping and other nontraditional index techniques is given in O'Neil and Quass [OQ97].

For work regarding the selection of materialized cuboids for efficient OLAP query processing, see Chaudhuri and Dayal [CD97], Harinarayan, Rajaraman, and Ullman [HRU96], and Sristava et al. [SDJL96]. Methods for cube size estimation can be found in Deshpande et al. [DNR+97], Ross and Srivastava [RS97], and Beyer and Ramakrishnan [BR99]. Agrawal, Gupta, and Sarawagi [AGS97] proposed operations for modeling multidimensional databases.

There are some recent studies on the implementation of discovery-oriented data cubes for data mining. This includes the discovery-driven exploration of OLAP data cubes by Sarawagi, Agrawal, and Megiddo [SAM98], and the construction of multifeature data cubes by Ross, Srivastava, and Chatziantoniou [RSC98]. Methods for answering queries quickly by on-line aggregation are described in Hellerstein, Haas, and Wang [HHW97] and Hellerstein et al. [HAC+99]. Techniques for estimating the top $N$ queries are proposed in Carey and Kossman [CK98] and Donjerkovic and Ramakrishnan [DR99]. For a discussion of methodologies for OLAM, see Han [Han98].

# Data Preprocessing

**Chapter 3**

**Today's real-world databases are highly susceptible** to noisy, missing, and inconsistent data due to their typically huge size, often several gigabytes or more. *"How can the data be preprocessed in order to help improve the quality of the data and, consequently, of the mining results?"* you may wonder. *"How can the data be preprocessed so as to improve the efficiency and ease of the mining process?"*

There are a number of data preprocessing techniques. *Data cleaning* can be applied to remove noise and correct inconsistencies in the data. *Data integration* merges data from multiple sources into a coherent data store, such as a data warehouse or a data cube. *Data transformations*, such as normalization, may be applied. For example, normalization may improve the accuracy and efficiency of mining algorithms involving distance measurements. *Data reduction* can reduce the data size by aggregating, eliminating redundant features, or clustering, for instance. These data processing techniques, when applied prior to mining, can substantially improve the overall quality of the patterns mined and/or the time required for the actual mining.

In this chapter, you will learn methods for data preprocessing. These methods are organized into the following categories: data cleaning, data integration and transformation, and data reduction. The use of concept hierarchies for data discretization, an alternative form of data reduction, is also discussed. Concept hierarchies can be further used to promote mining at multiple levels of abstraction. You will study how concept hierarchies can be generated automatically from the given data.

## 3.1 Why Preprocess the Data?

Imagine that you are a manager at *AllElectronics* and have been charged with analyzing the company's data with respect to the sales at your branch. You immediately set out to perform this task. You carefully inspect the company's database and data warehouse, identifying and selecting the attributes or dimensions to be included in your analysis, such as *item*, *price*, and *units_sold*. Alas! You notice that several of the attributes for various tuples have no recorded value. For your analysis, you would like to include information as to whether each item purchased was advertised as on sale, yet you discover that this information has not been recorded. Furthermore, users of your database system have reported errors, unusual values, and inconsistencies in the data recorded for some transactions. In other words, the data you wish to analyze by data mining techniques are **incomplete** (lacking attribute values or certain attributes of interest, or containing only aggregate data), **noisy** (containing errors, or *outlier* values that deviate from the expected), and **inconsistent** (e.g., containing discrepancies in the department codes used to categorize items). Welcome to the real world!

Incomplete, noisy, and inconsistent data are commonplace properties of large real-world databases and data warehouses. Incomplete data can occur for a number of reasons. Attributes of interest may not always be available, such as customer information for sales transaction data. Other data may not be included simply because it was not considered important at the time of entry. Relevant data may not be recorded due to a misunderstanding, or because of equipment malfunctions. Data that were inconsistent with other recorded data may have been deleted. Furthermore, the recording of the history or modifications to the data may have been overlooked. Missing data, particularly for tuples with missing values for some attributes, may need to be inferred.

There are many possible reasons for noisy data (having incorrect attribute values). The data collection instruments used may be faulty. There may have been human or computer errors occurring at data entry. Errors in data transmission can also occur. There may be technology limitations, such as limited buffer size for coordinating synchronized data transfer and consumption. Incorrect data may also result from inconsistencies in naming conventions or data codes used. Duplicate tuples also require data cleaning.

**Data cleaning** routines work to "clean" the data by filling in missing values, smoothing noisy data, identifying or removing outliers, and resolving inconsistencies. Dirty data can cause confusion for the mining procedure, resulting in unreliable output. Although most mining routines have some procedures for dealing with incomplete or noisy data, they are not always robust. Instead, they may concentrate on avoiding overfitting the data to the function being modeled. Therefore, a useful preprocessing step is to run your data through some data cleaning routines. Section 3.2 discusses methods for cleaning up your data.

Getting back to your task at *AllElectronics*, suppose that you would like to include data from multiple sources in your analysis. This would involve integrating multiple databases, data cubes, or files, that is, **data integration**. Yet some attributes representing a given concept may have different names in different databases, causing inconsistencies and redundancies. For example, the attribute for customer identification may be referred to as *customer_id* in one data store, and *cust_id* in another. Naming inconsistencies may also occur for attribute values. For example, the same first name could be registered as "Bill" in one database, but "William" in another, and "B." in the third. Furthermore, you suspect that some attributes may be inferred from others (e.g., annual revenue). Having a large amount of redundant data may slow down or confuse the knowledge discovery process. Clearly, in addition to data cleaning, steps must be taken to help avoid redundancies during data integration. Typically, data cleaning and data integration are performed as a preprocessing step when preparing the data for a data warehouse. Additional data cleaning may be performed to detect and remove redundancies that may have resulted from data integration.

Getting back to your data, you have decided, say, that you would like to use a distance-based mining algorithm for your analysis, such as neural networks, nearest-neighbor classifiers, or clustering.[1] Such methods provide better results if the data to be analyzed have been *normalized*, that is, scaled to a specific range such as [0.0, 1.0]. Your customer data, for example, contain the attributes *age* and *annual salary*. The *annual salary* attribute can take many more values than *age*. Therefore, if the attributes are left unnormalized, then distance measurements taken on *annual salary* will generally outweigh distance measurements taken on *age*. Furthermore, it would be useful for your analysis to obtain aggregate information as to the sales per customer region—something that is not part of any precomputed data cube in your data warehouse. You soon realize that **data transformation** operations, such as normalization and aggregation, are additional data preprocessing procedures that would contribute towards the success of the mining process. Data integration and data transformation are discussed in Section 3.3.

*"Hmmm,"* you wonder, as you consider your data even further. *"The data set I have selected for analysis is huge—it is sure to slow down the mining process. Is there any way I can reduce the size of my data set, without jeopardizing the data mining results?"* **Data reduction** obtains a reduced representation of the data set that is much smaller in volume, yet produces the same (or almost the same) analytical results. There are a number of strategies for data reduction. These include *data aggregation* (e.g., building a data cube), *dimension reduction* (e.g., removing irrelevant attributes through correlation analysis), *data compression* (e.g., using encoding schemes such as minimum length encoding or wavelets), and *numerosity reduction* (e.g., "replacing" the data by alternative, smaller representations such as clusters or parametric models). Data can also be "reduced" by *generalization*, where low-level concepts, such as *city* for customer location, are replaced with higher-level concepts, such as *region* or *province_or_state*. A concept hierarchy is used to organize the concepts into varying levels of abstraction. Data reduction is the topic of Section 3.4. Since concept hierarchies are so useful in mining at multiple levels of abstraction, we devote a separate section to the automatic generation of this important data structure. Section 3.5 discusses concept hierarchy generation, a form of data reduction by data discretization.

---

[1] Neural network and nearest-neighbor classifiers are described in Chapter 7, while clustering is discussed in Chapter 8.

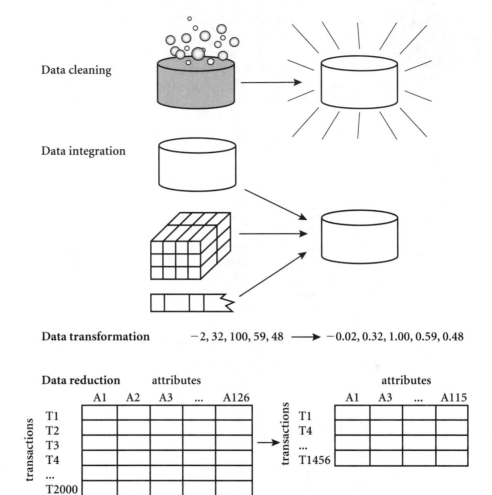

**Figure 3.1** Forms of data preprocessing.

Figure 3.1 summarizes the data preprocessing steps described here. Note that the above categorization is not mutually exclusive. For example, the removal of redundant data may be seen as a form of data cleaning, as well as data reduction.

In summary, real-world data tend to be dirty, incomplete, and inconsistent. Data preprocessing techniques can improve the quality of the data, thereby helping to improve the accuracy and efficiency of the subsequent mining process. Data preprocessing is an important step in the knowledge discovery process, since quality decisions must be based on quality data. Detecting data anomalies, rectifying them early, and reducing the data to be analyzed can lead to huge payoffs for decision making.

# 3.2 Data Cleaning

Real-world data tend to be incomplete, noisy, and inconsistent. *Data cleaning* routines attempt to fill in missing values, smooth out noise while identifying outliers, and correct inconsistencies in the data. In this section, you will study basic methods for data cleaning.

## 3.2.1 Missing Values

Imagine that you need to analyze *AllElectronics* sales and customer data. You note that many tuples have no recorded value for several attributes, such as customer *income*. How can you go about filling in the missing values for this attribute? Let's look at the following methods:

1. **Ignore the tuple:** This is usually done when the class label is missing (assuming the mining task involves classification or description). This method is not very effective, unless the tuple contains several attributes with missing values. It is especially poor when the percentage of missing values per attribute varies considerably.

2. **Fill in the missing value manually:** In general, this approach is time-consuming and may not be feasible given a large data set with many missing values.

3. **Use a global constant to fill in the missing value:** Replace all missing attribute values by the same constant, such as a label like "*Unknown*" or $-\infty$. If missing values are replaced by, say, "*Unknown,*" then the mining program may mistakenly think that they form an interesting concept, since they all have a value in common—that of "*Unknown.*" Hence, although this method is simple, it is not recommended.

4. **Use the attribute mean to fill in the missing value:** For example, suppose that the average income of *AllElectronics* customers is $28,000. Use this value to replace the missing value for *income*.

5. **Use the attribute mean for all samples belonging to the same class as the given tuple:** For example, if classifying customers according to *credit_risk*, replace the missing value with the average *income* value for customers in the same credit risk category as that of the given tuple.

6. **Use the most probable value to fill in the missing value:** This may be determined with regression, inference-based tools using a Bayesian formalism, or decision tree induction. For example, using the other customer attributes in your data set, you may construct a decision tree to predict the missing values for *income*. Decision trees are described in detail in Chapter 7.

Methods 3 to 6 bias the data. The filled-in value may not be correct. Method 6, however, is a popular strategy. In comparison to the other methods, it uses the most information from the present data to predict missing values. By considering the values of the other attributes in its estimation of the missing value for *income*, there is a greater chance that the relationships between *income* and the other attributes are preserved.

### 3.2.2 Noisy Data

"*What is noise?*" **Noise** is a random error or variance in a measured variable. Given a numeric attribute such as, say, *price*, how can we "smooth" out the data to remove the noise? Let's look at the following data smoothing techniques:

**1.** **Binning:** Binning methods smooth a sorted data value by consulting its "neighborhood," that is, the values around it. The sorted values are distributed into a number of "buckets," or *bins*. Because binning methods consult the neighborhood of values, they perform *local* smoothing. Figure 3.2 illustrates some binning techniques. In this example, the data for *price* are first sorted and then partitioned into *equidepth* bins of depth 3 (i.e., each bin contains three values). In **smoothing by bin means**, each value in a bin is replaced by the mean value of the bin. For example, the mean of the values 4, 8, and 15 in Bin 1 is 9. Therefore, each original value in this bin is replaced by the value 9. Similarly, **smoothing by bin medians** can be employed, in which each bin value is replaced by the bin median. In **smoothing by bin boundaries**, the minimum and maximum values in a given bin are identified as the *bin boundaries*. Each bin value is then replaced by the closest boundary value. In general, the larger the width, the greater the effect of the smoothing. Alternatively, bins may be equiwidth, where the interval range of values in each bin is constant. Binning is also used as a discretization technique and is further discussed in Section 3.5 and in Chapter 6.

Sorted data for *price* (in dollars): 4, 8, 15, 21, 21, 24, 25, 28, 34

Partition into (equidepth) bins:
    Bin 1: 4, 8, 15
    Bin 2: 21, 21, 24
    Bin 3: 25, 28, 34

Smoothing by bin means:
    Bin 1: 9, 9, 9
    Bin 2: 22, 22, 22
    Bin 3: 29, 29, 29

Smoothing by bin boundaries:
    Bin 1: 4, 4, 15
    Bin 2: 21, 21, 24
    Bin 3: 25, 25, 34

**Figure 3.2** Binning methods for data smoothing.

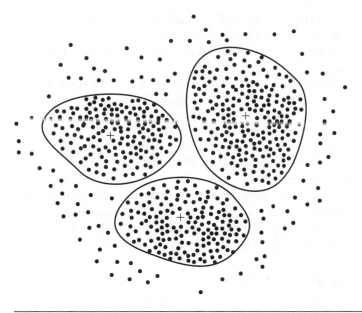

**Figure 3.3**   Outliers may be detected by clustering analysis.

2. **Clustering:** Outliers may be detected by clustering, where similar values are organized into groups, or "clusters." Intuitively, values that fall outside of the set of clusters may be considered outliers (Figure 3.3). Chapter 8 is dedicated to the topic of clustering.

3. **Combined computer and human inspection:** Outliers may be identified through a combination of computer and human inspection. In one application, for example, an information-theoretic measure was used to help identify outlier patterns in a handwritten character database for classification. The measure's value reflected the "surprise" content of the predicted character label with respect to the known label. Outlier patterns may be informative (e.g., identifying useful data exceptions, such as different versions of the characters "0" or "7") or "garbage" (e.g., mislabeled characters). Patterns whose surprise content is above a threshold are output to a list. A human can then sort through the patterns in the list to identify the actual garbage ones. This is much faster than having to manually search through the entire database. The garbage patterns can then be excluded from use in subsequent data mining.

4. **Regression:** Data can be smoothed by fitting the data to a function, such as with regression. *Linear regression* involves finding the "best" line to fit two variables, so that one variable can be used to predict the other. *Multiple linear regression* is an extension of linear regression, where more than two variables are involved

and the data are fit to a multidimensional surface. Using regression to find a mathematical equation to fit the data helps smooth out the noise. Regression is further described in Section 3.4.4, as well as in Chapter 7.

Many methods for data smoothing are also methods for data reduction involving discretization. For example, the binning techniques described above reduce the number of distinct values per attribute. This acts as a form of data reduction for logic-based data mining methods, such as decision tree induction, which repeatedly make value comparisons on sorted data. Concept hierarchies are a form of data discretization that can also be used for data smoothing. A concept hierarchy for *price*, for example, may map real *price* values into *inexpensive, moderately_priced*, and *expensive*, thereby reducing the number of data values to be handled by the mining process. Data discretization is discussed in Section 3.5. Some methods of classification, such as neural networks, have built-in data smoothing mechanisms. Classification is the topic of Chapter 7.

### 3.2.3 Inconsistent Data

There may be inconsistencies in the data recorded for some transactions. Some data inconsistencies may be corrected manually using external references. For example, errors made at data entry may be corrected by performing a paper trace. This may be coupled with routines designed to help correct the inconsistent use of codes. Knowledge engineering tools may also be used to detect the violation of known data constraints. For example, known functional dependencies between attributes can be used to find values contradicting the functional constraints.

There may also be inconsistencies due to data integration, where a given attribute can have different names in different databases. Redundancies may also exist. Data integration and the removal of redundant data are described in Section 3.3.1.

## 3.3 Data Integration and Transformation

Data mining often requires data integration—the merging of data from multiple data stores. The data may also need to be transformed into forms appropriate for mining. This section describes both data integration and data transformation.

### 3.3.1 Data Integration

It is likely that your data analysis task will involve *data integration*, which combines data from multiple sources into a coherent data store, as in data warehousing. These sources may include multiple databases, data cubes, or flat files.

There are a number of issues to consider during data integration. *Schema integration* can be tricky. How can equivalent real-world entities from multiple data sources be matched up? This is referred to as the **entity identification problem**. For example, how can the data analyst or the computer be sure that *customer_id* in one database and *cust_number* in another refer to the same entity? Databases and data warehouses typically have metadata—that is, data about the data. Such metadata can be used to help avoid errors in schema integration.

*Redundancy* is another important issue. An attribute may be redundant if it can be "derived" from another table, such as *annual revenue*. Inconsistencies in attribute or dimension naming can also cause redundancies in the resulting data set.

Some redundancies can be detected by **correlation analysis**. For example, given two attributes, such analysis can measure how strongly one attribute implies the other, based on the available data. The correlation between attributes $A$ and $B$ can be measured by

$$r_{A,B} = \frac{\Sigma (A - \bar{A})(B - \bar{B})}{(n - 1)\sigma_A \sigma_B} \tag{3.1}$$

where $n$ is the number of tuples, $\bar{A}$ and $\bar{B}$ are the respective mean values of $A$ and $B$, and $\sigma_A$ and $\sigma_B$ are the respective standard deviations of $A$ and $B$.[2] If the resulting value of Equation (3.1) is greater than 0, then $A$ and $B$ are positively correlated, meaning that the values of $A$ increase as the values of $B$ increase. The higher the value, the more each attribute implies the other. Hence, a high value may indicate that $A$ (or $B$) may be removed as a redundancy. If the resulting value is equal to 0, then $A$ and $B$ are independent and there is no correlation between them. If the resulting value is less than 0, then $A$ and $B$ are negatively correlated, where the values of one attribute increase as the values of the other attribute decrease. This means that each attribute discourages the other. Equation (3.1) may detect a correlation between the *customer_id* and *cust_number* attributes described above. Correlation analysis is further described in Section 6.5.2.

In addition to detecting redundancies between attributes, duplication should also be detected at the tuple level (e.g., where there are two or more identical tuples for a given unique data entry case).

A third important issue in data integration is the *detection and resolution of data value conflicts*. For example, for the same real-world entity, attribute values

---

[2] The mean of $A$ is

$$\bar{A} = \frac{\Sigma A}{n}.$$

The standard deviation of $A$ is

$$\sigma_A = \sqrt{\frac{\Sigma (A - \bar{A})^2}{n - 1}}.$$

from different sources may differ. This may be due to differences in representation, scaling, or encoding. For instance, a *weight* attribute may be stored in metric units in one system and British imperial units in another. The *price* of different hotels may involve not only different currencies but also different services (such as free breakfast) and taxes. Such semantic heterogeneity of data poses great challenges in data integration.

Careful integration of the data from multiple sources can help reduce and avoid redundancies and inconsistencies in the resulting data set. This can help improve the accuracy and speed of the subsequent mining process.

## 3.3.2 Data Transformation

In *data transformation*, the data are transformed or consolidated into forms appropriate for mining. Data transformation can involve the following:

- **Smoothing**, which works to remove the noise from data. Such techniques include binning, clustering, and regression.

- **Aggregation**, where summary or aggregation operations are applied to the data. For example, the daily sales data may be aggregated so as to compute monthly and annual total amounts. This step is typically used in constructing a data cube for analysis of the data at multiple granularities.

- **Generalization** of the data, where low-level or "primitive" (raw) data are replaced by higher-level concepts through the use of concept hierarchies. For example, categorical attributes, like *street*, can be generalized to higher-level concepts, like *city* or *country*. Similarly, values for numeric attributes, like *age*, may be mapped to higher-level concepts, like *young, middle-aged*, and *senior*.

- **Normalization**, where the attribute data are scaled so as to fall within a small specified range, such as −1.0 to 1.0, or 0.0 to 1.0.

- **Attribute construction** (or *feature construction*), where new attributes are constructed and added from the given set of attributes to help the mining process.

Smoothing is a form of data cleaning and was discussed in Section 3.2.2. Aggregation and generalization also serve as forms of data reduction and are discussed in Sections 3.4 and 3.5, respectively. In this section, we therefore discuss normalization and attribute construction.

An attribute is normalized by scaling its values so that they fall within a small specified range, such as 0.0 to 1.0. Normalization is particularly useful for classification algorithms involving neural networks, or distance measurements such as nearest neighbor classification and clustering. If using the neural network back-propagation algorithm for classification mining (Chapter 7), normalizing the input values for each attribute measured in the training samples will help speed up the learning phase. For distance-based methods, normalization helps prevent attributes with initially large ranges (e.g., *income*) from outweighing attributes with initially smaller ranges (e.g., binary attributes). There are many methods for data normalization. We study three: *min-max normalization, z-score normalization,* and *normalization by decimal scaling.*

**Min-max normalization** performs a linear transformation on the original data. Suppose that $min_A$ and $max_A$ are the minimum and maximum values of an attribute $A$. Min-max normalization maps a value $v$ of $A$ to $v'$ in the range $[new\_min_A, new\_max_A]$ by computing

$$v' = \frac{v - min_A}{max_A - min_A}(new\_max_A - new\_min_A) + new\_min_A. \tag{3.2}$$

Min-max normalization preserves the relationships among the original data values. It will encounter an "out of bounds" error if a future input case for normalization falls outside of the original data range for $A$.

**Example 3.1** Suppose that the minimum and maximum values for the attribute *income* are $12,000 and $98,000, respectively. We would like to map *income* to the range [0.0, 1.0]. By min-max normalization, a value of $73,600 for *income* is transformed to $\frac{73,600-12,000}{98,000-12,000}(1.0 - 0) + 0 = 0.716$. ∎

In **z-score normalization** (or *zero-mean normalization*), the values for an attribute $A$ are normalized based on the mean and standard deviation of $A$. A value $v$ of $A$ is normalized to $v'$ by computing

$$v' = \frac{v - \bar{A}}{\sigma_A} \tag{3.3}$$

where $\bar{A}$ and $\sigma_A$ are the mean and standard deviation, respectively, of attribute $A$. This method of normalization is useful when the actual minimum and maximum of attribute $A$ are unknown, or when there are outliers that dominate the min-max normalization.

**Example 3.2** Suppose that the mean and standard deviation of the values for the attribute *income* are $54,000 and $16,000, respectively. With z-score normalization, a value of $73,600 for *income* is transformed to $\frac{73,600-54,000}{16,000} = 1.225$. ∎

**Normalization by decimal scaling** normalizes by moving the decimal point of values of attribute $A$. The number of decimal points moved depends on the maximum absolute value of $A$. A value $v$ of $A$ is normalized to $v'$ by computing

$$v' = \frac{v}{10^j}, \tag{3.4}$$

where $j$ is the smallest integer such that $Max(|v'|) < 1$.

**Example 3.3** Suppose that the recorded values of $A$ range from $-986$ to $917$. The maximum absolute value of $A$ is $986$. To normalize by decimal scaling, we therefore divide each value by $1000$ (i.e., $j = 3$) so that $-986$ normalizes to $-0.986$. ∎

Note that normalization can change the original data quite a bit, especially the latter two methods shown above. It is also necessary to save the normalization parameters (such as the mean and standard deviation if using z-score normalization) so that future data can be normalized in a uniform manner.

In **attribute construction**, new attributes are constructed from the given attributes and added in order to help improve the accuracy and understanding of structure in high-dimensional data. For example, we may wish to add the attribute *area* based on the attributes *height* and *width*. Attribute construction can help alleviate the *fragmentation problem* when decision tree algorithms are used for classification, where an attribute is repeatedly tested along a path in the derived decision tree.[3] Examples of operators for attribute construction include **and** for binary attributes and **product** for nominal attributes. By combining attributes, attribute construction can discover missing information about the relationships between data attributes that can be useful for knowledge discovery.

## 3.4 Data Reduction

Imagine that you have selected data from the *AllElectronics* data warehouse for analysis. The data set will likely be huge! Complex data analysis and mining on huge amounts of data may take a very long time, making such analysis impractical or infeasible.

**Data reduction** techniques can be applied to obtain a reduced representation of the data set that is much smaller in volume, yet closely maintains the integrity of the original data. That is, mining on the reduced data set should be more efficient yet produce the same (or almost the same) analytical results.

Strategies for data reduction include the following:

1. **Data cube aggregation**, where aggregation operations are applied to the data in the construction of a data cube.

2. **Dimension reduction**, where irrelevant, weakly relevant, or redundant attributes or dimensions may be detected and removed.

3. **Data compression**, where encoding mechanisms are used to reduce the data set size.

---

[3] Decision trees are described in detail in Chapter 7.

4. **Numerosity reduction**, where the data are replaced or estimated by alternative, smaller data representations such as parametric models (which need store only the model parameters instead of the actual data), or nonparametric methods such as clustering, sampling, and the use of histograms.

5. **Discretization and concept hierarchy generation**, where raw data values for attributes are replaced by ranges or higher conceptual levels. Concept hierarchies allow the mining of data at multiple levels of abstraction and are a powerful tool for data mining. We therefore defer the discussion of automatic concept hierarchy generation to Section 3.5, which is devoted entirely to this topic.

Strategies 1 to 4 above are discussed in the remainder of this section. The computational time spent on data reduction should not outweigh or "erase" the time saved by mining on a reduced data set size.

### 3.4.1 Data Cube Aggregation

Imagine that you have collected the data for your analysis. These data consist of the *AllElectronics* sales per quarter, for the years 1997 to 1999. You are, however, interested in the annual sales (total per year), rather than the total per quarter. Thus the data can be *aggregated* so that the resulting data summarize the total sales per year instead of per quarter. This aggregation is illustrated in Figure 3.4. The resulting data set is smaller in volume, without loss of information necessary for the analysis task.

Data cubes were discussed in Chapter 2. For completeness, we briefly review some of that material here. Data cubes store multidimensional aggregated information. For example, Figure 3.5 shows a data cube for multidimensional

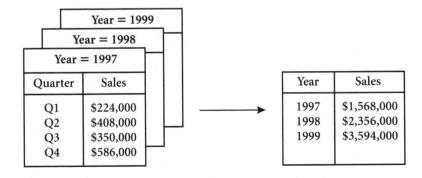

**Figure 3.4**  Sales data for a given branch of *AllElectronics* for the years 1997 to 1999. On the left, the sales are shown per quarter. On the right, the data are aggregated to provide the annual sales.

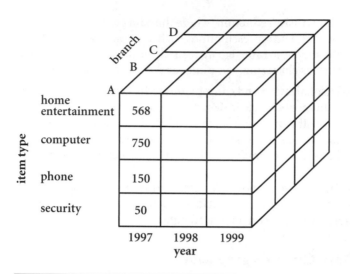

**Figure 3.5** A data cube for sales at *AllElectronics*.

analysis of sales data with respect to annual sales per item type for each *AllElectronics* branch. Each cell holds an aggregate data value, corresponding to the data point in multidimensional space. Concept hierarchies may exist for each attribute, allowing the analysis of data at multiple levels of abstraction. For example, a hierarchy for *branch* could allow branches to be grouped into regions, based on their address. Data cubes provide fast access to precomputed, summarized data, thereby benefiting on-line analytical processing as well as data mining.

The cube created at the lowest level of abstraction is referred to as the *base cuboid*. A cube for the highest level of abstraction is the *apex cuboid*. For the sales data of Figure 3.5, the apex cuboid would give one total—the total *sales* for all three years, for all item types, and for all branches. Data cubes created for varying levels of abstraction are often referred to as *cuboids*, so that a data cube may instead refer to a *lattice of cuboids*. Each higher level of abstraction further reduces the resulting data size.

The base cuboid should correspond to an individual entity of interest, such as *sales* or *customer*. In other words, the lowest level should be usable, or useful for the analysis. Since data cubes provide fast accessing to precomputed, summarized data, they should be used when possible to reply to queries regarding aggregated information. When replying to such OLAP queries or data mining requests, the *smallest* available cuboid relevant to the given task should be used. This issue is also addressed in Chapter 2.

## 3.4.2 Dimensionality Reduction

Data sets for analysis may contain hundreds of attributes, many of which may be irrelevant to the mining task, or redundant. For example, if the task is to classify customers as to whether or not they are likely to purchase a popular new CD at *AllElectronics* when notified of a sale, attributes such as the customer's telephone number are likely to be irrelevant, unlike attributes such as *age* or *music_taste*. Although it may be possible for a domain expert to pick out some of the useful attributes, this can be a difficult and time-consuming task, especially when the behavior of the data is not well known (hence, a reason behind its analysis!). Leaving out relevant attributes or keeping irrelevant attributes may be detrimental, causing confusion for the mining algorithm employed. This can result in discovered patterns of poor quality. In addition, the added volume of irrelevant or redundant attributes can slow down the mining process.

*Dimensionality reduction* reduces the data set size by removing such attributes (or dimensions) from it. Typically, methods of attribute subset selection are applied. The goal of **attribute subset selection** is to find a minimum set of attributes such that the resulting probability distribution of the data classes is as close as possible to the original distribution obtained using all attributes. Mining on a reduced set of attributes has an additional benefit. It reduces the number of attributes appearing in the discovered patterns, helping to make the patterns easier to understand.

*"How can we find a 'good' subset of the original attributes?"* For $d$ attributes, there are $2^d$ possible subsets. An exhaustive search for the optimal subset of attributes can be prohibitively expensive, especially as $d$ and the number of data classes increase. Therefore, heuristic methods that explore a reduced search space are commonly used for attribute subset selection. These methods are typically *greedy* in that, while searching through attribute space, they always make what looks to be the best choice at the time. Their strategy is to make a locally optimal choice in the hope that this will lead to a globally optimal solution. Such greedy methods are effective in practice and may come close to estimating an optimal solution.

The "best" (and "worst") attributes are typically determined using tests of statistical significance, which assume that the attributes are independent of one another. Many other attribute evaluation measures can be used, such as the *information gain* measure used in building decision trees for classification.[4]

Basic heuristic methods of attribute subset selection include the following techniques, some of which are illustrated in Figure 3.6.

1. **Stepwise forward selection:** The procedure starts with an empty set of attributes. The best of the original attributes is determined and added to the

---

[4] The information gain measure is described in detail in Sections 5.3.2 and 7.3.1. It is briefly described in Section 3.5.1 with respect to attribute discretization.

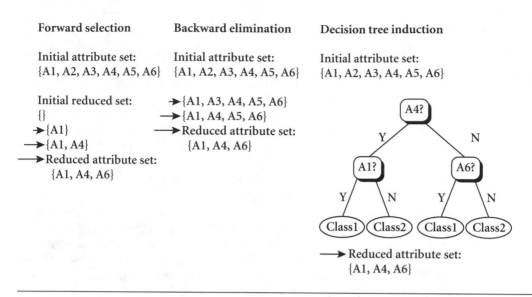

**Forward selection**

Initial attribute set:
{A1, A2, A3, A4, A5, A6}

Initial reduced set:
{}
➤{A1}
⟶{A1, A4}
⟶Reduced attribute set:
{A1, A4, A6}

**Backward elimination**

Initial attribute set:
{A1, A2, A3, A4, A5, A6}

➤{A1, A3, A4, A5, A6}
⟶{A1, A4, A5, A6}
⟶Reduced attribute set:
{A1, A4, A6}

**Decision tree induction**

Initial attribute set:
{A1, A2, A3, A4, A5, A6}

⟶Reduced attribute set:
{A1, A4, A6}

**Figure 3.6**  Greedy (heuristic) methods for attribute subset selection.

set. At each subsequent iteration or step, the best of the remaining original attributes is added to the set.

**2. Stepwise backward elimination:** The procedure starts with the full set of attributes. At each step, it removes the worst attribute remaining in the set.

**3. Combination of forward selection and backward elimination:** The stepwise forward selection and backward elimination methods can be combined so that, at each step, the procedure selects the best attribute and removes the worst from among the remaining attributes.

The stopping criteria for methods 1 to 3 may vary. The procedure may employ a threshold on the measure used to determine when to stop the attribute selection process.

▪ **Decision tree induction:** Decision tree algorithms, such as ID3 and C4.5, were originally intended for classification. Decision tree induction constructs a flow-chart-like structure where each internal (nonleaf) node denotes a test on an attribute, each branch corresponds to an outcome of the test, and each external (leaf) node denotes a class prediction. At each node, the algorithm chooses the "best" attribute to partition the data into individual classes.

When decision tree induction is used for attribute subset selection, a tree is constructed from the given data. All attributes that do not appear in the tree are assumed to be irrelevant. The set of attributes appearing in the tree form the reduced subset of attributes. This method of attribute selection is visited again in greater detail in Chapter 5.

If the mining task is classification, and the mining algorithm itself is used to determine the attribute subset, then this is called a **wrapper approach**; otherwise, it is a **filter approach**. In general, the wrapper approach leads to greater accuracy since it optimizes the evaluation measure of the algorithm while removing attributes. However, it requires much more computation than a filter approach.

### 3.4.3  Data Compression

In *data compression*, data encoding or transformations are applied so as to obtain a reduced or "compressed" representation of the original data. If the original data can be *reconstructed* from the compressed data without any loss of information, the data compression technique used is called **lossless**. If, instead, we can reconstruct only an approximation of the original data, then the data compression technique is called **lossy**. There are several well-tuned algorithms for string compression. Although they are typically lossless, they allow only limited manipulation of the data. In this section, we instead focus on two popular and effective methods of lossy data compression: *wavelet transforms* and *principal components analysis*.

#### Wavelet Transforms

The **discrete wavelet transform (DWT)** is a linear signal processing technique that, when applied to a data vector $D$, transforms it to a numerically different vector, $D'$, of **wavelet coefficients**. The two vectors are of the same length.

"Hmmm," you wonder. "How can this technique be useful for data reduction if the wavelet transformed data are of the same length as the original data?" The usefulness lies in the fact that the wavelet transformed data can be truncated. A compressed approximation of the data can be retained by storing only a small fraction of the strongest of the wavelet coefficients. For example, all wavelet coefficients larger than some user-specified threshold can be retained. The remaining coefficients is set to 0. The resulting data representation is therefore very sparse, so that operations that can take advantage of data sparsity are computationally very fast if performed in wavelet space. The technique also works to remove noise without smoothing out the main features of the data, making it effective for data cleaning as well. Given a set of coefficients, an approximation of the original data can be constructed by applying the *inverse* of the DWT used.

The DWT is closely related to the *discrete Fourier transform (DFT)*, a signal processing technique involving sines and cosines. In general, however, the DWT achieves better lossy compression. That is, if the same number of coefficients is retained for a DWT and a DFT of a given data vector, the DWT version will provide a more accurate approximation of the original data. Hence, for an equivalent approximation, the DWT requires less space than the DFT. Unlike the DFT,

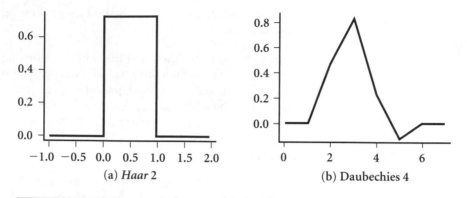

(a) *Haar* 2  (b) Daubechies 4

**Figure 3.7** Examples of wavelet families. The number next to a wavelet name is the number of *vanishing moments* of the wavelet. This is a set of mathematical relationships that the coefficients must satisfy and is related to the number of coefficients.

wavelets are quite localized in space, contributing to the conservation of local detail.

There is only one DFT, yet there are several families of DWTs. Figure 3.7 shows some wavelet families. Popular wavelet transforms include the Haar_2, Daubechies_4, and Daubechies_6 transforms. The general procedure for applying a discrete wavelet transform uses a hierarchical *pyramid algorithm* that halves the data at each iteration, resulting in fast computational speed. The method is as follows:

1. The length, $L$, of the input data vector must be an integer power of 2. This condition can be met by padding the data vector with zeros, as necessary.

2. Each transform involves applying two functions. The first applies some data smoothing, such as a sum or weighted average. The second performs a weighted difference, which acts to bring out the detailed features of the data.

3. The two functions are applied to pairs of the input data, resulting in two sets of data of length $L/2$. In general, these represent a smoothed or low frequency version of the input data, and the high frequency content of it, respectively.

4. The two functions are recursively applied to the sets of data obtained in the previous loop, until the resulting data sets obtained are of length 2.

5. A selection of values from the data sets obtained in the above iterations are designated the wavelet coefficients of the transformed data.

Equivalently, a matrix multiplication can be applied to the input data in order to obtain the wavelet coefficients, where the matrix used depends on the given DWT. The matrix must be **orthonormal**, meaning that the columns are unit vectors and are mutually orthogonal, so that the matrix inverse is just its transpose. Although we do not have room to discuss it here, this property allows the reconstruction of the data from the smooth and smooth-difference data sets. By factoring the matrix used into a product of a few sparse matrices, the resulting *"fast DWT"* algorithm has a complexity of $O(n)$ for an input vector of length $n$.

Wavelet transforms can be applied to multidimensional data, such as a data cube. This is done by first applying the transform to the first dimension, then to the second, and so on. The computational complexity involved is linear with respect to the number of cells in the cube. Wavelet transforms give good results on sparse or skewed data and on data with ordered attributes. Lossy compression by wavelets is reportedly better than JPEG compression, the current commercial standard. Wavelet transforms have many real-world applications, including the compression of fingerprint images, computer vision, analysis of time-series data, and data cleaning.

## Principal Components Analysis

In this subsection we provide an intuitive introduction to principal components analysis as a method of data compression. A detailed theoretical explanation is beyond the scope of this book.

Suppose that the data to be compressed consist of $N$ tuples or data vectors, from $k$ dimensions. **Principal components analysis**, or **PCA** (also called the Karhunen-Loeve, or K-L method), searches for $c$ $k$-dimensional orthogonal vectors that can best be used to represent the data, where $c \leq k$. The original data are thus projected onto a much smaller space, resulting in data compression. PCA can be used as a form of dimensionality reduction. However, unlike attribute subset selection, which reduces the attribute set size by retaining a subset of the initial set of attributes, PCA "combines" the essence of attributes by creating an alternative, smaller set of variables. The initial data can then be projected onto this smaller set.

The basic procedure is as follows:

1. The input data are normalized, so that each attribute falls within the same range. This step helps ensure that attributes with large domains will not dominate attributes with smaller domains.

2. PCA computes $c$ orthonormal vectors that provide a basis for the normalized input data. These are unit vectors that each point in a direction perpendicular to the others. These vectors are referred to as the *principal components*. The input data are a linear combination of the principal components.

3. The principal components are sorted in order of decreasing "significance" or strength. The principal components essentially serve as a new set of axes for the data, providing important information about variance. That is, the sorted axes are such that the first axis shows the most variance among the data, the second axis shows the next highest variance, and so on. For example, Figure 3.8

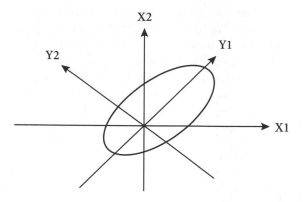

**Figure 3.8** Principal components analysis. $Y1$ and $Y2$ are the first two principal components for the given data.

shows the first two principal components, $Y1$ and $Y2$, for the given set of data originally mapped to the axes $X1$ and $X2$. This information helps identify groups or patterns within the data.

4. Since the components are sorted according to decreasing order of "significance," the size of the data can be reduced by eliminating the weaker components, that is, those with low variance. Using the strongest principal components, it should be possible to reconstruct a good approximation of the original data.

PCA is computationally inexpensive, can be applied to ordered and unordered attributes, and can handle sparse data and skewed data. Multidimensional data of more than two dimensions can be handled by reducing the problem to two dimensions. For example, a 3-D data cube for sales with the dimensions *item_type*, *branch*, and *year* must first be reduced to a 2-D cube, such as with the dimensions *item_type* and *branch* × *year*. In comparison with wavelet transforms for data compression, PCA tends to be better at handling sparse data, while wavelet transforms are more suitable for data of high dimensionality.

### 3.4.4 Numerosity Reduction

*"Can we reduce the data volume by choosing alternative, 'smaller' forms of data representation?"* Techniques of *numerosity reduction* can indeed be applied for this purpose. These techniques may be parametric or nonparametric. For *parametric methods*, a model is used to estimate the data, so that typically only the data parameters need be stored, instead of the actual data. (Outliers may also be stored.) Log-linear models, which estimate discrete multidimensional proba-

bility distributions, are an example. *Nonparametric methods* for storing reduced representations of the data include histograms, clustering, and sampling.

Let's have a look at each of the numerosity reduction techniques mentioned above.

### Regression and Log-Linear Models

Regression and log-linear models can be used to approximate the given data. In **linear regression**, the data are modeled to fit a straight line. For example, a random variable, $Y$ (called a *response variable*), can be modeled as a linear function of another random variable, $X$ (called a *predictor variable*), with the equation

$$Y = \alpha + \beta X, \tag{3.5}$$

where the variance of $Y$ is assumed to be constant. The coefficients $\alpha$ and $\beta$ (called *regression coefficients*) specify the $Y$-intercept and slope of the line, respectively. These coefficients can be solved for by the *method of least squares*, which minimizes the error between the actual line separating the data and the estimate of the line. **Multiple regression** is an extension of linear regression allowing a response variable $Y$ to be modeled as a linear function of a multidimensional feature vector.

**Log-linear models** approximate discrete multidimensional probability distributions. The method can be used to estimate the probability of each cell in a base cuboid for a set of discretized attributes, based on the smaller cuboids making up the data cube lattice. This allows higher-order data cubes to be constructed from lower-order ones. Log-linear models are therefore also useful for data compression (since the smaller-order cuboids together typically occupy less space than the base cuboid) and data smoothing (since cell estimates in the smaller-order cuboids are less subject to sampling variations than cell estimates in the base cuboid).

Regression and log-linear models can both be used on sparse data although their application may be limited. While both methods can handle skewed data, regression does exceptionally well. Regression can be computationally intensive when applied to high-dimensional data, while log-linear models show good scalability for up to 10 or so dimensions. Regression and log-linear models are further discussed in Section 7.8.

### Histograms

Histograms use binning to approximate data distributions and are a popular form of data reduction. A **histogram** for an attribute $A$ partitions the data distribution of $A$ into disjoint subsets, or *buckets*. The buckets are displayed on a horizontal axis, while the height (and area) of a bucket typically reflects the average frequency of the values represented by the bucket. If each bucket represents only a single attribute-value/frequency pair, the buckets are called *singleton buckets*. Often, buckets instead represent continuous ranges for the given attribute.

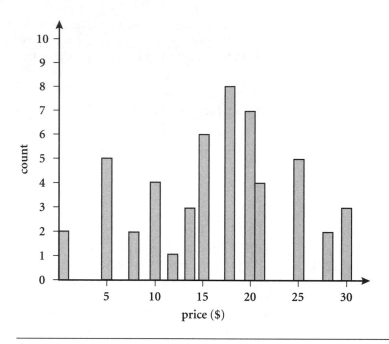

**Figure 3.9** A histogram for *price* using singleton buckets—each bucket represents one price-value/ frequency pair.

**Example 3.4** The following data are a list of prices of commonly sold items at *AllElectronics* (rounded to the nearest dollar). The numbers have been sorted: 1, 1, 5, 5, 5, 5, 5, 8, 8, 10, 10, 10, 10, 12, 14, 14, 14, 15, 15, 15, 15, 15, 15, 18, 18, 18, 18, 18, 18, 18, 18, 20, 20, 20, 20, 20, 20, 20, 21, 21, 21, 21, 25, 25, 25, 25, 25, 28, 28, 30, 30, 30.

Figure 3.9 shows a histogram for the data using singleton buckets. To further reduce the data, it is common to have each bucket denote a continuous range of values for the given attribute. In Figure 3.10, each bucket represents a different $10 range for *price*.    ∎

"*How are the buckets determined and the attribute values partitioned?*" There are several partitioning rules, including the following:

- **Equiwidth:** In an equiwidth histogram, the width of each bucket range is uniform (such as the width of $10 for the buckets in Figure 3.10).

- **Equidepth** (or equiheight): In an equidepth histogram, the buckets are created so that, roughly, the frequency of each bucket is constant (that is, each bucket contains roughly the same number of contiguous data samples).

- **V-Optimal:** If we consider all of the possible histograms for a given number of buckets, the V-Optimal histogram is the one with the least variance. Histogram

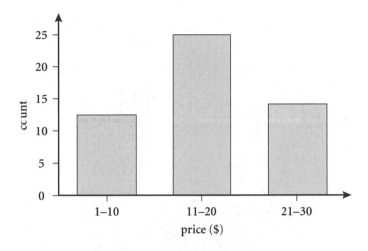

**Figure 3.10** An equiwidth histogram for *price*, where values are aggregated so that each bucket has a uniform width of $10.

variance is a weighted sum of the original values that each bucket represents, where bucket weight is equal to the number of values in the bucket.

- **MaxDiff:** In a MaxDiff histogram, we consider the difference between each pair of adjacent values. A bucket boundary is established between each pair for pairs having the $\beta - 1$ largest differences, where $\beta$ is user-specified.

V-Optimal and MaxDiff histograms tend to be the most accurate and practical. Histograms are highly effective at approximating both sparse and dense data, as well as highly skewed and uniform data. The histograms described above for single attributes can be extended for multiple attributes. *Multidimensional histograms* can capture dependencies between attributes. Such histograms have been found effective in approximating data with up to five attributes. More studies are needed regarding the effectiveness of multidimensional histograms for very high dimensions. Singleton buckets are useful for storing outliers with high frequency. Histograms are further described in Section 5.5.

### Clustering

Clustering techniques consider data tuples as objects. They partition the objects into groups or *clusters*, so that objects within a cluster are "similar" to one another and "dissimilar" to objects in other clusters. Similarity is commonly defined in terms of how "close" the objects are in space, based on a distance function. The "quality" of a cluster may be represented by its *diameter*, the maximum distance between any two objects in the cluster. *Centroid distance* is an alternative measure

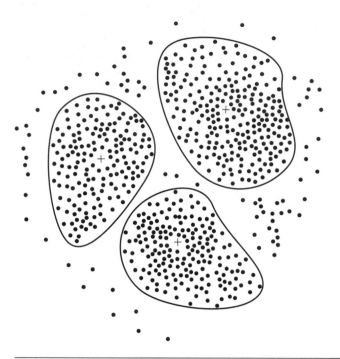

**Figure 3.11** A 2-D plot of customer data with respect to customer locations in a city, showing three data clusters. Each cluster centroid is marked with a "+".

of cluster quality and is defined as the average distance of each cluster object from the cluster centroid (denoting the "average object," or average point in space for the cluster). Figure 3.11 shows a 2-D plot of customer data with respect to customer locations in a city, where the centroid of each cluster is shown with a "+". Three data clusters are visible.

In data reduction, the cluster representations of the data are used to replace the actual data. The effectiveness of this technique depends on the nature of the data. It is much more effective for data that can be organized into distinct clusters than for smeared data.

In database systems, **multidimensional index trees** are primarily used for providing fast data access. They can also be used for hierarchical data reduction, providing a multiresolution clustering of the data. This can be used to provide approximate answers to queries. An index tree recursively partitions the multidimensional space for a given set of data objects, with the root node representing the entire space. Such trees are typically balanced, consisting of internal and leaf nodes. Each parent node contains keys and pointers to child nodes that, collectively, represent the space represented by the parent node. Each leaf node contains pointers to the data tuples they represent (or to the actual tuples).

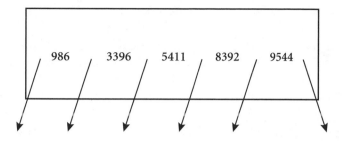

**Figure 3.12** The root of a B+-tree for a given set of data.

An index tree can therefore store aggregate and detail data at varying levels of resolution or abstraction. It provides a hierarchy of clusterings of the data set, where each cluster has a label that holds for the data contained in the cluster. If we consider each child of a parent node as a bucket, then an index tree can be considered as a *hierarchical histogram*. For example, consider the root of a B+-tree as shown in Figure 3.12, with pointers to the data keys 986, 3396, 5411, 8392, and 9544. Suppose that the tree contains 10,000 tuples with keys ranging from 1 to 9999. The data in the tree can be approximated by an equidepth histogram of six buckets for the key ranges 1 to 985, 986 to 3395, 3396 to 5410, 5411 to 8391, 8392 to 9543, and 9544 to 9999. Each bucket contains roughly 10,000/6 items. Similarly, each bucket is subdivided into smaller buckets, allowing for aggregate data at a finer-detailed level. The use of multidimensional index trees as a form of data reduction relies on an ordering of the attribute values in each dimension. Multidimensional index trees include R-trees, quad-trees, and their variations. They are well suited for handling both sparse and skewed data.

There are many measures for defining clusters and cluster quality. Clustering methods are further described in Chapter 8.

## Sampling

Sampling can be used as a data reduction technique since it allows a large data set to be represented by a much smaller random sample (or subset) of the data. Suppose that a large data set, $D$, contains $N$ tuples. Let's have a look at some possible samples for $D$.

- **Simple random sample without replacement (SRSWOR) of size $n$:** This is created by drawing $n$ of the $N$ tuples from $D$ ($n < N$), where the probability of drawing any tuple in $D$ is $1/N$, that is, all tuples are equally likely.
- **Simple random sample with replacement (SRSWR) of size $n$:** This is similar to SRSWOR, except that each time a tuple is drawn from $D$, it is recorded and

then *replaced*. That is, after a tuple is drawn, it is placed back in $D$ so that it may be drawn again.

▪ **Cluster sample:** If the tuples in $D$ are grouped into $M$ mutually disjoint "clusters," then an SRS of $m$ clusters can be obtained, where $m < M$. For example, tuples in a database are usually retrieved a page at a time, so that each page can be considered a cluster. A reduced data representation can be obtained by applying, say, SRSWOR to the pages, resulting in a cluster sample of the tuples.

▪ **Stratified sample:** If $D$ is divided into mutually disjoint parts called *strata,* a stratified sample of $D$ is generated by obtaining an SRS at each stratum. This helps to ensure a representative sample, especially when the data are skewed. For example, a stratified sample may be obtained from customer data, where a stratum is created for each customer age group. In this way, the age group having the smallest number of customers will be sure to be represented.

These samples are illustrated in Figure 3.13. They represent the most commonly used forms of sampling for data reduction.

An advantage of sampling for data reduction is that the cost of obtaining a sample *is proportional to the size of the sample*, $n$, as opposed to $N$, the data set size. Hence, sampling complexity is potentially *sublinear* to the size of the data. Other data reduction techniques can require at least one complete pass through $D$. For a fixed sample size, sampling complexity increases only linearly as the number of data dimensions, $d$, increases, while techniques using histograms, for example, increase exponentially in $d$.

When applied to data reduction, sampling is most commonly used to estimate the answer to an aggregate query. It is possible (using the central limit theorem) to determine a sufficient sample size for estimating a given function within a specified degree of error. This sample size, $n$, may be extremely small in comparison to $N$. Sampling is a natural choice for the progressive refinement of a reduced data set. Such a set can be further refined by simply increasing the sample size.

## 3.5   Discretization and Concept Hierarchy Generation

**Discretization techniques** can be used to reduce the number of values for a given continuous attribute, by dividing the range of the attribute into intervals. Interval labels can then be used to replace actual data values. Reducing the number of values for an attribute is especially beneficial if decision-tree-based methods of classification mining are to be applied to the preprocessed data. These methods are typically recursive, where a large amount of time is spent on sorting the data at each step. Hence, the smaller the number of distinct values to sort, the faster these methods should be. Many discretization techniques can be applied recursively in order to provide a hierarchical or multiresolution partitioning of the attribute

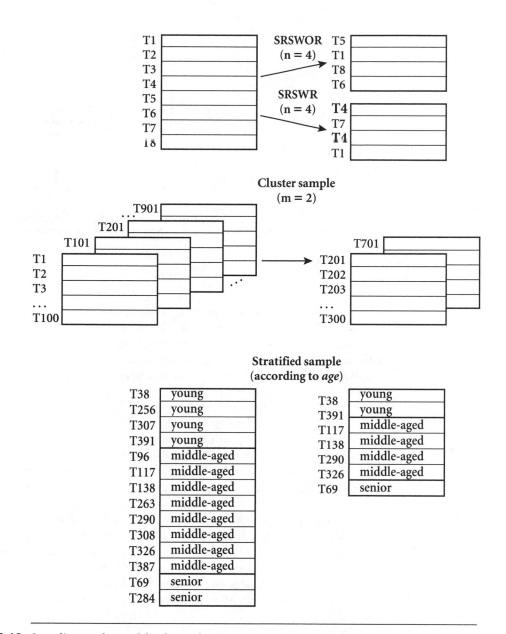

**Figure 3.13** Sampling can be used for data reduction.

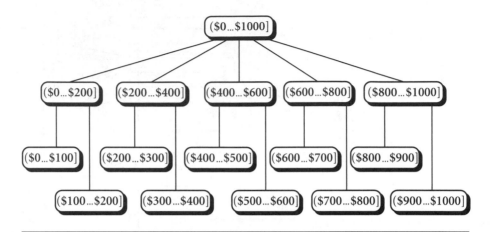

**Figure 3.14** A concept hierarchy for the attribute *price*.

values, known as a concept hierarchy. Concept hierarchies, introduced in Chapter 2, are useful for mining at multiple levels of abstraction.

A concept hierarchy for a given numeric attribute defines a discretization of the attribute. Concept hierarchies can be used to reduce the data by collecting and replacing low-level concepts (such as numeric values for the attribute *age*) by higher-level concepts (such as *young, middle-aged*, or *senior*). Although detail is lost by such data generalization, the generalized data may be more meaningful and easier to interpret, and will require less space than the original data. Mining on a reduced data set will require fewer input/output operations and be more efficient than mining on a larger, ungeneralized data set. An example of a concept hierarchy for the attribute *price* is given in Figure 3.14. More than one concept hierarchy can be defined for the same attribute in order to accommodate the needs of the various users.

Manual definition of concept hierarchies can be a tedious and time-consuming task for the user or domain expert. Fortunately, many hierarchies are implicit within the database schema and can be defined at the schema definition level. Concept hierarchies often can be automatically generated or dynamically refined based on statistical analysis of the data distribution.

Let's look at the generation of concept hierarchies for numeric and categorical data.

### 3.5.1 Discretization and Concept Hierarchy Generation for Numeric Data

It is difficult and laborious to specify concept hierarchies for numeric attributes due to the wide diversity of possible data ranges and the frequent updates of data values. Such manual specification can also be quite arbitrary.

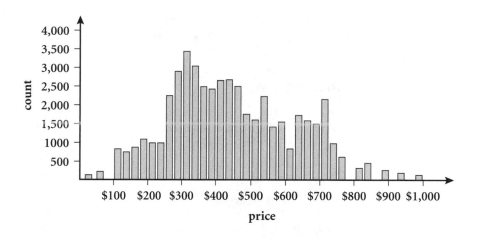

**Figure 3.15**   Histogram showing the distribution of values for the attribute *price*.

Concept hierarchies for numeric attributes can be constructed automatically based on data distribution analysis. We examine five methods for numeric concept hierarchy generation: *binning, histogram analysis, cluster analysis, entropy-based discretization,* and *data segmentation by "natural partitioning."*

### Binning

Section 3.2.2 discussed binning methods for data smoothing. These methods are also forms of discretization. For example, attribute values can be discretized by distributing the values into bins, and replacing each bin value by the bin mean or median, as in *smoothing by bin means* or *smoothing by bin medians*, respectively. These techniques can be applied recursively to the resulting partitions in order to generate concept hierarchies.

### Histogram Analysis

Histograms, as discussed in Section 3.4.4, can also be used for discretization. Figure 3.15 presents a histogram showing the data distribution of the attribute *price* for a given data set. For example, the most frequent price range is roughly $300–$325. Partitioning rules can be used to define the ranges of values. For instance, in an *equiwidth* histogram, the values are partitioned into equal-sized partions or ranges (e.g., ($0 . . . $100], ($100 . . . $200], . . . , ($900 . . . $1000]). With an *equidepth* histogram, the values are partitioned so that, ideally, each partition contains the same number of data samples. The histogram analysis algorithm can be applied recursively to each partition in order to automatically generate a multilevel concept hierarchy, with the procedure terminating once a prespecified number of concept levels has been reached. A *minimum interval size* can also be used per level to control the recursive procedure. This specifies the minimum width of a partition, or the minimum number of values for each partition at each level.

## Cluster Analysis

A clustering algorithm can be applied to partition data into clusters or groups. Each cluster forms a node of a concept hierarchy, where all nodes are at the same conceptual level. Each cluster may be further decomposed into several subclusters, forming a lower level of the hierarchy. Clusters may also be grouped together in order to form a higher conceptual level of the hierarchy. Clustering methods for data mining are studied in Chapter 8.

## Entropy-Based Discretization

An information-based measure called *entropy* can be used to recursively partition the values of a numeric attribute $A$, resulting in a hierarchical discretization. Such a discretization forms a numerical concept hierarchy for the attribute. Given a set of data tuples, $S$, the basic method for entropy-based discretization of $A$ is as follows:

1. Each value of $A$ can be considered a potential interval boundary or threshold $T$. For example, a value $v$ of $A$ can partition the samples in $S$ into two subsets satisfying the conditions $A < v$ and $A \geq v$, respectively, thereby creating a binary discretization.

2. Given $S$, the threshold value selected is the one that maximizes the information gain resulting from the subsequent partitioning. The information gain is

$$I(S, T) = \frac{|S_1|}{|S|} Ent(S_1) + \frac{|S_2|}{|S|} Ent(S_2), \tag{3.6}$$

where $S_1$ and $S_2$ correspond to the samples in $S$ satisfying the conditions $A < T$ and $A \geq T$, respectively. The entropy function $Ent$ for a given set is calculated based on the class distribution of the samples in the set. For example, given $m$ classes, the entropy of $S_1$ is

$$Ent(S_1) = - \sum_{i=1}^{m} p_i \log_2(p_i), \tag{3.7}$$

where $p_i$ is the probability of class $i$ in $S_1$, determined by dividing the number of samples of class $i$ in $S_1$ by the total number of samples in $S_1$. The value of $Ent(S_2)$ can be computed similarly.

**3.** The process of determining a threshold value is recursively applied to each partition obtained, until some stopping criterion is met, such as

$$Ent(S) - I(S, T) > \delta. \qquad (3.8)$$

Entropy-based discretization can reduce data size. Unlike the other methods mentioned here so far, entropy-based discretization uses class information. This makes it more likely that the interval boundaries are defined to occur in places that may help improve classification accuracy. The information gain and entropy measures described here are also used for decision tree induction. These measures are revisited in greater detail in Sections 5.3.2 and 7.3.1.

### Segmentation by Natural Partitioning

Although binning, histogram analysis, clustering, and entropy-based discretization are useful in the generation of numerical hierarchies, many users would like to see numerical ranges partitioned into relatively uniform, easy-to-read intervals that appear intuitive or "natural." For example, annual salaries broken into ranges like ($50,000, $60,000] are often more desirable than ranges like ($51,263.98, $60,872.34], obtained by some sophisticated clustering analysis.

The **3-4-5 rule** can be used to segment numeric data into relatively uniform, "natural" intervals. In general, the rule partitions a given range of data into 3, 4, or 5 relatively equiwidth intervals, recursively and level by level, based on the value range at the most significant digit. The rule is as follows:

- If an interval covers 3, 6, 7, or 9 distinct values at the most significant digit, then partition the range into 3 intervals (3 equiwidth intervals for 3, 6, 9, and 3 intervals in the grouping of 2-3-2 for 7).

- If it covers 2, 4, or 8 distinct values at the most significant digit, then partition the range into 4 equiwidth intervals.

- If it covers 1, 5, or 10 distinct values at the most significant digit, then partition the range into 5 equiwidth intervals.

The rule can be recursively applied to each interval, creating a concept hierarchy for the given numeric attribute. Since there could be some dramatically large positive or negative values in a data set, the top-level segmentation, based merely on the minimum and maximum values, may derive distorted results. For example, the assets of a few people could be several orders of magnitude higher than those of others in a data set. Segmentation based on the maximal asset values may lead to a highly biased hierarchy. Thus the top-level segmentation can be performed based on the range of data values representing the majority (e.g., 5th percentile to 95th percentile) of the given data. The extremely high or low values beyond the top-level segmentation will form distinct interval(s) that can be handled separately, but in a similar manner.

The following example illustrates the use of the 3-4-5 rule for the automatic construction of a numeric hierarchy.

**Example 3.5**  Suppose that profits at different branches of *AllElectronics* for the year 1999 cover a wide range, from −$351,976.00 to $4,700,896.50. A user wishes to have a concept hierarchy for *profit* automatically generated. For improved readability, we use the notation $(l...r]$ to represent the interval $(l, r]$. For example, $(−\$1,000,000...\$0]$ denotes the range from −$1,000,000 (exclusive) to $0 (inclusive).

Suppose that the data within the 5th percentile and 95th percentile are between −$159,876 and $1,838,761. The results of applying the 3-4-5 rule are shown in Figure 3.16.

1. Based on the above information, the minimum and maximum values are $MIN = −\$351,976.00$, and $MAX = \$4,700,896.50$. The low (5th percentile) and high (95th percentile) values to be considered for the top or first level of segmentation are $LOW = −\$159,876$, and $HIGH = \$1,838,761$.

2. Given LOW and HIGH, the most significant digit is at the million dollar digit position (i.e., $msd = 1,000,000$). Rounding LOW down to the million dollar digit, we get $LOW' = −\$1,000,000$; rounding HIGH up to the million dollar digit, we get $HIGH' = +\$2,000,000$.

3. Since this interval ranges over three distinct values at the most significant digit, that is, $(2,000,000 − (−1,000,000))/1,000,000 = 3$, the segment is partitioned into three equiwidth subsegments according to the 3-4-5 rule: $(−\$1,000,000 ... \$0]$, $(\$0 ... \$1,000,000]$, and $(\$1,000,000 ... \$2,000,000]$. This represents the top tier of the hierarchy.

4. We now examine the MIN and MAX values to see how they "fit" into the first-level partitions. Since the first interval $(−\$1,000,000 ... \$0]$ covers the *MIN* value, that is, $LOW' < MIN$, we can adjust the left boundary of this interval to make the interval smaller. The most significant digit of *MIN* is the hundred thousand digit position. Rounding *MIN* down to this position, we get $MIN' = −\$400,000$. Therefore, the first interval is redefined as $(−\$400,000 ... 0]$.

   Since the last interval, $(\$1,000,000 ... \$2,000,000]$, does not cover the *MAX* value, that is, $MAX > HIGH'$, we need to create a new interval to cover it. Rounding up *MAX* at its most significant digit position, the new interval is $(\$2,000,000 ... \$5,000,000]$. Hence, the topmost level of the hierarchy contains four partitions, $(−\$400,000 ... \$0]$, $(\$0 ... \$1,000,000]$, $(\$1,000,000 ... \$2,000,000]$, and $(\$2,000,000 ... \$5,000,000]$.

5. Recursively, each interval can be further partitioned according to the 3-4-5 rule to form the next lower level of the hierarchy:

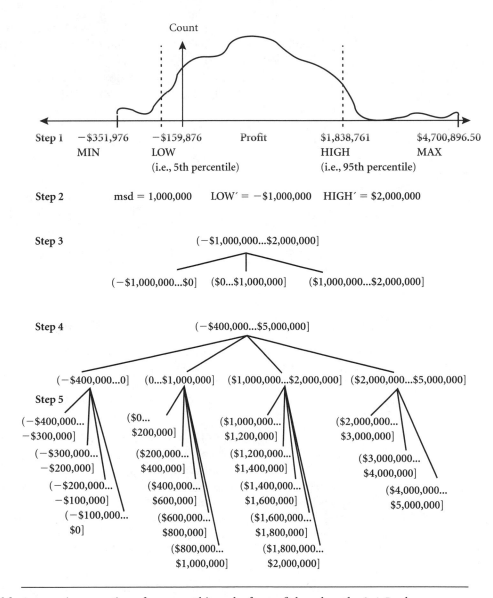

**Figure 3.16** Automatic generation of a concept hierarchy for *profit* based on the 3-4-5 rule.

- The first interval, (−$400,000 . . . $0], is partitioned into 4 subintervals: (−$400,000 . . . −$300,000], (−$300,000 . . . −$200,000], (−$200,000 . . . −$100,000], and (−$100,000 . . . $0].
- The second interval, ($0 . . . $1,000,000], is partitioned into 5 subintervals: ($0 . . . $200,000], ($200,000 . . . $400,000], ($400,000 . . . $600,000], ($600,000 . . . $800,000], and ($800,000 . . . $1,000,000].
- The third interval, ($1,000,000 . . . $2,000,000], is partitioned into 5 subintervals: ($1,000,000 . . . $1,200,000], ($1,200,000 . . . $1,400,000], ($1,400,000 . . . $1,600,000], ($1,600,000 . . . $1,800,000], and ($1,800,000 . . . $2,000,000].
- The last interval, ($2,000,000 . . . $5,000,000], is partitioned into 3 subintervals: ($2,000,000 . . . $3,000,000], ($3,000,000 . . . $4,000,000], and ($4,000,000 . . . $5,000,000].

Similarly, the 3-4-5 rule can be carried on iteratively at deeper levels, as necessary. ∎

## 3.5.2 Concept Hierarchy Generation for Categorical Data

Categorical data are discrete data. Categorical attributes have a finite (but possibly large) number of distinct values, with no ordering among the values. Examples include *geographic location*, *job category*, and *item type*. There are several methods for the generation of concept hierarchies for categorical data.

**Specification of a partial ordering of attributes explicitly at the schema level by users or experts:**  Concept hierarchies for categorical attributes or dimensions typically involve a group of attributes. A user or expert can easily define a concept hierarchy by specifying a partial or total ordering of the attributes at the schema level. For example, a relational database or a dimension *location* of a data warehouse may contain the following group of attributes: *street, city, province_or_state*, and *country*. A hierarchy can be defined by specifying the total ordering among these attributes at the schema level, such as *street < city < province_or_state < country*.

**Specification of a portion of a hierarchy by explicit data grouping:**  This is essentially the manual definition of a portion of a concept hierarchy. In a large database, it is unrealistic to define an entire concept hierarchy by explicit value enumeration. However, it is realistic to specify explicit groupings for a small portion of intermediate-level data. For example, after specifying that *province* and *country* form a hierarchy at the schema level, one may like to add some intermediate levels manually, such as defining explicitly "{*Alberta, Saskatchewan, Manitoba*} ⊂ *prairies_Canada*" and "{*British Columbia, prairies_Canada*} ⊂ *Western_Canada*".

Specification of a *set of attributes*, **but not of their partial ordering:**   A user may specify a set of attributes forming a concept hierarchy, but omit to explicitly state their partial ordering. The system can then try to automatically generate the attribute ordering so as to construct a meaningful concept hierarchy.

*"Without knowledge of data semantics, how can a hierarchical ordering for an arbitrary set of categorical attributes be found?"* you may ask. Consider the following observation that since higher-level concepts generally cover several subordinate lower-level concepts, an attribute defining a high concept level will usually contain a smaller number of distinct values than an attribute defining a lower concept level. Based on this observation, a concept hierarchy can be automatically generated based on the number of distinct values per attribute in the given attribute set. The attribute with the most distinct values is placed at the lowest level of the hierarchy. The lower the number of distinct values an attribute has, the higher it is in the generated concept hierarchy. This heuristic rule works well in many cases. Some local-level swapping or adjustments may be performed by users or experts, when necessary, after examination of the generated hierarchy.

Let's examine an example of this method.

**Example 3.6**  Suppose a user selects a set of attributes, *street, country, province_or_state*, and *city*, for a dimension *location* from the database *AllElectronics*, but does not specify the hierarchical ordering among the attributes.

The concept hierarchy for *location* can be generated automatically as follows. First, sort the attributes in ascending order based on the number of distinct values in each attribute. This results in the following (where the number of distinct values per attribute is shown in parentheses): *country* (15), *province_or_state* (365), *city* (3567), and *street* (674,339). Second, generate the hierarchy from the top down according to the sorted order, with the first attribute at the top level and the last attribute at the bottom level. The resulting hierarchy is shown in Figure 3.17. Finally, the user can examine the generated hierarchy, and when necessary, modify it to reflect desired semantic relationships among the attributes. In this example, it is obvious that there is no need to modify the generated hierarchy.                                                                      ■

Note that this heuristic rule cannot be pushed to the extreme since there are obvious cases that do not follow such a heuristic. For example, a time dimension in a database may contain 20 distinct years, 12 distinct months, and 7 distinct days of the week. However, this does not suggest that the time hierarchy should be *"year < month < days_of_the_week"*, with *days_of_the_week* at the top of the hierarchy.

Specification of only a partial set of attributes:   Sometimes a user can be sloppy when defining a hierarchy, or may have only a vague idea about what should be included in a hierarchy. Consequently, the user may have included only a small subset of the relevant attributes in a hierarchy specification. For example,

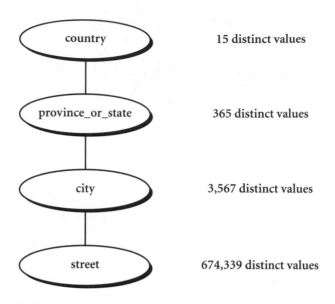

country                 15 distinct values

province_or_state       365 distinct values

city                    3,567 distinct values

street                  674,339 distinct values

**Figure 3.17** Automatic generation of a schema concept hierarchy based on the number of distinct attribute values.

instead of including all the hierarchically relevant attributes for *location*, the user may have specified only *street* and *city*. To handle such partially specified hierarchies, it is important to embed data semantics in the database schema so that attributes with tight semantic connections can be pinned together. In this way, the specification of one attribute may trigger a whole group of semantically tightly linked attributes to be "dragged in" to form a complete hierarchy. Users, however, should have the option to override this feature, as necessary.

**Example 3.7** Suppose that a database system has pinned together the five attributes *number, street, city, province_or_state*, and *country* because they are closely linked semantically, regarding the notion of *location*. If a user were to specify only the attribute *city* for a hierarchy defining *location*, the system may automatically drag in all of the above five semantically related attributes to form a hierarchy. The user may choose to drop any of these attributes, such as *number* and *street*, from the hierarchy, keeping *city* as the lowest conceptual level in the hierarchy.

∎

# 3.6 Summary

- **Data preprocessing** is an important issue for both data warehousing and data mining, as real-world data tend to be incomplete, noisy, and inconsistent. Data preprocessing includes data cleaning, data integration, data transformation, and data reduction.

- **Data cleaning** routines can be used to fill in missing values, smooth noisy data, identify outliers, and correct data inconsistencies.

- **Data integration** combines data from multiple sources to form a coherent data store. Metadata, correlation analysis, data conflict detection, and the resolution of semantic heterogeneity contribute towards smooth data integration.

- **Data transformation** routines convert the data into appropriate forms for mining. For example, attribute data may be **normalized** so as to fall between a small range, such as 0.0 to 1.0.

- **Data reduction** techniques such as data cube aggregation, dimension reduction, data compression, numerosity reduction, and discretization can be used to obtain a reduced representation of the data, while minimizing the loss of information content.

- **Automatic generation of concept hierarchies** for numeric data can involve techniques such as binning, histogram analysis, cluster analysis, entropy-based discretization, and segmentation by natural partitioning. For categoric data, concept hierarchies may be generated based on the number of distinct values of the attributes defining the hierarchy.

- Although several methods of data preprocessing have been developed, data preparation remains an active area of research.

## Exercises

**3.1** Data quality can be assessed in terms of accuracy, completeness, and consistency. Propose two other dimensions of data quality.

**3.2** In real-world data, tuples with missing values for some attributes are a common occurrence. Describe various methods for handling this problem.

**3.3** Suppose that the data for analysis include the attribute *age*. The *age* values for the data tuples are (in increasing order): 13, 15, 16, 16, 19, 20, 20, 21, 22, 22, 25, 25, 25, 25, 30, 33, 33, 35, 35, 35, 35, 36, 40, 45, 46, 52, 70.

(a) Use smoothing by bin means to smooth the above data, using a bin depth of 3. Illustrate your steps. Comment on the effect of this technique for the given data.

(b) How might you determine outliers in the data?

(c) What other methods are there for data smoothing?

**3.4** Discuss issues to consider during data integration.

**3.5** Using the data for *age* given in Exercise 3.3, answer the following:

(a) Use min-max normalization to transform the value 35 for *age* onto the range [0.0, 1.0].

(b) Use z-score normalization to transform the value 35 for *age*, where the standard deviation of *age* is 12.94 years.

(c) Use normalization by decimal scaling to transform the value 35 for *age*.

(d) Comment on which method you would prefer to use for the given data, giving reasons as to why.

**3.6** Use a flow chart to summarize the following procedures for attribute subset selection:

(a) Stepwise forward selection

(b) Stepwise backward elimination

(c) A combination of forward selection and backward elimination

**3.7** Using the data for *age* given in Exercise 3.3,

(a) Plot an equiwidth histogram of width 10.

(b) Sketch examples of each of the following sampling techniques: SRSWOR, SRSWR, cluster sampling, stratified sampling. Use samples of size 5 and the strata "young", "middle-aged", and "senior".

**3.8** Propose an algorithm, in pseudocode or in your favorite programming language, for the following:

(a) The automatic generation of a concept hierarchy for categorical data based on the number of distinct values of attributes in the given schema

(b) The automatic generation of a concept hierarchy for numeric data based on the *equiwidth* partitioning rule

(c) The automatic generation of a concept hierarchy for numeric data based on the *equidepth* partitioning rule

## Bibliographic Notes

Data preprocessing is discussed in a number of textbooks, including Kennedy, Lee, Van Roy, et al. [KLV+98], Weiss and Indurkhya [WI98], and Pyle [Pyl99]. More specific references to individual preprocessing techniques are given below.

For discussion regarding data quality, see Redman [Red92], Wang, Storey, and Firth [WSF95], Wand and Wang [WW96], and Ballou and Tayi [BT99]. The handling of missing attribute values is discussed in Friedman [Fri77], Breiman, Friedman, Olshen, and Stone [BFOS84], and Quinlan [Qui89]. A method for the detection of outlier or "garbage" patterns in a handwritten character database is given in Guyon, Matic, and Vapnik [GMV96]. Binning and data normalization are treated in many texts, including [KLV+98, WI98, Pyl99]. Systems that include attribute (or feature) construction include BACON by Langley, Simon,

Bradshaw, and Zytkow [LSBZ87], Stagger by Schlimmer [Schl87], FRINGE by Pagallo [Pag89], and AQ17-DCI by Bloedorn and Michalski [BM98]. Attribute construction is also described in Liu and Motoda [LM98a, LM98b].

A good survey of data reduction techniques can be found in Barbará et al. [BDF+97]. For algorithms on data cubes and their precomputation, see [SS94, AAD+96, HRU96, RS97, ZDN97]. Attribute subset selection (or *feature subset selection*) is described in many texts, such as Neter, Kutner, Nachtsheim, and Wasserman [NKNW96], Dash and Liu [DL97], and Liu and Motoda [LM98, LM98b]. A combination forward selection and backward elimination method was proposed in Siedlecki and Sklansky [SS88]. A wrapper approach to attribute selection is described in Kohavi and John [KJ97]. Unsupervised attribute subset selection is described in Dash, Liu, and Yao [DLY97]. For a description of wavelets for data compression, see Press, Teukolosky, Vetterling, and Flannery [PTVF96]. A general account of wavelets can be found in Hubbard [Hub96]. For a list of wavelet software packages, see Bruce, Donoho, and Gao [BDG96]. Daubechies transforms are described in Daubechies [Dau92]. The book by Press, et al. [PTVF96] includes an introduction to singular value decomposition for principal components analysis. Routines for PCA are included in most statistical software packages, such as SAS (*http://www.sas.com/SASHome.html*).

An introduction to regression and log-linear models can be found in several textbooks, such as [Jam85, Dob90, JW92, Dev95, NKNW96]. For log-linear models (known as *multiplicative models* in the computer science literature), see Pearl [Pea88]. For a general introduction to histograms, see Barbará et al. [BDF+97] and Devore and Peck [DP97]. For extensions of single attribute histograms to multiple attributes, see Muralikrishna and DeWitt [MD88] and Poosala and Ioannidis [PI97]. Several references to clustering algorithms are given in Chapter 8 of this book, which is devoted to the topic. A survey of multidimensional indexing structures is given in Gaede and Günther [GG98]. The use of multidimensional index trees for data aggregation is discussed in Aoki [Aok98]. Index trees include R-trees (Guttman [Gut84]), quad-trees (Finkel and Bentley [FB74]), and their variations. For discussion on sampling and data mining, see Kivinen and Mannila [KM94] and John and Langley [JL96].

ChiMerge by Kerber [Ker92] and Chi2 by Liu and Setiono [LS95] are methods for the automatic discretization of numeric attributes that both employ the $\chi^2$ statistic. Fayyad and Irani [FI93] apply the minimum description length principle to determine the number of intervals for numeric discretization. In Catlett [Cat91], the D-2 system binarizes a numeric feature recursively. Entropy-based discretization with the C4.5 algorithm is described in Quinlan [Qui93]. Concept hierarchies and their automatic generation from categorical data are described in Han and Fu [HF94].

# Data Mining Primitives, Languages, and System Architectures

**A popular misconception about data mining is to expect** that data mining systems can *autonomously* dig out *all* of the valuable knowledge that is embedded in a given large database, without human intervention or guidance. Although it may at first sound appealing to have an autonomous data mining system, in practice, such systems would uncover an overwhelmingly large set of patterns. The entire set of generated patterns may easily surpass the size of the given database! To let a data mining system "run loose" in its discovery of patterns, without providing it with any indication regarding the portions of the database that the user wants to probe or the kinds of patterns the user would find interesting, is to let loose a data mining "monster." Most of the patterns discovered would be irrelevant to the analysis task of the user. Furthermore, many of the patterns found, though related to the analysis task, may be difficult to understand or lack validity, novelty, or utility—making them uninteresting. Thus, it is neither realistic nor desirable to generate, store, or present all of the patterns that could be discovered from a given database.

A more realistic scenario is to expect that users can communicate with the data mining system using a set of *data mining primitives* designed in order to facilitate efficient and fruitful knowledge discovery. Such primitives include the specification of the portions of the database or the set of data in which the user is interested (including the database attributes or data warehouse dimensions of interest), the kinds of knowledge to be mined, background knowledge useful in guiding the discovery process, interestingness measures for pattern evaluation, and how the discovered knowledge should be visualized. These primitives allow the user to *interactively* communicate with the data mining system during discovery in order to examine the findings from different angles or depths, and direct the mining process.

A data mining query language can be designed to incorporate these primitives, allowing users to flexibly interact with data mining systems. Having a data mining query language provides a foundation on which user-friendly graphical interfaces can be built. In addition, it is important to have a well-designed system architecture for implementation of such data mining systems. This would facilitate a data mining system's communication with other information systems and its integration with the overall information processing environment.

In this chapter, you will learn about the data mining primitives and study the design of a data mining query language based on these principles. You will also learn about system architectures for data mining systems.

## 4.1 Data Mining Primitives: What Defines a Data Mining Task?

Each user will have a **data mining task** in mind, that is, some form of data analysis that she would like to have performed. A data mining task can be specified in the form of a **data mining query**, which is input to the data mining system. A data mining query is defined in terms of the following primitives, as illustrated in Figure 4.1.

- **Task-relevant data:** This is the database portion to be investigated. For example, suppose that you are a manager of *AllElectronics* in charge of sales in the United States and Canada. In particular, you would like to study the buying trends of customers in Canada. Rather than mining the entire database, you can specify that only the data relating to customer purchases in Canada need be retrieved, along with the related customer profile information. You can also specify attributes of interest to be considered in the mining process. These are referred to as **relevant attributes**.[1] For example, if you are interested only in studying possible relationships between, say, the items purchased and customer annual income and age, then the attributes *name* of the relation *item*, and *income* and *age* of the relation *customer,* can be specified as the relevant attributes for mining.

- **The kinds of knowledge to be mined:** This specifies the *data mining functions* to be performed, such as characterization, discrimination, association, classification, clustering, or evolution analysis. For instance, if studying the buying habits of customers in Canada, you may choose to mine associations between customer profiles and the items that these customers like to buy.

- **Background knowledge:** Users can specify *background knowledge*, or knowledge about the domain to be mined. This knowledge is useful for guiding the

---

[1] If mining is to be performed on data from a multidimensional data cube, the user can specify relevant dimensions.

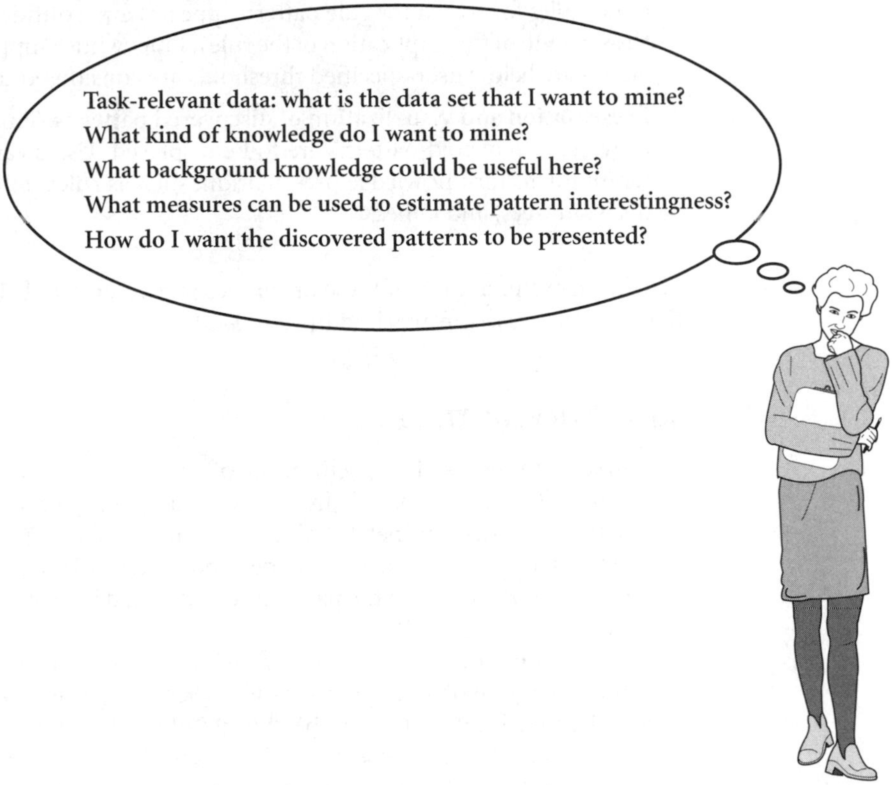

**Figure 4.1** Defining a data mining task or query.

knowledge discovery process and for evaluating the patterns found. There are several kinds of background knowledge. In this chapter, we focus our discussion on a popular form of background knowledge known as *concept hierarchies*. Concept hierarchies are useful in that they allow data to be mined at multiple levels of abstraction. Other examples include user beliefs regarding relationships in the data. These can be used to evaluate the discovered patterns according to their degree of unexpectedness (where unexpected patterns are deemed interesting) or expectedness (where patterns that confirm a user hypothesis are considered interesting).

■ **Interestingness measures:** These functions are used to separate uninteresting patterns from knowledge. They may be used to guide the mining process or, after discovery, to evaluate the discovered patterns. Different kinds of knowledge may have different interestingness measures. For example, interestingness measures for association rules include **support** (the percentage of task-relevant data tuples for which the rule pattern appears) and **confidence** (an estimate of the strength of the implication of the rule). Rules whose support and confidence values are below user-specified thresholds are considered uninteresting.

■ **Presentation and visualization of discovered patterns:** This refers to the form in which discovered patterns are to be displayed. Users can choose from different forms for knowledge presentation, such as rules, tables, charts, graphs, decision trees, and cubes.

Below, we examine each of these primitives in greater detail. The specification of these primitives is summarized in Figure 4.2.

## 4.1.1 Task-Relevant Data

The first primitive is the specification of the data on which mining is to be performed. Typically, a user is interested in only a subset of the database. It is impractical to indiscriminately mine the entire database, particularly since the number of patterns generated could be exponential with respect to the database size. Furthermore, many of the patterns found would be irrelevant to the interests of the user.

In a relational database, the set of task-relevant data can be collected via a relational query involving operations like selection, projection, join, and aggregation. This retrieval of data can be thought of as a "subtask" of the data mining task. The data collection process results in a new data relation, called the **initial data relation**. The initial data relation can be ordered or grouped according to the conditions specified in the query. The data may be cleaned or transformed (e.g., aggregated on certain attributes) prior to applying data mining analysis. The initial relation may or may not correspond to a physical relation in the database. Since virtual relations are called **views** in the field of databases, the set of task-relevant data for data mining is called a **minable view**.

**Example 4.1**   If the data mining task is to study associations between items frequently purchased at *AllElectronics* by customers in Canada, the task-relevant data can be specified by providing the following information:

■ The name of the *database* or *data warehouse* to be used (e.g., *AllElectronics_db*)

■ The names of the *tables* or *data cubes* containing the relevant data (e.g., *item*, *customer*, *purchases*, and *items_sold*)

■ *Conditions* for selecting the relevant data (e.g., retrieve data pertaining to purchases made in Canada for the current year)

■ The *relevant attributes or dimensions* (e.g., *name* and *price* from the *item* table, and *income* and *age* from the *customer* table)

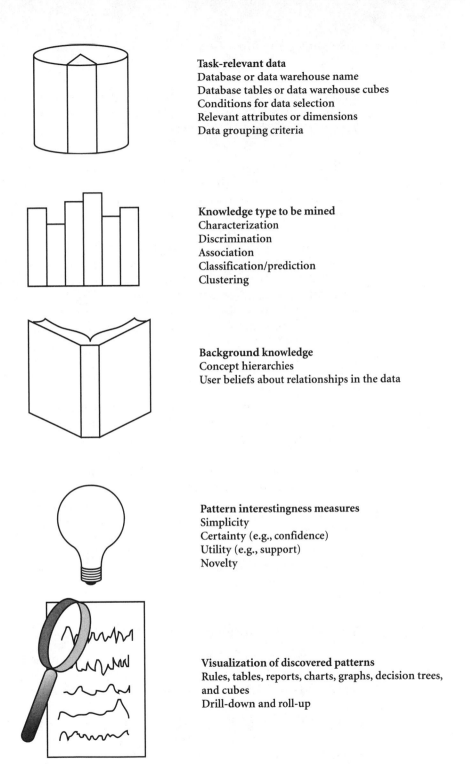

**Task-relevant data**
Database or data warehouse name
Database tables or data warehouse cubes
Conditions for data selection
Relevant attributes or dimensions
Data grouping criteria

**Knowledge type to be mined**
Characterization
Discrimination
Association
Classification/prediction
Clustering

**Background knowledge**
Concept hierarchies
User beliefs about relationships in the data

**Pattern interestingness measures**
Simplicity
Certainty (e.g., confidence)
Utility (e.g., support)
Novelty

**Visualization of discovered patterns**
Rules, tables, reports, charts, graphs, decision trees,
and cubes
Drill-down and roll-up

**Figure 4.2**  Primitives for specifying a data mining task.

In addition, the user may specify that the data retrieved be grouped by certain attributes, such as "**group by** *date*". Given this information, an SQL query can be used to retrieve the task-relevant data. ∎

In a data warehouse, data are typically stored in a multidimensional database, known as a **data cube**, which can be implemented using a multidimensional array structure, a relational structure, or a combination of both, as discussed in Chapter 2. The set of task-relevant data can be specified by condition-based data filtering, *slicing* (extracting data for a given attribute value, or "slice"), or *dicing* (extracting the intersection of several slices) of the data cube.

Notice that in a data mining query, the conditions provided for data selection can be at a level that is conceptually higher than the data in the database or data warehouse. For example, a user may specify a selection on items at *AllElectronics* using the concept *type* = *"home entertainment"*, even though individual items in the database may not be stored according to type, but rather, at a lower conceptual, such as *"TV"*, *"CD player"*, or *"VCR"*. A concept hierarchy on *item* that specifies that *"home entertainment"* is at a higher concept level, composed of the lower-level concepts {*"TV"*, *"CD player"*, *"VCR"*}, can be used in the collection of the task-relevant data.

Specification of the relevant attributes or dimensions can be a difficult task for users. A user may have only a rough idea of what the interesting attributes for exploration might be. Furthermore, when specifying the data to be mined, the user may overlook additional relevant data having strong semantic links to them. For example, the sales of certain items may be closely linked to particular events such as Christmas or Halloween, or to particular groups of customers, yet these factors may not be included in the general data analysis request. For such cases, mechanisms can be used that help give a more precise specification of the task-relevant data. These include functions to evaluate and rank attributes according to their relevance with respect to the operation specified. In addition, techniques that search for attributes with strong semantic ties can be used to enhance the initial data set specified by the user.

## 4.1.2 The Kind of Knowledge to be Mined

It is important to specify the kind of knowledge to be mined, as this determines the data mining function to be performed. The kinds of knowledge include concept description (characterization and discrimination), association, classification, prediction, clustering, and evolution analysis.

In addition to specifying the kind of knowledge to be mined for a given data mining task, the user can be more specific and provide pattern templates that all discovered patterns must match. These templates, or **metapatterns** (also called **metarules** or **metaqueries**), can be used to guide the discovery process. The use of metapatterns is illustrated in the following example.

**Example 4.2** A user studying the buying habits of *AllElectronics* customers may choose to mine *association rules* of the form

$$P(X : customer, W) \wedge Q(X, Y) \Rightarrow buys(X, Z)$$

where $X$ is a key of the *customer* relation; $P$ and $Q$ are **predicate variables** that can be instantiated to the relevant attributes or dimensions specified as part of the task relevant data, and $W$, $Y$, and $Z$ are object variables that can take on the values of their respective predicates for customers $X$.

The search for association rules is confined to those matching the given metarule, such as

$$age(X, ``30 \ldots 39") \wedge income(X, ``40K \ldots 49K") \Rightarrow buys(X, ``VCR")$$
$$[2.2\%, 60\%] \qquad (4.1)$$

and

$$occupation(X, ``student") \wedge age(X, ``20 \ldots 29") \Rightarrow buys(X, ``computer")$$
$$[1.4\%, 70\%]. \qquad (4.2)$$

The former rule states that customers in their thirties, with an annual income of between 40K and 49K, are likely (with 60% confidence) to purchase a VCR, and such cases represent about 2.2% of the total number of transactions. The latter rule states that customers who are students and in their twenties are likely (with 70% confidence) to purchase a computer, and such cases represent about 1.4% of the total number of transactions. ∎

## 4.1.3 Background Knowledge: Concept Hierarchies

Background knowledge is information about the domain to be mined that can be useful in the discovery process. In this section, we focus our attention on a simple yet powerful form of background knowledge known as *concept hierarchies*. Concept hierarchies allow the discovery of knowledge at multiple levels of abstraction.

As described in Chapter 2, a **concept hierarchy** defines a sequence of mappings from a set of low-level concepts to higher-level, more general concepts. A concept hierarchy for the dimension *location* is shown in Figure 4.3, mapping low-level concepts (i.e., cities) to more general concepts (i.e., countries).

Notice that this concept hierarchy is represented as a set of **nodes** organized in a tree, where each node, in itself, represents a concept. A special node, **all**, is reserved for the root of the tree. It denotes the most generalized value of the given dimension. If not explicitly shown, it is implied. This concept hierarchy consists of four **levels**. By convention, levels within a concept hierarchy are numbered from top to bottom, starting with level 0 for the **all** node. In our example, level 1 represents the concept *country*, while levels 2 and 3 represent the concepts *province_or_state* and *city*, respectively. The leaves of the hierarchy correspond to the dimension's raw data values (**primitive level data**). These are the most specific

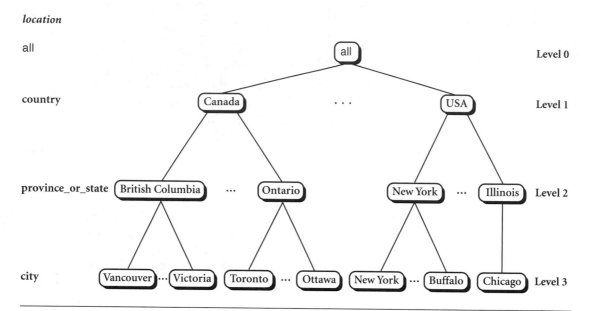

*location*

**Figure 4.3** A concept hierarchy for the dimension *location*.

values, or concepts, of the given attribute or dimension. Although a concept hierarchy often defines a taxonomy represented in the shape of a tree, it may also be in the form of a general lattice or partial order.

Concept hierarchies are a useful form of background knowledge in that they allow raw data to be handled at higher, generalized levels of abstraction. Generalization of the data, or **rolling up,** is achieved by replacing primitive-level data (such as city names for *location*, or numerical values for *age*) by higher-level concepts (such as continents for *location*, or ranges like "20...39", "40...59", "60+" for *age*). This allows the user to view the data at *more meaningful* and explicit abstractions, and makes the discovered patterns easier to understand. Generalization has an added advantage of compressing the data. Mining on a compressed data set will require fewer input/output operations and be more efficient than mining on a larger, uncompressed data set.

If the resulting data appear overgeneralized, concept hierarchies also allow specialization, or **drilling down,** whereby concept values are replaced by lower-level concepts. By rolling up and drilling down, users can view the data from different perspectives, gaining further insight into hidden data relationships.

Concept hierarchies can be provided by system users, domain experts, or knowledge engineers. The mappings are typically data- or application-specific. Concept hierarchies can often be automatically discovered or dynamically refined based on statistical analysis of the data distribution. The automatic generation of concept hierarchies is discussed in detail in Chapter 3.

There may be more than one concept hierarchy for a given attribute or dimension, based on different user viewpoints. For example, a regional sales manager of *AllElectronics* who is interested in studying the buying habits of customers at different locations may prefer the concept hierarchy of Figure 4.3. A marketing manager, however, may prefer to see *location* organized with respect to linguistic lines in order to facilitate the distribution of commercial ads.

There are four major types of concept hierarchies. Chapter 2 introduced the most common types—*schema hierarchies* and *set-grouping hierarchies*, which we review here. In addition, we also study *operation-derived hierarchies* and *rule-based hierarchies*.

**Schema hierarchies:**  A *schema hierarchy* (or more rigorously, a *schema-defined hierarchy*) is a total or partial order among attributes in the database schema. Schema hierarchies may formally express existing semantic relationships between attributes. Typically, a schema hierarchy specifies a data warehouse dimension.

**Example 4.3** Given the schema of a relation for *address* containing the attributes *street, city, province_or_state*, and *country*, we can define a *location* schema hierarchy by the following total order:

$$street < city < province\_or\_state < country$$

This means that *street* is at a conceptually lower level than *city*, which is lower than *province_or_state*, which is conceptually lower than *country*. A schema hierarchy provides metadata information, that is, data about the data. Its specification in terms of a total or partial order among attributes is more concise than an equivalent definition that lists all instances of streets, provinces or states, and countries.    ▪

**Set-grouping hierarchies:**  A *set-grouping hierarchy* organizes values for a given attribute or dimension into groups of constants or range values. A total or partial order can be defined among groups. Set-grouping hierarchies can be used to refine or enrich schema-defined hierarchies, when the two types of hierarchies are combined. They are typically used for defining small sets of object relationships.

**Example 4.4** A set-grouping hierarchy for the attribute *age* can be specified in terms of ranges, as in the following:

$$\{young, middle\_aged, senior\} \subset \textbf{all}(age)$$

$$\{20 \ldots 39\} \subset young$$

$$\{40 \ldots 59\} \subset middle\_aged$$

$$\{60 \ldots 89\} \subset senior$$

Notice that similar range specifications can also be generated automatically, as detailed in Chapter 3. ∎

**Operation-derived hierarchies:** An *operation-derived hierarchy* is based on operations specified by users, experts, or the data mining system. Operations can include the decoding of information-encoded strings, information extraction from complex data objects, and data clustering.

**Example 4.5** An e-mail address or a URL of the WWW may contain hierarchy information relating departments, universities (or companies), and countries. Decoding operations can be defined to extract such information in order to form concept hierarchies.

For example, the e-mail address *dmbook@cs.sfu.ca* gives the partial order "*login-name < department < university < country*", forming a concept hierarchy for e-mail addresses. Similarly, the URL address *http://www.cs.sfu.ca/research/DB/DBMiner* can be decoded so as to provide a partial order that forms the base of a concept hierarchy for URLs. ∎

Alternatively, mathematical and statistical operations, such as data clustering and data distribution analysis algorithms, can be used to form concept hierarchies, as discussed in Section 3.5.

**Rule-based hierarchies:** A *rule-based hierarchy* occurs when either a whole concept hierarchy or a portion of it is defined by a set of rules and is evaluated dynamically based on the current database data and the rule definition.

**Example 4.6** The following rules may be used to categorize *AllElectronics* items as *low_profit_margin* items, *medium_profit_margin* items, and *high_profit_margin* items, where the profit margin of an item $X$ is defined as the difference between the retail price and actual cost of $X$. Items having a profit margin of less than \$50 may be defined as *low_profit_margin* items, items earning a profit between \$50 and \$250 may be defined as *medium_profit_margin* items, and items earning a profit of more than \$250 may be defined as *high_profit_margin* items.

$$low\_profit\_margin(X) \Leftarrow price(X, P1) \wedge cost(X, P2) \wedge ((P1 - P2) < \$50)$$

$$medium\_profit\_margin(X) \Leftarrow price(X, P1) \wedge cost(X, P2) \wedge ((P1 - P2)$$
$$\geq \$50) \wedge ((P1 - P2) \leq \$250)$$

$$high\_profit\_margin(X) \Leftarrow price(X, P1) \wedge cost(X, P2) \wedge ((P1 - P2) > \$250)$$

∎

The use of concept hierarchies for data mining is described in the remaining chapters of this book.

## 4.1.4 Interestingness Measures

Although specification of the task-relevant data and of the kind of knowledge to be mined (e.g, characterization, association, etc.) may substantially reduce the number of patterns generated, a data mining process may still generate a large number of patterns. Typically, only a small fraction of these patterns will actually be of interest to the given user. Thus, users need to further confine the number of uninteresting patterns returned by the process. This can be achieved by specifying interestingness measures that estimate the simplicity, certainty, utility, and novelty of patterns.

In this section, we study some objective measures of pattern interestingness. Such objective measures are based on the structure of patterns and the statistics underlying them. In general, each measure is associated with a *threshold* that can be controlled by the user. Rules that do not meet the threshold are considered uninteresting, and hence are not presented to the user as knowledge.

**Simplicity:** A factor contributing to the interestingness of a pattern is the pattern's overall simplicity for human comprehension. Objective measures of pattern simplicity can be viewed as functions of the pattern structure, defined in terms of the pattern size in bits, or the number of attributes or operators appearing in the pattern. For example, the more complex the structure of a rule is, the more difficult it is to interpret, and, hence, the less interesting it is likely to be.

**Rule length**, for instance, is a simplicity measure. For rules expressed in conjunctive normal form (i.e., as a set of conjunctive predicates), rule length is typically defined as the number of conjuncts in the rule. Association, discrimination, or classification rules whose lengths exceed a user-defined threshold can be considered uninteresting. For patterns expressed as decision trees, simplicity may be a function of the number of tree leaves or tree nodes.

**Certainty:** Each discovered pattern should have a measure of certainty associated with it that assesses the validity or "trustworthiness" of the pattern. A certainty measure for association rules of the form "$A \Rightarrow B$", where $A$ and $B$ are sets of items, is **confidence**. Given a set of task-relevant data tuples (or transactions in a transaction database) the confidence of "$A \Rightarrow B$" is defined as

$$\text{confidence}(A \Rightarrow B) = \frac{\#\_tuples\_containing\_both\_A\_and\_B}{\#\_tuples\_containing\_A}. \qquad (4.3)$$

**Example 4.7** Suppose that the set of task-relevant data consists of transactions of items purchased from the computer department of *AllElectronics*. A confidence of 85% for the association rule

$$buys(X, \text{"computer"}) \Rightarrow buys(X, \text{"software"}) \qquad (4.4)$$

means that 85% of all customers who purchased a computer also bought software.                                                   ∎

A confidence value of 100%, or 1, indicates that the rule is always correct on the data analyzed. Such rules are called **exact**.

For classification rules, Equation 4.3 can easily be adapted to act as a measure of certainty referred to as **reliability** or **accuracy**. Classification rules propose a model for distinguishing objects, or tuples, of a target class (say, *bigSpenders*) from objects of contrasting classes (say, *budgetSpenders*). A low reliability value indicates that the rule in question incorrectly classifies a large number of contrasting class objects as target class objects. Rule reliability is also known as **rule strength, rule quality, certainty factor**, and **discriminating weight**.

Utility:   The potential usefulness of a pattern is a factor defining its interestingness. It can be estimated by a utility function, such as support. The **support** of an association pattern refers to the percentage of task-relevant data tuples (or transactions) for which the pattern is true. For association rules of the form "$A \Rightarrow B$" where $A$ and $B$ are sets of items, it is defined as

$$\text{support}(A \Rightarrow B) = \frac{\#\_tuples\_containing\_both\_A\_and\_B}{total\_\#\_of\_tuples}. \tag{4.5}$$

**Example 4.8**   Suppose that the set of task-relevant data consists of transactions from the computer department of *AllElectronics*. A support of 30% for the Association Rule (4.4) means that 30% of all customers in the computer department purchased both a computer and software.                                                   ∎

Association rules that satisfy both a user-specified *minimum confidence threshold* and user-specified *minimum support threshold* are referred to as **strong association rules** and are considered interesting. Rules with low support likely represent noise, or rare or exceptional cases.

The numerator of the support equation is also known as the rule **count**. Quite often, this number is displayed instead of support. Support can easily be derived from it.

Characteristic and discriminant descriptions are, in essence, generalized tuples. Any generalized tuple representing less than $Y\%$ of the total number of task-relevant tuples can be considered noise. Such tuples are not displayed to the user. The value of $Y$ is referred to as the **noise threshold**.

Novelty:   Novel patterns are those that contribute new information or increased performance to the given pattern set. For example, a data exception may be considered novel in that it differs from that expected based on a statistical model or user beliefs. Another strategy for detecting novelty is to remove redundant patterns. If a discovered rule can be implied by another rule that is already in the knowledge base or in the derived rule set, then either rule should be reexamined in order to remove the potential redundancy.

Mining with concept hierarchies can result in a large number of redundant rules. For example, suppose that the following association rules were mined from the *AllElectronics* database, using the concept hierarchy in Figure 4.3 for *location*:

$$location(X, \text{``Canada''}) \Rightarrow buys(X, \text{``SONY\_TV''}) \qquad [8\%, 70\%] \qquad (4.6)$$

$$location(X, \text{``Montreal''}) \Rightarrow buys(X, \text{``SONY\_TV''}) \qquad [2\%, 71\%] \qquad (4.7)$$

Suppose that Rule (4.6) has 8% support and 70% confidence. We might expect Rule (4.7) to have a confidence of around 70% as well, since all the tuples representing data objects for Montreal are also data objects for Canada. Rule (4.6) is more general than Rule (4.7), and therefore, we would expect the former rule to occur more frequently than the latter. Consequently, the two rules should not have the same support. Suppose that about one quarter of all sales in Canada come from Montreal. We would then expect the support of the rule involving Montreal to be one quarter of the support of the rule involving Canada. In other words, we expect the support of Rule (4.7) to be $8\% \times \frac{1}{4} = 2\%$. If the actual confidence and support of Rule (4.7) are as expected, then the rule is considered redundant since it does not offer any additional information and is less general than Rule (4.6). These ideas are further discussed in Chapter 6.

Data mining systems should allow users to flexibly and interactively specify, test, and modify interestingness measures and their respective thresholds. There are many other objective measures, apart from the basic ones studied above. Subjective measures exist as well, which consider user beliefs regarding relationships in the data, in addition to objective statistical measures. Interestingness measures are discussed in greater detail throughout the book.

## 4.1.5 Presentation and Visualization of Discovered Patterns

*"How can I 'see' the discovered patterns?"* For data mining to be effective, data mining systems should be able to display the discovered patterns in multiple forms, such as rules, tables, crosstabs (cross-tabulations), pie or bar charts, decision trees, cubes, or other visual representations (Figure 4.4). Allowing the visualization of discovered patterns in various forms can help users with different backgrounds to identify patterns of interest and to interact or guide the system in further discovery. A user should be able to specify the forms of presentation to be used for displaying the discovered patterns.

The use of concept hierarchies plays an important role in aiding the user to visualize the discovered patterns. Mining with concept hierarchies allows the representation of discovered knowledge in high-level concepts, which may be more understandable to users than rules expressed in terms of primitive (i.e., raw) data,

**Rules**

age(X, "young") and income(X, "high") => class(X, "A")
age(X, "young") and income(X, "low") => class(X, "B")
age(X, "old") => class(X, "C")

**Table**

| age | income | class | count |
|-----|--------|-------|-------|
| young | high | A | 1,402 |
| young | low | B | 1,038 |
| old | high | C | 786 |
| old | low | C | 1,374 |

**Crosstab**

| age | income | | class | | |
|-----|--------|-----|-------|-----|-----|
| | high | low | A | B | C |
| young | 1,402 | 1,038 | 1,402 | 1,038 | 0 |
| old | 786 | 1,374 | 0 | 0 | 2,160 |
| count | 2,188 | 2,412 | 1,402 | 1,038 | 2,160 |

**Pie chart**

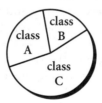

**Bar chart**

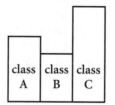

**Decision tree**

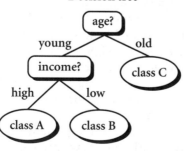

**Data cube**

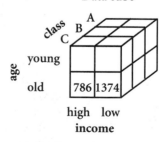

**Figure 4.4** Various forms of presenting and visualizing the discovered patterns.

such as functional or multivalued dependency rules, or integrity constraints. Furthermore, data mining systems should employ concept hierarchies to implement drill-down and roll-up operations, so that users may inspect discovered patterns at multiple levels of abstraction. In addition, pivoting (or rotating), slicing, and dicing operations aid the user in viewing generalized data and knowledge from different perspectives. These operations were discussed in detail in Chapter 2. A data mining system should provide such interactive operations for any dimension, as well as for individual values of each dimension.

Some representation forms may be better suited than others for particular kinds of knowledge. For example, generalized relations and their corresponding crosstabs or pie/bar charts are good for presenting characteristic descriptions, whereas decision trees are a common choice for classification. Interestingness measures such as those described in Section 4.1.4 can be displayed for each discovered pattern, in order to help users identify those patterns representing useful knowledge.

## 4.2 A Data Mining Query Language

*"Why is it important to have a data mining query language?"* Well, recall that a desired feature of data mining systems is the ability to *support ad hoc and interactive data mining* in order to facilitate flexible and effective knowledge discovery. Data mining query languages can be designed to support such a feature.

The importance of the design of a good data mining query language can also be seen from observing the history of relational database systems. Relational database systems have dominated the database market for decades. The standardization of relational query languages, which occurred at the early stages of relational database development, is widely credited for the success of the relational database field. Although each commercial relational database system has its own graphical user interace, the underlying core of each interface is a standardized relational query language. The standardization of relational query languages provided a foundation on which relational systems were developed and evolved. It facilitated information exchange and technology transfer, and promoted commercialization and wide acceptance of relational database technology. The recent standardization activities in database systems, such as work relating to SQL-3, and so on, further illustrate the importance of having a standard database language for success in the development and commercialization of database systems. Hence, having a good query language for data mining may help standardize the development of platforms for data mining systems.

Designing a comprehensive data mining language is challenging because data mining covers a wide spectrum of tasks, from data characterization to mining association rules, data classification, and evolution analysis. Each task has different requirements. The design of an effective data mining query language requires a deep understanding of the power, limitation, and underlying mechanisms of the various kinds of data mining tasks.

How would you design a data mining query language? Earlier in this chapter, we looked at primitives for defining a data mining task in the form of a data mining query. The primitives specify the following:

- The set of task-relevant data to be mined
- The kind of knowledge to be mined
- The background knowledge to be used in the discovery process
- The interestingness measures and thresholds for pattern evaluation
- The expected representation for visualizing the discovered patterns

Based on these primitives, we design a query language for data mining called **DMQL** (Data Mining Query Language). DMQL allows the ad hoc mining of several kinds of knowledge from relational databases and data warehouses at multiple levels of abstraction.[2]

The language adopts an SQL-like syntax, so that it can easily be integrated with the relational query language SQL. The syntax of DMQL is defined in an extended BNF grammar, where "[ ]" represents 0 or one occurrence, "{ }" represents 0 or more occurrences, and words in **sans serif** font represent keywords.

In Sections 4.2.1 to 4.2.5, we develop DMQL syntax for each of the data mining primitives. In Section 4.2.6, we show an example data mining query, specified in the proposed syntax. A top-level summary of the language is shown in Figure 4.5.

## 4.2.1 Syntax for Task-Relevant Data Specification

The first step in defining a data mining task is the specification of the task-relevant data, that is, the data on which mining is to be performed. This involves specifying the database and tables or data warehouse containing the relevant data, conditions for selecting the relevant data, the relevant attributes or dimensions for exploration, and instructions regarding the ordering or grouping of the data retrieved. DMQL provides clauses for the specification of such information, as follows:

- **use database** ⟨database_name⟩ or **use data warehouse** ⟨data_warehouse_name⟩: The **use** clause directs the mining task to the database or data warehouse specified.
- **from** ⟨relation(s)/cube(s)⟩ [**where** ⟨condition⟩]: The **from** and **where** clauses respectively specify the database tables or data cubes involved, and the conditions defining the data to be retrieved.

---

[2] DMQL syntax for defining data warehouses and data marts is given in Chapter 2.

⟨DMQL⟩              ::=  ⟨DMQL_Statement⟩; {⟨DMQL_Statement⟩}
⟨DMQL_Statement⟩ ::=  ⟨Data_Mining_Statment⟩
                    |  ⟨Concept_Hierarchy_Definition_Statement⟩
                    |  ⟨Visualization_and_Presentation⟩
⟨Data_Mining_Statement⟩ ::=
                        **use database** ⟨database_name⟩ | **use data warehouse** ⟨data_warehouse_name⟩
                        {**use hierarchy** ⟨hierarchy_name⟩ **for** ⟨attribute_or_dimension⟩}
                        ⟨Mine_Knowledge_Specification⟩
                        **in relevance to** ⟨attribute_or_dimension_list⟩
                        **from** ⟨relation(s)/cube(s)⟩
                        [**where** ⟨condition⟩]
                        [**order by** ⟨order_list⟩]
                        [**group by** ⟨grouping_list⟩]
                        [**having** ⟨condition⟩]
                        {**with** [⟨interest_measure_name⟩] **threshold** = ⟨threshold_value⟩
                        [**for** ⟨attribute(s)⟩]}
⟨Mine_Knowledge_Specification⟩ ::= ⟨Mine_Char⟩ | ⟨Mine_Discr⟩ | ⟨Mine_Assoc⟩ | ⟨Mine_Class⟩
⟨Mine_Char⟩ ::=         **mine characteristics** [**as** ⟨pattern_name⟩]
                        **analyze** ⟨measure(s)⟩
⟨Mine_Discr⟩ ::=        **mine comparison** [**as** ⟨pattern_name⟩]
                        **for** ⟨target_class⟩ **where** ⟨target_condition⟩
                        {**versus** ⟨contrast_class_*i*⟩ **where** ⟨contrast_condition_*i*⟩}
                        **analyze** ⟨measure(s)⟩
⟨Mine_Assoc⟩ ::=        **mine associations** [**as** ⟨pattern_name⟩]
                        [**matching** ⟨metapattern⟩]
⟨Mine_Class⟩ ::=        **mine classification** [**as** ⟨pattern_name⟩]
                        **analyze** ⟨classifying_attribute_or_dimension⟩
⟨Concept_Hierarchy_Definition_Statement⟩ ::=
                        **define hierarchy** ⟨hierarchy_name⟩
                        [**for** ⟨attribute_or_dimension⟩]
                        **on** ⟨relation_or_cube_or_hierarchy⟩
                        **as** ⟨hierarchy_description⟩
                        [**where** ⟨condition⟩]
⟨Visualization_and_Presentation⟩ ::=
                        **display as** ⟨result_form⟩ | {⟨Multilevel_Manipulation⟩}
⟨Multilevel_Manipulation⟩::= **roll up on** ⟨attribute_or_dimension ⟩
                        | **drill down on** ⟨attribute_or_dimension⟩
                        | **add** ⟨attribute_or_dimension⟩
                        | **drop** ⟨attribute_or_dimension⟩

**Figure 4.5**  Top-level syntax of the data mining query language DMQL.

  ▪ **in relevance to** ⟨attribute_or_dimension_list⟩: This clause lists the attributes or dimensions for exploration.

  ▪ **order by** ⟨order_list⟩: The **order by** clause specifies the sorting order of the task-relevant data.

  ▪ **group by** ⟨grouping_list⟩: The **group by** clause specifies criteria for grouping the data.

  ▪ **having** ⟨condition⟩: The **having** clause specifies the condition by which groups of data are considered relevant.

These clauses form an SQL query to collect the task-relevant data.

**Example 4.9** This example shows how to use DMQL to specify the task-relevant data described in Example 4.1 for the mining of associations between items frequently purchased at *AllElectronics* by Canadian customers, with respect to customer *income* and *age*. In addition, the user specifies that the data are to be grouped by date. The data are retrieved from a relational database.

> **use database** AllElectronics_db
> **in relevance to** I.name, I.price, C.income, C.age
> **from** customer C, item I, purchases P, items_sold S
> **where** I.item_ID = S.item_ID **and** S.trans_ID = P.trans_ID **and** P.cust_ID = C.cust_ID **and** C.country = "Canada"
> **group by** P.date ▪

## 4.2.2 Syntax for Specifying the Kind of Knowledge to be Mined

The ⟨Mine_Knowledge_Specification⟩ statement is used to specify the kind of knowledge to be mined. In other words, it indicates the data mining functionality to be performed. Its syntax is defined below for characterization, discrimination, association, and classification.

Characterization:

> ⟨Mine_Knowledge_Specification⟩ ::=
>     **mine characteristics** [**as** ⟨pattern_name⟩]
>     **analyze** ⟨measure(s)⟩

This specifies that characteristic descriptions are to be mined. The **analyze** clause, when used for characterization, specifies aggregate measures, such as count, sum, or count% (percentage count, i.e., the percentage of tuples in the relevant data set with the specified characteristics). These measures are to be computed for each data characteristic found.

**Example 4.10** The following specifies that the kind of knowledge to be mined is a characteristic description describing customer purchasing habits. For each characteristic, the percentage of task-relevant tuples satisfying that characteristic is to be displayed.

> **mine characteristics as** customerPurchasing
> **analyze** count% ∎

### Discrimination:

> ⟨Mine_Knowledge_Specification⟩ ::=
>     **mine comparison** [**as** ⟨pattern_name⟩]
>     **for** ⟨target_class⟩ **where** ⟨ target_condition⟩
>     {**versus** ⟨contrast_class_*i*⟩ **where** ⟨contrast_condition_*i*⟩}
>     **analyze** ⟨measure(s)⟩

This specifies that discriminant descriptions are to be mined. These descriptions compare a given target class of objects with one or more other contrasting classes. Hence, this kind of knowledge is referred to as a **comparison**. As for characterization, the **analyze** clause specifies aggregate measures, such as count, sum, or count%, to be computed and displayed for each description.

**Example 4.11** The user may define categories of customers, and then mine descriptions of each category. For instance, a user may define *bigSpenders* as customers who purchase items that cost $100 or more on average, and *budgetSpenders* as customers who purchase items at less than $100 on average. The mining of discriminant descriptions for customers from each of these categories can be specified in DMQL as shown below, where *I* refers to the *item* relation. The count of task-relevant tuples satisfying each description is to be displayed.

> **mine comparison as** purchaseGroups
> **for** bigSpenders **where** avg(I.price) ≥ $100
> **versus** budgetSpenders **where** avg(I.price) < $100
> **analyze** count ∎

### Association:

> ⟨Mine_Knowledge_Specification⟩ ::=
>     **mine associations** [**as** ⟨pattern_name⟩]
>     [**matching** ⟨metapattern⟩]

This specifies the mining of patterns of association. When specifying association mining, the user has the option of providing templates (also known as *metapatterns* or *metarules*) with the **matching** clause. The metapatterns can be used to focus the discovery towards the patterns that match the given meta-patterns, thereby enforcing additional syntactic constraints for the mining task. In addition to providing syntactic constraints, the metapatterns represent data hunches or hypotheses that the user finds interesting for investigation. Mining with the use of metapatterns, or **metarule-guided mining**, allows additional flexibility for ad hoc rule mining. While metapatterns may be used in the mining of other forms of knowledge, they are most useful for association mining due to the vast number of potentially generated associations.

**Example 4.12** The metapattern of Example 4.2 can be specified as follows to guide the mining of association rules describing customer buying habits.

> **mine associations as** buyingHabits
> **matching** $P(X : customer, W) \land Q(X, Y) \Rightarrow buys(X, Z)$

where $X$ is a key of the *customer* relation, $P$ and $Q$ are predicate variables that can be instantiated to the relevant attributes or dimensions specified as part of the task-relevant data, and $W$, $Y$, and $Z$ are object variables that can take on the values of their respective predicates for customers $X$. ∎

**Classification:**

> ⟨Mine_Knowledge_Specification⟩ ::=
>     **mine classification** [**as** ⟨pattern_name⟩]
>     **analyze** ⟨classifying_attribute_or_dimension⟩

This specifies that patterns for data classification are to be mined. The **analyze** clause specifies that the classification is performed according to the values of ⟨classifying_attribute_or_dimension⟩. For categorical attributes or dimensions, typically each value represents a class (such as "low-risk", "medium-risk", and "high-risk", for the attribute *credit_rating*). For numeric attributes or dimensions, each class may be defined by a range of values (such as "20-39", "40-59", "60-89" for *age*). Classification provides a concise framework that best describes the objects in each class and distinguishes them from other classes.

**Example 4.13** To mine patterns classifying customer credit rating where the classes are determined by the attribute *credit_rating*, the following DMQL specification is used:

> **mine classification as** classifyCustomerCreditRating
> **analyze** credit_rating ∎

The data mining language should also allow the specification of other kinds of knowledge to be mined, in addition to those shown above. These include the mining of data clusters, evolution rules or sequential patterns, and deviations.

### 4.2.3 Syntax for Concept Hierarchy Specification

Concept hierarchies allow the mining of knowledge at multiple levels of abstraction. In order to accommodate the different viewpoints of users with regard to the data, there may be more than one concept hierarchy per attribute or dimension. For instance, some users may prefer to organize branch locations by provinces and states, while others may prefer to organize them according to languages used. In such cases, a user can indicate which concept hierarchy is to be used with the statement

**use hierarchy** ⟨hierarchy_name⟩ **for** ⟨attribute_or_dimension⟩

Otherwise, a default hierarchy per attribute or dimension is used.

*"How can we define concept hierarchies using DMQL?"* In Section 4.1.3, we studied four types of concept hierarchies. Let's look at some examples of defining concept hierarchies with DMQL.

**Example 4.14** **Definition of a schema hierarchy:** Earlier, we defined a schema hierarchy for a relation *address* as the total order *street* < *city* < *province_or_state* < *country*. This can be defined in the data mining query language as

**define hierarchy** location_hierarchy **on** address **as**
[street, city, province_or_state, country]

The ordering of the listed attributes is important. In fact, a total order is defined that specifies that *street* is conceptually one level lower than *city*, which is in turn conceptually one level lower than *province_or_state*, and so on. ∎

**Example 4.15** **Definition of a set-grouping hierarchy.** The set-grouping hierarchy for *age* of Example 4.4 can be defined in terms of ranges as follows, where, by convention, the most general concept, **all**, is placed at the root of the hierarchy (i.e., at level 0).

**define hierarchy** age_hierarchy **for** age **on** customer **as**
level1: {*young, middle_aged, senior*} < level0: **all**
level2: {20 . . . 39} < level1: *young*
level2: {40 . . . 59} < level1: *middle_aged*
level2: {60 . . . 89} < level1: *senior*

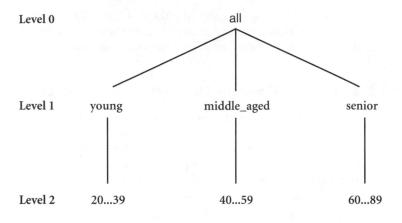

**Figure 4.6** A concept hierarchy for the attribute *age*.

The notation " . . . " implicitly specifies all the possible values within the given range. For example, "{20 . . . 39}" includes all integers within the range of the endpoints, 20 and 39. Ranges may also be specified with real numbers as endpoints. The corresponding concept hierarchy is shown in Figure 4.6. ∎

Additional examples are left as an exercise.

### 4.2.4 Syntax for Interestingness Measure Specification

The user can help control the number of uninteresting patterns returned by the data mining system by specifying measures of pattern interestingness and their corresponding thresholds. Interestingness measures include the confidence, support, noise, and novelty measures described in Section 4.1.4. Interestingness measures and thresholds can be specified by the user with the statement

**with** [⟨interest_measure_name⟩] **threshold** = ⟨threshold_value⟩

**Example 4.16** In mining association rules, a user can confine the rules to be found by specifying a minimum support and minimum confidence threshold of 5% and 70%, respectively, with the statements

**with** support **threshold** = 5%
**with** confidence **threshold** = 70% ∎

The interestingness measures and threshold values can be set and modified interactively.

## 4.2.5 Syntax for Pattern Presentation and Visualization Specification

*"How can users specify the forms of presentation and visualization to be used in displaying the discovered patterns?"* Our data mining query language needs syntax that allows users to specify the display of discovered patterns in one or more forms, including rules, tables, crosstabs, pie or bar charts, decision trees, cubes, curves, or surfaces. We define the DMQL **display** statement for this purpose:

> **display as** ⟨result_form⟩

where the ⟨result_form⟩ could be any of the knowledge presentation or visualization forms listed above.

Interactive mining should allow the discovered patterns to be viewed at different concept levels or from different angles. This can be accomplished with roll-up and drill-down operations, as described in Chapter 2. Patterns can be rolled up, or viewed at a more general level, by *climbing up* the concept hierarchy of an attribute or dimension (replacing lower-level concept values by higher-level values). Generalization can also be performed by dropping attributes or dimensions. For example, suppose that a pattern contains the attribute *city*. Given the *location* hierarchy *city < province_or_state < country < continent*, then dropping the attribute *city* from the patterns will generalize the data to the next highest level attribute, *province_or_state*. Patterns can be drilled down on, or viewed at a less general level, by *stepping down* the concept hierarchy of an attribute or dimension. Patterns can also be made less general by adding attributes or dimensions to their description. The attribute added must be one of the attributes listed in the **in relevance to** clause for task-relevant specification. The user can alternately view the patterns at different levels of abstractions with the use of the following DMQL syntax:

> ⟨Multilevel_Manipulation⟩ ::= **roll up on** ⟨attribute_or_dimension⟩
> | **drill down on** ⟨attribute_or_dimension⟩
> | **add** ⟨attribute_or_dimension⟩
> | **drop** ⟨attribute_or_dimension⟩

**Example 4.17** Suppose that descriptions are mined based on the dimensions *location*, *age*, and *income*. Users can "**roll up on** location" or "**drop** age" to generalize the discovered patterns. ∎

## 4.2.6 Putting It All Together—An Example of a DMQL Query

In the above discussion, we presented DMQL syntax for specifying data mining queries in terms of the five data mining primitives. For a given query, these primitives define the task-relevant data, the kind of knowledge to be mined, the concept hierarchies and interestingness measures to be used, and the representation forms for pattern visualization. Here we put these components together. Let's look at an example for the full specification of a DMQL query.

**Example 4.18** **Mining characteristic descriptions.** Suppose, as a marketing manager of *AllElectronics*, you would like to characterize the buying habits of customers who purchase items priced at no less than $100, with respect to the customer's age, the type of item purchased, and the place in which the item was made. For each characteristic discovered, you would like to know the percentage of customers having that characteristic. In particular, you are only interested in purchases made in Canada, and paid for with an American Express ("AmEx") credit card. You would like to view the resulting descriptions in the form of a table. This data mining query is expressed in DMQL as follows.

**use database** AllElectronics_db
**use hierarchy** location_hierarchy **for** B.address
**mine characteristics as** customerPurchasing
**analyze** count%
**in relevance to** C.age, I.type, I.place_made
**from** customer C, item I, purchases P, items_sold S, works_at W, branch B
**where** I.item_ID = S.item_ID **and** S.trans_ID = P.trans_ID **and** P.cust_ID = C.cust_ID
    **and** P.method_paid = "AmEx" **and** P.empl_ID = W.empl_ID
    **and** W.branch_ID = B.branch_ID **and** B.address = "Canada" **and** I.price $\geq$ 100
**with** noise threshold = 5%
**display as** table

The data mining query is parsed to form an SQL query that retrieves the set of task-relevant data from the *AllElectronics* database. The concept hierarchy *location_hierarchy*, corresponding to the concept hierarchy of Figure 4.3, is used to generalize branch locations to high-level concept levels such as "Canada". An algorithm for mining characteristic rules, which uses the generalized data, can then be executed. Algorithms for mining characteristic rules are introduced in Chapter 5. The mined characteristic descriptions, derived from the attributes *age, type,* and *place_made*, are displayed as a table, or generalized relation (Table 4.1). The percentage of task-relevant tuples satisfying each generalized tuple is shown as count%. If no visualization form is specified, a default form is used. The noise threshold of 5% means any generalized tuple found that represents less than 5% of the total count is omitted from display. ∎

Similarly, the complete DMQL specification of data mining queries for discrimination, association, classification, and prediction can be given. Example queries are presented in the following chapters that study the mining of these kinds of knowledge.

**Table 4.1** Characteristic descriptions in the form of a table, or generalized relation.

| age | type | place_made | count% |
|-----|------|------------|--------|
| 30 . . . 39 | home security system | USA | 19 |
| 40 . . . 49 | home security system | USA | 15 |
| 20 . . . 29 | CD player | Japan | 26 |
| 30 . . . 39 | CD player | USA | 13 |
| 40 . . . 49 | large screen TV | Japan | 8 |
| ⋮ | ⋮ | ⋮ | ⋮ |
| | | | 100% |

### 4.2.7 Other Data Mining Languages and the Standardization of Data Mining Primitives

*"You have introduced DMQL in this book. Are there other data mining languages?"* Besides DMQL, which is used to introduce data mining primitives and concepts in this book, there have been research efforts to design other data mining languages and industry efforts to standardize data mining primitives and languages. Here we introduce a few examples. Detailed information about these languages and standards can be found in the references listed in the bibliographic notes of this chapter.

**MSQL** is a data mining query language, proposed by Imielinski and Virmani [IV99]. The language uses SQL-like syntax and SQL primitives including sorting and group-by. Since an enormous number of rules can be generated in data mining, MSQL provides primitives like **GetRules** and **SelectRules** for both rule generation and rule selection. It treats data and rules uniformly and, therefore, optimization can be explored by either performing selective, query-based rule generation from data, or manipulating or querying the generated set of rules.

Other research efforts on data mining language design include the **MINE RULE** operator, proposed by Meo, Psaila, and Ceri [MPC96]. It follows SQL-like syntax and serves as rule generation queries for mining association rules. Another proposal, by Tsur, Ullman, Abitboul, Clifton, et al. [TUA+98], uses Datalog syntax to express query flocks, which facilitates both mining and testing rules.

*"Are there any standardization efforts in data mining?"* Recently, Microsoft proposed a data mining language called **OLE DB for Data Mining** (DM). This is a notable effort towards the standardization of data mining language primitives. Having a standard data mining language will help to strengthen the data mining industry by facilitating the development of data mining platforms and of data mining systems, and the sharing of data mining results.

OLE DB for DM, together with OLE DB and OLE DB for OLAP, constitute three important steps by Microsoft towards the standardization of database, database warehousing, and data mining languages. The specifications of OLE DB for

DM cover the primitives for creation and use of several important data mining modules, including association, predictive modeling (classification and prediction), and clustering. Since the details of OLE DB for DM have yet to be finalized at the time of this book's publication, we have chosen to use DMQL as the data mining language in this book. A short introduction to OLE DB for DM is compiled in Appendix A.

CRISP-DM (for "CRoss-Industry Standard Process for Data Mining") (*http://www.crisp-dm.org/*) is another standardization effort related to data mining. It moves away from the focus on technology by addressing the needs of all levels of users in deploying data mining technology to solve business problems. CRISP-DM is an international project that brings together a few data warehousing, data mining, and user companies, to work on providing a platform and process structure for effective data mining. The project is to define and validate a data mining process that is generally applicable in diverse industry sectors. It addresses issues like (1) mapping from business issues to data mining problems, (2) capturing and understanding data, (3) identifying and solving problems within the data, (4) applying data mining techniques, (5) interpreting data mining results within the business context, (6) deploying and maintaining data mining results, and (7) capturing and transfering expertise to ensure future projects benefit from experience. The project provides a process structure for carrying out data mining and provides guidance on potential problems that can occur in data mining projects.

With further developments of data mining systems and the standardization of data mining languages, it is expected that the data mining language used in future editions of this book will evolve towards primitives similar to OLE DB for DM, or eventually be replaced by a more complete standard data mining language, whatever such a language may be called by that time.

## 4.3 Designing Graphical User Interfaces Based on a Data Mining Query Language

A data mining query language provides necessary primitives that allow users to communicate with data mining systems. However, inexperienced users may find data mining query languages awkward to use and the syntax difficult to remember. Instead, users may prefer to communicate with data mining systems through a graphical user interface (GUI). In relational database technology, SQL serves as a standard "core" language for relational systems, on top of which GUIs can easily be designed. Similarly, a data mining query language may serve as a "core language" for data mining system implementations, providing a basis for the development of GUIs for effective data mining.

A data mining GUI may consist of the following functional components:

- **Data collection and data mining query composition:** This component allows the user to specify task-relevant data sets and to compose data mining queries. It is similar to GUIs used for the specification of relational queries.

- **Presentation of discovered patterns:** This component allows the display of the discovered patterns in various forms, including tables, graphs, charts, curves, and other visualization techniques.

- **Hierarchy specification and manipulation:** This component allows for concept hierarchy specification, either manually by the user or automatically (based on analysis of the data at hand). In addition, this component should allow concept hierarchies to be modified by the user or adjusted automatically based on a given data set distribution.

- **Manipulation of data mining primitives:** This component may allow the dynamic adjustment of data mining thresholds, as well as the selection, display, and modification of concept hierarchies. It may also allow the modification of previous data mining queries or conditions.

- **Interactive multilevel mining:** This component should allow roll-up or drill-down operations on discovered patterns.

- **Other miscellaneous information:** This component may include on-line help manuals, indexed search, debugging, and other interactive graphical facilities.

The design of a graphical user interface should also take into consideration different classes of users of a data mining system. In general, users of data mining systems can be classified into two categories: *business analysts* and *business executives*. A business analyst would like to have flexibility and convenience in selecting different portions of data, manipulating dimensions and levels, setting mining parameters, and tuning data mining processes. On the other hand, a business executive needs clear presentation and interpretation of data mining results, flexibility in viewing and comparing different data mining results, and easy integration of data mining results into report writing and presentation processes. A well-designed data mining system should provide friendly user interfaces for both kinds of users.

*"Will data mining query languages evolve to form a standard for designing data mining GUIs?"* If such an evolution is possible, the standard would facilitate data mining software development and system communication. Some GUI primitives, such as pointing to a particular point in a curve or graph, however, are difficult to specify using a text-based data mining query language like DMQL. Alternatively, a standardized GUI-based language may evolve and replace SQL-like data mining languages. Only time will tell.

# 4.4 Architectures of Data Mining Systems

With popular and diverse applications of data mining, it is expected that a good variety of data mining systems will be designed and developed in future years. Although rich and powerful data mining functions form the core of a data mining system, like most software systems, the architecture and design of a data mining system is critically important. A good system architecture will facilitate the system to make best use of the software environment, accomplish data mining tasks in an efficient and timely manner, interoperate and exchange information with other information systems, be adaptable to users' diverse requirements, and evolve with time.

*"What are the desired architectures for data mining systems?"* With decades of research and development in the database and information industry, *database systems* and *data warehouse systems* have become the mainstream information systems. Tremendous amounts of data and information have been stored and/or integrated in such systems. Moreover, comprehensive information processing and data analysis infrastructures have been or will be continuously and systematically constructed surrounding database systems and data warehouses. These include accessing, integration, consolidation, and transformation of multiple, heterogeneous databases, ODBC/OLE DB connections, Web-accessing and service facilities, and reporting and OLAP analysis tools.

Under this situation, a critical question in the design of a data mining system becomes whether we should couple or integrate a data mining (DM) system with a database (DB) system and/or a data warehouse (DW) system, and if we should, how to do it correctly. To answer these questions, we need to examine the possible ways of coupling or integrating a DM system and a DB/DW system. Based on different architecture designs, a DM system can be integrated with a DB/DW system using the following coupling schemes: *no coupling, loose coupling, semi-tight coupling*, and *tight coupling*. Let us examine these one by one.

**No coupling:**   *No coupling* means that a DM system will not utilize any function of a DB or DW system. It may fetch data from a particular source (such as a file system), process data using some data mining algorithms, and then store the mining results in another file.

Such a system, though simple, suffers from several drawbacks. First, a DB system provides a great deal of flexibility and efficiency at storing, organizing, accessing, and processing data. Without using a DB/DW system, a DM system may spend a substantial amount of time finding, collecting, cleaning, and transforming data. In DB and/or DW systems, data tend to be well organized, indexed, cleaned, integrated, or consolidated, so that finding the task-relevant, high-quality data becomes an easy task. Second, there are many tested, scalable algorithms and data structures implemented in DB and DW systems. It is feasible to realize efficient, scalable implementations using such systems. Moreover, most data have been or will be stored in DB/DW systems. Without any coupling of such systems, a DM system will need to use other tools to extract data, making it difficult to integrate such a system into an information processing environment. Thus, no coupling represents a poor design.

**Loose coupling:**   *Loose coupling* means that a DM system will use some facilities of a DB or DW system, fetching data from a data repository managed by these systems, performing data mining, and then storing the mining results either in a file or in a designated place in a database or data warehouse.

Loose coupling is better than no coupling since it can fetch any portion of data stored in databases or data warehouses by using query processing, indexing, and other system facilities. It incurs some advantages of the flexibility, efficiency, and other features provided by such systems. However, many loosely coupled mining systems are main memory–based. Since mining itself does not explore data structures and query optimization methods provided by DB or DW systems, it is difficult for loose coupling to achieve high scalability and good performance with large data sets.

**Semitight coupling:**   *Semitight coupling* means that besides linking a DM system to a DB/DW system, efficient implementations of a few essential data mining primitives (identified by the analysis of frequently encountered data mining functions) can be provided in the DB/DW system. These primitives can include sorting, indexing, aggregation, histogram analysis, multiway join, and precomputation of some essential statistical measures, such as sum, count, max, min, standard deviation, and so on. Moreover, some frequently used intermediate mining results can be precomputed and stored in the DB/DW system. Since these intermediate mining results are either precomputed or can be computed efficiently, this design will enhance the performance of a DM system.

**Tight coupling:**   *Tight coupling* means that a DM system is smoothly integrated into the DB/DW system. The data mining subsystem is treated as one functional component of an information system. Data mining queries and functions are optimized based on mining query analysis, data structures, indexing schemes, and query processing methods of a DB or DW system. With further technology advances, DM, DB, and DW systems will evolve and integrate together as one information system with multiple functionalities. This will provide a uniform information processing environment.

This approach is highly desirable since it facilitates efficient implementations of data mining functions, high system performance, and an integrated information processing environment.

With this analysis, one can see that a data mining system should be coupled with a DB/DW system. Loose coupling, though not efficient, is better than no coupling since it makes use of both data and system facilities of a DB/DW system. Tight coupling is highly desirable, but its implementation is nontrivial and more research is needed in this area. Semitight coupling is a compromise between loose and tight coupling. It is important to identify commonly used data mining primitives and provide efficient implementations of such primitives in DB or DW systems.

# 4.5 Summary

- We have studied five **primitives** for specifying a data mining task in the form of a **data mining query**. These primitives are the specification of task-relevant data (i.e., the data set to be mined), the kind of knowledge to be mined (e.g., characterization, discrimination, association, classification, or prediction), background knowledge (typically in the form of concept hierarchies), interestingness measures, and knowledge presentation and visualization techniques to be used for displaying the discovered patterns.

- In defining the **task-relevant data,** the user specifies the database and tables (or data warehouse and data cubes) containing the data to be mined, conditions for selecting and grouping such data, and the attributes (or dimensions) to be considered during mining.

- **Concept hierarchies** provide useful background knowledge for expressing discovered patterns in concise, high-level terms and facilitate the mining of knowledge at multiple levels of abstraction.

- Measures of **pattern interestingness** assess the simplicity, certainty, utility, or novelty of discovered patterns. Such measures can be used to help reduce the number of uninteresting patterns returned to the user.

- Users should be able to specify the desired form for **visualizing** the discovered patterns, such as rules, tables, charts, decision trees, cubes, graphs, or reports. Roll-up and drill-down operations should also be available for the inspection of patterns at multiple levels of abstraction.

- **Data mining query languages** can be designed to support ad hoc and interactive data mining. A data mining query language, such as DMQL, should provide commands for specifying each of the data mining primitives, as well as for concept hierarchy generation and manipulation. Such query languages are SQL-based and may eventually form a standard on which graphical user interfaces for data mining can be based.

- **Data mining system architecture** includes the consideration of coupling a data mining system with a database/data warehouse system. There are several possible designs: *no coupling, loose coupling, semitight coupling*, and *tight coupling*. A well-designed data mining system should offer tight or semitight coupling with a database and/or data warehouse system.

## Exercises

4.1 List and describe the five *primitives* for specifying a data mining task.

4.2 Describe why *concept hierarchies* are useful in data mining.

**4.3** The four major types of concept hierarchies are: *schema hierarchies, set-grouping hierarchies, operation-derived hierarchies,* and *rule-based hierarchies.*

(a) Briefly define each type of hierarchy.

(b) For each hierarchy type, provide an example that was not presented in this chapter.

**4.4** Suppose that the university course database for *Big-University* includes the following attributes describing students: *name, address, status* (e.g., undergraduate or graduate), *major,* and *GPA* (cumulative grade point average).

(a) Propose a concept hierarchy for the attributes *address, status, major,* and *GPA.*

(b) For each concept hierarchy that you have proposed above, what type of concept hierarchy is it?

(c) Define each hierarchy using DMQL syntax.

(d) Write a DMQL query to find the characteristics of students who have an excellent GPA.

(e) Write a DMQL query to compare students majoring in science with students majoring in arts.

(f) Write a DMQL query to find associations involving course instructors, student grades, and some other attribute of your choice. Use a *metarule* to specify the format of associations you would like to find. Specify minimum thresholds for the confidence and support of the association rules reported.

(g) Write a DMQL query to predict student grades in "Computing Science 101" based on student GPA and course instructor.

**4.5** Consider Association Rule (4.8) below, which was mined from the student database at *Big-University*:

$$major(X, \text{``science''}) \Rightarrow status(X, \text{``undergrad''}). \tag{4.8}$$

Suppose that the number of students at the university (that is, the number of task-relevant data tuples) is 5000, that 56% of undergraduates at the university major in science, that 64% of the students are registered in programs leading to undergraduate degrees, and that 70% of the students are majoring in science.

(a) Compute the *confidence* and *support* of Rule (4.8).

(b) Consider Rule (4.9) below:

$$major(X, \text{``biology''}) \Rightarrow status(X, \text{``undergrad''}) \quad [17\%, 80\%] \tag{4.9}$$

Suppose that 30% of science students are majoring in biology. Would you consider Rule (4.9) to be novel with respect to Rule (4.8)? Explain.

**4.6** The ⟨Mine_Knowledge_Specification⟩ statement can be used to specify the mining of characteristic, discriminant, association, and classification rules. Propose a syntax for the mining of clusters.

4.7 The following exercises concern DMQL syntax for defining concept hierarchies.

(a) A data mining system will typically have a predefined concept hierarchy for the schema *date* (*day, month, quarter, year*). Provide the definition of such a hierarchy using DMQL.

(b) Concept hierarchy definitions can involve several relations. For example, an *item_hierarchy* may involve two relations, *item* and *supplier*, defined by the following schema:

*item*(*item_ID, brand, type, place_made, supplier*)

*supplier*(*name, type, headquarter_location, owner, size, assets, revenue*)

Propose a DMQL definition for *item_hierarchy*. (Hint: You may use a **where** construct and dot ("∴") notation, as in SQL.)

(c) Use DMQL syntax for set-grouping hierarchies in order to refine the schema hierarchy of Example 4.14 for *location* by adding an additional concept level, *continent*.

(d) As an alternative to the set-grouping hierarchy for *age* in Example 4.15, a user may wish to define an operation-derived hierarchy based on data clustering routines. Propose DMQL syntax for such a hierarchy for *age*, based on the formation of, say, five clusters.

(e) A concept hierarchy can be defined based on a set of rules. Propose DMQL syntax for the definition of the rule-based hierarchy of Example 4.6 for *items* at *AllElectronics* based on profit margins.

4.8 Discuss the importance of establishing a *standardized data mining query language*. What are some of the potential benefits and challenges involved in such a task? List a few of the recent proposals in this area.

4.9 Describe the differences between the following architectures for the integration of a data mining system with a database or data warehouse system: *no coupling, loose coupling, semitight coupling,* and *tight coupling*. State which architecture you think is the most popular, and why.

## Bibliographic Notes

A number of objective interestingness measures have been proposed in the literature. Simplicity measures are given in Michalski [Mic83]. The confidence and support measures for association rule interestingness described in this chapter were proposed in Agrawal, Imielinski, and Swami [AIS93a]. The strategy we described for identifying redundant multilevel association rules was proposed by Srikant and Agrawal [SA95, SA96]. Other objective interestingness measures have been presented in [HM91, PS91ab, SG92 AIS93a, MM95, CHY96, KA96]. Subjective measures of interestingness, which consider user beliefs regarding relationships in the data, are discussed in [PSM94, MPSM96, ST96, LHC97].

The DMQL data mining query language was proposed by Han, Fu, Wang, et al. [HFW+96a] for the *DBMiner* data mining system.

*Discovery Board* (formerly *Data Mine*) was proposed by Imielinski, Virmani, and Abdulghani [IVA96] as an application development interface prototype involving an SQL-based operator for data mining query specification and rule retrieval. Its associated data mining query language, MSQL, was proposed by Imielinski and Virmani [IV99]. MINE RULE, an SQL-like operator for mining single-dimensional association rules, was proposed by Meo, Psaila, and Ceri [MPC96] and extended by Baralis and Psaila [BP97]. An association rule generation language, using Datalog syntax [RG00] and based on the concept of *query flocks*, was proposed by Tsur, Ullman, Abitboul, Clifton, et al. [TUA+98]. Mining with metarules is described in Klemettinen, Mannila, Ronkainen, et al. [KMR+94], Fu and Han [FH95], Shen, Ong, Mitbander, and Zaniolo [SOMZ96], and Kamber, Han, and Chiang [KHC97]. Other ideas involving the use of templates or predicate constraints in mining have been discussed in [AK93, DT93, LHC97, ST96, SVA97, NLHP98].

An important contributing factor to the success of the relational database systems [SH98] is the standardization of the relational database language SQL. The recent standardization activities in database systems, such as work relating to SQL-3 and so on, further illustrate the importance of having a standard database language for success in the development and commercialization of database systems. Microsoft Corporation has made a major data mining standardization effort by proposing *OLE DB for Data Mining (DM)* [Mic00]. An introduction to the data mining language primitives of *OLE DB for DM* can be found in Appendix A of this book. CRISP-DM (for "Cross-Industry Standard Process for Data Mining") (*http://www.crisp-dm.org/*) is another standardization effort related to data mining; however, it moves away from the focus on technology by addressing the needs of all levels of users in deploying data mining technology to solve business problems.

There have been many graphical user interfaces and visualization tools developed for data mining, which can be found in various data mining products. Several books on data mining, such as *Data Mining Solutions* by Westphal and Blaxton [WB98], present many good examples and visual snapshots. For a survey of visualization techniques, see "Visual techniques for exploring databases" by Keim [Kei97].

Architectures of data mining systems have been discussed by many researchers in conference panels and meetings. The recent design of data mining languages, such as [Mic00, IV99], the proposal of on-line analytical mining, such as [Han98], and the study of optimization of data mining queries, such as [NLHP98, STA98, LNHP99] can be viewed as steps toward tight integration of data mining systems with database systems and data warehouse systems. Some data mining primitives, proposed by Sarawagi, Thomas, and Agrawal [STA98], such as KWayJoin,

GatherPrune, and so on, can also be used as building blocks in relational or object-relational systems, for efficient implementation of data mining in such database systems.

# Concept Description: Characterization and Comparison

From a data analysis point of view, data mining can be classified into two categories: descriptive data mining and predictive data mining. *Descriptive data mining* describes the data set in a concise and summarative manner and presents interesting general properties of the data. *Predictive data mining* analyzes the data in order to construct one or a set of models, and attempts to predict the behavior of new data sets.

Databases usually store large amounts of data in great detail. However, users often like to view sets of *summarized* data in concise, descriptive terms. Such data descriptions may provide an overall picture of a class of data or distinguish it from a set of comparative classes. Moreover, users like the ease and flexibility of having data sets described at different levels of granularity and from different angles. Such descriptive data mining is called *concept description* and forms an important component of data mining.

In this chapter, you will learn how concept description can be performed efficiently and effectively.

## 5.1 What Is Concept Description?

The simplest kind of descriptive data mining is *concept description*. A concept usually refers to a collection of data such as *frequent_buyers, graduate_students*, and so on. As a data mining task, concept description is not a simple enumeration of the data. Instead, **concept description** generates descriptions for *characterization* and *comparison* of the data. It is sometimes called **class description**, when the concept to be described refers to a class of objects. **Characterization** provides a concise and succinct summarization of the given collection of data, while concept or class

**comparison** (also known as **discrimination**) provides descriptions comparing two or more collections of data. Since concept description involves both characterization and comparison, we will study techniques for accomplishing each of these tasks.

Concept description has close ties with *data generalization*. Given the large amount of data stored in databases, it is useful to be able to describe concepts in concise and succinct terms at generalized (rather than low) levels of abstraction. Allowing data sets to be generalized at multiple levels of abstraction facilitates users in examining the general behavior of the data. Given the *AllElectronics* database, for example, instead of examining individual customer transactions, sales managers may prefer to view the data generalized to higher levels, such as summarized by customer groups according to geographic regions, frequency of purchases per group, and customer income. Such multiple dimensional, multilevel data generalization is similar to multidimensional data analysis in data warehouses. In this context, concept description resembles *on-line analytical processing* (OLAP) in data warehouses, discussed in Chapter 2.

*"What are the differences between concept description in large databases and on-line analytical processing?"* The fundamental differences between the two involve the following.

**Complex data types and aggregation:**  Data warehouses and OLAP tools are based on a multidimensional data model that views data in the form of a data cube, consisting of dimensions (or attributes) and measures (aggregate functions). However, the possible data types of the dimensions and measures for most commercial versions of these systems are restricted. Many current OLAP systems confine dimensions to nonnumeric data.[1] Similarly, measures (such as `count()`, `sum()`, `average()`) in current OLAP systems apply only to numeric data. In contrast, for concept formation, the database attributes can be of various data types, including numeric, nonnumeric, spatial, text, or image. Furthermore, the aggregation of attributes in a database may include sophisticated data types, such as the collection of nonnumeric data, the merging of spatial regions, the composition of images, the integration of texts, and the grouping of object pointers. Therefore, OLAP, with its restrictions on the possible dimension and measure types, represents a simplified model for data analysis. Concept description in databases can handle complex data types of the attributes and their aggregations, as necessary.

**User-control versus automation:**  On-line analytical processing in data warehouses is a purely user-controlled process. The selection of dimensions and

---

[1] Note that in Chapter 3, we showed how concept hierarchies may be automatically generated from numeric data to form numeric dimensions. This feature, however, is a result of recent research in data mining and is not available in most commercial systems.

the application of OLAP operations, such as drill-down, roll-up, slicing, and dicing, are directed and controlled by the users. Although the control in most OLAP systems is quite user-friendly, users do require a good understanding of the role of each dimension. Furthermore, in order to find a satisfactory description of the data, users may need to specify a long sequence of OLAP operations. In contrast, concept description in data mining strives for a more automated process that helps users determine which dimensions (or attributes) should be included in the analysis, and the degree to which the given data set should be generalized in order to produce an interesting summarization of the data.

Recently, data warehousing and OLAP technology has been evolving towards handling more complex types of data and embedding more knowledge discovery mechanisms, as discussed in Chapter 2. As this technology continues to develop, it is expected that additional descriptive data mining features will be integrated into future OLAP systems.

In this chapter, you will learn methods for concept description, including multilevel generalization, summarization, characterization, and comparison. Such methods set the foundation for the implementation of two major functional modules in data mining: *multiple-level characterization* and *comparison*. In addition, you will also examine techniques for the presentation of concept descriptions in multiple forms, including tables, charts, graphs, and rules.

## 5.2 Data Generalization and Summarization-Based Characterization

Data and objects in databases often contain detailed information at primitive concept levels. For example, the *item* relation in a *sales* database may contain attributes describing low-level item information such as *item_ID, name, brand, category, supplier, place_made*, and *price*. It is useful to be able to summarize a large set of data and present it at a high conceptual level. For example, summarizing a large set of items relating to Christmas season sales provides a general description of such data, which can be very helpful for sales and marketing managers. This requires an important functionality in data mining: *data generalization*.

**Data generalization** is a process that abstracts a large set of task-relevant data in a database from a relatively low conceptual level to higher conceptual levels. Methods for the efficient and flexible generalization of large data sets can be categorized according to two approaches: (1) the data cube (or OLAP) approach and (2) the attribute-oriented induction approach. The data cube approach was described in Chapter 2. In this section, we describe the attribute-oriented induction approach.

## 5.2.1 **Attribute-Oriented Induction**

The attribute-oriented induction (AOI) approach to data generalization and summarization-based characterization was first proposed in 1989, a few years prior to the introduction of the data cube approach. The data cube approach can be considered as a data warehouse–based, precomputation-oriented, materialized-view approach. It performs *off-line* aggregation before an OLAP or data mining query is submitted for processing. On the other hand, the *attribute-oriented induction approach*, at least in its initial proposal, is a relational database query-oriented, generalization-based, *on-line* data analysis technique. However, there is no inherent barrier distinguishing the two approaches based on on-line aggregation versus off-line precomputation. Some aggregations in the data cube can be computed on-line, while off-line precomputation of multidimensional space can speed up attribute-oriented induction as well.

Let's first introduce the attribute-oriented induction approach. We will then perform a detailed analysis of the approach and its variations and extensions.

The general idea of attribute-oriented induction is to first collect the task-relevant data using a relational database query and then perform generalization based on the examination of the number of distinct values of each attribute in the relevant set of data. The generalization is performed by either *attribute removal* or *attribute generalization*. Aggregation is performed by merging identical generalized tuples and accumulating their respective counts. This reduces the size of the generalized data set. The resulting generalized relation can be mapped into different forms for presentation to the user, such as charts or rules.

The following series of examples illustrates the process of attribute-oriented induction.

**Example 5.1** Specifying a data mining query for characterization with DMQL:   Suppose that a user would like to describe the general characteristics of graduate students in the *Big-University* database, given the attributes *name, gender, major, birth_place, birth_date, residence, phone# (telephone number)*, and *gpa (grade_point_average)*. A data mining query for this characterization can be expressed in the data mining query language DMQL as follows:

> **use** Big_University_DB
> **mine characteristics as** "Science_Students"
> **in relevance to** name, gender, major, birth_place, birth_date, residence, phone#, gpa
> **from** student
> **where** status **in** "graduate"

We will see how this example of a typical data mining query can apply attribute-oriented induction for mining characteristic descriptions.   ■

"*What is the first step of attribute-oriented induction?*" First, **data focusing** should be performed *prior* to attribute-oriented induction. This step corresponds to the specification of the task-relevant data (or data for analysis) as described in Chapter 4. The data are collected based on the information provided in the data mining query. Since a data mining query is usually relevant to only a portion of the database, selecting the relevant set of data not only makes mining more efficient, but also derives more meaningful results than mining on the entire database.

Specifying the set of relevant attributes (i.e., attributes for mining, as indicated in DMQL with the **in relevance to** clause) may be difficult for the user. A user may select only a few attributes that she feels may be important, while missing others that could also play a role in the description. For example, suppose that the dimension *birth_place* is defined by the attributes *city*, *province_or_state*, and *country*. Of these attributes, the user has only thought to specify *city*. In order to allow generalization on the *birth_place* dimension, the other attributes defining this dimension should also be included. In other words, having the system automatically include *province_or_state* and *country* as relevant attributes allows *city* to be generalized to these higher conceptual levels during the induction process.

At the other extreme, a user may introduce too many attributes by specifying all of the possible attributes with the clause "**in relevance to** ∗". In this case, all of the attributes in the relation specified by the **from** clause would be included in the analysis. Many of these attributes are unlikely to contribute to an interesting description. Section 5.3 describes a method for handling such cases by filtering out statistically irrelevant or weakly relevant attributes from the descriptive mining process.

"*What does the* '**where** *status* **in** *"graduate"*' *clause mean?*" This **where** clause implies that a concept hierarchy exists for the attribute *status*. Such a concept hierarchy organizes primitive-level data values for *status*, such as "*M.Sc.*", "*M.A.*", "*M.B.A.*", "*Ph.D.*", "*B.Sc.*", "*B.A.*", into higher conceptual levels, such as "*graduate*" and "*undergraduate*". This use of concept hierarchies does not appear in traditional relational query languages, yet is a common feature in data mining query languages.

**Example 5.2** Transforming a data mining query to a relational query:  The data mining query presented in Example 5.1 is transformed into the following relational query for the collection of the task-relevant set of data:

> **use** Big_University_DB
> **select** name, gender, major, birth_place, birth_date, residence, phone#, gpa
> **from** student
> **where** status **in** {"*M.Sc.*", "*M.A.*", "*M.B.A.*", "*Ph.D.*"}

The transformed query is executed against the relational database, *Big_University_DB*, and returns the data shown in Table 5.1. This table is called the (task-relevant) **initial working relation**. It is the data on which induction will be performed. Note that each tuple is, in fact, a conjunction of attribute-value pairs.

**Table 5.1** Initial working relation: a collection of task-relevant data.

| name | gender | major | birth_place | birth_date | residence | phone# | gpa |
|---|---|---|---|---|---|---|---|
| Jim Woodman | M | CS | Vancouver, BC, Canada | 8-12-76 | 3511 Main St., Richmond | 687-4598 | 3.67 |
| Scott Lachance | M | CS | Montreal, Que, Canada | 28-7-75 | 345 1st Ave., Richmond | 253-9106 | 3.70 |
| Laura Lee | F | physics | Seattle, WA, USA | 25-8-70 | 125 Austin Ave., Burnaby | 420-5232 | 3.83 |
| . . . | . . . | . . . | . . . | . . . | . . . | . . . | . . . |

Hence, we can think of a tuple within a relation as a rule of conjuncts, and of induction on the relation as the generalization of these rules. ∎

"*Now that the data are ready for attribute-oriented induction, how is attribute-oriented induction performed?*" The essential operation of attribute-oriented induction is *data generalization*, which can be performed in either of two ways on the initial working relation: *attribute removal* and *attribute generalization*.

**Attribute removal** is based on the following rule: *If there is a large set of distinct values for an attribute of the initial working relation, but either (1) there is no generalization operator on the attribute (e.g., there is no concept hierarchy defined for the attribute), or (2) its higher-level concepts are expressed in terms of other attributes, then the attribute should be removed from the working relation.*

What is the reasoning behind this rule? An attribute-value pair represents a conjunct in a generalized tuple, or rule. The removal of a conjunct eliminates a constraint and thus generalizes the rule. If, as in case 1, there is a large set of distinct values for an attribute but there is no generalization operator for it, the attribute should be removed because it cannot be generalized, and preserving it would imply keeping a large number of disjuncts which contradicts the goal of generating concise rules. On the other hand, consider case 2, where the higher-level concepts of the attribute are expressed in terms of other attributes. For example, suppose that the attribute in question is *street*, whose higher-level concepts are represented by the attributes ⟨*city, province_or_state, country*⟩. The removal of *street* is equivalent to the application of a generalization operator. This rule corresponds to the generalization rule known as *dropping conditions* in the machine learning literature on *learning from examples*.

**Attribute generalization** is based on the following rule: *If there is a large set of distinct values for an attribute in the initial working relation, and there exists a set of generalization operators on the attribute, then a generalization operator should be selected and applied to the attribute.* This rule is based on the following reasoning. Use of a generalization operator to generalize an attribute value within a tuple, or rule, in the working relation will make the rule cover more of the original data tuples, thus generalizing the concept it represents. This corresponds to the generalization rule known as *climbing generalization trees* in *learning from examples*, or *concept tree ascension*.

Both rules, *attribute removal* and *attribute generalization*, claim that if there is a *large* set of distinct values for an attribute, further generalization should be applied. This raises the question: how large is "*a large set of distinct values for an attribute*" considered to be?

Depending on the attributes or application involved, a user may prefer some attributes to remain at a rather low abstraction level while others are generalized to higher levels. The control of how high an attribute should be generalized is typically quite subjective. The control of this process is called **attribute generalization control**. If the attribute is generalized "too high," it may lead to overgeneralization, and the resulting rules may not be very informative. On the other hand, if the attribute is not generalized to a "sufficiently high level," then undergeneralization may result, where the rules obtained may not be informative either. Thus, a balance should be attained in attribute-oriented generalization.

There are many possible ways to control a generalization process. We will describe two common approaches.

The first technique, called **attribute generalization threshold control**, either sets one generalization threshold for all of the attributes, or sets one threshold for each attribute. If the number of distinct values in an attribute is greater than the attribute threshold, further attribute removal or attribute generalization should be performed. Data mining systems typically have a default attribute threshold value (typically ranging from 2 to 8) and should allow experts and users to modify the threshold values as well. If a user feels that the generalization reaches too high a level for a particular attribute, the threshold can be increased. This corresponds to drilling down along the attribute. Also, to further generalize a relation, the user can reduce the threshold of a particular attribute, which corresponds to rolling up along the attribute.

The second technique, called **generalized relation threshold control**, sets a threshold for the generalized relation. If the number of (distinct) tuples in the generalized relation is greater than the threshold, further generalization should be performed. Otherwise, no further generalization should be performed. Such a threshold may also be preset in the data mining system (usually within a range of 10 to 30), or set by an expert or user, and should be adjustable. For example, if a user feels that the generalized relation is too small, she can increase the threshold, which implies drilling down. Otherwise, to further generalize a relation, she can reduce the threshold, which implies rolling up.

These two techniques can be applied in sequence: first apply the attribute threshold control technique to generalize each attribute, and then apply relation threshold control to further reduce the size of the generalized relation. No matter which generalization control technique is applied, the user should be allowed to adjust the generalization thresholds in order to obtain interesting concept descriptions.

In many database-oriented induction processes, users are interested in obtaining quantitative or statistical information about the data at different levels of abstraction. Thus, it is important to accumulate count and other aggregate values in the induction process. Conceptually, this is performed as follows. A special measure, or numerical attribute, that is associated with each database tuple is the aggregate function, `count`. Its value for each tuple in the initial working relation is initialized to 1. Through attribute removal and attribute generalization, tuples within the initial working relation may be generalized, resulting in groups of *identical tuples*. In this case, all of the identical tuples forming a group should be merged into one tuple. The count of this new, generalized tuple is set to the total number of tuples from the initial working relation that are represented by (i.e., were merged into) the new generalized tuple. For example, suppose that by attribute-oriented induction, 52 data tuples from the initial working relation are all generalized to the same tuple, $T$. That is, the generalization of these 52 tuples resulted in 52 identical instances of tuple $T$. These 52 identical tuples are merged to form one instance of $T$, whose count is set to 52. Other popular aggregate functions include `sum` and `avg`. For a given generalized tuple, `sum` contains the sum of the values of a given numeric attribute for the initial working relation tuples making up the generalized tuple. Suppose that tuple $T$ contained `sum`(*units_sold*) as an aggregate function. The sum value for tuple $T$ would then be set to the total number of units sold for each of the 52 tuples. The aggregate `avg` (average) is computed according to the formula, `avg` = `sum`/`count`.

**Example 5.3** **Attribute-oriented induction:** Here we show how attribute-oriented induction is performed on the initial working relation of Table 5.1, obtained in Example 5.2. For each attribute of the relation, the generalization proceeds as follows:

1. *name:* Since there are a large number of distinct values for *name* and there is no generalization operation defined on it, this attribute is removed.

2. *gender:* Since there are only two distinct values for *gender*, this attribute is retained and no generalization is performed on it.

3. *major:* Suppose that a concept hierarchy has been defined that allows the attribute *major* to be generalized to the values {*arts&science, engineering, business*}. Suppose also that the attribute generalization threshold is set to 5, and that there are over 20 distinct values for *major* in the initial working relation. By attribute generalization and attribute generalization control, *major* is therefore generalized by climbing the given concept hierarchy.

4. *birth_place:* This attribute has a large number of distinct values; therefore, we would like to generalize it. Suppose that a concept hierarchy exists for *birth_place*, defined as *city < province_or_state < country*. If the number of distinct values for *country* in the initial working relation is greater than the attribute generalization threshold, then *birth_place* should be removed, since even though a generalization operator exists for it, the generalization threshold would not be satisfied. If instead, the number of distinct values for *country* is less than the attribute generalization threshold, then *birth_place* should be generalized to *birth_country*.

**Table 5.2** A generalized relation obtained by attribute-oriented induction on the data of Table 5.1.

| gender | major | birth_country | age_range | residence_city | gpa | count |
|--------|-------|---------------|-----------|----------------|-----|-------|
| M | Science | Canada | 20 . . . 25 | Richmond | very_good | 16 |
| F | Science | Foreign | 25 . . . 30 | Burnaby | excellent | 22 |
| . . . | . . . | . . . | . . . | . . . | . . . | . . . |

5. *birth_date:* Suppose that a hierarchy exists that can generalize *birth_date* to *age*, and *age* to *age_range*, and that the number of age ranges (or intervals) is small with respect to the attribute generalization threshold. Generalization of *birth_date* should therefore take place.

6. *residence:* Suppose that *residence* is defined by the attributes *number, street, residence_city, residence_province_or_state*, and *residence_country*. The number of distinct values for *number* and *street* will likely be very high, since these concepts are quite low level. The attributes *number* and *street* should therefore be removed, so that *residence* is then generalized to *residence_city*, which contains fewer distinct values.

7. *phone#:* As with the attribute *name* above, this attribute contains too many distinct values and should therefore be removed in generalization.

8. *gpa:* Suppose that a concept hierarchy exists for *gpa* that groups values for grade point average into numerical intervals like {3.75–4.0, 3.5–3.75, . . . }, which in turn are grouped into descriptive values, such as {*excellent, very good,* . . . }. The attribute can therefore be generalized.

The generalization process will result in groups of identical tuples. For example, the first two tuples of Table 5.1 both generalize to the same identical tuple (namely, the first tuple shown in Table 5.2). Such identical tuples are then merged into one, with their counts accumulated. This process leads to the generalized relation shown in Table 5.2.

Based on the vocabulary used in OLAP, we may view count as a *measure*, and the remaining attributes as *dimensions*. Note that aggregate functions, such as sum, may be applied to numerical attributes, like *salary* and *sales*. These attributes are referred to as *measure attributes*.

Implementation techniques and methods of presenting the derived generalization are discussed in the following subsections.

## 5.2.2 Efficient Implementation of Attribute-Oriented Induction

"*How is attribute-oriented induction actually implemented?*" The previous subsection provided an introduction to attribute-oriented induction. The general

**Algorithm: Attribute_oriented_induction.** Mining generalized characteristics in a relational database given a user's data mining request.

**Input:**   (i) *DB*, a relational database; (ii) *DMQuery*, a data mining query; (iii) *a_list*, a list of attributes (containing attributes $a_i$); (iv) *Gen*($a_i$), a set of concept hierarchies or generalization operators on attributes $a_i$; (v) *a_gen_thresh*($a_i$), attribute generalization thresholds for each $a_i$.

**Output:**   *P*, a *Prime_generalized_relation*.

**Method:**   The method is outlined as follows.

1. $W \leftarrow$ **get_task_relevant_data**(*DMQuery*, *DB*); // Let $W$, the working relation, hold the task-relevant data.

2. **prepare_for_generalization**($W$); // This is implemented as follows.

   (a) Scan $W$ and collect the distinct values for each attribute $a_i$. (Note: If $W$ is very large, this may be done by examining a sample of $W$.)

   (b) For each attribute $a_i$, determine whether $a_i$ should be removed, and if not, compute its minimum desired level $L_i$ based on its given or default attribute threshold, and determine the mapping-pairs ($v$, $v'$), where $v$ is a distinct value of $a_i$ in $W$, and $v'$ is its corresponding generalized value at level $L_i$.

3. $P \leftarrow$ **generalization**($W$);

   The *Prime_generalized_relation*, $P$, is derived by replacing each value $v$ in $W$ by its corresponding $v'$ in the mapping while accumulating count and computing any other aggregate values.

   This step can be implemented efficiently using either of the two following variations:

   (a) For each generalized tuple, insert the tuple into a sorted prime relation $P$ by a binary search: if the tuple is already in $P$, simply increase its count and other aggregate values accordingly; otherwise, insert it into $P$.

   (b) Since in most cases the number of distinct values at the prime relation level is small, the prime relation can be coded as an $m$-dimensional array where $m$ is the number of attributes in $P$, and each dimension contains the corresponding generalized attribute values. Each array element holds the corresponding count and other aggregation values, if any. The insertion of a generalized tuple is performed by measure aggregation in the corresponding array element.

---

**Figure 5.1**   Basic algorithm for attribute-oriented induction.

procedure is summarized in Figure 5.1. The efficiency of this algorithm is analyzed as follows:

- Step 1 of the algorithm is essentially a relational query to collect the task-relevant data into the **working relation**, $W$. Its processing efficiency depends on the query processing methods used. Given the successful implementation and commercialization of database systems, this step is expected to have good performance.

- Step 2 collects statistics on the working relation. This requires scanning the relation at most once. The cost for computing the minimum desired level and determining the mapping pairs $(v, v')$ for each attribute is dependent on the number of distinct values for each attribute and is smaller than $n$, the number of tuples in the initial relation.

- Step 3 derives the **prime relation**, $P$. This is performed by inserting generalized tuples into $P$. There are a total of $n$ tuples in $W$ and $p$ tuples in $P$. For each tuple $t$ in $W$, we substitute its attribute values based on the derived mapping-pairs. This results in a generalized tuple $t'$. If variation (a) is adopted, each $t'$ takes $O(\log p)$ to find the location for count incrementation or tuple insertion. Thus the total time complexity is $O(n \times \log p)$ for all of the generalized tuples. If variation (b) is adopted, each $t'$ takes $O(1)$ to find the tuple for count incrementation. Thus the overall time complexity is $O(n)$ for all of the generalized tuples.

Many data analysis tasks need to examine a good number of dimensions or attributes. For example, an interactive data mining system may *dynamically* introduce and test additional attributes rather than just those specified in the mining query. Advanced descriptive data mining tasks, such as *analytical characterization* (to be discussed in Section 5.3), require attribute relevance analysis for a large set of attributes. Furthermore, a user with little knowledge of the *truly* relevant set of data may simply specify "**in relevance to** *" in the mining query. In these cases, the precomputation of aggregation values will speed up the analysis of a large number of dimensions or attributes. Hence, a data cube implementation is an attractive alternative to the database approach described above.

The *data cube implementation* of attribute-oriented induction can be performed in two ways.

**Construct a data cube on-the-fly for the given data mining query:**  This method constructs a data cube dynamically based on the task-relevant set of data. This is desirable if either the task-relevant data set is too specific to match any predefined data cube, or it is not very large. Since such a data cube is computed only after the query is submitted, the major motivation for constructing such a data cube is to facilitate efficient drill-down analysis. With such a data cube, drilling down below the level of the prime relation will simply require retrieving data from the cube, or performing minor generalization from some intermediate-level data stored in the cube instead of generalization from the primitive-level data. This will speed up the drill-down process. However, since the attribute-oriented data generalization involves the computation of a query-related data cube, it may involve more processing than simple computation of the prime relation and thus increase the response time. A balance between the two may be struck by computing a cube-structured "subprime" relation in which each dimension of the generalized relation is a few levels deeper than the level of the prime relation. This will facilitate drilling down to these levels with a reasonable storage and processing cost, although further drilling down beyond these levels will still require generalization from the primitive-level data. Notice that such further drilling down is more likely to be localized, rather than spread out over the full spectrum of the cube.

**Use a predefined data cube:**   An alternative method is to construct a data cube before a data mining query is posed to the system, and use this predefined cube for subsequent data mining. This is desirable if the granularity of the task-relevant data can match that of the predefined data cube and the set of task-relevant data is quite large. Since such a data cube is precomputed, it facilitates attribute relevance analysis, attribute-oriented induction, slicing and dicing, roll-up, and drill-down. The cost one must pay is the cost of cube computation and the nontrivial storage overhead. A balance between the computation/storage overheads and the accessing speed may be attained by precomputing a selected set of all of the possible materializable cuboids, as explored in Chapter 2.

## 5.2.3 **Presentation of the Derived Generalization**

*"Attribute-oriented induction generates one or a set of generalized descriptions. How can these descriptions be visualized?"* The descriptions can be presented to the user in a number of different ways. Generalized descriptions resulting from attribute-oriented induction are most commonly displayed in the form of a **generalized relation**.

**Example 5.4**   Suppose that attribute-oriented induction was performed on a *sales* relation of the *AllElectronics* database, resulting in the generalized description of Table 5.3 for sales in 1999. The description is shown in the form of a generalized relation. Table 5.2 of Example 5.3 is another example of a generalized relation.    ∎

Descriptions can also be visualized in the form of **cross-tabulations**, or **crosstabs**. In a two-dimensional crosstab, each row represents a value from an attribute, and each column represents a value from another attribute. In an $n$-dimensional crosstab (for $n > 2$), the columns may represent the values of more than one attribute, with subtotals shown for attribute-value groupings. This representation is similar to *spreadsheets*. It is easy to map directly from a data cube structure to a crosstab.

**Example 5.5**   The generalized relation shown in Table 5.3 can be transformed into the 3-D crosstabulation shown in Table 5.4.    ∎

**Table 5.3**  A generalized relation for the sales in 1999.

| location | item | sales (in million dollars) | count (in thousands) |
|---|---|---|---|
| Asia | TV | 15 | 300 |
| Europe | TV | 12 | 250 |
| North_America | TV | 28 | 450 |
| Asia | computer | 120 | 1000 |
| Europe | computer | 150 | 1200 |
| North_America | computer | 200 | 1800 |

**Table 5.4**  A crosstab for the sales in 1999.

| location\item | TV | | computer | | both_items | |
|---|---|---|---|---|---|---|
| | sales | count | sales | count | sales | count |
| Asia | 15 | 300 | 120 | 1000 | 135 | 1300 |
| Europe | 12 | 250 | 150 | 1200 | 162 | 1450 |
| North_America | 28 | 450 | 200 | 1800 | 228 | 2250 |
| all_regions | 55 | 1000 | 470 | 4000 | 525 | 5000 |

Generalized data can be presented graphically, using bar charts, pie charts, and curves. Visualization with graphs is popular in data analysis. Such graphs and curves can represent 2-D or 3-D data.

**Example 5.6**  The sales data of the crosstab shown in Table 5.4 can be transformed into the bar chart representation of Figure 5.2 and the pie chart representation of Figure 5.3. ∎

Finally, a 3-D generalized relation or crosstab can be represented by a 3-D data cube. Such a 3-D cube view is an attractive tool for cube browsing.

**Example 5.7**  Consider the data cube shown in Figure 5.4 for the dimensions *item, location,* and *cost*. The *size* of a cell (displayed as a tiny cube) represents the count of the corresponding cell, while the *brightness* of the cell can be used to represent another measure of the cell, such as sum(*sales*). Pivoting, drilling, and slicing-and-dicing operations can be performed on the data cube browser by mouse clicking. ∎

A generalized relation may also be represented in the form of logic rules. Typically, each generalized tuple represents a rule disjunct. Since data in a large database usually span a diverse range of distributions, a single generalized tuple is unlikely to *cover*, or represent, 100% of the initial working relation tuples, or *cases*.

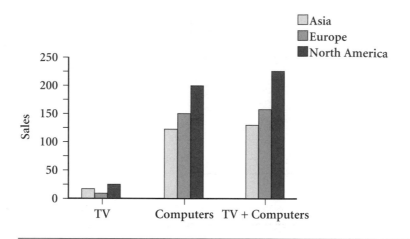

**Figure 5.2**  Bar chart representation of the sales in 1999.

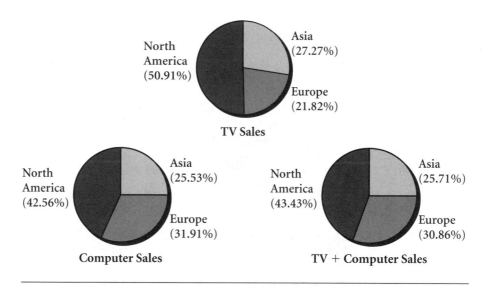

**Figure 5.3**  Pie chart representation of the sales in 1999.

Thus quantitative information, such as the percentage of data tuples that satisfy the left- and right-hand side of the rule, should be associated with each rule. A logic rule that is associated with quantitative information is called a **quantitative rule**.

To define a quantitative characteristic rule, we introduce the **t-weight** as an interestingness measure that describes the *typicality* of each *disjunct* in the rule,

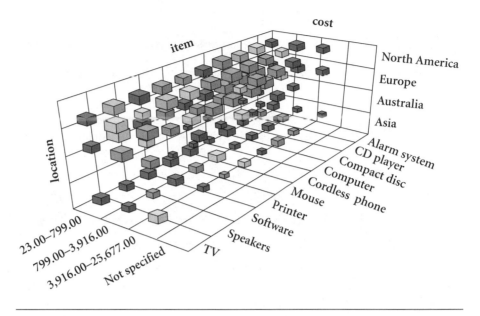

**Figure 5.4** A 3-D cube view representation of the sales in 1999.

or of each *tuple* in the corresponding generalized relation. The measure is defined as follows. Let the class of objects that is to be characterized (or described by the rule) be called the *target class*. Let $q_a$ be a generalized tuple describing the target class. The **t-weight** for $q_a$ is the percentage of tuples of the target class from the initial working relation that are covered by $q_a$. Formally, we have

$$t\_weight = count(q_a)/\Sigma_{i=1}^{n} count(q_i), \tag{5.1}$$

where $n$ is the number of tuples for the target class in the generalized relation; $q_1, \ldots, q_n$ are tuples for the target class in the generalized relation; and $q_a$ is in $q_1, \ldots, q_n$. Obviously, the range for the t-weight is [0.0, 1.0] or [0%, 100%].

A **quantitative characteristic rule** can then be represented either (1) in logic form by associating the corresponding t-weight value with each disjunct covering the target class, or (2) in the relational table or crosstab form by changing the count values in these tables for tuples of the target class to the corresponding t-weight values.

Each disjunct of a quantitative characteristic rule represents a condition. In general, the disjunction of these conditions forms a *necessary* condition of the target class, since the condition is derived based on all of the cases of the target class; that is, all tuples of the target class must satisfy this condition. However, the rule may not be a *sufficient* condition of the target class, since a tuple satisfying the same condition could belong to another class. Therefore, the rule should be expressed in the form

$$\forall X, \ target\_class(X) \Rightarrow condition_1(X)[t:w_1] \vee \cdots \vee condition_m(X)[t:w_m]. \quad (5.2)$$

The rule indicates that if $X$ is in the *target_class*, there is a probability of $w_i$ that $X$ satisfies *condition$_i$*, where $w_i$ is the t-weight value for condition or disjunct $i$, and $i$ is in $\{1, \ldots, m\}$.

**Example 5.8** The crosstab shown in Table 5.4 can be transformed into logic rule form. Let the target class be the set of computer items. The corresponding characteristic rule, in logic form, is

$$\forall X, \ item(X) = \text{``computer''} \Rightarrow$$

$$(location(X) = \text{``Asia''})[t:25.00\%] \vee (location(X) = \text{``Europe''})[t:30.00\%] \vee$$

$$(location(X) = \text{``North\_America''})[t:45.00\%] \qquad (5.3)$$

Notice that the first t-weight value of 25.00% is obtained by 1000, the value corresponding to the count slot for "(*Asia, computer*)", divided by 4000, the value corresponding to the count slot for "(*all_regions, computer*)". (That is, 4000 represents the total number of computer items sold.) The t-weights of the other two disjuncts were similarly derived. Quantitative characteristic rules for other target classes can be computed in a similar fashion. ∎

"*How can the t-weight and interestingness measures in general be used by the data mining system to display only the concept descriptions that it objectively evaluates as interesting?*" A threshold can be set for this purpose. For example, if the t-weight of a generalized tuple is lower than the threshold, then the tuple is considered to represent only a negligible portion of the database and can therefore be ignored as uninteresting. Ignoring such negligible tuples does not mean that they should be removed from the intermediate results (i.e., the prime generalized relation, or the data cube, depending on the implementation) since they may contribute to subsequent further exploration of the data by the user via interactive rolling up or drilling down of other dimensions and levels of abstraction. Such a threshold may be referred to as a **significance threshold** or **support threshold**, where the latter term is popularly used in association rule mining.

## 5.3 Analytical Characterization: Analysis of Attribute Relevance

"*What if I am not sure which attribute to include for class characterization and class comparison? I may end up specifying too many attributes, which could slow down the system considerably.*" Measures of attribute relevance analysis can be used to help identify irrelevant or weakly relevant attributes that can be excluded from the concept description process. The incorporation of this preprocessing step into class characterization or comparison is referred to as *analytical characterization* or *analytical comparison*, respectively. This section describes a general method of attribute relevance analysis and its integration with attribute-oriented induction.

## 5.3.1  Why Perform Attribute Relevance Analysis?

The first limitation of class characterization for multidimensional data analysis in data warehouses and OLAP tools is the handling of complex objects. This was discussed in Section 5.2. The second limitation is the *lack of an automated generalization process*: the user must explicitly tell the system which dimensions should be included in the class characterization and to how high a level each dimension should be generalized. Actually, each step of generalization or specialization on any dimension must be specified by the user.

Usually, it is not difficult for a user to instruct a data mining system regarding how high a level each dimension should be generalized. For example, users can set attribute generalization thresholds for this, or specify which level a given dimension should reach, such as with the command "**generalize dimension** *location* **to the** *country* **level**". Even without explicit user instruction, a default value such as 2 to 8 can be set by the data mining system, which would allow each dimension to be generalized to a level that contains only 2 to 8 distinct values. If the user is not satisfied with the current level of generalization, she can specify dimensions on which drill-down or roll-up operations should be applied.

It is nontrivial, however, for users to determine which dimensions should be included in the analysis of class characteristics. Data relations often contain 50 to 100 attributes, and a user may have little knowledge regarding which attributes or dimensions should be selected for effective data mining. A user may include too few attributes in the analysis, causing the resulting mined descriptions to be incomplete. On the other hand, a user may introduce too many attributes for analysis (e.g., by indicating "**in relevance to** *", which includes all the attributes in the specified relations).

Methods should be introduced to perform attribute (or dimension) relevance analysis in order to filter out statistically irrelevant or weakly relevant attributes, and retain or even rank the most relevant attributes for the descriptive mining task at hand. Class characterization that includes the analysis of attribute/dimension relevance is called **analytical characterization**. Class comparison that includes such analysis is called **analytical comparison**.

Intuitively, an attribute or dimension is considered *highly relevant* with respect to a given class if it is likely that the values of the attribute or dimension may be used to distinguish the class from others. For example, it is unlikely that the color of an automobile can be used to distinguish expensive from cheap cars, but the model, make, style, and number of cylinders are likely to be more relevant attributes. Moreover, even within the same dimension, different levels of concepts may have dramatically different powers for distinguishing a class from others. For example, in the *birth_date* dimension, *birth_day* and *birth_month* are unlikely to be relevant to the *salary* of employees. However, the *birth_decade* (i.e., age interval) may be highly relevant to the *salary* of employees. This implies that the analysis of dimension relevance should be performed at *multilevels of abstraction*, and only the most relevant levels of a dimension should be included in the analysis.

Above we said that attribute/dimension relevance is evaluated based on the ability of the attribute/dimension to distinguish objects of a class from others. When mining a class comparison (or discrimination), the target class and the contrasting classes are explicitly given in the mining query. The relevance analysis should be performed by comparison of these classes, as we shall see below. However, when mining class characteristics, there is only one class to be characterized. That is, no contrasting class is specified. It is therefore not obvious what the contrasting class should be for use in the relevance analysis. In this case, typically, the contrasting class is taken to be the *set of comparable data in the database that excludes the set of data to be characterized*. For example, to characterize graduate students, the contrasting class can be composed of the set of undergraduate students.

## 5.3.2 Methods of Attribute Relevance Analysis

There have been many studies in machine learning, statistics, fuzzy and rough set theories, and so on, on attribute relevance analysis. The general idea behind attribute relevance analysis is to compute some measure that is used to quantify the relevance of an attribute with respect to a given class or concept. Such measures include information gain, the Gini index, uncertainty, and correlation coefficients.

Here we introduce a method that integrates an *information gain* analysis technique (such as that presented in the ID3 and C4.5 algorithms for learning decision trees[2]) with a dimension-based data analysis method. The resulting method removes the less informative attributes, collecting the more informative ones for use in concept description analysis.

*"How does the information gain calculation work?"* Let $S$ be a set of *training samples*, where the class label of each sample is known. Each sample is in fact a tuple. One attribute is used to determine the class of the training samples. For instance, the attribute *status* can be used to define the class label of each sample as either *"graduate"* or *"undergraduate"*. Suppose that there are $m$ classes. Let $S$ contain $s_i$ samples of class $C_i$, for $i = 1, \ldots, m$. An arbitrary sample belongs to class $C_i$ with probability $s_i/s$, where $s$ is the total number of samples in set $S$. The **expected information** needed to classify a given sample is

---

[2] A **decision tree** is a flow-chart-like tree structure, where each node denotes a test on an attribute, each branch represents an outcome of the test, and tree leaves represent classes or class distributions. Decision trees are useful for classification and can easily be converted to logic rules. Decision tree induction is described in Chapter 7.

$$I(s_1, s_2, \ldots, s_m) = -\sum_{i=1}^{m} \frac{s_i}{s} \log_2 \frac{s_i}{s}. \tag{5.4}$$

An attribute $A$ with values $\{a_1, a_2, \cdots, a_v\}$ can be used to partition $S$ into the subsets $\{S_1, S_2, \cdots, S_v\}$, where $S_j$ contains those samples in $S$ that have value $a_j$ of $A$. Let $S_j$ contain $s_{ij}$ samples of class $C_i$. The expected information based on this partitioning by $A$ is known as the entropy of $A$. It is the weighted average:

$$E(A) = \sum_{j=1}^{v} \frac{s_{1j} + \cdots + s_{mj}}{s} I(s_{1j}, \ldots, s_{mj}). \tag{5.5}$$

The **information gain** obtained by this partitioning on $A$ is defined by

$$Gain(A) = I(s_1, s_2, \ldots, s_m) - E(A). \tag{5.6}$$

In this approach to relevance analysis, we can compute the information gain for each of the attributes defining the samples in $S$. The attribute with the highest information gain is considered the most discriminating attribute of the given set. By computing the information gain for each attribute, we therefore obtain a ranking of the attributes. This ranking can be used for relevance analysis to select the attributes to be used in concept description.

Attribute relevance analysis for concept description is performed as follows:

1. **Data collection:** Collect data for both the target class and the contrasting class by query processing. For class comparison, both the *target class* and the *contrasting class* are provided by the user in the data mining query. For class characterization, the *target class* is the class to be characterized, whereas the *contrasting class* is the set of comparable data that are not in the target class.

2. **Preliminary relevance analysis using conservative AOI:** This step identifies a set of dimensions and attributes on which the selected relevance measure is to be applied. Since different levels of a dimension may have dramatically different relevance with respect to a given class, each attribute defining the conceptual levels of the dimension should be included in the relevance analysis in principle. Attribute-oriented induction (AOI) can be used to perform some preliminary relevance analysis on the data by removing or generalizing attributes having a very large number of distinct values (such as *name* and *phone#*). Such attributes are unlikely to be found useful for concept description. To be conservative, the AOI performed here should employ attribute generalization thresholds that are set reasonably large so as to allow more (but not all) attributes to be considered in further relevance analysis by the selected measure (Step 3 below). The relation obtained by such an application of AOI is called the **candidate relation** of the mining task.

3. **Remove irrelevant and weakly relevant attributes using the selected relevance analysis measure:** Evaluate each attribute in the candidate relation using the selected relevance analysis measure. The relevance measure used in this step may be built into the data mining system or provided by the user. For example, the information gain measure described above may be used. The attributes are then sorted (i.e., ranked) according to their computed relevance to the data mining task. Attributes that are not relevant or are weakly relevant to the task are then removed. A threshold may be set to define "weakly relevant." This step results in an **initial target class working relation** and an **initial contrasting class working relation**.

4. **Generate the concept description using AOI:** Perform AOI using a less conservative set of attribute generalization thresholds. If the descriptive mining task is class characterization, only the initial target class working relation is included here. If the descriptive mining task is class comparison, both the initial target class working relation and the initial contrasting class working relation are included.

The complexity of this procedure is similar to the algorithm in Figure 5.1 since the induction process is performed twice, that is, in preliminary relevance analysis (Step 2) and on the initial working relation (Step 4). The statistics used in attribute relevance analysis with the selected measure (Step 3) may be collected during the scanning of the database in Step 2.

### 5.3.3 Analytical Characterization: An Example

If the mined concept descriptions involve many attributes, analytical characterization should be performed. This procedure first removes irrelevant or weakly relevant attributes prior to performing generalization. Let's examine an example of such an analytical mining process.

**Example 5.9** Suppose that we would like to mine the general characteristics describing graduate students at *Big-University* using analytical characterization. Given are the attributes *name, gender, major, birth_place, birth_date, phone#*, and *gpa*.

"*How is the analytical characterization performed?*" In Step 1, the target class data are collected, consisting of the set of graduate students. Data for a contrasting class are also required in order to perform relevance analysis. This is taken to be the set of undergraduate students.

In Step 2, preliminary relevance analysis is performed via attribute removal and attribute generalization by applying attribute-oriented induction with conservative attribute generalization thresholds. Similar to Example 5.3, the attributes *name* and *phone#* are removed because their number of distinct values exceeds their respective attribute analytical thresholds. Also as in Example 5.3, concept hierarchies are used to generalize *birth_place* to *birth_country*, and *birth_date* to *age_range*. The attributes *major* and *gpa* are also generalized to

**Table 5.5** Candidate relation obtained for analytical characterization: target class (graduate students).

| gender | major | birth_country | age_range | gpa | count |
|--------|-------|---------------|-----------|-----|-------|
| M | Science | Canada | 21 . . . 25 | very_good | 16 |
| F | Science | Foreign | 26 . . . 30 | excellent | 22 |
| M | Engineering | Foreign | 26 . . . 30 | excellent | 18 |
| F | Science | Foreign | 26 . . . 30 | excellent | 25 |
| M | Science | Canada | 21 . . . 25 | excellent | 21 |
| F | Engineering | Canada | 21 . . . 25 | excellent | 18 |

**Table 5.6** Candidate relation obtained for analytical characterization: contrasting class (undergraduate students).

| gender | major | birth_country | age_range | gpa | count |
|--------|-------|---------------|-----------|-----|-------|
| M | Science | Foreign | <=20 | very_good | 18 |
| F | Business | Canada | <=20 | fair | 20 |
| M | Business | Canada | <=20 | fair | 22 |
| F | Science | Canada | 21 . . . 25 | fair | 24 |
| M | Engineering | Foreign | 21 . . . 25 | very_good | 22 |
| F | Engineering | Canada | <= 20 | excellent | 24 |

higher abstraction levels using the concept hierarchies described in Example 5.3. Hence, the attributes remaining for the candidate relation are *gender, major, birth_country, age_range*, and *gpa*. The resulting relation is shown in Tables 5.5 and 5.6.

In Step 3, the attributes in the candidate relation are evaluated using the selected relevance analysis measure, such as information gain. Let $C_1$ correspond to the class *graduate* and $C_2$ correspond to the class *undergraduate*. There are 120 samples of class *graduate* and 130 samples of class *undergraduate*. To compute the information gain of each attribute, we first use Equation (5.4) to compute the expected information needed to classify a given sample:

$$I(s_1, s_2) = I(120, 130) = -\frac{120}{250} \log_2 \frac{120}{250} - \frac{130}{250} \log_2 \frac{130}{250} = 0.9988.$$

Next, we need to compute the entropy of each attribute. Let's try the attribute *major*. We need to look at the distribution of *graduate* and *undergraduate* students for each value of *major*. We compute the expected information for each of these distributions.

For *major* = *"Science"*:

$$s_{11} = 84 \quad s_{21} = 42 \quad I(s_{11}, s_{21}) = 0.9183$$

For *major* = *"Engineering"*:

$$s_{12} = 36 \quad s_{22} = 46 \quad I(s_{12}, s_{22}) = 0.9892$$

For *major* = *"Business"*:

$$s_{13} = 0 \quad s_{23} = 42 \quad I(s_{13}, s_{23}) = 0$$

Using Equation (5.5), the expected information needed to classify a given sample if the samples are partitioned according to *major* is

$$E(major) = \frac{126}{250}I(s_{11}, s_{21}) + \frac{82}{250}I(s_{12}, s_{22}) + \frac{42}{250}I(s_{13}, s_{23}) = 0.7873.$$

Hence, the gain in information from such a partitioning would be

$$Gain(major) = I(s_1, s_2) - E(major) = 0.2115.$$

Similarly, we can compute the information gain for each of the remaining attributes. The information gain for each attribute, sorted in increasing order, is 0.0003 for *gender*, 0.0407 for *birth_country*, 0.2115 for *major*, 0.4490 for *gpa*, and 0.5971 for *age_range*. Suppose that we use an attribute relevance threshold of 0.1 to identify weakly relevant attributes. The information gain of the attributes *gender* and *birth_country* are below the threshold, and therefore considered weakly relevant. Thus, they are removed. The contrasting class is also removed, resulting in the initial target class working relation.

In Step 4, attribute-oriented induction is applied to the initial target class working relation, following the algorithm in Figure 5.1.    ∎

## 5.4  Mining Class Comparisons: Discriminating between Different Classes

In many applications, users may not be interested in having a single class (or concept) described or characterized, but rather would prefer to mine a description that compares or distinguishes one class (or concept) from other comparable classes (or concepts). Class discrimination or comparison (hereafter referred to as **class comparison**) mines descriptions that distinguish a target class from its contrasting classes. Notice that the target and contrasting classes must be *comparable* in the sense that they share similar dimensions and attributes. For example, the three classes *person, address,* and *item* are not comparable. However, the sales in the last three years are comparable classes, and so are computer science students versus physics students.

Our discussions on class characterization in the previous sections handle multilevel data summarization and characterization in a single class. The techniques developed can be extended to handle class comparison across several comparable classes. For example, the attribute generalization process described for class characterization can be modified so that the generalization is performed *synchronously* among all the classes compared. This allows the attributes in all of the classes to be generalized to the *same* levels of abstraction. Suppose, for instance, that we are given the *AllElectronics* data for sales in 1998 and sales in 1999 and would like to compare these two classes. Consider the dimension *location* with abstractions at the *city*, *province_or_state*, and *country* levels. Each class of data should be generalized to the same *location* level. That is, they are synchronously all generalized to either the *city* level, or the *province_or_state* level, or the *country* level. Ideally, this is more useful than comparing, say, the sales in Vancouver in 1998 with the sales in the United States in 1999 (i.e., where each set of sales data is generalized to a different level). The users, however, should have the option to overwrite such an automated, synchronous comparison with their own choices, when preferred.

## 5.4.1 Class Comparison Methods and Implementations

*"How is class comparison performed?"* In general, the procedure is as follows:

1. **Data collection:** The set of relevant data in the database is collected by query processing and is partitioned respectively into a *target class* and one or a set of *contrasting class(es)*.

2. **Dimension relevance analysis:** If there are many dimensions and *analytical comparison* is desired, then dimension relevance analysis should be performed on these classes as described in Section 5.3, and only the highly relevant dimensions are included in the further analysis.

3. **Synchronous generalization:** Generalization is performed on the target class to the level controlled by a user- or expert-specified dimension threshold, which results in a **prime target class relation/cuboid**. The concepts in the contrasting class(es) are generalized to the same level as those in the prime target class relation/cuboid, forming the **prime contrasting class(es) relation/cuboid**.

4. **Presentation of the derived comparison:** The resulting class comparison description can be visualized in the form of tables, graphs, and rules. This presentation usually includes a "contrasting" measure (such as count%) that reflects the comparison between the target and contrasting classes. The user can adjust the comparison description by applying drill-down, roll-up, and other OLAP operations to the target and contrasting classes, as desired.

The above discussion outlines a general algorithm for mining analytical comparisons in databases. In comparison with analytical characterization, the above algorithm involves synchronous generalization of the target class with the contrasting classes so that classes are simultaneously compared at the same levels of abstraction.

*"Can class comparison mining be implemented efficiently using data cube techniques?"* Yes—the procedure is similar to the implementation for mining data characterizations discussed in Section 5.2.2. A flag can be used to indicate whether or not a tuple represents a target or contrasting class, where this flag is viewed as an additional dimension in the data cube. Since all of the other dimensions of the target and contrasting classes share the same portion of the cube, the synchronous generalization and specialization are realized automatically by rolling up and drilling down in the cube.

The following example mines a class comparison describing the graduate students and the undergraduate students at *Big-University*.

**Example 5.10** **Mining a class comparison.** Suppose that you would like to compare the general properties between the graduate students and the undergraduate students at *Big-University*, given the attributes *name, gender, major, birth_place, birth_date, residence, phone#*, and *gpa*.

This data mining task can be expressed in DMQL as follows:

```
use Big_University_DB
mine comparison as "grad_vs_undergrad_students"
in relevance to name, gender, major, birth_place, birth_date, residence, phone#, gpa
for "graduate_students"
where status in "graduate"
versus "undergraduate_students"
where status in "undergraduate"
analyze count%
from student
```

Let's see how this typical example of a data mining query for mining comparison descriptions can be processed.

First, the query is transformed into two relational queries that collect two sets of task-relevant data: one for the *initial target class working relation*, and the other for the *initial contrasting class working relation*, as shown in Tables 5.7 and 5.8. This can also be viewed as the construction of a data cube, where the status {*graduate, undergraduate*} serves as one dimension, and the other attributes form the remaining dimensions.

Second, dimension relevance analysis is performed on the two classes of data. After this analysis, irrelevant or weakly relevant dimensions, such as *name, gender, birth_place, residence*, and *phone#*, are removed from the resulting classes. Only the highly relevant attributes are included in the subsequent analysis.

Third, synchronous generalization is performed: Generalization is performed on the target class to the levels controlled by user- or expert-specified dimension

**Table 5.7**  Initial target class working relation (graduate students).

| name | gender | major | birth_place | birth_date | residence | phone# | gpa |
|------|--------|-------|-------------|------------|-----------|--------|-----|
| Jim Woodman | M | CS | Vancouver, BC, Canada | 8-12-76 | 3511 Main St., Richmond | 687-4598 | 3.67 |
| Scott Lachance | M | CS | Montreal, Que, Canada | 28-7-75 | 345 1st Ave., Vancouver | 253-9106 | 3.70 |
| Laura Lee | F | Physics | Seattle, WA, USA | 25-8-70 | 125 Austin Ave., Burnaby | 420-5232 | 3.83 |
| . . . | . . . | . . . | . . . | . . . | . . . | . . . | . . . |

**Table 5.8**  Initial contrasting class working relation (undergraduate students).

| name | gender | major | birth_place | birth_date | residence | phone# | gpa |
|------|--------|-------|-------------|------------|-----------|--------|-----|
| Bob Schumann | M | Chemistry | Calgary, Alt, Canada | 10-1-78 | 2642 Halifax St., Burnaby | 294-4291 | 2.96 |
| Amy Eau | F | Biology | Golden, BC, Canada | 30-3-76 | 463 Sunset Cres., Vancouver | 681-5417 | 3.52 |
| . . . | . . . | . . . | . . . | . . . | . . . | . . . | . . . |

**Table 5.9**  Prime generalized relation for the target class (graduate students).

| major | age_range | gpa | count% |
|-------|-----------|-----|--------|
| Science | 21 . . . 25 | good | 5.53% |
| Science | 26 . . . 30 | good | 5.02% |
| Science | over_30 | very_good | 5.86% |
| . . . | . . . | . . . | . . . |
| Business | over_30 | excellent | 4.68% |

thresholds, forming the *prime target class relation/cuboid*. The contrasting class is generalized to the same levels as those in the prime target class relation/cuboid, forming the *prime contrasting class(es) relation/cuboid*, as presented in Tables 5.9 and 5.10. In comparison with undergraduate students, graduate students tend to be older and have a higher GPA, in general.

Finally, the resulting class comparison is presented in the form of tables, graphs, and/or rules. This visualization includes a contrasting measure (such as count%) that compares between the target class and the contrasting class. For example, 5.02% of the graduate students majoring in Science are between 26 and 30 years of age and have a "good" GPA, while only 2.32% of undergraduates have these same characteristics. Drilling and other OLAP operations may be performed on the target and contrasting classes as deemed necessary by the user in order to adjust the abstraction levels of the final description.  ∎

**Table 5.10** Prime generalized relation for the contrasting class (undergraduate students).

| major | age_range | gpa | count% |
|---|---|---|---|
| Science | 16 . . . 20 | fair | 5.53% |
| Science | 16 . . . 20 | good | 4.53% |
| . . . | . . . | . . . | . . . |
| Science | 26 . . . 30 | good | 2.32% |
| . . . | . . . | . . . | . . . |
| Business | over_30 | excellent | 0.68% |

## 5.4.2 Presentation of Class Comparison Descriptions

*"How can class comparison descriptions be visualized?"* As with class characterizations, class comparisons can be presented to the user in various forms, including generalized relations, crosstabs, bar charts, pie charts, curves, and rules. With the exception of logic rules, these forms are used in the same way for characterization as for comparison. In this section, we discuss the visualization of class comparisons in the form of discriminant rules.

As is similar with characterization descriptions, the discriminative features of the target and contrasting classes of a comparison description can be described quantitatively by a *quantitative discriminant rule*, which associates a statistical interestingness measure, *d-weight*, with each generalized tuple in the description.

Let $q_a$ be a generalized tuple, and $C_j$ be the target class, where $q_a$ covers some tuples of the target class. Note that it is possible that $q_a$ also covers some tuples of the contrasting classes, particularly since we are dealing with a comparison description. The **d-weight** for $q_a$ is the ratio of the number of tuples from the initial target class working relation that are covered by $q_a$ to the total number of tuples in both the initial target class and contrasting class working relations that are covered by $q_a$. Formally, the d-weight of $q_a$ for the class $C_j$ is defined as

$$d\_weight = count(q_a \in C_j) / \Sigma_{i=1}^{m} count(q_a \in C_i), \tag{5.7}$$

where $m$ is the total number of the target and contrasting classes, $C_j$ is in $\{C_1, \ldots, C_m\}$, and $count(q_a \in C_i)$ is the number of tuples of class $C_i$ that are covered by $q_a$. The range for the d-weight is [0.0, 1.0] (or [0%, 100%]).

A high d-weight in the target class indicates that the concept represented by the generalized tuple is primarily derived from the target class, whereas a low d-weight implies that the concept is primarily derived from the contrasting classes. A threshold can be set to control the display of interesting tuples based on the d-weight or other measures used, as described in Section 5.2.3.

**Table 5.11** Count distribution between graduate and undergraduate students for a generalized tuple.

| status | major | age_range | gpa | count |
|---|---|---|---|---|
| graduate | Science | 21 . . . 25 | good | 90 |
| undergraduate | Science | 21 . . . 25 | good | 210 |

**Example 5.11** In Example 5.10, suppose that the count distribution for the generalized tuple *major = "Science" and age_range = "21 . . . 25" and gpa = "good"* from Tables 5.9 and 5.10 is as shown in Table 5.11.

The d-weight for the given generalized tuple is 90/(90 + 210) = 30% with respect to the target class, and 210/(90 + 210) = 70% with respect to the contrasting class. That is, *if a student majoring in Science is 21 to 25 years old and has a "good" gpa, then based on the data, there is a 30% probability that she is a graduate student, versus a 70% probability that she is an undergraduate student*. Similarly, the d-weights for the other generalized tuples in Tables 5.9 and 5.10 can be derived. ∎

A **quantitative discriminant rule** for the target class of a given comparison description is written in the form

$$\forall X, \ target\_class(X) \Leftarrow condition(X) \quad [d : d\_weight], \quad (5.8)$$

where the condition is formed by a generalized tuple of the description. This is different from rules obtained in class characterization where the arrow of implication is from left to right.

**Example 5.12** Based on the generalized tuple and count distribution in Example 5.11, a quantitative discriminant rule for the target class *graduate_student* can be written as follows:

$$\forall X, status(X) = \text{``graduate\_student"} \Leftarrow$$
$$major(X) = \text{``Science"} \wedge age\_range(X) = \text{``21 . . . 25"} \wedge gpa(X) = \text{``good"}$$
$$[d : 30\%]. \quad (5.9)$$

∎

Notice that a discriminant rule provides a *sufficient* condition, but not a *necessary* one, for an object (or tuple) to be in the target class. For example, Rule (5.9) implies that if $X$ satisfies the condition, then the probability that $X$ is a graduate student is 30%. However, it does not imply the probability that $X$ meets the condition, given that $X$ is a graduate student. This is because although the tuples that meet the condition are in the target class, other tuples that do not necessarily

**Table 5.12** A crosstab for the total number (*count*) of TVs and computers sold in thousands in 1999.

| location\item | TV | computer | both_items |
|---|---|---|---|
| Europe | 80 | 240 | 320 |
| North_America | 120 | 560 | 680 |
| *both_regions* | 200 | 800 | 1000 |

satisfy this condition may also be in the target class, since the rule may not cover *all* of the examples of the target class in the database. Therefore, the condition is sufficient, but not necessary.

### 5.4.3 Class Description: Presentation of Both Characterization and Comparison

*"Since class characterization and class comparison are two aspects forming a class description, can we present both in the same table or in the same rule?"* Actually, as long as we have a clear understanding of the meaning of the t-weight and d-weight measures and can interpret them correctly, there is no additional difficulty in presenting both aspects in the same table. Let's examine an example of expressing both class characterization and class discrimination in the same crosstab.

**Example 5.13** Let Table 5.12 be a crosstab showing the total number (in thousands) of TVs and computers sold at *AllElectronics* in 1999.

Let *Europe* be the target class and *North_America* be the contrasting class. The t-weights and d-weights of the sales distribution between the two classes are presented in Table 5.13. According to the table, the t-weight of a generalized tuple or object (e.g., *item* = "*TV*") for a given class (e.g., the target class *Europe*) shows how typical the tuple is of the given class (e.g., what proportion of these sales in Europe are for TVs?). The d-weight of a tuple shows how distinctive the tuple is in the given (target or contrasting) class in comparison with its rival class (e.g., how do the TV sales in Europe compare with those in North America?).

For example, the t-weight for "*(Europe, TV)*" is 25% because the number of TVs sold in Europe (80,000) represents only 25% of the European sales for both items (320,000). The d-weight for "*(Europe, TV)*" is 40% because the number of TVs sold in Europe (80,000) represents 40% of the number of TVs sold in both the target and the contrasting classes of Europe and North America, respectively (which is 200,000). ∎

Notice that the *count* measure in the crosstab of Table 5.13 obeys the general property of a crosstab (i.e., the *count* values per row and per column, when totaled, match the corresponding totals in the *both_items* and *both_regions* slots, respectively, for *count*). However, this property is not observed by the t-weight

**Table 5.13** The same crosstab as in Table 5.12, but here the t-weight and d-weight values associated with each class are shown.

| location\item | TV | | | computer | | | both_items | | |
|---|---|---|---|---|---|---|---|---|---|
| | count | t-weight | d-weight | count | t-weight | d-weight | count | t-weight | d-weight |
| Europe | 80 | 25% | 40% | 240 | 75% | 30% | 320 | 100% | 32% |
| North_America | 120 | 17.65% | 60% | 560 | 82.35% | 70% | 680 | 100% | 68% |
| both_regions | 200 | 20% | 100% | 800 | 80% | 100% | 1000 | 100% | 100% |

and d-weight measures. This is because the semantic meaning of each of these measures is different from that of *count*, as we explained in Example 5.13.

"*Can a quantitative characteristic rule and a quantitative discriminant rule be expressed together in the form of one rule?*" The answer is yes—a quantitative characteristic rule and a quantitative discriminant rule for the same class can be combined to form a *quantitative description rule* for the class, which displays the t-weights *and* d-weights associated with the corresponding characteristic and discriminant rules. To see how this is done, let's quickly review how quantitative characteristic and discriminant rules are expressed.

As discussed in Section 5.2.3, a quantitative characteristic rule provides a necessary condition for the given target class since it presents a probability measurement for each property that can occur in the target class. Such a rule is of the form

$$\forall X, \ target\_class(X) \Rightarrow condition_1(X)[t:w_1] \vee \cdots \vee condition_m(X)[t:w_m], \quad (5.10)$$

where each condition represents a property of the target class. The rule indicates that if $X$ is in the *target_class*, the probability that $X$ satisfies $condition_i$ is the value of the t-weight, $w_i$, where $i$ is in $\{1, \ldots, m\}$.

As previously discussed in Section 5.4.1, a quantitative discriminant rule provides a sufficient condition for the target class since it presents a quantitative measurement of the properties that occur in the target class versus those that occur in the contrasting classes. Such a rule is of the form

$$\forall X, \ target\_class(X) \Leftarrow condition_1(X)[d:w_1] \vee \cdots \vee condition_m(X)[d:w_m].$$

The rule indicates that if $X$ satisfies $condition_i$, there is a probability of $w_i$ (the d-weight value) that $x$ is in the *target_class*, where $i$ is in $\{1, \ldots, m\}$.

A quantitative characteristic rule and a quantitative discriminant rule for a given class can be combined as follows to form a **quantitative description rule**: (1) For each condition, show both the associated t-weight and d-weight, and (2) a bidirectional arrow should be used between the given class and the conditions. That is, a quantitative description rule is of the form

$$\forall X, \ \textit{target\_class}(X) \Leftrightarrow \textit{condition}_1(X)[t:w_1, d:w_1'] \vee \cdots \vee \textit{condition}_m(X)$$

$$[t:w_m, d:w_m']. \tag{5.11}$$

This form indicates that for *i* from 1 to *m*, if *X* is in the *target_class*, there is a probability of $w_i$ that *X* satisfies *condition$_i$*; and if *X* satisfies *condition$_i$*, there is a probability of $w_i'$ that *X* is in the *target_class*.

**Example 5.14** It is straightforward to transform the crosstab of Table 5.13 in Example 5.13 into a class description in the form of quantitative description rules. For example, the quantitative description rule for the target class, *Europe*, is

$$\forall X, \textit{location}(X) = \text{``Europe''} \Leftrightarrow$$

$$(\textit{item}(X) = \text{``TV''})[t:25\%, d:40\%] \vee (\textit{item}(X) = \text{``computer''})$$

$$[t:75\%, d:30\%] \tag{5.12}$$

The rule states that for the sales of TVs and computers at *AllElectronics* in 1999, if the sale of one of these items occurred in Europe, then the probability of the item being a TV is 25%, while that of being a computer is 75%. On the other hand, if we compare the sales of these items in Europe and North America, then 40% of the TVs were sold in Europe (and therefore we can deduce that 60% of the TVs were sold in North America). Furthermore, regarding computer sales, 30% of these sales took place in Europe. ∎

## 5.5 Mining Descriptive Statistical Measures in Large Databases

Earlier in this chapter, we discussed class description in terms of popular measures, such as *count, sum,* and *average*. Relational database systems provide five built-in aggregate functions: `count()`, `sum()`, `avg()`, `max()`, and `min()`. These functions can also be computed efficiently (in incremental and distributed manners) in data cubes. Thus, there is no problem in including these aggregate functions as basic measures in the descriptive mining of multidimensional data.

For many data mining tasks, however, users would like to learn more data characteristics regarding both central tendency and data dispersion. Measures of central tendency include *mean, median, mode,* and *midrange*, while measures of data dispersion include *quartiles, outliers,* and *variance*. These descriptive statistics are of great help in understanding the distribution of the data. Such measures have been studied extensively in the statistical literature. From the data mining point of view, we need to examine how they can be computed efficiently in large multidimensional databases.

### 5.5.1 Measuring the Central Tendency

The most common and most effective numerical measure of the "center" of a set of data is the *(arithmetic) mean*. Let $x_1, x_2, \ldots, x_n$ be a set of $n$ values or observations. The **mean** of this set of values is

$$\bar{x} = \frac{1}{n} \sum_{i=1}^{n} x_i. \tag{5.13}$$

This corresponds to the built-in aggregate function, *average* (avg() in SQL), provided in relational database systems. In most data cubes, *sum* and *count* are saved in precomputation. Thus, the derivation of *average* is straightforward, using the formula *average = sum/count*.

Sometimes, each value $x_i$ in a set may be associated with a weight $w_i$, for $i = 1, \ldots, n$. The weights reflect the significance, importance, or occurrence frequency attached to their respective values. In this case, we can compute

$$\bar{x} = \frac{\sum_{i=1}^{n} w_i x_i}{\sum_{i=1}^{n} w_i}. \tag{5.14}$$

This is called the **weighted arithmetic mean** or the **weighted average**.

In Chapter 2, a measure was defined as *algebraic* if it can be computed from distributive aggregate measures. Since avg() can be computed by sum()/count(), where both sum() and count() are distributive aggregate measures in the sense that they can be computed in a distributive manner, then avg() is an algebraic measure. One can verify that the weighted average is also an algebraic measure.

Although the mean is the single most useful quantity that we use to describe a set of data, it is not the only, or even always the best, way of measuring the center of a set of data. For skewed data, a better measure of the center of data is the *median*, $M$. Suppose that the values forming a given set of data are in numerical order. The **median** is *the middle value* of the ordered set if the number of values $n$ is an odd number; otherwise (i.e., if $n$ is even), it is *the average of the middle two values*.

Based on the categorization of measures in Chapter 2, the median is neither a distributive measure nor an algebraic measure—it is a holistic measure in the sense that it cannot be computed by partitioning a set of values arbitrarily into smaller subsets, computing their medians independently, and merging the median values of each subset. On the contrary, count(), sum(), max(), and min() can be computed in this manner (being distributive measures) and are therefore easier to compute than the median.

Although it is not easy to compute the exact median value in a large database, an approximate median can be efficiently computed. For example, for grouped data, the median, obtained by interpolation, is given by

$$median = L_1 + \left(\frac{n/2 - (\sum f)_l}{f_{median}}\right)c, \tag{5.15}$$

where $L_1$ is the lower class boundary of (i.e., lowest value for) the class containing the median, $n$ is the number of values in the data, $(\sum f)_l$ is the sum of the frequencies of all of the classes that are lower than the median class, $f_{median}$ is the frequency of the median class, and $c$ is the size of the median class interval.

Another measure of central tendency is the *mode*. The **mode** for a set of data is the value that occurs most frequently in the set. It is possible for the greatest frequency to correspond to several different values, which results in more than one mode. Data sets with one, two, or three modes are respectively called **unimodal**, **bimodal**, and **trimodal**. In general, a data set with two or more modes is **multimodal**. At the other extreme, if each data value occurs only once, then there is no mode.

For unimodal frequency curves that are moderately skewed (asymmetrical), we have the following empirical relation:

$$mean - mode = 3 \times (mean - median). \tag{5.16}$$

This implies that the mode for unimodal frequency curves that are moderately skewed can easily be computed if the mean and median values are known.

The **midrange**, that is, *the average of the largest and smallest values in a data set*, can be used to measure the central tendency of the set of data. It is trivial to compute the midrange using the SQL aggregate functions, `max()` and `min()`.

## 5.5.2 Measuring the Dispersion of Data

The degree to which numeric data tend to spread is called the **dispersion**, or **variance** of the data. The most common measures of data dispersion are the *five-number summary* (based on *quartiles*), the *interquartile range*, and the *standard deviation*. The plotting of *boxplots* (which show outlier values) also serves as a useful graphical method.

### Quartiles, Outliers, and Boxplots

The *k*th **percentile** of a set of data in numerical order is the value $x$ having the property that $k$ percent of the data entries lie at or below $x$. Values at or below the *median M* (discussed in the previous subsection) correspond to the 50th percentile.

The most commonly used percentiles other than the median are **quartiles**. The **first quartile**, denoted by $Q_1$, is the 25th percentile; the **third quartile**, denoted by $Q_3$, is the 75th percentile. The quartiles, including the median, give some indication of the center, spread, and shape of a distribution. The distance between the first and third quartiles is a simple measure of spread that gives the range covered by the middle half of the data. This distance is called the **interquartile range** (*IQR*) and is defined as

$$IQR = Q_3 - Q_1. \tag{5.17}$$

We should be aware that no single numerical measure of spread, such as *IQR*, is very useful for describing skewed distributions. The spreads of two sides of a skewed distribution are unequal. Therefore, it is more informative to also provide the two quartiles $Q_1$ and $Q_3$, along with the median, $M$. One common rule of thumb for identifying suspected **outliers** is to single out values falling at least $1.5 \times IQR$ above the third quartile or below the first quartile.

Because $Q_1$, $M$, and $Q_3$ contain no information about the endpoints (e.g., tails) of the data, a fuller summary of the shape of a distribution can be obtained by providing the highest and lowest data values as well. This is known as the *five-number summary*. The **five-number summary** of a distribution consists of the median $M$, the quartiles $Q_1$ and $Q_3$, and the smallest and largest individual observations, written in the order *Minimum, $Q_1$, M, $Q_3$, Maximum*.

A popularly used visual representation of a distribution is the **boxplot**. In a boxplot:

- Typically, the ends of the box are at the quartiles, so that the box length is the interquartile range, *IQR*.
- The median is marked by a line within the box.
- Two lines (called *whiskers*) outside the box extend to the smallest (*Minimum*) and largest (*Maximum*) observations.

When dealing with a moderate number of observations, it is worthwhile to plot potential outliers individually. To do this in a boxplot, the whiskers are extended to the extreme high and low observations *only if* these values are less than $1.5 \times IQR$ beyond the quartiles. Otherwise, the whiskers terminate at the most extreme observations occurring within $1.5 \times IQR$ of the quartiles. The remaining cases are plotted individually. Boxplots can be used in the comparisons of several sets of compatible data. Figure 5.5 shows boxplots for unit price data for items sold at four branches of *AllElectronics* during a given time period. For branch 1, we see that the median price of items sold is $80, $Q_1$ is $60, $Q_3$ is $100.

Based on similar reasoning as in our analysis of the median in Section 5.5.1, we can conclude that $Q_1$ and $Q_3$ are holistic measures, as is *IQR*. The efficient computation of boxplots or even *approximate boxplots* is interesting regarding the mining of large data sets.

### Variance and Standard Deviation

The **variance** of $n$ observations $x_1, x_2, \ldots, x_n$ is

$$s^2 = \frac{1}{n-1} \sum_{i=1}^{n} (x_i - \bar{x})^2 = \frac{1}{n-1} [\sum x_i^2 - \frac{1}{n}(\sum x_i)^2]. \tag{5.18}$$

The **standard deviation** $s$ is the square root of the variance $s^2$.

The basic properties of the standard deviation $s$ as a measure of spread are

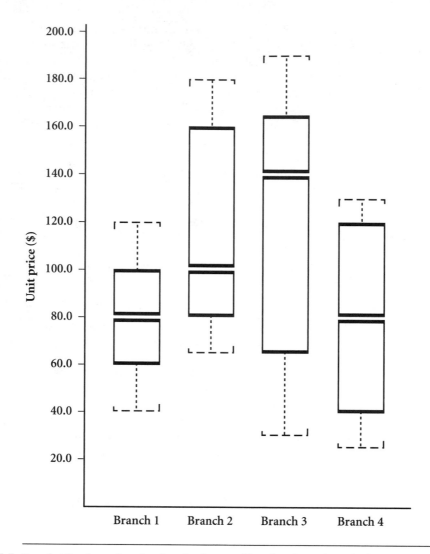

**Figure 5.5** Boxplot for the unit price data for items sold at four branches of *AllElectronics* during a given time period.

- $s$ measures spread about the mean and should be used only when the mean is chosen as the measure of center.

- $s = 0$ only when there is no spread, that is, when all observations have the same value. Otherwise $s > 0$.

Notice that variance and standard deviation are algebraic measures because $n$ (which is count() in SQL), $\sum x_i$ (which is the sum() of $x_i$), and $\sum x_i^2$ (which

**Table 5.14**  A set of unit price data for items sold at a branch of *AllElectronics*.

| Unit price ($) | Number of items sold |
|---|---|
| 40 | 275 |
| 43 | 300 |
| 47 | 250 |
| .. | .. |
| 74 | 360 |
| 75 | 515 |
| 78 | 540 |
| .. | .. |
| 115 | 320 |
| 117 | 270 |
| 120 | 350 |

is the sum() of $x_i^2$) can be computed in any partition and then merged to feed into the algebraic equation (5.18). Thus the computation of the two measures is scalable in large databases.

### 5.5.3 Graph Displays of Basic Statistical Class Descriptions

Aside from the bar charts, pie charts, and line graphs discussed earlier in this chapter, there are also a few additional popularly used graphs for the display of data summaries and distributions. These include *histograms, quantile plots, q-q plots, scatter plots,* and *loess curves.*

Plotting **histograms**, or **frequency histograms**, is a univariate graphical method. A histogram consists of a set of rectangles that reflect the counts or frequencies of the classes present in the given data. The base of each rectangle is on the horizontal axis, centered at a "class" mark, and the base length is equal to the class width. Typically, the class width is uniform, with classes being defined as the values of a categoric attribute, or equiwidth ranges of a discretized continuous attribute. In these cases, the height of each rectangle is equal to the count or relative frequency of the class it represents, and the histogram is generally referred to as a **bar chart**. Alternatively, classes for a continuous attribute may be defined by ranges of nonuniform width. In this case, for a given class, the class width is equal to the range width, and the height of the rectangle is the class density (i.e., the count or relative frequency of the class, divided by the class width). Partitioning rules for constructing histograms were discussed in Chapter 3.

Figure 5.6 shows a histogram for the data set of Table 5.14, where classes are defined by equiwidth ranges representing $20 increments and the frequency is the number of items sold. Histograms are at least a century old and are a widely

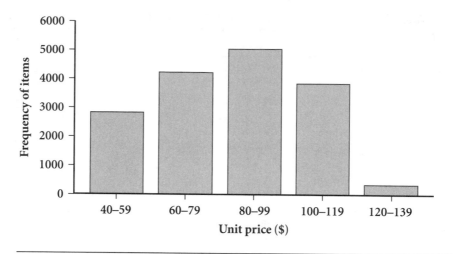

**Figure 5.6**   A histogram for the data set of Table 5.14.

used univariate graphical method. However, they may not be as effective as the quantile plot, q-q plot, and boxplot methods for comparing groups of univariate observations.

A **quantile plot** is a simple and effective way to have a first look at a univariate data distribution. First, it displays all of the data (allowing the user to assess both the overall behavior and unusual occurrences). Second, it plots quantile information. The mechanism used in this step is slightly different from the percentile computation. Let $x_{(i)}$, for $i = 1$ to $n$, be the data sorted in increasing order so that $x_{(1)}$ is the smallest observation and $x_{(n)}$ is the largest. Each observation $x_{(i)}$ is paired with a percentage, $f_i$, which indicates that approximately $100f_i\%$ of the data are below or equal to the value $x_{(i)}$. We say "approximately" because there may not be a value with exactly a fraction $f_i$ of the data below or equal to $x_{(i)}$. Note that the 0.25 quantile corresponds to quartile $Q_1$, the 0.50 quantile is the median, and the 0.75 quantile is $Q_3$. Let

$$f_i = \frac{i - 0.5}{n}.$$

These numbers increase in equal steps of $1/n$, ranging from $1/2n$ (which is slightly above zero) to $1 - 1/2n$ (which is slightly below one). On a quantile plot, $x_{(i)}$ is graphed against $f_i$. This allows us to compare different distributions based on their quantiles. For example, given the quantile plots of sales data for two different time periods, we can compare their $Q_1$, median, $Q_3$, and other $f_i$ values at a glance. Figure 5.7 shows a quantile plot for the *unit price* data of Table 5.14.

A **quantile-quantile plot**, or **q-q plot**, graphs the quantiles of one univariate distribution against the corresponding quantiles of another. It is a powerful vi-

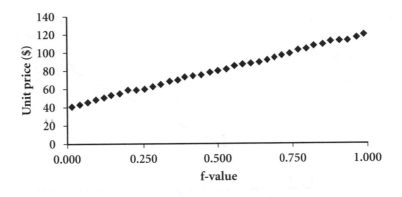

**Figure 5.7** A quantile plot for the unit price data of Table 5.14.

sualization tool in that it allows the user to view whether there is a shift in going from one distribution to another.

Suppose that we have two sets of observations for the variable *unit price*, taken from two different branch locations. Let $x_{(1)}, \ldots, x_{(n)}$ be the data from the first branch, and $y_{(1)}, \ldots, y_{(m)}$ be the data from the second, where each data set is sorted in increasing order. If $m = n$ (i.e., the number of points in each set is the same), then we simply plot $y_{(i)}$ against $x_{(i)}$, where $y_{(i)}$ and $x_{(i)}$ are both $(i - 0.5)/n$ quantiles of their respective data sets. If $m < n$ (i.e., the second branch has fewer observations than the first), there can be only $m$ points on the q-q plot. Here, $y_{(i)}$ is the $(i - 0.5)/m$ quantile of the $y$ data, which is plotted against the $(i - 0.5)/m$ quantile of the $x$ data. This computation typically involves interpolation.

Figure 5.8 shows a quantile-quantile plot for *unit price* data of items sold at two different branches of *AllElectronics* during a given time period. The lowest point in the left corner corresponds to the same quantile, 0.03, for each data set. (To aid in comparison, we also show a straight line that represents the case of when, for each given quantile, the unit price at each branch is the same. In addition, the darker points correspond to the data for $Q_1$, the median, and $Q_3$, respectively.) For example, we see that at this quantile, the unit price of items sold at branch 1 was slightly less than that at branch 2. In other words, 3% of items sold at branch 1 were less than or equal to $40, while 3% of items at branch 2 were less than or equal to $42. At the highest quantile, we see that the unit price of items at branch 2 was slightly less than that at branch 1. In general, we note that there is a shift in the distribution of branch 1 with respect to branch 2 in that the unit prices of items sold at branch 1 tend to be lower than those at branch 2.

A **scatter plot** is one of the most effective graphical methods for determining if there appears to be a relationship, pattern, or trend between two quantitative variables. To construct a scatter plot, each pair of values is treated as a pair of coordinates in an algebraic sense and plotted as points in the plane. The scatter

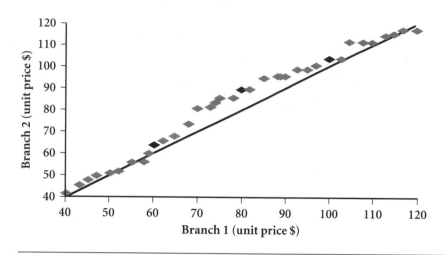

**Figure 5.8** A quantile-quantile plot for unit price data from two different branches.

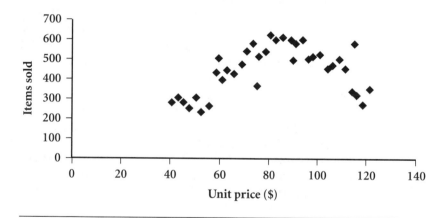

**Figure 5.9** A scatter plot for the data set of Table 5.14.

plot is a useful exploratory method for providing a first look at bivariate data to see how they are distributed throughout the plane, for example, and to see clusters of points, outliers, and so forth. Figure 5.9 shows a scatter plot for the set of data in Table 5.14.

A **loess curve** is another important exploratory graphic aid that adds a smooth curve to a scatter plot in order to provide better perception of the pattern of dependence. The word *loess* is short for "local regression." Figure 5.10 shows a loess curve for the set of data in Table 5.14.

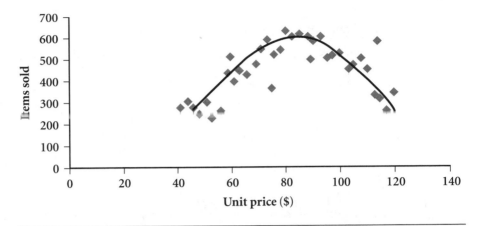

**Figure 5.10**   A loess curve for the data set of Table 5.14.

To fit a loess curve, values need to be set for two parameters—$\alpha$, a smoothing parameter, and $\lambda$, the degree of the polynomials that are fitted by the regression. While $\alpha$ can be any positive number (typical values are between 1/4 and 1), $\lambda$ can be 1 or 2. The goal in choosing $\alpha$ is to produce a fit that is as smooth as possible without unduly distorting the underlying pattern in the data. The curve becomes smoother as $\alpha$ increases. There may be some lack of fit, however, indicating possible "missing" data patterns. If $\alpha$ is very small, the underlying pattern is tracked, yet overfitting of the data may occur, where local "wiggles" in the curve may not be supported by the data. If the underlying pattern of the data has a "gentle" curvature with no local maxima and minima, then local linear fitting is usually sufficient ($\lambda = 1$). However, if there are local maxima or minima, then local quadratic fitting ($\lambda = 2$) typically does a better job of following the pattern of the data and maintaining local smoothness.

# 5.6 Discussion

We have presented a set of scalable methods for mining concept or class descriptions in large databases. In this section, we discuss related issues regarding such descriptions. These include a comparison of the cube-based and attribute-oriented induction approaches to data generalization with typical machine learning methods, the implementation of incremental and parallel mining of concept descriptions, and interestingness measures for concept descriptions.

### 5.6.1 Concept Description: A Comparison with Typical Machine Learning Methods

In this chapter, we studied database-oriented methods for mining concept descriptions in large databases. These methods include a data cube-based and an attribute-oriented induction approach to data generalization for concept description. Other influential concept description methods have been proposed and studied in the machine learning literature since the 1980s. Typical machine learning methods for concept description follow a *learning-from-examples* paradigm. In general, such methods work on sets of concept or class-labeled training samples that are examined in order to derive or learn a hypothesis describing the class under study.

*"What are the major differences between methods of learning from examples and the data mining methods presented here?"* First, there are differences in the *philosophies* of the machine learning and data mining approaches, and their *basic assumptions* regarding the concept description problem. In most of the learning-from-examples algorithms developed in machine learning, the set of samples to be analyzed is partitioned into two sets: *positive* samples and *negative* ones, representing target and contrasting classes, respectively. The learning process selects one positive sample at random and uses it to form a hypothesis describing objects of that class. The learning process then performs *generalization* on the hypothesis using the remaining positive samples, and *specialization* using the negative samples. In general, the resulting hypothesis covers all the positive samples, but none of the negative samples.

A database usually does not store the negative data explicitly. Thus no explicitly specified negative samples can be used for specialization. This is why, for analytical characterization mining and for comparison mining in general, data mining methods must collect a set of comparable data that are not in the target (positive) class for use as negative data (Sections 5.3 and 5.4). Most database-oriented methods also therefore tend to be generalization-based. Even though most provide the drill-down (specialization) operation, this operation is essentially implemented by backtracking the generalization process to a previous state.

Second, another major difference between machine learning and database-oriented techniques for concept description concerns the *size of the set of training samples.* For traditional machine learning methods, the training set is typically relatively small in comparison with the data analyzed by database-oriented techniques. Hence, for machine learning methods, it is easier to find descriptions that cover all of the positive samples without covering any negative samples. However, considering the diversity and huge amount of data stored in real-world databases, it is unlikely for analysis of such data to derive a rule or pattern that covers all of the positive samples but none of the negative ones. Instead, what one may expect to find is a set of features or rules that cover a *majority* of the data in the positive class, *maximally* distinguishing the positive from the negative samples. (This can also be described as a *probability distribution.*)

Third, distinctions between the machine learning and database-oriented approaches also exist regarding the *methods of generalization used*. Both approaches do employ attribute removal and attribute generalization as their main generalization techniques. Consider the set of training samples as a set of tuples. The machine learning approach performs generalization *tuple by tuple*, whereas the database-oriented approach performs generalization on an *attribute-by-attribute* (or entire dimension) basis.

In the tuple-by-tuple strategy of the machine learning approach, the training samples are examined one at a time in order to induce generalized concepts. In order to form the most specific hypothesis (or concept description) that is consistent with all of the positive samples and none of the negative ones, the algorithm must search every node in the search space representing all of the possible concepts derived from generalization on each training sample. Since different attributes of a tuple may be generalized to various levels of abstraction, the number of nodes searched for a given training sample may involve a huge number of possible combinations.

On the other hand, a database approach employing an attribute-oriented strategy performs generalization on each attribute or dimension uniformly for all of the tuples in the data relation at the *early* stages of generalization. Such an approach essentially focuses its attention on individual attributes, rather than on combinations of attributes. This is referred to as *factoring the version space*, where **version space** is defined as the subset of hypotheses consistent with the training samples. Factoring the version space can substantially improve the computational efficiency. Suppose there are $k$ concept hierarchies used in the generalization and there are $p$ nodes in each concept hierarchy. The total size of $k$ factored version spaces is $p \times k$. In contrast, the size of the unfactored version space searched by the machine learning approach is $p^k$ for the same concept tree.

Notice that algorithms that, during the early generalization stages, explore many possible combinations of different attribute-value conditions given a large number of tuples cannot be productive since such combinations will eventually be merged during further generalizations. Different possible combinations should be explored only when the relation has first been generalized to a relatively smaller relation, as is done in the database-oriented approaches described in this chapter.

Another obvious advantage of the attribute-oriented approach over many other machine learning algorithms is the *integration of the data mining process with set-oriented database operations*. In contrast to most existing learning algorithms, which do not take full advantage of database facilities, the attribute-oriented induction approach primarily adopts relational operations, such as selection, join, projection (extracting task-relevant data and removing attributes), tuple substitution (ascending concept trees), and sorting (discovering common tuples among classes). Such relational operations are set-oriented and have typically been optimized in most existing database systems. Therefore, the attribute-oriented approach is not only efficient but can also easily be exported to other relational systems. This comment applies to data cube-based generalization algorithms as well. The data cube-based approach explores more optimization techniques than traditional database query processing techniques by incorporating sparse cube techniques, various methods of cube computation, as well as indexing and accessing techniques. Therefore, a high performance gain of database-oriented algorithms over machine learning techniques is expected when handling large data sets.

### 5.6.2 Incremental and Parallel Mining of Concept Description

Given the huge amount of data in a database, it is highly preferable to update data mining results *incrementally* rather than mining from scratch on each database update. Thus incremental data mining is an attractive goal for many kinds of mining in large databases or data warehouses. Fortunately, it is straightforward to extend the database-oriented concept description mining algorithms for incremental data mining.

*"How could we extend attribute-oriented induction for use in incremental data mining?"* Suppose that a generalized relation $R$ is stored in the database. When a set of new tuples, $\Delta DB$, is inserted into the database, attribute-oriented induction can be performed on $\Delta DB$ in order to generalize the attributes to the same conceptual levels as the respective corresponding attributes in the generalized relation, $R$. The associated aggregation information, such as count, sum, and so on, can be calculated by applying the generalization algorithm to $\Delta DB$. The generalized relation so derived, $\Delta R$, on $\Delta DB$, can then easily be merged into the generalized relation $R$, since $R$ and $\Delta R$ share the same dimensions and exist at the same abstraction levels for each dimension. The union, $R \cup \Delta R$, becomes a new generalized relation, $R'$. Minor adjustments, such as dimension generalization or specialization, can be performed on $R'$ as specified by the user, if desired. Incremental deletion can be performed in a similar manner. The details are left as an exercise.

Data sampling methods, parallel algorithms, and distributed algorithms can be explored for concept description mining, based on the same philosophy. For example, attribute-oriented induction can be performed by *sampling* a subset of data from a huge set of task-relevant data or by first performing induction *in parallel* on several partitions of the task-relevant data set, and then merging the generalized results.

## 5.7 Summary

- Data mining can be classified into *descriptive data mining* and *predictive data mining*. **Concept description** is the most basic form of descriptive data mining. It describes a given set of task-relevant data in a concise and summarative manner, presenting interesting general properties of the data.

- Concept (or class) description consists of **characterization** and **comparison** (or **discrimination**). The former summarizes and describes a collection of data, called the **target class**, whereas the latter summarizes and distinguishes one collection of data, called the **target class**, from other collection(s) of data, collectively called the **contrasting class(es)**.

- There are two general approaches to concept characterization: the **data cube OLAP-based approach** and the **attribute-oriented induction approach**. Both are attribute- or dimension-based generalization approaches. The attribute-oriented induction approach can be implemented using either relational or data cube structures.

- The **attribute-oriented induction approach** consists of the following techniques: *data focusing*, *data generalization by attribute removal or attribute generalization*, *count and aggregate value accumulation*, *attribute generalization control*, and *generalization data visualization*.

- Generalized data can be **visualized** in multiple forms, including generalized relations, crosstabs, bar charts, pie charts, cube views, curves, and rules. Drill-down and roll-up operations can be performed on the generalized data interactively.

- **Analytical characterization/comparison** performs attribute and dimension relevance analysis in order to filter out irrelevant or weakly relevant attributes prior to the induction process.

- **Concept comparison** can be performed using the attribute-oriented induction or data cube approach in a manner similar to concept characterization. Generalized tuples from the target and contrasting classes can be quantitatively compared and contrasted.

- Characterization and comparison descriptions (which form a concept description) can both be visualized in the *same* generalized relation, crosstab, or quantitative rule form, although they are displayed with different interestingness measures. These measures include the **t-weight** (for tuple typicality) and **d-weight** (for tuple discriminability).

- From the descriptive statistics point of view, additional **statistical measures** can be used in describing central tendency and data dispersion. Quartiles, variations, and outliers are useful additional information that can be mined in databases. Boxplots, quantile plots, scatter plots, and quantile-quantile plots are useful visualization tools in descriptive data mining.

- In comparison with machine learning algorithms, database-oriented concept description leads to efficiency and scalability in large databases and data warehouses.

- Concept description mining can be performed **incrementally**, in **parallel**, or in a **distributed** manner, by making minor extensions to the basic methods involved.

## Exercises

5.1 For *class characterization*, what are the major differences between a data cube-based implementation and a relational implementation such as attribute-oriented induction? Discuss which method is most efficient and under what conditions this is so.

5.2 Suppose that the following table is derived by *attribute-oriented induction*.

| class | birth_place | count |
|-------|-------------|-------|
| | Canada | 180 |
| Programmer | others | 120 |
| | Canada | 20 |
| DBA | others | 80 |

(a) Transform the table into a crosstab showing the associated t-weights and d-weights.

(b) Map the class *Programmer* into a (bidirectional) *quantitative descriptive rule*, for example, $\forall X$, *Programmer*$(X) \Leftrightarrow$ (*birth_place*$(X) =$ "*Canada*" $\wedge \ldots$) $[t : x\%, d : y\%] \ldots \vee (\ldots)[t : w\%, d : z\%]$.

5.3 Discuss why *analytical characterization* is needed and how it can be performed. Compare the result of two induction methods: (1) with relevance analysis and (2) without relevance analysis.

5.4 Give three additional commonly used statistical measures (i.e., not illustrated in this chapter) for the characterization of *data dispersion*, and discuss how they can be computed efficiently in large databases.

5.5 Suppose that the data for analysis includes the attribute *age*. The *age* values for the data tuples are (in increasing order) 13, 15, 16, 16, 19, 20, 20, 21, 22, 22, 25, 25, 25, 25, 30, 33, 33, 35, 35, 35, 35, 36, 40, 45, 46, 52, 70.

(a) What is the *mean* of the data? What is the *median*?

(b) What is the *mode* of the data ? Comment on the data's modality (i.e., bimodal, trimodal, etc.).

(c) What is the *midrange* of the data?

(d) Can you find (roughly) the first quartile ($Q1$) and the third quartile ($Q3$) of the data?

(e) Give the *five-number summary* of the data.

(f) Show a *boxplot* of the data.

(g) How is a *quantile-quantile plot* different from a *quantile plot*?

5.6  Given a generalized relation $R$ derived from a database $DB$, suppose that a set $\Delta DB$ of tuples needs to be deleted from $DB$. Outline an *incremental* updating procedure for applying the necessary deletions to $R$.

5.7  Outline a data cube-based *incremental* algorithm for mining analytical class comparisons.

5.8  Outline a method for (1) *parallel* and (2) *distributed* mining of statistical measures of data dispersion in a data cube environment.

## Bibliographic Notes

Generalization and summarization methods have been studied in the statistics literature long before the onset of computers. Good summaries of statistical descriptive data mining methods include Cleveland [Cle93] and Devore [Dev95]. Generalization-based induction techniques, such as learning from examples, were proposed and studied in the machine learning literature before data mining became active. A theory and methodology of inductive learning was proposed by Michalski [Mic83]. The learning-from-examples method was proposed by Michalski [Mic83]. Version space was proposed by Mitchell [Mit77, Mit82]. The method of factoring the version space described in Section 5.6.1 was presented by Subramanian and Feigenbaum [SF86b]. Overviews of machine learning techniques can be found in Dieterich and Michalski [DM83], Michalski, Carbonell, and Mitchell [MCM86], and Mitchell [Mit97].

The data cube-based generalization technique was initially proposed by Codd, Codd, and Salley [CCS93] and has been implemented in many OLAP-based data warehouse systems. Gray, Bosworth, Layman, and Pirahesh [GCB+97] proposed a cube operator for computing aggregations in data cubes. Recently, there have been many studies on the efficient computation of data cubes, which contribute to the efficient computation of data generalization. A comprehensive survey on the topic can be found in Chaudhuri and Dayal [CD97].

Database-oriented methods for concept description explore scalable and efficient techniques for describing large sets of data in databases and data warehouses. The attribute-oriented induction method described in this chapter was first proposed by Cai, Cercone, and Han [CCH91] and further extended by Han, Cai, and Cercone [HCC93], Han and Fu [HF96], Carter and Hamilton [CH98], and Han, Nishio, Kawano, and Wang [HNKW98].

There are many methods for assessing attribute relevance. Each has its own bias. The information gain measure is biased towards attributes with many values. Many alternatives have been proposed, such as gain ratio (Quinlan [Qui93]), which considers the probability of each attribute value. Other relevance measures include the Gini index (Breiman, Friedman, Olshen, and Stone [BFOS84]), the

$\chi^2$ contingency table statistic, and the uncertainty coefficient (Johnson and Wichern [JW92]). For a comparison of attribute selection measures for decision tree induction, see Buntine and Niblett [BN92]. For additional methods, see Liu and Motoda [LM98ab], Dash and Liu [DL97], and Almuallim and Dietterich [AD91].

For statistics-based visualization of data using boxplots, quantile plots, quantile-quantile plots, scatter plots, and loess curves, see Cleveland [Cle93] and Devore [Dev95]. Knorr and Ng [KN98] studied a unified approach for defining and computing outliers.

# Mining Association Rules in Large Databases

**6**

Association rule mining finds interesting association or correlation relationships among a large set of data items. With massive amounts of data continuously being collected and stored, many industries are becoming interested in mining association rules from their databases. The discovery of interesting association relationships among huge amounts of business transaction records can help in many business decision making processes, such as catalog design, cross-marketing, and loss-leader analysis.

A typical example of association rule mining is **market basket analysis**. This process analyzes customer buying habits by finding associations between the different items that customers place in their "shopping baskets" (Figure 6.1). The discovery of such associations can help retailers develop marketing strategies by gaining insight into which items are frequently purchased together by customers. For instance, if customers are buying milk, how likely are they to also buy bread (and what kind of bread) on the same trip to the supermarket? Such information can lead to increased sales by helping retailers do selective marketing and plan their shelf space. For example, placing milk and bread within close proximity may further encourage the sale of these items together within single visits to the store.

How can we find association rules from large amounts of data, where the data are either transactional or relational? Which association rules are the most interesting? How can we help or guide the mining procedure to discover interesting associations? What language constructs are useful in defining a data mining query language for association rule mining? In this chapter, we will delve into each of these questions.

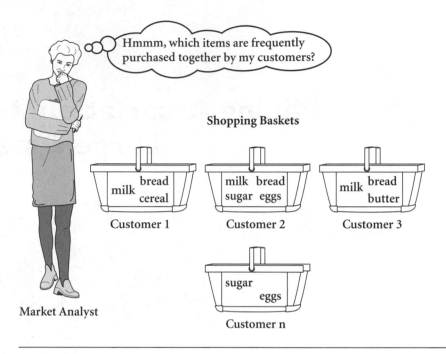

**Figure 6.1** Market basket analysis.

# 6.1 Association Rule Mining

Association rule mining searches for interesting relationships among items in a given data set. This section provides an introduction to association rule mining. We begin in Section 6.1.1 by presenting an example of market basket analysis, the earliest form of association rule mining. The basic concepts of mining associations are given in Section 6.1.2. Section 6.1.3 presents a road map to the different kinds of association rules that can be mined.

## 6.1.1 Market Basket Analysis: A Motivating Example for Association Rule Mining

Suppose, as manager of an *AllElectronics* branch, you would like to learn more about the buying habits of your customers. Specifically, you wonder, *"Which groups or sets of items are customers likely to purchase on a given trip to the store?"* To answer your question, market basket analysis may be performed on the retail data of customer transactions at your store. The results may be used to plan marketing or advertising strategies, as well as catalog design. For instance, market basket analysis may help managers design different store layouts. In one strategy, items that are frequently purchased together can be placed in close proximity in order to further encourage the sale of such items together. If customers who purchase computers also tend to buy financial management software at the same time, then placing the hardware display close to the software display may help to increase the sales of both of these items. In an alternative strategy, placing hardware and software at opposite ends of the store may entice customers who purchase such items to pick up other items along the way. For instance, after deciding on an expensive computer, a customer may observe security systems for sale while heading towards the software display to purchase financial management software and may decide to purchase a home security system as well. Market basket analysis can also help retailers to plan which items to put on sale at reduced prices. If customers tend to purchase computers and printers together, then having a sale on printers may encourage the sale of printers *as well as* computers.

If we think of the universe as the set of items available at the store, then each item has a Boolean variable representing the presence or absence of that item. Each basket can then be represented by a Boolean vector of values assigned to these variables. The Boolean vectors can be analyzed for buying patterns that reflect items that are frequently *associated* or purchased together. These patterns can be represented in the form of **association rules**. For example, the information that customers who purchase computers also tend to buy financial management software at the same time is represented in Association Rule (6.1) below:

$$computer \Rightarrow financial\_management\_software$$

$$[support = 2\%, confidence = 60\%] \tag{6.1}$$

Rule **support** and **confidence** are two measures of rule interestingness that were described earlier in Section 4.1.4. They respectively reflect the usefulness and certainty of discovered rules. A support of 2% for Association Rule (6.1) means that 2% of all the transactions under analysis show that computer and financial management software are purchased together. A confidence of 60% means that 60% of the customers who purchased a computer also bought the software. Typically, association rules are considered interesting if they satisfy both a **minimum support threshold** and a **minimum confidence threshold**. Such thresholds can be set by users or domain experts.

## 6.1.2 Basic Concepts

Let $\mathcal{I} = \{i_1, i_2, \ldots, i_m\}$ be a set of items. Let $D$, the task-relevant data, be a set of database transactions where each transaction $T$ is a set of items such that $T \subseteq \mathcal{I}$. Each transaction is associated with an identifier, called TID. Let $A$ be a set of items. A transaction $T$ is said to contain $A$ if and only if $A \subseteq T$. An association rule is an implication of the form $A \Rightarrow B$, where $A \subset \mathcal{I}$, $B \subset \mathcal{I}$, and $A \cap B = \phi$. The rule $A \Rightarrow B$ holds in the transaction set $D$ with **support** $s$, where $s$ is the percentage of transactions in $D$ that contain $A \cup B$ (i.e., both $A$ and $B$). This is taken to be the probability, $P(A \cup B)$. The rule $A \Rightarrow B$ has **confidence** $c$ in the transaction set $D$ if $c$ is the percentage of transactions in $D$ containing $A$ that also contain $B$. This is taken to be the conditional probability, $P(B|A)$. That is,

$$support(A \Rightarrow B) = P(A \cup B) \tag{6.2}$$

$$confidence(A \Rightarrow B) = P(B|A). \tag{6.3}$$

Rules that satisfy both a minimum support threshold (*min_sup*) and a minimum confidence threshold (*min_conf*) are called **strong**. By convention, we write support and confidence values so as to occur between 0% and 100%, rather than 0 to 1.0.

A set of items is referred to as an **itemset**.[1] An itemset that contains $k$ items is a $k$-**itemset**. The set {*computer, financial_management_software*} is a 2-itemset. The **occurrence frequency of an itemset** is the number of transactions that contain the itemset. This is also known, simply, as the **frequency**, **support count**, or **count** of the itemset. An itemset satisfies **minimum support** if the occurrence frequency of the itemset is greater than or equal to the product of *min_sup* and the total number of transactions in $D$. The number of transactions required for the itemset to satisfy minimum support is therefore referred to as the **minimum support count**. If an itemset satisfies minimum support, then it is a **frequent** itemset.[2] The set of frequent $k$-itemsets is commonly denoted by $L_k$.[3]

"*How are association rules mined from large databases?*" Association rule mining is a two-step process:

1. **Find all frequent itemsets:** By definition, each of these itemsets will occur at least as frequently as a pre-determined minimum support count.

2. **Generate strong association rules from the frequent itemsets:** By definition, these rules must satisfy minimum support and minimum confidence.

Additional interestingness measures can be applied, if desired. The second step is the easiest of the two. The overall performance of mining association rules is determined by the first step.

---

[1] In the data mining research literature, "itemset" is more commonly used than "item set."

[2] In early work, itemsets satisfying minimum support were referred to as **large**. This term, however, is somewhat confusing as it has connotations to the number of items in an itemset rather than the frequency of occurrence of the set. Hence, we use the more recent term **frequent**.

[3] Although the term **frequent** is preferred over **large**, for historical reasons frequent $k$-itemsets are still denoted as $L_k$.

### 6.1.3 **Association Rule Mining: A Road Map**

Market basket analysis is just one form of association rule mining. In fact, there are many kinds of association rules. Association rules can be classified in various ways, based on the following criteria:

- **Based on the *types of values* handled in the rule:** If a rule concerns associations between the presence or absence of items, it is a **Boolean association rule**. For example, Rule (6.1) above is a Boolean association rule obtained from market basket analysis.

  If a rule describes associations between quantitative items or attributes, then it is a **quantitative association rule**. In these rules, quantitative values for items or attributes are partitioned into intervals. The following rule is an example of a quantitative association rule, where $X$ is a variable representing a customer:

  $$age(X, \text{``}30 \ldots 39\text{''}) \wedge income(X, \text{``}42K \ldots 48K\text{''})$$
  $$\Rightarrow buys(X, high \; resolution \; TV) \qquad (6.4)$$

  Note that the quantitative attributes, *age* and *income*, have been discretized.

- **Based on the *dimensions* of data involved in the rule:** If the items or attributes in an association rule reference only one dimension, then it is a **single-dimensional association rule**. Note that Rule (6.1) could be rewritten as

  $$buys(X, \text{``}computer\text{''}) \Rightarrow buys(X, \text{``}financial\_management\_software\text{''}) \quad (6.5)$$

  Rule (6.1) is a single-dimensional association rule since it refers to only one dimension, *buys*.[4] If a rule references two or more dimensions, such as the dimensions *buys, time_of_transaction*, and *customer_category*, then it is a **multidimensional association rule**. Rule (6.4) is considered a multidimensional association rule since it involves three dimensions: *age, income*, and *buys*.

- **Based on the *levels of abstractions* involved in the rule set:** Some methods for association rule mining can find rules at differing levels of abstraction. For example, suppose that a set of association rules mined includes the following rules:

  $$age(X, \text{``}30 \ldots 39\text{''}) \Rightarrow buys(X, \text{``}laptop \; computer\text{''}) \qquad (6.6)$$

  $$age(X, \text{``}30 \ldots 39\text{''}) \Rightarrow buys(X, \text{``}computer\text{''}) \qquad (6.7)$$

  In Rules (6.6) and (6.7), the items bought are referenced at different levels of abstraction. (e.g., "*computer*" is a higher-level abstraction of "*laptop computer*".) We refer to the rule set mined as consisting of **multilevel association rules**. If,

---

[4] Following the terminology used in multidimensional databases, we refer to each distinct predicate in a rule as a *dimension*.

instead, the rules within a given set do not reference items or attributes at different levels of abstraction, then the set contains **single-level association rules**.

- **Based on *various extensions* to association mining:** Association mining can be extended to correlation analysis, where the absence or presence of correlated items can be identified. It can also be extended to mining *maxpatterns* (i.e., maximal frequent patterns) and *frequent closed itemsets*. A **maxpattern** is a frequent pattern, $p$, such that any proper superpattern[5] of $p$ is not frequent. A **frequent closed itemset** is a *frequent* closed itemset where an itemset $c$ is *closed* if there exists no proper superset of $c$, $c'$, such that every transaction containing $c$ also contains $c'$. Maxpatterns and frequent closed itemsets can be used to substantially reduce the number of frequent itemsets generated in mining.

Throughout the rest of this chapter, you will study methods for mining each of the association rule types described.

## 6.2 Mining Single-Dimensional Boolean Association Rules from Transactional Databases

In this section, you will learn methods for mining the simplest form of association rules—*single-dimensional, single-level, Boolean association rules*, such as those discussed for market basket analysis in Section 6.1.1. We begin by presenting **Apriori**, a basic algorithm for finding frequent itemsets (Section 6.2.1). A procedure for generating strong association rules from frequent itemsets is discussed in Section 6.2.2. Section 6.2.3 describes several variations to the Apriori algorithm for improved efficiency and scalability. Section 6.2.4 presents methods for mining association rules that, unlike Apriori, do not involve the generation of "candidate" frequent itemsets. Section 6.2.5 describes how principles from Apriori can be applied to improve the efficiency of answering *iceberg queries,* which are common in market basket analysis.

### 6.2.1 The Apriori Algorithm: Finding Frequent Itemsets Using Candidate Generation

**Apriori** is an influential algorithm for mining frequent itemsets for Boolean association rules. The name of the algorithm is based on the fact that the algorithm uses *prior knowledge* of frequent itemset properties, as we shall see below. Apriori employs an iterative approach known as a *level-wise* search, where $k$-itemsets are used to explore $(k + 1)$-itemsets. First, the set of frequent 1-itemsets is found. This set is denoted $L_1$. $L_1$ is used to find $L_2$, the set of frequent 2-itemsets, which is used

---

[5] $q$ is a superpattern of $p$ if $p$ is a subpattern of $q$, that is, if $q$ contains $p$.

to find $L_3$, and so on, until no more frequent $k$-itemsets can be found. The finding of each $L_k$ requires one full scan of the database.

To improve the efficiency of the level-wise generation of frequent itemsets, an important property called the **Apriori property**, presented below, is used to reduce the search space. We will first describe this property, and then show an example illustrating its use.

*Apriori property:* All nonempty subsets of a frequent itemset must also be frequent. The Apriori property is based on the following observation. By definition, if an itemset $I$ does not satisfy the minimum support threshold, *min_sup*, then $I$ is not frequent, that is, $P(I) <$ *min_sup*. If an item $A$ is added to the itemset $I$, then the resulting itemset (i.e., $I \cup A$) cannot occur more frequently than $I$. Therefore, $I \cup A$ is not frequent either, that is, $P(I \cup A) <$ *min_sup*.

This property belongs to a special category of properties called **anti-monotone** in the sense that *if a set cannot pass a test, all of its supersets will fail the same test as well*. It is called *anti-monotone* because the property is monotonic in the context of failing a test.

*"How is the Apriori property used in the algorithm?"* To understand this, let us look at how $L_{k-1}$ is used to find $L_k$. A two-step process is followed, consisting of **join** and **prune** actions.

1. **The join step:** To find $L_k$, a set of **candidate** $k$-itemsets is generated by joining $L_{k-1}$ with itself. This set of candidates is denoted $C_k$. Let $l_1$ and $l_2$ be itemsets in $L_{k-1}$. The notation $l_i[j]$ refers to the $j$th item in $l_i$ (e.g., $l_1[k-2]$ refers to the second to the last item in $l_1$). By convention, Apriori assumes that items within a transaction or itemset are sorted in lexicographic order. The join, $L_{k-1} \bowtie L_{k-1}$, is performed, where members of $L_{k-1}$ are joinable if their first $(k-2)$ items are in common. That is, members $l_1$ and $l_2$ of $L_{k-1}$ are joined if $(l_1[1] = l_2[1]) \wedge (l_1[2] = l_2[2]) \wedge \ldots \wedge (l_1[k-2] = l_2[k-2]) \wedge (l_1[k-1] < l_2[k-1])$. The condition $l_1[k-1] < l_2[k-1]$ simply ensures that no duplicates are generated. The resulting itemset formed by joining $l_1$ and $l_2$ is $l_1[1]l_1[2] \ldots l_1[k-1]l_2[k-1]$.

2. **The prune step:** $C_k$ is a superset of $L_k$, that is, its members may or may not be frequent, but all of the frequent $k$-itemsets are included in $C_k$. A scan of the database to determine the count of each candidate in $C_k$ would result in the determination of $L_k$ (i.e., all candidates having a count no less than the minimum support count are frequent by definition, and therefore belong to $L_k$). $C_k$, however, can be huge, and so this could involve heavy computation. To reduce the size of $C_k$, the Apriori property is used as follows. Any $(k-1)$-itemset that is not frequent cannot be a subset of a frequent $k$-itemset. Hence, if any $(k-1)$-subset of a candidate $k$-itemset is not in $L_{k-1}$, then the candidate cannot be frequent either and so can be removed from $C_k$. This subset testing can be done quickly by maintaining a hash tree of all frequent itemsets.

| TID | List of item_IDs |
|------|------------------|
| T100 | I1, I2, I5 |
| T200 | I2, I4 |
| T300 | I2, I3 |
| T400 | I1, I2, I4 |
| T500 | I1, I3 |
| T600 | I2, I3 |
| T700 | I1, I3 |
| T800 | I1, I2, I3, I5 |
| T900 | I1, I2, I3 |

**Figure 6.2** Transactional data for an *AllElectronics* branch.

**Example 6.1** Let's look at a concrete example of Apriori, based on the *AllElectronics* transaction database, $D$, of Figure 6.2. There are nine transactions in this database, that is, $|D| = 9$. We use Figure 6.3 to illustrate the Apriori algorithm for finding frequent itemsets in $D$.

1. In the first iteration of the algorithm, each item is a member of the set of candidate 1-itemsets, $C_1$. The algorithm simply scans all of the transactions in order to count the number of occurrences of each item.

2. Suppose that the minimum transaction support count required is 2 (i.e., $min\_sup = 2/9 = 22\%$). The set of frequent 1-itemsets, $L_1$, can then be determined. It consists of the candidate 1-itemsets satisfying minimum support.

3. To discover the set of frequent 2-itemsets, $L_2$, the algorithm uses $L_1 \bowtie L_1$ to generate a candidate set of 2-itemsets, $C_2$.[6] $C_2$ consists of $\binom{|L_1|}{2}$ 2-itemsets.

4. Next, the transactions in $D$ are scanned and the support count of each candidate itemset in $C_2$ is accumulated, as shown in the middle table of the second row in Figure 6.3.

5. The set of frequent 2-itemsets, $L_2$, is then determined, consisting of those candidate 2-itemsets in $C_2$ having minimum support.

6. The generation of the set of candidate 3-itemsets, $C_3$, is detailed in Figure 6.4. First, let $C_3 = L_2 \bowtie L_2 = \{\{I1,I2,I3\}, \{I1,I2,I5\}, \{I1,I3,I5\}, \{I2,I3,I4\}, \{I2,I3,I5\}, \{I2,I4,I5\}\}$. Based on the Apriori property that all subsets of a frequent itemset must also be frequent, we can determine that the four latter candidates cannot

---

[6] $L_1 \bowtie L_1$ is equivalent to $L_1 \times L_1$ since the definition of $L_k \bowtie L_k$ requires the two joining itemsets to share $k - 1 = 0$ items.

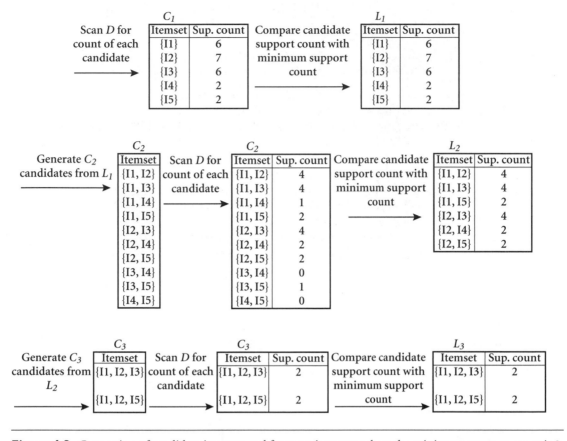

**Figure 6.3** Generation of candidate itemsets and frequent itemsets, where the minimum support count is 2.

possibly be frequent. We therefore remove them from $C_3$, thereby saving the effort of unnecessarily obtaining their counts during the subsequent scan of $D$ to determine $L_3$. Note that when given a candidate $k$-itemset, we only need to check if its $(k-1)$-subsets are frequent since the Apriori algorithm uses a level-wise search strategy.

**7.** The transactions in $D$ are scanned in order to determine $L_3$, consisting of those candidate 3-itemsets in $C_3$ having minimum support (Figure 6.3).

**8.** The algorithm uses $L_3 \bowtie L_3$ to generate a candidate set of 4-itemsets, $C_4$. Although the join results in $\{\{I1,I2,I3,I5\}\}$, this itemset is pruned since its subset $\{\{I2,I3,I5\}\}$ is not frequent. Thus, $C_4 = \phi$, and the algorithm terminates, having found all of the frequent itemsets.  ∎

**1.** Join: $C_3 = L_2 \bowtie L_2 = \{\{I1,I2\}, \{\{I1,I3\}, \{\{I1,I5\}, \{I2,I3\}, \{I2,I4\}, \{I2,I5\}\} \bowtie \{\{I1,I2\}, \{\{I1,I3\}, \{\{I1,I5\}, \{I2,I3\}, \{I2,I4\}, \{I2,I5\}\} = \{\{I1,I2,I3\}, \{I1,I2,I5\}, \{I1,I3,I5\}, \{I2,I3,I4\}, \{I2,I3,I5\}, \{I2,I4,I5\}\}$.

**2.** Prune using the Apriori property: All nonempty subsets of a frequent itemset must also be frequent. Do any of the candidates have a subset that is not frequent?

- The 2-item subsets of $\{I1,I2,I3\}$ are $\{I1,I2\}$, $\{I1,I3\}$, and $\{I2,I3\}$. All 2-item subsets of $\{I1,I2,I3\}$ are members of $L_2$. Therefore, keep $\{I1,I2,I3\}$ in $C_3$.

- The 2-item subsets of $\{I1,I2,I5\}$ are $\{I1,I2\}$, $\{I1,I5\}$, and $\{I2,I5\}$. All 2-item subsets of $\{I1,I2,I5\}$ are members of $L_2$. Therefore, keep $\{I1,I2,I5\}$ in $C_3$.

- The 2-item subsets of $\{I1,I3,I5\}$ are $\{I1,I3\}$, $\{I1,I5\}$, and $\{I3,I5\}$. $\{I3,I5\}$ is not a member of $L_2$, and so it is not frequent. Therefore, remove $\{I1,I3,I5\}$ from $C_3$.

- The 2-item subsets of $\{I2,I3,I4\}$ are $\{I2,I3\}$, $\{I2,I4\}$, and $\{I3,I4\}$. $\{I3,I4\}$ is not a member of $L_2$, and so it is not frequent. Therefore, remove $\{I2,I3,I4\}$ from $C_3$.

- The 2-item subsets of $\{I2,I3,I5\}$ are $\{I2,I3\}$, $\{I2,I5\}$, and $\{I3,I5\}$. $\{I3,I5\}$ is not a member of $L_2$, and so it is not frequent. Therefore, remove $\{I2,I3,I5\}$ from $C_3$.

- The 2-item subsets of $\{I2,I4,I5\}$ are $\{I2,I4\}$, $\{I2,I5\}$, and $\{I4,I5\}$. $\{I4,I5\}$ is not a member of $L_2$, and so it is not frequent. Therefore, remove $\{I2,I4,I5\}$ from $C_3$.

**3.** Therefore, $C_3 = \{\{I1,I2,I3\}, \{I1,I2,I5\}\}$ after pruning.

---

**Figure 6.4** Generation of candidate 3-itemsets, $C_3$, from $L_2$ using the Apriori property.

Figure 6.5 shows pseudocode for the Apriori algorithm and its related procedures. Step 1 of Apriori finds the frequent 1-itemsets, $L_1$. In steps 2–10, $L_{k-1}$ is used to generate candidates $C_k$ in order to find $L_k$. The `apriori_gen` procedure generates the candidates and then uses the Apriori property to eliminate those having a subset that is not frequent (step 3). This procedure is described below. Once all the candidates have been generated, the database is scanned (step 4). For each transaction, a `subset` function is used to find all subsets of the transaction that are candidates (step 5), and the count for each of these candidates is accumulated (steps 6 and 7). Finally, all those candidates satisfying minimum support form the set of frequent itemsets, $L$. A procedure can then be called to generate association rules from the frequent itemsets. Such a procedure is described in Section 6.2.2.

The `apriori_gen` procedure performs two kinds of actions, namely, **join** and **prune**, as described above. In the join component, $L_{k-1}$ is joined with $L_{k-1}$ to generate potential candidates (steps 1–4). The prune component (steps 5–7) employs the Apriori property to remove candidates that have a subset that is not frequent. The test for infrequent subsets is shown in procedure `has_infrequent_subset`.

**Algorithm:** **Apriori.** Find frequent itemsets using an iterative level-wise approach based on candidate generation.

**Input:** Database, $D$, of transactions; minimum support threshold, *min_sup*.

**Output:** $L$, frequent itemsets in $D$.

**Method:**

(1)    $L_1$ = find_frequent_1 itemsets(D);
(2)    for $(k = 2; L_{k-1} \neq \phi; k++)$ {
(3)        $C_k = $ **apriori_gen**$(L_{k-1}, min\_sup)$;
(4)        for each transaction $t \in D$ { // scan $D$ for counts
(5)            $C_t = $ subset$(C_k, t)$; // get the subsets of $t$ that are candidates
(6)            for each candidate $c \in C_t$
(7)                c.count++;
(8)        }
(9)        $L_k = \{c \in C_k | c.count \geq min\_sup\}$
(10)    }
(11)    return $L = \cup_k L_k$;

**procedure apriori_gen**$(L_{k-1}$: frequent $(k-1)$-itemsets; *min_sup*: minimum support threshold)
(1)    for each itemset $l_1 \in L_{k-1}$
(2)        for each itemset $l_2 \in L_{k-1}$
(3)            if $(l_1[1] = l_2[1]) \wedge (l_1[2] = l_2[2]) \wedge ... \wedge (l_1[k-2] = l_2[k-2]) \wedge (l_1[k-1] < l_2[k-1])$ then {
(4)                $c = l_1 \bowtie l_2$; // join step: generate candidates
(5)                if **has_infrequent_subset**$(c, L_{k-1})$ then
(6)                    delete $c$; // prune step: remove unfruitful candidate
(7)                else add $c$ to $C_k$;
(8)            }
(9)    return $C_k$;

**procedure has_infrequent_subset**$(c$: candidate $k$-itemset; $L_{k-1}$: frequent $(k-1)$-itemsets);
            // use prior knowledge
(1)    for each $(k-1)$-subset $s$ of $c$
(2)        if $s \notin L_{k-1}$ then
(3)            return TRUE;
(4)    return FALSE;

---

**Figure 6.5** The Apriori algorithm for discovering frequent itemsets for mining Boolean association rules.

## 6.2.2 Generating Association Rules from Frequent Itemsets

Once the frequent itemsets from transactions in a database $D$ have been found, it is straightforward to generate strong association rules from them (where *strong* association rules satisfy both minimum support and minimum confidence). This can be done using the following equation for confidence, where the conditional probability is expressed in terms of itemset support count:

$$confidence(A \Rightarrow B) = P(B|A) = \frac{support\_count(A \cup B)}{support\_count(A)}, \tag{6.8}$$

where $support\_count(A \cup B)$ is the number of transactions containing the itemsets $A \cup B$, and $support\_count(A)$ is the number of transactions containing the itemset $A$. Based on this equation, association rules can be generated as follows:

- For each frequent itemset $l$, generate all nonempty subsets of $l$.

- For every nonempty subset $s$ of $l$, output the rule "$s \Rightarrow (l - s)$" if $\frac{support\_count(l)}{support\_count(s)} \geq$ $min\_conf$, where $min\_conf$ is the minimum confidence threshold.

Since the rules are generated from frequent itemsets, each one automatically satisfies minimum support. Frequent itemsets can be stored ahead of time in hash tables along with their counts so that they can be accessed quickly.

**Example 6.2** Let's try an example based on the transactional data for *AllElectronics* shown in Figure 6.2. Suppose the data contain the frequent itemset $l = \{I1,I2,I5\}$. What are the association rules that can be generated from $l$? The nonempty subsets of $l$ are $\{I1,I2\}$, $\{I1,I5\}$, $\{I2,I5\}$, $\{I1\}$, $\{I2\}$, and $\{I5\}$. The resulting association rules are as shown below, each listed with its confidence:

$$
\begin{aligned}
&I1 \wedge I2 \Rightarrow I5, &&confidence= 2/4 = 50\% \\
&I1 \wedge I5 \Rightarrow I2, &&confidence= 2/2 = 100\% \\
&I2 \wedge I5 \Rightarrow I1, &&confidence= 2/2 = 100\% \\
&I1 \Rightarrow I2 \wedge I5, &&confidence= 2/6 = 33\% \\
&I2 \Rightarrow I1 \wedge I5, &&confidence= 2/7 = 29\% \\
&I5 \Rightarrow I1 \wedge I2, &&confidence= 2/2 = 100\%
\end{aligned}
$$

If the minimum confidence threshold is, say, 70%, then only the second, third, and last rules above are output, since these are the only ones generated that are strong. ∎

## 6.2.3 Improving the Efficiency of Apriori

*"How might the efficiency of Apriori be improved?"* Many variations of the Apriori algorithm have been proposed that focus on improving the efficiency of the original algorithm. Several of these variations are enumerated below.

Create hash table $H_2$
using hash function
$h(x, y) = ((order\ of\ x) \times 10 + (order\ of\ y))\ mod\ 7$
⟶

$H_2$

| bucket address | 0 | 1 | 2 | 3 | 4 | 5 | 6 |
|---|---|---|---|---|---|---|---|
| bucket count | 2 | 2 | 4 | 2 | 2 | 4 | 4 |
| bucket contents | {I1, I4} {I3, I5} | {I1, I5} {I1, I5} | {I2, I3} {I2, I3} {I2, I3} {I2, I3} | {I2, I4} {I2, I4} | {I2, I5} {I2, I5} | {I1, I2} {I1, I2} {I1, I2} {I1, I2} | {I1, I3} {I1, I3} {I1, I3} {I1, I3} |

**Figure 6.6** Hash table, $H_2$, for candidate 2-itemsets: This hash table was generated by scanning the transactions of Figure 6.2 while determining $L_1$ from $C_1$. If the minimum support count is, say, 3, then the itemsets in buckets 0, 1, 3, and 4 cannot be frequent and so they should not be included in $C_2$.

**Hash-based technique (hashing itemset counts):** A hash-based technique can be used to reduce the size of the candidate $k$-itemsets, $C_k$, for $k > 1$. For example, when scanning each transaction in the database to generate the frequent 1-itemsets, $L_1$, from the candidate 1-itemsets in $C_1$, we can generate all of the 2-itemsets for each transaction, hash (i.e., map) them into the different *buckets* of a *hash table* structure, and increase the corresponding bucket counts (Figure 6.6). A 2-itemset whose corresponding bucket count in the hash table is below the support threshold cannot be frequent and thus should be removed from the candidate set. Such a hash-based technique may substantially reduce the number of the candidate $k$-itemsets examined (especially when $k = 2$).

**Transaction reduction (reducing the number of transactions scanned in future iterations):** A transaction that does not contain any frequent $k$-itemsets cannot contain any frequent $(k + 1)$-itemsets. Therefore, such a transaction can be marked or removed from further consideration since subsequent scans of the database for $j$-itemsets, where $j > k$, will not require it.

**Partitioning (partitioning the data to find candidate itemsets):** A partitioning technique can be used that requires just two database scans to mine the frequent itemsets (Figure 6.7). It consists of two phases. In Phase I, the algorithm subdivides the transactions of $D$ into $n$ nonoverlapping partitions. If the minimum support threshold for transactions in $D$ is *min_sup*, then the minimum itemset support count for a partition is *min_sup* × *the number of transactions in that partition*. For each partition, all frequent itemsets within the partition are found. These are referred to as **local frequent itemsets**. The procedure employs a special data structure that, for each itemset, records the TIDs of the transactions containing the items in the itemset. This allows it to find all of the local frequent $k$-itemsets, for $k = 1, 2, \ldots$, in just one scan of the database.

A local frequent itemset may or may not be frequent with respect to the entire database, $D$. *Any itemset that is potentially frequent with respect to $D$ must occur as a frequent itemset in at least one of the partitions.* Therefore, all

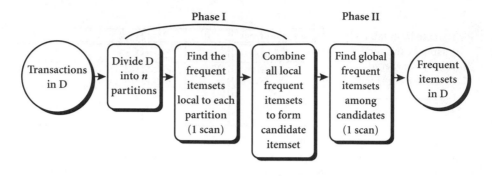

**Figure 6.7** Mining by partitioning the data.

local frequent itemsets are candidate itemsets with respect to $D$. The collection of frequent itemsets from all partitions forms the **global candidate itemsets** with respect to $D$. In Phase II, a second scan of $D$ is conducted in which the actual support of each candidate is assessed in order to determine the global frequent itemsets. Partition size and the number of partitions are set so that each partition can fit into main memory and therefore be read only once in each phase.

**Sampling (mining on a subset of the given data):**    The basic idea of the sampling approach is to pick a random sample $S$ of the given data $D$, and then search for frequent itemsets in $S$ instead of $D$. In this way, we trade off some degree of accuracy against efficiency. The sample size of $S$ is such that the search for frequent itemsets in $S$ can be done in main memory, and so only one scan of the transactions in $S$ is required overall. Because we are searching for frequent itemsets in $S$ rather than in $D$, it is possible that we will miss some of the global frequent itemsets. To lessen this possibility, we use a lower support threshold than minimum support to find the frequent itemsets local to $S$ (denoted $L^S$). The rest of the database is then used to compute the actual frequencies of each itemset in $L^S$. A mechanism is used to determine whether all of the global frequent itemsets are included in $L^S$. If $L^S$ actually contains all of the frequent itemsets in $D$, then only one scan of $D$ is required. Otherwise, a second pass can be done in order to find the frequent itemsets that were missed in the first pass. The sampling approach is especially beneficial when efficiency is of utmost importance, such as in computationally intensive applications that must be run on a very frequent basis.

**Dynamic itemset counting (adding candidate itemsets at different points during a scan):**    A dynamic itemset counting technique was proposed in which the database is partitioned into blocks marked by start points. In this variation, new candidate itemsets can be added at any start point, unlike in Apriori, which determines new candidate itemsets only immediately prior to each complete database scan. The technique is dynamic in that it estimates the support of all of the itemsets that have been counted so far, adding new candidate itemsets if all of their subsets are estimated to be frequent. The resulting algorithm requires fewer database scans than Apriori.

Other variations involving the mining of multilevel and multidimensional association rules are discussed in the rest of this chapter. The mining of associations related to spatial data, time-series data, and multimedia data are discussed in Chapter 9.

## 6.2.4 Mining Frequent Itemsets without Candidate Generation

As we have seen, in many cases the Apriori candidate generate-and-test method reduces the size of candidate sets significantly and leads to good performance gain. However, it may suffer from two nontrivial costs.

- **It may need to generate a huge number of candidate sets.** For example, if there are $10^4$ frequent 1-itemsets, the Apriori algorithm will need to generate more than $10^7$ candidate 2-itemsets and accumulate and test their occurrence frequencies. Moreover, to discover a frequent pattern of size 100, such as $\{a_1, \ldots, a_{100}\}$, it must generate more than $2^{100} \approx 10^{30}$ candidates in total.

- **It may need to repeatedly scan the database and check a large set of candidates by pattern matching.** This is especially the case for mining long patterns.

*"Can we design a method that mines the complete set of frequent itemsets without candidate generation?"* An interesting method in this attempt is called **frequent-pattern growth,** or simply **FP-growth,** which adopts a *divide-and-conquer* strategy as follows: compress the database representing frequent items into a **frequent-pattern tree,** or **FP-tree,** but retain the itemset association information, and then divide such a compressed database into a set of *conditional databases* (a special kind of projected database), each associated with one frequent item, and mine each such database separately. Let's look at an example.

**Example 6.3** We reexamine the mining of transaction database, $D$, of Figure 6.2 in Example 6.1 using the frequent-pattern growth approach.

The first scan of the database is the same as Apriori, which derives the set of frequent items (1-itemsets) and their support counts (frequencies). Let the minimum support count be 2. The set of frequent items is sorted in the order of descending support count. This resulting set or *list* is denoted $L$. Thus, we have $L = [I2: 7, I1: 6, I3: 6, I4: 2, I5: 2]$.

An FP-tree is then constructed as follows. First, create the root of the tree, labeled with "null". Scan database $D$ a second time. The items in each transaction are processed in $L$ order (i.e., sorted according to descending support count) and a branch is created for each transaction. For example, the scan of the first transaction, "T100: I1, I2, I5", which contains three items (I2, I1, I5) in *L* order, leads to the construction of the first branch of the tree with three nodes: $\langle$(I2: 1), (I1: 1), (I5: 1)$\rangle$, where I2 is linked as a child of the root, I1 is linked to I2, and I5 is linked to I1. The second transaction, T200, contains the items I2 and I4 in *L* order, which would result in a branch where I2 is linked to the root and I4 is linked to I2. However, this branch would share a common **prefix**, $\langle$I2$\rangle$, with the existing path for T100. Therefore, we instead increment the count of the I2 node by 1, and create a new node, (I4: 1), which is linked as a child of (I2: 2). In general, when considering the branch to be added for a transaction, the count of each node along a common prefix is incremented by 1, and nodes for the items following the prefix are created and linked accordingly.

To facilitate tree traversal, an item header table is built so that each item points to its occurrences in the tree via a chain of **node-links**. The tree obtained after scanning all of the transactions is shown in Figure 6.8 with the associated node-links. Therefore, the problem of mining frequent patterns in databases is transformed to that of mining the FP-tree.

The mining of the FP-tree proceeds as follows. Start from each frequent length-1 pattern (as an initial **suffix pattern**), construct its **conditional pattern base** (a "subdatabase" which consists of the set of *prefix paths* in the FP-tree co-occurring with the suffix pattern), then construct its (*conditional*) FP-tree, and perform mining recursively on such a tree. The pattern growth is achieved by the concatenation of the suffix pattern with the frequent patterns generated from a conditional FP-tree.

Mining of the FP-tree is summarized in Table 6.1 and detailed as follows. Let's first consider I5 which is the last item in *L*, rather than the first. The reasoning behind this will become apparent as we explain the FP-tree mining process. I5

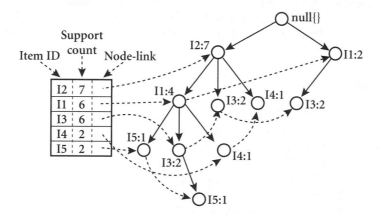

**Figure 6.8** An FP-tree that registers compressed, frequent pattern information.

**Table 6.1** Mining the FP-tree by creating conditional (sub)pattern bases.

| item | conditional pattern base | conditional FP-tree | frequent patterns generated |
|------|--------------------------|---------------------|-----------------------------|
| I5 | {(I2 I1: 1), (I2 I1 I3: 1)} | ⟨I2: 2, I1: 2⟩ | I2 I5: 2, I1 I5: 2, I2 I1 I5: 2 |
| I4 | {(I2 I1: 1), (I2: 1)} | ⟨I2: 2⟩ | I2 I4: 2 |
| I3 | {(I2 I1: 2), (I2: 2), (I1: 2)} | ⟨I2: 4, I1: 2⟩, ⟨I1: 2⟩ | I2 I3: 4, I1 I3: 4, I2 I1 I3: 2 |
| I1 | {(I2: 4)} | ⟨I2: 4⟩ | I2 I1: 4 |

occurs in two branches of the FP-tree of Figure 6.8. (The occurrences of I5 can easily be found by following its chain of node-links.) The paths formed by these branches are ⟨(I2 I1 I5: 1)⟩ and ⟨(I2 I1 I3 I5: 1)⟩. Therefore, considering I5 as a suffix, its corresponding two prefix paths are ⟨(I2 I1: 1)⟩ and ⟨(I2 I1 I3: 1)⟩, which form its conditional pattern base. Its conditional FP-tree contains only a single path, ⟨I2: 2, I1: 2⟩; I3 is not included because its support count of 1 is less than the minimum support count. The single path generates all the combinations of frequent patterns: I2 I5: 2, I1 I5: 2, I2 I1 I5: 2.

For I4, its two prefix paths form the conditional pattern base, {(I2 I1: 1), (I2: 1)}, which generates a single-node conditional FP-tree ⟨I2: 2⟩ and derives one frequent pattern, I2 I1: 2. Notice that although I5 follows I4 in the first branch, there is no need to include I5 in the analysis here since any frequent pattern involving I5 has been analyzed in the examination of I5. This is the reason that we started processing at the end of $L$, rather than at the front.

Similar to the above analysis, I3's conditional pattern base is {(I2 I1: 2), (I2: 2), (I1: 2)}. Its conditional FP-tree has two branches, ⟨I2: 4, I1: 2⟩ and ⟨I1: 2⟩, as shown in Figure 6.9, which generates the set of patterns: {I2 I3: 4, I1 I3: 2, I2 I1 I3: 2}. Finally, I1's conditional pattern base is {(I2: 4)}, whose FP-tree contains only one node ⟨I2: 4⟩, which generates one frequent pattern, I2 I1: 4. This mining process is summarized in Figure 6.10. ∎

The FP-growth method transforms the problem of finding long frequent patterns to looking for shorter ones recursively and then concatenating the suffix.

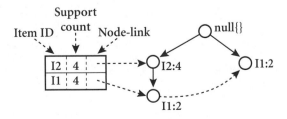

**Figure 6.9** The conditional FP-tree associated with the conditional node I3.

**Algorithm: FP_growth.** Mine frequent patterns using an FP-tree by pattern fragment growth.

**Input:** A transaction database, $D$; minimum support threshold, *min_sup*.

**Output:** The complete set of frequent patterns.

**Method:**

1. The FP-tree is constructed in the following steps.

   (a) Scan the transaction database $D$ once. Collect the set of frequent items $F$ and their supports. Sort $F$ in support descending order as $L$, the *list* of frequent items.

   (b) Create the root of an FP-tree, and label it as "null". For each transaction *Trans* in $D$ do the following.

      Select and sort the frequent items in *Trans* according to the order of $L$. Let the sorted frequent item list in *Trans* be $[p|P]$, where $p$ is the first element and $P$ is the remaining list. Call **insert_tree**($[p|P]$, $T$), which is performed as follows. If $T$ has a child $N$ such that $N.item\text{-}name = p.item\text{-}name$, then increment $N$'s count by 1; else create a new node $N$, and let its count be 1, its parent link be linked to $T$, and its node-link to the nodes with the same *item-name* via the node-link structure. If $P$ is nonempty, call **insert_tree**($P$, $N$) recursively.

2. Mining of an FP-tree is performed by calling **FP_growth**($FP\_tree$, *null*), which is implemented as follows.

   **procedure FP_growth**($Tree$, $\alpha$)
   (1)    **if** $Tree$ contains a single path $P$ **then**
   (2)        **for each** combination (denoted as $\beta$) of the nodes in the path $P$
   (3)           generate pattern $\beta \cup \alpha$ with *support = minimum support of nodes in $\beta$*;
   (4)    **else for each** $a_i$ in the header of $Tree$ {
   (5)        generate pattern $\beta = a_i \cup \alpha$ with *support = $a_i.support$*;
   (6)        construct $\beta$'s conditional pattern base and then $\beta$'s conditional
                 FP_tree $Tree_\beta$;
   (7)        **if** $Tree_\beta \neq \emptyset$ **then**
   (8)           call **FP_growth**($Tree_\beta$, $\beta$); }

---

**Figure 6.10** The FP-growth algorithm for discovering frequent itemsets without candidate generation.

It uses the least frequent items as a suffix, offering good selectivity. The method substantially reduces the search costs.

When the database is large, it is sometimes unrealistic to construct a main memory-based FP-tree. An interesting alternative is to first partition the database into a set of projected databases, and then construct an FP-tree and mine it in each projected database. Such a process can be recursively applied to any projected database if its FP-tree still cannot fit in main memory.

A study on the performance of the FP-growth method shows that it is efficient and scalable for mining both long and short frequent patterns, and is about an order of magnitude faster than the Apriori algorithm. It is also faster than a Tree-Projection algorithm which projects a database into a tree of projected databases recursively.

## 6.2.5 Iceberg Queries

The Apriori algorithm can be used to improve the efficiency of answering *iceberg queries*. Iceberg queries are commonly used in data mining, particularly for market basket analysis. An **iceberg query** computes an aggregate function over an attribute or set of attributes in order to find aggregate values above some specified threshold. Given a relation $R$ with attributes $a\_1, a\_2, \ldots, a\_n$ and $b$, and an aggregate function, *agg_f*, an iceberg query is of the form

| | |
|---|---|
| **select** | R.a\_1, R.a\_2, . . . , R.a\_n, agg_f(R.b) |
| **from** | relation R |
| **group by** | R.a\_1, R.a\_2, . . . , R.a\_n |
| **having** | agg_f(R.b) >= threshold |

Given the large quantity of input data tuples, the number of tuples that will satisfy the threshold in the **having** clause is relatively small. The output result is seen as the "tip of the iceberg," where the "iceberg" is the set of input data.

**Example 6.4** **An iceberg query:** Suppose that, given sales data, you would like to generate a list of customer-item pairs for customers who have purchased items in a quantity of three or more. This can be expressed with the following iceberg query.

| | |
|---|---|
| **select** | P.cust_ID, P.item_ID, SUM(P.qty) |
| **from** | Purchases P |
| **group by** | P.cust_ID, P.item_ID |
| **having** | SUM(P.qty) >= 3 |

∎

*"How can the query of Example 6.4 be answered?"* you ask. A common strategy is to apply hashing or sorting to compute the value of the aggregate function, SUM, for all of the customer-item groups, and then remove those for which the quantity of items purchased by the given customer was less than three. The number of tuples satisfying this condition is likely to be small with respect to the total number of tuples processed, leaving room for improvements in efficiency. Alternatively, we can use a variation of the Apriori property to prune the number of customer-item pairs considered. That is, instead of looking at the quantities of each item purchased by each customer, we can do the following:

■ Generate *cust_list*, a list of customers who bought three or more items in total, for example,

```
select      P.cust_ID
from        Purchases P
group by    P.cust_ID
having      SUM(P.qty) >= 3
```

■ Generate *item_list*, a list of items that were purchased by any customer in quantities of three or more, for example,

```
select      P.item_ID
from        Purchases P
group by    P.item_ID
having      SUM(P.qty) >= 3
```

From this a priori knowledge, we can eliminate many of the customer-item pairs that would otherwise have been generated in the hashing/sorting approach: only generate candidate customer-item pairs for customers in *cust_list* and items in *item_list*. A count is maintained for such pairs. While the approach improves efficiency by pruning many pairs or groups a priori, the resulting number of customer-item pairs may still be so large that it does not fit into main memory. Hashing and sampling strategies may be integrated into the process to help improve the overall efficiency of this query answering technique.

## 6.3 Mining Multilevel Association Rules from Transaction Databases

In this section, you will learn methods for mining multilevel association rules, that is, rules involving items at different levels of abstraction. Methods for checking for redundant multilevel rules are also discussed.

### 6.3.1 Multilevel Association Rules

For many applications, it is difficult to find strong associations among data items at low or primitive levels of abstraction due to the sparsity of data in multidimensional space. Strong associations discovered at high concept levels may represent common sense knowledge. However, what may represent common sense to one user may seem novel to another. Therefore, data mining systems should provide capabilities to mine association rules at multiple levels of abstraction and traverse easily among different abstraction spaces.

Let's examine the following example.

**Table 6.2**  Task-relevant data, $D$.

| TID | Items purchased |
| --- | --- |
| T1 | IBM desktop computer, Sony b/w printer |
| T2 | Microsoft educational software, Microsoft financial management software |
| T3 | Logitech mouse computer accessory, Ergoway wrist pad computer accessory |
| T4 | IBM desktop computer, Microsoft financial management software |
| T5 | IBM desktop computer |
| ⋮ | ⋮ |

**Example 6.5**  Suppose we are given the task-relevant set of transactional data in Table 6.2 for sales at the computer department of an *AllElectronics* branch, showing the items purchased for each transaction TID. The concept hierarchy for the items is shown in Figure 6.11. A concept hierarchy defines a sequence of mappings from a set of low-level concepts to higher-level, more general concepts. Data can be generalized by replacing low-level concepts within the data by their higher-level concepts, or *ancestors*, from a concept hierarchy.[7] The concept hierarchy of Figure 6.11 has four levels, referred to as levels 0, 1, 2, and 3. By convention, levels within a concept hierarchy are numbered from top to bottom, starting with level 0 at the root node for **all** (the most general abstraction level). Here, level 1 includes *computer, software, printer,* and *computer accessory*, level 2 includes *desktop computer, laptop computer, educational software, financial management software, . . . ,* and level 3 includes *IBM desktop computer, . . . , Microsoft educational software,* and so on. Level 3 represents the most specific abstraction level of this hierarchy. Concept hierarchies may be specified by users familiar with the data or may exist implicitly in the data.

The items in Table 6.2 are at the lowest level of the concept hierarchy of Figure 6.11. It is difficult to find interesting purchase patterns at such raw or primitive-level data. For instance, if *"IBM desktop computer"* or *"Sony b/w (black and white) printer"* each occurs in a very small fraction of the transactions, then it may be difficult to find strong associations involving such items. Few people may buy such items together, making it unlikely that the itemset *"{IBM desktop computer, Sony b/w printer}"* will satisfy minimum support. However, consider the generalization of *"Sony b/w printer"* to *"b/w printer"*. One would expect that it is easier to find strong associations between *"IBM desktop computer"* and *"b/w printer"* than between *"IBM desktop computer"* and *"Sony b/w printer"*. Similarly, many people may purchase *"computer"* and *"printer"* together, rather than specifically

---

[7] Concept hierarchies were described in detail in Chapters 2 and 4. In order to make the chapters of this book as self-contained as possible, we offer their definition again here. Generalization was described in Chapter 5.

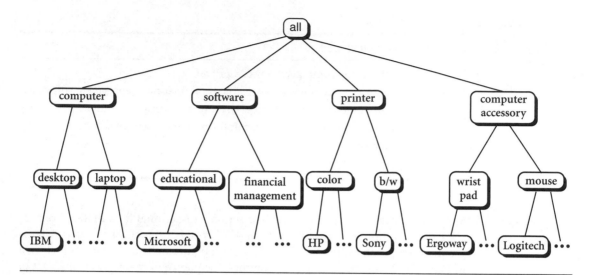

**Figure 6.11**    A concept hierarchy for *AllElectronics* computer items.

purchasing *"IBM desktop computer"* and *"Sony b/w printer"* together. In other words, itemsets containing generalized items, such as *"{IBM desktop computer, b/w printer}"* and *"{computer, printer}"* are more likely to have minimum support than itemsets containing only primitive-level data, such as *"{IBM desktop computer, Sony b/w printer}"*. Hence, it is easier to find interesting associations among items at *multiple* concept levels, rather than only among low-level data.  ■

Rules generated from association rule mining with concept hierarchies are called **multiple-level** or **multilevel association rules**, since they consider more than one concept level.

## 6.3.2  Approaches to Mining Multilevel Association Rules

*"How can we mine multilevel association rules efficiently using concept hierarchies?"* Let's look at some approaches based on a support-confidence framework. In general, a top-down strategy is employed, where counts are accumulated for the calculation of frequent itemsets at each concept level, starting at the concept level 1 and working towards the lower, more specific concept levels, until no more frequent itemsets can be found. That is, once all frequent itemsets at concept level 1 are found, then the frequent itemsets at level 2 are found, and so on. For each level, any algorithm for discovering frequent itemsets may be used, such as Apriori or its variations. A number of variations to this approach are described below and illustrated in Figures 6.12 to 6.16, where nodes indicate an item or itemset that

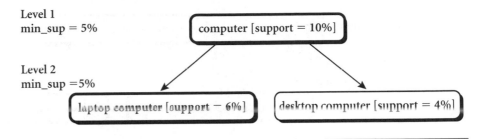

**Figure 6.12**  Multilevel mining with uniform support.

has been examined, and nodes with thick borders indicate that an examined item or itemset is frequent.

- **Using uniform minimum support for all levels** (referred to as **uniform support**): The same minimum support threshold is used when mining at each level of abstraction. For example, in Figure 6.12, a minimum support threshold of 5% is used throughout (e.g., for mining from "*computer*" down to "*laptop computer*"). Both "*computer*" and "*laptop computer*" are found to be frequent, while "*desktop computer*" is not.

  When a uniform minimum support threshold is used, the search procedure is simplified. The method is also simple in that users are required to specify only one minimum support threshold. An optimization technique can be adopted, based on the knowledge that an ancestor is a superset of its descendents: the search avoids examining itemsets containing any item whose ancestors do not have minimum support.

  The uniform support approach, however, has some difficulties. It is unlikely that items at lower levels of abstraction will occur as frequently as those at higher levels of abstraction. If the minimum support threshold is set too high, it could miss several meaningful associations occurring at low abstraction levels. If the threshold is set too low, it may generate many uninteresting associations occurring at high abstraction levels. This provides the motivation for the following approach.

- **Using reduced minimum support at lower levels** (referred to as **reduced support**): Each level of abstraction has its own minimum support threshold. The lower the abstraction level, the smaller the corresponding threshold. For example, in Figure 6.13, the minimum support thresholds for levels 1 and 2 are 5% and 3%, respectively. In this way, "*computer*", "*laptop computer*", and "*desktop computer*" are all considered frequent.

For mining multiple-level associations with *reduced support*, there are a number of alternative search strategies:

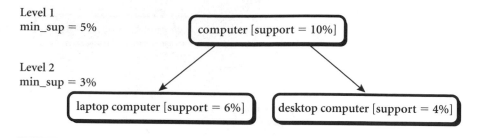

**Figure 6.13** Multilevel mining with reduced support.

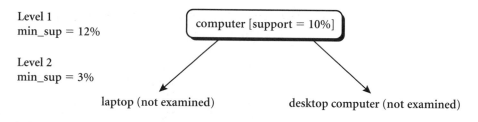

**Figure 6.14** Multilevel mining with reduced support, using level-cross filtering by a single item.

- **Level-by-level independent:** This is a full-breadth search, where no background knowledge of frequent itemsets is used for pruning. Each node is examined, regardless of whether or not its parent node is found to be frequent.

- **Level-cross filtering by single item:** An item at the $i$th level is examined if and only if its parent node at the $(i - 1)$th level is frequent. In other words, we investigate a more specific association from a more general one. If a node is frequent, its children will be examined; otherwise, its descendents are pruned from the search. For example, in Figure 6.14, the descendent nodes of *"computer"* (i.e., *"laptop computer"* and *"desktop computer"*) are not examined, since *"computer"* is not frequent.

- **Level-cross filtering by $k$-itemset:** A $k$-itemset at the $i$th level is examined if and only if its corresponding parent $k$-itemset at the $(i - 1)$th level is frequent. For example, in Figure 6.15, the 2-itemset *"{computer, printer}"* is frequent, therefore the nodes *"{laptop computer, b/w printer}"*, *"{laptop computer, color printer}"*, *"{desktop computer, b/w printer}"*, and *"{desktop computer, color printer}"* are examined.

*"How do these methods compare?"* The *level-by-level independent* strategy is very relaxed in that it may lead to examining numerous infrequent items at low levels, finding associations between items of little importance. For example, if *"computer*

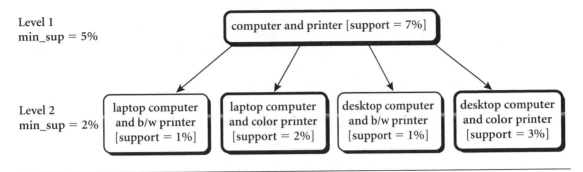

**Figure 6.15**  Multilevel mining with reduced support, using level-cross filtering by a $k$-itemset. Here, $k = 2$.

*furniture*" is rarely purchased, it may not be beneficial to examine whether the more specific "*computer chair*" is associated with "*laptop*". However, if "*computer accessories*" are sold frequently, it may be beneficial to see whether there is an associated purchase pattern between "*laptop*" and "*mouse*".

The *level-cross filtering by k-itemset* strategy allows the mining system to examine only the children of frequent $k$-itemsets. This restriction is very strong in that there usually are not many $k$-itemsets that, when combined, are also frequent (especially when $k > 2$). Hence, many valuable patterns may be filtered out using this approach.

The *level-cross filtering by single item* strategy represents a compromise between the two extremes. However, this method may miss associations between low-level items that are frequent based on a reduced minimum support, but whose ancestors do not satisfy minimum support (since the support thresholds at each level can be different). For example, if "*color monitor*" occurring at concept level $i$ is frequent based on the minimum support threshold of level $i$, but its parent "*monitor*" at level $(i - 1)$ is not frequent according to the minimum support threshold of level $(i - 1)$, then frequent associations such as "*desktop computer* $\Rightarrow$ *color monitor*" will be missed.

A modified version of the *level-cross filtering by single item* strategy, known as the **controlled level-cross filtering by single item** strategy, addresses the above concern as follows. A threshold, called the **level passage threshold**, can be set up for "passing down" relatively frequent items (called **subfrequent items**) to lower levels. In other words, this method allows the children of items that do not satisfy the minimum support threshold to be examined if these items satisfy the level passage threshold. Each concept level can have its own level passage threshold. The level passage threshold for a given level is typically set to a value between the minimum support threshold of the next lower level and the minimum support threshold of the given level. Users may choose to "slide down" or lower the level passage threshold at high concept levels to allow the descendents of the subfrequent items at lower levels to be examined. Sliding the level passage

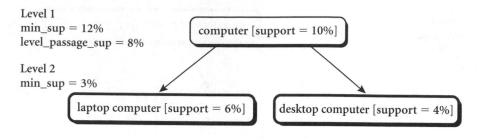

**Figure 6.16** Multilevel mining with controlled level-cross filtering by single item.

threshold down to the minimum support threshold of the lowest level would allow the descendents of all of the items to be examined. For example, in Figure 6.16, setting the level passage threshold (*level_passage_sup*) of level 1 to 8% allows the nodes "*laptop computer*" and "*desktop computer*" at level 2 to be examined and found frequent, even though their parent node, "*computer*", is not frequent. By adding this mechanism, users have the flexibility to further control the mining process at multiple abstraction levels, as well as reduce the number of meaningless associations that would otherwise be examined and generated.

So far, our discussion has focused on finding frequent itemsets where all items within the itemset must belong to the same concept level. This may result in rules such as "*computer* ⟹ *printer*" (where "*computer*" and "*printer*" are both at concept level 1) and "*desktop computer* ⟹ *b/w printer*" (where "*desktop computer*" and "*b/w printer*" are both at level 2 of the given concept hierarchy). Suppose, instead, that we would like to find rules that *cross concept level boundaries*, such as "*computer* ⟹ *b/w printer*", where items within the rule are not required to belong to the same concept level. These rules are called **cross-level association rules**.

"*How can cross-level associations be mined?*" If mining associations from concept levels $i$ and $j$, where level $j$ is more specific (i.e., at a lower abstraction level) than $i$, then the reduced minimum support threshold of level $j$ should be used overall so that items from level $j$ can be included in the analysis.

## 6.3.3 Checking for Redundant Multilevel Association Rules

Concept hierarchies are useful in data mining since they permit the discovery of knowledge at different levels of abstraction, such as multilevel association rules. However, when multilevel association rules are mined, some of the rules found will be redundant due to "ancestor" relationships between items. For example, consider the following rules where "*desktop computer*" is an ancestor of "*IBM desktop computer*" based on the concept hierarchy of Figure 6.11.

$$desktop\ computer \Rightarrow b/w\ printer \quad [support = 8\%, confidence = 70\%] \quad (6.9)$$

$$IBM\ desktop\ computer \Rightarrow b/w\ printer$$

$$[support = 2\%, confidence = 72\%] \quad (6.10)$$

*"If Rules (6.9) and (6.10) are both mined, then how useful is the latter rule?"* you may wonder. *"Does it really provide any novel information?"* If the latter, less general rule does not provide new information, it should be removed. Let's have a look at how this may be determined. A rule, $R1$, is an **ancestor** of a rule, $R2$, if $R1$ can be obtained by replacing the items in $R2$ by their ancestors in a concept hierarchy. For example, Rule (6.9) is an ancestor of Rule (6.10) since *"desktop computer"* is an ancestor of *"IBM desktop computer"*. Based on this definition, a rule can be considered redundant if its support and confidence are close to their "expected" values, based on an ancestor of the rule. As an illustration, suppose that Rule (6.9) has a 70% confidence and 8% support, and that about one quarter of all *"desktop computer"* sales are for *"IBM desktop computers"*. One may expect Rule (6.10) to have a confidence of around 70% (since all data samples of *"IBM desktop computer"* are also samples of *"desktop computer"*) and a support of around 2% (i.e., $8\% \times \frac{1}{4}$). If this is indeed the case, then Rule (6.10) is not interesting since it does not offer any additional information and is less general than Rule (6.9).

# 6.4 Mining Multidimensional Association Rules from Relational Databases and Data Warehouses

In this section, you will learn methods for mining multidimensional association rules, that is, rules involving more than one dimension or predicate (e.g., rules relating what a customer *buys* as well as the customer's *age*). These methods can be organized according to their treatment of quantitative attributes.

## 6.4.1 Multidimensional Association Rules

So far in this chapter, we have studied association rules that imply a single predicate, that is, the predicate *buys*. For instance, in mining our *AllElectronics* database, we may discover the Boolean association rule *"IBM desktop computer $\Rightarrow$ Sony b/w printer"*, which can also be written as

$$buys(X, ``IBM\ desktop\ computer") \Rightarrow buys(X, ``Sony\ b/w\ printer") \quad (6.11)$$

where $X$ is a variable representing customers who purchased items in *AllElectronics* transactions. Following the terminology used in multidimensional databases, we refer to each distinct predicate in a rule as a dimension. Hence, we can refer to Rule (6.11) as a **single-dimensional** or **intradimension association rule** since it contains a single distinct predicate (e.g., *buys*) with multiple occurrences (i.e., the predicate occurs more than once within the rule). As we have seen in the previous sections of this chapter, such rules are commonly mined from transactional data.

Suppose, however, that rather than using a transactional database, sales and related information are stored in a relational database or data warehouse. Such data stores are multidimensional, by definition. For instance, in addition to keeping track of the items purchased in sales transactions, a relational database may record other attributes associated with the items, such as the quantity purchased or the price, or the branch location of the sale. Additional relational information regarding the customers who purchased the items, such as customer age, occupation, credit rating, income, and address, may also be stored. Considering each database attribute or warehouse dimension as a predicate, it can therefore be interesting to mine association rules containing *multiple* predicates, such as

$$age(X, ``20 \dots 29") \wedge occupation(X, ``student") \Rightarrow buys(X, ``laptop") \quad (6.12)$$

Association rules that involve two or more dimensions or predicates can be referred to as **multidimensional association rules**. Rule (6.12) contains three predicates (*age, occupation*, and *buys*), each of which occurs *only once* in the rule. Hence, we say that it has **no repeated predicates**. Multidimensional association rules with no repeated predicates are called **interdimension association rules**. We may also be interested in mining multidimensional association rules with repeated predicates, which contain multiple occurrences of some predicates. These rules are called **hybrid-dimension association rules**. An example of such a rule is the following, where the predicate *buys* is repeated:

$$age(X, ``20 \dots 29") \wedge buys(X, ``laptop") \Rightarrow buys(X, ``b/w printer") \quad (6.13)$$

Note that database attributes can be categorical or quantitative. **Categorical** attributes have a finite number of possible values, with no ordering among the values (e.g., *occupation, brand, color*). Categorical attributes are also called **nominal** attributes, since their values are "names of things." **Quantitative** attributes are numeric and have an implicit ordering among values (e.g., *age, income, price*). Techniques for mining multidimensional association rules can be categorized according to three basic approaches regarding the treatment of quantitative attributes.

In the first approach, *quantitative attributes are discretized using predefined concept hierarchies*. This discretization occurs prior to mining. For instance, a concept hierarchy for *income* may be used to replace the original numeric values of this attribute by ranges, such as "0 . . . 20K", "21K . . . 30K", "31K . . . 40K", and so on. Here, discretization is *static* and predetermined. The discretized numeric attributes, with their range values, can then be treated as categorical attributes (where each range is considered a category). We refer to this as **mining multidimensional association rules using static discretization of quantitative attributes**.

In the second approach, *quantitative attributes are discretized into "bins" based on the distribution of the data*. These bins may be further combined during the mining process. The discretization process is *dynamic* and established so as to satisfy some mining criteria, such as maximizing the confidence of the rules mined. Because this strategy treats the numeric attribute values as quantities rather than as predefined ranges or categories, association rules mined from this approach are also referred to as **quantitative association rules**.

In the third approach, *quantitative attributes are discretized so as to capture the semantic meaning of such interval data*. This dynamic discretization procedure considers the distance between data points. Hence, such quantitative association rules are also referred to as **distance-based association rules**.

Let's study each of these approaches for mining multidimensional association rules. For simplicity, we confine our discussion to interdimension association rules. Note that rather than searching for frequent itemsets (as is done for single-dimensional association rule mining), in multidimensional association rule mining we search for frequent *predicate sets*. A *k*-**predicate set** is a set containing $k$ conjunctive predicates. For instance, the set of predicates {*age, occupation, buys*} from Rule (6.12) is a 3-predicate set. Similar to the notation used for itemsets, we use the notation $L_k$ to refer to the set of frequent $k$-predicate sets.

## 6.4.2 Mining Multidimensional Association Rules Using Static Discretization of Quantitative Attributes

Quantitative attributes, in this case, are discretized prior to mining using predefined concept hierarchies, where numeric values are replaced by ranges. Categorical attributes may also be generalized to higher conceptual levels if desired. If the resulting task-relevant data are stored in a relational table, then the Apriori algorithm requires just a slight modification so as to find all frequent predicate sets rather than frequent itemsets (i.e., by searching through all of the relevant attributes, instead of searching only one attribute, like *buys*). Finding all frequent $k$-predicate sets will require $k$ or $k + 1$ scans of the table. Other strategies, such as hashing, partitioning, and sampling may be employed to improve the performance.

Alternatively, the transformed task-relevant data may be stored in a *data cube*. Data cubes are well suited for the mining of multidimensional association rules, since they are multidimensional by definition. Data cubes and their computation were discussed in detail in Chapter 2. To review, a data cube consists of a lattice of cuboids that are multidimensional data structures. These structures can hold the given task-relevant data, as well as aggregate, group-by information. Figure 6.17 shows the lattice of cuboids defining a data cube for the dimensions *age*, *income*, and *buys*. The cells of an *n*-dimensional cuboid are used to store the support counts of the corresponding *n*-predicate sets. The base cuboid aggregates the task-relevant data by *age, income*, and *buys*; the 2-D cuboid, *(age, income)*, aggregates by *age* and *income*; the 0-D (apex) cuboid contains the total number of transactions in the task-relevant data, and so on.

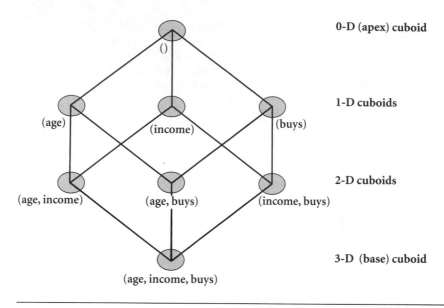

**Figure 6.17** Lattice of cuboids, making up a 3-D data cube. Each cuboid represents a different group-by. The base cuboid contains the three predicates *age, income*, and *buys*.

Due to the ever-increasing use of data warehousing and OLAP technology, it is possible that a data cube containing the dimensions of interest to the user may already exist, fully materialized. *"If this is the case, how can we go about finding the frequent predicate sets?"* A strategy similar to that employed in Apriori can be used, based on prior knowledge that *every subset of a frequent predicate set must also be frequent*. This property can be used to reduce the number of candidate predicate sets generated.

In cases where no relevant data cube exists for the mining task, one must be created. Chapter 2 describes algorithms for fast, efficient computation of data cubes. These can be modified to search for frequent itemsets during cube construction.

### 6.4.3 Mining Quantitative Association Rules

Quantitative association rules are multidimensional association rules in which the numeric attributes are *dynamically* discretized during the mining process so as to satisfy some mining criteria, such as maximizing the confidence or compactness of the rules mined. In this section, we will focus specifically on how to mine quantitative association rules having two quantitative attributes on the left-hand side of the rule, and one categorical attribute on the right-hand side of the rule, for example,

$$A_{quan1} \wedge A_{quan2} \Rightarrow A_{cat}$$

where $A_{quan1}$ and $A_{quan2}$ are tests on quantitative attribute ranges (where the ranges are dynamically determined), and $A_{cat}$ tests a categorical attribute from the task-relevant data. Such rules have been referred to as **two-dimensional quantitative association rules**, since they contain two quantitative dimensions. For instance, suppose you are curious about the association relationship between pairs of quantitative attributes, like customer age and income, and the type of television that customers like to buy. An example of such a 2-D quantitative association rule is

$$age(X, \text{``}30 \ldots 39\text{''}) \land income(X, \text{``}42K \ldots 48K\text{''})$$

$$\Rightarrow buys(X, \text{``}high\ resolution\ TV\text{''}) \tag{6.14}$$

*"How can we find such rules?"* Let's look at an approach used in a system called **ARCS** (Association Rule Clustering System), which borrows ideas from image processing. Essentially, this approach maps pairs of quantitative attributes onto a 2-D grid for tuples satisfying a given categorical attribute condition. The grid is then searched for clusters of points, from which the association rules are generated. The following steps are involved in ARCS:

**Binning:**  Quantitative attributes can have a very wide range of values defining their domain. Just think about how big a 2-D grid would be if we plotted *age* and *income* as axes, where each possible value of *age* was assigned a unique position on one axis, and similarly, each possible value of *income* was assigned a unique position on the other axis! To keep grids down to a manageable size, we instead partition the ranges of quantitative attributes into intervals. These intervals are dynamic in that they may later be further combined during the mining process. The partitioning process is referred to as **binning**, that is, where the intervals are considered "bins." Three common binning strategies are

- **Equiwidth binning**, where the interval size of each bin is the same,
- **Equidepth binning**, where each bin has approximately the same number of tuples assigned to it, and
- **Homogeneity-based binning**, where bin size is determined so that the tuples in each bin are uniformly distributed.

ARCS uses equiwidth binning, where the bin size for each quantitative attribute is input by the user. A 2-D array for each possible bin combination involving both quantitative attributes is created. Each array cell holds the corresponding count distribution for each possible class of the categorical attribute of the rule right-hand side. By creating this data structure, the task-relevant data need only be scanned once. The same 2-D array can be used to generate rules for any value of the categorical attribute, based on the same two quantitative attributes. Binning is also discussed in Chapter 3.

**Finding frequent predicate sets:**  Once the 2-D array containing the count distribution for each category is set up, this can be scanned in order to find the

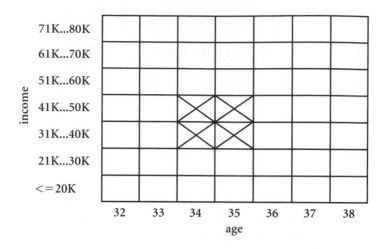

**Figure 6.18** A 2-D grid for tuples representing customers who purchase high-resolution TVs.

frequent predicate sets (those satisfying minimum support) that also satisfy minimum confidence. Strong association rules can then be generated from these predicate sets, using a rule generation algorithm like that described in Section 6.2.2.

**Clustering the association rules:** The strong association rules obtained in the previous step are then mapped to a 2-D grid. Figure 6.18 shows a 2-D grid for 2-D quantitative association rules predicting the condition *buys(X, "high resolution TV")* on the rule right-hand side, given the quantitative attributes *age* and *income*. The four Xs correspond to the rules

$$age(X, 34) \wedge income(X, \text{"31K} \ldots \text{40K"}) \Rightarrow buys(X, \text{"high resolution TV"}) \quad (6.15)$$

$$age(X, 35) \wedge income(X, \text{"31K} \ldots \text{40K"}) \Rightarrow buys(X, \text{"high resolution TV"}) \quad (6.16)$$

$$age(X, 34) \wedge income(X, \text{"41K} \ldots \text{50K"}) \Rightarrow buys(X, \text{"high resolution TV"}) \quad (6.17)$$

$$age(X, 35) \wedge income(X, \text{"41K} \ldots \text{50K"}) \Rightarrow buys(X, \text{"high resolution TV"}) \quad (6.18)$$

*"Can we find a simpler rule to replace the above four rules?"* Notice that these rules are quite "close" to one another, forming a rule cluster on the grid. Indeed, the four rules can be combined or "clustered" together to form the following simpler rule, which subsumes and replaces the above four rules:

$$age(X, \text{"34} \ldots \text{35"}) \wedge income(X, \text{"31K} \ldots \text{50K"})$$

$$\Rightarrow buys(X, \text{"high resolution TV"}) \quad (6.19)$$

| Price ($) | Equiwidth (width $10) | Equidepth (depth 2) | Distance-based |
|-----------|-----------------------|---------------------|----------------|
| 7 | [0, 10] | [7, 20] | [7, 7] |
| 20 | [11, 20] | [22, 50] | [20, 22] |
| 22 | [21, 30] | [51, 53] | [50, 53] |
| 50 | [31, 40] | | |
| 51 | [41, 50] | | |
| 53 | [51, 60] | | |

**Table 6.3** Binning methods like equiwidth and equidepth do not always capture the semantics of interval data.

ARCS employs a clustering algorithm for this purpose. The algorithm scans the grid, searching for rectangular clusters of rules. In this way, bins of the quantitative attributes occurring within a rule cluster may be further combined, and hence, further dynamic discretization of the quantitative attributes occurs.

The grid-based technique described here assumes that the initial association rules can be clustered into rectangular regions. Prior to performing the clustering, smoothing techniques can be used to help remove noise and outliers from the data. Rectangular clusters may oversimplify the data. Alternative approaches have been proposed, based on other shapes of regions that tend to better fit the data, yet require greater computation effort.

A non-grid-based technique has been proposed to find quantitative association rules that are more general, where any number of quantitative and categorical attributes can appear on either side of the rules. In this technique, quantitative attributes are dynamically partitioned using equidepth binning, and the partitions are combined based on a measure of *partial completeness*, which quantifies the information lost due to partitioning. For references on these alternatives to ARCS, see the bibliographic notes.

## 6.4.4 Mining Distance-Based Association Rules

The previous section described quantitative association rules where quantitative attributes are discretized initially by binning methods, and the resulting intervals are then combined. Such an approach, however, may not capture the semantics of interval data since they do not consider the relative distance between data points or between intervals.

Consider, for example, Table 6.3 which shows data for the attribute *price*, partitioned according to equiwidth and equidepth binning versus a distance-based partitioning. The distance-based partitioning seems the most intuitive, since it groups values that are close together within the same interval (e.g., [20, 22]). In contrast, equidepth partitioning groups distant values together (e.g., [22, 50]). Equiwidth may split values that are close together and create intervals for which there are no data. Clearly, a distance-based partitioning that considers the density or number of points in an interval, as well as the "closeness" of points in an interval, helps produce a more meaningful discretization. Intervals for each quantitative attribute can be established by *clustering* the values for the attribute.

A disadvantage of association rules is that they do not allow for approximations of attribute values. Consider the following association rule:

$$item\_type(X, \text{``electronic''}) \wedge manufacturer(X, \text{``foreign''})$$

$$\Rightarrow price(X, \$200) \tag{6.20}$$

where $X$ is a variable describing items at *AllElectronics*. In reality, it is more likely that the prices of foreign electronic items are *close to or approximately* $200, rather than exactly $200. It would be useful to have association rules that can express such a notion of closeness. Note that the support and confidence measures do not consider the closeness of values for a given attribute. This motivates the mining of **distance-based association rules,** which capture the semantics of interval data while allowing for approximation in data values. A two-phase algorithm can be used to mine distance-based association rules. The first phase employs clustering to find the intervals or clusters, adapting to the amount of available memory. The second phase obtains distance-based association rules by searching for groups of clusters that occur frequently together.

*"How are clusters formed in the first phase?"* Here, we give an intuitive description of how clusters can be formed. Interested readers may wish to read Chapter 8, as well as the references for distance-based association rules given in the bibliographic notes of this chapter. Let $S[X]$ be a set of $N$ tuples $t_1, t_2, \ldots, t_N$ projected on the attribute set $X$. A **diameter** measure is defined to assess the closeness of tuples. The diameter of $S[X]$ is the average pairwise distance between the tuples projected on $X$. Distance measures such as the Euclidean distance or Manhattan distance may be used.[8] The smaller the diameter of $S[X]$ is, the "closer" its tuples are when projected on $X$. Hence, the diameter metric assesses the *density* of a cluster. A **cluster** $C_X$ is a set of tuples defined on an attribute set $X$, where the tuples satisfy a **density threshold**, as well as a **frequency threshold,** which specifies the minimum number of tuples in a cluster. Clustering methods such as those described in Chapter 8 may be modified for use in this first phase of the mining process.

---

[8] The Euclidean and Manhattan distances between two tuples $t_1 = (x_{11}, x_{12}, \ldots, x_{1m})$ and $t_2 = (x_{21}, x_{22}, \ldots, x_{2m})$ are, respectively, $Euclidean\_d(t_1, t_2) = \sqrt{\sum_{i=1}^{m}(x_{1i} - x_{2i})^2}$ and $Manhattan\_d(t_1, t_2) = \sum_{i=1}^{m} |x_{1i} - x_{2i}|$.

In the second phase, clusters are combined to form distance-based association rules. Consider a simple distance-based association rule of the form $C_X \Rightarrow C_Y$. Suppose that $X$ is the attribute set *{age}* and $Y$ is the attribute set *{income}*. We want to ensure that the implication between the cluster $C_X$ for *age* and $C_Y$ for *income* is strong. This means that when the age-clustered tuples $C_X$ are projected onto the attribute *income*, their corresponding *income* values lie within the income-cluster $C_Y$, or close to it. A cluster $C_X$ projected onto the attribute set $Y$ is denoted $C_X[Y]$. Therefore, the distance between $C_X[Y]$ and $C_Y[Y]$ must be small. This distance measures the *degree of association* between $C_X$ and $C_Y$. The smaller the distance between $C_X[Y]$ and $C_Y[Y]$ the stronger the degree of association between $C_X$ and $C_Y$. The degree of association measure can be defined using standard statistical measures, such as the average intercluster distance, or the centroid Manhattan distance, where the centroid of a cluster represents the "average" tuple of the cluster.

In general, clusters can be combined to find distance-based association rules of the form

$$C_{X_1} C_{X_2} \ldots C_{X_x} \Rightarrow C_{Y_1} C_{Y_2} \ldots C_{Y_y}$$

where $X_i$ and $Y_j$ are pairwise disjoint sets of attributes, and the following three conditions are met: (1) The clusters in the rule antecedent are each strongly associated with each cluster in the consequent; (2) the clusters in the antecedent collectively occur together; and (3) the clusters in the consequent collectively occur together. The degree of association replaces the confidence framework in non-distance-based association rules, while the density threshold replaces the notion of support.

## 6.5 From Association Mining to Correlation Analysis

*"When mining association rules, how can the data mining system tell which rules are likely to be interesting to the user?"* Most association rule mining algorithms employ a support-confidence framework. In spite of using minimum support and confidence thresholds to help weed out or exclude the exploration of uninteresting rules, many rules that are not interesting to the user may still be produced. In this section, we first look at how even strong association rules can be uninteresting and misleading, and then discuss additional measures based on statistical independence and correlation analysis.

### 6.5.1 Strong Rules Are Not Necessarily Interesting: An Example

*"In data mining, are all of the* strong *association rules discovered (i.e., those rules satisfying the minimum support and minimum confidence thresholds) interesting enough to present to the user?"* Not necessarily. Whether a rule is interesting or not

can be judged either subjectively or objectively. Ultimately, only the user can judge if a given rule is interesting or not, and this judgment, being subjective, may differ from one user to another. However, objective interestingness measures, based on the statistics "behind" the data, can be used as one step towards the goal of weeding out uninteresting rules from presentation to the user.

"*So, how can we tell which strong association rules are really interesting?*" Let's examine the following example.

**Example 6.6** Suppose we are interested in analyzing transactions at *AllElectronics* with respect to the purchase of computer games and videos. Let *game* refer to the transactions containing computer games, and *video* refer to those containing videos. Of the 10,000 transactions analyzed, the data show that 6000 of the customer transactions included computer games, while 7500 included videos, and 4000 included both computer games and videos. Suppose that a data mining program for discovering association rules is run on the data, using a minimum support of, say, 30% and a minimum confidence of 60%. The following association rule is discovered:

$$buys(X, \text{``computer games''}) \Rightarrow buys(X, \text{``videos''})$$

$$[support = 40\%, confidence = 66\%] \tag{6.21}$$

Rule (6.21) is a strong association rule and would therefore be reported, since its support value of $\frac{4000}{10,000} = 40\%$ and confidence value of $\frac{4000}{6000} = 66\%$ satisfy the minimum support and minimum confidence thresholds, respectively. However, Rule (6.21) is misleading since the probability of purchasing videos is 75%, which is even larger than 66%. In fact, computer games and videos are negatively associated because the purchase of one of these items actually decreases the likelihood of purchasing the other. Without fully understanding this phenomenon, one could make unwise business decisions based on the rule derived. ■

The above example also illustrates that the confidence of a rule $A \Rightarrow B$ can be deceiving in that it is only an *estimate* of the conditional probability of itemset $B$ given itemset $A$. It does not measure the real strength (or lack of strength) of the implication between $A$ and $B$. Hence, alternatives to the support-confidence framework can be useful in mining interesting data relationships.

## 6.5.2 From Association Analysis to Correlation Analysis

Association rules mined using a support-confidence framework are useful for many applications. However, the support-confidence framework can be misleading in that it may identify a rule $A \Rightarrow B$ as interesting when, in fact, the occurrence of $A$ does not imply the occurrence of $B$. In this section, we consider an alternative framework for finding interesting relationships between data itemsets based on correlation.

The occurrence of itemset $A$ is **independent** of the occurrence of itemset $B$ if $P(A \cup B) = P(A)P(B)$; otherwise itemsets $A$ and $B$ are **dependent** and **correlated** as events. This definition can easily be extended to more than two itemsets. The **correlation** between the occurrence of $A$ and $B$ can be measured by computing

$$\text{corr}_{A,B} = \frac{P(A \cup B)}{P(A)P(B)}. \tag{6.22}$$

If the resulting value of Equation (6.22) is less than 1, then the occurrence of $A$ is negatively correlated with (or discourages) the occurrence of $B$. If the resulting value is greater than 1, then $A$ and $B$ are positively correlated, meaning the occurrence of one implies the occurrence of the other. If the resulting value is equal to 1, then $A$ and $B$ are independent and there is no correlation between them.

Equation (6.22) is equivalent to $P(B|A)/P(B)$, which is also called the **lift** of the association rule $A \Rightarrow B$. For example, if $A$ corresponds to the sale of computer games and $B$ corresponds to the sale of videos, then given the current market conditions, the sale of games is said to increase or "lift" the likelihood of the sale of videos by a factor of the value returned by Equation (6.22).

Let's go back to the computer game and video data of Example 6.6.

**Example 6.7** To help filter out misleading "strong" associations of the form $A \Rightarrow B$, we need to study how the two itemsets, $A$ and $B$, are correlated. Let $\overline{game}$ refer to the transactions of Example 6.6 that do not contain computer games, and $\overline{video}$ refer to those that do not contain videos. The transactions can be summarized in a **contingency table**. A contingency table for the data of Example 6.6 is shown in Table 6.4. From the table, we can see that the probability of purchasing a computer game is $P(\{game\}) = 0.60$, the probability of purchasing a video is $P(\{video\}) = 0.75$, and the probability of purchasing both is $P(\{game, video\}) = 0.40$. By Equation (6.22), $P(\{game, video\})/(P(\{game\}) \times P(\{video\})) = 0.40/(0.60 \times 0.75) = 0.89$. Since this value is less than 1, there is a negative correlation between the occurrence of $\{game\}$ and $\{video\}$. The numerator is the likelihood of a customer purchasing both, while the denominator is what the likelihood would have been if the two

**Table 6.4** A 2 × 2 contingency table summarizing the transactions with respect to computer game and video purchases.

|  | *game* | $\overline{game}$ | $\Sigma$ *row* |
|---|---|---|---|
| *video* | 4,000 | 3,500 | 7,500 |
| $\overline{video}$ | 2,000 | 500 | 2,500 |
| $\Sigma_{col}$ | 6,000 | 4,000 | 10,000 |

purchases were completely independent. Such a negative correlation cannot be identified by a support-confidence framework.  ∎

This motivates the mining of rules that identify correlations, or *correlation rules*. A **correlation rule** is of the form $\{i_1, i_2, \ldots, i_m\}$ where the occurrences of the items $\{i_1, i_2, \ldots, i_m\}$ are correlated. Given a correlation value determined by Equation (6.22), the $\chi^2$ statistic can be used to determine if the correlation is statistically significant. The $\chi^2$ statistic can also determine negative implication.

An advantage of correlation is that it is *upward closed*. This means that if a set $S$ of items is correlated (i.e., the items in $S$ are correlated), then every superset of $S$ is also correlated. In other words, adding items to a set of correlated items does not remove the existing correlation. The $\chi^2$ statistic is also upward closed within each significance level.

When searching for sets of correlations to form correlation rules, the upward closure property of correlation and $\chi^2$ can be used. Starting with the empty set, we may explore the itemset space (or *itemset lattice*), adding one item at a time, looking for **minimal correlated itemsets**—itemsets that are correlated although no subset of them is correlated. These itemsets form a **border** within the lattice. Because of closure, no itemset below this border will be correlated. Since all supersets of a minimal correlated itemset are correlated, we can stop searching upward. An algorithm that performs a series of such "walks" through itemset space is called a **random walk algorithm**. Such an algorithm can be combined with tests of support in order to perform additional pruning. Random walk algorithms can easily be implemented using data cubes. It is an open problem to adapt the procedure described here to very large databases. Another limitation is that the $\chi^2$ statistic is less accurate when the contingency table data are sparse, and can be misleading for contingency tables larger than $2 \times 2$. Proposed alternatives to the support-confidence framework for assessing the interestingness of association rules are given in the bibliographic notes.

## 6.6 Constraint-Based Association Mining

For a given set of task-relevant data, the data mining process may uncover thousands of rules, many of which are uninteresting to the user. In **constraint-based mining**, mining is performed under the guidance of various kinds of constraints provided by the user. These constraints include the following:

- **Knowledge type constraints:** These specify the type of knowledge to be mined, such as association.
- **Data constraints:** These specify the set of task-relevant data.
- **Dimension/level constraints:** These specify the dimension of the data, or levels of the concept hierarchies, to be used.

- **Interestingness constraints:** These specify thresholds on statistical measures of rule interestingness, such as support and confidence.

- **Rule constraints:** These specify the form of rules to be mined. Such constraints may be expressed as metarules (rule templates), as the maximum or minimum number of predicates that can occur in the rule antecedent or consequent, or as relationships among attributes, attribute values, and/or aggregates.

The above constraints can be specified using a high-level declarative data mining query language, such as that described in Chapter 4.

The first four of the above types of constraints have already been addressed in earlier parts of this book and chapter. In this section, we discuss the use of *rule constraints* to focus the mining task. This form of constraint-based mining allows users to specify the rules to be mined according to their intention, thereby making the data mining process more *effective*. In addition, a sophisticated mining query optimizer can be used to exploit the constraints specified by the user, thereby making the mining process more *efficient*. Constraint-based mining encourages interactive exploratory mining and analysis. In Section 6.6.1, you will study metarule-guided mining, where syntactic rule constraints are specified in the form of rule templates. Section 6.6.2 discusses the use of additional rule constraints, specifying set/subset relationships, constant initiation of variables, and aggregate functions.

## 6.6.1 Metarule-Guided Mining of Association Rules

*"How are metarules useful?"* Metarules allow users to specify the syntactic form of rules that they are interested in mining. The rule forms can be used as constraints to help improve the efficiency of the mining process. Metarules may be based on the analyst's experience, expectations, or intuition regarding the data, or automatically generated based on the database schema.

**Example 6.8** Suppose that as a market analyst for *AllElectronics*, you have access to the data describing customers (such as customer age, address, and credit rating) as well as the list of customer transactions. You are interested in finding associations between customer traits and the items that customers buy. However, rather than finding *all* of the association rules reflecting these relationships, you are particularly interested only in determining which pairs of customer traits promote the sale of educational software. A metarule can be used to specify this information describing the form of rules you are interested in finding. An example of such a metarule is

$$P_1(X, Y) \wedge P_2(X, W) \Rightarrow buys(X, \text{``educational software''}) \tag{6.23}$$

where $P_1$ and $P_2$ are **predicate variables** that are instantiated to attributes from the given database during the mining process, $X$ is a variable representing a customer, and $Y$ and $W$ take on values of the attributes assigned to $P_1$ and $P_2$, respectively.

Typically, a user will specify a list of attributes to be considered for instantiation with $P_1$ and $P_2$. Otherwise, a default set may be used.

In general, a metarule forms a hypothesis regarding the relationships that the user is interested in probing or confirming. The data mining system can then search for rules that match the given metarule. For instance, Rule (6.24) matches or **complies with** Metarule (6.23).

$$age(X, \text{"30} \dots \text{39"}) \wedge income(X, \text{"41K} \dots \text{60K"})$$

$$\Rightarrow buys(X, \text{"educational software"}) \tag{6.24}$$

■

*"How can metarules be used to guide the mining process?"* Let's examine this problem closely. Suppose that we wish to mine interdimension association rules, such as in the example above. A metarule is a rule template of the form

$$P_1 \wedge P_2 \wedge \dots \wedge P_l \Rightarrow Q_1 \wedge Q_2 \wedge \dots \wedge Q_r \tag{6.25}$$

where $P_i$ $(i = 1, \dots, l)$ and $Q_j$ $(j = 1, \dots, r)$ are either instantiated predicates or predicate variables. Let the number of predicates in the metarule be $p = l + r$. In order to find interdimension association rules satisfying the template,

■ We need to find all frequent $p$-predicate sets, $L_p$.

■ We must also have the support or count of the $l$-predicate subsets of $L_p$ in order to compute the confidence of rules derived from $L_p$.

This is a typical case of mining multidimensional association rules, which was described in Section 6.4. As shown there, data cubes are well suited to the mining of multidimensional association rules owing to their ability to store aggregate dimension values. Owing to the popularity of OLAP and data warehousing, it is possible that a fully materialized $n$-D data cube suitable for the given mining task already exists, where $n$ is the number of attributes to be considered for instantiation with the predicate variables plus the number of predicates already instantiated in the given metarule, and $n \geq p$. Such an $n$-D cube is typically represented by a lattice of cuboids, similar to that shown in Figure 6.17. In this case, we need only scan the $p$-D cuboids, comparing each cell count with the minimum support count, in order to find $L_p$. Since the $l$-D cuboids have already been computed and contain the counts of the $l$-D predicate subsets of $L_p$, a rule generation procedure can then be called to return strong rules that comply with the given metarule. We call this approach an **abridged $n$-D cube search**, since rather than searching the entire $n$-D data cube, only the $p$-D and $l$-D cuboids are ever examined.

If a relevant $n$-D data cube does not exist for the metarule-guided mining task, then one must be constructed and searched. Rather than constructing the entire cube, only the *p*-D and *l*-D cuboids need be computed. Methods for cube construction are discussed in Chapter 2.

## 6.6.2 Mining Guided by Additional Rule Constraints

Rule constraints specifying set/subset relationships, constant initiation of variables, and aggregate functions can be specified by the user. These may be used together with, or as an alternative to, metarule-guided mining. In this section, we examine rule constraints as to how they can be used to make the mining process more efficient. Let us study an example where rule constraints are used to mine hybrid-dimension association rules.

**Example 6.9** Suppose that *AllElectronics* has a sales multidimensional database with the following interrelated relations:

- *sales(customer_name, item_name, transaction_id)*
- *lives(customer_name, region, city)*
- *item(item_name, category, price)*
- *transaction(transaction_id, day, month, year)*

where *lives, item,* and *transaction* are three dimension tables, linked to the fact table *sales* via three keys, *customer_name, item_name,* and *transaction_id,* respectively.

Our association mining query is to *"Find the sales of what cheap items (where the sum of the prices is less than \$100) that may promote the sales of what expensive items (where the minimum price is \$500) in the same category for Vancouver customers in 1999".* This can be expressed in the DMQL data mining query language as follows, where each line of the query has been enumerated to aid in our discussion.

$$
\begin{aligned}
&(1) \quad \textbf{mine associations as} \\
&(2) \qquad lives(C, \_, \text{``Vancouver''}) \wedge sales^+(C, ?\{I\}, \{S\}) \Rightarrow sales^+(C, ?\{J\}, \{T\}) \\
&(3) \quad \textbf{from } sales \\
&(4) \quad \textbf{where } \text{S.year} = 1999 \textbf{ and } \text{T.year} = 1999 \textbf{ and } \text{I.category} = \text{J.category} \\
&(5) \quad \textbf{group by } C, \text{I.category} \\
&(6) \quad \textbf{having } \text{sum(I.price)} \leq 100 \textbf{ and } \text{min(J.price)} \geq 500 \\
&(7) \quad \textbf{with } \text{support } \textbf{threshold} = 1\% \\
&(8) \quad \textbf{with } \text{confidence } \textbf{threshold} = 50\%
\end{aligned}
$$

Before we discuss the rule constraints, let us have a closer look at the above query. Line 1 is a knowledge type constraint, where association patterns are to be discovered. Line 2 specifies a metarule. This is an abbreviated form for the following metarule for hybrid-dimension association rules (multidimensional association rules where the repeated predicate here is *sales*):

$lives(C, \_, \text{``Vancouver''})$

$\qquad \land\ sales(C, ?I_1, S_1) \land \cdots \land sales(C, ?I_k, S_k) \land I = \{I_1, \ldots, I_k\} \land S$

$\qquad = \{S_1, \ldots, S_k\}$

$\qquad \Rightarrow sales(C, ?J_1, T_1) \land \cdots \land sales(C, ?J_m, T_m) \land J = \{J_1, \ldots, J_m\} \land T$

$\qquad = \{T_1, \ldots, T_m\}$

which means that one or more *sales* records in the form of "$sales(C, ?I_1, S_1) \land$ $\ldots sales(C, ?I_k, S_k)$" will reside at the rule antecedent (left-hand side), and the question mark "?" means that only *item_name*, $I_1, \ldots, I_k$ need be printed out. "$I = \{I_1, \ldots, I_k\}$" means that all the *I*s at the antecedent are taken from a set *I*, obtained from the SQL-like **where** clause of line 4. Similar notational conventions are used at the consequent (right-hand side).

The metarule may allow the generation of association rules like the following:

$lives(C, \_, \text{``Vancouver''}) \land sales(C, \text{``Census\_CD''}, \_) \land sales(C, \text{``MS/Office''}, \_)$

$\qquad \Rightarrow sales(C, \text{``MS/SQLServer''}, \_), \qquad [1.5\%, 68\%] \qquad\qquad (6.26)$

which means that if a customer in Vancouver bought "Census_CD" and "MS/ Office", it is likely (with a probability of 68%) that the customer also bought "MS/SQLServer", and 1.5% of all of the customers bought all three.

Data constraints are specified in the "*lives*(_, _, "*Vancouver*")" portion of the metarule (i.e., all the customers whose city is Vancouver), and in line 3, which specifies that only the fact table, *sales*, need be explicitly referenced. In such a multidimensional database, variable reference is simplified. For example, "*S.year* = 1999" is equivalent to the SQL statement "**from** *sales S, transaction R* **where** *S.transaction_id = R.transaction_id* **and** *R.year = 1999*". All three dimensions (*lives*, *item*, and *transaction*) are used. Level constraints are as follows: for *lives*, we consider just *customer_name* since only *city* = "*Vancouver*" is used in the selection; for *item*, we consider the levels *item_name* and *category* since they are used in the query; and for *transaction*, we are only concerned with *transaction_id* since *day* and *month* are not referenced and *year* is used only in the selection.

Rule constraints include most portions of the **where** (line 4) and **having** (line 6) clauses, such as "*S.year = 1999*", "*T.year = 1999*", "*I.category = J.category*", "*sum(I.price)* ≤ *100*", and "*min(J.price)* ≥ *500*". Finally, lines 7 and 8 specify two interestingness constraints (i.e., thresholds), namely, a minimum support of 1% and a minimum confidence of 50%. ∎

Knowledge type and data constraints are applied before mining. The remaining constraint types could be used after mining, to filter out discovered rules. This, however, may make the mining process very inefficient and expensive. Dimension/level constraints were discussed in Section 6.3.2, and interestingness constraints have been discussed throughout this chapter. Let's focus now on rule constraints.

*"What kind of constraints can be used during the mining process to prune the rule search space?"* you ask. *"More specifically, what kind of rule constraints can be 'pushed' deep into the mining process and still ensure the completeness of the answers to a mining query?"*

Rule constraints can be classified into the following five categories with respect to frequent itemset mining: (1) *antimonotone,* (2) *monotone,* (3) *succinct,* (4) *convertible,* and (5) *inconvertible.* For each category, we will use an example to show its characteristics and explain how such kinds of constraints can be used in the mining process.

The first category of constraints is *antimonotone.* Consider the rule constraint "*sum(I.price)* $\leq$ 100" of Example 6.9. Suppose we are using the Apriori framework, which at each iteration $k$, explores itemsets of size $k$. If the price summation of the items in an itemset is no less than 100, this itemset can be pruned from the search space, since adding more items into the set will only make it more expensive and thus will never satisfy the constraint. In other words, if an itemset does not satisfy this rule constraint, none of its supersets can satisfy the constraint. If a rule constraint obeys this property, it is called **antimonotone.** Pruning by antimonotone constraints can be applied at each iteration of Apriori-style algorithms to help improve the efficiency of the overall mining process while guaranteeing completeness of the data mining task.

Note that the Apriori property, which states that all nonempty subsets of a frequent itemset must also be frequent, is also antimonotone. If a given itemset does not satisfy minimum support, none of its supersets can. This property is used at each iteration of the Apriori algorithm to reduce the number of candidate itemsets examined, thereby reducing the search space for association rules.

Other examples of antimonotone constraints include "*min(J.price)* $\geq$ 500", "*count(I)* $\leq$ 10", and so on. Any itemset that violates either of these constraints can be discarded since adding more items to such itemsets can never satisfy the constraints. A constraint such as "*avg(I.price)* $\leq$ 100" is not antimonotone. For a given set that does not satisfy this constraint, a superset created by adding some (cheap) items may result in satisfying the constraint. Hence, pushing this constraint inside the mining process will not guarantee completeness of the data mining task. A list of SQL-primitives-based constraints, characterized on the notion of antimonotonicity, is given in the second column of Table 6.5. To simplify our discussion, only existence operators (e.g., $=$, $\in$, but not $\neq$, $\notin$) and comparison (or containment) operators with equality (e.g., $\leq$, $\subseteq$) are given.

The second category of constraints is *monotone.* If the rule constraint in Example 6.9 were "*sum(I.price)* $\geq$ 100", the constraint-based processing method would be quite different. If an itemset $I$ satisfies the constraint, that is, the sum of the prices in the set is no less than 100, further addition of more items to $I$ will increase cost and will always satisfy the constraint. Therefore, further testing of this constraint on itemset $I$ becomes redundant. In other words, if an itemset satisfies this rule constraint, so do all of its supersets. If a rule constraint obeys this property, it is called **monotone.** Similar rule monotone constraints include "*min(I.price)* $\leq$ 10,"

**Table 6.5** Characterization of commonly used SQL-based constraints.

| Constraint | Antimonotone | Monotone | Succinct |
|---|---|---|---|
| $v \in S$ | no | yes | yes |
| $S \supseteq V$ | no | yes | yes |
| $S \subseteq V$ | yes | no | yes |
| $min(S) \leq v$ | no | yes | yes |
| $min(S) \geq v$ | yes | no | yes |
| $max(S) \leq v$ | yes | no | yes |
| $max(S) \geq v$ | no | yes | yes |
| $count(S) \leq v$ | yes | no | weakly |
| $count(S) \geq v$ | no | yes | weakly |
| $sum(S) \leq v \ (\forall a \in S, a \geq 0)$ | yes | no | no |
| $sum(S) \geq v \ (\forall a \in S, a \geq 0)$ | no | yes | no |
| $range(S) \leq v$ | yes | no | no |
| $range(S) \geq v$ | no | yes | no |
| $avg(S) \, \theta v, \theta \in \{\leq, \geq\}$ | convertible | convertible | no |
| $support(S) \geq \xi$ | yes | no | no |
| $support(S) \leq \xi$ | no | yes | no |

"$count(I) \geq 10$", and so on. A list of SQL-primitives-based constraints, characterized on the notion of monotonicity, is given in the third column of Table 6.5.

The third category is *succinct constraints*. For this category of constraints, we can *enumerate all and only those sets that are guaranteed to satisfy the constraint.* That is, if a rule constraint is **succinct**, we can directly generate precisely the sets that satisfy it, even before support counting begins. This avoids the substantial overhead of the generate-and-test paradigm. In other words, such constraints are *precounting prunable.* For example, the constraint "$min(J.price) \geq 500$" in Example 6.9 is succinct. This is because we can explicitly and precisely generate all the sets of items satisfying the constraint. Specifically, such a set must contain at least one item whose price is no less than $500. It is of the form $S_1 \cup S_2$, where $S_1 \neq \emptyset$ is a subset of the set of all those items with prices no less than $500, and $S_2$, possibly empty, is a subset of the set of all those items with prices no greater than $500. Because there is a precise "formula" to generate all the sets satisfying a succinct constraint, there is no need to iteratively check the rule constraint during the mining process. A list of SQL-primitives-based constraints, characterized on the notion of succinctness, is given in the fourth column of Table 6.5.

The fourth category is **convertible constraints**. Some constraints belong to none of the above three categories. However, if the items in the itemset are arranged in a particular order, the constraint may become monotone or antimonotone with regard to a frequent itemset mining process. For example, the constraint

"$avg(I.price) \leq 100$" is neither antimonotone nor monotone. However, if items in a transaction are added to an itemset in price-ascending order, the constraint becomes *antimonotone*, because if an itemset $I$ violates the constraint (i.e., with an average price greater than $100), further addition of more expensive items into the itemset will never make it satisfy the constraint. Similarly, if items in a transaction are added to an itemset in price-descending order, it becomes *monotone,* because if the itemset satisfies the constraint (i.e., with an average price no greater than $100), adding cheaper items into the current itemset will still make the average price no greater than $100. Aside from "$avg(S) \leq v$," and $avg(S) \geq v$," given in Table 6.5, there are many other convertible constraints, such as "$variance(S) \geq v$," "$standard\_deviation(S) \geq v$," and so on.

Note that the above discussion does not imply that every constraint is convertible. For example, "$sum(S)\ \theta v$," where $\theta \in \{\leq, \geq\}$ and each element in $S$ could be of any real value, is not convertible. Therefore, there is yet a fifth category of constraints, called **inconvertible constraints.** The good news is that although there still exist some tough constraints that are not convertible, most simple SQL expressions with built-in SQL aggregates belong to one of the first four categories to which efficient constraint mining methods can be applied.

## 6.7 Summary

- The discovery of association relationships among huge amounts of data is useful in selective marketing, decision analysis, and business management. A popular area of application is **market basket analysis,** which studies the buying habits of customers by searching for sets of items that are frequently purchased together (or in sequence). **Association rule mining** consists of first finding **frequent** itemsets (set of items, such as $A$ and $B$, satisfying a *minimum support threshold*, or percentage of the task-relevant tuples), from which **strong** association rules in the form of $A \Rightarrow B$ are generated. These rules also satisfy a *minimum confidence threshold* (a prespecified probability of satisfying $B$ under the condition that $A$ is satisfied).

- Association rules can be classified into several categories based on different criteria, such as the following:

  (1) Based on the *types of values* handled in the rule, associations can be classified into **Boolean** versus **quantitative**. A *Boolean* association shows relationships between discrete (categorical) objects. A *quantitative* association is a multidimensional association that involves numeric attributes that are discretized dynamically. It may involve categorical attributes as well.

  (2) Based on the *dimensions* of data involved in the rules, associations can be classified into **single-dimensional** versus **multidimensional**. Single-dimensional association involves a single predicate or dimension, such

as *buys*; multidimensional association involves multiple (distinct) predicates or dimensions. Single-dimensional association shows **intraattribute** relationships (i.e., associations within one attribute or dimension); multidimensional association shows **interattribute** relationships (i.e., between or among attributes/dimensions).

(3) Based on the *levels of abstractions* involved in the rule, associations can be classified into **single-level** versus **multilevel**. In a *single-level* association, the items or predicates mined are not considered at different levels of abstraction; a *multilevel* association does consider multiple levels of abstraction.

(4) Based on *various extensions* to association mining, association mining can be extended to **correlation analysis**, and the mining of **maximal frequent patterns** ("max-patterns") and **frequent closed itemsets**. Correlation analysis indicates the absence or presence of correlated items. A *max-pattern* is a frequent pattern $p$ such that any proper superpattern of $p$ is not frequent. A *frequent closed itemset* is where an itemset $c$ is *closed* if there exists no proper superset of $c$, $c'$, such that every transaction that contains a subpattern of $c$ also contains $c'$.

- The **Apriori algorithm** is an efficient association rule mining algorithm that explores the level-wise mining Apriori property: *all nonempty subsets of a frequent itemset must also be frequent.* At the $k$th iteration (for $k > 1$), it forms frequent $(k + 1)$-itemset candidates based on the frequent $k$-itemsets, and scans the database once to find the *complete* set of frequent $(k + 1)$-itemsets, $L_{k+1}$.

  Variations involving hashing and transaction reduction can be used to make the procedure more efficient. Other variations include partitioning the data (mining on each partition and then combining the results), and sampling the data (mining on a subset of the data). These variations can reduce the number of data scans required to as little as two or one.

- **Frequent pattern growth (FP-growth)** is a method of mining frequent itemsets without candidate generation. It constructs a highly compact data structure (an *FP-tree*) to compress the original transaction database. Rather than employing the generate-and-test strategy of Apriori-like methods, it focuses on frequent pattern (fragment) growth which avoids costly candidate generation, resulting in greater efficiency.

- **Multilevel association rules** can be mined using several strategies, based on how minimum support thresholds are defined at each level of abstraction. When using **reduced minimum support** at lower levels, pruning approaches include *level-cross filtering by single item* and *level-cross filtering by k-itemset*. Redundant multilevel (descendent) association rules can be eliminated from presentation to the user if their support and confidence are close to their expected values, based on their corresponding ancestor rules.

- Techniques for mining **multidimensional association rules** can be categorized according to their treatment of quantitative attributes. First, quantitative attributes may be *discretized statically*, based on predefined concept hierarchies. Data cubes are well suited to this approach, since both the data cube and quantitative attributes can make use of concept hierarchies. Second, **quantitative association rules** can be mined where quantitative attributes are discretized dynamically based on binning, where "adjacent" association rules may be combined by clustering. Third, **distance-based association rules** can be mined to capture the semantics of interval data, where intervals are defined by clustering.

- Not all strong association rules are interesting. **Correlation rules** can be mined for items that are statistically correlated.

- **Constraint-based rule mining** allow users to focus the search for rules by providing metarules (i.e., pattern templates) and additional mining constraints. Such mining is facilitated with the use of a declarative data mining query language and user interface, and poses great challenges for mining query optimization. Rule constraints can be classified into five categories: **antimonotone, monotone, succinctness, convertible,** and **inconvertible.** Constraints belonging to the first four of these categories can be used during association mining to guide the process, leading to more efficient and effective mining.

- Association rules should not be used directly for prediction without further analysis or domain knowledge. They do not necessarily indicate causation. They are, however, a helpful starting point for further exploration, making them a popular tool for understanding data.

## Exercises

**6.1** The Apriori algorithm makes use of *prior knowledge* of subset support properties.

(a) Prove that all nonempty subsets of a frequent itemset must also be frequent.

(b) Prove that the support of any nonempty subset $s'$ of itemset $s$ must be as great as the support of $s$.

(c) Given frequent itemset $l$ and subset $s$ of $l$, prove that the confidence of the rule "$s' \Rightarrow (l - s')$" cannot be more than the confidence of "$s \Rightarrow (l - s)$", where $s'$ is a subset of $s$.

(d) A *partitioning* variation of Apriori subdivides the transactions of a database $D$ into $n$ nonoverlapping partitions. Prove that any itemset that is frequent in $D$ must be frequent in at least one partition of $D$.

**6.2** Section 6.2.2 describes a method for *generating association rules* from frequent itemsets. Propose a more efficient method. Explain why it is more efficient than the one proposed in Section 6.2.2. (*Hint:* Consider incorporating the properties of Exercise 6.1(b) and 6.1(c) into your design.)

**6.3** A database has four transactions. Let $min\_sup = 60\%$ and $min\_conf = 80\%$.

| TID | date | items_bought |
|-----|------|--------------|
| T100 | 10/15/99 | {K, A, D, B} |
| T200 | 10/15/99 | {D, A, C, E, B} |
| T300 | 10/19/99 | {C, A, B, E } |
| T400 | 10/22/99 | {B, A, D} |

(a) Find all frequent itemsets using Apriori and FP-growth, respectively. Compare the efficiency of the two mining processes.

(b) List all of the *strong* association rules (with support *s* and confidence *c*) matching the following metarule, where $X$ is a variable representing customers, and $item_i$ denotes variables representing items (e.g., "A", "B", etc.):

$$\forall x \in transaction, \quad buys(X, item_1) \wedge buys(X, item_2) \Rightarrow buys(X, item_3) \quad [s, c]$$

**6.4** A database has four transactions. Let $min\_sup = 60\%$ and $min\_conf = 80\%$.

| cust_ID | TID | items_bought (in the form of brand-item_category) |
|---------|-----|---------------------------------------------------|
| 01 | T100 | {King's-Crab, Sunset-Milk, Dairyland-Cheese, Best-Bread} |
| 02 | T200 | {Best-Cheese, Dairyland-Milk, Goldenfarm-Apple, Tasty-Pie, Wonder-Bread} |
| 01 | T300 | {Westcoast-Apple, Dairyland-Milk, Wonder-Bread, Tasty-Pie} |
| 03 | T400 | {Wonder-Bread, Sunset-Milk, Dairyland-Cheese} |

(a) At the granularity of *item_category* (e.g., $item_i$ could be "*Milk*"), for the following rule template,

$$\forall X \in transaction, \quad buys(X, item_1) \wedge buys(X, item_2) \Rightarrow buys(X, item_3) \quad [s, c]$$

list the frequent $k$-itemset for the largest $k$, and *all* of the *strong* association rules (with their support *s* and confidence *c*) containing the frequent $k$-itemset for the largest $k$.

(b) At the granularity of *brand-item_category* (e.g., $item_i$ could be "*Sunset-Milk*"), for the following rule template,

$$\forall X \in customer, \quad buys(X, item_1) \wedge buys(X, item_2) \Rightarrow buys(X, item_3)$$

list the frequent $k$-itemset for the largest $k$. Note: Do not print any rules.

**6.5** Suppose that a large store has a transaction database that is *distributed* among four locations. Transactions in each component database have the same format, namely $T_j : \{i_1, \ldots, i_m\}$, where $T_j$ is a transaction identifier, and $i_k$ $(1 \le k \le m)$ is the identifier of an item purchased in the transaction. Propose an efficient

**Table 6.6** Generalized relation for Exercise 6.7.

| major | status | age | nationality | gpa | count |
|-------|--------|-----|-------------|-----|-------|
| French | M.A | over_30 | Canada | 2.8 ... 3.2 | 3 |
| cs | junior | 16 ... 20 | Europe | 3.2 ... 3.6 | 29 |
| physics | M.S | 26 ... 30 | Latin_America | 3.2 ... 3.6 | 18 |
| engineering | Ph.D | 26 ... 30 | Asia | 3.6 ... 4.0 | 78 |
| philosophy | Ph.D | 26 ... 30 | Europe | 3.2 ... 3.6 | 5 |
| French | senior | 16 ... 20 | Canada | 3.2 ... 3.6 | 40 |
| chemistry | junior | 21 ... 25 | USA | 3.6 ... 4.0 | 25 |
| cs | senior | 16 ... 20 | Canada | 3.2 ... 3.6 | 70 |
| philosophy | M.S | over_30 | Canada | 3.6 ... 4.0 | 15 |
| French | junior | 16 ... 20 | USA | 2.8 ... 3.2 | 8 |
| philosophy | junior | 26 ... 30 | Canada | 2.8 ... 3.2 | 9 |
| philosophy | M.S | 26 ... 30 | Asia | 3.2 ... 3.6 | 9 |
| French | junior | 16 ... 20 | Canada | 3.2 ... 3.6 | 52 |
| math | senior | 16 ... 20 | USA | 3.6 ... 4.0 | 32 |
| cs | junior | 16 ... 20 | Canada | 3.2 ... 3.6 | 76 |
| philosophy | Ph.D | 26 ... 30 | Canada | 3.6 ... 4.0 | 14 |
| philosophy | senior | 26 ... 30 | Canada | 2.8 ... 3.2 | 19 |
| French | Ph.D | over_30 | Canada | 2.8 ... 3.2 | 1 |
| engineering | junior | 21 ... 25 | Europe | 3.2 ... 3.6 | 71 |
| math | Ph.D | 26 ... 30 | Latin_America | 3.2 ... 3.6 | 7 |
| chemistry | junior | 16 ... 20 | USA | 3.6 ... 4.0 | 46 |
| engineering | junior | 21 ... 25 | Canada | 3.2 ... 3.6 | 96 |
| French | M.S | over_30 | Latin_America | 3.2 ... 3.6 | 4 |
| philosophy | junior | 21 ... 25 | USA | 2.8 ... 3.2 | 8 |
| math | junior | 16 ... 20 | Canada | 3.6 ... 4.0 | 59 |

algorithm to mine global association rules (without considering multilevel associations). You may present your algorithm in the form of an outline. Your algorithm should not require shipping all of the data to one site and should not cause excessive network communication overhead.

**6.6** Suppose that frequent itemsets are saved for a large transaction database, *DB*. Discuss how to efficiently mine the (global) association rules under the same minimum support threshold, if a set of new transactions, denoted as $\Delta DB$, is *(incrementally) added in*?

**6.7** Suppose that a data relation describing students at *Big-University* has been generalized to the generalized relation *R* in Table 6.6.

Let the concept hierarchies be as follows:

| | |
|---|---|
| *status* : | {*freshman, sophomore, junior, senior*} ∈ *undergraduate*. |
| | {*M.Sc., M.A., Ph.D.*} ∈ *graduate*. |
| *major* : | {*physics, chemistry, math*} ∈ *science*. |
| | {*cs, engineering*} ∈ *appl_sciences*. |
| | {*French, philosophy*} ∈ *arts*. |
| *age* : | {16 . . . 20, 21 . . . 25} ∈ *young*. |
| | {26 . . . 30, *over_30*} ∈ *old*. |
| *nationality* : | {*Asia, Europe, Latin_America*} ∈ *foreign*. |
| | {*Canada, U.S.A.*} ∈ *North_America*. |

Let the minimum support threshold be 20% and the minimum confidence threshold be 50% (at each of the levels).

(a) Draw the concept hierarchies for *status, major, age,* and *nationality*.

(b) Find the set of strong multilevel association rules in *R* using *uniform support* for all levels, for the following rule template,

$$\forall S \in R, \; P(S, x) \wedge Q(S, y) \Rightarrow gpa(S, z) \quad [s, c]$$

where $P, Q \in \{status, major, age, nationality\}$.

(c) Find the set of strong multilevel association rules in *R* using *level-cross filtering by single items*, where a reduced support of 10% is used for the lowest abstraction level, for the preceding rule template.

6.8 Propose and outline a **level-shared mining** approach to mining multilevel association rules in which each item is encoded by its level position, and an initial scan of the database collects the count for each item *at each concept level*, identifying frequent and subfrequent items. Comment on the processing cost of mining multilevel associations with this method in comparison to mining single-level associations.

6.9 Show that the support of an itemset *H* that contains both an item *h* and its ancestor $\hat{h}$ will be the same as the support for the itemset $H - \hat{h}$. Explain how this can be used in *cross-level* association rule mining.

6.10 When mining cross-level association rules, suppose it is found that the itemset "{*IBM desktop computer, printer*}" does not satisfy minimum support. Can this information be used to *prune* the mining of a "descendent" itemset such as "{*IBM desktop computer, b/w printer*}"? Give a general rule explaining how this information may be used for pruning the search space.

6.11 Propose a method for mining *hybrid-dimension* association rules (multidimensional association rules with repeating predicates).

6.12 Give a short example to show that items in a strong association rule may actually be *negatively correlated*.

6.13 The following contingency table summarizes supermarket transaction data, where *hot dogs* refers to the transactions containing hot dogs, $\overline{hotdogs}$ refers to the transactions that do not contain hot dogs, *hamburgers* refers to the transactions containing hamburgers, and $\overline{hamburgers}$ refers to the transactions that do not contain hamburgers.

|  | *hotdogs* | $\overline{hotdogs}$ | $\Sigma_{row}$ |
|---|---|---|---|
| *hamburgers* | 2000 | 500 | 2500 |
| $\overline{hamburgers}$ | 1000 | 1500 | 2500 |
| $\Sigma_{col}$ | 3000 | 2000 | 5000 |

(a) Suppose that the association rule "*hot dogs $\Rightarrow$ hamburgers*" is mined. Given a minimum support threshold of 25% and a minimum confidence threshold of 50%, is this association rule strong?

(b) Based on the given data, is the purchase of *hot dogs* independent of the purchase of *hamburgers*? If not, what kind of *correlation* relationship exists between the two?

**6.14** Sequential patterns can be mined in methods similar to the mining of association rules. Design an efficient algorithm to mine **multilevel sequential patterns** from a transaction database. An example of such a pattern is the following: "*A customer who buys a PC will buy Microsoft software within three months*", on which one may drill down to find a more refined version of the pattern, such as "*A customer who buys a Pentium PC will buy Microsoft Office within three months*".

**6.15** Prove that each entry in the following table correctly characterizes its corresponding rule constraint for frequent itemset mining.

|  | Rule Constraint | Antimonotone | Monotone | Succinct |
|---|---|---|---|---|
| (a) | $v \in S$ | no | yes | yes |
| (b) | $S \subseteq V$ | yes | no | yes |
| (c) | $min(S) \leq v$ | no | yes | yes |
| (d) | $range(S) \leq v$ | yes | no | no |
| (e) | $avg(S) \geq v$ | convertible | convertible | no |

**6.16** The price of each item in a store is nonnegative. The store manager is only interested in rules of the form: "*one free item may trigger $200 total purchases in the same transaction*". State how to mine such rules *efficiently*.

**6.17** The price of each item in a store is nonnegative. For each of the following cases, identify the kinds of constraint they represent and briefly discuss how to mine such association rules *efficiently*.

(a) Containing at least one Nintendo game

(b) Containing items whose sum of the prices is less than $150

(c) Containing one free item and other items whose sum of the prices is at least $200

(d) Where the average price of all the items is between $100 and $500

## Bibliographic Notes

Association rule mining was first proposed by Agrawal, Imielinski, and Swami [AIS93b]. The Apriori algorithm discussed in Section 6.2.1 was done by Agrawal and Srikant [AS94]. A variation of the algorithm using the similar pruning heuristic was developed independently by Mannila, Tiovonen, and Verkamo [MTV94]. A joint publication combining these works later appeared in Agrawal, Mannila, Srikant, Toivonen, and Verkamo [AMS+96]. A method for generating association rules is described in Agrawal and Srikant [AS94a]. References for the variations of Apriori described in Section 6.2.3 include the following. The use of hash tables to improve association mining efficiency was studied by Park, Chen, and Yu [PCY95a]. Transaction reduction techniques are described in Agrawal and Srikant [AS94b], Han and Fu [HF95], and Park, Chen, and Yu [PCY95a]. The partitioning technique was proposed by Savasere, Omiecinski, and Navathe [SON95]. The sampling approach is discussed in Toivonen [Toi96]. A dynamic itemset counting approach is given in Brin, Motwani, Ullman, and Tsur [BMUT97]. Association rule mining has various extensions, including sequential pattern mining (Agrawal and Srikant [AS95]), espisodes mining (Mannila, Toivonen, and Verkamo [MTV97]), mining spatial association rules (Koperski and Han [KH95]), mining cyclic association rules (Özden, Ramaswamy, and Silberschatz [ORS98]), mining negative association rules (Savasere, Omiecinski and Navathe [SON98]), mining intertransaction association rules (Lu, Han, and Feng [LHF98]), and calendric market basket analysis (Ramaswamy, Mahajan, and Silberschatz [RMS98]). The mining of max-patterns is described in Bayardo [Bay98]. The mining of frequent closed itemsets was proposed in Pasquier, Bastide, Taouil, and Lakhal [PBTL99] and an efficient mining algorithm is proposed by Pei, Han, and Mao [PHM00]. Iceberg query computation was studied in Fang, Shivakumar, Garcia-Molina, et al. [FSGM+98], and an efficient iceberg cube computation method was developed by Beyer and Ramakrishnan [BR99]. A depth-first generation of frequent itemsets was proposed by Agarwal, Aggarwal, and Prasad [AAP00]. A method for mining frequent patterns without candidate generation was proposed by Han, Pei, and Yin [HPY00].

Multilevel association mining was studied in Han and Fu [HF95], and Srikant and Agrawal [SA95]. In Srikant and Agrawal [SA95], such mining was studied in the context of *generalized association rules*, and an R-interest measure is proposed for removing redundant rules.

The ARCS system described in Section 6.4.3 for mining quantitative association rules based on rule clustering was proposed by Lent, Swami, and Widom [LSW97]. Techniques for mining quantitative rules based on x-monotone and rectilinear regions were presented by Fukuda, Morimoto, Morishita, and Tokuyama [FMMT96], and Yoda, Fukuda, Morimoto, et al. [YFM+97]. A non-grid-based technique for mining quantitative association rules, which uses a measure of partial completeness, was proposed by Srikant and Agrawal [SA96]. The approach described in Section 6.4.4 for mining (distance-based) association rules over interval data was proposed by Miller and Yang [MY97]. Mining multidimensional association rules using static discretization of quantitative attributes and data cubes was studied by Kamber, Han, and Chiang [KHC97].

The statistical independence of rules in data mining was studied by Piatetski-Shapiro [PS91b]. The interestingness problem of strong association rules is discussed in Chen, Han, and Yu [CHY96], Brin, Motwani, and Silverstein [BMS97], and Aggarwal and Yu [AY99]. An efficient method for generalizing associations to correlations is given in Brin, Motwani, and Silverstein [BMS97], and briefly summarized in Section 6.5.2. Other alternatives to the support-confidence framework for assessing the interestingness of association rules are proposed in Brin, Motwani, Ullman, and Tsur [BMUT97] and Ahmed, El-Makky, and Taha [AEMT00]. Silverstein, Brin, Motwani, and Ullman [SBMU98] studied the problem of mining causal structures over transaction databases.

The use of metarules as syntactic or semantic filters defining the form of interesting single-dimensional association rules was proposed in Klemettinen, Mannila, Ronkainen, et al. [KMR+94]. Metarule-guided mining, where the metarule consequent specifies an action (such as Bayesian clustering or plotting) to be applied to the data satisfying the metarule antecedent, was proposed in Shen, Ong, Mitbander, and Zaniolo [SOMZ96]. A relation-based approach to metarule-guided mining of association rules was studied in Fu and Han [FH95]. A data cube–based approach was studied in Kamber, Han, and Chiang [KHC97]. The constraint-based association rule mining of Section 6.6.2 was studied in Ng, Lakshmanan, Han, and Pang [NLHP98], Lakshmanan, Ng, Han, and Pang [LNHP99], and Pei and Han [PH00]. An efficient method for mining constrained correlated sets was given in Grahne, Lakshmanan, and Wang [GLW00]. Other ideas involving the use of templates or predicate constraints in mining have been discussed in [AK93, DT93, HK91, LHC97, ST96, SVA97].

The association mining language presented in this chapter was based on an extension of the data mining query language, DMQL, proposed in Han, Fu, Wang, et al. [HFW+96], by incorporation of the spirit of the SQL-like operator for mining single-dimensional association rules proposed by Meo, Psaila, and Ceri [MPC96]. It is expected that our future revision will follow the syntax of *OLE DB for Data Mining (DM)*, proposed by Microsoft Corporation [Mic00].

An efficient incremental updating of mined association rules was proposed by Cheung, Han, Ng, and Wong [CHNW96]. Parallel and distributed association data mining under the Apriori framework was studied by Park, Chen, and Yu [PCY95b], Agrawal and Shafer [AS96], and Cheung, Han, Ng, et al. [CHN+96]. Another parallel association mining method which explores itemset clustering using a vertical database layout was proposed in Zaki, Parthasarathy, Ogihara, and Li [ZPOL97].

# Classification and Prediction

Databases are rich with hidden information that can be used for making intelligent business decisions. Classification and prediction are two forms of data analysis that can be used to extract models describing important data classes or to predict future data trends. Whereas *classification* predicts categorical labels, *prediction* models continuous-valued functions. For example, a classification model may be built to categorize bank loan applications as either safe or risky, while a prediction model may be built to predict the expenditures of potential customers on computer equipment given their income and occupation. Many classification and prediction methods have been proposed by researchers in machine learning, expert systems, statistics, and neurobiology. Most algorithms are memory resident, typically assuming a small data size. Recent database mining research has built on such work, developing scalable classification and prediction techniques capable of handling large disk-resident data. These techniques often consider parallel and distributed processing.

In this chapter, you will learn basic techniques for data classification such as decision tree induction, Bayesian classification and Bayesian belief networks, and neural networks. The integration of data warehousing technology with classification is also discussed, as well as association-based classification. Other approaches to classification, such as *k*-nearest neighbor classifiers, case-based reasoning, genetic algorithms, rough sets, and fuzzy logic techniques are introduced. Methods for prediction, including linear, nonlinear, and generalized linear regression models, are briefly discussed. Where applicable, you will learn of modifications, extensions, and optimizations to these techniques for their application to data classification and prediction for large databases.

## 7.1 What Is Classification? What Is Prediction?

**Data classification** is a two-step process (Figure 7.1). In the first step, a model is built describing a predetermined set of data classes or concepts. The model is

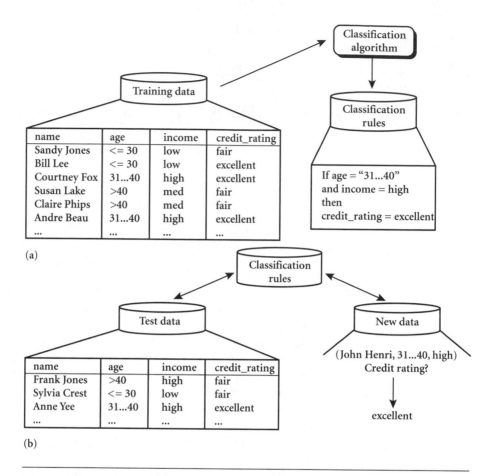

**Figure 7.1** The data classification process: (a) *Learning:* Training data are analyzed by a classification algorithm. Here, the class label attribute is *credit_rating*, and the learned model or classifier is represented in the form of classification rules. (b) *Classification:* Test data are used to estimate the accuracy of the classification rules. If the accuracy is considered acceptable, the rules can be applied to the classification of new data tuples.

constructed by analyzing database tuples described by attributes. Each tuple is assumed to belong to a predefined class, as determined by one of the attributes, called the **class label attribute**. In the context of classification, data tuples are also referred to as *samples, examples,* or *objects.* The data tuples analyzed to build the model collectively form the **training data set.** The individual tuples making up the training set are referred to as **training samples** and are randomly selected from the sample population. Since the class label of each training sample *is provided,* this step is also known as **supervised learning** (i.e., the learning of the model is "supervised" in that it is told to which class each training sample belongs). It contrasts with **unsupervised learning** (or **clustering**), in which the class label of each training sample is not known, and the number or set of classes to be learned may not be known in advance. Clustering is the topic of Chapter 8.

Typically, the learned model is represented in the form of classification rules, decision trees, or mathematical formulae. For example, given a database of customer credit information, classification rules can be learned to identify customers as having either excellent or fair credit ratings (Figure 7.1(a)). The rules can be used to categorize future data samples, as well as provide a better understanding of the database contents.

In the second step (Figure 7.1(b)), the model is used for classification. First, the predictive accuracy of the model (or classifier) is estimated. Section 7.9 describes several methods for estimating classifier accuracy. The **holdout method** is a simple technique that uses a **test set** of class-labeled samples. These samples are randomly selected and are independent of the training samples. The **accuracy** of a model on a given test set is the percentage of test set samples that are correctly classified by the model. For each test sample, the known class label is compared with the learned model's class prediction for that sample. Note that if the accuracy of the model were estimated based on the training data set, this estimate could be optimistic since the learned model tends to **overfit** the data (that is, it may have incorporated some particular anomalies of the training data that are not present in the overall sample population). Therefore, a test set is used.

If the accuracy of the model is considered acceptable, the model can be used to classify future data tuples or objects for which the class label is not known. (Such data are also referred to in the machine learning literature as "unknown" or "previously unseen" data.) For example, the classification rules learned in Figure 7.1(a) from the analysis of data from existing customers can be used to predict the credit rating of new or future (i.e., previously unseen) customers.

"*How is prediction different from classification?*" **Prediction** can be viewed as the construction and use of a model to assess the class of an unlabeled sample, or to assess the value or value ranges of an attribute that a given sample is likely to have. In this view, classification and regression are the two major types of prediction problems, where classification is used to predict discrete or nominal values, while regression is used to predict continuous or ordered values. In our view, however, we refer to the use of prediction to predict class labels as *classification*, and the use of prediction to predict continuous values (e.g., using regression techniques) as *prediction*. This view is commonly accepted in data mining.

Classification and prediction have numerous applications including credit approval, medical diagnosis, performance prediction, and selective marketing.

**Example 7.1**   Suppose that we have a database of customers on the *AllElectronics* mailing list. The mailing list is used to send out promotional literature describing new products and upcoming price discounts. The database describes attributes of the customers, such as their name, age, income, occupation, and credit rating. The customers can be classified as to whether or not they have purchased a computer at *AllElectronics*.

Suppose that new customers are added to the database and that you would like to notify these customers of an upcoming computer sale. To send out promotional literature to every new customer in the database can be quite costly. A more cost-efficient method would be to target only those new customers who are likely to purchase a new computer. A classification model can be constructed and used for this purpose.

Suppose instead that you would like to predict the number of major purchases that a customer will make at *AllElectronics* during a fiscal year. Since the predicted value here is ordered, a prediction model can be constructed for this purpose. ∎

## 7.2 Issues Regarding Classification and Prediction

This section describes issues regarding preprocessing the data for classification and prediction. Criteria for the comparison and evaluation of classification methods are also described.

### 7.2.1 Preparing the Data for Classification and Prediction

The following preprocessing steps may be applied to the data in order to help improve the accuracy, efficiency, and scalability of the classification or prediction process.

- **Data cleaning:** This refers to the preprocessing of data in order to remove or reduce *noise* (by applying smoothing techniques, for example) and the treatment of *missing values* (e.g., by replacing a missing value with the most commonly occurring value for that attribute, or with the most probable value based on statistics). Although most classification algorithms have some mechanisms for handling noisy or missing data, this step can help reduce confusion during learning.

- **Relevance analysis:** Many of the attributes in the data may be *irrelevant* to the classification or prediction task. For example, data recording the day of the week on which a bank loan application was filed is unlikely to be relevant to the success of the application. Furthermore, other attributes may be *redundant*. Hence, relevance analysis may be performed on the data with the aim of removing any irrelevant or redundant attributes from the learning process. In machine learning, this step is known as *feature selection*. Including such attributes may otherwise slow down, and possibly mislead, the learning step.

    Ideally, the time spent on relevance analysis, when added to the time spent on learning from the resulting "reduced" feature subset, should be less than the time that would have been spent on learning from the original set of features. Hence, such analysis can help improve classification efficiency and scalability.

- **Data transformation:** The data can be *generalized* to higher-level concepts. Concept hierarchies may be used for this purpose. This is particularly useful for continuous-valued attributes. For example, numeric values for the attribute *income* may be generalized to discrete ranges such as *low, medium,* and *high*. Similarly, nominal-valued attributes, like *street*, can be generalized to higher-level concepts, like *city*. Since generalization compresses the original training data, fewer input/output operations may be involved during learning.

  The data may also be normalized, particularly when neural networks or methods involving distance measurements are used in the learning step. **Normalization** involves scaling all values for a given attribute so that they fall within a small specified range, such as −1.0 to 1.0, or 0.0 to 1.0. In methods that use distance measurements, for example, this would prevent attributes with initially large ranges (like, say, *income*) from outweighing attributes with initially smaller ranges (such as binary attributes).

Data cleaning, relevance analysis, and data transformation are described in greater detail in Chapter 3 of this book. Relevance analysis is also described in Chapter 5.

## 7.2.2 Comparing Classification Methods

Classification and prediction methods can be compared and evaluated according to the following criteria:

- **Predictive accuracy:** This refers to the ability of the model to correctly predict the class label of new or previously unseen data.
- **Speed:** This refers to the computation costs involved in generating and using the model.
- **Robustness:** This is the ability of the model to make correct predictions given noisy data or data with missing values.
- **Scalability:** This refers to the ability to construct the model efficiently given large amounts of data.
- **Interpretability:** This refers to the level of understanding and insight that is provided by the model.

These issues are discussed throughout the chapter. The database research community's contributions to classification and prediction for data mining have emphasized the scalability aspect, particularly with respect to decision tree induction.

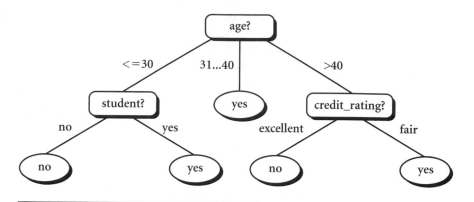

**Figure 7.2** A decision tree for the concept *buys_computer*, indicating whether or not a customer at *AllElectronics* is likely to purchase a computer. Each internal (nonleaf) node represents a test on an attribute. Each leaf node represents a class (either *buys_computer = yes* or *buys_computer = no*).

## 7.3 Classification by Decision Tree Induction

*"What is a decision tree?"* A **decision tree** is a flow-chart-like tree structure, where each *internal node* denotes a test on an attribute, each *branch* represents an outcome of the test, and *leaf nodes* represent classes or class distributions. The topmost node in a tree is the *root* node. A typical decision tree is shown in Figure 7.2. It represents the concept *buys_computer*, that is, it predicts whether or not a customer at *AllElectronics* is likely to purchase a computer. Internal nodes are denoted by rectangles, and leaf nodes are denoted by ovals.

In order to classify an unknown sample, the attribute values of the sample are tested against the decision tree. A path is traced from the root to a leaf node that holds the class prediction for that sample. Decision trees can easily be converted to classification rules.

In Section 7.3.1, we describe a basic algorithm for learning decision trees. When decision trees are built, many of the branches may reflect noise or outliers in the training data. *Tree pruning* attempts to identify and remove such branches, with the goal of improving classification accuracy on unseen data. Tree pruning is described in Section 7.3.2. The extraction of classification rules from decision trees is discussed in Section 7.3.3. Enhancements of the basic decision tree algorithm are given in Section 7.3.4. Scalability issues for the induction of decision trees from large databases are discussed in Section 7.3.5. Section 7.3.6 describes the integration of decision tree induction with data warehousing facilities, such as data cubes, allowing the mining of decision trees at multiple levels of granularity. Decision trees have been used in many application areas ranging from medicine to

**Algorithm: Generate_decision_tree.** Generate a decision tree from the given training data.

**Input:** The training samples, *samples*, represented by discrete-valued attributes; the set of candidate attributes, *attribute-list*.

**Output:** A decision tree.

**Method:**

(1)     create a node $N$;
(2)     **if** *samples* are all of the same class, $C$ **then**
(3)         return $N$ as a leaf node labeled with the class $C$;
(4)     **if** *attribute-list* is empty **then**
(5)         return $N$ as a leaf node labeled with the most common class in *samples*; // majority voting
(6)     select *test-attribute*, the attribute among *attribute-list* with the highest information gain;
(7)     label node $N$ with *test-attribute*;
(8)     **for each** known value $a_i$ **of** *test-attribute* // partition the samples
(9)         grow a branch from node $N$ for the condition *test-attribute* $= a_i$;
(10)     let $s_i$ be the set of samples in *samples* for which *test-attribute* $= a_i$; // a partition
(11)     **if** $s_i$ is empty **then**
(12)         attach a leaf labeled with the most common class in *samples*;
(13)     **else** attach the node returned by Generate_decision_tree($s_i$, *attribute-list–test-attribute*);

---

**Figure 7.3** Basic algorithm for inducing a decision tree from training samples.

game theory and business. They are the basis of several commercial rule induction systems.

## 7.3.1 Decision Tree Induction

The basic algorithm for decision tree induction is a greedy algorithm that constructs decision trees in a top-down recursive divide-and-conquer manner. The algorithm, summarized in Figure 7.3, is a version of ID3, a well-known decision tree induction algorithm. Extensions to the algorithm are discussed in Sections 7.3.2 to 7.3.6. The basic strategy is as follows.

- The tree starts as a single node representing the training samples (step 1).

- If the samples are all of the same class, then the node becomes a leaf and is labeled with that class (steps 2 and 3).

- Otherwise, the algorithm uses an entropy-based measure known as *information gain* as a heuristic for selecting the attribute that will best separate the samples into individual classes (step 6). This attribute becomes the "test" or "decision" attribute at the node (step 7). In this version of the algorithm, all attributes are categorical, that is, discrete-valued. Continuous-valued attributes must be discretized.

- A branch is created for each known value of the test attribute, and the samples are partitioned accordingly (steps 8-10).

- The algorithm uses the same process recursively to form a decision tree for the samples at each partition. Once an attribute has occurred at a node, it need not be considered in any of the node's descendents (step 13).

- The recursive partitioning stops only when any one of the following conditions is true:

  (a) All samples for a given node belong to the same class (steps 2 and 3), or
  (b) There are no remaining attributes on which the samples may be further partitioned (step 4). In this case, **majority voting** is employed (step 5). This involves converting the given node into a leaf and labeling it with the class in majority among *samples*. Alternatively, the class distribution of the node samples may be stored.
  (c) There are no samples for the branch *test-attribute* = $a_i$ (step 11). In this case, a leaf is created with the majority class in *samples* (step 12).

### Attribute Selection Measure

The **information gain** measure is used to select the test attribute at each node in the tree. Such a measure is referred to as an *attribute selection measure* or a *measure of the goodness of split*. The attribute with the highest information gain (or greatest *entropy* reduction) is chosen as the test attribute for the current node. This attribute minimizes the information needed to classify the samples in the resulting partitions and reflects the least randomness or "impurity" in these partitions. Such an information-theoretic approach minimizes the expected number of tests needed to classify an object and guarantees that a simple (but not necessarily the simplest) tree is found.

Let $S$ be a set consisting of $s$ data samples. Suppose the class label attribute has $m$ distinct values defining $m$ distinct classes, $C_i$ (for $i = 1, \ldots, m$). Let $s_i$ be the number of samples of $S$ in class $C_i$. The expected information needed to classify a given sample is given by

$$I(s_1, s_2, \ldots, s_m) = -\sum_{i=1}^{m} p_i \log_2(p_i), \tag{7.1}$$

where $p_i$ is the probability that an arbitrary sample belongs to class $C_i$ and is estimated by $s_i/s$. Note that a log function to the base 2 is used since the information is encoded in bits.

Let attribute $A$ have $v$ distinct values, $\{a_1, a_2, \cdots, a_v\}$. Attribute $A$ can be used to partition $S$ into $v$ subsets, $\{S_1, S_2, \cdots, S_v\}$, where $S_j$ contains those samples in $S$

that have value $a_j$ of $A$. If $A$ were selected as the test attribute (i.e., the best attribute for splitting), then these subsets would correspond to the branches grown from the node containing the set $S$. Let $s_{ij}$ be the number of samples of class $C_i$ in a subset $S_j$. The **entropy**, or expected information based on the partitioning into subsets by $A$, is given by

$$E(A) = \sum_{j=1}^{v} \frac{s_{1j} + \cdots + s_{mj}}{s} I(s_{1j}, \ldots, s_{mj}). \tag{7.2}$$

The term $\frac{s_{1j} + \cdots + s_{mj}}{s}$ acts as the weight of the $j$th subset and is the number of samples in the subset (i.e., having value $a_j$ of $A$) divided by the total number of samples in $S$. The smaller the entropy value, the greater the purity of the subset partitions. Note that for a given subset $S_j$,

$$I(s_{1j}, s_{2j}, \ldots, s_{mj}) = -\sum_{i=1}^{m} p_{ij} \log_2(p_{ij}) \tag{7.3}$$

where $p_{ij} = \frac{s_{ij}}{|S_j|}$ and is the probability that a sample in $S_j$ belongs to class $C_i$.

The encoding information that would be gained by branching on $A$ is

$$Gain(A) = I(s_1, s_2, \ldots, s_m) - E(A). \tag{7.4}$$

In other words, $Gain(A)$ is the expected reduction in entropy caused by knowing the value of attribute $A$.

The algorithm computes the information gain of each attribute. The attribute with the highest information gain is chosen as the test attribute for the given set $S$. A node is created and labeled with the attribute, branches are created for each value of the attribute, and the samples are partitioned accordingly.

**Example 7.2** **Induction of a decision tree.**    Table 7.1 presents a training set of data tuples taken from the *AllElectronics* customer database. (The data are adapted from [Qui86].) The class label attribute, *buys_computer*, has two distinct values (namely, {*yes, no*}); therefore, there are two distinct classes ($m = 2$). Let class $C_1$ correspond to *yes* and class $C_2$ correspond to *no*. There are 9 samples of class *yes* and 5 samples of class *no*. To compute the information gain of each attribute, we first use Equation (7.1) to compute the expected information needed to classify a given sample:

$$I(s_1, s_2) = I(9, 5) = -\frac{9}{14} \log_2 \frac{9}{14} - \frac{5}{14} \log_2 \frac{5}{14} = 0.940.$$

Next, we need to compute the entropy of each attribute. Let's start with the attribute *age*. We need to look at the distribution of *yes* and *no* samples for each value of *age*. We compute the expected information for each of these distributions.

**Table 7.1**    Training data tuples from the *AllElectronics* customer database.

| RID | age | income | student | credit_rating | Class: buys_computer |
|-----|-----|--------|---------|---------------|----------------------|
| 1 | <=30 | high | no | fair | no |
| 2 | <=30 | high | no | excellent | no |
| 3 | 31 ... 40 | high | no | fair | yes |
| 4 | >40 | medium | no | fair | yes |
| 5 | >40 | low | yes | fair | yes |
| 6 | >40 | low | yes | excellent | no |
| 7 | 31 ... 40 | low | yes | excellent | yes |
| 8 | <=30 | medium | no | fair | no |
| 9 | <=30 | low | yes | fair | yes |
| 10 | >40 | medium | yes | fair | yes |
| 11 | <=30 | medium | yes | excellent | yes |
| 12 | 31 ... 40 | medium | no | excellent | yes |
| 13 | 31 ... 40 | high | yes | fair | yes |
| 14 | >40 | medium | no | excellent | no |

For *age* = "<=30":

$s_{11} = 2$    $s_{21} = 3$    $I(s_{11}, s_{21}) = 0.971$

For *age* = "31 ... 40":

$s_{12} = 4$    $s_{22} = 0$    $I(s_{12}, s_{22}) = 0$

*For* age = ">40":

$s_{13} = 3$    $s_{23} = 2$    $I(s_{13}, s_{23}) = 0.971$

Using Equation (7.2), the expected information needed to classify a given sample if the samples are partitioned according to *age* is

$$E(age) = \frac{5}{14}I(s_{11}, s_{21}) + \frac{4}{14}I(s_{12}, s_{22}) + \frac{5}{14}I(s_{13}, s_{23}) = 0.694.$$

Hence, the gain in information from such a partitioning would be

$$Gain(age) = I(s_1, s_2) - E(age) = 0.246.$$

Similarly, we can compute *Gain(income)* = 0.029, *Gain(student)* = 0.151, and *Gain(credit_rating)* = 0.048. Since *age* has the highest information gain among the attributes, it is selected as the test attribute. A node is created and labeled with *age*, and branches are grown for each of the attribute's values. The samples are then partitioned accordingly, as shown in Figure 7.4. Notice that the samples

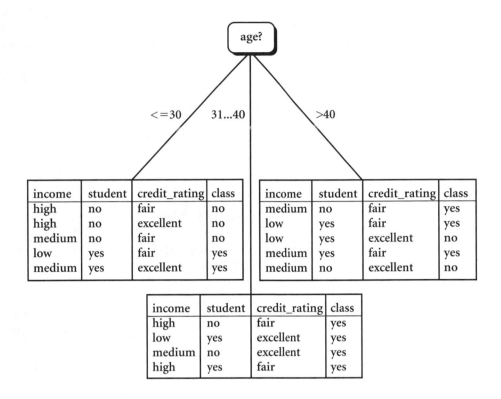

**Figure 7.4** The attribute *age* has the highest information gain and therefore becomes a test attribute at the root node of the decision tree. Branches are grown for each value of *age*. The samples are shown partitioned according to each branch.

falling into the partition for *age* = "*31 . . . 40*" all belong to the same class. Since they all belong to class *yes*, a leaf should therefore be created at the end of this branch and labeled with *yes*. The final decision tree returned by the algorithm is shown in Figure 7.2. ∎

In summary, decision tree induction algorithms have been used for classification in a wide range of application domains. Such systems do not use domain knowledge. The learning and classification steps of decision tree induction are generally fast.

### 7.3.2 Tree Pruning

When a decision tree is built, many of the branches will reflect anomalies in the training data due to noise or outliers. Tree pruning methods address this problem of *overfitting* the data. Such methods typically use statistical measures to remove the least reliable branches, generally resulting in faster classification and an improvement in the ability of the tree to correctly classify independent test data.

*"How does tree pruning work?"* There are two common approaches to tree pruning.

In the **prepruning** approach, a tree is "pruned" by halting its construction early (e.g., by deciding not to further split or partition the subset of training samples at a given node). Upon halting, the node becomes a leaf. The leaf may hold the most frequent class among the subset samples or the probability distribution of those samples.

When constructing a tree, measures such as statistical significance, $\chi^2$, information gain, and so on, can be used to assess the goodness of a split. If partitioning the samples at a node would result in a split that falls below a prespecified threshold, then further partitioning of the given subset is halted. There are difficulties, however, in choosing an appropriate threshold. High thresholds could result in oversimplified trees, while low thresholds could result in very little simplification.

The second approach, **postpruning**, removes branches from a "fully grown" tree. A tree node is pruned by removing its branches. The *cost complexity* pruning algorithm is an example of the postpruning approach. The lowest unpruned node becomes a leaf and is labeled by the most frequent class among its former branches. For each nonleaf node in the tree, the algorithm calculates the expected error rate that would occur if the subtree at that node were pruned. Next, the expected error rate occurring if the node were not pruned is calculated using the error rates for each branch, combined by weighting according to the proportion of observations along each branch. If pruning the node leads to a greater expected error rate, then the subtree is kept. Otherwise, it is pruned. After generating a set of progressively pruned trees, an independent test set is used to estimate the accuracy of each tree. The decision tree that minimizes the expected error rate is preferred.

Rather than pruning trees based on expected error rates, we can prune trees based on the number of bits required to encode them. The "best pruned tree" is the one that minimizes the number of encoding bits. This method adopts the Minimum Description Length (MDL) principle, which follows the notion that the simplest solution is preferred. Unlike cost complexity pruning, it does not require an independent set of samples.

Alternatively, prepruning and postpruning may be interleaved for a combined approach. Postpruning requires more computation than prepruning, yet generally leads to a more reliable tree.

### 7.3.3 Extracting Classification Rules from Decision Trees

*"Can I get classification rules out of my decision tree? If so, how?"* The knowledge represented in decision trees can be extracted and represented in the form of classification IF-THEN rules. One rule is created for each path from the root to a

leaf node. Each attribute-value pair along a given path forms a conjunction in the rule antecedent ("IF" part). The leaf node holds the class prediction, forming the rule consequent ("THEN" part). The IF-THEN rules may be easier for humans to understand, particularly if the given tree is very large.

**Example 7.3**    **Generating classification rules from a decision tree.** The decision tree of Figure 7.2 can be converted to classification IF-THEN rules by tracing the path from the root node to each leaf node in the tree. The rules extracted from Figure 7.2 are

IF *age* = "<=30" AND *student* = "no"          THEN *buys_computer* = "no"

IF *age* = "<=30" AND *student* = "yes"         THEN *buys_computer* = "yes"

IF *age* = "31 . . . 40"                        THEN *buys_computer* = "yes"

IF *age* = ">40" AND *credit_rating* = "excellent"   THEN *buys_computer* = "no"

IF *age* = ">40" AND *credit_rating* = "fair"        THEN *buys_computer* = "yes"    ■

C4.5, a later version of the ID3 algorithm, uses the training samples to estimate the accuracy of each rule. Since this would result in an optimistic estimate of rule accuracy, C4.5 employs a pessimistic estimate to compensate for the bias. Alternatively, a set of test samples independent from the training set can be used to estimate rule accuracy.

A rule can be "pruned" by removing any condition in its antecedent that does not improve the estimated accuracy of the rule. For each class, rules within a class may then be ranked according to their estimated accuracy. Since it is possible that a given test sample will not satisfy any rule antecedent, a default rule assigning the majority class is typically added to the resulting rule set.

## 7.3.4 Enhancements to Basic Decision Tree Induction

*"What are some enhancements to basic decision tree induction?"* Many enhancements to the basic decision tree induction algorithm of Section 7.3.1 have been proposed. In this section, we discuss several major enhancements, many of which are incorporated into C4.5, a successor algorithm to ID3.

The basic decision tree induction algorithm of Section 7.3.1 requires all attributes to be categorical or discretized. The algorithm can be modified to allow for attributes that have a whole range of discrete or continuous values. A test on such an attribute $A$ results in two branches, corresponding to the conditions $A \leq V$ and $A > V$ for some numeric value, $V$, of $A$. Given $v$ values of $A$, then $v - 1$ possible splits are considered in determining $V$. Typically, the midpoints between each pair of adjacent values are considered. If the values are sorted in advance, then this requires only one pass through the values.

The information gain measure is biased in that it tends to prefer attributes with many values. Many alternatives have been proposed, such as gain ratio, which considers the probability of each attribute value. Various other selection measures exist, including the Gini index, the $\chi^2$ contingency table statistic, and the G-statistic.

Many methods have been proposed for handling missing attribute values. A missing or unknown value for an attribute $A$ may be replaced by the most common value for $A$, for example. Alternatively, the apparent information gain of attribute $A$ can be reduced by the proportion of samples with unknown values of $A$. In this way, "fractions" of a sample having a missing value can be partitioned into more than one branch at a test node. Other methods may look for the most probable value of $A$, or make use of known relationships between $A$ and other attributes.

By repeatedly splitting the data into smaller and smaller partitions, decision tree induction is prone to the problems of *fragmentation*, *repetition*, and *replication*. In **fragmentation**, the number of samples at a given branch becomes so small as to be statistically insignificant. One solution to this problem is to allow for the grouping of categorical attribute values. A tree node may test whether the value of an attribute belongs to a given set of values, such as $A_i \in \{a_1, a_2, \ldots, a_n\}$. Another alternative is to create binary decision trees, where each branch holds a Boolean test on an attribute. Binary trees result in less fragmentation of the data. Some empirical studies have found that binary decision trees tend to be more accurate than traditional decision trees. **Repetition** occurs when an attribute is repeatedly tested along a given branch of the tree. In **replication**, duplicate subtrees exist within the tree. These situations can impede the accuracy and comprehensibility of the resulting tree. **Attribute** (or feature) **construction** is an approach for preventing these three problems, where the limited representation of the given attributes is improved by creating new attributes based on the existing ones. Attribute construction is also discussed in Chapter 3, as a form of data transformation.

**Incremental** versions of decision tree induction have been proposed. When given new training data, these restructure the decision tree acquired from learning on previous training data, rather than relearning a new tree from scratch.

Additional enhancements to basic decision tree induction that address scalability and the integration of data warehousing techniques are discussed in Sections 7.3.5 and 7.3.6, respectively.

## 7.3.5 Scalability and Decision Tree Induction

*"How scalable is decision tree induction?"* The efficiency of existing decision tree algorithms, such as ID3 and C4.5, has been well established for relatively small data sets. Efficiency and scalability become issues of concern when these algorithms are applied to the mining of very large real-world databases. Most decision tree algorithms have the restriction that the training samples should reside in main memory. In data mining applications, very large training sets of millions of samples are common. Hence, this restriction limits the scalability of such algorithms, where the decision tree construction can become inefficient due to swapping of the training samples in and out of main and cache memories.

**Table 7.2**  Sample data for the class *buys_computer*.

| RID | credit_rating | age | buys_computer |
|-----|---------------|-----|---------------|
| 1 | excellent | 38 | yes |
| 2 | excellent | 26 | yes |
| 3 | fair | 35 | no |
| 4 | excellent | 49 | no |

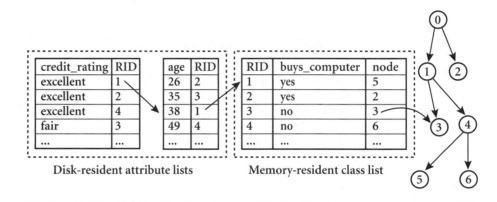

**Figure 7.5**  Attribute list and class list data structures used in SLIQ for the sample data of Table 7.2.

Early strategies for inducing decision trees from large databases include discretizing continuous attributes and sampling data at each node. These, however, still assume that the training set can fit in memory. An alternative method first partitions the data into subsets that individually can fit into memory, and then builds a decision tree from each subset. The final output classifier combines each classifier obtained from the subsets. Although this method allows for the classification of large data sets, its classification accuracy is not as high as the single classifier that would have been built using all of the data at once.

More recent decision tree algorithms that address the scalability issue have been proposed. Algorithms for the induction of decision trees from very large training sets include SLIQ and SPRINT, both of which can handle categorical and continuous-valued attributes. Both algorithms propose presorting techniques on disk-resident data sets that are too large to fit in memory. Both define the use of new data structures to facilitate the tree construction. SLIQ employs disk-resident *attribute lists* and a single memory-resident *class list*. The attribute lists and class list generated by SLIQ for the sample data of Table 7.2 are shown in Figure 7.5. Each attribute has an associated attribute list, indexed by *RID* (a record identifier). Each tuple is represented by a linkage of one entry from each attribute list to an

| credit_rating | buys_computer | RID |
|---|---|---|
| excellent | yes | 1 |
| excellent | yes | 2 |
| excellent | no | 4 |
| fair | no | 3 |
| ... | ... | ... |

| age | buys_computer | RID |
|---|---|---|
| 26 | yes | 2 |
| 35 | no | 3 |
| 38 | yes | 1 |
| 49 | no | 4 |
| ... | ... | ... |

**Figure 7.6**   Attribute list data structure used in SPRINT for the sample data of Table 7.2.

entry in the class list (holding the class label of the given tuple), which in turn is linked to its corresponding leaf node in the decision tree. The class list remains in memory since it is often accessed and modified in the building and pruning phases. The size of the class list grows proportionally with the number of tuples in the training set. When a class list cannot fit into memory, the performance of SLIQ decreases.

SPRINT uses a different *attribute list* data structure that holds the class and *RID* information, as shown in Figure 7.6. When a node is split, the attribute lists are partitioned and distributed among the resulting child nodes accordingly. When a list is partitioned, the order of the records in the list is maintained. Hence, partitioning lists does not require resorting. SPRINT was designed to be easily parallelized, further contributing to its scalability.

While both SLIQ and SPRINT handle disk-resident data sets that are too large to fit into memory, the scalability of SLIQ is limited by the use of its memory-resident data structure. SPRINT removes all memory restrictions, yet requires the use of a hash tree proportional in size to the training set. This may become expensive as the training set size grows.

RainForest is a framework for the scalable induction of decision trees. The method adapts to the amount of main memory available and applies to any decision tree induction algorithm. It maintains an AVC-set (Attribute-Value, Class label) indicating the class distribution for each attribute. RainForest reports a speed-up over SPRINT.

## 7.3.6  Integrating Data Warehousing Techniques and Decision Tree Induction

Decision tree induction can be integrated with data warehousing techniques for data mining. In this section, we discuss how a multidimensional data cube approach and attribute-oriented induction can be integrated with decision tree induction in order to facilitate interactive multilevel mining. In general, the techniques described here are applicable to other forms of learning as well.

The data cube approach can be integrated with decision tree induction to provide interactive multilevel mining of decision trees. The data cube and knowledge stored in the concept hierarchies can be used to induce decision trees at different levels of abstraction. Furthermore, once a decision tree has been derived, the concept hierarchies can be used to generalize or specialize individual nodes in the tree, allowing attribute roll-up or drill-down, and reclassification of the data for the newly specified abstraction level. This interactive feature allows users to focus their attention on areas of the tree or data that they find interesting.

Attribute-oriented induction (AOI) uses concept hierarchies to generalize the training data by replacing lower-level data with higher-level concepts (Chapter 5). When integrating AOI with decision tree induction, generalization to a very low (specific) concept level can result in quite large and bushy trees. Generalization to a very high concept level can result in decision trees of little use, where interesting and important subconcepts are lost due to overgeneralization. Instead, generalization should be to some intermediate concept level, set by a domain expert or controlled by a user-specified threshold. Hence, the use of AOI may result in classification trees that are more understandable, smaller, and therefore easier to interpret than trees obtained from methods operating on ungeneralized (larger) sets of low-level data (such as SLIQ or SPRINT).

A criticism of typical decision tree generation is that, because of the recursive partitioning, some resulting data subsets may become so small that partitioning them further would have no statistically significant basis. The maximum size of such "insignificant" data subsets can be statistically determined. To deal with this problem, an **exception threshold** may be introduced. If the portion of samples in a given subset is less than the threshold, further partitioning of the subset is halted. Instead, a leaf node is created that stores the subset and class distribution of the subset samples.

Owing to the large amount and wide diversity of data in large databases, it may not be reasonable to assume that each leaf node will contain samples belonging to the same class. This problem may be addressed by employing a **precision** or **classification threshold**. Further partitioning of the data subset at a given node is terminated if the percentage of samples belonging to any given class at that node exceeds this threshold.

A data mining query language may be used to specify and facilitate the enhanced decision tree induction method. Suppose that the data mining task is to predict the credit risk of customers in their thirties, based on their income and occupation. This may be specified as the following data mining query:

**mine classification**
**analyze** credit_risk
**in relevance to** income, occupation
**from** Customer_db
**where** (age >= 30) **and** (age < 40)
**display as** rules

The above query, expressed in DMQL, executes a relational query on *Customer_ db* to retrieve the task-relevant data. Tuples not satisfying the **where** clause are ignored, and only the data concerning the attributes specified in the **in relevance to** clause and the class label attribute (*credit_risk*) are collected. AOI is then performed on this data. Since the query has not specified which concept hierarchies to employ, default hierarchies are used. A graphical user interface may be designed to facilitate user specification of data mining tasks via such a data mining query language. In this way, the user can help guide the automated data mining process.

## 7.4 Bayesian Classification

*"What are Bayesian classifiers?"* Bayesian classifiers are statistical classifiers. They can predict class membership probabilities, such as the probability that a given sample belongs to a particular class.

Bayesian classification is based on Bayes theorem, described below. Studies comparing classification algorithms have found a simple Bayesian classifier known as the *naive Bayesian classifier* to be comparable in performance with decision tree and neural network classifiers. Bayesian classifiers have also exhibited high accuracy and speed when applied to large databases.

Naive Bayesian classifiers assume that the effect of an attribute value on a given class is independent of the values of the other attributes. This assumption is called *class conditional independence*. It is made to simplify the computations involved and, in this sense, is considered "naive." *Bayesian belief networks* are graphical models, which unlike naive Bayesian classifiers, allow the representation of dependencies among subsets of attributes. Bayesian belief networks can also be used for classification.

Section 7.4.1 reviews basic probability notation and Bayes theorem. You will then learn naive Bayesian classification in Section 7.4.2. Bayesian belief networks are described in Section 7.4.3.

### 7.4.1 Bayes Theorem

Let $X$ be a data sample whose class label is unknown. Let $H$ be some hypothesis, such as that the data sample $X$ belongs to a specified class $C$. For classification problems, we want to determine $P(H|X)$, the probability that the hypothesis $H$ holds given the observed data sample $X$.

$P(H|X)$ is the **posterior probability**, or *a posteriori probability*, of $H$ conditioned on $X$. For example, suppose the world of data samples consists of fruits, described by their color and shape. Suppose that $X$ is red and round, and that $H$ is the hypothesis that $X$ is an apple. Then $P(H|X)$ reflects our confidence that $X$ is an apple given that we have seen that $X$ is red and round. In contrast, $P(H)$ is the **prior probability**, or *a priori probability,* of $H$. For our example, this is the probability that any given data sample is an apple, regardless of how the data sample looks. The posterior probability, $P(H|X)$, is based on more information (such as background knowledge) than the prior probability, $P(H)$, which is independent of $X$.

Similarly, $P(X|H)$ is the posterior probability of $X$ conditioned on $H$. That is, it is the probability that $X$ is red and round given that we know that it is true that $X$ is an apple. $P(X)$ is the prior probability of $X$. Using our example, it is the probability that a data sample from our set of fruits is red and round.

"*How are these probabilities estimated?*" $P(X)$, $P(H)$, and $P(X|H)$ may be estimated from the given data, as we shall see below. **Bayes theorem** is useful in that it provides a way of calculating the posterior probability, $P(H|X)$, from $P(H)$, $P(X)$, and $P(X|H)$. Bayes theorem is

$$P(H|X) = \frac{P(X|H)P(H)}{P(X)}. \tag{7.5}$$

In the next section, you will learn how Bayes theorem is used in the naive Bayesian classifier.

## 7.4.2 Naive Bayesian Classification

The **naive Bayesian** classifier, or **simple Bayesian** classifier, works as follows:

1. Each data sample is represented by an $n$-dimensional feature vector, $X = (x_1, x_2, \ldots, x_n)$, depicting $n$ measurements made on the sample from $n$ attributes, respectively, $A_1, A_2, \ldots, A_n$.

2. Suppose that there are $m$ classes, $C_1, C_2, \ldots, C_m$. Given an unknown data sample, $X$ (i.e., having no class label), the classifier will predict that $X$ belongs to the class having the highest posterior probability, conditioned on $X$. That is, the naive Bayesian classifier assigns an unknown sample $X$ to the class $C_i$ if and only if

$$P(C_i|X) > P(C_j|X) \quad \text{for } 1 \leq j \leq m, j \neq i.$$

Thus we maximize $P(C_i|X)$. The class $C_i$ for which $P(C_i|X)$ is maximized is called the *maximum posteriori hypothesis*. By Bayes theorem (Equation (7.5)),

$$P(C_i|X) = \frac{P(X|C_i)P(C_i)}{P(X)}. \tag{7.6}$$

3. As $P(X)$ is constant for all classes, only $P(X|C_i)P(C_i)$ need be maximized. If the class prior probabilities are not known, then it is commonly assumed that the classes are equally likely, that is, $P(C_1) = P(C_2) = \ldots = P(C_m)$, and we would therefore maximize $P(X|C_i)$. Otherwise, we maximize $P(X|C_i)P(C_i)$. Note that the class prior probabilities may be estimated by $P(C_i) = \frac{s_i}{s}$, where $s_i$ is the number of training samples of class $C_i$, and $s$ is the total number of training samples.

**4.** Given data sets with many attributes, it would be extremely computationally expensive to compute $P(X|C_i)$. In order to reduce computation in evaluating $P(X|C_i)$, the naive assumption of **class conditional independence** is made. This presumes that the values of the attributes are conditionally independent of one another, given the class label of the sample, that is, there are no dependence relationships among the attributes. Thus,

$$P(X|C_i) = \prod_{k=1}^{n} P(x_k|C_i). \tag{7.7}$$

The probabilities $P(x_1|C_i), P(x_2|C_i), \ldots, P(x_n|C_i)$ can be estimated from the training samples, where

(a) If $A_k$ is categorical, then $P(x_k|C_i) = \frac{s_{ik}}{s_i}$, where $s_{ik}$ is the number of training samples of class $C_i$ having the value $x_k$ for $A_k$, and $s_i$ is the number of training samples belonging to $C_i$.

(b) If $A_k$ is continuous-valued, then the attribute is typically assumed to have a Gaussian distribution so that

$$P(x_k|C_i) = g(x_k, \mu_{C_i}, \sigma_{C_i}) = \frac{1}{\sqrt{2\pi}\sigma_{C_i}} e^{-\frac{(x_k - \mu_{C_i})^2}{2\sigma_{C_i}^2}}, \tag{7.8}$$

where $g(x_k, \mu_{C_i}, \sigma_{C_i})$ is the **Gaussian (normal) density function** for attribute $A_k$, while $\mu_{C_i}$ and $\sigma_{C_i}$ are the mean and standard deviation, respectively, given the values for attribute $A_k$ for training samples of class $C_i$.

**5.** In order to classify an unknown sample $X$, $P(X|C_i)P(C_i)$ is evaluated for each class $C_i$. Sample $X$ is then assigned to the class $C_i$ if and only if

$$P(X|C_i)P(C_i) > P(X|C_j)P(C_j) \quad \text{for } 1 \le j \le m, j \ne i.$$

In other words, it is assigned to the class $C_i$ for which $P(X|C_i)P(C_i)$ is the maximum.

*"How effective are Bayesian classifiers?"* In theory, Bayesian classifiers have the minimum error rate in comparison to all other classifiers. However, in practice this is not always the case owing to inaccuracies in the assumptions made for its use, such as class conditional independence, and the lack of available probability data. However, various empirical studies of this classifier in comparison to decision tree and neural network classifiers have found it to be comparable in some domains.

Bayesian classifiers are also useful in that they provide a theoretical justification for other classifiers that do not explicitly use Bayes theorem. For example, under certain assumptions, it can be shown that many neural network and curve-fitting algorithms output the *maximum posteriori* hypothesis, as does the naive Bayesian classifier.

**Example 7.4** **Predicting a class label using naive Bayesian classification:**   We wish to predict the class label of an unknown sample using naive Bayesian classification, given the same training data as in Example 7.2 for decision tree induction. The training data are in Table 7.1. The data samples are described by the attributes *age*, *income*, *student*, and *credit_rating*. The class label attribute, *buys_computer*, has two distinct values (namely, {*yes, no*}). Let $C_1$ correspond to the class *buys_computer* = "*yes*" and $C_2$ correspond to *buys_computer* = "*no*". The unknown sample we wish to classify is

$$X = (age = \text{"<=30"}, income = \text{"medium"}, student = \text{"yes"}, credit\_rating$$
$$= \text{"fair"}).$$

We need to maximize $P(X|C_i)P(C_i)$, for $i$ = 1, 2. $P(C_i)$, the prior probability of each class, can be computed based on the training samples:

$$P(buys\_computer = \text{"yes"}) = 9/14 = 0.643$$

$$P(buys\_computer = \text{"no"}) = 5/14 = 0.357$$

To compute $P(X|C_i)$, for $i$ = 1, 2, we compute the following conditional probabilities:

| | |
|---|---|
| *P(age = "<30"* \| *buys_computer = "yes")* | $= 2/9 = 0.222$ |
| *P(age = "<30"* \| *buys_computer = "no")* | $= 3/5 = 0.600$ |
| *P(income = "medium"* \| *buys_computer = "yes")* | $= 4/9 = 0.444$ |
| *P(income = "medium"* \| *buys_computer = "no")* | $= 2/5 = 0.400$ |
| *P(student = "yes"* \| *buys_computer = "yes")* | $= 6/9 = 0.667$ |
| *P(student = "yes"* \| *buys_computer = "no")* | $= 1/5 = 0.200$ |
| *P(credit_rating = "fair"* \| *buys_computer = "yes")* | $= 6/9 = 0.667$ |
| *P(credit_rating = "fair"* \| *buys_computer = "no")* | $= 2/5 = 0.400$ |

Using the above probabilities, we obtain

$$P(X|buys\_computer = \text{"yes"}) = 0.222 \times 0.444 \times 0.667 \times 0.667 = 0.044$$
$$P(X|buys\_computer = \text{"no"}) = 0.600 \times 0.400 \times 0.200 \times 0.400 = 0.019$$
$$P(X|buys\_computer = \text{"yes"})P(buys\_computer = \text{"yes"}) = 0.044 \times 0.643 = 0.028$$
$$P(X|buys\_computer = \text{"no"})P(buys\_computer = \text{"no"}) = 0.019 \times 0.357 = 0.007$$

Therefore, the naive Bayesian classifier predicts *buys_computer* = "*yes*" for sample $X$. ∎

### 7.4.3 Bayesian Belief Networks

The naive Bayesian classifier makes the assumption of class conditional independence, that is, given the class label of a sample, the values of the attributes are

(a)                                                      (b)

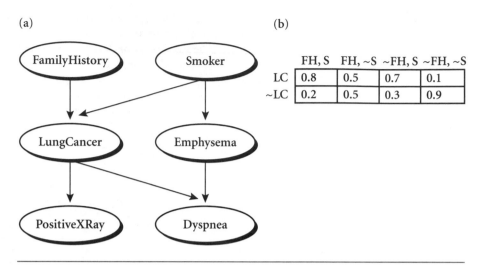

**Figure 7.7** (a) A simple Bayesian belief network. (b) The conditional probability table for the values of the variable *LungCancer (LC)* showing each possible combination of the values of its parent nodes, *FamilyHistory (FH)* and *Smoker (S)*. Figure is adapted from [RN95].

conditionally independent of one another. This assumption simplifies computation. When the assumption holds true, then the naive Bayesian classifier is the most accurate in comparison with all other classifiers. In practice, however, dependencies can exist between variables. **Bayesian belief networks** specify joint conditional probability distributions. They allow class conditional independencies to be defined between subsets of variables. They provide a graphical model of causal relationships, on which learning can be performed. These networks are also known as **belief networks**, **Bayesian networks**, and **probabilistic networks**. For brevity, we will refer to them as belief networks.

A belief network is defined by two components. The first is a *directed acyclic graph*, where each node represents a random variable and each arc represents a probabilistic dependence. If an arc is drawn from a node $Y$ to a node $Z$, then $Y$ is a **parent** or **immediate predecessor** of $Z$, and $Z$ is a **descendent** of $Y$. Each variable is conditionally independent of its nondescendents in the graph, given its parents. The variables may be discrete or continuous-valued. They may correspond to actual attributes given in the data or to "hidden variables" believed to form a relationship (such as medical syndromes in the case of medical data).

Figure 7.7(a) shows a simple belief network, adapted from [RN95] for six Boolean variables. The arcs allow a representation of causal knowledge. For example, having lung cancer is influenced by a person's family history of lung cancer, as well as whether or not the person is a smoker. Furthermore, the arcs also show that the variable *LungCancer* is conditionally independent of *Emphysema*, given its parents, *FamilyHistory* and *Smoker*. This means that once the values of *Fami-*

*lyHistory* and *Smoker* are known, then the variable *Emphysema* does not provide any additional information regarding *LungCancer*.

The second component defining a belief network consists of one *conditional probability table (CPT)* for each variable. The CPT for a variable $Z$ specifies the conditional distribution $P(Z|Parents(Z))$, where $Parents(Z)$ are the parents of $Z$. Figure 7.7(b) shows a CPT for *LungCancer*. The conditional probability for each value of *LungCancer* is given for each possible combination of values of its parents. For instance, from the upper leftmost and bottom rightmost entries, respectively, we see that

$$P(LungCancer = \text{"yes"} \mid FamilyHistory = \text{"yes"}, \ Smoker = \text{"yes"}) = 0.8$$

$$P(LungCancer = \text{"no"} \mid FamilyHistory = \text{"no"}, \ Smoker = \text{"no"}) = 0.9$$

The joint probability of any tuple $(z_1, \ldots, z_n)$ corresponding to the variables or attributes $Z_1, \ldots, Z_n$ is computed by

$$P(z_1, \ldots, z_n) = \prod_{i=1}^{n} P(z_i|Parents(Z_i)), \tag{7.9}$$

where the values for $P(z_i|Parents(Z_i))$ correspond to the entries in the CPT for $Z_i$.

A node within the network can be selected as an "output" node, representing a class label attribute. There may be more than one output node. Inference algorithms for learning can be applied on the network. The classification process, rather than returning a single class label, can return a probability distribution for the class label attribute, that is, predicting the probability of each class.

## 7.4.4 Training Bayesian Belief Networks

*"How does a Bayesian belief network learn?"* In the learning or training of a belief network, a number of scenarios are possible. The network structure may be given in advance or inferred from the data. The network variables may be *observable* or *hidden* in all or some of the training samples. The case of hidden data is also referred to as *missing values* or *incomplete data*.

If the network structure is known and the variables are observable, then training the network is straightforward. It consists of computing the CPT entries, as is similarly done when computing the probabilities involved in naive Bayesian classification.

When the network structure is given and some of the variables are hidden, then a method of gradient descent can be used to train the belief network. The object is to learn the values for the CPT entries. Let $S$ be a set of $s$ training samples, $X_1, X_2, \ldots, X_s$. Let $w_{ijk}$ be a CPT entry for the variable $Y_i = y_{ij}$ having the parents $U_i = u_{ik}$. For example, if $w_{ijk}$ is the upper leftmost CPT entry of Figure 7.7(b), then $Y_i$ is *LungCancer*; $y_{ij}$ is its value, "yes"; $U_i$ lists the parent nodes of $Y_i$, namely, {*FamilyHistory, Smoker*}; and $u_{ik}$ lists the values of the parent nodes, namely, {"yes", "yes"}. The $w_{ijk}$ are viewed as weights, analogous to the weights in hidden units of neural networks (Section 7.5). The set of weights is collectively referred to as $w$. The weights are initialized to random probability values. The gradient descent strategy performs greedy hill-climbing. At each iteration, the weights are updated and will eventually converge to a local optimum solution.

The method searches for the $w_{ijk}$ values that best model the data, based on the assumption that each possible setting of $w$ is equally likely. The goal is thus to maximize $P_w(S) = \prod_{d=1}^{s} P_w(X_d)$. This is done by following the gradient of $\ln P_w(S)$, which makes the problem simpler. Given the network structure and initialized $w_{ijk}$, the algorithm proceeds as follows:

1. **Compute the gradients:** For each $i, j, k$, compute

$$\frac{\partial \ln P_w(S)}{\partial w_{ijk}} = \sum_{d=1}^{s} \frac{P(Y_i = y_{ij}, U_i = u_{ik} | X_d)}{w_{ijk}} \qquad (7.10)$$

The probability in the right-hand side of Equation (7.10) is to be calculated for each training sample $X_d$ in $S$. For brevity, let's refer to this probability simply as $p$. When the variables represented by $Y_i$ and $U_i$ are hidden for some $X_d$, then the corresponding probability $p$ can be computed from the observed variables of the sample using standard algorithms for Bayesian network inference (such as those available in the commercial software package Hugin (*http://www.hugin.dk*)).

2. **Take a small step in the direction of the gradient:** The weights are updated by

$$w_{ijk} \leftarrow w_{ijk} + (l)\frac{\partial \ln P_w(S)}{\partial w_{ijk}}, \qquad (7.11)$$

where $l$ is the **learning rate** representing the step size, and $\frac{\partial \ln P_w(S)}{\partial w_{ijk}}$ is computed from Equation (7.10). The learning rate is set to a small constant.

3. **Renormalize the weights:** Because the weights $w_{ijk}$ are probability values, they must be between 0.0 and 1.0, and $\sum_j w_{ijk}$ must equal 1 for all $i, k$. These criteria are achieved by renormalizing the weights after they have been updated by Equation (7.11).

Several algorithms exist for learning the network structure from the training data given observable variables. The problem is one of discrete optimization. For solutions, please see the bibliographic notes at the end of this chapter.

# 7.5 Classification by Backpropagation

*"What is backpropagation?"* Backpropagation is a neural network learning algorithm. The field of neural networks was originally kindled by psychologists and neurobiologists who sought to develop and test computational analogues of neurons. Roughly speaking, a **neural network** is a set of connected input/output units where each connection has a weight associated with it. During the learning phase, the network learns by adjusting the weights so as to be able to predict the correct class label of the input samples. Neural network learning is also referred to as *connectionist learning* due to the connections between units.

Neural networks involve long training times and are therefore more suitable for applications where this is feasible. They require a number of parameters that are typically best determined empirically, such as the network topology or "structure." Neural networks have been criticized for their poor interpretability, since it is difficult for humans to interpret the symbolic meaning behind the learned weights. These features initially made neural networks less desirable for data mining.

Advantages of neural networks, however, include their high tolerance to noisy data as well as their ability to classify patterns on which they have not been trained. In addition, several algorithms have recently been developed for the extraction of rules from trained neural networks. These factors contribute towards the usefulness of neural networks for classification in data mining.

The most popular neural network algorithm is the backpropagation algorithm, proposed in the 1980s. In Section 7.5.1 you will learn about multilayer feed-forward networks, the type of neural network on which the backpropagation algorithm performs. Section 7.5.2 discusses defining a network topology. The backpropagation algorithm is described in Section 7.5.3. Rule extraction from trained neural networks is discussed in Section 7.5.4.

## 7.5.1 A Multilayer Feed-Forward Neural Network

The backpropagation algorithm performs learning on a **multilayer feed-forward** neural network. An example of such a network is shown in Figure 7.8. The inputs correspond to the attributes measured for each training sample. The inputs are fed simultaneously into a layer of units making up the **input layer**. The weighted outputs of these units are, in turn, fed simultaneously to a second layer of "neuronlike" units, known as a **hidden layer**. The hidden layer's weighted outputs can be input to another hidden layer, and so on. The number of hidden layers is arbitrary, although in practice, usually only one is used. The weighted outputs of the last hidden layer are input to units making up the **output layer**, which emits the network's prediction for given samples.

The units in the hidden layers and output layer are sometimes referred to as **neurodes**, due to their symbolic biological basis, or as **output units**. The multi-

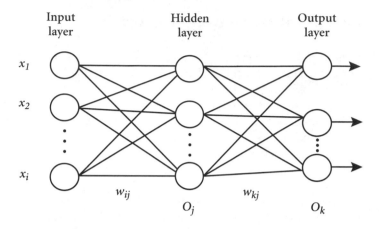

**Figure 7.8**   A multilayer feed-forward neural network: A training sample, $X = (x_1, x_2, \ldots, x_i)$, is fed to the input layer. Weighted connections exist between each layer, where $w_{ij}$ denotes the weight from a unit $j$ in one layer to a unit $i$ in the previous layer.

layer neural network shown in Figure 7.8 has two layers of output units. Therefore, we say that it is a **two-layer** neural network. Similarly, a network containing two hidden layers is called a *three-layer* neural network, and so on. The network is **feed-forward** in that none of the weights cycles back to an input unit or to an output unit of a previous layer. It is **fully connected** in that each unit provides input to each unit in the next forward layer.

Multilayer feed-forward networks of linear threshold functions, given enough hidden units, can closely approximate any function.

## 7.5.2 Defining a Network Topology

*"How can I design the topology of the neural network?"* Before training can begin, the user must decide on the network topology by specifying the number of units in the input layer, the number of hidden layers (if more than one), the number of units in each hidden layer, and the number of units in the output layer.

Normalizing the input values for each attribute measured in the training samples will help speed up the learning phase. Typically, input values are normalized so as to fall between 0.0 and 1.0. Discrete-valued attributes may be encoded such that there is one input unit per domain value. For example, if the domain of an attribute $A$ is $\{a_0, a_1, a_2\}$, then we may assign three input units to represent $A$. That is, we may have, say, $I_0, I_1, I_2$ as input units. Each unit is initialized to 0. If $A = a_0$, then $I_0$ is set to 1. If $A = a_1$, $I_1$ is set to 1, and so on. One output unit may be used to represent two classes (where the value 1 represents one class, and the value 0 represents the other). If there are more than two classes, then one output unit per class is used.

There are no clear rules as to the "best" number of hidden layer units. Network design is a trial-and-error process and may affect the accuracy of the resulting trained network. The initial values of the weights may also affect the resulting accuracy. Once a network has been trained and its accuracy is not considered acceptable, it is common to repeat the training process with a different network topology or a different set of initial weights.

### 7.5.3 **Backpropagation**

*"How does backpropagation work?"* Backpropagation learns by iteratively processing a set of training samples, comparing the network's prediction for each sample with the actual known class label. For each training sample, the weights are modified so as to minimize the mean squared error between the network's prediction and the actual class. These modifications are made in the "backwards" direction, that is, from the output layer, through each hidden layer down to the first hidden layer (hence the name *backpropagation*). Although it is not guaranteed, in general the weights will eventually converge, and the learning process stops. The algorithm is summarized in Figure 7.9. Each step is described below.

**Initialize the weights:**  The weights in the network are initialized to small random numbers (e.g., ranging from $-1.0$ to $1.0$, or $-0.5$ to $0.5$). Each unit has a *bias* associated with it, as explained below. The biases are similarly initialized to small random numbers.

Each training sample, $X$, is processed by the following steps.

**Propagate the inputs forward:**  In this step, the net input and output of each unit in the hidden and output layers are computed. First, the training sample is fed to the input layer of the network. Note that for unit $j$ in the input layer, its output is equal to its input, that is, $O_j = I_j$ for input unit $j$. The net input to each unit in the hidden and output layers is computed as a linear combination of its inputs. To help illustrate this, a hidden layer or output layer unit is shown in Figure 7.10. The inputs to the unit are, in fact, the outputs of the units connected to it in the previous layer. To compute the net input to the unit, each input connected to the unit is multiplied by its corresponding weight, and this is summed. Given a unit $j$ in a hidden or output layer, the net input, $I_j$, to unit $j$ is

$$I_j = \sum_i w_{ij}O_i + \theta_j, \tag{7.12}$$

where $w_{ij}$ is the weight of the connection from unit $i$ in the previous layer to unit $j$; $O_i$ is the output of unit $i$ from the previous layer; and $\theta_j$ is the **bias** of the unit. The bias acts as a threshold in that it serves to vary the activity of the unit.

**Algorithm:   Backpropagation.** Neural network learning for classification, using the backpropagation algorithm.

**Input:**  The training samples, *samples*; the learning rate, *l*; a multilayer feed-forward network, *network*.

**Output:**   A neural network trained to classify the samples.

**Method:**

(1)   Initialize all weights and biases in *network*;
(2)   **while** terminating condition is not satisfied {
(3)        **for** each training sample *X* in *samples* {
(4)            // Propagate the inputs forward:
(5)            **for** each hidden or output layer unit *j* {
(6)                $I_j = \sum_i w_{ij} O_i + \theta_j$; //compute the net input of unit *j* with respect to the previous layer, *i*
(7)                $O_j = \frac{1}{1+e^{-I_j}}$; } // compute the output of each unit *j*
(8)            // Backpropagate the errors:
(9)            **for** each unit *j* in the output layer
(10)               $Err_j = O_j(1 - O_j)(T_j - O_j)$; // compute the error
(11)           **for** each unit *j* in the hidden layers, from the last to the first hidden layer
(12)               $Err_j = O_j(1 - O_j) \sum_k Err_k w_{jk}$; // compute the error with respect to the next higher layer, *k*
(13)           **for** each weight $w_{ij}$ in *network* {
(14)               $\Delta w_{ij} = (l)Err_j O_i$; // weight increment
(15)               $w_{ij} = w_{ij} + \Delta w_{ij}$; } // weight update
(16)           **for** each bias $\theta_j$ in *network* {
(17)               $\Delta\theta_j = (l)Err_j$; // bias increment
(18)               $\theta_j = \theta_j + \Delta\theta_j$; } // bias update
(19)       } }

---

**Figure 7.9**   Backpropagation algorithm.

Each unit in the hidden and output layers takes its net input and then applies an **activation** function to it, as illustrated in Figure 7.10. The function symbolizes the activation of the neuron represented by the unit. The **logistic**, or **sigmoid**, function is used. Given the net input $I_j$ to unit *j*, then $O_j$, the output of unit *j*, is computed as

$$O_j = \frac{1}{1 + e^{-I_j}}. \tag{7.13}$$

This function is also referred to as a *squashing function*, since it maps a large input domain onto the smaller range of 0 to 1. The logistic function is non-

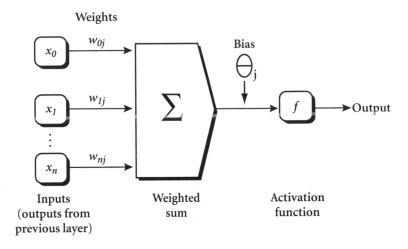

**Figure 7.10**  A hidden or output layer unit $j$: The inputs to unit $j$ are outputs from the previous layer. These are multiplied by their corresponding weights in order to form a weighted sum, which is added to the bias associated with unit $j$. A nonlinear activation function is applied to the net input.

linear and differentiable, allowing the backpropagation algorithm to model classification problems that are linearly inseparable.

**Backpropagate the error:**  The error is propagated backwards by updating the weights and biases to reflect the error of the network's prediction. For a unit $j$ in the output layer, the error $Err_j$ is computed by

$$Err_j = O_j(1 - O_j)(T_j - O_j) \tag{7.14}$$

where $O_j$ is the actual output of unit $j$, and $T_j$ is the *true* output, based on the known class label of the given training sample. Note that $O_j(1 - O_j)$ is the derivative of the logistic function.

To compute the error of a hidden layer unit $j$, the weighted sum of the errors of the units connected to unit $j$ in the next layer are considered. The error of a hidden layer unit $j$ is

$$Err_j = O_j(1 - O_j) \sum_k Err_k w_{jk}, \tag{7.15}$$

where $w_{jk}$ is the weight of the connection from unit $j$ to a unit $k$ in the next higher layer, and $Err_k$ is the error of unit $k$.

The weights and biases are updated to reflect the propagated errors. Weights are updated by the following equations, where $\Delta w_{ij}$ is the change in weight $w_{ij}$:

$$\Delta w_{ij} = (l)Err_j O_i \tag{7.16}$$

$$w_{ij} = w_{ij} + \Delta w_{ij} \tag{7.17}$$

*"What is the 'l' in Equation (7.16)?"* The variable $l$ is the **learning rate**, a constant typically having a value between 0.0 and 1.0. Backpropagation learns using a method of gradient descent to search for a set of weights that can model the given classification problem so as to minimize the mean squared distance between the network's class prediction and the actual class label of the samples. The learning rate helps to avoid getting stuck at a local minimum in decision space (i.e., where the weights appear to converge, but are not the optimum solution) and encourages finding the global minimum. If the learning rate is too small, then learning will occur at a very slow pace. If the learning rate is too large, then oscillation between inadequate solutions may occur. A rule of thumb is to set the learning rate to $1/t$, where $t$ is the number of iterations through the training set so far.

Biases are updated by the following equations below, where $\Delta\theta_j$ is the change in bias $\theta_j$:

$$\Delta\theta_j = (l)Err_j \tag{7.18}$$

$$\theta_j = \theta_j + \Delta\theta_j \tag{7.19}$$

Note that here we are updating the weights and biases after the presentation of each sample. This is referred to as **case updating**. Alternatively, the weight and bias increments could be accumulated in variables, so that the weights and biases are updated after all of the samples in the training set have been presented. This latter strategy is called **epoch updating**, where one iteration through the training set is an **epoch**. In theory, the mathematical derivation of backpropagation employs epoch updating, yet in practice, case updating is more common since it tends to yield more accurate results.

**Terminating condition:**   Training stops when

- all $\Delta w_{ij}$ in the previous epoch were so small as to be below some specified threshold, or
- the percentage of samples misclassified in the previous epoch is below some threshold, or
- a prespecified number of epochs has expired.

In practice, several hundreds of thousands of epochs may be required before the weights will converge.

**Example 7.5**  **Sample calculations for learning by the backpropagation algorithm:**   Figure 7.11 shows a multilayer feed-forward neural network. Let the learning rate be 0.9. The initial weight and bias values of the network are given in Table 7.3, along with the first training sample, $X = (1, 0, 1)$, whose class label is 1.

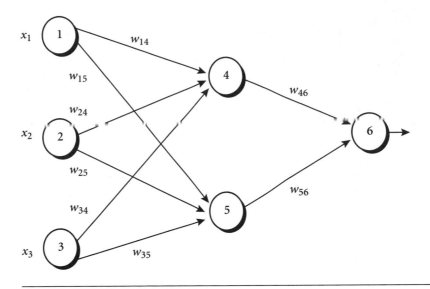

**Figure 7.11** An example of a multilayer feed-forward neural network.

**Table 7.3** Initial input, weight, and bias values.

| $x_1$ | $x_2$ | $x_3$ | $w_{14}$ | $w_{15}$ | $w_{24}$ | $w_{25}$ | $w_{34}$ | $w_{35}$ | $w_{46}$ | $w_{56}$ | $\theta_4$ | $\theta_5$ | $\theta_6$ |
|------|------|------|------|------|------|------|------|------|------|------|------|------|------|
| 1 | 0 | 1 | 0.2 | −0.3 | 0.4 | 0.1 | −0.5 | 0.2 | −0.3 | −0.2 | −0.4 | 0.2 | 0.1 |

**Table 7.4** The net input and output calculations.

| Unit $j$ | Net input, $I_j$ | Output, $O_j$ |
|------|------|------|
| 4 | $0.2 + 0 − 0.5 − 0.4 = −0.7$ | $1/(1 + e^{0.7}) = 0.332$ |
| 5 | $−0.3 + 0 + 0.2 + 0.2 = 0.1$ | $1/(1 + e^{-0.1}) = 0.525$ |
| 6 | $(−0.3)(0.332) − (0.2)(0.525) + 0.1 = −0.105$ | $1/(1 + e^{0.105}) = 0.474$ |

This example shows the calculations for backpropagation, given the first training sample, $X$. The sample is fed into the network, and the net input and output of each unit are computed. These values are shown in Table 7.4. The error of each unit is computed and propagated backwards. The error values are shown in Table 7.5. The weight and bias updates are shown in Table 7.6. ∎

**Table 7.5** Calculation of the error at each node.

| Unit $j$ | $Err_j$ |
|---|---|
| 6 | $(0.474)(1 - 0.474)(1 - 0.474) = 0.1311$ |
| 5 | $(0.525)(1 - 0.525)(0.1311)(-0.2) = -0.0065$ |
| 4 | $(0.332)(1 - 0.332)(0.1311)(-0.3) = -0.0087$ |

**Table 7.6** Calculations for weight and bias updating.

| Weight or bias | New value |
|---|---|
| $w_{46}$ | $-0.3 + (0.9)(0.1311)(0.332) = -0.261$ |
| $w_{56}$ | $-0.2 + (0.9)(0.1311)(0.525) = -0.138$ |
| $w_{14}$ | $0.2 + (0.9)(-0.0087)(1) = 0.192$ |
| $w_{15}$ | $-0.3 + (0.9)(-0.0065)(1) = -0.306$ |
| $w_{24}$ | $0.4 + (0.9)(-0.0087)(0) = 0.4$ |
| $w_{25}$ | $0.1 + (0.9)(-0.0065)(0) = 0.1$ |
| $w_{34}$ | $-0.5 + (0.9)(-0.0087)(1) = -0.508$ |
| $w_{35}$ | $0.2 + (0.9)(-0.0065)(1) = 0.194$ |
| $\theta_6$ | $0.1 + (0.9)(0.1311) = 0.218$ |
| $\theta_5$ | $0.2 + (0.9)(-0.0065) = 0.194$ |
| $\theta_4$ | $-0.4 + (0.9)(-0.0087) = -0.408$ |

Several variations and alternatives to the backpropagation algorithm have been proposed for classification in neural networks. These may involve the dynamic adjustment of the network topology and of the learning rate or other parameters, or the use of different error functions.

## 7.5.4 Backpropagation and Interpretability

*"How can I 'understand' what the backpropagation network has learned?"* A major disadvantage of neural networks lies in their knowledge representation. Acquired knowledge in the form of a network of units connected by weighted links is difficult for humans to interpret. This factor has motivated research in extracting the knowledge embedded in trained neural networks and in representing that knowledge symbolically. Methods include extracting rules from networks and sensitivity analysis.

Various algorithms for the extraction of rules have been proposed. The methods typically impose restrictions regarding procedures used in training the given neural network, the network topology, and the discretization of input values.

Fully connected networks are difficult to articulate. Hence, often the first step towards extracting rules from neural networks is **network pruning**. This consists of simplifying the network structure by removing weighted links that have the least effect on the trained network. For example, a weighted link may be deleted if such removal does not result in a decrease in the classification accuracy of the network.

Once the trained network has been pruned, some approaches will then perform link, unit, or activation value clustering. In one method, for example, clustering is used to find the set of common activation values for each hidden unit in a given trained two-layer neural network (Figure 7.12). The combinations of these activation values for each hidden unit are analyzed. Rules are derived relating combinations of activation values with corresponding output unit values. Similarly, the sets of input values and activation values are studied to derive rules describing the relationship between the input and hidden unit layers. Finally, the two sets of rules may be combined to form IF-THEN rules. Other algorithms may derive rules of other forms, including $M$-of-$N$ rules (where $M$ out of a given $N$ conditions in the rule antecedent must be true in order for the rule consequent to be applied), decision trees with $M$-of-$N$ tests, fuzzy rules, and finite automata.

**Sensitivity analysis** is used to assess the impact that a given input variable has on a network output. The input to the variable is varied while the remaining input variables are fixed at some value. Meanwhile, changes in the network output are monitored. The knowledge gained from this form of analysis can be represented in rules such as "*IF X decreases 5% THEN Y increases 8%*".

# 7.6 Classification Based on Concepts from Association Rule Mining

"*Can any ideas from association rule mining be applied to classification?*" Association rule mining is an important and highly active area of data mining research. Chapter 6 of this book described many algorithms for association rule mining. Recently, data mining techniques have been developed that apply concepts used in association rule mining to the problem of classification. In this section, we study three methods in historical order. The first two, *ARCS* and *associative classification*, use association rules for classification. The third method, *CAEP*, mines "emerging patterns" that consider the concept of support used in mining associations.

The first method mines association rules based on clustering and then employs the rules for classification. The **ARCS**, or Association Rule Clustering System (Section 6.4.3), mines association rules of the form $A_{quan1} \wedge A_{quan2} \Rightarrow A_{cat}$, where $A_{quan1}$ and $A_{quan2}$ are tests on quantitative attribute ranges (where the ranges are dynamically determined), and $A_{cat}$ assigns a class label for a categorical attribute from the given training data. Association rules are plotted on a 2-D grid. The algorithm scans the grid, searching for rectangular clusters of rules. In this way, adjacent ranges of the quantitative attributes occurring within a rule cluster may be combined. The clustered association rules generated by ARCS were applied to classification, and their accuracy was compared to C4.5. In general, ARCS was

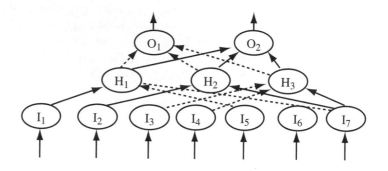

Identify sets of common activation values for
each hidden node, $H_i$:
  for $H_1$: $(-1,0,1)$
  for $H_2$: $(0.1)$
  for $H_3$: $(-1,0.24,1)$

---

Derive rules relating common activation values
with output nodes, $O_j$:
  IF ($H_2 = 0$ and $H_3 = -1$) OR
    ($H_1 = -1$ and $H_2 = 1$ and $H_3 = -1$) OR
    ($H_1 = -1$ and $H_2 = 0$ and $H_3 = 0.24$)
  THEN $O_1 = 1, O_2 = 0$
  ELSE $O_1 = 0, O_2 = 1$

---

Derive rules relating input nodes, $I_i$, to
output nodes, $O_j$:
  IF ($I_2 = 0$ AND $I_7 = 0$) THEN $H_2 = 0$
  IF ($I_4) = 1$ AND $I_6 = 1$) THEN $H_3 = -1$
  IF ($I_5 = 0$) THEN $H_3 = -1$

---

Obtain rules relating inputs and output classes:
  IF ($I_2 = 0$ AND $I_7 = 0$ AND $I_4 = 1$ AND
  $I_6 = 1$) THEN class = 1
  IF ($I_2 = 0$ AND $I_7 = 0$ and $I_5 = 0$) THEN
  class = 1

**Figure 7.12** Rules can be extracted from training neural networks. Adapted from [LSL95].

empirically found to be slightly more accurate than C4.5 when there are outliers in the data. The accuracy of ARCS is related to the degree of discretization used. In terms of scalability, ARCS requires a constant amount of memory, regardless of the database size. C4.5 has exponentially higher execution times than ARCS, requiring the entire database, multiplied by some factor, to fit entirely in main memory.

The second method is referred to as **associative classification.** It mines rules of the form *condset* $\Rightarrow y$, where *condset* is a set of *items* (or attribute-value pairs) and $y$ is a class label. Rules that satisfy a prespecified minimum support are **frequent**, where a rule has **support** $s$ if $s$% of the samples in the given data set contain *condset* and belong to class $y$. A rule satisfying minimum confidence is called **accurate**, where a rule has **confidence** $c$ if $c$% of the samples in the given data set that contain *condset* belong to class $y$. If a set of rules has the same condset, then the rule with the highest confidence is selected as the **possible rule** (**PR**) to represent the set.

The association classification method consists of two steps. The first step finds the set of all PRs that are both frequent and accurate. It uses an iterative approach, similar to that described for Apriori in Section 6.2.1, where prior knowledge is used to prune the rule search. The second step uses a heuristic method to construct the classifier, where the discovered rules are organized according to decreasing precedence based on their confidence and support. The algorithm may require several passes over the data set, depending on the length of the longest rule found. When classifying a new sample, the first rule satisfying the sample is used to classify it. The classifier also contains a default rule, having lowest precedence, which specifies a default class for any new sample that is not satisfied by any other rule in the classifier. In general, the associative classification method was empirically found to be more accurate than C4.5 on several data sets. Each of the above two steps was shown to have linear scale-up.

The third method, **CAEP** (classification by aggregating emerging patterns), uses the notion of itemset support to mine **emerging patterns** (EPs), which are used to construct a classifier. Roughly speaking, an **EP** is an itemset (or set of items) whose support increases significantly from one class of data to another. The ratio of the two supports is called the **growth rate** of the EP. For example, suppose that we have a data set of customers with the classes *buys_computer* = *"yes"*, or $C_1$, and *buys_computer* = *"no"*, or $C_2$. The itemset {*age* = *"$\leq$ 30"*, *student* = *"no"*} is a typical EP, whose support increases from 0.2% in $C_1$ to 57.6% in $C_2$, at a growth rate of $\frac{57.6\%}{0.2\%} = 288$. Note that an item is either a simple equality test on a categorical attribute, or a membership test checking whether a numerical attribute is in an interval. Each EP is a multiattribute test and can be very strong at differentiating instances of one class from another. For instance, if a new sample $X$ contains the above EP, then with odds of 99.6% we can claim that $X$ belongs to $C_2$. In general, the differentiating power of an EP is roughly proportional to its growth rate and its support in the target class.

*"How does CAEP use EPs to build a classifier?"* For each class $C$, CAEP finds EPs satisfying given support and growth rate thresholds, where growth rate is computed with respect to the set of all non-$C$ samples versus the target set of all $C$ samples. "Border-based" algorithms can be used for this purpose. When classifying a new sample, $X$, for each class $C$, the differentiating power of the EPs of class $C$ that occur in $X$ are aggregated to derive a score for $C$ that is then normalized. The class with the largest normalized score determines the class label of $X$.

CAEP has been found to be more accurate than C4.5 and association-based classification on several data sets. It also performs well on data sets where the main class of interest is in the minority. It scales up on data volume and dimensionality. An alternative classifier, called the *JEP-classifier*, was proposed based on **jumping emerging patterns** (JEPs). A **JEP** is a special type of EP, defined as an itemset whose support increases abruptly from zero in one data set to nonzero in another data set. The two classifiers are considered complementary.

# 7.7 Other Classification Methods

In this section, we give a brief description of a number of other classification methods. These methods include $k$-nearest neighbor classification, case-based reasoning, genetic algorithms, rough set, and fuzzy set approaches. In general, these methods are less commonly used for classification in commercial data mining systems than the methods described earlier in this chapter. Nearest neighbor classification, for example, stores all training samples, which may present difficulties when learning from very large data sets. Furthermore, many applications of case-based reasoning, genetic algorithms, and rough sets for classification are still in the prototype phase. These methods, however, are enjoying increasing popularity, and hence we include them here.

## 7.7.1 *k*-Nearest Neighbor Classifiers

Nearest neighbor classifiers are based on learning by analogy. The training samples are described by $n$-dimensional numeric attributes. Each sample represents a point in an $n$-dimensional space. In this way, all of the training samples are stored in an $n$-dimensional pattern space. When given an unknown sample, a **$k$-nearest neighbor classifier** searches the pattern space for the $k$ training samples that are closest to the unknown sample. These $k$ training samples are the $k$ "nearest neighbors" of the unknown sample. "Closeness" is defined in terms of Euclidean distance, where the Euclidean distance between two points, $X = (x_1, x_2, \ldots, x_n)$ and $Y = (y_1, y_2, \ldots, y_n)$ is

$$d(X, Y) = \sqrt{\sum_{i=1}^{n} (x_i - y_i)^2}. \tag{7.20}$$

The unknown sample is assigned the most common class among its $k$ nearest neighbors. When $k = 1$, the unknown sample is assigned the class of the training sample that is closest to it in pattern space.

Nearest neighbor classifiers are **instance-based** or **lazy learners** in that they store all of the training samples and do not build a classifier until a new (unlabeled) sample needs to be classified. This contrasts with **eager learning** methods, such as decision tree induction and backpropagation, which construct a generalization model before receiving new samples to classify. Lazy learners can incur expensive computational costs when the number of potential neighbors (i.e., stored training samples) with which to compare a given unlabeled sample is great. Therefore, they require efficient indexing techniques. As expected, lazy learning methods are faster at training than eager methods, but slower at classification since all computation is delayed to that time. Unlike decision tree induction and backpropagation, nearest neighbor classifiers assign equal weight to each attribute. This may cause confusion when there are many irrelevant attributes in the data.

Nearest neighbor classifiers can also be used for prediction, that is, to return a real-valued prediction for a given unknown sample. In this case, the classifier returns the average value of the real-valued labels associated with the $k$ nearest neighbors of the unknown sample.

## 7.7.2 Case-Based Reasoning

**Case-based reasoning** (CBR) classifiers are instanced-based. Unlike nearest neighbor classifiers, which store training samples as points in Euclidean space, the samples or "cases" stored by CBR are complex symbolic descriptions. Business applications of CBR include problem resolution for customer service help desks, for example, where cases describe product-related diagnostic problems. CBR has also been applied to areas such as engineering and law, where cases are either technical designs or legal rulings, respectively.

When given a new case to classify, a case-based reasoner will first check if an identical training case exists. If one is found, then the accompanying solution to that case is returned. If no identical case is found, then the case-based reasoner will search for training cases having components that are similar to those of the new case. Conceptually, these training cases may be considered as neighbors of the new case. If cases are represented as graphs, this involves searching for subgraphs that are similar to subgraphs within the new case. The case-based reasoner tries to combine the solutions of the neighboring training cases in order to propose a solution for the new case. If incompatibilities arise with the individual solutions, then backtracking to search for other solutions may be necessary. The case-based reasoner may employ background knowledge and problem-solving strategies in order to propose a feasible combined solution.

Challenges in case-based reasoning include finding a good similarity metric (e.g., for matching subgraphs), developing efficient techniques for indexing training cases, and methods for combining solutions.

### 7.7.3 Genetic Algorithms

**Genetic algorithms** attempt to incorporate ideas of natural evolution. In general, genetic learning starts as follows. An initial **population** is created consisting of randomly generated rules. Each rule can be represented by a string of bits. As a simple example, suppose that samples in a given training set are described by two Boolean attributes, $A_1$ and $A_2$, and that there are two classes, $C_1$ and $C_2$. The rule "*IF $A_1$ AND NOT $A_2$ THEN $C_2$*" can be encoded as the bit string "100", where the two leftmost bits represent attributes $A_1$ and $A_2$, respectively, and the rightmost bit represents the class. Similarly, the rule "*IF NOT $A_1$ AND NOT $A_2$ THEN $C_1$*" can be encoded as "001". If an attribute has $k$ values, where $k > 2$, then $k$ bits may be used to encode the attribute's values. Classes can be encoded in a similar fashion.

Based on the notion of survival of the fittest, a new population is formed to consist of the *fittest* rules in the current population, as well as *offspring* of these rules. Typically, the **fitness** of a rule is assessed by its classification accuracy on a set of training samples.

Offspring are created by applying genetic operators such as crossover and mutation. In **crossover**, substrings from pairs of rules are swapped to form new pairs of rules. In **mutation**, randomly selected bits in a rule's string are inverted.

The process of generating new populations based on prior populations of rules continues until a population $P$ "evolves" where each rule in $P$ satisfies a prespecified fitness threshold.

Genetic algorithms are easily parallelizable and have been used for classification as well as other optimization problems. In data mining, they may be used to evaluate the fitness of other algorithms.

### 7.7.4 Rough Set Approach

Rough set theory can be used for classification to discover structural relationships within imprecise or noisy data. It applies to discrete-valued attributes. Continuous-valued attributes must therefore be discretized prior to its use.

Rough set theory is based on the establishment of **equivalence classes** within the given training data. All of the data samples forming an equivalence class are indiscernible, that is, the samples are identical with respect to the attributes describing the data. Given real-world data, it is common that some classes cannot be distinguished in terms of the available attributes. Rough sets can be used to approximately or "roughly" define such classes. A rough set definition for a given

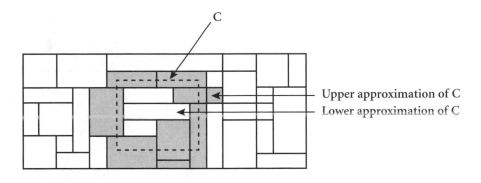

**Figure 7.13** A rough set approximation of the set of samples of the class $C$ using lower and upper approximation sets of $C$. The rectangular regions represent equivalence classes.

class $C$ is approximated by two sets—a **lower approximation** of $C$ and an **upper approximation** of $C$. The lower approximation of $C$ consists of all of the data samples that, based on the knowledge of the attributes, are certain to belong to $C$ without ambiguity. The upper approximation of $C$ consists of all of the samples that, based on the knowledge of the attributes, cannot be described as not belonging to $C$. The lower and upper approximations for a class $C$ are shown in Figure 7.13, where each rectangular region represents an equivalence class. Decision rules can be generated for each class. Typically, a decision table is used to represent the rules.

Rough sets can also be used for feature reduction (where attributes that do not contribute towards the classification of the given training data can be identified and removed) and relevance analysis (where the contribution or significance of each attribute is assessed with respect to the classification task). The problem of finding the minimal subsets (**reducts**) of attributes that can describe all of the concepts in the given data set is NP-hard. However, algorithms to reduce the computation intensity have been proposed. In one method, for example, a **discernibility matrix** is used that stores the differences between attribute values for each pair of data samples. Rather than searching on the entire training set, the matrix is instead searched to detect redundant attributes.

## 7.7.5 Fuzzy Set Approaches

Rule-based systems for classification have the disadvantage that they involve sharp cutoffs for continuous attributes. For example, consider the following rule for customer credit application approval. The rule essentially says that applications for customers who have had a job for two or more years and who have a high income (i.e., of at least $50K) are approved:

$$IF\ (years\_employed >= 2) \wedge (income \geq 50K)\ THEN\ credit = \text{``approved''} \quad (7.21)$$

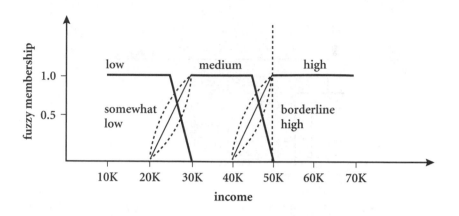

**Figure 7.14** Fuzzy values for *income*.

By Rule (7.21), a customer who has had a job for at least two years will receive credit if her income is, say, $50K, but not if it is $49K. Such harsh thresholding may seem unfair. Instead, fuzzy logic can be introduced into the system to allow "fuzzy" thresholds or boundaries to be defined. Rather than having a precise cutoff between categories or sets, fuzzy logic uses truth values between 0.0 and 1.0 to represent the degree of membership that a certain value has in a given category. Hence, with fuzzy logic, we can capture the notion that an income of $49K is, to some degree, high, although not as high as an income of $50K.

Fuzzy logic is useful for data mining systems performing classification. It provides the advantage of working at a high level of abstraction. In general, the use of fuzzy logic in rule-based systems involves the following:

- Attribute values are converted to fuzzy values. Figure 7.14 shows how values for the continuous attribute *income* are mapped into the discrete categories {*low, medium, high*}, as well as how the fuzzy membership or truth values are calculated. Fuzzy logic systems typically provide graphical tools to assist users in this step.

- For a given new sample, more than one fuzzy rule may apply. Each applicable rule contributes a vote for membership in the categories. Typically, the truth values for each predicted category are summed.

- The sums obtained above are combined into a value that is returned by the system. This process may be done by weighting each category by its truth sum and multiplying by the mean truth value of each category. The calculations involved may be more complex, depending on the complexity of the fuzzy membership graphs.

Fuzzy logic systems have been used in numerous areas for classification, including health care and finance.

# 7.8 Prediction

*"What if we would like to predict a continuous value, rather than a categorical label?"* The prediction of continuous values can be modeled by statistical techniques of *regression*. For example, we may like to develop a model to predict the salary of college graduates with 10 years of work experience, or the potential sales of a new product given its price. Many problems can be solved by *linear regression*, and even more can be tackled by applying transformations to the variables so that a nonlinear problem can be converted to a linear one. For reasons of space, we cannot give a fully detailed treatment of regression. Instead, this section provides an intuitive introduction to the topic. By the end of this section, you will be familiar with the ideas of linear, multiple, and nonlinear regression, as well as generalized linear models.

Several software packages exist to solve regression problems. Examples include SAS (*http://www.sas.com*), SPSS (*http://www.spss.com*), and S-Plus (*http://www.mathsoft.com*).

## 7.8.1 Linear and Multiple Regression

*"What is linear regression?"* In **linear regression**, data are modeled using a straight line. Linear regression is the simplest form of regression. Bivariate linear regression models a random variable, $Y$ (called a **response variable**), as a linear function of another random variable, $X$ (called a **predictor variable**), that is,

$$Y = \alpha + \beta X, \tag{7.22}$$

where the variance of $Y$ is assumed to be constant, and $\alpha$ and $\beta$ are **regression coefficients** specifying the Y-intercept and slope of the line, respectively. These coefficients can be solved for by the **method of least squares**, which minimizes the error between the actual data and the estimate of the line. Given $s$ samples or data points of the form $(x_1, y_1), (x_2, y_2), \ldots, (x_s, y_s)$, then the regression coefficients can be estimated using this method with the following equations:

$$\beta = \frac{\sum_{i=1}^{s}(x_i - \bar{x})(y_i - \bar{y})}{\sum_{i=1}^{s}(x_i - \bar{x})^2} \tag{7.23}$$

$$\alpha = \bar{y} - \beta\bar{x} \tag{7.24}$$

where $\bar{x}$ is the average of $x_1, x_2, \ldots, x_s$, and $\bar{y}$ is the average of $y_1, y_2, \ldots, y_s$. The coefficients $\alpha$ and $\beta$ often provide good approximations to otherwise complicated regression equations.

**Table 7.7**  Salary data.

| X Years experience | Y Salary (in $1000s) |
|---|---|
| 3 | 30 |
| 8 | 57 |
| 9 | 64 |
| 13 | 72 |
| 3 | 36 |
| 6 | 43 |
| 11 | 59 |
| 21 | 90 |
| 1 | 20 |
| 16 | 83 |

**Example 7.6**  **Linear regression using the method of least squares:**  Table 7.7 shows a set of paired data where $X$ is the number of years of work experience of a college graduate and $Y$ is the corresponding salary of the graduate. A plot of the data is shown in Figure 7.15, suggesting a linear relationship between the two variables, $X$ and $Y$. We model the relationship that salary may be related to the number of years of work experience with the equation $Y = \alpha + \beta X$.

Given the above data, we compute $\bar{x} = 9.1$ and $\bar{y} = 55.4$. Substituting these values into Equation (7.23), we get

$$\beta = \frac{(3 - 9.1)(30 - 55.4) + (8 - 9.1)(57 - 55.4) + \cdots + (16 - 9.1)(83 - 55.4)}{(3 - 9.1)^2 + (8 - 9.1)^2 + \cdots + (16 - 9.1)^2} = 3.5$$

$$\alpha = 55.4 - (3.5)(9.1) = 23.6$$

Thus, the equation of the least squares line is estimated by $Y = 23.6 + 3.5X$. Using this equation, we can predict that the salary of a college graduate with, say, 10 years of experience is $58.6K. ∎

**Multiple regression** is an extension of linear regression involving more than one predictor variable. It allows response variable $Y$ to be modeled as a linear function of a multidimensional feature vector. An example of a multiple regression model based on two predictor attributes or variables, $X_1$ and $X_2$, is

$$Y = \alpha + \beta_1 X_1 + \beta_2 X_2. \tag{7.25}$$

The method of least squares can also be applied here to solve for $\alpha$, $\beta_1$, and $\beta_2$.

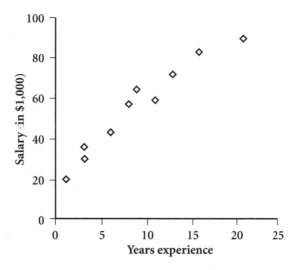

**Figure 7.15**   Plot of the data in Table 7.7 for Example 7.6. Although the points do not fall on a straight line, the overall pattern suggests a linear relationship between $X$ (*years experience*) and $Y$ (*salary*).

## 7.8.2 Nonlinear Regression

*"How can we model data that does not show a linear dependence? For example, what if a given response variable and predictor variables have a relationship that may be modeled by a polynomial function?"* **Polynomial regression** can be modeled by adding polynomial terms to the basic linear model. By applying transformations to the variables, we can convert the nonlinear model into a linear one that can then be solved by the method of least squares.

**Example 7.7**   **Transformation of a polynomial regression model to a linear regression model:** Consider a cubic polynomial relationship given by

$$Y = \alpha + \beta_1 X + \beta_2 X^2 + \beta_3 X^3. \tag{7.26}$$

To convert this equation to linear form, we define new variables:

$$X_1 = X \qquad X_2 = X^2 \qquad X_3 = X^3 \tag{7.27}$$

Equation (7.26) can then be converted to linear form by applying the above assignments, resulting in the equation $Y = \alpha + \beta_1 X_1 + \beta_2 X_2 + \beta_3 X_3$, which is solvable by the method of least squares.   ∎

In Exercise 7.9, you are asked to find the transformations required to convert a nonlinear model involving a power function into a linear regression model.

Some models are intractably nonlinear (such as the sum of exponential terms, for example) and cannot be converted to a linear model. For such cases, it may be possible to obtain least square estimates through extensive calculations on more complex formulae.

### 7.8.3 Other Regression Models

Linear regression is used to model continuous-valued functions. It is widely used, owing largely to its simplicity. *"Can it also be used to predict categorical labels?"* **Generalized linear models** represent the theoretical foundation on which linear regression can be applied to the modeling of categorical response variables. In generalized linear models, the variance of the response variable $Y$ is a function of the mean value of $Y$, unlike in linear regression, where the variance of $Y$ is constant. Common types of generalized linear models include **logistic regression** and **Poisson regression**. Logistic regression models the probability of some event occurring as a linear function of a set of predictor variables. Count data frequently exhibit a Poisson distribution and are commonly modeled using Poisson regression.

**Log-linear models** approximate *discrete* multidimensional probability distributions. They may be used to estimate the probability value associated with data cube cells. For example, suppose we are given data for the attributes *city, item, year*, and *sales*. In the log-linear method, all attributes must be categorical; hence continuous-valued attributes (like *sales*) must first be discretized. The method can then be used to estimate the probability of each cell in the 4-D base cuboid for the given attributes, based on the 2-D cuboids for *city* and *item*, *city* and *year*, *city* and *sales*, and the 3-D cuboid for *item, year*, and *sales*. In this way, an iterative technique can be used to build higher-order data cubes from lower-order ones. The technique scales up well to allow for many dimensions. Aside from prediction, the log-linear model is useful for data compression (since the smaller-order cuboids together typically occupy less space than the base cuboid) and data smoothing (since cell estimates in the smaller-order cuboids are less subject to sampling variations than cell estimates in the base cuboid).

## 7.9 Classifier Accuracy

Estimating classifier accuracy is important in that it allows one to evaluate how accurately a given classifier will label future data, that is, data on which the classifier has not been trained. For example, if data from previous sales are used to train a classifier to predict customer purchasing behavior, we would like some estimate of how accurately the classifier can predict the purchasing behavior of future customers. Accuracy estimates also help in the comparison of different classifiers. In Section 7.9.1, we discuss techniques for estimating classifier accuracy, such as the *holdout* and k-*fold cross-validation* methods. Section 7.9.2 describes *bagging* and *boosting*, two strategies for increasing classifier accuracy. Section 7.9.3 discusses additional issues relating to classifier accuracy and selection.

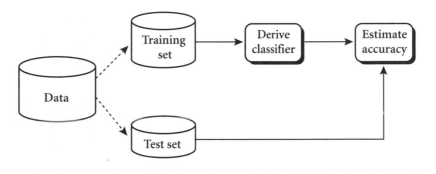

**Figure 7.16** Estimating classifier accuracy with the holdout method.

## 7.9.1 Estimating Classifier Accuracy

Using training data to derive a classifier and then to estimate the accuracy of the classifier can result in misleading overoptimistic estimates due to over-specialization of the learning algorithm (or model) to the data. Holdout and cross-validation are two common techniques for assessing classifier accuracy, based on randomly sampled partitions of the given data.

In the **holdout** method, the given data are randomly partitioned into two independent sets, a *training set* and a *test set*. Typically, two thirds of the data are allocated to the training set, and the remaining one third is allocated to the test set. The training set is used to derive the classifier, whose accuracy is estimated with the test set (Figure 7.16). The estimate is pessimistic since only a portion of the initial data is used to derive the classifier. **Random subsampling** is a variation of the holdout method in which the holdout method is repeated $k$ times. The overall accuracy estimate is taken as the average of the accuracies obtained from each iteration.

In $k$-**fold cross-validation**, the initial data are randomly partitioned into $k$ mutually exclusive subsets or "folds," $S_1, S_2, \ldots, S_k$, each of approximately equal size. Training and testing is performed $k$ times. In iteration $i$, the subset $S_i$ is reserved as the test set, and the remaining subsets are collectively used to train the classifier. That is, the classifier of the first iteration is trained on subsets $S_2, \ldots, S_k$ and tested on $S_1$; the classifier of the second iteration is trained on subsets $S_1, S_3, \ldots, S_k$ and tested on $S_2$; and so on. The accuracy estimate is the overall number of correct classifications from the $k$ iterations, divided by the total number of samples in the initial data. In **stratified cross-validation**, the folds are stratified so that the class distribution of the samples in each fold is approximately the same as that in the initial data.

Other methods of estimating classifier accuracy include **bootstrapping**, which samples the given training instances uniformly *with replacement*, and **leave-one-out**, which is $k$-fold cross-validation with $k$ set to $s$, the number of initial samples.

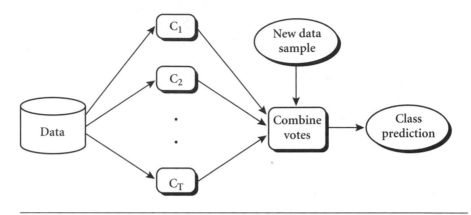

**Figure 7.17** Increasing classifier accuracy: Bagging and boosting each generate a set of classifiers, $C_1, C_2, \ldots, C_T$. Voting strategies are used to combine the class predictions for a given unknown sample.

In general, stratified 10-fold cross-validation is recommended for estimating classifier accuracy (even if computation power allows using more folds) due to its relatively low bias and variance.

The use of such techniques to estimate classifier accuracy increases the overall computation time, yet is useful for selecting among several classifiers.

## 7.9.2 Increasing Classifier Accuracy

In the previous section, we studied methods of estimating classifier accuracy. In Section 7.3.2, we saw how pruning can be applied to decision tree induction to help improve the accuracy of the resulting decision trees. Are there *general* techniques for improving classifier accuracy?

The answer is yes. **Bagging** (or *bootstrap aggregation*) and **boosting** are two such techniques (Figure 7.17). Each combines a series of $T$ learned classifiers, $C_1, C_2, \ldots, C_T$, with the aim of creating an improved composite classifier, $C*$.

*"How do these methods work?"* Suppose that you are a patient and would like to have a diagnosis made based on your symptoms. Instead of asking one doctor, you may choose to ask several. If a certain diagnosis occurs more than the others, you may choose this as the final or best diagnosis. Now replace each doctor by a classifier, and you have the intuition behind bagging. Suppose instead, you assign weights to the "value" or worth of each doctor's diagnosis, based on the accuracies of previous diagnoses they have made. The final diagnosis is then a combination of the weighted diagnoses. This is the essence behind boosting. Let us have a closer look at these two techniques.

Given a set $S$ of $s$ samples, bagging works as follows. For iteration $t$ ($t = 1, 2, \ldots, T$), a training set $S_t$ is sampled with replacement from the original set of samples, $S$. Since sampling with replacement is used, some of the original samples of $S$ may not be included in $S_t$, while others may occur more than once. A classifier $C_t$ is learned for each training set $S_t$. To classify an unknown sample, $X$, each classifier $C_t$ returns its class prediction, which counts as one vote. The bagged classifier, $C*$, counts the votes and assigns the class with the most votes to $X$. Bagging can be applied to the prediction of continuous values by taking the average value of each classifier prediction.

In boosting, weights are assigned to each training sample. A series of classifiers is learned. After a classifier $C_t$ is learned, the weights are updated to allow the subsequent classifier, $C_{t+1}$, to "pay more attention" to the misclassification errors made by $C_t$. The final boosted classifier, $C*$, combines the votes of each individual classifier, where the weight of each classifier's vote is a function of its accuracy. The boosting algorithm can be extended for the prediction of continuous values.

## 7.9.3 Is Accuracy Enough to Judge a Classifier?

In addition to accuracy, classifiers can be compared with respect to their speed, robustness (e.g., accuracy on noisy data), scalability, and interpretability. Scalability can be evaluated by assessing the number of I/O operations involved for a given classification algorithm on data sets of increasingly large size. Interpretability is subjective, although we may use objective measurements such as the complexity of the resulting classifier (e.g., number of tree nodes for decision trees, or number of hidden units for neural networks, etc.) in assessing it.

*"Are there alternatives to the accuracy measure?"* Suppose that you have trained a classifier to classify medical data samples as either *"cancer"* or *"not_cancer"*. An accuracy rate of, say, 90% may make the classifier seem quite accurate, but what if only, say, 3–4% of the training samples are actually *"cancer"*? Clearly, an accuracy rate of 90% may not be acceptable—the classifier could be correctly labeling only the *"not_cancer"* samples, for instance. Instead, we would like to be able to access how well the classifier can recognize *"cancer"* samples (referred to as **positive samples**) and how well it can recognize *"not_cancer"* samples (referred to as **negative samples**). The **sensitivity** and **specificity** measures can be used, respectively, for this purpose. In addition, we may use **precision** to access the percentage of samples labeled as *"cancer"* that actually are *"cancer"* samples. These measures are defined as

$$sensitivity = \frac{t\_pos}{pos} \qquad (7.28)$$

$$specificity = \frac{t\_neg}{neg} \qquad (7.29)$$

$$precision = \frac{t\_pos}{(t\_pos + f\_pos)} \qquad (7.30)$$

where $t\_pos$ is the number of **true positives** (*"cancer"* samples that were correctly classified as such), $pos$ is the number of positive (*"cancer"*) samples, $t\_neg$ is the number of **true negatives** (*"not_cancer"* samples that were correctly classified as such), $neg$ is the number of negative (*"not_cancer"*) samples, and $f\_pos$ is the number of **false positives** (*"not_cancer"* samples that were incorrectly labeled as *"cancer"*). It can be shown that accuracy is a function of sensitivity and specificity:

$$accuracy = sensitivity \frac{pos}{(pos + neg)} + specificity \frac{neg}{(pos + neg)}. \tag{7.31}$$

*"Are there other cases where accuracy may not be appropriate?"* In classification problems, it is commonly assumed that all samples are uniquely classifiable, that is, that each training sample can belong to only one class. Yet, owing to the wide diversity of data in large databases, it is not always reasonable to assume that all samples are uniquely classifiable. Rather, it is more probable to assume that each sample may belong to more than one class. How then can the accuracy of classifiers on large databases be measured? The accuracy measure is not appropriate, since it does not take into account the possibility of samples belonging to more than one class.

Rather than returning a class label, it is useful to return a probability class distribution. Accuracy measures may then use a **second guess** heuristic, whereby a class prediction is judged as correct if it agrees with the first or second most probable class. Although this does take into consideration, to some degree, the nonunique classification of samples, it is not a complete solution.

# 7.10 Summary

- Classification and prediction are two forms of data analysis that can be used to extract models describing important data classes or to predict future data trends. While **classification** predicts categorical labels (classes), **prediction** models continuous-valued functions.

- Preprocessing of the data in preparation for classification and prediction can involve **data cleaning** to reduce noise or handle missing values, **relevance analysis** to remove irrelevant or redundant attributes, and **data transformation**, such as generalizing the data to higher-level concepts or normalizing the data.

- Predictive accuracy, computational speed, robustness, scalability, and interpretability are five **criteria** for the evaluation of classification and prediction methods.

- **ID3** and **C4.5** are greedy algorithms for the induction of decision trees. Each algorithm uses an information-theoretic measure to select the attribute tested for each nonleaf node in the tree. **Pruning** algorithms attempt to improve accuracy by removing tree branches reflecting noise in the data. Early decision tree algorithms typically assume that the data are memory resident—a limitation to data mining on large databases. Since then, several scalable algorithms have been proposed to address this issue, such as SLIQ, SPRINT, and RainForest. Decision trees can easily be converted to classification IF-THEN rules.

- **Naive Bayesian classification** and **Bayesian belief networks** are based on Bayes theorem of posterior probability. Unlike naive Bayesian classification (which assumes class conditional independence), Bayesian belief networks allow class conditional independencies to be defined between subsets of variables.

- **Backpropagation** is a neural network algorithm for classification that employs a method of gradient descent. It searches for a set of weights that can model the data so as to minimize the mean squared distance between the network's class prediction and the actual class label of data samples. Rules may be extracted from trained neural networks in order to help improve the interpretability of the learned network.

- **Association mining** techniques, which search for frequently occurring patterns in large databases, can be adapted for classification.

- Nearest neighbor classifiers and case-based reasoning classifiers are **instance-based** methods of classification in that they store all of the training samples in pattern space. Hence, both require efficient indexing techniques. In **genetic algorithms**, populations of rules "evolve" via operations of crossover and mutation until all rules within a population satisfy a specified threshold. **Rough set theory** can be used to approximately define classes that are not distinguishable based on the available attributes. **Fuzzy set** approaches replace "brittle" threshold cutoffs for continuous-valued attributes with degree of membership functions.

- Linear, nonlinear, and generalized linear models of **regression** can be used for prediction. Many nonlinear problems can be converted to linear problems by performing transformations on the predictor variables.

- Data warehousing techniques, such as attribute-oriented induction and the use of multidimensional data cubes, can be integrated with classification methods in order to allow fast **multilevel mining**. Classification tasks may be specified using a data mining query language, promoting interactive data mining.

- **Stratified $k$-fold cross-validation** is a recommended method for estimating classifier accuracy. **Bagging** and **boosting** methods can be used to increase overall classification accuracy by learning and combining a series of individual classifiers. **Sensitivity**, **specificity**, and **precision** are useful alternatives to the accuracy measure, particularly when the main class of interest is in the minority.

- There have been numerous comparisons on the different classification methods, and the matter remains a research topic. No single method has been found to be superior over all others for all data sets. Issues such as accuracy, training time, robustness, interpretability, and scalability must be considered and can involve trade-offs, further complicating the quest for an overall superior method. Empirical studies show that the accuracies of many algorithms are sufficiently similar that their differences are statistically insignificant, while training times may differ substantially. In general, most neural network and statistical classification methods involving splines tend to be more computationally intensive than most decision tree methods.

## Exercises

**7.1** Briefly outline the major steps of *decision tree classification*.

**7.2** Why is *tree pruning* useful in decision tree induction? What is a drawback of using a separate set of samples to evaluate pruning?

**7.3** Given a decision tree, you have the option of (a) converting the decision tree to rules and then pruning the resulting rules, or (b) pruning the decision tree and then converting the pruned tree to rules. What advantage does (a) have over (b)?

**7.4** Why is *naive Bayesian classification* called "naive"? Briefly outline the major ideas of naive Bayesian classification.

**7.5** Compare the advantages and disadvantages of *eager* classification (e.g., decision tree, Bayesian, neural network) versus *lazy* classification (e.g., $k$-nearest neighbor, case-based reasoning).

**7.6** The following table consists of training data from an employee database. The data have been generalized. For a given row entry, *count* represents the number of data tuples having the values for *department, status, age,* and *salary* given in that row.

| department | status | age | salary | count |
|---|---|---|---|---|
| sales | senior | 31 . . . 35 | 46K . . . 50K | 30 |
| sales | junior | 26 . . . 30 | 26K . . . 30K | 40 |
| sales | junior | 31 . . . 35 | 31K . . . 35K | 40 |
| systems | junior | 21 . . . 25 | 46K . . . 50K | 20 |
| systems | senior | 31 . . . 35 | 66K . . . 70K | 5 |
| systems | junior | 26 . . . 30 | 46K . . . 50K | 3 |
| systems | senior | 41 . . . 45 | 66K . . . 70K | 3 |
| marketing | senior | 36 . . . 40 | 46K . . . 50K | 10 |
| marketing | junior | 31 . . . 35 | 41K . . . 45K | 4 |
| secretary | senior | 46 . . . 50 | 36K . . . 40K | 4 |
| secretary | junior | 26 . . . 30 | 26K . . . 30K | 6 |

Let *status* be the class label attribute.

(a) How would you modify the ID3 algorithm to take into consideration the *count* of each generalized data tuple (i.e., of each row entry)?

(b) Use your modified version of ID3 to construct a decision tree from the given data.

(c) Given a data sample with the values *"systems", "46–50K"*, and *"26 . . . 30"* for the attributes *department, status*, and *age*, respectively, what would a naive Bayesian classification of the *junior* for the sample be?

(d) Design a multilayer feed-forward neural network for the given data. Label the nodes in the input and output layers.

(e) Using the multilayer feed-forward neural network obtained above, show the weight values after one iteration of the backpropagation algorithm given the training instance *"(sales, senior, 31 . . . 35, 46K . . . 50K)"*. Indicate your initial weight values and biases, and the learning rate used.

**7.7** Write an algorithm for $k$-nearest neighbor classification given $k$ and $n$, the number of attributes describing each sample.

**7.8** The following table shows the midterm and final exam grades obtained for students in a database course.

| X <br> Midterm exam | Y <br> Final exam |
|---|---|
| 72 | 84 |
| 50 | 63 |
| 81 | 77 |
| 74 | 78 |
| 94 | 90 |
| 86 | 75 |
| 59 | 49 |
| 83 | 79 |
| 65 | 77 |
| 33 | 52 |
| 88 | 74 |
| 81 | 90 |

(a) Plot the data. Do $X$ and $Y$ seem to have a linear relationship?

(b) Use the *method of least squares* to find an equation for the prediction of a student's final exam grade based on the student's midterm grade in the course.

(c) Predict the final exam grade of a student who received an 86 on the midterm exam.

**7.9** Some *nonlinear regression* models can be converted to linear models by applying transformations to the predictor variables. Show how the nonlinear regression equation $Y = \alpha X^{\beta}$ can be converted to a linear regression equation solvable by the method of least squares.

**7.10** What is *boosting*? State why it may improve the accuracy of decision tree induction.

**7.11** Show that accuracy is a function of sensitivity and specificity, that is, prove Equation (7.31).

**7.12** It is difficult to assess classification accuracy when individual data objects may belong to more than one class at a time. In such cases, comment on what criteria you would use to compare different classifiers modeled after the same data.

## Bibliographic Notes

Classification from a machine learning perspective is described in several books, such as Weiss and Kulikowski [WK91], Michie, Spiegelhalter, and Taylor [MST94], Langley [Lan96], and Mitchell [Mit97]. Weiss and Kulikowski [WK91] compare classification and prediction methods from many different fields, in addition to describing practical techniques for the evaluation of classifier performance. Many of these books describe each of the basic methods of classification discussed in this chapter. Edited collections containing seminal articles on machine learning can be found in Michalski, Carbonell, and Mitchell [MCM83, MCM86], Kodratoff and Michalski [KM90], Shavlik and Dietterich [SD90], and Michalski and Tecuci [MT94]. For a presentation of machine learning with respect to data mining applications, see Michalski, Bratko, and Kubat [MBK98].

The C4.5 algorithm is described in a book by Quinlan [Qui93]. The book gives an excellent presentation of many of the issues regarding decision tree induction, as does a comprehensive survey on decision tree induction by Murthy [Mur98]. Other algorithms for decision tree induction include the predecessor of C4.5, namely, ID3 (Quinlan [Qui86]), CART (Breiman, Friedman, Olshen, and Stone [BFOS84]), FACT (Loh and Vanichsetakul [LV88]), QUEST (Loh and Shih [LS97]), PUBLIC (Rastogi and Shim [RS98]), and CHAID (Kass [Kas80] and Magidson [Mag94]). Incremental versions of ID3 include ID4 (Schlimmer and Fisher [SF86a]) and ID5 (Utgoff [Utg88]). In addition, INFERULE (Uthurusamy, Fayyad, and Spangler [UFS91]) learns decision trees from inconclusive data. KATE (Manago and Kodratoff [MK91]) learns decision trees from complex structured data. Decision tree algorithms that address the scalability issue in data mining include SLIQ (Mehta, Agrawal, and Rissanen [MAR96]), SPRINT (Shafer, Agrawal, and Mehta [SAM96]), RainForest (Gehrke, Ramakrishnan, and Ganti [GRG98]), BOAT (Gehrke, Ganti, Ramakrishnan, and Loh [GGRL99]), and Kamber, Winstone, Gong, et al. [KWG+97]. Earlier approaches described include [Cat91, CS93a, CS93b]. For a comparison of attribute selection measures for decision tree induction, see Buntine and Niblett [BN92], Murthy [Mur98], and Shih [Shi00]. For a detailed discussion on such measures, see Kononenko and

Hong [KH97]. Attribute (or feature) construction is described in Liu and Motoda [LM98a, LM98b]. Examples of systems with attribute construction include BACON by Langley, Simon, Bradshaw, Zytko [LSBZ87], Stagger by Schlimmer [Schl87], FRINGE by Pagallo [Pag89], and AQ17-DCI by Bloedorn and Michalski [BM98].

There are numerous algorithms for decision tree pruning, including cost complexity pruning (Breiman, Friedman, Olshen, and Stone [BFOS84]), reduced error pruning (Quinlan [Qui87]), and pessimistic pruning (Quinlan [Qui86]). PUBLIC (Rastogi and Shim [RS98]) integrates decision tree construction with tree pruning. MDL-based pruning methods can be found in Quinlan and Rivest [QR89], Mehta, Agrawal, and Rissanen [MRA95], and Rastogi and Shim [RS98]. Others methods include Niblett and Bratko [NB86], and Hosking, Pednault, and Sudan [HPS97]. For an empirical comparison of pruning methods, see Mingers [Min89] and Malerba, Floriana, and Semeraro [MFS95]. For a survey on simplifying decision trees, see Breslow and Aha [BA97].

For the extraction of rules from decision trees, see Quinlan [Qui87, Qui93]. Rather than generating rules by extracting them from decision trees, it is also possible to induce rules directly from the training data. Rule induction algorithms include CN2 (Clark and Niblett [CN89]), AQ15 (Hong, Mozetic, and Michalski [HMM86]), ITRULE (Smyth and Goodman [SG92]), FOIL (Quinlan [Qui90]), and Swap-1 (Weiss and Indurkhya [WI98]). Rule refinement strategies that identify the most interesting rules among a given rule set can be found in Major and Mangano [MM95]. The integration of attribution-oriented induction with decision tree induction is proposed in Kamber, Winstone, Gong, et al. [KWG+97]. The precision or classification threshold described in Section 7.3.6 is used in Agrawal, Ghosh, Imielinski, et al. [AGI+92] and Kamber et al. [KWG+97].

Thorough presentations of Bayesian classification can be found in Duda and Hart [DH73], a classic textbook on pattern recognition, as well as machine learning textbooks such as Weiss and Kulikowski [WK91] and Mitchell [Mit97]. For an analysis of the predictive power of naive Bayesian classifiers when the class conditional independence assumption is violated, see Domingos and Pazzani [DP96]. Experiments with kernel density estimation for continuous-valued attributes, rather than Gaussian estimation, have been reported for naive Bayesian classifiers in John [Joh97]. For an introduction to Bayesian belief networks, see Heckerman [Hec96]. Algorithms for inference on belief networks can be found in Russell and Norvig [RN95] and Jensen [Jen96]. The method of gradient descent, described in Section 7.4.4 for training Bayesian belief networks, is given in Russell, Binder, Koller, and Kanazawa [RBKK95]. The example given in Figure 7.8 is adapted from Russell et al. [RBKK95]. Alternative strategies for learning belief networks with hidden variables include the EM algorithm (Lauritzen [Lau95]). Solutions for learning the belief network structure from training data given observable variables are proposed in [CH92, Bun94, HGC95].

The backpropagation algorithm was presented in Rumelhart, Hinton, and Williams [RHW86]. Since then, many variations have been proposed involving, for example, alternative error functions (Hanson and Burr [HB88]), dynamic adjustment of the network topology (Fahlman and Lebiere [FL90] and Le Cun, Denker, and Solla [LDS90]), and dynamic adjustment of the learning rate and momentum parameters (Jacobs [Jac88]). Other variations are discussed in Chauvin and Rumelhart [CR95]. Books on neural networks include [RM86, HN90, HKP91, Fu94, CR95, Bis95, Rip96]. Many books on machine learning, such as [WK91, Mit97], also contain good explanations of the backpropagation algorithm. There are several techniques for extracting rules from neural networks, such as [SN88, Gal93, TS93, Fu94, Avn95, LSL95, CS96b, LGT97]. The method of rule extraction described in Section 7.5.4 is based on Lu, Setiono, and Liu [LSL95]. Critiques of techniques for rule extraction from neural networks can be found in Craven and Shavlik [CS97]. Roy [Roy00] proposes that the theoretical foundations of neural networks are flawed with respect to assumptions made regarding how connectionist learning models the brain. An extensive survey of applications of neural networks in industry, business, and science is provided in Widrow, Rumelhart, and Lehr [WRL94].

The ARCS system described in Section 7.6 is proposed in Lent, Swami, and Widom [LSW97] and is also described in Chapter 6. The method of associative classification is proposed in Liu, Hsu, and Ma [LHM98]. The CAEP classifier, using emerging patterns, is proposed in Dong and Li [DL99]. The JEP-classifier, using jumping emerging patterns, is described in Li, Dong, and Ramamohanarao [LDR00]. Meretakis and Wüthrich [MW99] propose constructing a naive Bayesian classifier by mining long itemsets.

Nearest neighbor methods are discussed in many statistical texts on classification, such as Duda and Hart [DH73] and James [Jam85]. Additional information can be found in Cover and Hart [CH67] and Fukunaga and Hummels [FH87]. References on case-based reasoning (CBR) include the texts [RS89, Kol93, Lea96], as well as [AP94]. For texts on genetic algorithms, see [Gol89, Mic92, Mit96]. Rough sets were introduced in Pawlak [Paw91]. Concise summaries of rough set theory in data mining include [Zia91, CPS98]. Rough sets have been used for feature reduction and expert system design in many applications, including [Zia91, LP97, Swi98]. Algorithms to reduce the computation intensity in finding reducts have been proposed in [SR92]. General descriptions of fuzzy logic can be found in [Zad65, BS97, CPS98].

There are many good textbooks that cover the techniques of regression. Examples include [Jam85, Dob90, JW92, Dev95, HC95, NKNW96, Agr96]. The book by Press, Teukolsky, Vetterling, and Flannery [PTVF96] and accompanying source code contain many statistical procedures, such as the method of least squares for both linear and multiple regression. Recent nonlinear regression models include projection pursuit and MARS (Friedman [Fri91]). Log-linear models are also known in the computer science literature as *multiplicative models*. For log-linear models from a computer science perspective, see Pearl [Pea88]. Regression trees (Breiman, Friedman, Olshen, and Stone [BFOS84]) are often comparable in performance with other regression methods, particularly when there exist many higher-order dependencies among the predictor variables.

Methods for data cleaning and data transformation are discussed in Kennedy, Lee, Van Roy, et al. [KLV$^+$98], Weiss and Indurkhya [WI98], Pyle [Pyl99], and Chapter 3 of this book. Issues involved in estimating classifier accuracy are described in Weiss and Kulikowski [WK91]. The use of stratified 10-fold cross-validation for estimating classifier accuracy is recommended over the holdout, cross-validation, leave-one-out (Stone [Sto74]) and bootstrapping (Efron and Tibshirani [ET93]) methods, based on a theoretical and empirical study by Kohavi [Koh95]. Bagging is proposed in Breiman [Bre96]. The boosting technique of Freund and Schapire [FS97] has been applied to several different classifiers, including decision tree induction (Quinlan [Qui96]) and naive Bayesian classification (Elkan [Elk97]). Sensitivity, specificity, and precision are discussed in Frakes and Baeza-Yates [FBY92].

The University of California at Irvine (UCI) maintains a Machine Learning Repository of data sets for the development and testing of classification algorithms. For information on this repository, see *http://www.ics.uci.edu/~mlearn/MLRepository.html*.

No classification method is superior over all others for all data types and domains. Empirical comparisons of classification methods include [Qui88, SMT91, BCP93, CM94, MST94, BU95, LLS00].

# Cluster Analysis

**Imagine that you are given a set of data objects for analysis where,** unlike in classification, the class label of each object is not known. *Clustering* is the process of grouping the data into classes or *clusters* so that objects within a cluster have high similarity in comparison to one another, but are very dissimilar to objects in other clusters. Dissimilarities are assessed based on the attribute values describing the objects. Often, distance measures are used. Clustering has its roots in many areas, including data mining, statistics, biology, and machine learning.

In this chapter, you will learn the requirements of clustering methods for operating on large amounts of data. You will also study how to compute dissimilarities between objects represented by various attribute or variable types. You will study several clustering techniques, organized into the following categories: *partitioning methods*, *hierarchical methods*, *density-based methods*, *grid-based methods*, and *model-based methods*. Clustering can also be used for *outlier detection*, which forms the final topic of this chapter.

## 8.1 What Is Cluster Analysis?

The process of grouping a set of physical or abstract objects into classes of *similar* objects is called **clustering**. A **cluster** is a collection of data objects that are *similar* to one another within the same cluster and are *dissimilar* to the objects in other clusters. A cluster of data objects can be treated collectively as one group in many applications.

Cluster analysis is an important human activity. Early in childhood, one learns how to distinguish between cats and dogs, or between animals and plants, by continuously improving subconscious clustering schemes. Cluster analysis has been widely used in numerous applications, including pattern recognition, data analysis, image processing, and market research. By clustering, one can identify dense and sparse regions and, therefore, discover overall distribution patterns and interesting correlations among data attributes.

*"What are some typical applications of clustering?"* In business, clustering can help marketers discover distinct groups in their customer bases and characterize customer groups based on purchasing patterns. In biology, it can be used to derive plant and animal taxonomies, categorize genes with similar functionality, and gain insight into structures inherent in populations. Clustering may also help in the identification of areas of similar land use in an earth observation database, and in the identification of groups of automobile insurance policy holders with a high average claim cost, as well as the identification of groups of houses in a city according to house type, value, and geographical location. It can also be used to help classify documents on the Web for information discovery. As a data mining function, cluster analysis can be used as a stand-alone tool to gain insight into the distribution of data, to observe the characteristics of each cluster, and to focus on a particular set of clusters for further analysis. Alternatively, it may serve as a preprocessing step for other algorithms, such as characterization and classification, which would then operate on the detected clusters.

Data clustering is under vigorous development. Contributing areas of research include data mining, statistics, machine learning, spatial database technology, biology, and marketing. Owing to the huge amounts of data collected in databases, cluster analysis has recently become a highly active topic in data mining research.

As a branch of statistics, cluster analysis has been studied extensively for many years, focusing mainly on *distance-based cluster analysis*. Cluster analysis tools based on $k$-means, $k$-medoids, and several other methods have also been built into many statistical analysis software packages or systems, such as S-Plus, SPSS, and SAS. In machine learning, clustering is an example of **unsupervised learning**. Unlike classification, clustering and unsupervised learning do not rely on predefined classes and class-labeled training examples. For this reason, clustering is a form of **learning by observation**, rather than *learning by examples*. In **conceptual clustering**, a group of objects forms a class only if it is describable by a concept. This differs from conventional clustering, which measures similarity based on geometric distance. Conceptual clustering consists of two components: (1) it discovers the appropriate classes, and (2) it forms descriptions for each class, as in classification. The guideline of striving for high intraclass similarity and low interclass similarity still applies.

In data mining, efforts have focused on finding methods for efficient and effective cluster analysis in *large databases*. Active themes of research focus on the *scalability* of clustering methods, the effectiveness of methods for clustering *complex shapes and types of data*, *high-dimensional* clustering techniques, and methods for clustering *mixed numerical and categorical data* in large databases.

Clustering is a challenging field of research where its potential applications pose their own special requirements. The following are typical requirements of clustering in data mining:

- **Scalability:** Many clustering algorithms work well on small data sets containing fewer than 200 data objects; however, a large database may contain millions of objects. Clustering on a *sample* of a given large data set may lead to biased results. Highly scalable clustering algorithms are needed.

- **Ability to deal with different types of attributes:** Many algorithms are designed to cluster interval-based (numerical) data. However, applications may require clustering other types of data, such as binary, categorical (nominal), and ordinal data, or mixtures of these data types.

- **Discovery of clusters with arbitrary shape:** Many clustering algorithms determine clusters based on Euclidean or Manhattan distance measures. Algorithms based on such distance measures tend to find spherical clusters with similar size and density. However, a cluster could be of any shape. It is important to develop algorithms that can detect clusters of arbitrary shape.

- **Minimal requirements for domain knowledge to determine input parameters:** Many clustering algorithms require users to input certain parameters in cluster analysis (such as the number of desired clusters). The clustering results can be quite sensitive to input parameters. Parameters are often hard to determine, especially for data sets containing high-dimensional objects. This not only burdens users, but also makes the quality of clustering difficult to control.

- **Ability to deal with noisy data:** Most real-world databases contain outliers or missing, unknown, or erroneous data. Some clustering algorithms are sensitive to such data and may lead to clusters of poor quality.

- **Insensitivity to the order of input records:** Some clustering algorithms are sensitive to the order of input data; for example, the same set of data, when presented with different orderings to such an algorithm, may generate dramatically different clusters. It is important to develop algorithms that are insensitive to the order of input.

- **High dimensionality:** A database or a data warehouse can contain several dimensions or attributes. Many clustering algorithms are good at handling low-dimensional data, involving only two to three dimensions. Human eyes are good at judging the quality of clustering for up to three dimensions. It is challenging to cluster data objects in high-dimensional space, especially considering that such data can be very sparse and highly skewed.

- **Constraint-based clustering:** Real-world applications may need to perform clustering under various kinds of constraints. Suppose that your job is to choose the locations for a given number of new automatic cash-dispensing machines (i.e., ATMs) in a city. To decide upon this, you may cluster households while considering constraints such as the city's rivers and highway networks, and customer requirements per region. A challenging task is to find groups of data with good clustering behavior that satisfy specified constraints.

- **Interpretability and usability**: Users expect clustering results to be interpretable, comprehensible, and usable. That is, clustering may need to be tied up with specific semantic interpretations and applications. It is important to study how an application goal may influence the selection of clustering methods.

With these requirements in mind, our study of cluster analysis proceeds as follows. First, we study different types of data and how they can influence clustering methods. Second, we present a general categorization of clustering methods. We then study each clustering method in detail, including partitioning methods, hierarchical methods, density-based methods, grid-based methods, and model-based methods. We also examine clustering in high-dimensional space and outlier analysis.

## 8.2 Types of Data in Cluster Analysis

In this section, we study the types of data that often occur in cluster analysis and how to preprocess them for such an analysis. Suppose that a data set to be clustered contains $n$ objects, which may represent persons, houses, documents, countries, and so on. Main memory-based clustering algorithms typically operate on either of the following two data structures.

- **Data matrix** (or *object-by-variable structure*): This represents $n$ objects, such as persons, with $p$ **variables** (also called *measurements* or *attributes*), such as age, height, weight, gender, race, and so on. The structure is in the form of a relational table, or $n$-by-$p$ matrix ($n$ objects $\times$ $p$ variables):

$$\begin{bmatrix} x_{11} & \cdots & x_{1f} & \cdots & x_{1p} \\ \vdots & \vdots & \vdots & \vdots & \vdots \\ x_{i1} & \cdots & x_{if} & \cdots & x_{ip} \\ \vdots & \vdots & \vdots & \ddots & \vdots \\ x_{n1} & \cdots & x_{nf} & \cdots & x_{np} \end{bmatrix} \tag{8.1}$$

- **Dissimilarity matrix** (or *object-by-object structure*): This stores a collection of proximities that are available for all pairs of $n$ objects. It is often represented by an $n$-by-$n$ table:

$$\begin{bmatrix} 0 & & & & \\ d(2,1) & 0 & & & \\ d(3,1) & d(3,2) & 0 & & \\ \vdots & \vdots & \vdots & & \\ d(n,1) & d(n,2) & \cdots & \cdots & 0 \end{bmatrix} \tag{8.2}$$

where $d(i,j)$ is the measured **difference** or **dissimilarity** between objects $i$ and $j$. In general, $d(i,j)$ is a nonnegative number that is close to 0 when objects

$i$ and $j$ are highly similar or "near" each other, and becomes larger the more they differ. Since $d(i, j) = d(j, i)$, and $d(i, i) = 0$, we have the matrix in (8.2). Measures of dissimilarity are discussed throughout this section.

The data matrix is often called a **two-mode** matrix, whereas the dissimilarity matrix is called a **one-mode** matrix, since the rows and columns of the former represent different entities, while those of the latter represent the same entity. Many clustering algorithms operate on a dissimilarity matrix. If the data are presented in the form of a data matrix, it can first be transformed into a dissimilarity matrix before applying such clustering algorithms.

"*How can dissimilarity,* d(i,j), *be assessed?*" you may wonder. In this section, we discuss how object dissimilarity can be computed for objects described by *interval-scaled* variables; by *binary* variables; by *nominal, ordinal,* and *ratio-scaled* variables; or combinations of these variable types. The dissimilarity data can later be used to compute clusters of objects.

## 8.2.1 Interval-Scaled Variables

This section discusses *interval-scaled variables* and their standardization. It then describes distance measures that are commonly used for computing the dissimilarity of objects described by such variables. These measures include the *Euclidean, Manhattan,* and *Minkowski distances*.

"*What are interval-scaled variables?*" **Interval-scaled variables** are continuous measurements of a roughly linear scale. Typical examples include weight and height, latitude and longitude coordinates (e.g., when clustering houses), and weather temperature.

The measurement unit used can affect the clustering analysis. For example, changing measurement units from meters to inches for height, or from kilograms to pounds for weight, may lead to a very different clustering structure. In general, expressing a variable in smaller units will lead to a larger range for that variable, and thus a larger effect on the resulting clustering structure. To help avoid dependence on the choice of measurement units, the data should be standardized. Standardizing measurements attempts to give all variables an equal weight. This is particularly useful when given no prior knowledge of the data. However, in some applications, users may intentionally want to give more weight to a certain set of variables than to others. For example, when clustering basketball player candidates, we may prefer to give more weight to the variable height.

"*How can the data for a variable be standardized?*" To standardize measurements, one choice is to convert the original measurements to unitless variables. Given measurements for a variable $f$, this can be performed as follows.

**1.** Calculate the **mean absolute deviation**, $s_f$:

$$s_f = \frac{1}{n}(|x_{1f} - m_f| + |x_{2f} - m_f| + \cdots + |x_{nf} - m_f|), \tag{8.3}$$

where $x_{1f}, \ldots, x_{nf}$ are $n$ measurements of $f$, and $m_f$ is the *mean* value of $f$, that is, $m_f = \frac{1}{n}(x_{1f} + x_{2f} + \cdots + x_{nf})$.

2. Calculate the **standardized measurement**, or **z-score**:

$$z_{if} = \frac{x_{if} - m_f}{s_f}.$$ (8.4)

The mean absolute deviation, $s_f$, is more robust to outliers than the standard deviation, $\sigma_f$. When computing the mean absolute deviation, the deviations from the mean (i.e., $|x_{if} - m_f|$) are not squared; hence, the effect of outliers is somewhat reduced. There are more robust measures of dispersion, such as the *median absolute deviation*. However, the advantage of using the mean absolute deviation is that the z-scores of outliers do not become too small; hence, the outliers remain detectable.

Standardization may or may not be useful in a particular application. Thus the choice of whether and how to perform standardization should be left to the user. Methods of standardization are also discussed in Chapter 3 under normalization techniques for data preprocessing.

"OK," you now ask, "*once I have standardized the data, how can I compute the dissimilarity between objects?*" After standardization, or without standardization in certain applications, the dissimilarity (or similarity) between the objects described by interval-scaled variables is typically computed based on the distance between each pair of objects. The most popular distance measure is **Euclidean distance**, which is defined as

$$d(i, j) = \sqrt{|x_{i1} - x_{j1}|^2 + |x_{i2} - x_{j2}|^2 + \cdots + |x_{ip} - x_{jp}|^2},$$ (8.5)

where $i = (x_{i1}, x_{i2}, \ldots, x_{ip})$ and $j = (x_{j1}, x_{j2}, \ldots, x_{jp})$ are two $p$-dimensional data objects.

Another well-known metric is **Manhattan (or city block) distance**, defined as

$$d(i, j) = |x_{i1} - x_{j1}| + |x_{i2} - x_{j2}| + \cdots + |x_{ip} - x_{jp}|.$$ (8.6)

Both the Euclidean distance and Manhattan distance satisfy the following mathematic requirements of a distance function:

1. $d(i, j) \geq 0$: Distance is a nonnegative number.
2. $d(i, i) = 0$: The distance of an object to itself is 0.
3. $d(i, j) = d(j, i)$: Distance is a symmetric function.
4. $d(i, j) \leq d(i, h) + d(h, j)$: Going directly from object $i$ to object $j$ in space is no more than making a detour over any other object $h$ (*triangular inequality*).

**Minkowski distance** is a generalization of both Euclidean distance and Manhattan distance. It is defined as

$$d(i, j) = (|x_{i1} - x_{j1}|^q + |x_{i2} - x_{j2}|^q + \cdots + |x_{ip} - x_{jp}|^q)^{1/q},$$

(8.7)

where $q$ is a positive integer. It represents the Manhattan distance when $q = 1$, and Euclidean distance when $q = 2$.

It each variable is assigned a weight according to its perceived importance, the *weighted* Euclidean distance can be computed as

$$d(i, j) = \sqrt{w_1|x_{i1} - x_{j1}|^2 + w_2|x_{i2} - x_{j2}|^2 + \cdots + w_p|x_{ip} - x_{jp}|^2}.$$

(8.8)

Weighting can also be applied to the Manhattan and Minkowski distances.

## 8.2.2 Binary Variables

This section describes how to compute the dissimilarity between objects described by either *symmetric* or *asymmetric binary variables.*

A **binary variable** has only two states: 0 or 1, where 0 means that the variable is absent, and 1 means that it is present. Given the variable *smoker* describing a patient, for instance, 1 indicates that the patient smokes, while 0 indicates that the patient does not. Treating binary variables as if they are interval-scaled can lead to misleading clustering results. Therefore, methods specific to binary data are necessary for computing dissimilarities.

"*So, how can I compute the dissimilarity between two binary variables?*" One approach involves computing a dissimilarity matrix from the given binary data. If all binary variables are thought of as having the same weight, we have the 2-by-2 contingency table of Table 8.1, where $q$ is the number of variables that equal 1 for both objects $i$ and $j$, $r$ is the number of variables that equal 1 for object $i$ but that are 0 for object $j$, $s$ is the number of variables that equal 0 for object $i$ but equal 1 for object $j$, and $t$ is the number of variables that equal 0 for both objects $i$ and $j$. The total number of variables is $p$, where $p = q + r + s + t$.

**Table 8.1**  A contingency table for binary variables.

|          |     | Object j |       |       |
|----------|-----|----------|-------|-------|
|          |     | 1        | 0     | Sum   |
|          | 1   | $q$      | $r$   | $q + r$ |
| Object i | 0   | $s$      | $t$   | $s + t$ |
|          | Sum | $q + s$  | $r + t$ | $p$   |

*"What is the difference between symmetric and asymmetric binary variables?"* A binary variable is **symmetric** if both of its states are equally valuable and carry the same weight; that is, there is no preference on which outcome should be coded as 0 or 1. One such example could be the attribute *gender* having the states *male* and *female*. Similarity that is based on symmetric binary variables is called **invariant similarity** in that the result does not change when some or all of the binary variables are coded differently. For invariant similarities, the most well-known coefficient for assessing the dissimilarity between objects $i$ and $j$ is the **simple matching coefficient**, defined as

$$d(i, j) = \frac{r + s}{q + r + s + t}. \tag{8.9}$$

A binary variable is **asymmetric** if the outcomes of the states are not equally important, such as the *positive* and *negative* outcomes of a disease *test*. By convention, we shall code the most important outcome, which is usually the rarest one, by 1 (e.g., *HIV positive*), and the other by 0 (e.g., *HIV negative*). Given two asymmetric binary variables, the agreement of two 1s (a positive match) is then considered more significant than that of two 0s (a negative match). Therefore, such binary variables are often considered "monary" (as if having one state). The similarity based on such variables is called **noninvariant similarity**. For noninvariant similarities, the most well-known coefficient is the **Jaccard coefficient**, where the number of negative matches, $t$, is considered unimportant and thus is ignored in the computation:

$$d(i, j) = \frac{r + s}{q + r + s}. \tag{8.10}$$

When both symmetric and asymmetric binary variables occur in the same data set, the mixed variables approach described in Section 8.2.4 can be applied.

**Example 8.1** **Dissimilarity between binary variables:** Suppose that a patient record table (Table 8.2) contains the attributes *name, gender, fever, cough, test-1, test-2, test-3,* and *test-4*, where *name* is an object-id, *gender* is a symmetric attribute, and the remaining attributes are asymmetric binary.

For asymmetric attribute values, let the values $Y$ (*yes*) and $P$ (*positive*) be set to 1, and the value $N$ (*no* or *negative*) be set to 0. Suppose that the distance between objects (patients) is computed based only on the asymmetric variables. According to the Jaccard coefficient formula (8.10), the distance between each pair of the three patients, Jack, Mary, and Jim, should be

**Table 8.2** A relational table containing mostly binary attributes.

| name | gender | fever | cough | test-1 | test-2 | test-3 | test-4 |
|------|--------|-------|-------|--------|--------|--------|--------|
| Jack | M | Y | N | P | N | N | N |
| Mary | F | Y | N | P | N | P | N |
| Jim | M | Y | Y | N | N | N | N |
| $\vdots$ | $\vdots$ | $\vdots$ | $\vdots$ | $\vdots$ | $\vdots$ | $\vdots$ | $\vdots$ |

$$d(jack, mary) = \frac{0 + 1}{2 + 0 + 1} = 0.33 \tag{8.11}$$

$$d(jack, jim) = \frac{1 + 1}{1 + 1 + 1} = 0.67 \tag{8.12}$$

$$d(jim, mary) = \frac{1 + 2}{1 + 1 + 2} = 0.75 \tag{8.13}$$

These measurements suggest that Jim and Mary are unlikely to have a similar disease since they have the highest dissimilarity value among the three pairs. Of the three patients, Jack and Mary are the most likely to have a similar disease. ■

## 8.2.3 Nominal, Ordinal, and Ratio-Scaled Variables

This section discusses how to compute the dissimilarity between objects described by *nominal, ordinal,* and *ratio-scaled* variables.

### Nominal Variables

A nominal variable is a generalization of the binary variable in that it can take on more than two states. For example, *map_color* is a nominal variable that may have, say, five states: *red, yellow, green, pink,* and *blue.*

Let the number of states of a nominal variable be $M$. The states can be denoted by letters, symbols, or a set of integers, such as $1, 2, \ldots, M$. Notice that such integers are used just for data handling and do not represent any specific ordering.

*"How is dissimilarity computed between objects described by nominal variables?"* The dissimilarity between two objects $i$ and $j$ can be computed using the **simple matching** approach:

$$d(i, j) = \frac{p - m}{p}, \tag{8.14}$$

where $m$ is the number of *matches* (i.e., the number of variables for which $i$ and $j$ are in the same state), and $p$ is the total number of variables. Weights can be assigned to increase the effect of $m$ or to assign greater weight to the matches in variables having a larger number of states.

Nominal variables can be encoded by asymmetric binary variables by creating a new binary variable for each of the $M$ nominal states. For an object with a given state value, the binary variable representing that state is set to 1, while the remaining binary variables are set to 0. For example, to encode the nominal variable *map_color*, a binary variable can be created for each of the five colors listed above. For an object having the color *yellow*, the *yellow* variable is set to 1, while the remaining four variables are set to 0. The dissimilarity coefficient for this form of encoding can be calculated using the methods discussed in Section 8.2.2.

### Ordinal Variables

A **discrete ordinal variable** resembles a nominal variable, except that the $M$ states of the ordinal value are ordered in a meaningful sequence. Ordinal variables are very useful for registering subjective assessments of qualities that cannot be measured objectively. For example, professional ranks are often enumerated in a sequential order, such as assistant, associate, and full. A **continuous ordinal variable** looks like a set of continuous data of an unknown scale; that is, the relative ordering of the values is essential but their actual magnitude is not. For example, the relative ranking in a particular sport (e.g., gold, silver, bronze) is often more essential than the actual values of a particular measure. Ordinal variables may also be obtained from the discretization of interval-scaled quantities by splitting the value range into a finite number of classes. The values of an ordinal variable can be mapped to *ranks*. For example, suppose that an ordinal variable $f$ has $M_f$ states. These ordered states define the ranking $1, \ldots, M_f$.

*"How are ordinal variables handled?"* The treatment of ordinal variables is quite similar to that of interval-scaled variables when computing the dissimilarity between objects. Suppose that $f$ is a variable from a set of ordinal variables describing $n$ objects. The dissimilarity computation with respect to $f$ involves the following steps:

1. The value of $f$ for the $i$th object is $x_{if}$, and $f$ has $M_f$ ordered states, representing the ranking $1, \ldots, M_f$. Replace each $x_{if}$ by its corresponding rank, $r_{if} \in \{1, \ldots, M_f\}$.

2. Since each ordinal variable can have a different number of states, it is often necessary to map the range of each variable onto [0.0,1.0] so that each variable has equal weight. This can be achieved by replacing the rank $r_{if}$ of the $i$th object in the $f$th variable by

$$z_{if} = \frac{r_{if} - 1}{M_f - 1}. \tag{8.15}$$

**3.** Dissimilarity can then be computed using any of the distance measures described in Section 8.2.1 for interval-scaled variables, using $z_{if}$ to represent the $f$ value for the $i$th object.

### Ratio-Scaled Variables

A ratio-scaled variable makes a positive measurement on a nonlinear scale, such as an exponential scale, approximately following the formula

$$Ae^{Bt} \quad \text{or} \quad Ae^{-Bt}, \tag{8.16}$$

where $A$ and $B$ are positive constants. Typical examples include the growth of a bacteria population, or the decay of a radioactive element.

*"How can I compute the dissimilarity between objects described by ratio-scaled variables?"* There are three methods to handle ratio-scaled variables for computing the dissimilarity between objects.

- Treat ratio-scaled variables like interval-scaled variables. This, however, is not usually a good choice since it is likely that the scale may be distorted.

- Apply **logarithmic transformation** to a ratio-scaled variable $f$ having value $x_{if}$ for object $i$ by using the formula $y_{if} = \log(x_{if})$. The $y_{if}$ values can be treated as interval-valued, as described in Section 8.2.1. Notice that for some ratio-scaled variables, log-log or other transformations may be applied, depending on the definition and application.

- Treat $x_{if}$ as continuous ordinal data and treat their ranks as interval-valued.

The latter two methods are the most effective, although the choice of method used may be dependent on the given application.

## 8.2.4 Variables of Mixed Types

Sections 8.2.1 to 8.2.3 discussed how to compute the dissimilarity between objects described by variables of the same type, where these types may be either *interval-scaled*, *symmetric binary*, *asymmetric binary*, *nominal*, *ordinal*, or *ratio-scaled*. However, in many real databases, objects are described by a *mixture* of variable types. In general, a database can contain all of the six variable types listed above.

*"So, how can we compute the dissimilarity between objects of mixed variable types?"* One approach is to group each kind of variable together, performing a separate cluster analysis for each variable type. This is feasible if these analyses derive compatible results. However, in real applications, it is unlikely that a separate cluster analysis per variable type will generate compatible results.

A more preferable approach is to process all variable types together, performing a single cluster analysis. One such technique combines the different variables into a single dissimilarity matrix, bringing all of the meaningful variables onto a common scale of the interval [0.0,1.0].

Suppose that the data set contains $p$ variables of mixed type. The dissimilarity $d(i, j)$ between objects $i$ and $j$ is defined as

$$d(i, j) = \frac{\Sigma_{f=1}^{p} \delta_{ij}^{(f)} d_{ij}^{(f)}}{\Sigma_{f=1}^{p} \delta_{ij}^{(f)}}, \tag{8.17}$$

where the indicator $\delta_{ij}^{(f)} = 0$ if either (1) $x_{if}$ or $x_{jf}$ is missing (i.e., there is no measurement of variable $f$ for object $i$ or object $j$), or (2) $x_{if} = x_{jf} = 0$ and variable $f$ is asymmetric binary; otherwise, $\delta_{ij}^{(f)} = 1$. The contribution of variable $f$ to the dissimilarity between $i$ and $j$, $d_{ij}^{(f)}$, is computed dependent on its type:

- If $f$ is binary or nominal: $d_{ij}^{(f)} = 0$ if $x_{if} = x_{jf}$; otherwise $d_{ij}^{(f)} = 1$.

- If $f$ is interval-based: $d_{ij}^{(f)} = \frac{|x_{if} - x_{jf}|}{max_h x_{hf} - min_h x_{hf}}$, where $h$ runs over all nonmissing objects for variable $f$.

- If $f$ is ordinal or ratio-scaled: compute the ranks $r_{if}$ and $z_{if} = \frac{r_{if} - 1}{M_f - 1}$, and treat $z_{if}$ as interval-scaled.

Thus, the dissimilarity between objects can be computed even when the variables describing the objects are of different types.

## 8.3 A Categorization of Major Clustering Methods

There exist a large number of clustering algorithms in the literature. The choice of clustering algorithm depends both on the type of data available and on the particular purpose and application. If cluster analysis is used as a descriptive or exploratory tool, it is possible to try several algorithms on the same data to see what the data may disclose.

In general, major clustering methods can be classified into the following categories.

**Partitioning methods:** Given a database of $n$ objects or data tuples, a partitioning method constructs $k$ partitions of the data, where each partition represents a cluster and $k \leq n$. That is, it classifies the data into $k$ groups, which together satisfy the following requirements: (1) each group must contain at least one object, and (2) each object must belong to exactly one group. Notice that the second requirement can be relaxed in some fuzzy partitioning techniques. References to such techniques are given in the bibliographic notes.

Given $k$, the number of partitions to construct, a partitioning method creates an initial partitioning. It then uses an **iterative relocation technique** that attempts to improve the partitioning by moving objects from one group to another. The general criterion of a good partitioning is that objects in the same cluster are "close" or related to each other, whereas objects of different clusters are "far apart" or very different. There are various kinds of other criteria for judging the quality of partitions.

To achieve global optimality in partitioning-based clustering would require the exhaustive enumeration of all of the possible partitions. Instead, most applications adopt one of two popular heuristic methods: (1) the k-*means* algorithm, where each cluster is represented by the mean value of the objects in the cluster, and (2) the k-*medoids* algorithm, where each cluster is represented by one of the objects located near the center of the cluster. These heuristic clustering methods work well for finding spherical-shaped clusters in small to medium-sized databases. To find clusters with complex shapes and for clustering very large data sets, partitioning-based methods need to be extended. Partitioning-based clustering methods are studied in depth in Section 8.4.

**Hierarchical methods:**    A hierarchical method creates a hierarchical decomposition of the given set of data objects. A hierarchical method can be classified as being either *agglomerative* or *divisive*, based on how the hierarchical decomposition is formed. The *agglomerative approach*, also called the *bottom-up* approach, starts with each object forming a separate group. It successively merges the objects or groups close to one another, until all of the groups are merged into one (the topmost level of the hierarchy), or until a termination condition holds. The *divisive approach*, also called the *top-down* approach, starts with all the objects in the same cluster. In each successive iteration, a cluster is split up into smaller clusters, until eventually each object is in one cluster, or until a termination condition holds.

Hierarchical methods suffer from the fact that once a step (merge or split) is done, it can never be undone. This rigidity is useful in that it leads to smaller computation costs by not worrying about a combinatorial number of different choices. However, a major problem of such techniques is that they cannot correct erroneous decisions. There are two approaches to improving the quality of hierarchical clustering: (1) perform careful analysis of object "linkages" at each hierarchical partitioning, such as in CURE and Chameleon, or (2) integrate hierarchical agglomeration and iterative relocation by first using a hierarchical agglomerative algorithm and then refining the result using iterative relocation, as in BIRCH. Hierarchical clustering methods are studied in Section 8.5.

**Density-based methods:**    Most partitioning methods cluster objects based on the distance between objects. Such methods can find only spherical-shaped clusters and encounter difficulty at discovering clusters of arbitrary shapes. Other clustering methods have been developed based on the notion of *density*. Their general idea is to continue growing the given cluster as long as the density (number of objects or data points) in the "neighborhood" exceeds some threshold; that is, for each data point within a given cluster, the neighborhood of a given radius has to contain at least a minimum number of points. Such a method can be used to filter out noise (outliers) and discover clusters of arbitrary shape.

DBSCAN is a typical density-based method that grows clusters according to a density threshold. OPTICS is a density-based method that computes an augmented clustering ordering for automatic and interactive cluster analysis. Density-based clustering methods are studied in Section 8.6.

**Grid-based methods:**   Grid-based methods quantize the object space into a finite number of cells that form a grid structure. All of the clustering operations are performed on the grid structure (i.e., on the quantized space). The main advantage of this approach is its fast processing time, which is typically independent of the number of data objects and dependent only on the number of cells in each dimension in the quantized space.

STING is a typical example of a grid-based method. CLIQUE and Wave-Cluster are two clustering algorithms that are both grid-based and density-based. Grid-based clustering methods are studied in Section 8.7.

**Model-based methods:**   Model-based methods hypothesize a model for each of the clusters and find the best fit of the data to the given model. A model-based algorithm may locate clusters by constructing a density function that reflects the spatial distribution of the data points. It also leads to a way of automatically determining the number of clusters based on standard statistics, taking "noise" or outliers into account and thus yielding robust clustering methods. Model-based clustering methods are studied in Section 8.8.

Some clustering algorithms integrate the ideas of several clustering methods, so that it is sometimes difficult to classify a given algorithm as uniquely belonging to only one clustering method category. Furthermore, some applications may have clustering criteria that require the integration of several clustering techniques.

In the following sections, we examine each of the above five clustering methods in detail. We also introduce algorithms that integrate the ideas of several clustering methods. Outlier analysis, which typically involves clustering, is described in Section 8.9.

# 8.4  Partitioning Methods

Given a database of *n* objects and *k*, the number of clusters to form, a partitioning algorithm organizes the objects into *k* partitions ($k \leq n$), where each partition represents a cluster. The clusters are formed to optimize an objective partitioning criterion, often called a *similarity function*, such as distance, so that the objects within a cluster are "similar," whereas the objects of different clusters are "dissimilar" in terms of the database attributes.

**Algorithm:**   *k*-**means.** The *k*-means algorithm for partitioning based on the mean value of the objects in the cluster.

**Input:**   The number of clusters *k* and a database containing *n* objects.

**Output:**   A set of *k* clusters that minimizes the squared-error criterion.

**Method:**

> (1)   arbitrarily choose *k* objects as the initial cluster centers;
> (2)   repeat
> (3)     (re)assign each object to the cluster to which the object is the most similar,
>         based on the mean value of the objects in the cluster;
> (4)     update the cluster means, i.e., calculate the mean value of the objects for each cluster;
> (5)   until no change;

**Figure 8.1**   The *k*-means algorithm.

## 8.4.1  Classical Partitioning Methods: *k*-Means and *k*-Medoids

The most well-known and commonly used partitioning methods are k-*means*, k-*medoids*, and their variations.

### Centroid-Based Technique: The *k*-Means Method

The *k*-**means algorithm** takes the input parameter, *k*, and partitions a set of *n* objects into *k* clusters so that the resulting intracluster similarity is high but the intercluster similarity is low. Cluster similarity is measured in regard to the *mean* value of the objects in a cluster, which can be viewed as the cluster's *center of gravity*.

"*How does the* k-*means algorithm work?*" The *k*-means algorithm proceeds as follows. First, it randomly selects *k* of the objects, each of which initially represents a cluster mean or center. For each of the remaining objects, an object is assigned to the cluster to which it is the most similar, based on the distance between the object and the cluster mean. It then computes the new mean for each cluster. This process iterates until the criterion function converges. Typically, the **squared-error criterion** is used, defined as

$$E = \Sigma_{i=1}^{k} \Sigma_{p \in C_i} |p - m_i|^2, \tag{8.18}$$

where *E* is the sum of square-error for all objects in the database, *p* is the point in space representing a given object, and $m_i$ is the mean of cluster $C_i$ (both *p* and $m_i$ are multidimensional). This criterion tries to make the resulting *k* clusters as compact and as separate as possible. The *k*-means procedure is summarized in Figure 8.1.

The algorithm attempts to determine $k$ partitions that minimize the squared-error function. It works well when the clusters are compact clouds that are rather well separated from one another. The method is relatively scalable and efficient in processing large data sets because the computational complexity of the algorithm is $O(nkt)$, where $n$ is the total number of objects, $k$ is the number of clusters, and $t$ is the number of iterations. Normally, $k \ll n$ and $t \ll n$. The method often terminates at a local optimum.

The $k$-means method, however, can be applied only when the mean of a cluster is defined. This may not be the case in some applications, such as when data with categorical attributes are involved. The necessity for users to specify $k$, the number of clusters, in advance can be seen as a disadvantage. The $k$-means method is not suitable for discovering clusters with nonconvex shapes or clusters of very different size. Moreover, it is sensitive to noise and outlier data points since a small number of such data can substantially influence the mean value.

**Example 8.2** Suppose that there is a set of objects located in space as depicted in the rectangle shown in Figure 8.2(a). Let $k = 3$; that is, the user would like to cluster the objects into three clusters.

According to the algorithm in Figure 8.1, we arbitrarily choose three objects as the three initial cluster centers, where cluster centers are marked by a "+". Each object is distributed to a cluster based on the cluster center to which it is the nearest. Such a distribution forms silhouettes encircled by dotted curves, as shown in Figure 8.2(a).

This kind of grouping will update the cluster centers. That is, the mean value of each cluster is recalculated based on the objects in the cluster. Relative to these new centers, objects are redistributed to the cluster domains based on which cluster center is the nearest. Such a redistribution forms new silhouettes encircled by dashed curves, as shown in Figure 8.2(b).

This process iterates, leading to Figure 8.2(c). Eventually, no redistribution of the objects in any cluster occurs and so the process terminates. The resulting clusters are returned by the clustering process. ■

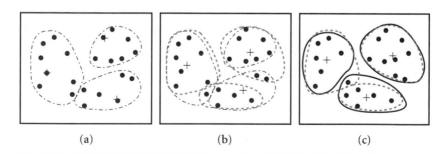

|     (a)     |     (b)     |     (c)     |

**Figure 8.2** Clustering of a set of objects based on the $k$-means method. (The mean of each cluster is marked by a "+".)

There are quite a few variants of the $k$-means method. These can differ in the selection of the initial $k$ means, the calculation of dissimilarity, and the strategies for calculating cluster means. An interesting strategy that often yields good results is to first apply a hierarchical agglomeration algorithm to determine the number of clusters and to find an initial clustering, and then use iterative relocation to improve the clustering.

Another variant to $k$-means is the **$k$-modes method,** which extends the $k$-means paradigm to cluster categorical data by replacing the means of clusters with modes, using new dissimilarity measures to deal with categorical objects, and using a frequency-based method to update modes of clusters. The $k$-means and the $k$-modes methods can be integrated to cluster data with mixed numeric and categorical values, resulting in the $k$-**prototypes** method.

The **EM (Expectation Maximization)** algorithm extends the $k$-means paradigm in a different way. Instead of assigning each object to a dedicated cluster, it assigns each object to a cluster according to a weight representing the probability of membership. In other words, there are no strict boundaries between clusters. Therefore, new means are computed based on weighted measures.

*"How can we make the k-means algorithm more scalable?"* A recent effort on scaling the $k$-means algorithm is based on the idea of identifying three kinds of regions in data: regions that are compressible, regions that must be maintained in main memory, and regions that are discardable. An object is *discardable* if its membership in a cluster is ascertained. An object is *compressible* if it is not discardable but belongs to a tight subcluster. A data structure known as a *clustering feature* is used to summarize objects that have been discarded or compressed. If an object is neither discardable nor compressible, then it should be *retained in main memory*. To achieve scalability, the iterative clustering algorithm only includes the clustering features of the compressible objects and the objects that must be retained in main memory, thereby turning a secondary-memory-based algorithm into a main-memory-based algorithm.

## Representative Object-Based Technique: The $k$-Medoids Method

The $k$-means algorithm is sensitive to outliers since an object with an extremely large value may substantially distort the distribution of data.

*"How might the algorithm be modified to diminish such sensitivity?"* you may wonder. Instead of taking the mean value of the objects in a cluster as a reference point, the **medoid** can be used, which is the most centrally located object in a cluster. Thus the partitioning method can still be performed based on the principle of minimizing the sum of the dissimilarities between each object and its corresponding reference point. This forms the basis of the $k$-**medoids method.**

The basic strategy of $k$-medoids clustering algorithms is to find $k$ clusters in $n$ objects by first arbitrarily finding a representative object (the medoid) for each cluster. Each remaining object is clustered with the medoid to which it is the most similar. The strategy then iteratively replaces one of the medoids by one of the non-medoids as long as the quality of the resulting clustering is improved. This quality

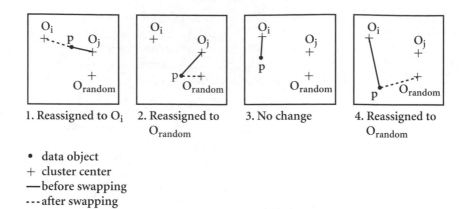

**Figure 8.3** Four cases of the cost function for *k*-medoids clustering.

is estimated using a cost function that measures the average dissimilarity between an object and the medoid of its cluster. To determine whether a nonmedoid object, $o_{random}$, is a good replacement for a current medoid, $o_j$, the following four cases are examined for each of the nonmedoid objects, $p$.

▪ **Case 1:** $p$ currently belongs to medoid $o_j$. If $o_j$ is replaced by $o_{random}$ as a medoid and $p$ is closest to one of $o_i$, $i \neq j$, then $p$ is reassigned to $o_i$.

▪ **Case 2:** $p$ currently belongs to medoid $o_j$. If $o_j$ is replaced by $o_{random}$ as a medoid and $p$ is closest to $o_{random}$, then $p$ is reassigned to $o_{random}$.

▪ **Case 3:** $p$ currently belongs to medoid $o_i$, $i \neq j$. If $o_j$ is replaced by $o_{random}$ as a medoid and $p$ is still closest to $o_i$, then the assignment does not change.

▪ **Case 4:** $p$ currently belongs to medoid $o_i$, $i \neq j$. If $o_j$ is replaced by $o_{random}$ as a medoid and $p$ is closest to $o_{random}$, then $p$ is reassigned to $o_{random}$.

Figure 8.3 illustrates the four cases. Each time a reassignment occurs, a difference in square-error $E$ is contributed to the cost function. Therefore, the cost function calculates the *difference* in square-error value if a current medoid is replaced by a nonmedoid object. The total cost of swapping is the sum of costs incurred by all nonmedoid objects. If the total cost is negative, then $o_j$ is replaced or swapped with $o_{random}$ since the actual square-error $E$ would be reduced. If the total cost is positive, the current medoid $o_j$ is considered acceptable, and nothing is changed in the iteration. A typical *k*-medoids algorithm is presented in Figure 8.4.

PAM (Partitioning around Medoids) was one of the first *k*-medoids algorithms introduced. It attempts to determine *k* partitions for *n* objects. After an initial

**Algorithm:**   $k$-**medoids.** A typical $k$-medoids algorithm for partitioning based on medoid or central objects.

**Input:**   The number of clusters $k$ and a database containing $n$ objects.

**Output:**   A set of $k$ clusters that minimizes the sum of the dissimilarities of all the objects to their nearest medoid.

**Method:**

> (1)    arbitrarily choose $k$ objects as the initial medoids;
> (2)    repeat
> (3)        assign each remaining object to the cluster with the nearest medoid;
> (4)        randomly select a nonmedoid object, $o_{random}$;
> (5)        compute the total cost, $S$, of swapping $o_j$ with $o_{random}$;
> (6)        **if** $S < 0$ **then** swap $o_j$ with $o_{random}$ to form the new set of $k$ medoids;
> (7)    until no change;

---

**Figure 8.4**  The $k$-medoids algorithm.

random selection of $k$ medoids, the algorithm repeatedly tries to make a better choice of medoids. All of the possible pairs of objects are analyzed, where one object in each pair is considered a medoid and the other is not. The quality of the resulting clustering is calculated for each such combination. An object, $o_j$, is replaced with the object causing the greatest reduction in square-error. The set of best objects for each cluster in one iteration forms the medoids for the next iteration. For large values of $n$ and $k$, such computation becomes very costly.

"*Which method is more robust—k-means or k-medoids?*" The $k$-medoids method is more robust than $k$-means in the presence of noise and outliers because a medoid is less influenced by outliers or other extreme values than a mean. However, its processing is more costly than the $k$-means method. Both methods require the user to specify $k$, the number of clusters.

## 8.4.2 Partitioning Methods in Large Databases: From *k*-Medoids to CLARANS

"*How efficient is the* k-*medoids algorithm on large data sets?*" A typical $k$-medoids partitioning algorithm like PAM works effectively for small data sets, but does not scale well for large data sets. To deal with larger data sets, a *sampling*-based method, called **CLARA** (Clustering LARge Applications) can be used.

The idea behind CLARA is as follows: Instead of taking the whole set of data into consideration, a small portion of the actual data is chosen as a representative of the data. Medoids are then chosen from this sample using PAM. If the sample is selected in a fairly random manner, it should closely represent the original data set. The representative objects (medoids) chosen will likely be similar to those that would have been chosen from the whole data set. CLARA draws multiple samples of the data set, applies PAM on each sample, and returns its best clustering as the output. As expected, CLARA can deal with larger data sets than PAM. The complexity of each iteration now becomes $O(ks^2 + k(n - k))$, where $s$ is the size of the sample, $k$ is the number of clusters, and $n$ is the total number of objects.

The effectiveness of CLARA depends on the sample size. Notice that PAM searches for the best $k$ medoids among a given data set, whereas CLARA searches for the best $k$ medoids among the *selected* sample of the data set. CLARA cannot find the best clustering if any sampled medoid is not among the best $k$ medoids. For example, if an object $o_i$ is one of the medoids in the best $k$ medoids but it is not selected during sampling, CLARA will never find the best clustering. This is, therefore, a trade-off for efficiency. A good clustering based on samples will not necessarily represent a good clustering of the whole data set if the sample is biased.

*"How might we improve the quality and scalability of CLARA?"* A $k$-medoids type algorithm called **CLARANS** (Clustering Large Applications based upon RANdomized Search) was proposed that combines the sampling technique with PAM. However, unlike CLARA, CLARANS does not confine itself to any sample at any given time. While CLARA has a fixed sample at each stage of the search, CLARANS draws a sample with some randomness in each step of the search. The clustering process can be presented as searching a graph where every node is a potential solution, that is, a set of $k$ medoids. The clustering obtained after replacing a single medoid is called the *neighbor* of the current clustering. The number of neighbors to be randomly tried is restricted by a user-specified parameter. If a better neighbor is found (i.e., having a lower square-error), CLARANS moves to the neighbor's node and the process starts again; otherwise the current clustering produces a local optimum. If the local optimum is found, CLARANS starts with new randomly selected nodes in search for a new local optimum.

CLARANS has been experimentally shown to be more effective than both PAM and CLARA. It can be used to find the most "natural" number of clusters using a *silhouette coefficient*—a property of an object that specifies how much the object truly belongs to the cluster. CLARANS also enables the detection of outliers. However, the computational complexity of CLARANS is about $O(n^2)$, where $n$ is the number of objects. Furthermore, its clustering quality is dependent on the sampling method used. The performance of CLARANS can be further improved by exploring spatial data structures, such as R*-trees, and some focusing techniques.

## 8.5  Hierarchical Methods

A hierarchical clustering method works by grouping data objects into a tree of clusters. Hierarchical clustering methods can be further classified into *agglomerative* and *divisive* hierarchical clustering, depending on whether the hierarchical decomposition is formed in a bottom-up or top-down fashion. The quality of

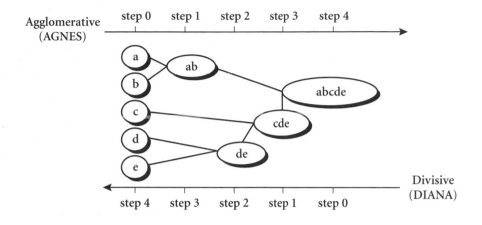

**Figure 8.5** Agglomerative and divisive hierarchical clustering on data objects $\{a, b, c, d, e\}$.

a pure hierarchical clustering method suffers from its inability to perform adjustment once a merge or split decision has been executed. Recent studies have emphasized the integration of hierarchical agglomeration with iterative relocation methods.

## 8.5.1 Agglomerative and Divisive Hierarchical Clustering

In general, there are two types of hierarchical clustering methods:

- **Agglomerative hierarchical clustering:** This bottom-up strategy starts by placing each object in its own cluster and then merges these atomic clusters into larger and larger clusters, until all of the objects are in a single cluster or until certain termination conditions are satisfied. Most hierarchical clustering methods belong to this category. They differ only in their definition of intercluster similarity.

- **Divisive hierarchical clustering:** This top-down strategy does the reverse of agglomerative hierarchical clustering by starting with all objects in one cluster. It subdivides the cluster into smaller and smaller pieces, until each object forms a cluster on its own or until it satisfies certain termination conditions, such as a desired number of clusters is obtained or the distance between the two closest clusters is above a certain threshold distance.

**Example 8.3** Figure 8.5 shows the application of **AGNES** (AGglomerative NESting), an agglomerative hierarchical clustering method, and **DIANA** (DIvisive ANAlysis), a divisive hierarchical clustering method, to a data set of five objects, $\{a, b, c, d, e\}$. Initially, AGNES places each object into a cluster of its own. The clusters are then merged step-by-step according to some criterion. For example, clusters $C_1$ and $C_2$ may be merged if an object in $C_1$ and an object in $C_2$ form the minimum Euclidean distance between any two objects from different clusters. This is a **single-link** approach in that each cluster is represented by all of the objects in the cluster, and the similarity between two clusters is measured by the similarity of the *closest* pair of data points belonging to different clusters. The cluster merging process repeats until all of the objects are eventually merged to form one cluster.

In DIANA, all of the objects are used to form one initial cluster. The cluster is split according to some principle, such as the maximum Euclidean distance between the closest neighboring objects in the cluster. The cluster splitting process repeats until, eventually, each new cluster contains only a single object. ∎

In either agglomerative or divisive hierarchical clustering, the user can specify the desired number of clusters as a termination condition.

Four widely used measures for distance between clusters are as follows, where $|p - p'|$ is the distance between two objects or points $p$ and $p'$, $m_i$ is the mean for cluster $C_i$, and $n_i$ is the number of objects in $C_i$.

- **Minimum distance:** $d_{min}(C_i, C_j) = min_{p \in C_i, p' \in C_j} |p - p'|$
- **Maximum distance:** $d_{max}(C_i, C_j) = max_{p \in C_i, p' \in C_j} |p - p'|$
- **Mean distance:** $d_{mean}(C_i, C_j) = |m_i - m_j|$
- **Average distance:** $d_{avg}(C_i, C_j) = \frac{1}{n_i n_j} \Sigma_{p \in C_i} \Sigma_{p' \in C_j} |p - p'|$

*"What are some of the difficulties with hierarchical clustering?"* The hierarchical clustering method, though simple, often encounters difficulties regarding the selection of merge or split points. Such a decision is critical because once a group of objects is merged or split, the process at the next step will operate on the newly generated clusters. It will neither undo what was done previously, nor perform object swapping between clusters. Thus merge or split decisions, if not well chosen at some step, may lead to low-quality clusters. Moreover, the method does not scale well since the decision of merge or split needs to examine and evaluate a good number of objects or clusters.

One promising direction for improving the clustering quality of hierarchical methods is to integrate hierarchical clustering with other clustering techniques for multiple phase clustering. A few such methods are introduced in the following subsections. The first, called BIRCH, begins by partitioning objects hierarchically using tree structures, and then applies other clustering algorithms to refine the clusters. The second, called CURE, represents each cluster by a certain fixed number of representative objects and then shrinks them toward the center of the cluster by a specified fraction. The third, called ROCK, merges clusters based on their interconnectivity. The fourth, called Chameleon, explores dynamic modeling in hierarchical clustering.

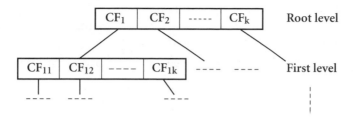

**Figure 8.6**  A CF tree structure.

## 8.5.2 **BIRCH: Balanced Iterative Reducing and Clustering Using Hierarchies**

BIRCH is an integrated hierarchical clustering method. It introduces two concepts, **clustering feature** and **clustering feature tree** (**CF tree**), which are used to summarize cluster representations. These structures help the clustering method achieve good speed and scalability in large databases. BIRCH is also effective for incremental and dynamic clustering of incoming objects. Let's have a closer look at the above-mentioned structures. A **clustering feature** (**CF**) is a triplet summarizing information about subclusters of objects. Given $N$ $d$-dimensional points or objects $\{o_i\}$ in a subcluster, then the CF of the subcluster is defined as

$$CF = (N, \vec{LS}, SS), \tag{8.19}$$

where $N$ is the number of points in the subcluster, $\vec{LS}$ is the linear sum on N points (i.e., $\sum_{i=1}^{N} \vec{o}_i$), and $SS$ is the square sum of data points (i.e., $\sum_{i=1}^{N} \vec{o}_i^2$).

A clustering feature is essentially a summary of the statistics for the given subcluster: the zeroth, first, and second moments of the subcluster from a statistical point of view. It registers crucial measurements for computing clusters and utilizes storage efficiently since it summarizes the information about the subclusters of objects instead of storing all objects.

A **CF tree** is a height-balanced tree that stores the clustering features for a hierarchical clustering. An example is shown in Figure 8.6. By definition, a nonleaf node in a tree has descendents or "children." The nonleaf nodes store sums of the CFs of their children, and thus summarize clustering information about their children. A CF tree has two parameters: *branching factor*, $B$, and *threshold*, $T$. The branching factor specifies the maximum number of children per nonleaf node. The threshold parameter specifies the maximum diameter of subclusters stored at the leaf nodes of the tree. These two parameters influence the size of the resulting tree.

*"How does the BIRCH algorithm work?"* It consists of two phases:

■ **Phase 1:** BIRCH scans the database to build an initial in-memory CF tree, which can be viewed as a multilevel compression of the data that tries to preserve the inherent clustering structure of the data.

■ **Phase 2:** BIRCH applies a (selected) clustering algorithm to cluster the leaf nodes of the CF tree.

For Phase 1, the CF tree is built dynamically as objects are inserted. Thus, the method is incremental. An object is inserted to the closest leaf entry (subcluster). If the diameter of the subcluster stored in the leaf node after insertion is larger than the threshold value, then the leaf node and possibly other nodes are split. After the insertion of the new object, information about it is passed toward the root of the tree. The size of the CF tree can be changed by modifying the threshold. If the size of the memory that is needed for storing the CF tree is larger than the size of the main memory, then a smaller threshold value can be specified and the CF tree is rebuilt. The rebuild process is performed by building a new tree from the leaf nodes of the old tree. Thus, the process of rebuilding the tree is done without the necessity of rereading all of the objects or points. This is similar to the insertion and node split in the construction of B+-trees. Therefore, for building the tree, data has to be read just once. Some heuristics and methods have been introduced to deal with outliers and improve the quality of CF trees by additional scans of the data. After the CF tree is built, any clustering algorithm, such as a typical partitioning algorithm, can be used with the CF tree in Phase 2.

BIRCH tries to produce the best clusters with the available resources. Given a limited amount of main memory, an important consideration is to minimize the time required for I/O. BIRCH applies a multiphase clustering technique: a single scan of the data set yields a basic good clustering, and one or more additional scans can (optionally) be used to further improve the quality. The computation complexity of the algorithm is $O(n)$, where $n$ is the number of objects to be clustered.

"*How effective is BIRCH?*" Experiments have shown the linear scalability of the algorithm with respect to the number of objects, and good quality of clustering of the data. However, since each node in a CF tree can hold only a limited number of entries due to its size, a CF tree node does not always correspond to what a user may consider a natural cluster. Moreover, if the clusters are not spherical in shape, BIRCH does not perform well because it uses the notion of radius or diameter to control the boundary of a cluster.

## 8.5.3  CURE: Clustering Using REpresentatives

Most clustering algorithms either favor clusters with spherical shape and similar sizes, or are fragile in the presence of outliers. CURE overcomes the problem of favoring clusters with spherical shape and similar sizes and is more robust with respect to outliers.

CURE employs a novel hierarchical clustering algorithm that adopts a middle ground between centroid-based and representative-object-based approaches. Instead of using a single centroid or object to represent a cluster, a fixed number of representative points in space are chosen. The representative points of a cluster are generated by first selecting well-scattered objects for the cluster and then "shrinking" or moving them toward the cluster center by a specified fraction, or *shrinking factor*. At each step of the algorithm, the two clusters with the closest pair of representative points (where each point in the pair is from a different cluster) are merged.

Having more than one representative point per cluster allows CURE to adjust well to the geometry of nonspherical shapes. The shrinking or condensing of clusters helps dampen the effects of outliers. Therefore, CURE is more robust to outliers and identifies clusters having nonspherical shapes and wide variance in size. It scales well for large databases without sacrificing clustering quality.

To handle large databases, CURE employs a combination of random sampling and partitioning: a random sample is first partitioned, and each partition is partially clustered. The partial clusters are then clustered in a second pass to yield the desired clusters.

The following steps outline the spirit of the CURE algorithm.

1. Draw a random sample, $S$, of the original objects.

2. Partition sample $S$ into a set of partitions.

3. Partially cluster each partition.

4. Eliminate outliers by random sampling. If a cluster grows too slowly, remove it.

5. Cluster the partial clusters. The representative points falling in each newly formed cluster are "shrinked" or moved toward the cluster center by a user-specified fraction, or shrinking factor, $\alpha$. These points then represent and capture the shape of the cluster.

6. Mark the data with the corresponding cluster labels.

Let's look at an example.

**Example 8.4** Imagine that there are a set of points (or objects) located in a rectangular region. A random sample of the objects is shown in Figure 8.7(a). These objects are distributed into two partitions, which are partially clustered based on minimal mean distance. The partial clusters are indicated by dashed curves, as shown in Figure 8.7(b). Each cluster representative is marked by a "+". The partial clusters are further clustered, resulting in the two clusters illustrated by solid curves in Figure 8.7(c). Each new cluster is "shrinked" or condensed by moving its representative points toward the cluster center by a fraction, $\alpha$. The representative

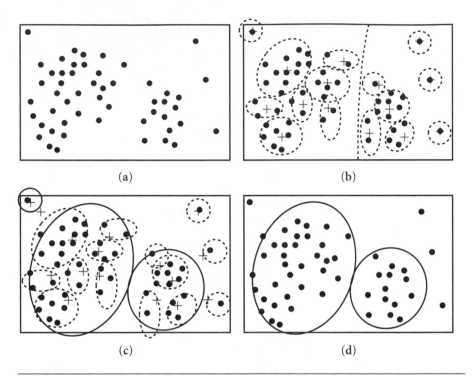

**Figure 8.7**    Clustering of a set of points (or objects) by CURE.  (a) A random sample of objects. (b) The objects are partitioned and partially clustered. Representative points for each cluster are marked by a "+". (c) The partial clusters are further clustered. For each new cluster, the representative points are "shrinked" or moved toward the cluster center. (d) The final clusters are of nonspherical shape.

points capture the shape of each cluster. Thus, the initial objects are partitioned into two clusters, with the outliers excluded, as shown in Figure 8.7(d).    ■

CURE produces high-quality clusters in the existence of outliers, allowing clusters of complex shapes and different sizes. The algorithm requires one scan of the entire database. Given $n$ objects, the complexity of CURE is of $O(n)$. "*How sensitive is CURE to its user-specified parameters, such as the sample size, number of desired clusters, and shrinking fraction, $\alpha$?*" A sensitivity analysis showed that although some parameters can be varied without impacting the quality of clustering, the parameter setting in general does have a significant influence on the results.

CURE does not handle categorical attributes. ROCK is an alternative agglomerative hierarchical clustering algorithm that is suited for clustering categorical attributes. It measures the similarity of two clusters by comparing the *aggregate interconnectivity* of two clusters against a user-specified static *interconnectivity model*, where the **interconnectivity** of two clusters $C_1$ and $C_2$ is defined by the number of *cross links* between the two clusters, and $link(p_i, p_j)$ is the number of common neighbors between two points $p_i$ and $p_j$. In other words, cluster similarity is based on the number of points from different clusters who have neighbors in common.

ROCK first constructs a sparse graph from a given data similarity matrix using a similarity threshold and the concept of shared neighbors. It then performs a hierarchical clustering algorithm on the sparse graph.

### 8.5.4 Chameleon: A Hierarchical Clustering Algorithm Using Dynamic Modeling

**Chameleon** is a clustering algorithm that explores dynamic modeling in hierarchical clustering. In its clustering process, two clusters are merged if the interconnectivity and closeness (proximity) between two clusters are highly related to the internal interconnectivity and closeness of objects within the clusters. The merge process based on the dynamic model facilitates the discovery of natural and homogeneous clusters and applies to all types of data as long as a similarity function is specified.

Chameleon is derived based on the observation of the weakness of two hierarchical clustering algorithms: CURE and ROCK. CURE and related schemes ignore information about the aggregate interconnectivity of objects in two different clusters, whereas ROCK and related schemes ignore information about the closeness of two clusters while emphasizing their interconnectivity.

*"How does Chameleon work?"* The main approach of Chameleon is illustrated in Figure 8.8. Chameleon first uses a graph partitioning algorithm to cluster the data objects into a large number of relatively small subclusters. It then uses an agglomerative hierarchical clustering algorithm to find the genuine clusters by

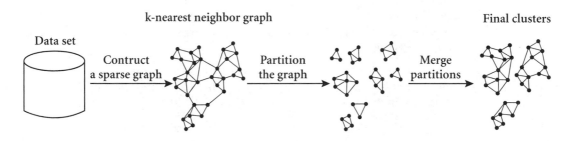

**Figure 8.8** Chameleon: Hierarchical clustering based on *k*-nearest neighbors and dynamic modeling. Based on [KHK99].

repeatedly combining or merging the subclusters. To determine the pairs of most similar subclusters, it takes into account both the interconnectivity as well as the closeness of the clusters, especially the internal characteristics of the clusters themselves. Thus it does not depend on a static, user-supplied model and can automatically adapt to the internal characteristics of the clusters being merged.

Let's look at Chameleon in closer detail. As shown in Figure 8.8, Chameleon represents its objects based on the commonly used *k-nearest neighbor graph approach*. Each vertex of the *k*-nearest neighbor graph represents a data object, and there exists an edge between two vertices (objects) if one object is among the *k*-most similar objects of the other. The *k*-nearest neighbor graph $G_k$ captures the concept of neighborhood dynamically: the neighborhood radius of an object is determined by the *density* of the region in which this object resides. In a dense region, the neighborhood is defined narrowly; in a sparse region, it is defined more widely. This tends to result in more natural clusters, in comparison with density-based methods such as DBSCAN (described in Section 8.6) that instead use a global neighborhood. Moreover, the density of the region is recorded as the weight of the edges. That is, the edge of a dense region tends to weigh more than that of a sparse region.

Chameleon determines the similarity between each pair of clusters $C_i$ and $C_j$ according to their *relative interconnectivity* $RI(C_i, C_j)$ and their *relative closeness* $RC(C_i, C_j)$:

- The **relative interconnectivity** $RI(C_i, C_j)$ between two clusters $C_i$ and $C_j$ is defined as the absolute interconnectivity between $C_i$ and $C_j$, normalized with respect to the internal interconnectivity of the two clusters $C_i$ and $C_j$. That is,

$$RI(C_i, C_j) = \frac{|EC_{\{C_i, C_j\}}|}{\frac{1}{2}(|EC_{C_i}| + |EC_{C_j}|)}, \tag{8.20}$$

  where $EC_{\{C_i, C_j\}}$ is the *edge-cut* of the cluster containing both $C_i$ and $C_j$ so that the cluster is broken into $C_i$ and $C_j$, and similarly, $EC_{C_i}$ (or $EC_{C_j}$) is the *size of its min-cut bisector* (i.e., the weighted sum of edges that partition the graph into two roughly equal parts).

- The **relative closeness** $RC(C_i, C_j)$ between a pair of clusters $C_i$ and $C_j$ is the absolute closeness between $C_i$ and $C_j$, normalized with respect to the internal closeness of the two clusters $C_i$ and $C_j$. It is defined as

$$RC(C_i, C_j) = \frac{\overline{S}_{EC_{\{C_i, C_j\}}}}{\frac{|C_i|}{|C_i| + |C_j|}\overline{S}_{EC_{C_i}} + \frac{|C_j|}{|C_i| + |C_j|}\overline{S}_{EC_{C_j}}}, \tag{8.21}$$

where $\overline{S}_{EC_{\{C_i,C_j\}}}$ is the average weight of the edges that connect vertices in $C_i$ to vertices in $C_j$, and $\overline{S}_{EC_{C_i}}$ (or $\overline{S}_{EC_{C_j}}$) is the average weight of the edges that belong to the min-cut bisector of cluster $C_i$ (or $C_j$).

It has been shown that Chameleon has more power at discovering arbitrarily shaped clusters of high quality than CURE and DBSCAN. However, the processing cost for high dimensional data may require $O(n^2)$ time for $n$ objects in the worst case.

## 8.6 Density-Based Methods

To discover clusters with arbitrary shape, density-based clustering methods have been developed. These typically regard clusters as dense regions of objects in the data space that are separated by regions of low density (representing noise).

### 8.6.1 DBSCAN: A Density-Based Clustering Method Based on Connected Regions with Sufficiently High Density

**DBSCAN** (Density-Based Spatial Clustering of Applications with Noise) is a density-based clustering algorithm. The algorithm grows regions with sufficiently high density into clusters and discovers clusters of arbitrary shape in spatial databases with noise. It defines a cluster as a maximal set of *density-connected* points.

The basic ideas of density-based clustering involve a number of new definitions. We intuitively present these definitions, and then follow up with an example.

- The neighborhood within a radius $\epsilon$ of a given object is called the $\epsilon$-**neighborhood** of the object.

- If the $\epsilon$-neighborhood of an object contains at least a minimum number, *MinPts*, of objects, then the object is called a **core object**.

- Given a set of objects, $D$, we say that an object $p$ is **directly density-reachable** from object $q$ if $p$ is within the $\epsilon$-neighborhood of $q$, and $q$ is a core object.

- An object $p$ is **density-reachable** from object $q$ with respect to $\epsilon$ and *MinPts* in a set of objects, $D$, if there is a chain of objects $p_1, \ldots, p_n$, $p_1 = q$ and $p_n = p$ such that $p_{i+1}$ is directly density-reachable from $p_i$ with respect to $\epsilon$ and *MinPts*, for $1 \leq i \leq n$, $p_i \in D$.

- An object $p$ is **density-connected** to object $q$ with respect to $\epsilon$ and *MinPts* in a set of objects, $D$, if there is an object $o \in D$ such that both $p$ and $q$ are density-reachable from $o$ with respect to $\epsilon$ and *MinPts*.

Density reachability is the transitive closure of direct density reachability, and this relationship is asymmetric. Only core objects are mutually density reachable. Density connectivity, however, is a symmetric relation.

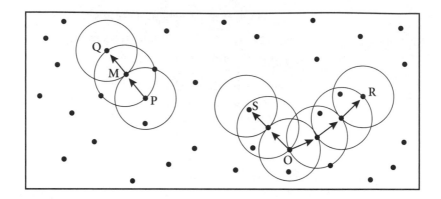

**Figure 8.9** Density reachability and density connectivity in density-based clustering.    Based on [EKSX96].

**Example 8.5**    Consider Figure 8.9 for a given $\epsilon$ represented by the radius of the circles, and, say, let *MinPts* = 3. Based on the above definitions:

- Of the labeled points, $M$, $P$, $O$, and $R$ are core objects since each is in an $\epsilon$-neighborhood containing at least three points.

- $Q$ is directly density-reachable from $M$. $M$ is directly density-reachable from $P$ and vice versa.

- $Q$ is (indirectly) density-reachable from $P$ since $Q$ is directly density-reachable from $M$ and $M$ is directly density-reachable from $P$. However, $P$ is not density-reachable from $Q$ since $Q$ is not a core object. Similarly, $R$ and $S$ are density-reachable from $O$ and $O$ is density-reachable from $R$.

- $O$, $R$, and $S$ are all density-connected. ∎

A **density-based cluster** is a set of density-connected objects that is maximal with respect to density-reachability. Every object not contained in any cluster is considered to be *noise*.

"*How does DBSCAN find clusters?*" DBSCAN searches for clusters by checking the $\epsilon$-neighborhood of each point in the database. If the $\epsilon$-neighborhood of a point $p$ contains more than *MinPts*, a new cluster with $p$ as a core object is created. DBSCAN then iteratively collects directly density-reachable objects from these core objects, which may involve the merge of a few density-reachable clusters. The process terminates when no new point can be added to any cluster.

If a spatial index is used, the computational complexity of DBSCAN is $O(n \log n)$, where $n$ is the number of database objects. Otherwise, it is $O(n^2)$. The algorithm is sensitive to the user-defined parameters. DBSCAN is further discussed in the following section, where it is compared to an alternative density-based clustering method called OPTICS.

## 8.6.2 **OPTICS: Ordering Points To Identify the Clustering Structure**

Although DBSCAN (the density-based clustering algorithm described in Section 8.6.1) can cluster objects given input parameters such as $\epsilon$ and *MinPts*, it still leaves the user with the responsibility of selecting parameter values that will lead to the discovery of acceptable clusters. Actually, this is a problem associated with many other clustering algorithms. Such parameter settings are usually empirically set and difficult to determine, especially for real-world, high-dimensional data sets. Most algorithms are very sensitive to such parameter values: slightly different settings may lead to very different clusterings of the data. Moreover, high-dimensional real data sets often have very skewed distributions such that their intrinsic clustering structure may not be characterized by *global* density parameters.

To help overcome this difficulty, a cluster analysis method called **OPTICS** was proposed. Rather than produce a data set clustering explicitly, OPTICS computes an augmented *cluster ordering* for automatic and interactive cluster analysis. This ordering represents the density-based clustering structure of the data. It contains information that is equivalent to density-based clustering obtained from a wide range of parameter settings.

By examining DBSCAN, we can easily see that for a constant *MinPts* value, density-based clusters with respect to a higher density (i.e., a lower value for $\epsilon$) are *completely contained* in density-connected sets obtained with respect to a lower density. Recall that the parameter $\epsilon$ is a distance—it is the neighborhood radius. Therefore, in order to produce a set or ordering of density-based clusters, we can extend the DBSCAN algorithm to process a set of distance parameter values at the same time. To construct the different clusterings simultaneously, the objects should be processed in a specific order. This order selects an object that is density-reachable with respect to the lowest $\epsilon$ value so that clusters with higher density (lower $\epsilon$) will be finished first. Based on this idea, two values need to be stored for each object—*core-distance* and *reachability-distance*:

- The **core-distance** of an object $p$ is the smallest $\epsilon'$ value that makes $p$ a core object. If $p$ is not a core object, the core-distance of $p$ is undefined.

- The **reachability-distance** of an object $q$ with respect to another object $p$ is the greater value of the core-distance of $p$ and the Euclidean distance between $p$ and $q$. If $p$ is not a core object, the reachability-distance between $p$ and $q$ is undefined.

**Example 8.6** Figure 8.10 illustrates the concepts of core-distance and reachability-distance. Suppose that $\epsilon = 6$ mm and *MinPts* = 5. The core-distance of $p$ is the distance, $\epsilon'$,

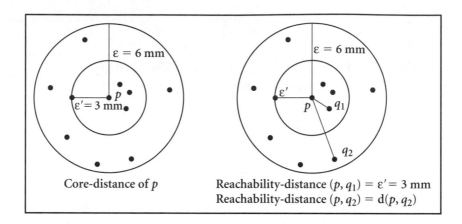

**Figure 8.10** OPTICS terminology. Based on [ABKS99].

between $p$ and the fourth closest data object. The reachability-distance of $q_1$ with respect to $p$ is the core-distance of $p$ (i.e., $\epsilon' = 3$ mm) since this is greater than the Euclidean distance from $p$ to $q_1$. The reachability-distance of $q_2$ with respect to $p$ is the Euclidean distance from $p$ to $q_2$ since this is greater than the core-distance of $p$. ∎

*"How are these values used?"* The OPTICS algorithm creates an ordering of the objects in a database, additionally storing the core-distance and a suitable reachability-distance for each object. An algorithm was proposed to extract clusters based on the ordering information produced by OPTICS. Such information is sufficient for the extraction of all density-based clusterings with respect to any distance $\epsilon'$ that is smaller than the distance $\epsilon$ used in generating the order.

The cluster ordering of a data set can be represented graphically, which helps in its understanding. For example, Figure 8.11 is the reachability plot for a simple two-dimensional data set, which presents a general overview of how the data are structured and clustered. Methods have also been developed for viewing clustering structures of high-dimensional data at various levels of detail.

Because of the structural equivalence of the OPTICS algorithm to DBSCAN, the OPTICS algorithm has the same run-time complexity as that of DBSCAN, that is, $O(n \log n)$ if a spatial index is used.

### 8.6.3 DENCLUE: Clustering Based on Density Distribution Functions

DENCLUE (DENsity-based CLUstEring) is a clustering method based on a set of density distribution functions. The method is built on the following ideas: (1) the influence of each data point can be formally modeled using a mathematical function, called an *influence function*, that describes the impact of a data point

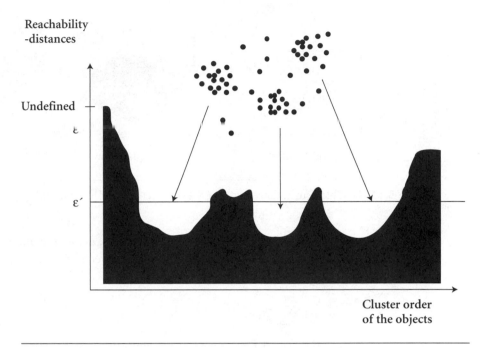

**Figure 8.11**  Cluster ordering in OPTICS.  Figure is based on [ABKS99].

within its neighborhood; (2) the overall density of the data space can be modeled analytically as the sum of the influence functions of all data points; and (3) clusters can then be determined mathematically by identifying *density attractors*, where density attractors are local maxima of the overall density function.

Let $x$ and $y$ be objects in $F^d$, a $d$-dimensional feature space. The **influence function** of data object $y$ on $x$ is a function $f_B^y : F^d \to R_0^+$, which is defined in terms of a basic influence function $f_B$:

$$f_B^y(x) = f_B(x, y). \tag{8.22}$$

In principle, the influence function can be an arbitrary function that can be determined by the distance between two objects in a neighborhood. The distance function $d(x, y)$ should be reflexive and symmetric, such as the Euclidean distance function (Section 8.2.1). It is used to compute a *square wave influence function*,

$$f_{Square}(x, y) = \begin{cases} 0 & \text{if } d(x, y) > \sigma \\ 1 & \text{otherwise} \end{cases} \tag{8.23}$$

or a *Gaussian influence function*,

$$f_{Gauss}(x, y) = e^{-\frac{d(x,y)^2}{2\sigma^2}}. \tag{8.24}$$

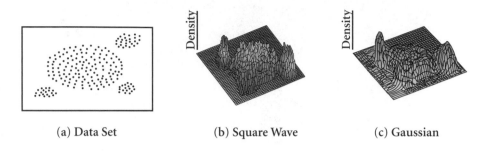

(a) Data Set        (b) Square Wave        (c) Gaussian

**Figure 8.12** Possible density functions for a 2-D data set. From [HK98].

The **density function** at an object $x \in F^d$ is defined as the sum of influence functions of all data points. Given $n$ data objects, $D = \{x_1, \ldots, x_n\} \subset F^d$, the density function at $x$ is defined as

$$f_B^D(x) = \sum_{i=1}^{n} f_B^{x_i}(x). \tag{8.25}$$

For example, the density function that results from the Gaussian influence function (8.24) is

$$f_{Gauss}^D(x) = \sum_{i=1}^{n} e^{-\frac{d(x,x_i)^2}{2\sigma^2}}. \tag{8.26}$$

From the density function, we can define the *gradient* of the function and the *density attractor*, the local maxima of the overall density function. For a continuous and differentiable influence function, a hill-climbing algorithm guided by the gradient can be used to determine the density attractor of a set of data points. Figure 8.12 shows a Gaussian density function and a density attractor for a 2-D data set.

From the density function, we can define the *gradient* of the function and the *density attractor,* the local maxima of the overall density function. A point $x$ is said to be *density attracted* to a density attractor $x^*$ if there exists a set of points $x_0, x_1, \ldots, x_k$ such that $x_0 = x$, $s_k = x^*$ and the gradient of $x_{i-1}$ is in the direction of $x_i$ for $0 < i < k$. For a continuous and differentiable influence function, a hill-climbing algorithm guided by the gradient can be used to determine the density attractor of a set of data points. Figure 8.12 shows a 2-D data set, Gaussian density functions for the data set, and the density attractor.

Based on these notions, both *center-defined cluster* and *arbitrary-shape cluster* can be formally defined. A **center-defined cluster** for a density extractor $x^*$ is a

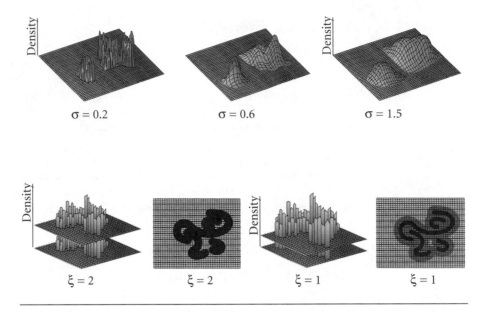

**Figure 8.13** Examples of center-defined clusters (top row) and arbitrary-shape clusters (bottom row). From [HK98].

subset $C$ that is *density-extracted* by $x^*$, and the density function at $x^*$ is no less than a threshold $\xi$; otherwise (i.e., if its density function value is less than $\xi$), it is considered an outlier. An **arbitrary-shape cluster** is a set of $C$s, each being density-extracted, with the density function value no less than a threshold $\xi$, and where there exists a path $P$ from each region to another, and the density function value for each point along the path is no less than $\xi$. Examples of center-defined and arbitrary-shape clusters are shown in Figure 8.13.

"*What major advantages does DENCLUE have in comparison with other clustering algorithms, in general?*" There are several: (1) it has a solid mathematical foundation and generalizes other clustering methods, including partition-based, hierarchical, and locality-based methods, (2) it has good clustering properties for data sets with large amounts of noise, (3) it allows a compact mathematical description of arbitrarily shaped clusters in high-dimensional data sets, and (4) it uses grid cells yet only keeps information about grid cells that do actually contain data points. It manages these cells in a tree-based access structure, and thus is significantly faster than some influential algorithms, such as DBSCAN (by a factor of up to 45). However, the method requires careful selection of the density parameter $\sigma$ and noise threshold $\xi$, as the selection of such parameters may significantly influence the quality of the clustering results.

# 8.7 Grid-Based Methods

The grid-based clustering approach uses a multiresolution grid data structure. It quantizes the space into a finite number of cells that form a grid structure on which all of the operations for clustering are performed. The main advantage of the approach is its fast processing time, which is typically independent of the number of data objects, yet dependent on only the number of cells in each dimension in the quantized space.

Some typical examples of the grid-based approach include STING, which explores statistical information stored in the grid cells; WaveCluster, which clusters objects using a wavelet transform method; and CLIQUE, which represents a grid- and density-based approach for clustering in high-dimensional data space.

## 8.7.1 STING: STatistical INformation Grid

STING is a grid-based multiresolution clustering technique in which the spatial area is divided into rectangular cells. There are usually several levels of such rectangular cells corresponding to different levels of resolution, and these cells form a hierarchical structure: each cell at a high level is partitioned to form a number of cells at the next lower level. Statistical information regarding the attributes in each grid cell (such as the mean, maximum, and minimum values) are precomputed and stored. These statistical parameters are useful for query processing, as described below.

Figure 8.14 shows a hierarchical structure for STING clustering. Statistical parameters of higher-level cells can easily be computed from the parameters of the lower-level cells. These parameters include the following: the attribute-independent parameter, *count*; and the attribute-dependent parameters, *m* (mean), *s* (standard deviation), *min* (minimum), *max* (maximum), and the type of *distribution* that the attribute value in the cell follows, such as *normal, uniform, exponential*, or *none* (if the distribution is unknown). When the data are loaded into the database, the parameters *count, m, s, min*, and *max* of the bottom-level cells are calculated directly from the data. The value of *distribution* may either be assigned by the user if the distribution type is known beforehand or obtained by hypothesis tests such as the $\chi^2$ test. The type of distribution of a higher-level cell can be computed based on the majority of distribution types of its corresponding lower-level cells in conjunction with a threshold filtering process. If the distributions of the lower-level cells disagree with each other and fail the threshold test, the distribution type of the high-level cell is set to *none*.

*"How is this statistical information useful for query-answering?"* The statistical parameters can be used in a top-down, grid-based method as follows. First, a layer within the hierarchical structure is determined from which the query-answering process is to start. This layer typically contains a small number of cells. For each

cell in the current layer, we compute the confidence interval (or estimated range of probability) reflecting the cell's relevancy to the given query. The irrelevant cells are removed from further consideration. Processing of the next lower level examines only the remaining relevant cells. This process is repeated until the bottom layer is reached. At this time, if the query specification is met, the regions of relevant cells that satisfy the query are returned. Otherwise, the data that fall into the relevant cells are retrieved and further processed until they meet the requirements of the query.

*"What advantages does STING offer over other clustering methods?"* STING offers several advantages: (1) the grid-based computation is *query-independent* since the statistical information stored in each cell represents the summary information of the data in the grid cell, independent of the query; (2) the grid structure facilitates parallel processing and incremental updating; and (3) the method's efficiency is a major advantage: STING goes through the database once to compute the statistical parameters of the cells, and hence the time complexity of generating clusters is $O(n)$, where $n$ is the total number of objects. After generating the hierarchical structure, the query processing time is $O(g)$, where $g$ is the total number of grid cells at the lowest level, which is usually much smaller than $n$.

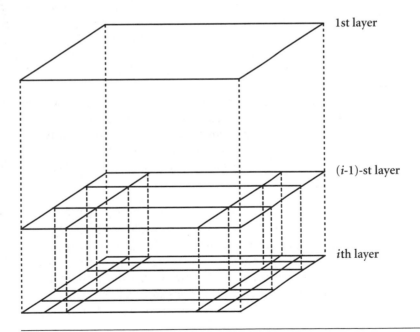

**Figure 8.14** A hierarchical structure for STING clustering.

Since STING uses a multiresolution approach to perform cluster analysis, the quality of STING clustering depends on the granularity of the lowest level of the grid structure. If the granularity is very fine, the cost of processing will increase substantially; however, if the bottom level of the grid structure is too coarse, it may reduce the quality of cluster analysis. Moreover, STING does not consider the spatial relationship between the children and their neighboring cells for construction of a parent cell. As a result, the shapes of the resulting clusters are isothetic, that is, all of the cluster boundaries are either horizontal or vertical, and no diagonal boundary is detected. This may lower the quality and accuracy of the clusters despite the fast processing time of the technique.

## 8.7.2 WaveCluster: Clustering Using Wavelet Transformation

**WaveCluster** is a multiresolution clustering algorithm that first summarizes the data by imposing a multidimensional grid structure onto the data space. It then uses a *wavelet transformation* to transform the original feature space, finding dense regions in the transformed space.

In this approach, each grid cell summarizes the information of a group of points that map into the cell. This summary information typically fits into main memory for use by the multiresolution wavelet transform and the subsequent cluster analysis.

*"But what is a wavelet transform?"* A **wavelet transform** is a signal processing technique that decomposes a signal into different frequency subbands. The wavelet model can be applied to $n$-dimensional signals by applying a one-dimensional wavelet transform $n$ times. In applying a wavelet transform, data are transformed so as to preserve the relative distance between objects at different levels of resolution. This allows the natural clusters in the data to become more distinguishable. Clusters can then be identified by searching for dense regions in the new domain. Wavelet transforms are also discussed in Chapter 3, where they are used for data reduction by compression. Additional references to the technique are given in the bibliographic notes.

*"Why is wavelet transformation useful for clustering?"* It offers the following advantages:

- It provides unsupervised clustering. It uses hat-shape filters that emphasize regions where the points cluster, while at the same time suppressing weaker information outside of the cluster boundaries. Thus, dense regions in the original feature space act as attractors for nearby points and as inhibitors for points that are further away. This means that the clusters in the data automatically stand out and "clear" the regions around them. Thus, another advantage is that wavelet transformation can automatically result in the removal of outliers.

- The multiresolution property of wavelet transformations can help in the detection of clusters at varying levels of accuracy. For example, Figure 8.15 shows a sample of two-dimensional feature space, where each point in the image

**Figure 8.15**  A sample of two-dimensional feature space.  From [SCZ98].

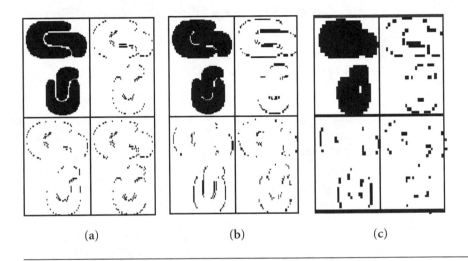

(a)                    (b)                    (c)

**Figure 8.16**  Multiresolution of the feature space in Figure 8.15 at (a) scale 1 (high resolution); (b) scale 2 (medium resolution); (c) scale 3 (low resolution). From [SCZ98].

represents the attribute or feature values of one object in the spatial data set. Figure 8.16 shows the resulting wavelet transformation at different resolutions, from a fine scale (scale 1) to a coarse scale (scale 3). At each level, the four subbands into which the original data are decomposed are shown. The subband shown in the upper-left quadrant emphasizes the average neighborhood around each data point The subband in the upper-right quadrant emphasizes the horizontal edges of the data. The subband in the lower-left quadrant emphasizes the vertical edges, while the subband in the lower-right quadrant emphasizes the corners.

- Wavelet-based clustering is very fast, with a computational complexity of $O(n)$, where $n$ is the number of objects in the database. The algorithm implementation can be made parallel.

WaveCluster is a grid-based and density-based algorithm. it conforms with many of the requirements of a good clustering algorithm: It handles large data sets efficiently, discovers clusters with arbitrary shape, successfully handles outliers, is insensitive to the order of input, and does not require the specification of input parameters such as the number of clusters or a neighborhood radius. In experimental studies, WaveCluster was found to outperform BIRCH, CLARANS, and DBSCAN in terms of both efficiency and clustering quality. The study also found WaveCluster capable of handling data with up to 20 dimensions.

### 8.7.3 CLIQUE: Clustering High-Dimensional Space

The CLIQUE (CLustering In QUEst) clustering algorithm integrates density-based and grid-based clustering. It is useful for clustering high-dimensional data in large databases. CLIQUE is based on the following:

- Given a large set of multidimensional data points, the data space is usually not uniformly occupied by the data points. CLIQUE's clustering identifies the sparse and the "crowded" *areas in space* (or **units**), thereby discovering the overall distribution patterns of the data set.

- A unit is **dense** if the fraction of total data points contained in it exceeds an input model parameter. In CLIQUE, a cluster is defined as a maximal set of *connected dense units*.

*"How does CLIQUE work?"* CLIQUE performs multidimensional clustering in two steps.

In the first step, CLIQUE partitions the $n$-dimensional data space into nonoverlapping rectangular units, identifying the dense units among these. This is done (in 1-D) for each dimension. For example, Figure 8.17 shows dense rectangular units found with respect to *age* for the dimensions *salary* and (number of weeks of) *vacation*. The subspaces representing these dense units are intersected to form a *candidate* search space in which dense units of higher dimensionality may exist.

*"Why does CLIQUE confine its search for dense units of higher dimensionality to the intersection of the dense units in the subspaces?"* The identification of the candidate search space is based on the *Apriori property* used in association rule mining.[1] In general, the property employs prior knowledge of items in the search space so that portions of the space can be pruned. The property, adapted for

---

[1] Association rule mining is described in detail in Chapter 6. In particular, the Apriori property is described in Section 6.2.1.

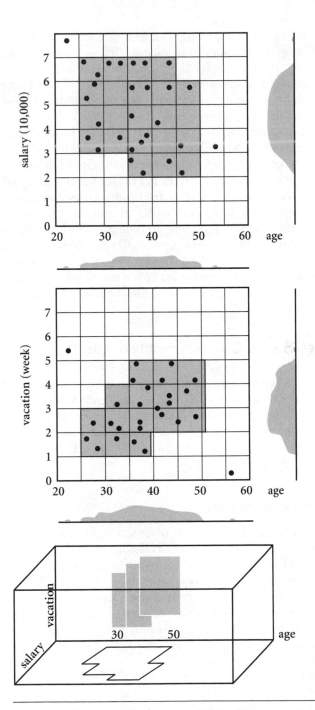

**Figure 8.17** Dense units found with respect to *age* for the dimensions *salary* and *vacation* are intersected in order to provide a candidate search space for dense units of higher dimensionality.

CLIQUE, states the following: *If a k-dimensional unit is dense, then so are its projections in* $(k-1)$*-dimensional space*. That is, given a $k$-dimensional candidate dense unit, if we check its $(k-1)$-th projection units and find any that are not dense, then we know that the $k$th dimensional unit cannot be dense either. Therefore, we can generate potential or candidate dense units in $k$-dimensional space from the dense units found in $(k-1)$-dimensional space. In general, the resulting space searched is much smaller than the original space. The dense units are then examined in order to determine the clusters.

In the second step, CLIQUE generates a minimal description for each cluster as follows. For each cluster, it determines the maximal region that covers the cluster of connected dense units. It then determines a minimal cover for each cluster.

*"How effective is CLIQUE?"* CLIQUE automatically finds subspaces of the highest dimensionality such that high-density clusters exist in those subspaces. It is insensitive to the order of input tuples and does not presume any canonical data distribution. It scales linearly with the size of input and has good scalability as the number of dimensions in the data is increased. However, the accuracy of the clustering result may be degraded at the expense of the simplicity of the method.

## 8.8 Model-Based Clustering Methods

Model-based clustering methods attempt to optimize the fit between the given data and some mathematical model. Such methods are often based on the assumption that the data are generated by a mixture of underlying probability distributions. Model-based clustering methods follow two major approaches: a *statistical approach* or a *neural network approach*. Examples of each approach are described in this section.

### 8.8.1 Statistical Approach

**Conceptual clustering** is a form of clustering in machine learning that, given a set of unlabeled objects, produces a classification scheme over the objects. Unlike conventional clustering, which primarily identifies groups of like objects, conceptual clustering goes one step further by also finding characteristic descriptions for each group, where each group represents a concept or class. Hence, conceptual clustering is a two-step process: first, clustering is performed, followed by characterization. Here, clustering quality is not solely a function of the individual objects. Rather, it incorporates factors such as the generality and simplicity of the derived concept descriptions.

Most methods of conceptual clustering adopt a statistical approach that uses probability measurements in determining the concepts or clusters. Probabilistic descriptions are typically used to represent each derived concept.

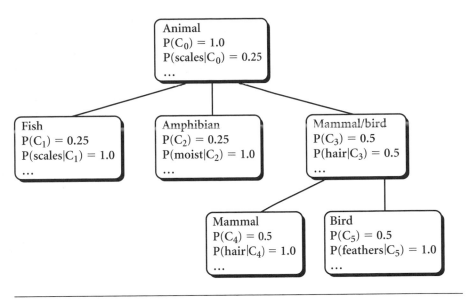

**Figure 8.18**  A classification tree. Figure is based on [Fis87].

COBWEB is a popular and simple method of incremental conceptual cluster-ing. Its input objects are described by categorical attribute-value pairs. COBWEB creates a hierarchical clustering in the form of a **classification tree**.

*"But, what is a classification tree? Is it the same as a decision tree?"* Figure 8.18 shows a classification tree for animal data, based on [Fis87]. A classification tree differs from a decision tree. Each node in a classification tree refers to a concept and contains a probabilistic description of that concept which summarizes the objects classified under the node. The probabilistic description includes the probability of the concept and conditional probabilities of the form $P(A_i = V_{ij}|C_k)$, where $A_i = V_{ij}$ is an attribute-value pair and $C_k$ is the concept class. (Counts are accumulated and stored at each node for computation of the probabilities.) This is unlike decision trees, which label branches rather than nodes and use logical rather than probabilistic descriptors.[2] The sibling nodes at a given level of a classification tree are said to form a **partition**. To classify an object using a classification tree, a partial matching function is employed to descend the tree along a path of "best" matching nodes.

COBWEB uses a heuristic evaluation measure called *category utility* to guide construction of the tree. **Category utility (CU)** is defined as

---

[2] Decision trees are described in Chapter 7.

$$\frac{\Sigma_{k=1}^n P(C_k)[\Sigma_i\Sigma_j P(A_i = V_{ij}|C_k)^2 - \Sigma_i\Sigma_j P(A_i = V_{ij})^2]}{n}, \tag{8.27}$$

where $n$ is the number of nodes, concepts, or "categories" forming a partition $\{C_1, C_2, \ldots, C_n\}$ at the given level of the tree. In other words, category utility is the increase in the expected number of attribute values that can be correctly guessed given a partition (where this expected number corresponds to the term $P(C_k)\Sigma_i\Sigma_j P(A_i = V_{ij}|C_k)^2$) over the expected number of correct guesses with no such knowledge (corresponding to the term $\Sigma_i\Sigma_j P(A_i = V_{ij})^2$). Although we do not have room to show the derivation, category utility rewards intraclass similarity and interclass dissimilarity where

- **Intraclass similarity** is the probability $P(A_i = V_{ij}|C_k)$. The larger this value is, the greater the proportion of class members that share this attribute-value pair, and the more predictable the pair is of class members.
- **Interclass dissimilarity** is the probability $P(C_k|A_i = V_{ij})$. The larger this value is, the fewer the objects in contrasting classes that share this attribute-value pair, and the more predictive the pair is of the class.

Let's have a look at how COBWEB works. COBWEB incrementally incorporates objects into a classification tree.

"*Given a new object,*" you wonder, "*how does COBWEB decide where to incorporate it into the classification tree?*" COBWEB descends the tree along an appropriate path, updating counts along the way, in search of the "best host" or node at which to classify the object. This decision is based on temporarily placing the object in each node and computing the category utility of the resulting partition. The placement that results in the highest category utility should be a good host for the object.

"*Hmm, but what if the object does not really belong to any of the concepts represented in the tree so far? What if it is better to create a new node for the given object?*" That is a good point. In fact, COBWEB also computes the category utility of the partition that would result if a new node were to be created for the object. This is compared to the above computation based on the existing nodes. The object is then placed in an existing class, or a new class is created for it, based on the partition with the highest category utility value. Notice that COBWEB has the ability to automatically adjust the number of classes in a partition. It does not need to rely on the user to provide such an input parameter.

The two operators mentioned above are highly sensitive to the input order of the object. COBWEB has two additional operators that help make it less sensitive to input order. These are **merging** and **splitting**. When an object is incorporated, the two best hosts are considered for merging into a single class. Furthermore, COBWEB considers splitting the children of the best host among the existing categories. These decisions are based on category utility. The merging and splitting operators allow COBWEB to perform a bidirectional search—for example, a merge can undo a previous split.

*"What are the limitations of COBWEB?"* COBWEB has a number of limitations. First, it is based on the assumption that probability distributions on separate attributes are statistically independent of one other. This assumption is, however, not always true since correlation between attributes often exists. Moreover, the probability distribution representation of clusters makes it quite expensive to update and store the clusters. This is especially so when the attributes have a large number of values since their time and space complexities depend not only on the number of attributes, but also on the number of values for each attribute. Furthermore, the classification tree is not height-balanced for skewed input data, which may cause the time and space complexity to degrade dramatically.

CLASSIT is an extension of COBWEB for incremental clustering of continuous (or real valued) data. It stores a continuous normal distribution (i.e., mean and standard deviation) for each individual attribute in each node and uses a modified category utility measure that is an integral over continuous attributes instead of a sum over discrete attributes as in COBWEB. However, it suffers similar problems as COBWEB and thus is not suitable for clustering large database data.

In industry, AutoClass is a popular clustering method that uses Bayesian statistical analysis to estimate the number of clusters. Additional research is needed in the application of conceptual clustering methods to data mining. Further references are provided in the bibliographic notes.

## 8.8.2 Neural Network Approach

The neural network approach to clustering tends to represent each cluster as an *exemplar*. An exemplar acts as a "prototype" of the cluster and does not necessarily have to correspond to a particular data example or object. New objects can be distributed to the cluster whose exemplar is the most similar, based on some distance measure. The attributes of an object assigned to a cluster can be predicted from the attributes of the cluster's exemplar.

In this section, we discuss two prominent methods of the neural network approach to clustering. The first is *competitive learning*, and the second is *self-organizing feature maps*, both of which involve competing neural units.

**Competitive learning** involves a hierarchical architecture of several units (or artificial "neurons") that compete in a "winner-takes-all" fashion for the object that is currently being presented to the system. Figure 8.19 shows an example of a competitive learning system. Each circle represents a unit. The winning unit within a cluster becomes *active* (indicated by a filled circle), while the others are *inactive* (indicated by empty circles). Connections between layers are *excitatory*— a unit in a given layer can receive inputs from all of the units in the next lower level. The configuration of active units in a layer represents the input pattern to the next higher layer. The units within a cluster at a given layer compete with one another to respond to the pattern that is output from the layer below. Connections within

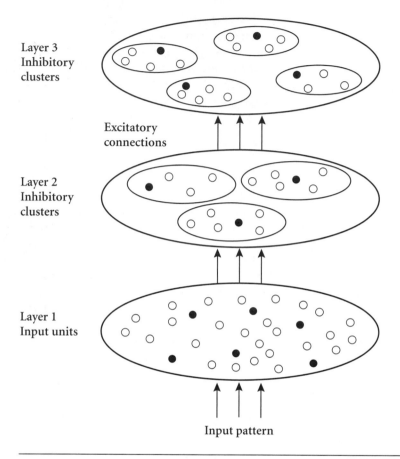

**Figure 8.19** An architecture for competitive learning. The number of layers can be arbitrary. Based on [RZ85].

layers are *inhibitory* so that only one unit in any given cluster may be active. The winning unit adjusts the weights on its connections between other units in the cluster so that it will respond even more strongly to future objects that are the same or similar to the current one. If we view the weights as defining an exemplar, then new objects are assigned to the cluster with the closest exemplar. The number of clusters and the number of units per cluster are input parameters.

At the end of the clustering (or any clustering, in general), each cluster can be thought of as a new "feature" that detects some regularity in the objects. Thus, the resulting clusters can be viewed as a mapping of low-level features to higher-level features.

With **self-organizing feature maps (SOMs)**, clustering is also performed by having several units compete for the current object. The unit whose weight vector is closest to the current object becomes the winning or active unit. So as to move even closer to the input object, the weights of the winning unit are adjusted, as well as those of its nearest neighbors. SOMs assume that there is some topology or ordering among the input objects, and that the units will eventually take on this structure in space. The organization of units is said to form a feature map. SOMs are believed to resemble processing that can occur in the brain and are useful for visualizing high-dimensional data in 2- or 3-D space.

The neural network approach to clustering has strong theoretical links with actual brain processing. Further research is required in making it readily applicable to large databases due to long processing times and the intricacies of complex data.

## 8.9 Outlier Analysis

*"What is an outlier?"* Very often, there exist data objects that do not comply with the general behavior or model of the data. Such data objects, which are grossly different from or inconsistent with the remaining set of data, are called **outliers**.

Outliers can be caused by measurement or execution error. For example, the display of a person's age as −999 could be caused by a program default setting of an unrecorded age. Alternatively, outliers may be the result of inherent data variability. The salary of the chief executive officer of a company, for instance, could naturally stand out as an outlier among the salaries of the other employees in the firm.

Many data mining algorithms try to minimize the influence of outliers or eliminate them all together. This, however, could result in the loss of important hidden information since *one person's noise could be another person's signal*. In other words, the outliers themselves may be of particular interest, such as in the case of fraud detection, where outliers may indicate fraudulent activity. Thus, outlier detection and analysis is an interesting data mining task, referred to as **outlier mining**.

Outlier mining has wide applications. As mentioned above, it can be used in fraud detection, for example, by detecting unusual usage of credit cards or telecommunication services. In addition, it is useful in customized marketing for identifying the spending behavior of customers with extremely low or extremely high incomes, or in medical analysis for finding unusual responses to various medical treatments.

Outlier mining can be described as follows: Given a set of $n$ data points or objects, and $k$, the expected number of outliers, find the top $k$ objects that are considerably dissimilar, exceptional, or inconsistent with respect to the remaining data. The outlier mining problem can be viewed as two subproblems: (1) define what data can be considered as inconsistent in a given data set, and (2) find an efficient method to mine the outliers so defined.

The problem of defining outliers is nontrivial. If a regression model is used for data modeling, analysis of the residuals can give a good estimation for data "extremeness." The task becomes tricky, however, when finding outliers in time-series data as they may be hidden in trend, seasonal, or other cyclic changes. When multidimensional data are analyzed, not any particular one, but rather a *combination* of dimension values may be extreme. For nonnumeric (i.e., categorical data), the definition of outliers requires special consideration.

*"What about using data visualization methods for outlier detection?"* you may wonder. This may seem to be an obvious choice, since human eyes are very fast and effective at noticing data inconsistencies. However, this does not apply to data containing cyclic plots, where apparently outlying values could be perfectly valid values in reality. Data visualization methods are weak in detecting outliers in data with many categorical attributes or in data of high dimensionality, since human eyes are good at visualizing numeric data of only two to three dimensions.

In this section, we instead examine computer-based methods for outlier detection. These can be categorized into three approaches: the *statistical approach*, the *distance-based approach*, and the *deviation-based approach*, each of which are studied here. Notice that while clustering algorithms discard outliers as noise, they can be modified to include outlier detection as a byproduct of their execution. In general, users must check that each outlier discovered by these approaches is indeed a "real" outlier.

### 8.9.1   Statistical-Based Outlier Detection

The statistical approach to outlier detection assumes a distribution or probability model for the given data set (e.g., a normal distribution) and then identifies outliers with respect to the model using a *discordancy test*. Application of the test requires knowledge of the data set parameters (such as the assumed data distribution), knowledge of distribution parameters (such as the mean and variance), and the expected number of outliers.

*"How does the discordancy testing work?"* A statistical discordancy test examines two hypotheses: a *working hypothesis* and an *alternative hypothesis*. A **working hypothesis**, $H$, is a statement that the entire data set of $n$ objects comes from an initial distribution model, $F$, that is,

$$H : o_i \in F, \quad \text{where } i = 1, 2, \ldots, n.$$

The hypothesis is retained if there is no statistically significant evidence supporting its rejection. A **discordancy test** verifies whether an object $o_i$ is significantly large (or small) in relation to the distribution $F$. Different test statistics have been proposed for use as a discordancy test, depending on the available knowledge of the data. Assuming that some statistic $T$ has been chosen for discordancy testing, and the value of the statistic for object $o_i$ is $v_i$, then the distribution of $T$ is constructed. Significance probability $SP(v_i) = Prob(T > v_i)$ is evaluated. If some $SP(v_i)$ is sufficiently small, then $o_i$ is discordant and the working hypothesis is rejected. An **alternative hypothesis**, $\overline{H}$, which states that $o_i$ comes from another distribution model, $G$, is adopted. The result is very much dependent on which model $F$ is chosen since $o_i$ may be an outlier under one model and a perfectly valid value under another.

The alternative distribution is very important in determining the power of the test, that is, the probability that the working hypothesis is rejected when $o_i$ is really an outlier. There are different kinds of alternative distributions.

- **Inherent alternative distribution:** In this case, the working hypothesis that all of the objects come from distribution $F$ is rejected in favor of the alternative hypothesis that all of the objects arise from another distribution, $G$:

$$\overline{H} : o_i \in G, \quad \text{where } i = 1, 2, \ldots, n.$$

F and $G$ may be different distributions or differ only in parameters of the same distribution. There are constraints on the form of the $G$ distribution in that it must have potential to produce outliers. For example, it may have a different mean or dispersion, or a longer tail.

- **Mixture alternative distribution:** The mixture alternative states that discordant values are not outliers in the $F$ population, but contaminants from some other population, $G$. In this case, the alternative hypothesis is

$$\overline{H} : o_i \in (1 - \lambda)F + \lambda G, \quad \text{where } i = 1, 2, \ldots, n.$$

- **Slippage alternative distribution:** This alternative states that all of the objects (apart from some prescribed small number) arise independently from the initial model $F$ with its given parameters, while the remaining objects are independent observations from a modified version of $F$ in which the parameters have been shifted.

There are two basic types of procedures for detecting outliers:

- **Block procedures:** In this case, either all of the suspect objects are treated as outliers, or all of them are accepted as consistent.

- **Consecutive (or sequential) procedures:** An example of such a procedure is the *inside-out* procedure. Its main idea is that the object that is least "likely" to be an outlier is tested first. If it is found to be an outlier, then all of the more extreme values are also considered outliers; otherwise, the next most extreme object is tested, and so on. This procedure tends to be more effective than block procedures.

*"How effective is the statistical approach at outlier detection?"* A major drawback is that most tests are for single attributes, yet many data mining problems require finding outliers in multidimensional space. Moreover, the statistical approach

requires knowledge about parameters of the data set, such as the data distribution. However, in many cases, the data distribution may not be known. Statistical methods do not guarantee that all outliers will be found for the cases where no specific test was developed, or the observed distribution cannot be adequately modeled with any standard distribution.

## 8.9.2 Distance-Based Outlier Detection

The notion of distance-based outliers was introduced to counter the main limitations imposed by statistical methods.

*"What is a distance-based outlier?"* An object $o$ in a data set $S$ is a **distance-based (DB) outlier** with parameters $p$ and $d$, that is, $DB(p, d)$, if at least a fraction $p$ of the objects in $S$ lie at a distance greater than $d$ from $o$. In other words, rather than relying on statistical tests, we can think of distance-based outliers as those objects who do not have "enough" neighbors, where neighbors are defined based on distance from the given object. In comparison with statistical-based methods, distance-based outlier detection generalizes the ideas behind discordancy testing for various standard distributions. Distance-based outlier detection avoids the excessive computation that can be associated with fitting the observed distribution into some standard distribution and in selecting discordancy tests.

For many discordancy tests, it can be shown that if an object $o$ is an outlier according to the given test, then $o$ is also a $DB(p, d)$ outlier for some suitably defined $p$ and $d$. For example, if objects that lie 3 or more standard deviations from the mean are considered to be outliers, assuming a normal distribution, then this definition can be generalized by a $DB(0.9988, 0.13\sigma)$ outlier.[3]

Several efficient algorithms for mining distance-based outliers have been developed. These are outlined as follows.

**Index-based algorithm:** Given a data set, the index-based algorithm uses multidimensional indexing structures, such as R-trees or k-d trees, to search for neighbors of each object $o$ within radius $d$ around that object. Let $M$ be the maximum number of objects within the $d$-neighborhood of an outlier. Therefore, once $M + 1$ neighbors of object $o$ are found, it is clear that $o$ is not an outlier. This algorithm has a worst-case complexity of $O(k * n^2)$, where $k$ is the dimensionality and $n$ is the number of objects in the data set. The index-based algorithm scales well as $k$ increases. However, this complexity evaluation takes only the search time into account even though the task of building an index, in itself, can be computationally intensive.

---

[3] The parameters $p$ and $d$ are computed using the normal curve's probability density function to satisfy the probability condition $(P|X - 3| \le d) < 1 - p$, i.e., $P(3 - d \le X \le 3 + d) < -p$. (Note that the solution may not be unique.) A $d$-neighborhood of radius 0.13 indicates a spread of $\pm 0.13$ units around the 3 $\sigma$ mark (i.e., [2.87, 3.13]). For a complete proof of the derivation, see [KN97].

**Nested-loop algorithm:**   The nested-loop algorithm has the same computational complexity as the index-based algorithm but avoids index structure construction and tries to minimize the number of I/Os. It divides the memory buffer space into two halves, and the data set into several logical blocks. By carefully choosing the order in which blocks are loaded into each half, I/O efficiency can be achieved.

**Cell-based algorithm:**   To avoid $O(n^2)$ computational complexity, a cell-based algorithm was developed for memory-resident data sets. Its complexity is $O(c^k + n)$, where $c$ is a constant depending on the number of cells and $k$ is the dimensionality. In this method, the data space is partitioned into cells with a side length equal to $\frac{d}{2\sqrt{k}}$. Each cell has two *layers* surrounding it. The first layer is one cell thick, while the second is $\lceil 2\sqrt{k} - 1 \rceil$ cells thick, rounded up to the closest integer. The algorithm counts outliers on a *cell-by-cell* rather than an object-by-object basis. For a given cell, it accumulates three counts—the number of objects in the cell, in the cell and the first layer together, and in the cell and both layers together. Let's refer to these counts as *cell_count*, *cell_+_1_layer_count*, and *cell_+_2_layers_count*, respectively.

"*How are outliers determined in this method?*" Let $M$ be the maximum number of outliers that can exist in the $d$-neighborhood of an outlier.

- An object $o$ in the current cell is considered an outlier only if *cell_+_1_layer_count* is less than or equal to $M$. If this condition does not hold, then all of the objects in the cell can be removed from further investigation as they cannot be outliers.

- If *cell_+_2_layers_count* is less than or equal to $M$, then *all* of the objects in the cell are considered outliers. Otherwise, if this number is more than $M$, then it is possible that some of the objects in the cell may be outliers. To detect these outliers, object-by-object processing is used where, for each object $o$ in the cell, objects in the second layer of $o$ are examined. For objects in the cell, only those objects having no more than $M$ points in their $d$-neighborhoods are outliers. The $d$-neighborhood of an object consists of the object's cell, all of its first layer, and some of its second layer.

A variation to the algorithm is linear with respect to $n$ and guarantees that no more than three passes over the data set are required. It can be used for large disk-resident data sets, yet does not scale well for high dimensions.

Distance-based outlier detection requires the user to set both the $p$ and $d$ parameters. Finding suitable settings for these parameters can involve much trial and error.

### 8.9.3 Deviation-Based Outlier Detection

Deviation-based outlier detection does not use statistical tests or distance-based measures to identify exceptional objects. Instead, it identifies outliers by examining the main characteristics of objects in a group. Objects that "deviate" from this description are considered outliers. Hence, in this approach the term *deviations* is typically used to refer to outliers. In this section, we study two techniques for deviation-based outlier detection. The first sequentially compares objects in a set, while the second employs an OLAP data cube approach.

#### Sequential Exception Technique

The sequential exception technique simulates the way in which humans can distinguish unusual objects from among a series of supposedly like objects. It uses implicit redundancy of the data. Given a set $S$ of $n$ objects, it builds a sequence of subsets, $\{S_1, S_2, \ldots, S_m\}$, of these objects with $2 \leq m \leq n$ such that

$$S_{j-1} \subset S_j, \quad \text{where } S_j \subseteq S.$$

Dissimilarities are assessed between subsets in the sequence. The technique introduces the following key terms.

- **Exception set:** This is the set of deviations or outliers. It is defined as the smallest subset of objects whose removal results in the greatest reduction of dissimilarity in the residual set.[4]

- **Dissimilarity function:** This function does not require a metric distance between the objects. It is any function that, if given a set of objects, returns a low value if the objects are similar to one another. The greater the dissimilarity among the objects, the higher the value returned by the function. The dissimilarity of a subset is incrementally computed based on the subset prior to it in the sequence. Given a subset of $n$ numbers $\{x_1, \ldots, x_n\}$, a possible dissimilarity function is the variance of the numbers in the set, that is,

$$\frac{1}{n}\Sigma_{i=1}^{n}(x_i - \overline{x})^2, \tag{8.28}$$

where $\overline{x}$ is the mean of the $n$ numbers in the set. For character strings, the dissimilarity function may be in the form of a pattern string (e.g., containing wildcard characters) that is used to cover all of the patterns seen so far. The dissimilarity increases when the pattern covering all of the strings in $S_{j-1}$ does not cover any string in $S_j$ that is not in $S_{j-1}$.

---

[4] For interested readers, this is equivalent to the greatest reduction in *Kolmogorov complexity* for the amount of data discarded.

- ▪ **Cardinality function**: This is typically the count of the number of objects in a given set.

- ▪ **Smoothing factor**: This is a function that is computed for each subset in the sequence. It assesses how much the dissimilarity can be reduced by removing the subset from the original set of objects. This value is scaled by the cardinality of the set. The subset whose smoothing factor value is the largest is the exception set.

The general task of finding an exception set can be NP-hard (i.e., intractable). A sequential approach is computationally feasible and can be implemented using a linear algorithm.

*"How does this technique work?"* Instead of assessing the dissimilarity of the current subset with respect to its complementary set, the algorithm selects a sequence of subsets from the set for analysis. For every subset, it determines the dissimilarity difference of the subset with respect to the *preceding* subset in the sequence.

*"Can't the order of the subsets in the sequence affect the results?"* To help alleviate any possible influence of the input order on the results, the above process can be repeated several times, each with a different random ordering of the subsets. The subset with the largest smoothing factor value, among all of the iterations, becomes the exception set.

### OLAP Data Cube Technique

An OLAP approach to deviation detection uses data cubes to identify regions of anomalies in large multidimensional data. This technique was described in detail in Chapter 2. For added efficiency, the deviation detection process is overlapped with cube computation. The approach is a form of *discovery-driven exploration* where precomputed measures indicating data exceptions are used to guide the user in data analysis, at all levels of aggregation. A cell value in the cube is considered an exception if it is significantly different from the expected value, based on a statistical model. The method uses visual cues such as background color to reflect the degree of exception of each cell. The user can choose to drill down on cells that are flagged as exceptions. The measure value of a cell may reflect exceptions occurring at more detailed or *lower levels* of the cube, where these exceptions are not visible from the current level.

The model considers variations and patterns in the measure value across *all of the dimensions* to which a cell belongs. For example, suppose that you have a data cube for sales data and are viewing the sales summarized per month. With the help of the visual cues, you notice an increase in sales in December in comparison to all other months. This may seem like an exception in the time dimension. However, by drilling down on the month of December to reveal the sales per item in that month, you note that there is a similar increase in sales for other items during December. Therefore, an increase in total sales in December is not an exception if the item dimension is considered. The model considers exceptions hidden at all aggregated group-by's of a data cube. Manual detection of such exceptions is difficult since the search space is typically very large, particularly when there are many dimensions involving concept hierarchies with several levels.

## 8.10 Summary

- A **cluster** is a collection of data objects that are *similar* to one another within the same cluster and are *dissimilar* to the objects in other clusters. The process of grouping a set of physical or abstract objects into classes of *similar* objects is called **clustering**.

- Cluster analysis has wide **applications** including market or customer segmentation, pattern recognition, biological studies, spatial data analysis, Web document classification, and many others. Cluster analysis can be used as a standalone data mining tool to gain insight into the data distribution, or serve as a preprocessing step for other data mining algorithms operating on the detected clusters.

- The quality of clustering can be assessed based on a measure of **dissimilarity** of objects, which can be computed for **various types of data**, including *interval-scaled*, *binary*, *nominal*, *ordinal*, and *ratio-scaled* variables, or combinations of these variable types.

- Clustering is a dynamic field of research in data mining. Many clustering algorithms have been developed. These can be **categorized** into *partitioning methods, hierarchical methods, density-based methods, grid-based methods*, and *model-based methods*.

- A **partitioning method** first creates an initial set of $k$ partitions, where parameter $k$ is the number of partitions to construct; then it uses an *iterative relocation technique* that attempts to improve the partitioning by moving objects from one group to another. Typical partitioning methods include $k$-means, $k$-medoids, CLARANS, and their improvements.

- A **hierarchical method** creates a hierarchical decomposition of the given set of data objects. The method can be classified as being either *agglomerative* (*bottom-up*) or *divisive* (*top-down*), based on how the hierarchical decomposition is formed. To compensate for the rigidity of merge or split, the quality of hierarchical agglomeration can be improved by analyzing object linkages at each hierarchical partitioning (such as in CURE and Chameleon) or integrating other clustering techniques, such as iterative relocation (as in BIRCH).

- A **density-based method** clusters objects based on the notion of density. It either grows clusters according to the density of neighborhood objects (such as in DBSCAN) or according to some density function (such as in DENCLUE).

OPTICS is a density-based method that generates an augmented ordering of the clustering structure of the data.

- A **grid-based method** first quantizes the object space into a finite number of cells that form a grid structure, and then performs clustering on the grid structure. STING is a typical example of a grid-based method based on statistical information stored in grid cells. CLIQUE and WaveCluster are two clustering algorithms that are both grid-based and density-based.

- A **model-based method** hypothesizes a model for each of the clusters and finds the best fit of the data to that model. Typical model-based methods involve statistical approaches (such as COBWEB, CLASSIT, and AutoClass) or neural network approaches (such as competitive learning and self-organizing feature maps).

- *One person's noise could be another person's signal.* **Outlier detection and analysis** are very useful for fraud detection, customized marketing, medical analysis, and many other tasks. Computer-based outlier analysis methods typically follow either a *statistical approach*, a *distance-based approach*, or a *deviation-based approach*.

## Exercises

8.1 Briefly outline how to compute the dissimilarity between objects described by the following types of variables:

(a) Asymmetric binary variables
(b) Nominal variables
(c) Ratio-scaled variables
(d) Numerical (interval-scaled) variables

8.2 Given the following measurements for the variable *age*:

18, 22, 25, 42, 28, 43, 33, 35, 56, 28,

standardize the variable by the following:

(a) Compute the mean absolute deviation of *age*.
(b) Compute the z-score for the first four measurements.

8.3 Given two objects represented by the tuples (22, 1, 42, 10) and (20, 0, 36, 8):

(a) Compute the *Euclidean distance* between the two objects.
(b) Compute the *Manhattan distance* between the two objects.
(c) Compute the *Minkowski distance* between the two objects, using $q = 3$.

8.4 The following table contains the attributes *name, gender, trait-1, trait-2, trait-3,* and *trait-4*, where *name* is an object-id, *gender* is a symmetric attribute, and the remaining *trait* attributes are asymmetric, describing personal traits of individuals who desire a penpal. Suppose that a service exists that attempts to find pairs of compatible penpals.

| name | gender | trait-1 | trait-2 | trait-3 | trait-4 |
|------|--------|---------|---------|---------|---------|
| Kevan | M | N | P | P | N |
| Caroline | F | N | P | P | N |
| Erik | M | P | N | N | P |
| ⋮ | ⋮ | ⋮ | ⋮ | ⋮ | ⋮ |

For asymmetric attribute values, let the value *P* be set to 1 and the value *N* be set to 0.

Suppose that the distance between objects (potential penpals) is computed based only on the asymmetric variables.

(a) Show the *contingency matrix* for each pair given Kevan, Caroline, and Erik.

(b) Compute the *simple matching coefficient* for each pair.

(c) Compute the *Jaccard coefficient* for each pair.

(d) Who do you suggest would make the best pair of penpals? Which pair of individuals would be the least compatible?

(e) Suppose that we are to include the symmetric variable *gender* in our analysis. Based on the Jaccard coefficient, who would be the most compatible pair, and why?

8.5 What is clustering? Briefly describe the following approaches to clustering methods: *partitioning* methods, *hierarchical* methods, *density-based* methods, *grid-based* methods, and *model-based* methods. Give examples in each case.

8.6 Suppose that the data mining task is to cluster the following eight points (with $(x, y)$ representing location) into three clusters.

$$A_1(2, 10), A_2(2, 5), A_3(8, 4), B_1(5, 8), B_2(7, 5), B_3(6, 4), C_1(1, 2), C_2(4, 9).$$

The distance function is Euclidean distance. Suppose initially we assign $A_1$, $B_1$, and $C_1$ as the center of each cluster, respectively. Use the *k-means* algorithm to show *only*

(a) the three cluster centers after the first round execution, and

(b) the final three clusters.

8.7 Use a diagram to illustrate how, for a constant *MinPts* value, *density-based clusters* with respect to a higher density (i.e., a lower value for $\epsilon$, the neighborhood radius) are completely contained in density-connected sets obtained with respect to a lower density.

**8.8** Human eyes are fast and effective at judging the quality of clustering methods for two-dimensional data. Can you design a data visualization method that may help humans visualize data clusters and judge the clustering quality for three-dimensional data? What about for even higher dimensional data?

**8.9** Give an example of how specific clustering methods may be *integrated*, for example, where one clustering algorithm is used as a preprocessing step for another.

**8.10** Clustering has been popularly recognized as an important data mining task with broad applications. Give one application example for each of the following cases:

(a) An application that takes clustering as a major data mining function

(b) An application that takes clustering as a preprocessing tool for data preparation for other data mining tasks

**8.11** Data cubes and multidimensional databases contain categorical, ordinal, and numerical data in hierarchical or aggregate forms. Based on what you have learned about the clustering methods, design a clustering method that finds clusters in large data cubes effectively and efficiently.

**8.12** Suppose that you are to allocate a number of automatic teller machines (ATMs) in a given region so as to satisfy a number of constraints. Households or places of work may be clustered so that typically one ATM is assigned per cluster. The clustering, however, may be constrained by factors involving the location of bridges, rivers, and highways that can affect ATM accessibility. Additional constraints may involve limitations on the number of ATMs per district forming the region. Given such constraints, how can clustering algorithms be modified to allow for *constraint-based clustering*?

**8.13** Why is outlier mining important? Briefly describe the different approaches behind *statistical-based outlier detection*, *distanced-based outlier detection*, and *deviation-based outlier detection*.

## Bibliographic Notes

Clustering methods are discussed in several textbooks, such as Hartigan [Har75], Jain and Dubes [JD88], and Kaufman and Rousseeuw [KR90]. A recent survey on clustering by Jain, Murty, and Flynn can be found in [JMF99]. Methods for combining variables of different types into a single dissimilarity matrix were introduced by Kaufman and Rousseeuw [KR90].

For partitioning methods, the $k$-means algorithm was first introduced by MacQueen [Mac67]. The $k$-medoids algorithms of PAM and CLARA were proposed by Kaufman and Rousseeuw [KR90]. The $k$-modes (for clustering categorical data) and $k$-prototypes (for clustering hybrid data) algorithms were proposed by Huang [Hua98], while the EM (Expectation Maximization) algorithm was introduced by Lauritzen [Lau95]. The CLARANS algorithm was proposed by Ng and Han [NH94]. Ester, Kriegel, and Xu [EKX95] proposed techniques for further improvement of the performance of CLARANS using efficient spatial access methods, such as R*-tree and focusing techniques. Another *k*-means-based scalable clustering algorithm was proposed by Bradley, Fayyad, and Reina [BFR98].

Agglomerative hierarchical clustering, such as AGNES, and divisive hierarchical clustering, such as DIANA, were introduced by Kaufman and Rousseeuw [KR90]. An interesting direction for improving the clustering quality of hierarchical clustering methods is to integrate hierarchical clustering with distance-based iterative relocation or other nonhierarchical clustering methods. For example, BIRCH, by Zhang, Ramakrishnan, and Livny [ZRL96], first performs hierarchical clustering with a CF tree before applying other techniques. Hierarchical clustering can also be performed by sophisticated linkage analysis, transformation, or nearest neighbor analysis, such as CURE by Guha, Rastogi, and Shim [GRS98], ROCK (for clustering categorical attributes) by Guha, Rastogi, and Shim [GRS99], and Chameleon by Karypis, Han, and Kumar [KHK99].

For density-based clustering methods, DBSCAN was proposed by Ester, Kriegel, Sander, and Xu [EKSX96]. Ankerst, Breunig, Kriegel, and Sander [ABKS99] developed a cluster ordering method, OPTICS, that facilitates density-based clustering without worrying about parameter specification. The DENCLUE algorithm, based on a set of density distribution functions, was proposed by Hinneburg and Keim [HK98].

A grid-based multiresolution approach, STING, which collects statistical information in grid cells, was proposed by Wang, Yang, and Muntz [WYM97]. WaveCluster, developed by Sheikholeslami, Chatterjee, and Zhang [SCZ98], is a multiresolution clustering approach that transforms the original feature space by wavelet transform. CLIQUE, developed by Agrawal, Gehrke, Gunopulos, and Raghavan [AGGR98], is an integrated, density-based and grid-based clustering method for clustering high-dimensional data.

For a set of seminal papers on model-based clustering, see Shavlik and Dietterich [SD90]. Conceptual clustering was first introduced by Michalski and Stepp [MS83]. Other examples of the statistical clustering approach include COBWEB by Fisher [Fis87], CLASSIT by Gennari, Langley, and Fisher [GLF89], and AutoClass by Cheeseman and Stutz [CS96a]. Studies of the neural network approach include competitive learning by Rumelhart and Zipser [RZ85], and SOM (self-organizing feature maps) by Kohonen [Koh82].

Scalable methods for clustering categorical data were studied by Gibson, Kleinberg, and Raghavan [GKR98], by Guha, Rastogi, and Shim [GRS99], and by Ganti, Gehrke, and Ramakrishnan [GGR99]. There are also many other clustering paradigms. For example, fuzzy clustering methods are discussed in Kaufman and Rousseeuw [KR90] and Bezdek and Pal [BP92].

Outlier detection and analysis can be categorized into three approaches: the statistical approach, the distance-based approach, and the deviation-based approach. The statistical approach and discordancy tests are described in Barnett and Lewis [BL94]. Distance-based outlier detection is described in Knorr and Ng [KN97, KN98]. The sequential problem approach to deviation-based outlier detection was introduced in Arning, Agrawal, and Raghavan [AAR96]. Sarawagi, Agrawal, and Megiddo [SAM98] introduced a discovery-driven method for identifying exceptions in large multidimensional data using OLAP data cubes. Jagadish, Koudas, and Muthukrishnan [JKM99] introduced an efficient method for mining deviants in time-series databases.

# Mining Complex Types of Data

**9**

**Our previous studies on data mining techniques** have focused on mining relational databases, transactional databases, and data warehouses formed by the transformation and integration of structured data. Vast amounts of data in various complex forms (e.g., structured and unstructured, hypertext and multimedia) have been growing explosively owing to the rapid progress of data collection tools, advanced database system technologies, and World-Wide Web (WWW) technologies. Therefore, an increasingly important task in data mining is to mine complex types of data, including *complex objects*, *spatial data*, *multimedia data*, *time-series data*, *text data*, and the *World-Wide Web*.[1]

In this chapter, we examine how to further develop the essential data mining techniques (such as characterization, association, classification, and clustering), and how to develop new ones to cope with complex types of data and perform fruitful knowledge mining in complex information repositories. The chapter is organized as follows. Section 9.1 is devoted to the multidimensional analysis and descriptive mining of complex data objects. Section 9.2 describes spatial data mining. Section 9.3 describes multimedia data mining. Section 9.4 is on time-series data mining. Section 9.5 describes mining text databases, and Section 9.6 describes mining the World-Wide Web. Since research into mining such complex databases has been evolving at a hasty pace, our discussion covers only some preliminary issues. We expect that many books dedicated to the mining of complex kinds of data will become available in the future.

---

[1] For a brief introduction to these forms of complex data, see Section 1.3.4.

# 9.1 Multidimensional Analysis and Descriptive Mining of Complex Data Objects

A major limitation of many commercial data warehouse and OLAP tools for multidimensional database analysis is their restriction on the allowable data types for dimensions and measures. Most data cube implementations confine dimensions to nonnumeric data, and measures to simple, aggregated values. To introduce data mining and multidimensional data analysis for complex objects, this section examines how to perform generalization on complex structured objects and construct object cubes for OLAP and mining in object databases.

The storage and access of **complex structured data** have been studied in object-relational and object-oriented database systems. These systems organize a large set of complex data objects into *classes*, which are in turn organized into *class/subclass* hierarchies. Each **object** in a class is associated with (1) an *object-identifier*, (2) a *set of attributes* that may contain sophisticated data structures, set- or list-valued data, class composition hierarchies, multimedia data, and so on, and (3) a *set of methods* that specify the computational routines or rules associated with the object class.

To facilitate generalization and induction in object-relational and object-oriented databases, it is important to study how each component of such databases can be generalized, and how the generalized data can be used for multidimensional data analysis and data mining.

## 9.1.1 Generalization of Structured Data

An important feature of object-relational and object-oriented databases is their capability of storing, accessing, and modeling **complex structure-valued data**, such as set-valued and list-valued data, and data with nested structures.

*"How can generalization be performed on such data?"* Let's start by having a look at the generalization of set-valued and list-valued attributes.

A **set-valued attribute** may be of homogeneous or heterogeneous type. Typically, set-valued data can be generalized by (1) *generalization of each value in the set into its corresponding higher-level concepts*, or (2) *derivation of the general behavior of the set*, such as the number of elements in the set, the types or value ranges in the set, or the weighted average for numerical data. Moreover, generalization can be performed by *applying different generalization operators to explore alternative generalization paths*. In this case, the result of generalization is a heterogeneous set.

**Example 9.1** Suppose that the *hobby* of a person is a set-valued attribute containing the set of values {*tennis, hockey, chess, violin, nintendo_games*}. This set can be generalized into a set of high-level concepts, such as {*sports, music, video_games*} or into the number 5 (i.e., the number of hobbies in the set). Moreover, a *count* can be associated with a generalized value to indicate how many elements are generalized to that value, as in {*sports(3), music(1), video_games(1)*}, where *sports(3)* indicates *three kinds of sports*, and so on.    ∎

A set-valued attribute may be generalized into a set-valued or a single-valued attribute; a single-valued attribute may be generalized into a set-valued attribute if the values form a lattice or "hierarchy," or the generalization follows different paths. Further generalizations on such a generalized set-valued attribute should follow the generalization path of each value in the set.

A **list-valued or a sequence-valued attribute** can be *generalized in a manner similar to that for set-valued attributes except that the order of the elements in the sequence should be observed in the generalization.* Each value in the list can be generalized into its corresponding higher-level concept. Alternatively, a list can be generalized according to its general behavior, such as the length of the list, the type of list elements, the value range, the weighted average value for numerical data, or by dropping unimportant elements in the list. A list may be generalized into a list, a set, or a single value.

**Example 9.2** Consider the following list or sequence of data for a person's education record: "*((B.Sc. in Electrical Engineering, U.B.C., Dec., 1990), (M.Sc. in Computer Engineering, U. Maryland, May, 1993), (Ph.D. in Computer Science, UCLA, Aug., 1997))*". This can be generalized by dropping less important descriptions (subattributes) of each tuple in the list, such as "*((B.Sc., U.B.C., 1990), · · ·)*", and/or by retaining only the most important tuple(s) in the list, e.g., "*(Ph.D. in Computer Science, UCLA, 1997)*".    ∎

A complex structure-valued attribute may contain sets, tuples, lists, trees, records, and so on, and their combinations, where one structure may be *nested* in another at any level. In general, a structure-valued attribute can be generalized in several ways, such as (1) generalizing each attribute in the structure while maintaining the shape of the structure, (2) flattening the structure and generalizing the flattened structure, (3) summarizing the low-level structures by high-level concepts or aggregation, and (4) returning the type or an overview of the structure.

## 9.1.2 Aggregation and Approximation in Spatial and Multimedia Data Generalization

Aggregation and approximation should be considered another important means of generalization, which is especially useful for generalizing attributes with large sets of values, complex structures, and spatial or multimedia data.

Let's take **spatial data** as an example. We would like to generalize detailed geographic points into clustered regions, such as business, residential, industrial, or agricultural areas, according to land usage. Such generalization often requires the merge of a set of geographic areas by spatial operations, such as spatial union or spatial clustering methods. Aggregation and approximation are important techniques for this form of generalization. In a **spatial merge**, it is necessary to not only merge the regions of similar types within the same general class but also compute the total areas, average density, or other aggregate functions while ignoring some scattered regions with different types if they are unimportant to the study. Other spatial operators, such as *spatial-union, spatial-overlapping,* and *spatial-intersection*, which may require the merging of scattered small regions into large, clustered regions, can also use spatial aggregation and approximation as data generalization operators.

**Example 9.3** Suppose that we have different pieces of land for various purposes of agricultural usage, such as the planting of vegetables, grains, and fruits. These pieces can be merged or *aggregated* into one large piece of agricultural land by a spatial merge. However, such a piece of agricultural land may contain highways, houses, small stores, and so on. If the majority of the land is used for agriculture, the scattered regions for other purposes can be ignored, and the whole region can be claimed as an agricultural area by *approximation*. ∎

A **multimedia database** may contain complex texts, graphics, images, video fragments, maps, voice, music, and other forms of audio/video information. Multimedia data are typically stored as sequences of bytes with variable lengths, and segments of data are linked together or indexed in a multidimensional way for easy reference.

Generalization on multimedia data can be performed by recognition and extraction of the essential features and/or general patterns of such data. There are many ways to extract such information. For an *image*, the size, color, shape, texture, orientation, and relative positions and structures of the contained objects or regions in the image can be extracted by aggregation and/or approximation. For a segment of *music*, its melody can be summarized based on the approximate patterns that repeatedly occur in the segment, while its style can be summarized based on its tone, tempo, or the major musical instruments played. For an *article*, its abstract or general organizational structure (e.g., the table of contents, the subject and index terms that frequently occur in the article, etc.) may serve as its generalization.

In general, it is a challenging task to generalize spatial data and multimedia data in order to extract interesting knowledge implicitly stored in the data. Technologies developed in spatial databases and multimedia databases such as spatial data accessing and analysis techniques, and content-based image retrieval and multidimensional indexing methods, should be integrated with data generalization and data mining techniques to achieve satisfactory results. Techniques for mining such data are further discussed in the following sections.

### 9.1.3 Generalization of Object Identifiers and Class/Subclass Hierarchies

*"How can object identifiers be generalized, if their role is to uniquely identify objects?"* At first glance, it may seem impossible to generalize an object identifier. It remains unchanged even after structural reorganization of the data. However, since objects in an object-oriented database are organized into classes, which in turn are organized into class/subclass hierarchies, the generalization of an object can be performed by referring to its associated hierarchy. Thus, an object identifier can be generalized as follows. First, the object identifier is generalized to the identifier of the *lowest subclass* to which the object belongs. The identifier of this subclass can then, in turn, be generalized to a higher-level class/subclass identifier by *climbing up* the class/subclass hierarchy. Similarly, a class or a subclass can be generalized to its corresponding superclass(es) by climbing up its associated class/subclass hierarchy.

*"Can inherited properties of objects be generalized?"* Since object-oriented databases are organized into class/subclass hierarchies, some attributes or methods of an object class are not explicitly specified in the class itself but are inherited from higher-level classes of the object. Some object-oriented database systems allow **multiple inheritance**, where properties can be inherited from more than one superclass when the class/subclass "hierarchy" is organized in the shape of a lattice. The inherited properties of an object can be derived by query processing in the object-oriented database. From the data generalization point of view, it is unnecessary to distinguish which data are stored within the class and which are inherited from its superclass. As long as the set of relevant data are collected by query processing, the data mining process will treat the inherited data in the same manner as the data stored in the object class, and perform generalization accordingly.

*Methods* are an important component of object-oriented databases. Many behavioral data of objects can be derived by the application of methods. Since a method is usually defined by a computational procedure/function or by a set of deduction rules, it is impossible to perform generalization on the method itself. However, generalization can be performed on *the data derived* by application of the method. That is, once the set of task-relevant data is derived by application of the method, generalization can then be performed on these data.

### 9.1.4 Generalization of Class Composition Hierarchies

An attribute of an object may be composed of or described by another object, some of whose attributes may be in turn composed of or described by other objects, thus forming a **class composition hierarchy**. Generalization on a class composition hierarchy can be viewed as generalization on a set of nested structured data (which are possibly infinite, if the nesting is recursive).

In principle, the reference to a composite object may traverse via a long sequence of references along the corresponding class composition hierarchy. However, in most cases, the longer the sequence of references traversed, the weaker the semantic linkage between the original object and the referenced composite object. For example, an attribute *vehicles_owned* of an object class *student* could refer to another object class *car*, which may contain an attribute *auto_dealer*, which may refer to attributes describing the dealer's *manager* and *children*. Obviously, it is unlikely that any interesting general regularities exist between a student and her car dealer's manager's children. Therefore, generalization on a class of objects should be performed on the descriptive attribute values and methods of the class, with limited reference to its closely related components via its closely related linkages in the class composition hierarchy. That is, in order to discover interesting knowledge, generalization should be performed on the objects in the class composition hierarchy that are *closely related in semantics* to the currently focused class(es), but not on those that have only remote and rather weak semantic linkages.

## 9.1.5 Construction and Mining of Object Cubes

In an object database, data generalization and multidimensional analysis are not applied to individual objects but to classes of objects. Since a set of objects in a class may share many attributes and methods, and the generalization of each attribute and method may apply a sequence of generalization operators, the major issue becomes how to make the generalization processes cooperate among different attributes and methods in the class(es).

*"So, how can class-based generalization be performed for a large set of objects?"* For class-based generalization, the *attribute-oriented induction method* developed in Chapter 5 for mining characteristics of relational databases can be extended to mine data characteristics in object databases. Consider that a generalization-based data mining process can be viewed as the application of a sequence of class-based generalization operators on different attributes. Generalization can continue until the resulting class contains a small number of generalized objects that can be summarized as a concise, generalized rule in high-level terms. For efficient implementation, the generalization of multidimensional attributes of a complex object class can be performed by examining each attribute (or dimension), generalizing each attribute to simple-valued data, and constructing a multidimensional data cube, called an **object cube**. Once an object cube is constructed, multidimensional analysis and data mining can be performed on it in a manner similar to that for relational data cubes.

Notice that from the application point of view, it is not always desirable to generalize a set of values to single-valued data. Consider the attribute *keyword*, which may contain a set of keywords describing a book. It does not make much sense to generalize this set of keywords to one single value. In this context, it is difficult to construct an object cube containing the *keyword* dimension. We will address some progress in this direction in the next section when discussing spatial data cube construction. However, it remains a challenging research issue to develop techniques for handling set-valued data effectively in object cube construction and object-based data mining.

## 9.1.6 Generalization-Based Mining of Plan Databases by Divide-and-Conquer

To show how generalization can play an important role in mining complex data-bases, we examine a case of mining significant patterns of successful actions in a plan database using a divide-and-conquer strategy.

A **plan** consists of a variable sequence of *actions*. A **plan database**, or simply a **planbase**, is a large collection of plans. **Plan mining** is the task of mining significant patterns or knowledge from a planbase. Plan mining can be used to discover travel patterns of business passengers in an air flight database, or find significant patterns from the sequences of actions in the repair of automobiles. Plan mining is different from sequential pattern mining, where a large number of frequently occurring sequences are mined at a very detailed level. Instead, plan mining is the extraction of important or significant *generalized* (sequential) patterns from a planbase.

Let's examine the plan mining process using an air travel example.

**Example 9.4** **An air flight planbase:** Suppose that the air travel planbase shown in Table 9.1 stores customer flight sequences, where each record corresponds to an *action* in a sequential database, and a *sequence* of records sharing the same plan number is considered as one plan with a sequence of actions. The columns *departure* and *arrival* specify the codes of the airports involved. Table 9.2 stores information about each airport.

There could be many patterns mined from a planbase like Table 9.1. For example, we may discover that most flights from cities in the Atlantic United States to midwestern cities have a stopover at ORD in Chicago, which could be due to the fact that ORD is the principal hub for several major airlines. Notice that the

**Table 9.1**  A database of travel plans: a travel planbase.

| plan# | action# | departure | departure_time | arrival | arrival_time | airline | · · · |
|-------|---------|-----------|----------------|---------|--------------|---------|-------|
| 1 | 1 | ALB | 800 | JFK | 900 | TWA | · · · |
| 1 | 2 | JFK | 1000 | ORD | 1230 | UA | · · · |
| 1 | 3 | ORD | 1300 | LAX | 1600 | UA | · · · |
| 1 | 4 | LAX | 1710 | SAN | 1800 | DAL | · · · |
| 2 | 1 | SPI | 900 | ORD | 950 | AA | · · · |
| ⋮ | ⋮ | ⋮ | ⋮ | ⋮ | ⋮ | ⋮ | ⋮ |

**Table 9.2** An airport information table.

| airport_code | city | state | region | airport_size | ... |
|---|---|---|---|---|---|
| ORD | Chicago | Illinois | Midwest | 100000 | ... |
| SPI | Springfield | Illinois | Midwest | 10000 | ... |
| LAX | Los Angeles | California | Pacific | 80000 | ... |
| ALB | Albany | New York | Atlantic | 20000 | ... |
| ⋮ | ⋮ | ⋮ | ⋮ | ⋮ | ⋮ |

airports that act as airline hubs (such as LAX in Los Angeles, ORD in Chicago, and JFK in New York) can easily be derived from Table 9.2 based on *airport_size*. However, there could be hundreds of hubs in a travel database. Indiscriminate mining may result in a large number of "rules" that lack substantial support, without providing a clear overall picture.

"*So, how should we go about mining a planbase?*" you ask. What we would like to find is a small number of general (sequential) patterns that cover a substantial portion of the plans, and then we can divide our search efforts based on such mined sequences. The key to mining such patterns is to generalize the plans in the planbase to a sufficiently high level. A multidimensional database model, such as the one shown in Figure 9.1 for the air flight planbase, can be used to facilitate such plan generalization. Since low-level information may never share enough commonality to form succinct plans, we should do the following: (1) generalize the planbase in different directions using the multidimensional model, (2) observe when the generalized plans share common, interesting, sequential patterns having substantial support, and (3) derive high-level, concise plans.

Let's examine this planbase. By combining tuples with the same plan number, the sequences of actions (shown in terms of airport codes) may appear as follows:

**ALB - JFK - ORD - LAX - SAN**

**SPI - ORD - JFK - SYR**

  . . .

These sequences may look very different. However, they can be generalized in multiple dimensions. When they are generalized based on the *airport_size* dimension, we observe some interesting sequential patterns like *S-L-L-S*, where *L* represents a large airport (i.e., a hub), and *S* represents a relatively small regional airport, as shown in Table 9.3.

The generalization of a large number of air travel plans may lead to some rather general but highly regular patterns. This is often the case if the **merge** and **optional** operators are applied to the generalized sequences, where the former merges (and collapses) consecutive identical symbols into one using the transitive

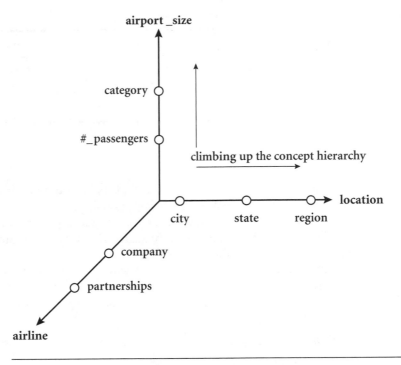

**Figure 9.1**   A multidimensional view of a database.

**Table 9.3**   Multidimensional generalization of a planbase.

| Plan# | Loc-Seq | Size-Seq | State-Seq | Region-Seq | $\cdots$ |
|-------|---------|----------|-----------|------------|------|
| 1 | ALB-JFK-ORD-LAX-SAN | S-L-L-L-S | N-N-I-C-C | E-E-M-P-P | $\cdots$ |
| 2 | SPI-ORD-JFK-SYR | S-L-L-S | I-I-N-N | M-M-E-E | $\cdots$ |
| $\vdots$ | $\vdots$ | $\vdots$ | $\vdots$ | $\vdots$ | $\vdots$ |

closure notation "+" to represent a sequence of actions of the same type, whereas the latter uses the notation "[ ]" to indicate that the object or action inside the square brackets "[ ]" is optional. Table 9.4 shows the result of applying the *merge* operator to the plans of Table 9.3.

By merging and collapsing similar actions, we can derive generalized sequential patterns, such as Pattern (9.1):

$$[S] - l^+ - [S] \qquad [98.5\%] \tag{9.1}$$

**Table 9.4** Merging consecutive, identical actions in plans.

| Plan# | Size-Seq | State-Seq | Region-Seq | $\cdots$ |
|---|---|---|---|---|
| 1 | $S$-$L^+$-$S$ | $N^+$-$I$-$C^+$ | $E^+$-$M$-$P^+$ | $\cdots$ |
| 2 | $S$-$L^+$-$S$ | $I^+$-$N^+$ | $M^+$-$E^+$ | $\cdots$ |
| $\vdots$ | $\vdots$ | $\vdots$ | $\vdots$ | $\vdots$ |

The pattern states that 98.5% of travel plans have the pattern $[S] - L^+ - [S]$, where $[S]$ indicates that action $S$ is optional, and $L^+$ indicates one or more repetitions of $L$. In other words, the travel pattern consists of flying first from possibly a small airport, hopping through one to many large airports, and finally reaching a large (or possibly, a small) airport.

After a sequential pattern is found with sufficient support, it can be used to partition the planbase. We can then mine each partition to find common characteristics. For example, from a partitioned planbase, we may find

$$flight(x, y) \wedge airport\_size(x, S) \wedge airport\_size(y, L)$$

$$\Rightarrow region(x) = region(y) \quad [75\%] \tag{9.2}$$

which means that for a direct flight from a small airport $x$ to a large airport $y$, there is a 75% probability that $x$ and $y$ belong to the same region. ∎

This example demonstrates a *divide-and-conquer strategy*, which first finds interesting, high-level concise sequences of plans by multidimensional generalization of a planbase, and then partitions the planbase based on mined patterns to discover the corresponding characteristics of subplanbases. This mining approach can be applied to many other applications. For example, in Weblog mining we can study general access patterns from the Web to identify popular Web portals and common paths before digging into detailed subordinate patterns.

The plan mining technique can be further developed in several aspects. For instance, a *minimum support threshold* similar to that in association rule mining can be used to determine the level of generalization and ensure that a pattern covers a sufficient number of cases. Additional operators in plan mining can be explored, such as *less_than*. Other variations include extracting associations from subsequences, or mining sequence patterns involving multidimensional attributes, for example, the patterns involving both airport size and countries. Such dimension-combined mining also requires the generalization of each dimension to a high level before examination of the combined sequence patterns.

# 9.2 Mining Spatial Databases

A **spatial database** stores a large amount of space-related data, such as maps, preprocessed remote sensing or medical imaging data, and VLSI chip layout data. Spatial databases have many features distinguishing them from relational databases. They carry topological and/or distance information, usually organized by sophisticated, multidimensional spatial indexing structures that are accessed by spatial data access methods and often require spatial reasoning, geometric computation, and spatial knowledge representation techniques.

**Spatial data mining** refers to the extraction of knowledge, spatial relationships, or other interesting patterns not explicitly stored in spatial databases. Such mining demands an integration of data mining with spatial database technologies. It can be used for understanding spatial data, discovering spatial relationships and relationships between spatial and nonspatial data, constructing spatial knowledge bases, reorganizing spatial databases, and optimizing spatial queries. It is expected to have wide applications in geographic information systems, geomarketing, remote sensing, image database exploration, medical imaging, navigation, traffic control, environmental studies, and many other areas where spatial data are used. A crucial challenge to spatial data mining is the exploration of *efficient* spatial data mining techniques due to the huge amount of spatial data and the complexity of spatial data types and spatial access methods.

*"What about using statistical techniques for spatial data mining?"* Statistical spatial data analysis has been a popular approach to analyzing spatial data. The approach handles numerical data well and usually proposes realistic models of spatial phenomena. However, it typically assumes statistical independence among the spatially distributed data, although in reality, spatial objects are often interrelated. Moreover, most statistical modeling can only be performed by experts having a fair amount of domain knowledge and statistical expertise. Furthermore, statistical methods do not work well with symbolic values, or incomplete or inconclusive data, and are computationally expensive in large databases. Spatial data mining allows the extension of traditional spatial analysis methods by placing emphasis on efficiency, scalability, cooperation with database systems, improved interaction with the user, and the discovery of new types of knowledge.

## 9.2.1 Spatial Data Cube Construction and Spatial OLAP

*"Can we construct a* spatial *data warehouse?"* Yes, as with relational data, we can integrate spatial data to construct a data warehouse that facilitates spatial data mining. A **spatial data warehouse** is a *subject-oriented, integrated, time-variant,* and *nonvolatile* collection of both spatial and nonspatial data in support of spatial data mining and spatial-data-related decision-making processes.

Let's have a look at the following example.

**Example 9.5** There are about 3000 weather probes distributed in British Columbia (BC), each recording daily temperature and precipitation for a designated small area and transmitting signals to a provincial weather station. With a spatial data warehouse that supports spatial OLAP, a user can view weather patterns on a map by month, by region, and by different combinations of temperature and precipitation, and can dynamically drill down or roll up along any dimension to explore desired patterns, such as "wet and hot regions in the Fraser Valley in Summer 1999." ■

There are several challenging issues regarding the construction and utilization of spatial data warehouses. The first challenge is the integration of spatial data from heterogeneous sources and systems. Spatial data are usually stored in different industry firms and government agencies using various data formats. Data formats are not only structure-specific (e.g., raster- vs. vector-based spatial data, object-oriented vs. relational models, different spatial storage and indexing structures, etc.), but also vendor-specific (e.g., ESRI, MapInfo, Intergraph, etc.). There has been a great deal of work on the integration and exchange of heterogeneous spatial data, which has paved the way for spatial data integration and spatial data warehouse construction.

The second challenge is the realization of fast and flexible on-line analytical processing in spatial data warehouses. The star schema model introduced in Chapter 2 is a good choice for modeling spatial data warehouses since it provides a concise and organized warehouse structure and facilitates OLAP operations. However, in a spatial warehouse, both dimensions and measures may contain spatial components.

There are three types of *dimensions* in a spatial data cube:

■ A **nonspatial dimension** contains only nonspatial data. Nonspatial dimensions *temperature* and *precipitation* can be constructed for the warehouse in Example 9.5, since each contains nonspatial data whose generalizations are nonspatial (such as "*hot*" for *temperature* and "*wet*" for *precipitation*).

■ A **spatial-to-nonspatial dimension** is a dimension whose primitive-level data are spatial but whose generalization, starting at a certain high level, becomes nonspatial. For example, the spatial dimension *city* relays geographic data for the U.S. map. Suppose that the dimension's spatial representation of, say, Seattle is generalized to the string "*pacific_northwest*". Although "*pacific_northwest*" is a spatial concept, its representation is not spatial (since, in our example, it is a string). It therefore plays the role of a nonspatial dimension.

■ A **spatial-to-spatial dimension** is a dimension whose primitive level and all of its high-level generalized data are spatial. For example, the dimension *equi_temperature_region* contains spatial data, as do all of its generalizations, such as with regions covering *0-5_degrees* (Celsius), *5-10_degrees*, and so on.

We distinguish two types of *measures* in a spatial data cube.

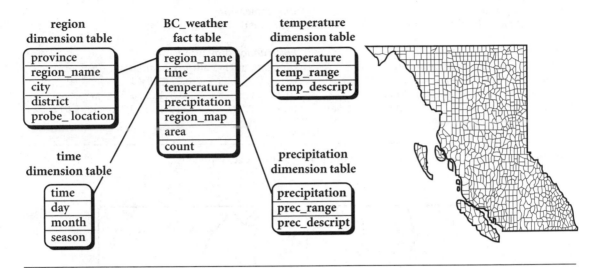

**Figure 9.2** A star schema of the *BC_weather* spatial data warehouse and corresponding BC weather probes map.

- A **numerical measure** contains only numerical data. For example, one measure in a spatial data warehouse could be the *monthly_revenue* of a region, so that a roll-up may compute the total revenue by year, by county, and so on. Numerical measures can be further classified into *distributive*, *algebraic*, and *holistic*, as discussed in Chapter 2.

- A **spatial measure** contains a collection of pointers to spatial objects. For example, in a generalization (or roll-up) in the spatial data cube of Example 9.5, the regions with the same range of *temperature* and *precipitation* will be grouped into the same cell, and the measure so formed contains a collection of pointers to those regions.

A nonspatial data cube contains only nonspatial dimensions and numerical measures. If a spatial data cube contains spatial dimensions but no spatial measures, its OLAP operations, such as drilling or pivoting, can be implemented in a manner similar to that for nonspatial data cubes.

*"But what if I need to use spatial measures in a spatial data cube?"* This notion raises some challenging issues on efficient implementation, as shown in the following example.

**Example 9.6** A star schema for the *BC_weather* warehouse of Example 9.5 is shown in Figure 9.2. It consists of four dimensions: *region temperature*, *time*, and *precipitation*, and three measures: *region_map*, *area*, and *count*. A concept hierarchy for each dimension can be created by users or experts, or generated automatically by data

*region_name* dimension:
*probe_location* < *district* < *city* < *region* < *province*

*temperature* dimension:
(*cold, mild, hot*) ⊂ **all**(*temperature*)
(*below_−20, −20 . . . −11, −10 . . . 0*) ⊂ *cold*
(*0 . . . 10, 11 . . . 15, 16 . . . 20*) ⊂ *mild*
(*20 . . . 25, 26 . . . 30, 31 . . . 35, above_35*) ⊂ *hot*

*time* dimension:
*hour* < *day* < *month* < *season*

*precipitation* dimension:
(*dry, fair, wet*) ⊂ **all**(*precipitation*)
(*0 . . . 0.05, 0.06 . . . 0.2*) ⊂ *dry*
(*0.2 . . . 0.5, 0.6 . . . 1.0, 1.1 . . . 1.5*) ⊂ *fair*
(*1.5 . . . 2.0, 2.1 . . . 3.0, 3.1 . . . 5.0, above_5.0*) ⊂ *wet*

**Figure 9.3**  Hierarchies for each dimension of the *BC_weather* data warehouse.

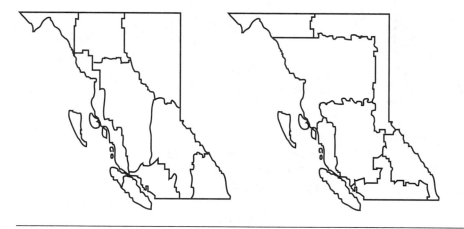

**Figure 9.4**  Generalized regions after different roll-up operations.

clustering analysis. Figure 9.3 presents hierarchies for each of the dimensions in the *BC_weather* warehouse.

Of the three measures, *area* and *count* are *numerical* measures that can be computed similarly to that for nonspatial data cubes; *region_map* is a *spatial* measure that represents a collection of spatial pointers to the corresponding regions. Since different spatial OLAP operations result in different collections of spatial objects in *region_map*, it is a major challenge to compute the merges of a large number of regions flexibly and dynamically. For example, two different roll-ups on the BC weather map data (Figure 9.2) may produce two different generalized region maps, as shown in Figure 9.4, each being the result of merging a large number of small (probe) regions from Figure 9.2.                                         ∎

"*Can we precompute all of the possible spatial merges and store them in the corresponding cuboid cells of a spatial data cube?*" The answer is—probably not. Unlike a numerical measure where each aggregated value requires only a few bytes of space, a merged region map of BC may require megabytes of storage. Thus, we face a dilemma for balancing the cost of on-line computation and the space overhead of storing computed measures: the substantial computation cost for on-the-fly computation of spatial aggregations calls for precomputation, yet substantial overhead for storing aggregated spatial values discourages it.

There are at least three possible choices in regard to the computation of spatial measures in spatial data cube construction.

- *Collect and store the corresponding spatial object pointers but do not perform precomputation of spatial measures in the spatial data cube.* This can be implemented by storing, in the corresponding cube cell, a pointer to a collection of spatial object pointers, and invoking and performing the spatial merge (or other computation) of the corresponding spatial objects, when necessary, on-the-fly. This method is a good choice if only spatial display is required (i.e., no real spatial merge has to be performed), or if there are not many regions to be merged in any pointer collection (so that the on-line merge is not very costly), or if on-line spatial merge computation is fast (recently, some efficient spatial merge methods have been developed for fast spatial OLAP). Since OLAP results are often used for on-line spatial analysis and mining, it is still recommended to precompute some of the spatially connected regions to speed up such analysis.

- *Precompute and store a rough approximation of the spatial measures in the spatial data cube.* This choice is good for a rough view or coarse estimation of spatial merge results under the assumption that it requires little storage space. For example, a *minimum bounding rectangle* (MBR), represented by two points, can be taken as a rough estimate of a merged region. Such a precomputed result is small and can be presented quickly to users. If higher precision is needed for specific cells, the application can either fetch precomputed high-quality results, if available, or compute them on-the-fly.

- *Selectively precompute some spatial measures in the spatial data cube.* This can be a smart choice. The question becomes, "Which portion of the cube should be selected for materialization?" The selection can be performed at the cuboid level, that is, either precompute and store *each* set of mergeable spatial regions for *each* cell of a selected cuboid, or precompute none if the cuboid is not selected. Since a cuboid usually consists of a large number of spatial objects, it may involve precomputation and storage of a large number of mergeable spatial objects, some of which may be rarely used. Therefore, it is recommended to perform selection at a finer granularity level: examining each group of mergeable spatial objects in a cuboid to determine whether such a merge should be precomputed. Decision should be based on the utility (such as access frequency or access priority), sharability of merged regions, and the balanced overall cost of space and on-line computation.

With efficient implementation of spatial data cubes and spatial OLAP, generalization-based descriptive spatial mining, such as spatial characterization and discrimination, can be performed efficiently.

## 9.2.2 Spatial Association Analysis

*"What about mining spatial* association *rules?"* Similar to the mining of association rules in transactional and relational databases, *spatial association rules* can be mined in spatial databases. A **spatial association rule** is of the form $A \Rightarrow B$ [$s\%$, $c\%$], where $A$ and $B$ are sets of spatial or nonspatial predicates, $s\%$ is the support of the rule, and $c\%$ is the confidence of the rule. For example, the following is a spatial association rule:

$$is\_a(X, \text{``school''}) \wedge close\_to(X, \text{``sports\_center''}) \Rightarrow close\_to(X, \text{``park''}) \quad [0.5\%, 80\%]$$

This rule states that 80% of schools that are close to sports centers are also close to parks, and 0.5% of the data belongs to such a case.

Various kinds of spatial predicates can constitute a spatial association rule. Examples include distance information (such as *close_to* and *far_away*), topological relations (like *intersect, overlap,* and *disjoint*), and spatial orientations (like *left_of* and *west_of*).

Since spatial association mining needs to evaluate multiple spatial relationships among a large number of spatial objects, the process could be quite costly. An interesting mining optimization method called **progressive refinement** can be adopted in spatial association analysis. The method first mines large data sets *roughly* using a fast algorithm and then improves the quality of mining in a pruned data set using a more expensive algorithm.

To ensure that the pruned data set covers the complete set of answers when applying the high-quality data mining algorithms at a later stage, an important requirement for the rough mining algorithm applied in the early stage is the **superset coverage property**: that is, it preserves all of the potential answers. In other words, it should allow a *false positive test*, which might include some data sets that do not belong to the answer sets, but it should not allow a *false negative test*, which might exclude some potential answers.

For mining spatial associations related to the spatial predicate *close_to*, we can first collect the candidates that pass the minimum support threshold by

- applying certain rough spatial evaluation algorithms, for example, using a minimum bounding rectangle structure (which registers only two spatial points rather than a set of complex polygons), and

- evaluating the relaxed spatial predicate, *g_close_to*, which is a generalized *close_to* covering a broader context that includes *close_to, touch,* and *intersect*.

If two spatial objects are closely located, their enclosing minimum bounding rectangles must be closely located, matching *g_close_to*. However, the reverse is not always true: if the enclosing minimum bounding rectangles are closely located, the two spatial objects may or may not be located so closely. Thus, the minimum bounding rectangle pruning is a false positive testing tool for closeness: only those that pass the *rough* test need to be further examined using more expensive spatial computation algorithms. With this preprocessing, only the patterns that are frequent at the approximation level will need to be examined by more detailed and finer, yet more expensive, spatial computation.

## 9.2.3 Spatial Clustering Methods

Spatial data clustering identifies clusters, or densely populated regions, according to some distance measurement in a large, multidimensional data set. Spatial clustering methods were thoroughly studied in Chapter 8 since cluster analysis usually considers spatial data clustering in examples and applications. Therefore, readers interested in spatial clustering should refer to Chapter 8.

## 9.2.4 Spatial Classification and Spatial Trend Analysis

**Spatial classification** analyzes spatial objects to derive classification schemes in relevance to certain spatial properties, such as the *neighborhood* of a district, highway, or river.

**Example 9.7** **Spatial classification:** Suppose that you would like to classify regions in a province into *rich* versus *poor* according to the average family income. In doing so, you would like to identify the important spatial-related factors that determine a region's classification. There are many properties associated with spatial objects, such as hosting a university, containing interstate highways, being near a lake or ocean, and so on. These properties can be used for relevance analysis and to find interesting classification schemes. Such classification schemes may be represented in the form of decision trees or rules, for example, as described in Chapter 7. ∎

**Spatial trend analysis** deals with another issue: the detection of changes and trends along a spatial dimension. Typically, trend analysis detects changes with time, such as the changes of temporal patterns in time-series data. Spatial trend analysis replaces time with space and studies the trend of nonspatial or spatial data changing with space. For example, we may observe the trend of changes in economic situation when moving away from the center of a city, or the trend of changes of the climate or vegetation with the increasing distance from an ocean. For such analyses, regression and correlation analysis methods are often applied by utilization of spatial data structures and spatial access methods.

There are also many applications where patterns are changing with *both space and time*. For example, traffic flows on highways and in cities are both time and space related. Weather patterns are also closely related to both time and space. Although there have been a few interesting studies on spatial classification and spatial trend analysis, the investigation of spatio-temporal data mining is still in its infancy. More methods and applications of spatial classification and trend analysis, especially those associated with time, need to be explored in the future.

### 9.2.5 Mining Raster Databases

Spatial database systems usually handle vector data that consist of points, lines, polygons (regions), and their compositions, such as networks or partitions. Typical examples of such data include maps, design graphs, and 3-D representations of the arrangement of the chains of protein molecules. However, a huge amount of space-related data are in **digital raster (image) forms**, such as satellite images, remote sensing data, and computer tomography. It is important to explore data mining in raster or image databases. Methods for mining raster and image data are examined in the following section regarding the mining of multimedia data.

## 9.3 Mining Multimedia Databases

*"What is a multimedia database?"* A **multimedia database system** stores and manages a large collection of *multimedia objects*, such as audio data, image data, video data, sequence data, and hypertext data, which contain text, text markups, and linkages. Multimedia database systems are increasingly common owing to the popular use of audio-video equipment, CD-ROMs, and the Internet. Typical multimedia database systems include NASA's EOS (Earth Observation System), various kinds of image and audio-video databases, human genome databases, and Internet databases.

In this section, our study of multimedia data mining focuses on image data mining. Mining sequence data is studied in Section 9.4 and in Chapter 10 with respect to data mining applications in bioinformatics. Mining hypertext data is studied in Section 9.6 on mining the World-Wide Web. Here we introduce multimedia data mining methods, including similarity search in multimedia data, multidimensional analysis, classification and prediction analysis, and mining associations in multimedia data.

### 9.3.1 Similarity Search in Multimedia Data

*"When searching for similarities in multimedia data, I suppose we can search based on either the data description or the data content?"* That is correct. For similarity searching in multimedia data, we consider two main families of multimedia indexing and retrieval systems: (1) **description-based retrieval** systems, which build indices and perform object retrieval based on image descriptions, such as keywords, captions, size, and time of creation; and (2) **content-based retrieval** systems, which support retrieval based on the image content, such as color histogram, texture, shape, objects, and wavelet transforms. Description-based retrieval is

labor-intensive if performed manually. If automated, the results are typically of poor quality; for example, the assignment of keywords to images can be a tricky and arbitrary task. Content-based retrieval uses visual features to index images and promotes object retrieval based on feature similarity, which is highly desirable in many applications.

In a content-based retrieval system, there are often two kinds of queries: *image-sample-based queries* and *image feature specification queries*. **Image sample-based queries** find all of the images that are similar to the given image sample. This search compares the **feature vector** (or **signature**) extracted from the sample with the feature vectors of images that have already been extracted and indexed in the image database. Based on this comparison, images that are close to the sample image are returned. **Image feature specification queries** specify or sketch image features like color, texture, or shape, which are translated into a feature vector to be matched with the feature vectors of the images in the database. Content-based retrieval has wide applications, including medical diagnosis, weather prediction, TV production, Web search engines for images, and e-commerce. Some systems, such as *QBIC* (*Query By Image Content*), support both sample-based and image feature specification queries. There are also systems that support both content-based and description-based retrieval.

Several approaches have been proposed and studied for similarity-based retrieval in image databases, based on image signature:

- **Color histogram-based signature**: In this approach, the signature of an image includes color histograms based on the color composition of an image regardless of its scale or orientation. Since this method does not contain any information about shape, location, or texture, two images with similar color composition may contain very different shapes or textures, and thus could be completely unrelated in semantics.

- **Multifeature composed signature**: In this approach, the signature of an image includes a composition of multiple features: color histogram, shape, location, and texture. Often, separate distance functions can be defined for each feature and subsequently combined to derive the overall results. Multiple dimensional content-based search often uses one or a few probe features to search for images containing such (similar) features. It can therefore be used to search for similar images.

- **Wavelet-based signature**: This approach uses the dominant wavelet coefficients of an image as its signature. Wavelets capture shape, texture, and location information in a single unified framework.[2] This improves efficiency and reduces the need for providing multiple search primitives (unlike the second method above). However, since this method computes a single signature for an entire

---

[2] Wavelet analysis was described in Section 3.4.3.

image, it may fail to identify images containing similar objects where the objects *differ* in location or size.

- **Wavelet-based signature with region-based granularity**: In this approach, the computation and comparison of signatures are at the granularity of regions, not the entire image. This is based on the observation that similar images may contain similar regions, but a region in one image could be a translation or scaling of a matching region in the other. Therefore, a similarity measure between the query image $Q$ and a target image $T$ can be defined in terms of the fraction of the area of the two images covered by matching pairs of regions from $Q$ and $T$. Such a region-based similarity search can find images containing similar objects, but where these objects may be translated or scaled.

## 9.3.2 Multidimensional Analysis of Multimedia Data

*"Can we construct a data cube for multimedia data analysis?"* To facilitate the multidimensional analysis of large multimedia databases, multimedia data cubes can be designed and constructed in a manner similar to that for traditional data cubes from relational data. A **multimedia data cube** can contain additional dimensions and measures for multimedia information, such as color, texture, and shape.

Let's examine a multimedia data mining system prototype called MultiMedia-Miner, which extends the DBMiner system by handling multimedia data. The example database tested in the MultiMediaMiner system is constructed as follows. Each image contains two descriptors: a *feature descriptor* and a *layout descriptor*. The original image is not stored directly in the database; only its descriptors are stored. The description information encompasses fields like image file name, image URL, image type (e.g., gif, jpeg, bmp, avi, mpeg, etc.), a list of all known Web pages referring to the image (i.e., parent URLs), a list of keywords, and a thumbnail used by the user interface for image and video browsing. The **feature descriptor** is a set of vectors for each visual characteristic. The main vectors are a color vector containing the color histogram quantized to 512 colors ($8 \times 8 \times 8$ for $R \times G \times B$), a MFC (Most Frequent Color) vector, and a MFO (Most Frequent Orientation) vector. The MFC and MFO contain five color centroids and five edge orientation centroids for the five most frequent colors and five most frequent orientations, respectively. The edge orientations used are $0°$, $22.5°$, $45°$, $67.5°$, $90°$, and so on. The **layout descriptor** contains a color layout vector and an edge layout vector. Regardless of their original size, all images are assigned an $8 \times 8$ grid. The most frequent color for each of the 64 cells is stored in the color layout vector, and the number of edges for each orientation in each of the cells is stored in the edge layout vector. Other sizes of grids, like $4 \times 4$, $2 \times 2$ and $1 \times 1$, can easily be derived.

The *Image Excavator* component of MultiMediaMiner uses image contextual information, like HTML tags in Web pages, to derive keywords. By traversing on-line directory structures, like the Yahoo! directory, it is possible to create

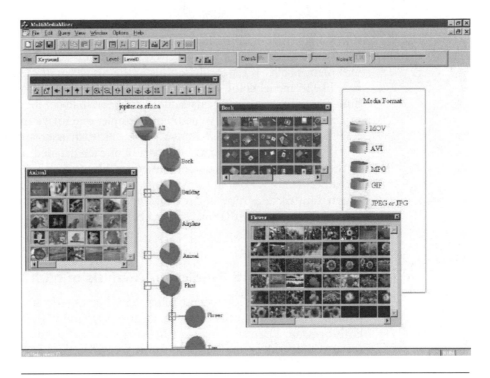

**Figure 9.5** An output of the *Classifier* module of **MultiMediaMiner**.

hierarchies of keywords mapped onto the directories in which the image was found. These graphs are used as concept hierarchies for the dimension *keyword* in the multimedia data cube.

"*What kind of dimensions can a multimedia data cube have?*" A multimedia data cube can have many dimensions. The following are some examples: the size of the image or video in bytes; the width and height of the frames (or picture), constituting two dimensions; the date on which the image or video was created (or last modified); the format type of the image or video; the frame sequence duration in seconds; the image or video Internet domain; the Internet domain of pages referencing the image or video (parent URL); the keywords; a color dimension; an edge-orientation dimension; and so on. Concept hierarchies for many numerical dimensions may be automatically defined. For other dimensions, such as for Internet domains or color, predefined hierarchies may be used.

The construction of a multimedia data cube will facilitate multiple dimensional analysis of multimedia data primarily based on visual content, and the mining of multiple kinds of knowledge, including summarization, comparison, classification, association, and clustering. The *Classifier* module of MultiMediaMiner and its output is presented in Figure 9.5.

The multimedia data cube seems to be an interesting model for multidimensional analysis of multimedia data. However, we should note that it is difficult to implement a data cube efficiently given a large number of dimensions. This curse of dimensionality is especially serious in the case of multimedia data cubes. We may like to model color, orientation, texture, keywords, and so on, as multiple dimensions in a multimedia data cube. However, many of these attributes are set-oriented instead of single-valued. For example, one image may correspond to a set of keywords. It may contain a set of objects, each associated with a set of colors. If we use each keyword as a dimension or each detailed color as a dimension in the design of the data cube, it will create a huge number of dimensions. On the other hand, not doing so may lead to the modeling of an image at a rather rough, limited, and imprecise scale. More research is needed on how to design a multimedia data cube that may strike a balance between efficiency and the power of representation.

## 9.3.3 Classification and Prediction Analysis of Multimedia Data

Classification and predictive modeling have been used for mining multimedia data, especially in scientific research, such as astronomy, seismology, and geoscientific research. Decision tree classification is an essential data mining method in reported image data mining applications.[3]

**Example 9.8**  Taking sky images that have been carefully classified by astronomers as the training set, we can construct models for the recognition of galaxies, stars, and other stellar objects, based on properties like magnitudes, areas, intensity, image moments, and orientation. A large number of sky images taken by telescopes or space probes can then be tested against the constructed models in order to identify new celestial bodies. Similar studies have successfully been performed to identify volcanoes on Venus.   ∎

*Data preprocessing* is important when mining such image data and can include data cleaning, data focusing, and feature extraction. Aside from standard methods used in pattern recognition such as edge detection and Hough transformations, techniques can be explored such as the decomposition of images to eigenvectors or the adoption of probabilistic models to deal with uncertainty. Since the image data are often in huge volumes and may require substantial processing power, parallel and distributed processing are useful.

Image data mining classification and clustering are closely linked to image analysis and scientific data mining, and thus many image analysis techniques and scientific data analysis methods can be applied to image data mining.

---

[3] Classification methods, including classification with decision trees, are discussed in Chapter 7.

### 9.3.4 **Mining Associations in Multimedia Data**

*"What kinds of associations can be mined in multimedia data?"* Association rules involving multimedia objects can be mined in image and video databases. At least three categories can be observed:

- **Associations between image content and nonimage content features:** A rule like *"If at least 50% of the upper part of the picture is blue, it is likely to represent sky"* belongs to this category since it links the image content to the keyword *sky*.

- **Associations among image contents that are not related to spatial relationships:** A rule like *"If a picture contains two blue squares, it is likely to contain one red circle as well"* belongs to this category since the associations are all regarding image contents.

- **Associations among image contents related to spatial relationships:** A rule like *"If a red triangle is in between two yellow squares, it is likely there is a big oval-shaped object underneath"* belongs to this category since it associates objects in the image with spatial relationships.

To mine associations among multimedia objects, we can treat each image as a transaction and find frequently occurring patterns among different images.

*"What are the differences between mining association rules in multimedia databases versus in transaction databases?"* There are some subtle differences. First, an image may contain multiple objects, each with many features such as color, shape, texture, keyword, and spatial location, so that there could be a large number of possible associations. In many cases, a feature may be considered as the same in two images at a certain level of resolution, but different at a finer resolution level. Therefore, it is essential to promote a **progressive resolution refinement** approach. That is, we can first mine frequently occurring patterns at a relatively rough resolution level, and then focus only on those that have passed the minimum support threshold when mining at a finer resolution level. This is because the patterns that are not frequent at a rough level cannot be frequent at finer resolution levels. Such a multiresolution mining strategy substantially reduces the overall data mining cost without loss of the quality and completeness of data mining results. This leads to an efficient methodology for mining frequent itemsets and associations in large multimedia databases.

Second, since a picture containing multiple recurrent objects is an important feature in image analysis, recurrence of the same objects should not be ignored in association analysis. For example, a picture containing two golden circles is treated quite differently from that containing only one. This is quite different from that in a transaction database, where the fact that a person buys one gallon of milk or two may often be treated the same as *"buys_milk"*. Therefore, the definition of multimedia association and its measurements, such as support and confidence, should be adjusted accordingly.

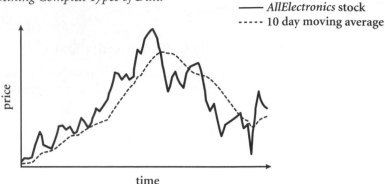

**Figure 9.6**   Time-series data: Stock price of *AllElectronic* over time.

Third, there often exist important relative spatial relationships among multi-media objects, such as *above*, *beneath*, *between*, *nearby*, *left-of*, and so on. These features are very useful for exploring object associations and correlations. Spatial relationships together with other content-based multimedia features, such as color, shape, texture, and keywords, may form interesting associations. Thus, spatial data mining methods and properties of topological spatial relationships become quite important for multimedia mining.

## 9.4  Mining Time-Series and Sequence Data

*"What is a time-series database? What is a sequence database?"* A **time-series database** consists of sequences of values or events changing with time. The values are typically measured at equal time intervals. Time-series databases are popular in many applications, such as studying daily fluctuations of a stock market, traces of a dynamic production process, scientific experiments, medical treatments, and so on. A time-series database is also a sequence database. However, a **sequence database** is any database that consists of sequences of ordered events, with or without concrete notions of time. For example, Web page traversal sequences are sequence data, but may not be time-series data.

In this section, we examine several important aspects of mining time-series databases and sequence databases, including trend analysis, similarity search, and the mining of sequential patterns and periodic patterns in time-related data.

### 9.4.1  Trend Analysis

A time series involving a variable $Y$, representing, say, the daily closing price of a share in a stock market, can be viewed as a function of time $t$, that is, $Y = F(t)$. Such a function can be illustrated as a time-series graph, as shown in Figure 9.6, which describes a point moving with the passage of time.

*"How can we study time-series data?"* There are four major **components** or **movements** that are used to characterize time-series data:

- **Long-term or trend movements:** These indicate the general direction in which a time-series graph is moving over a long interval of time. This movement is displayed by a **trend curve**, or a **trend line**. For example, the trend curve of Figure 9.6 is indicated by a dashed curve. Typical methods for determining a trend curve or trend line include the weighted moving average method and the least squares method, discussed further below.

- **Cyclic movements or cyclic variations:** These refer to the *cycles*, that is, the long-term oscillations about a trend line or curve, which may or may not be periodic. That is, the cycles need not necessarily follow exactly similar patterns after equal intervals of time.

- **Seasonal movements or seasonal variations:** These movements are due to events that recur annually, such as the sudden increase in sales of chocolates and flowers before Valentine's Day, or of department store items before Christmas. In other words, seasonal movements are the identical or nearly identical patterns that a time series appears to follow during corresponding months of successive years.

- **Irregular or random movements:** These characterize the sporadic motion of time series due to random or chance events, such as labor disputes, floods, or announced personnel changes within companies.

The above trend, cyclic, seasonal, and irregular movements are represented by the variables $T, C, S, I$, respectively. Time-series analysis is also referred to as the **decomposition** of a time series into these four basic movements. The time-series variable $Y$ can be modeled as either the product of the four variables (i.e., $Y = T \times C \times S \times I$) or their sum. This choice is typically empirical.

*"Given a set of values for $Y$ (i.e., $y_1, y_2, y_3, \ldots$), how can we determine the trend of the data?"* A common method for determining trend is to calculate a **moving average of order** $n$ as the following sequence of arithmetic means:

$$\frac{y_1 + y_2 + \cdots + y_n}{n}, \frac{y_2 + y_3 + \cdots + y_{n+1}}{n}, \frac{y_3 + y_4 + \cdots + y_{n+2}}{n}, \ldots \quad (9.3)$$

A moving average tends to reduce the amount of variation present in the data set. Thus the process of replacing the time series by its moving average eliminates unwanted fluctuations and is therefore also referred to as the **smoothing of time series**. If weighted arithmetic means are used in Sequence (9.3), the resulting sequence is called a **weighted moving average of order** $n$.

**Example 9.9** Given a sequence of nine values, we can compute its moving average of order 3, and its weighted moving average of order 3 using the weights (1, 4, 1). This information can be displayed in tabular form, where each value in the moving average is the mean of the three values immediately above it, and each value in the weighted moving average is the weighted average of the three values immediately above it.

| Original data: | | 3 | 7 | 2 | 0 | 4 | 5 | 9 | 7 | 2 |
|---|---|---|---|---|---|---|---|---|---|---|
| Moving average of order 3: | | | 4 | 3 | 2 | 3 | 6 | 7 | 6 | |
| Weighted (1, 4, 1) | | | | | | | | | | |
| moving average of order 3: | | | 5.5 | 2.5 | 1 | 3.5 | 5.5 | 8 | 6.5 | |

The first weighted average value is calculated as $\frac{1 \times 3 + 4 \times 7 + 1 \times 2}{1+4+1} = 5.5$. The weighted average typically assigns greater weights to the central elements in order to offset the smoothing effect. ∎

A moving average loses the data at the beginning and end of a series, may sometimes generate cycles or other movements that are not present in the original data, and may be strongly affected by the presence of extreme values. Notice that the influence of extreme values can be reduced by employing a weighted moving average with appropriate weights as shown in Example 9.9.

By using a weighted moving average of appropriate orders, the cyclic, seasonal, and irregular patterns in the data can be eliminated, resulting in only the trend movement.

*"Are there other ways to estimate the trend?"* Yes, one such method is the **free-hand method**, where an approximate curve or line is drawn to fit a set of data based on the user's own judgment. This method is costly and barely reliable for any large-scale data mining. An alternative is the **least squares method**, where we consider the best fitting curve $C$ as the *least squares curve*, that is, the curve having the minimum of $\Sigma_{i=1}^{n} d_i^2$, where the *deviation* or *error* $d_i$ is the difference between the value $y_i$ of a point $(x_i, y_i)$ and the corresponding value as determined from the curve $C$.

*"Is there any way to adjust the data for seasonal fluctuations?"* In many business transactions, there are expected regular seasonal fluctuations, such as higher sales volumes during the Christmas season. Therefore, it is important to identify such seasonal variations and "deseasonalize" the data for trend and cyclic data analysis. For this purpose, the concept of **seasonal index** is introduced, as a set of numbers showing the relative values of a variable during the months of a year. For example, if the sales during October, November, and December are 80%, 120%, and 140% of the average monthly sales for the whole year, respectively, then 80, 120, and 140 are the **seasonal index numbers** for the year. If the original monthly data are divided by the corresponding seasonal index numbers, the resulting data are said to be **deseasonalized**, or *adjusted for seasonal variations*. Such data still include trend, cyclic, and irregular movements.

The deseasonalized data can be adjusted for trend by dividing the data by their corresponding trend values. Furthermore, an appropriate moving average will smooth out the irregular variations and leave only cyclic variations for further analysis. If periodicity or approximate periodicity of cycles occurs, **cyclic indexes** can be constructed in a manner similar to that for seasonal indexes.

Finally, irregular or random movements can be estimated by adjusting data for the trend, seasonal, and cyclic variations. In general, small deviations tend to occur with large frequency, whereas large deviations tend to occur with small frequency, following a normal distribution.

In practice, it is often beneficial to first graph the time series and qualitatively estimate the presence of long-term trends, seasonal variations, and cyclic variation. This may help in selecting a suitable method for analysis and in comprehending its results.

With the systematic analysis of the movements of *trend, cyclic, seasonal*, and *irregular* components, it is possible to make long-term or short-term predictions (**forecasting the time series**) with reasonable quality.

## 9.4.2 Similarity Search in Time-Series Analysis

*"What is a similarity search?"* Unlike normal database queries, which find data that match the given query *exactly*, a **similarity search** finds data sequences that *differ only slightly* from the given query sequence. Given a set of time-series sequences, there are two types of similarity search. **Subsequence matching** finds all of the data sequences that are similar to the given sequence, while **whole sequence matching** finds those sequences that are similar to one other. Similarity search in time-series analysis is useful for the analysis of financial markets (e.g., stock data analysis), medical diagnosis (e.g., cardiogram analysis), and in scientific or engineering databases (e.g., power consumption analysis).

### Data Transformation: From Time Domain to Frequency Domain

For similarity analysis of time-series data, Euclidean distance is typically used as a similarity measure.

*"Do I need to transform the data?"* Many techniques for signal analysis require the data to be in the frequency domain. Therefore, distance-preserving orthonormal transformations are often used to transform the data from the time domain to the frequency domain. Usually, data-independent transformation is applied where the transformation matrix is determined a priori, independent of the input data. Two popular data-independent transformations are the *discrete Fourier transform (DFT)* and the *discrete wavelet transform (DWT)*.[4] Since the distance between two signals in the time domain is the same as their Euclidean distance in the frequency domain, the DFT does a good job of preserving essentials in the

---

[4] Discrete Fourier transforms and wavelet transforms were briefly discussed in Section 3.4.3.

first few coefficients. By keeping only the first few (i.e., "strongest") coefficients of the DFT, we can compute the lower bounds of the actual distance.

*"Once the data are transformed by, say, a DFT, how is a similarity search performed?"* For efficient accessing, a multidimensional index can be constructed using the first few Fourier coefficients. When a similarity query is submitted to the system, the index can be used to retrieve the sequences that are at most a certain small distance away from the query sequence. Postprocessing is then performed by computing the actual distance between sequences in the time domain and discarding any false matches.

*"What about subsequence matching?"* For subsequence matching, each sequence is first broken down into a set of "pieces" of *window* with length $w$. The features of the subsequence inside each window are then extracted. Each sequence is mapped to a "trail" in the feature space. For subsequence analysis, we divide the trail of each sequence into "subtrails," each represented by a minimum bounding rectangle. A multipiece assembly algorithm can then be used to search for longer sequence matches.

### Enhanced Similarity Search Methods to Handle Gaps and Differences in Offsets and Amplitudes

Most real-world applications do not require the matching subsequences to be perfectly aligned along the time axis. In other words, we should allow for pairs of subsequences to match if they are of the *same shape*, but differ due to the presence of gaps within a sequence or differences in offsets or amplitudes. This is particularly useful in many similar sequence analyses, such as stock market analysis and cardiogram analysis.

*"How can an enhanced similarity search be performed that allows for such differences?"* In an enhanced similarity model, users or experts can specify parameters such as a sliding window size, the width of an envelope for similarity, the maximum gap, a matching fraction, and so on. Consider Figure 9.7, showing two time sequences, from which gaps are removed. The resulting sequences are normalized with respect to offset translation and amplitude scaling, allowing subsequences with different scalings or offsets to be matched. Two subsequences are considered *similar* and can be matched if one lies within an envelope of $\epsilon$ width around the other (where $\epsilon$ is a small number, specified by a user or expert), ignoring outliers. Two sequences are *similar* if they have enough nonoverlapping time-ordered pairs of similar subsequences.

Based on the above, a similarity search that handles gaps and differences in offsets and amplitudes can be performed by the following steps:

1. **Atomic matching**: Find all pairs of gap-free windows of a small length that are similar.

2. **Window stitching**: Stitch similar windows to form pairs of large similar subsequences, allowing gaps between atomic matches.

**(1) Original sequences**

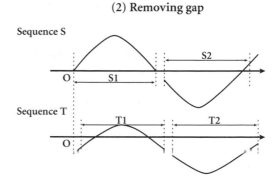

**(2) Removing gap**

**(3) Offset translation**

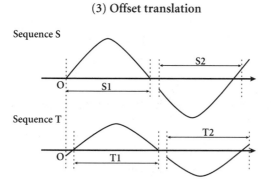

**(4) Amplitude scaling**

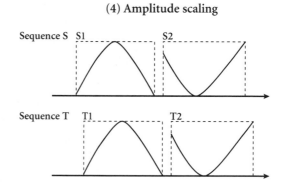

**(5) Subsequence matching**

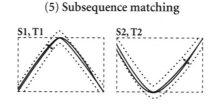

**Figure 9.7** Subsequence matching in time-series data: The original sequences are of the same shape, yet adjustments need to be made to deal with differences in gaps, offsets, and amplitudes. These adjustments allow subsequences to be matched within an envelope of width $\epsilon$.

**3. Subsequence ordering**: Linearly order the subsequence matches to determine whether enough similar pieces exist.

With such processing, sequences of similar shape but with gaps or differences in offsets or amplitudes can be found to match each other or to match query templates.

### Indexing Methods for Similarity Search

*"Are there any strategies for efficient implementation?"* To efficiently implement similarity search in large databases, various kinds of indexing methods have been explored. For example, *R-trees* and *R\*-trees* have been used to store minimal bounding rectangles so as to speed up the similarity search. In addition, the $\epsilon$-*kdB tree* has been developed for faster spatial similarity joins on high-dimensional points, and *suffix trees* have also been explored.

### Query Languages for Time Sequences

*"How can I specify the similarity search to be performed?"* It is important to design and develop powerful query languages to facilitate the specification of similarity searches in time sequences. A **time-sequence query language** should be able to specify not only simple similarity queries like *"Find all of the sequences similar to a given subsequence Q,"* but also sophisticated queries like *"Find all of the sequences that are similar to some sequence in class A, but not similar to any sequence in class B."* Moreover, it should be able to support various kinds of queries, such as range queries, all-pair queries, and nearest neighbor queries.

Another interesting kind of time-sequence query language is a shape definition language. It allows users to define and query the *overall shape* of time sequences using human-readable series of sequence transitions or macros, while ignoring the specific details.

**Example 9.10** The pattern *up, Up, UP* can be used to describe increasing degrees of rising slopes. A macro, such as *spike*, can denote a sequence like (*SteepUps, flat, SteepDowns*), where *SteepUps* is defined as ({*Up, UP*}, {*Up, UP*}, {*Up, UP*}), which means that one *SteepUps* consists of three steep up-slopes, each corresponding to either *Up* or *UP*. *SteepDowns* is similarly defined. ∎

Such a shape definition language increases the users' flexibility at specifying queries of desired shapes for sequence similarity search.

## 9.4.3 Sequential Pattern Mining

*"What is sequential pattern mining?"* **Sequential pattern mining** is the mining of frequently occurring patterns related to time or other sequences. An example of a sequential pattern is *"A customer who bought a Pentium PC nine months ago is*

*likely to order a new CPU chip within one month".* Since many business transactions, telecommunications records, weather data, and production processes are time sequence data, sequential pattern mining is useful in the analysis of such data for targeted marketing, customer retention, weather prediction, and so on.

### Cases and Parameters for Sequential Pattern Mining

Most studies of sequential pattern mining concentrate on *symbolic patterns*, since numerical curve patterns usually belong to the scope of trend analysis and prediction in statistical time-series analysis, as discussed in Section 9.4.1.

There are several parameters whose setting may strongly influence the results of sequential pattern mining. The first parameter is the **duration** of a time sequence $T$. The duration may be the entire available sequence in the database, or a user-selected subsequence such as that corresponding to the year 1999. Sequential pattern mining can then be confined to the data within a specified duration. Durations may also be defined as sets of partitioned sequences, such as every year, or every week after stock crashes, or every two weeks before and after a volcano eruption. In such cases, *periodic patterns* can be discovered.

The second parameter is the **event folding window**, $w$. A set of events occurring within a specified period of time can be viewed as occurring together in certain analyses. If $w$ is set to be as long as the duration $T$, it finds time-insensitive frequent patterns—these are essentially association patterns, such as "*In 1999, customers who bought a PC bought a digital camera as well*" (not even caring which was bought first). If $w$ is set to 0 (i.e., no event sequence folding), sequential patterns are found where each event occurs at a distinct time instant, such as "*A customer who bought a PC and then a memory chip is likely to buy a CD-ROM later on*". If $w$ is set to be something in between (e.g., for transactions occurring within the same month or within a slide window of 24 hours), then these transactions are considered as occurring within the same period, and such sequences are folded in the analysis.

The third parameter is the time **interval**, *int*, between events in the discovered pattern. This parameter may have the following settings:

- $int = 0$: This means that no interval gap is allowed; that is, it finds strictly consecutive sequences, such as sequential patterns like $a_{i-1}a_ia_{i+1}$, where $a_i$ is an event occurring at time $i$. The event folding window, $w$, can be taken into consideration in such a case. For example, if the event folding window is set to a week, this will find frequent patterns occurring in consecutive weeks. DNA analysis often requires the discovery of consecutive sequences without any interval gap.

- *min_interval* $\leq$ *int* $\leq$ *max_interval*: This means that we want to find patterns that are separated by at least *min_interval* but at most *max_interval*. For example, the pattern "*If a person rents movie A, it is likely she will rent movie B within 30 days*" implies *int* $\leq$ 30 (days).

- $int = c \neq 0$: Users may like to find patterns carrying an exact interval, *int*. For example, the query *"Every time the Dow Jones drops more than 5%, what will happen exactly two days later?"* will search for sequential patterns with $int = 2$ (days).

The user can specify constraints on the kinds of sequential patterns to be mined by providing "pattern templates" in the form of *serial episodes* and *parallel episodes,* or regular expressions. A **serial episode** is a set of events that occurs in a total order, whereas a **parallel episode** is a set of events whose occurrence ordering is trivial. Let the notation $(E, t)$ represent *event type E* at *time t*. Consider the data $(A,1)$, $(C,2)$, and $(B,5)$ with an event folding window width of 2, where the serial episode $A \rightarrow B$ and the parallel episode $A \& C$ both occur in the data. The user can also specify constraints in the form of a regular expression, such as $(A|B)C * (D|E)$, which indicates that the user would like to find patterns where event $A$ and $B$ first occur (but their relative ordering is unimportant), followed by one or a set of events $C$, followed by the events $D$ and $E$ (where $D$ can occur either before or after $E$). Notice that other events can occur in between those specified in the regular expression.

### Methods for Sequential Pattern Mining

The *Apriori property* employed in association rule mining can be applied to mining sequential patterns because if a sequential pattern of length $k$ is infrequent, its superset (of length $k + 1$) cannot be frequent. Therefore, most of the methods for mining sequential patterns adopt variations of Apriori-like algorithms although they may consider different parameter settings and constraints. Another approach for mining such patterns is to explore a database projection-based sequential pattern growth technique, similar to the frequent-pattern growth (FP-growth) method for mining frequent patterns without candidate generation (discussed in Section 6.2.4).

## 9.4.4 Periodicity Analysis

*"What is periodicity analysis?"* **Periodicity analysis** is the mining of periodic patterns, that is, the search for recurring patterns in time-series databases. Periodicity analysis can be applied to many important areas. For example, seasons, tides, planet trajectories, daily power consumptions, daily traffic patterns, and weekly TV programs all present certain periodic patterns.

As indicated in our discussion of the previous section, mining periodic patterns can be viewed as mining sequential patterns by taking durations as a set of partitioned sequences, such as every year, every slot after or before the occurrence of certain events, and so on.

The problem of mining periodic patterns can be partitioned into three categories:

- Mining **full periodic patterns**, where every point in time contributes (precisely or approximately) to the cyclic behavior of the time series. For example, all of the days in the year *approximately* contribute to the season cycle of the year.

- Mining **partial periodic patterns**, which specify the periodic behavior of the time series at some but not all of the points in time. For example, Sandy reads the *New York Times* from 7:00 to 7:30 every weekday morning, but her activities at other times do not have much regularity. Partial periodicity is a looser form of periodicity than full periodicity, and it also occurs more commonly in the real world.

- Mining **cyclic or periodic association rules,** which are rules that associate a set of events that occur periodically. An example of a periodic association rule is *"Based on day-to-day transactions, if afternoon tea is well received between 3:00–5:00 pm, dinner will sell well between 7:00–9:00 pm on weekends".*

Techniques for full periodicity analysis have been studied in signal analysis and statistics. Methods like FFT (Fast Fourier Transformation) have been popularly used to transform data from the time domain to the frequency domain in order to facilitate such analysis.

*"Can methods for finding full periodic patterns also be applied for the mining of partial periodic patterns?"* The efficient mining of partial periodicity has been studied in recent data mining research. Most methods for mining full periodic patterns are either inapplicable to or prohibitively expensive for mining partial periodic patterns owing to the latter's mixture of periodic events and nonperiodic events in the same period. For instance, FFT cannot be used for mining partial periodicity because it treats the time series as an inseparable flow of values. Some periodicity detection methods can uncover some partial periodic patterns, but only if the period, length, and timing of the segment in the partial patterns with certain behaviors are explicitly specified. For the newspaper reading example, we need to explicitly specify details such as "Find the regular activities of Sandy during the half-hour after 7:00 for a period of 24 hours." A naive adaptation of such methods to the partial periodic pattern mining problem would be prohibitively expensive, requiring their application to a huge number of possible combinations of the three parameters of period, length, and timing.

Most of the studies on mining partial periodic patterns and cyclic association rules apply the Apriori property heuristic and adopt some variations of Apriori-like mining methods. Constraints can also be pushed deep into the sequential pattern and periodic pattern mining process. The Apriori property, variations of the Apriori algorithm, and the use of mining constraints are discussed in Chapter 6.

# 9.5 Mining Text Databases

Most previous studies of data mining have focused on structured data, such as relational, transactional, and data warehouse data. However, in reality, a substantial portion of the available information is stored in **text databases** (or **document databases**), which consist of large collections of documents from various sources, such as news articles, research papers, books, digital libraries, e-mail messages, and Web pages. Text databases are rapidly growing due to the increasing amount of information available in electronic forms, such as electronic publications, e-mail, CD-ROMs, and the World-Wide Web (which can also be viewed as a huge, interconnected, dynamic text database).

Data stored in most text databases are *semistructured data* in that they are neither completely unstructured nor completely structured. For example, a document may contain a few structured fields, such as *title*, *authors*, *publication_date*, *length*, *category*, and so on, but also contain some largely unstructured text components, such as *abstract* and *contents*. There have been a great deal of studies on the modeling and implementation of semistructured data in recent database research. Moreover, information retrieval techniques, such as text indexing methods, have been developed to handle unstructured documents.

Traditional information retrieval techniques become inadequate for the increasingly vast amounts of text data. Typically, only a small fraction of the many available documents will be relevant to a given individual or user. Without knowing what could be in the documents, it is difficult to formulate effective queries for analyzing and extracting useful information from the data. Users need tools to compare different documents, rank the importance and relevance of the documents, or find patterns and trends across multiple documents. Thus, text mining has become an increasingly popular and essential theme in data mining.

## 9.5.1 Text Data Analysis and Information Retrieval

*"What is information retrieval?"* **Information retrieval** (**IR**) is a field that has been developing in parallel with database systems for many years. Unlike the field of database systems, which has focused on query and transaction processing of structured data, information retrieval is concerned with the organization and retrieval of information from a large number of text-based documents. A typical information retrieval problem is to locate relevant documents based on user input, such as keywords or example documents. Typical information retrieval systems include on-line library catalog systems and on-line document management systems.

Since information retrieval and database systems each handle different kinds of data, there are some database system problems that are usually not present in information retrieval systems, such as concurrency control, recovery, transaction management, and update. There are also some common information retrieval problems that are usually not encountered in traditional database systems, such as

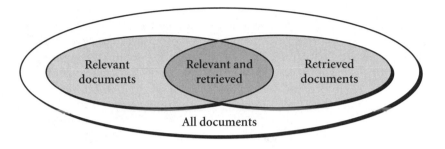

**Figure 9.8**  Relationship between the set of relevant documents and the set of retrieved documents.

unstructured documents, approximate search based on keywords, and the notion of relevance.

### Basic Measures for Text Retrieval

*"Suppose that a text retrieval system has just retrieved a number of documents for me based on my input in the form of a query. How can we assess how 'accurate' or 'correct' the system was?"* Let the set of documents relevant to a query be denoted as {*Relevant*}, and the set of documents retrieved be denoted as {*Retrieved*}. The set of documents that are both relevant and retrieved is denoted as {*Relevant*} ∩ {*Retrieved*}, as shown in the Venn diagram of Figure 9.8. There are two basic measures for assessing the quality of text retrieval:

- **Precision:** This is the percentage of retrieved documents that are in fact relevant to the query (i.e., "correct" responses). It is formally defined as

$$precision = \frac{|\{Relevant\} \cap \{Retrieved\}|}{|\{Retrieved\}|}. \tag{9.4}$$

- **Recall:** This is the percentage of documents that are relevant to the query and were, in fact, retrieved. It is formally defined as

$$recall = \frac{|\{Relevant\} \cap \{Retrieved\}|}{|\{Relevant\}|}. \tag{9.5}$$

### Keyword-Based and Similarity-Based Retrieval

*"What methods are there for information retrieval?"* Most information retrieval systems support *keyword-based* and/or *similarity-based* retrieval. In **keyword-based information retrieval**, a document is represented by a string, which can be identified by a set of keywords. A user provides a keyword or an expression formed out of a set of keywords, such as *"car **and** repair shops"*, *"tea **or** coffee"*, or *"database systems **but not** Oracle"*. A good information retrieval system should

consider synonyms when answering such queries. For example, given the keyword *car*, synonyms such as *automobile* and *vehicle* should be considered in the search as well. Keyword-based retrieval is a simple model that can encounter two major difficulties. The first is the **synonymy problem**: a keyword, such as *software product*, may not appear anywhere in the document, even though the document is closely related to *software product*. The second is the **polysemy problem**: the same keyword, such as *mining*, may mean different things in different contexts.

**Similarity-based retrieval** finds similar documents based on a set of common keywords. The output of such retrieval should be based on the *degree of relevance*, where relevance is measured based on the closeness of the keywords, the relative frequency of the keywords, and so on. Notice that in many cases, it is difficult to provide a precise measure of the degree of relevance between a set of keywords, such as the distance between *data mining* and *data analysis*.

*"How do keyword-based and similarity-based information retrieval systems work?"* A text retrieval system often associates a *stop list* with a set of documents. A **stop list** is a set of words that are deemed "irrelevant." For example, *a*, *the*, *of*, *for*, *with*, and so on are **stop words** even though they may appear frequently. Stop lists may vary when the document sets vary. For example, *database systems* could be an important keyword in a newspaper. However, it may be considered as a stop word in a set of research papers presented in a database systems conference.

A group of different words may share the same **word stem**. A text retrieval system needs to identify groups of words where the words in a group are small syntactic variants of one another, and collect only the common word stem per group. For example, the group of words *drug, drugged*, and *drugs*, share a common word stem, *drug*, and can be viewed as different occurrences of the same word.

*"How can we model a document to facilitate information retrieval?"* Starting with a set of $d$ documents and a set of $t$ terms, we can model each document as a vector $v$ in the $t$ dimensional space $\mathcal{R}^t$. The $j$th coordinate of $v$ is a number that measures the association of the $j$th term with respect to the given document: it is generally defined as 0 if the document does not contain the term, and nonzero otherwise. There are many ways to define the term-weighting for the nonzero entries in such a vector. For example, we can simply define $v_j = 1$ as long as the $j$th term occurs in the document, or let $v_j$ be the **term frequency**, that is, the number of occurrences of term $t_i$ in the document, or the **relative term frequency**, that is, the term frequency versus the total number of occurrences of all the terms in the document.

**Example 9.11** **A term frequency matrix:** In Table 9.5, each row represents a term, each column represents a document vector, and each entry, *frequency_matrix*$(i, j)$, registers the number of occurrences of term $t_i$ in document $d_j$. ∎

*"How can we determine if two documents are similar?"* Since similar documents are expected to have similar relative term frequencies, we can measure the similarity among a set of documents or between a document and a query (often defined

**Table 9.5**  A term frequency matrix showing the frequency of terms per document.

| Term/document | $d_1$ | $d_2$ | $d_3$ | $d_4$ | $d_5$ | $d_6$ | $d_7$ |
|---|---|---|---|---|---|---|---|
| $t_1$ | 321 | 84 | 31 | 68 | 72 | 15 | 430 |
| $t_2$ | 354 | 91 | 71 | 56 | 82 | 6 | 392 |
| $t_3$ | 15 | 32 | 167 | 46 | 289 | 225 | 17 |
| $t_4$ | 22 | 143 | 72 | 203 | 51 | 15 | 54 |
| $t_5$ | 74 | 87 | 85 | 92 | 25 | 54 | 121 |

as a set of keywords), based on similar relative term occurrences in the frequency table.

Alternatively, many metrics have been proposed for measuring document similarity. A representative metric is the **cosine measure**, defined as follows. Let $v_1$ and $v_2$ be two document vectors. Their cosine similarity is defined as

$$sim(v_1, v_2) = \frac{v_1 \cdot v_2}{|v_1||v_2|}, \tag{9.6}$$

where the inner product $v_1 \cdot v_2$ is the standard vector dot product, defined as $\Sigma_{i=1}^{t} v_{1i} v_{2i}$, and the norm $|v_1|$ in the denominator is defined as $|v_1| = \sqrt{v_1 \cdot v_1}$.

"*How can we use the similarity metrics?*" With the use of numeric similarity metrics for documents, we can construct similarity-based indices on such documents. Text-based queries can then be represented as vectors, which can be used to search for their nearest neighbors in a document collection. However, for any nontrivial document database, the number of terms $T$ and the number of documents $D$ are usually quite large. Such high dimensionality leads to the problem of inefficient computation, since the resulting frequency table will have size $T \times D$. Furthermore, the high dimensionality also leads to very sparse vectors and increases the difficulty in detecting and exploiting the relationships among terms (e.g., synonymy). To overcome these problems, a *latent semantic indexing* method has been developed that effectively reduces the size of the frequency table for analysis.

### Latent Semantic Indexing

"*How does latent semantic indexing reduce the size of the term frequency matrix?*" The **latent semantic indexing** method uses *singular value decomposition (SVD)*, a well-known technique in matrix theory, to reduce the size of the term frequency matrix. Given a $T \times D$ term frequency matrix representing $T$ terms and $D$ documents, the SVD method removes rows and columns to reduce the matrix to size $K \times K$, where $K$ is usually taken to be around a few hundred (e.g., 200) for large document collections. To minimize the amount of information loss, only the least significant parts of the frequency matrix are omitted.

The method for matrix transformation by SVD construction is rather sophisticated and is beyond the scope of this chapter. However, well-known SVD algorithms are available freely through software packages such as MATLAB (*www.mathworks.com*) and LAPACK (*www.netlib.org/lapack++*).

In general, the latent semantic indexing method consists of the following basic steps:

**1.** Create a term frequency matrix, *frequency_matrix*.

**2.** Compute singular valued decompositions of *frequency_matrix* by splitting the matrix into three smaller matrices, $U$, $S$, $V$, where $U$ and $V$ are orthogonal matrices (i.e., $U^T U = I$), and $S$ is a diagonal matrix of singular values. Matrix $S$ is of size $K \times K$ and is the reduced version of the original frequency matrix.

**3.** For each document $d$, replace its original document vector by a new one that excludes the terms eliminated during SVD.

**4.** Store the set of all vectors, and create indices for them using advanced multidimensional indexing techniques.

By singular value decomposition and multidimensional indexing, the transformed document vectors can be used to compare the similarity between two documents or to find the top $N$ matches for a query.

### Other Text Retrieval Indexing Techniques

There are several other popularly adopted text retrieval indexing techniques, including *inverted indices* and *signature files*.

An **inverted index** is an index structure that maintains two hash indexed or B+-tree indexed tables: *document_table* and *term_table*, where

- *document_table* consists of a set of document records, each containing two fields: *doc_id* and *posting_list*, where *posting_list* is a list of terms (or pointers to terms) that occur in the document, sorted according to some relevance measure.

- *term_table* consists of a set of term records, each containing two fields: *term_id* and *posting_list*, where *posting_list* specifies a list of document identifiers in which the term appears.

With such organization, it is easy to answer queries like "*Find all of the documents associated with a given set of terms*", or "*Find all of the terms associated with a given set of documents*". For example, to find all of the documents associated with a set of terms, we can first find a list of document identifiers in *term_table* for each term, and then intersect them to obtain the set of relevant documents. Inverted indices are widely used in industry. They are easy to implement, but are not satisfactory at handling synonymy and polysemy. The *posting_list*s could be rather long, making the storage requirement quite large.

A **signature file** is a file that stores a *signature* record for each document in the database. Each signature has a fixed size of *b* bits representing terms. A simple encoding scheme goes as follows. Each bit of a document signature is initialized to 0. A bit is set to 1 if the term it represents appears in the document. A signature $S_1$ matches another signature $S_2$ if each bit that is set in signature $S_2$ is also set in $S_1$. Since there are usually more terms than available bits, there may be multiple terms mapped into the same bit. Such multiple-to-one mappings make the search expensive since a document that matches the signature of a query does not necessarily contain the set of keywords of the query. The document has to be retrieved, parsed, stemmed, and checked. Improvements can be made by first performing frequency analysis, stemming, and by filtering stop words, and then using a hashing technique and superimposed coding technique to encode the list of terms into bit representation. Nevertheless, the problem of multiple-to-one mappings still exists, which is the major disadvantage of this approach.

## 9.5.2 Text Mining: Keyword-Based Association and Document Classification

*"What about mining associations in text databases? Can we also generate document classification schemes?"* This subsection addresses both of these questions.

### Keyword-Based Association Analysis

*"What is keyword-based association analysis?"* Such analysis collects sets of keywords or terms that occur frequently together and then finds the association or correlation relationships among them.

Like most of the analyses in text databases, association analysis first preprocesses the text data by parsing, stemming, removing stop words, and so on, and then evokes association mining algorithms. In a document database, each document can be viewed as a transaction, while a set of keywords in the document can be considered as a set of items in the transaction. That is, the database is in the format

{*document_id, a_set_of_keywords*}.

The problem of keyword association mining in document databases is thereby mapped to item association mining in transaction databases, where many interesting methods have been developed, as described in Chapter 6.

Notice that a set of frequently occurring consecutive or closely located keywords may form a *term* or a *phrase*. The association mining process can help detect *compound associations*, that is, domain-dependent terms or phrases, such as [Stanford, University] or [U.S., president, Bill, Clinton], or *noncompound associations*, such as [dollars, shares, exchange, total, commission, stake, securities].

Mining based on these associations is referred to as "term *level* association mining" (as opposed to mining on individual words). Term recognition and term level association mining enjoy two advantages in text analysis: (1) terms and phrases are automatically tagged so that there is no need for human effort in tagging documents, and (2) the number of meaningless results is greatly reduced, as is the execution time of the mining algorithms.

With such term and phrase recognition, term level mining can be evoked to find associations among a set of detected terms and keywords. Some users may like to find associations between pairs of keywords or terms from a given set of keywords or phrases, whereas others may wish to find the maximal set of terms occurring together. Therefore, based on user mining requirements, standard association mining or max-pattern mining algorithms may be evoked.

## Document Classification Analysis

Automated document classification is an important text mining task since, with the existence of a tremendous number of on-line documents, it is tedious yet essential to be able to automatically organize such documents into classes so as to facilitate document retrieval and subsequent analysis.

*"How can automated document classification be performed?"* A general procedure is as follows: First, a set of preclassified documents is taken as the training set. The training set is then analyzed in order to derive a classification scheme. Such a classification scheme often needs to be refined with a testing process. The so-derived classification scheme can be used for classification of other on-line documents.

This process appears similar to the classification of relational data. However, there is a fundamental difference. Relational data are well structured: each tuple is defined by a set of attribute-value pairs. For example, in the tuple {*sunny*, *warm*, *dry*, *not_windy*, *play_tennis*}, the value "*sunny*" corresponds to the attribute *weather_outlook*, "*warm*" corresponds to the attribute *temperature*, and so on. The classification analysis decides which set of attribute-value pairs has the greatest discriminating power in determining whether or not a person is going to play tennis. On the other hand, document databases are not structured according to attribute-value pairs. That is, a set of keywords associated with a set of documents is not organized into a fixed set of attributes or dimensions. Therefore, commonly used relational data-oriented classification methods, such as decision tree analysis, cannot be used to classify document databases.

An effective method for document classification is to explore association-based classification, which classifies documents based on a set of associated, frequently occurring text patterns. Such an association-based classification method proceeds as follows: First, keywords and terms can be extracted by information retrieval and simple association analysis techniques. Second, concept hierarchies of keywords and terms can be obtained using available term classes, such as WordNet, or relying on expert knowledge, or some keyword classification systems. Documents in the training set can also be classified into class hierarchies. A term association mining method can then be applied to discover sets of associated terms that can be used to maximally distinguish one class of documents from others. This derives a set of association rules associated with each document class. Such classification rules can be ordered based on their occurrence frequency and discriminative power, and used to classify new documents. Such a kind of association-based document classifier has been proven effective. For Web document classification, the Web page linkage information can be used to further assist the identification of document classes. Web linkage analysis methods are discussed in the next section.

## 9.6 Mining the World Wide Web

The World Wide Web serves as a huge, widely distributed, global information service center for news, advertisements, consumer information, financial management, education, government, e-commerce, and many other information services. The Web also contains a rich and dynamic collection of hyperlink information and Web page access and usage information, providing rich sources for data mining. However, based on the following observations, the Web also poses great challenges for effective resource and knowledge discovery.

- *The Web seems to be too huge for effective data warehousing and data mining.* The size of the Web is in the order of hundreds of terabytes and is still growing rapidly. Many organizations and societies put most of their public accessible information on the Web. It is barely possible to set up a data warehouse to replicate, store, or integrate all of the data on the Web.[5]

- *The complexity of Web pages is far greater than that of any traditional text document collection.* Web pages lack a unifying structure. They contain far more authoring style and content variations than any set of books or other traditional text-based documents. The Web is considered a huge digital library; however, the tremendous number of documents in this library are not arranged according to any particular sorted order. There is no index by category, nor by title, author, cover page, table of contents, and so on. It can be very challenging to search for the information you desire in such a library!

- *The Web is a highly dynamic information source.* Not only does the Web grow at a rapid pace, its information is also constantly updated. News, stock markets, company advertisements, and Web service centers update their Web pages regularly. Linkage information and access records are also updated frequently.

---

[5] Recently, there have been efforts to store or integrate all of the data on the Web. For example, a huge Internet archive in the order of tens of terabytes can be accessed at *http://www.archive.org/index1 .html*.

■ *The Web serves a broad diversity of user communities.* The Internet currently connects about 50 million workstations, and its user community is still expanding rapidly. Users may have very different backgrounds, interests, and usage purposes. Most users may not have good knowledge of the structure of the information network, may not be aware of the heavy cost of a particular search, may easily get lost by groping in the "darkness" of the network, and may easily get bored by taking many access "hops" and waiting impatiently for a piece of information.

■ *Only a small portion of the information on the Web is truly relevant or useful.* It is said that 99% of the Web information is useless to 99% of Web users. Although this may not seem obvious, it is true that a particular person is generally interested in only a tiny portion of the Web, while the rest of the Web contains information that is uninteresting to the user and may swamp desired search results. How can the portion of the Web that is truly relevant to your interest be determined? How can we find high-quality Web pages on a specified topic?

These challenges have promoted research into efficient and effective discovery and use of resources on the Internet.

There are many index-based **Web search engines** that search the Web, index Web pages, and build and store huge keyword-based indices that help locate sets of Web pages containing certain keywords. With such search engines, an experienced user may be able to quickly locate documents by providing a set of tightly constrained keywords and phrases. However, current keyword-based search engines suffer from several deficiencies. First, a topic of any breadth may easily contain hundreds of thousands of documents. This can lead to a huge number of document entries returned by a search engine, many of which are only marginally relevant to the topic or may contain materials of poor quality. Second, many documents that are highly relevant to a topic may not contain keywords defining them. This is referred to as the *polysemy* problem, discussed in the previous section on text mining. For example, the keyword *data mining* may turn up many Web pages related to other mining industries, yet fail to identify relevant papers on knowledge discovery, statistical analysis, or machine learning because they did not contain the keyword *data mining*. As another example, a search based on the keyword *search engine* may not find even the most popular Web search engines like Yahoo!, AltaVista, or America On-Line if these services do not claim to be search engines on their Web pages. This indicates that the current Web search engines are not sufficient for Web resource discovery.

*"If Web search engines are not sufficient for Web resource discovery, how can we even think of doing Web mining?"* **Web mining** is an even more challenging task that searches for Web access patterns, Web structures, and the regularity and dynamics of Web contents. In general, Web mining tasks can be classified into three categories: *Web content mining*, *Web structure mining*, and *Web usage*

*mining*. Alternatively, Web structures can be treated as a part of Web contents so that Web mining can instead be simply classified into *Web content mining* and *Web usage mining*.

In the following subsections, we discuss several important issues related to Web mining: *mining the Web's link structures* (Section 9.6.1), *automatic classification of Web documents* (Section 9.6.2), *building a multilayered Web information base* (Section 9.6.3), and *Weblog mining* (Section 9.6.4).

## 9.6.1 Mining the Web's Link Structures to Identify Authoritative Web Pages

*"What is meant by 'authoritative' Web pages?"* Suppose you would like to search for Web pages relating to a given topic, such as financial investing. In addition to retrieving pages that are relevant, you also hope that the pages retrieved will be of high quality, or *authoritative* on the topic.

*"But how can a search engine automatically identify authoritative Web pages for my topic?"* Interestingly, the secrecy of authority is hiding in Web page linkages. The Web consists not only of pages, but also of *hyperlinks* pointing from one page to another. These hyperlinks contain an enormous amount of latent human annotation that can help to automatically infer the notion of authority. When an author of a Web page creates a hyperlink pointing to another Web page, this can be considered as the author's endorsement of the other page. The collective endorsement of a given page by different authors on the Web may indicate the importance of the page and may naturally lead to the discovery of authoritative Web pages. Therefore, the tremendous amount of Web linkage information provides rich information about the relevance, the quality, and the structure of the Web's contents, and thus is a rich source for Web mining.

This idea has motivated some interesting studies on mining authoritative pages on the Web. In the 1970s, researchers in information retrieval proposed methods of using citations among journal articles to evaluate the quality of research papers. However, unlike journal citations, the Web linkage structure has some unique features. First, not every hyperlink represents the endorsement we seek. Some links are created for other purposes, such as for navigation or for paid advertisements. Yet overall, if the majority of hyperlinks are for endorsement, the collective opinion will still dominate. Second, for commercial or competitive interests, one authority will seldom have its Web page point to its rival authorities in the same field. For example, *CocaCola* may prefer not to endorse its competitor *Pepsi* by not linking to *Pepsi*'s Web pages. Third, authoritative pages are seldom particularly descriptive. For example, the main Web page of Yahoo! may not contain the explicit self-description *"Web search engine"*.

These properties of Web link structures have led researchers to consider another important category of Web pages called a *hub*. A **hub** is one or a set of Web pages that provides collections of links to authorities. Hub pages may not be prominent themselves, or there may exist few links pointing to them; however, they provide links to a collection of prominent sites on a common topic. Such pages could be lists of recommended links on individual home pages, such as recommended reference sites from a course home page, or professionally assembled resource lists on commercial sites. Hub pages play the role of implicitly conferring authorities on a focused topic. In general, a good hub is a page that points to many good authorities; a good authority is a page pointed to by many good hubs. Such a mutual reinforcement relationship between hubs and authorities helps the mining of authoritative Web pages and automated discovery of high-quality Web structures and resources.

"*So, how can we use hub pages to find authoritative pages?*" An algorithm using hubs, called HITS (Hyperlink-Induced Topic Search), was developed as follows.

First, HITS uses the query terms to collect a starting set of, say, 200 pages from an index-based search engine. These pages form the **root set**. Since many of these pages are presumably relevant to the search topic, some of them should contain links to most of the prominent authorities. Therefore, the root set can be expanded into a **base set** by including all of the pages that the root-set pages link to, and all of the pages that link to a page in the root set, up to a designated size cutoff, such as 1000 to 5000 pages (to be included in the base set).

Second, a weight-propagation phase is initiated. This is an iterative process that determines numerical estimates of hub and authority weights. Notice that since the links between two pages with the same Web domain (i.e., sharing the same first level in their URLs) often serve as a navigation function and thus do not confer authority, such links are excluded from the weight-propagation analysis.

We first associate a nonnegative **authority weight** $a_p$ and a nonnegative **hub weight** $h_p$ with each page $p$ in the base set, and initialize all $a$ and $h$ values to a uniform constant. The weights are normalized and an invariant is maintained that the squares of all weights sum to 1. The authority and hub weights are updated based on the following equations:

$$a_p = \sum_{(q \text{ such that } q \rightarrow p)} h_q \tag{9.7}$$

$$h_p = \sum_{(q \text{ such that } q \leftarrow p)} a_q \tag{9.8}$$

Equation (9.7) implies that if a page is pointed to by many good hubs, its authority weight should increase (i.e., it is the sum of the current hub weights of all of the pages pointing to it). Equation (9.8) implies that if a page is pointing to many good authorities, its hub weight should increase (i.e., it is the sum of the current authority weights of all of the pages it points to).

These equations can be written in matrix form as follows. Let us number the pages $\{1, 2, \ldots, n\}$ and define their **adjacency matrix** $A$ to be an $n \times n$ matrix where $A(i, j)$ is 1 if page $i$ links to page $j$, or 0 otherwise. Similarly, we define the **authority weight vector** $a = (a_1, a_2, \ldots, a_n)$, and the **hub weight vector** $h = (h_1, h_2, \ldots, h_n)$. Thus, we have

$$h = A \cdot a \tag{9.9}$$

$$a = A^T \cdot h \tag{9.10}$$

where $A^T$ is the transposition of matrix $A$. Unfolding these two equations $k$ times, we have

$$h = A \cdot a = AA^T h = (AA^T)h = (AA^T)^2 h = \cdots = (AA^T)^k h \tag{9.11}$$

$$a = A^T \cdot h = A^T A a = (A^T A)a = (A^T A)^2 a = \cdots = (A^T A)^k a \tag{9.12}$$

According to linear algebra, these two sequences of iterations, when normalized, converge to the principal eigenvectors of $AA^T$ and $A^T A$, respectively. This also proves that the authority and hub weights are intrinsic features of the linked pages collected, and are not influenced by the initial weight settings.

Finally, the HITS algorithm outputs a short list of the pages with large hub weights, and the pages with large authority weights for the given search topic. Many experiments have shown that HITS provides surprisingly good search results for a wide range of queries.

Although relying extensively on links can lead to encouraging results, the method may encounter some difficulties by ignoring textual contexts. For example, HITS sometimes drifts when hubs contain multiple topics. It may also cause "topic hijacking" when many pages from a single Web site point to the same single popular site, giving the site too large a share of the authority weight. Such problems can be overcome by replacing the sums of Equations (9.7) and (9.8) with weighted sums, scaling down the weights of multiple links from within the same site, using *anchor text* (the text surrounding hyperlink definitions in Web pages) to adjust the weight of the links along which authority is propagated, and breaking large hub pages into smaller units.

Systems based on the HITS algorithm include Clever and another system, Google, based on a similar principle. By analyzing Web links and textual context information, it has been reported that such systems can achieve better quality search results than those generated by term-index engines such as AltaVista and those created by human ontologists such as Yahoo!.

## 9.6.2 Automatic Classification of Web Documents

In the automatic classification of Web documents, each document is assigned a class label from a set of predefined topic categories, based on a set of examples of preclassified documents. For example, Yahoo!'s taxonomy and its associated documents can be used as training and test sets in order to derive a Web document classification scheme. This scheme may then be used to classify new Web documents by assigning categories from the same taxonomy.

Keyword-based document classification methods were discussed in Section 9.5.2, as well as keyword-based association analysis. These methods can be used for Web document classification. Such a term-based classification scheme has shown good results in Web page classification. Since hyperlinks contain high-quality semantic clues to a page's topic, it is beneficial to make good use of such semantic information in order to achieve even better accuracy than pure keyword-based classification. However, since the hyperlinks surrounding a document may be quite noisy, naive use of terms in a documents' hyperlink neighborhood can even *degrade* accuracy. The use of robust statistical models such as Markov random fields (MRFs), together with relaxation labeling, has been explored. Such a method has experimentally been shown to substantially improve the accuracy of Web document classification.

### 9.6.3 Construction of a Multilayered Web Information Base

As discussed in Chapter 2, a data warehouse can be constructed from a relational database to provide a multidimensional, hierarchical view of the data.

*"Can we construct a multilayered Web information base to provide a multidimensional, hierarchical view of the Web?"* you may wonder. Let us try to design such a multilayered Web information base to see whether it is realistic or beneficial.

First, it is unrealistic to create a Web warehouse containing a copy of every page on the Web, since this would just lead to a huge, duplicated WWW. This indicates that the bottom (most detailed) layer of such a multilayered Web information base must be the Web itself. It cannot be a separate warehouse. We will refer to this layer as *layer-0*.

Second, we can define *layer-1* to be the *Web page descriptor layer*, containing descriptive information for pages on the Web. Hence, *layer-1* is an abstraction of *layer-0*. It should be substantially smaller than *layer-0* but still rich enough to preserve most of the interesting, general information for keyword-based or multidimensional search or mining.

Based on the variety of Web page contents, *layer-1* can be organized into dozens of semistructured classes, such as *document, person, organization, advertisement, directory, sales, software, game, stocks, library_catalog, geographic_data, scientific_data*, and so on. For example, we may define class *document* as follows:

- **document**(*file_addr, doc_category, authoritative_rank, key_words, authors, title, publication, publication_date, abstract, language, table_of_contents, category_description, index, links_out, multimedia_attached, num_pages, form, size_doc, time_stamp, . . . , access_frequency*), where each entry is an abstraction of a *document* Web page. The first attribute, *file_addr*, registers the file name and the URL network address. The attributes *doc_category* and *authoritative_rank* contain crucial information that may be obtained by Web linkage analysis and document classification methods, as discussed in the previous two subsections. Many of the attributes contain major semantic information related to the document, such as *key_words, authors, title, publication, publication_date, abstract, language, table_of_contents, index, links_out, multimedia_attached*, and *num_pages*. Other attributes provide formatting information, such as *form*, which indicates the file format (e.g., .ps, .pdf, .tex, .doc, .html, text, compressed, uuencoded, etc.). Several attributes register information directly associated with the file, such as *size_doc* (size of the document file) and *time_stamp* (time last modified). The attribute *access_frequency* registers how frequently the entry is being accessed.

Third, various *higher-layer* Web directory services can be constructed on top of *layer-1* in order to provide multidimensional, application-specific services. For example, we may construct yellow page services for database-system-oriented research. Such a directory may contain hierarchical structures for a few dimensions, such as theme category, geographical location, date of publication, and so on.

*"Do we really want to include information about* every *Web page?"* Using Web page ranking and page or document classification services, we can choose to retain only the information necessary for relatively high-quality, highly relevant Web pages in the construction of *layer-1* and/or higher layers of the information base.

With the popular acceptance and adoption of the structured Web page markup language, XML, it is expected that a large number of future Web pages will be written in XML and possibly share a good set of common DTDs (Document Type Declarations).[6] Standardization with a language such as XML would greatly facilitate information exchange among different Web sites and information extraction for the construction of a multilayered Web information base. Furthermore, Web-based information search and knowledge discovery languages can be designed and implemented for such a purpose.

In summary, based on the above, it should be possible to construct a multi-layered Web information base to facilitate resource discovery, multidimensional analysis, and data mining on the Internet. It is expected that Web-based multidimensional analysis and data mining will form an important part of Internet-based information services.

## 9.6.4 Web Usage Mining

*"What is Web usage mining?"* Besides mining Web contents and Web linkage structures, another important task for Web mining is **Web usage mining**, which

---

[6] A DTD is a set of rules or "grammar" for the specification of elements, attributes, and entities. It indicates what tags are allowed, in what order they can appear, and how they can be nested.

mines Web log records to discover user access patterns of Web pages. Analyzing and exploring regularities in Web log records can identify potential customers for electronic commerce, enhance the quality and delivery of Internet information services to the end user, and improve Web server system performance.

A Web server usually registers a (Web) log entry, or **Weblog entry**, for every access of a Web page. It includes the URL requested, the IP address from which the request originated, and a timestamp. For Web-based e-commerce servers, a huge number of Web access log records are being collected. Popular Web sites may register the Weblog records in the order of hundreds of megabytes every day. Weblog databases provide rich information about Web dynamics. Thus it is important to develop sophisticated Weblog mining techniques.

In developing techniques for Web usage mining, we may consider the following. First, although it is encouraging and exciting to imagine the various potential applications of Weblog file analysis, it is important to know that the success of such applications depends on what and how much valid and reliable knowledge can be discovered from the large raw log data. Often, raw Weblog data need to be *cleaned, condensed, and transformed* in order to retrieve and analyze significant and useful information. In principle, these preprocessing methods are similar to those discussed in Chapter 3, although Weblog customized preprocessing is often needed.

Second, with the available URL, time, IP address, and Web page content information, a multidimensional view can be constructed on the Weblog database, and *multidimensional OLAP analysis* can be performed to find the top $N$ users, top $N$ accessed Web pages, most frequently accessed time periods, and so on, which will help discover potential customers, users, markets, and others.

Third, *data mining* can be performed on Weblog records to find association patterns, sequential patterns, and trends of Web accessing. For Web access pattern mining, it is often necessary to take further measures to obtain additional information of user traversal to facilitate detailed Weblog analysis. Such additional information may include user browsing sequences of the Web pages in the Web server buffer, and so on.

With the use of such Weblog files, studies have been conducted on analyzing system performance, improving system design by Web caching, Web page prefetching, and Web page swapping; understanding the nature of Web traffic; and understanding user reaction and motivation. For example, some studies have proposed adaptive sites: Web sites that improve themselves by learning from user access patterns. Weblog analysis may also help build customized Web services for individual users.

Since Weblog data provide information about what kind of users will access what kind of Web pages, Weblog information can be integrated with Web content and Web linkage structure mining to help Web page ranking, Web document classification, and the construction of a multilayered Web information base as well.

# 9.7 Summary

- Vast amounts of data are stored in various complex forms, such as structured or unstructured, hypertext, and multimedia. Thus, **mining complex types of data**, including *object data, spatial data, multimedia data, time-series data, text data*, and *Web data*, has become an increasingly important task in data mining.

- Multidimensional analysis and data mining can be performed in **object-relational and object-oriented databases**, by (1) *class-based generalization of complex objects*, including set-valued, list-valued, and other sophisticated types of data, class/subclass hierarchies, and class composition hierarchies; (2) constructing *object data cubes*; and (3) performing *generalization-based mining*. A **plan database** can be mined by a generalization-based, divide-and-conquer approach in order to find interesting general patterns at different levels of abstraction.

- **Spatial data mining** is the discovery of interesting patterns from large geospatial databases. *Spatial data cubes* that contain spatial dimensions and measures can be constructed. *Spatial OLAP* can be implemented to facilitate *multidimensional spatial data analysis*. Spatial data mining includes *spatial data description, classification, association, clustering*, and *spatial trend and outlier analysis*.

- **Multimedia data mining** is the discovery of interesting patterns from multimedia databases that store and manage large collections of multimedia objects, including audio data, image data, video data, sequence data, and hypertext data containing text, text markups, and linkages. Issues in multimedia data mining studies include *content-based retrieval and similarity search, generalization and multidimensional analysis, classification and prediction analysis*, and *mining associations* in multimedia data.

- A time-series database consists of sequences of values or events changing with time, such as stock market data, business transaction sequences, dynamic production processes, medical treatments, Web page access sequences, and so on. Research into **time-series and sequence data mining** covers issues on *trend analysis, similarity search in time-series analysis*, and *mining sequential patterns and periodic patterns in time-related data*.

- A substantial portion of the available information is stored in text or document databases that consist of large collections of documents, such as news articles, technical papers, books, digital libraries, e-mail messages, and Web pages. Text data mining has thus become increasingly important. **Text mining** goes one step beyond keyword-based and similarity-based information retrieval and discovers knowledge from semistructured text data using methods such as *keyword-based association* and *document classification*.

- The World Wide Web serves as a huge, widely distributed, global information service center for news, advertisements, consumer information, financial management, education, government, e-commerce, and many other services. It also contains a rich and dynamic collection of hyperlink information, and access and usage information, providing rich sources for data mining. **Web mining** includes mining *Web linkage structures, Web contents*, and *Web access patterns*. This involves mining Web link structures to identify *authoritative Web pages*, the *automatic classification* of Web documents, building a *multilayered Web information base*, and *Weblog mining*.

## Exercises

**9.1** A *heterogeneous database system* consists of multiple database systems that are defined independently, but that need to exchange and transform information among themselves and answer local and global queries. Discuss how to process a descriptive mining query in such a system using a generalization-based approach.

**9.2** An *object cube* can be constructed by generalization of an object-oriented database into relatively structured data prior to performing multidimensional generalization. Discuss how to handle set-oriented data in an object cube.

**9.3** *Spatial association mining* can be implemented in at least two ways: (1) dynamic computation of spatial association relationships among different spatial objects, based on the mining query, and (2) precomputation of spatial distances between spatial objects, where the association mining is based on such precomputed results. Discuss (1) how to implement each approach efficiently, and (2) which approach is preferable under what situation.

**9.4** Suppose that a city transportation department would like to perform data analysis on highway traffic for the planning of highway construction based on the city traffic data collected at different hours every day.

(a) Design a spatial data warehouse that stores the highway traffic information so that people can easily see the average and peak time traffic flow by highway, by time of day, and by weekdays, and the traffic situation when a major accident occurs.

(b) What information can we mine from such a spatial data warehouse to help city planners?

(c) This data warehouse contains both spatial and temporal data. Propose one mining technique that can efficiently mine interesting patterns from such a spatio-temporal data warehouse.

**9.5** *Similarity search in multimedia* has been a major theme in developing multimedia data retrieval systems. However, many *multimedia data mining* methods are based on the analysis of isolated simple multimedia features, such as color, shape, description, keywords, and so on.

(a) Can you show that an integration of similarity-based search with data mining may bring important progress in multimedia data mining? You may take any one mining task, such as multidimensional analysis, classification, association, or clustering, as an example.

(b) Outline an implementation technique that applies a similarity-based search method to enhance the quality of clustering in multimedia data.

**9.6** Suppose that a power station stores data about power consumption levels by time and by region, and power usage information per customer in each region. Discuss how to solve the following problems in such a *time-series database*.

(a) Find similar power consumption curve fragments for a given region on Fridays.

(b) Every time a power consumption curve rises sharply, what may happen within 20 minutes?

(c) How can we find the most influential features that distinguish a stable power consumption region from an unstable one?

**9.7** Suppose that a chain restaurant would like to mine customers' consumption behavior related to major sport events, such as *"Every time there is a Canucks hockey game on TV, the sales of Kentucky Fried Chicken will go up 20% one hour before the match"*.

(a) Describe a method to find such patterns efficiently.

(b) Most time-related association mining algorithms use Apriori-like algorithms to mine such patterns. An alternative database projection-based frequent-pattern (FP) growth method, introduced in Section 6.2.4, is efficient at mining frequent itemsets. Can you extend the FP-growth method to find such time-related patterns efficiently?

**9.8** An *e-mail database* is a database that stores a large number of electronic mail (e-mail) messages. It can be viewed as a semistructured database consisting mainly of text data. Discuss the following.

(a) How can such an e-mail database be structured so as to facilitate multidimensional search, such as by sender, by receiver, by subject, by time, and so on?

(b) What can be mined from such an e-mail database?

(c) Suppose you have roughly classified a set of your previous e-mail messages as *junk, unimportant, normal,* or *important.* Describe how a data mining system may take this as the training set to automatically classify new e-mail messages or unclassified ones.

**9.9** It is difficult to construct a global data warehouse for the World Wide Web due to its dynamic nature and the huge amounts of data stored in it. However, it is still interesting and useful to construct data warehouses for summarized, localized, multidimensional information on the Internet. Suppose that an Internet information service company would like to set up an Internet-based data warehouse to help tourists choose local hotels and restaurants.

(a) Can you design a Web-based tourist data warehouse that would facilitate such a service?

(b) Suppose each hotel and/or restaurant contains a Web page of its own. Discuss how to locate such Web pages, and what methods should be used to extract information from these Web pages in order to populate your Web-based tourist data warehouse.

(c) Discuss how to implement a mining method that may provide additional associated information, such as *"90% of customers who stay at the Downtown Hilton dine at the Emperor Garden Restaurant at least twice"*, each time a search returns a new Web page.

9.10 Each scientific or engineering discipline has its own subject index classification standard that is often used for classifying documents in its discipline.

(a) Design a Web document classification method that can take such a subject index to classify a set of Web documents automatically.

(b) Discuss how to use Web linkage information to improve the quality of such classification.

(c) Discuss how to use Web usage information to improve the quality of such classification.

9.11 Weblog records provide rich Web usage information for data mining.

(a) Mining Weblog access sequences may help prefetch certain Web pages into a Web server buffer such as those pages that are likely to be requested in the next several clicks. Design an efficient implementation method that may help mining such access sequences.

(b) Mining Weblog access records can help cluster users into separate groups to facilitate customized marketing. Discuss how to develop an efficient implementation method that may help user clustering.

## Bibliographic Notes

Mining complex types of data has been a fast developing, popular research field, with many research papers and tutorials appearing in conferences and journals on data mining and database systems. This chapter covers a few important themes, including multidimensional analysis and mining of complex data objects, spatial data mining, multimedia data mining, time-series and other time-related data mining, text mining, and Web mining.

Zaniolo, Ceri, Faloutsos, et al. [ZCF+97] present a systematic introduction of advanced database systems for handling complex types of data. For multidimensional analysis and mining of complex data objects, Han, Nishio, Kawano, and Wang [HNKW98] proposed a method for the design and construction of object cubes by multidimensional generalization and its use for mining complex types of data in object-oriented and object-relational databases. A method for the construction of multiple layered databases by generalization-based data mining techniques for handling semantic heterogeneity was proposed by Han, Ng, Fu, and Dao [HNFD98]. A generalization-based method for mining plan databases by divide-and-conquer was proposed by Han, Yang, and Kim [HYK99].

Some introductory materials about spatial database can be found in Maguire, Goodchild, and Rhind [MGR92], Güting [Güt94], and Egenhofer [Ege89]. For geospatial data mining, a comprehensive survey on spatial data mining methods can be found in Ester, Kriegel, and Sander [EKS97]. A collection of research contributions on geographic data mining and knowledge discovery are in Miller and Han [MH00]. Lu, Han, and Ooi [LHO93] proposed a generalization-based spatial data mining method by attribute-oriented induction. Ng and Han [NH94] proposed to perform descriptive spatial data analysis based on clustering results instead of on predefined concept hierarchies. Han, Stefanovic, and Koperski [HSK98] studied the problems associated with the design and construction of spatial data cubes. Zhou, Truffet, and Han proposed efficient polygon amalgamation methods for on-line multidimensional spatial analysis and spatial data mining [ZTH99]. Koperski and Han [KH95] proposed a progressive refinement method for mining spatial association rules. Knorr and Ng [KN96] presented a method for mining aggregate proximity relationships and commonalities in spatial databases. Spatial classification and trend analysis methods have been developed by Ester, Kriegel, Sander, and Xu [EKSX97] and Ester, Frommelt, Kriegel, and Sander [EFKS98]. A two-step method for classification of spatial data was proposed by Koperski, Han, and Stefanovic [KHS98]. Spatial clustering is a highly active area of recent research into geospatial data mining. For a detailed list of references on spatial clustering methods, please see the bibliographic notes of Chapter 8. A spatial data mining system prototype, GeoMiner, was developed by Han, Koperski, and Stefanovic [HKS97].

The theory and practice of multimedia database systems have been introduced in many textbooks and surveys, including Subramanian [Sub98] and Yu and Meng [YM97]. The IBM QBIC (Query by Image and Video Content) system was introduced by Flickner, Sawhney, Niblack, Ashley, et al. [FSN+95]. Faloutsos and Lin [FL95] developed a fast algorithm, FastMap, for indexing, data mining, and visualization of traditional and multimedia datasets. Natsev, Rastogi, and Shim [NRS99] developed WALRUS, a similarity retrieval algorithm for image databases that explores wavelet-based signatures with region-based granularity. Fayyad and Smyth [FS93] developed a classification method to analyze high-resolution radar images for identification of volcanoes on Venus. Fayyad, Djorgovski, and Weir [FDW96] applied decision tree methods to the classification of galaxies, stars, and other stellar objects in the Palomar Observatory Sky Survey (POSS-II) project. Stolorz and Dean [SD96] developed a data mining system, Quakefinder, for detecting earthquakes from remote sensing imagery. Zaïane, Han, and Zhu [ZHZ00] proposed a progressive deepening method for mining object and feature associations in large multimedia databases. A multimedia data mining system prototype, MultiMediaMiner, was developed by Zaïane, Han, Li, et al. [ZHL$^+$98].

Statistical methods for time-series analysis have been proposed and studied extensively in statistics, such as by Chatfield [Cha84] and by Shumway [Shu88]. Efficient similarity search in sequence databases was studied by Agrawal, Faloutsos, and Swami [AFS93]. A fast subsequence matching method in time-series databases was presented by Faloutsos, Ranganathan, and Manolopoulos [FRM94]. Agrawal, Lin, Sawhney, and Shim [ALSS95] developed a method for fast similarity search in the presence of noise, scaling, and translation in time-series databases. Language primitives for querying shapes of histories were proposed by Agrawal, Psaila, Wimmers, and Zait [APWZ95]. Other works on similarity-based search of time-series data include Rafiei and Mendelzon [RM97], Yi, Jagadish, and Faloutsos [YJF98], Park, Chu, Yoon, and Hsu [PCYH00], and Perng, Wang, Zhang, and Parker [PWZP00].

For mining sequential patterns, Agrawal and Srikant [AS95, SA96] developed an Apriori-like technique and a general sequential pattern mining algorithm, GSP. Mannila, Toivonen, and Verkamo [MTV97] consider frequent episodes in sequences, where episodes are essentially acyclic graphs of events whose edges specify the temporal before-and-after relationship but without timing-interval restrictions. Lu, Han, and Feng [LHF98] proposed intertransaction association rules, which are implication rules whose two sides are totally ordered episodes with timing-interval restrictions (on the events in the episodes and on the two sides). Bettini, Wang, and Jajodia [BWJ98] consider a generalization of intertransaction association rules. Özden, Ramaswamy, and Silberschatz [ORS98] studied methods for mining cyclic association rules. Sequence pattern mining for plan failures was proposed by Zaki, Lesh, and Ogihara [ZLO98]. A max-subpattern hit set method for mining partial periodicity was proposed by Han, Dong, and Yin [HDY99]. Garofalakis, Rastogi, and Shim [GRS99] proposed an efficient method for constraint-based mining of sequential patterns. Han, Pei, Mortazavi-Asl, et al. [HPMA$^+$00] developed an efficient sequential pattern mining method, FreeSpan, based on an approach of database projection and partitioned mining. Yi, Sidiropoulos, Johnson, Jagadish, et al. [YSJ$^+$00] introduced a method for online mining for coevolving time sequences.

Text data analysis has been studied extensively in information retrieval and text analysis, with many good textbooks and survey articles, such as Salton and McGill [SM83], Faloutsos [Fal85], Salton [Sal89], van Rijsbergen [vR90], Yu and Meng [YM97], Raghavan [Rag97], Subramanian [Sub98], and Kleinberg and Tomkins [KT99]. Recent information retrieval methods are systematically introduced in the book by Baeza-Yates and Riberio-Neto [BYRN99] The latent semantic indexing method for document similarity analysis was developed by Deerwester, Dumais, Furnas, et al. [DDF$^+$90]. The use of signature files is described in Tsichritzis and Christodoulakis [TC83]. Feldman and Hirsh [FH98] studied methods for mining association rules in text databases. A method for automated document classification based on association mining was proposed by Wang, Zhou, and Liew [WZL99].

There has been a lot of work on Web data modeling and Web query systems, such as W3QS by Konopnicki and Shmueli [KS95], WebSQL by Mendelzon, Mihaila, and Milo [MMM97], Lorel by Abiteboul, Quass, McHugh, et al. [AQM$^+$97], Weblog by Lakshmanan, Sadri, and Subramanian [LSS96], WebOQL by Arocena and Mendelzon [AM98], and NiagraCQ by Chen, DeWitt, Tian, and Wang [CDTW00]. Florescu, Levy, and Mendelzon [FLM98] present a comprehensive overview of research on Web databases.

Mining the Web's link structures to recognize authoritative Web pages was introduced by Chakrabarti, Dom, Kumar, et al. [CDK$^+$99] and Kleinberg and Tomkins [KT99]. The HITS algorithm was developed by Kleinberg [Kle99]. A page rank algorithm was developed by Brin and Page [BP98]. Web page classification was studied by Chakrabarti, Dom, and Indyk [CDI98] and Wang, Zhou, and Liew [WZL99]. A Web mining language, WebML, was proposed by Zaïane and Han [ZH98]. A multilayer database approach for constructing a Web warehouse was studied by Zaïane and Han [ZH95]. A tutorial survey on data mining for hypertext and the Web can be found in Chakrabarti [Cha00].

Web usage mining has been promoted and implemented by many industry firms. Automatic construction of adaptive Web sites based on learning from Weblog user access patterns was proposed by Perkowitz and Etzioni [PE99]. The use of Weblog access patterns for exploring Web usability was studied by Tauscher and Greenberg [TG97]. A research prototype system, WebLogMiner, was reported by Zaïane, Xin, and Han [ZXH98]. Srivastava, Cooley, Deshpande, and Tan [SCDT00] presented a survey of Web usage mining and its applications.

# Applications and Trends in Data Mining

*"What are some specific examples* of the use of data mining for applications in science and business? Where will data mining be in the future?" These are some of the questions you may have after reading the previous chapters of this book. In this final chapter, we discuss data mining applications and provide tips on what to consider when purchasing a data mining software system. Additional themes in data mining are described, such as visual and audio mining, statistical techniques for data mining, theoretical foundations of data mining, and intelligent query answering by the incorporation of data mining techniques. The social impacts of data mining and future trends are also discussed.

## 10.1 Data Mining Applications

In the previous chapters of this book, we have studied principles and methods for mining relational data, data warehouses, and complex types of data (including spatial data, multimedia data, time-series data, text data, and Web data). Since data mining is a young discipline with wide and diverse applications, there is still a nontrivial gap between general principles of data mining and domain-specific, effective data mining tools for particular applications. In this section, we examine a few application domains and discuss how customized data mining tools should be developed for such applications.

### 10.1.1 Data Mining for Biomedical and DNA Data Analysis

The past decade has seen an explosive growth in biomedical research, ranging from the development of new pharmaceuticals and advances in cancer therapies to the identification and study of the human genome by discovering large-scale sequencing patterns and gene functions. Since a great deal of biomedical research has focused on DNA data anlysis, we study this application here. Recent research in DNA analysis has led to the discovery of genetic causes for many diseases and disabilities, as well as the discovery of new medicines and approaches for disease diagnosis, prevention, and treatment.

An important focus in genome research is the study of DNA sequences since such sequences form the foundation of the genetic codes of all living organisms. All DNA sequences are comprised of four basic building blocks (called *nucleotides*): adenine (A), cytosine (C), guanine (G), and thymine (T). These four nucleotides are combined to form long sequences or chains that resemble a twisted ladder.

Human beings have around 100,000 genes. A gene is usually comprised of hundreds of individual nucleotides arranged in a particular order. There are almost an unlimited number of ways that the nucleotides can be ordered and sequenced to form distinct genes. It is challenging to identify particular gene sequence patterns that play roles in various diseases. Since many interesting sequential pattern analysis and similarity search techniques have been developed in data mining, data mining has become a powerful tool and contributes substantially to DNA analysis in the following ways.

**Semantic integration of heterogeneous, distributed genome databases:** Due to the highly distributed, uncontrolled generation and use of a wide variety of DNA data, the semantic integration of such heterogeneous and widely distributed genome databases becomes an important task for systematic and coordinated analysis of DNA databases. This has promoted the development of integrated data warehouses and distributed federated databases to store and manage the primary and derived genetic data. Data cleaning and data integration methods developed in data mining will help the integration of genetic data and the construction of data warehouses for genetic data analysis.

**Similarity search and comparison among DNA sequences:** We have studied similarity search methods in time-series data mining. One of the most important search problems in genetic analysis is similarity search and comparison among DNA sequences. Gene sequences isolated from diseased and healthy tissues can be compared to identify critical differences between the two classes of genes. This can be done by first retrieving the gene sequences from the two tissue classes, and then finding and comparing the frequently occurring patterns of each class. Usually, sequences occurring more frequently in the diseased samples than in the healthy samples might indicate the genetic factors of the disease; on the other hand, those occurring only more frequently in the healthy samples might indicate mechanisms that protect the body from the disease. Notice that although genetic analysis requires similarity search, the technique needed here is quite different from that used for time-series data. For example, data transformation methods such as scaling, normalization, and window stitching, which are popularly used in the analysis of time-series data, are ineffective for genetic data since such data are nonnumeric data and the precise interconnections between different kinds of nucleotides play an important role in their function. On the other hand, the analysis of frequent sequential patterns is important in the analysis of similarity and dissimilarity in genetic sequences.

**Association analysis: identification of co-occurring gene sequences:** Currently, many studies have focused on the comparison of one gene to another. However, most diseases are not triggered by a single gene but by a combination of genes acting together. Association analysis methods can be used to help determine the kinds of genes that are likely to co-occur in target samples. Such analysis would facilitate the discovery of groups of genes and the study of interactions and relationships between them.

**Path analysis: linking genes to different stages of disease development:** While a group of genes may contribute to a disease process, different genes may become active at different stages of the disease. If the sequence of genetic activities across the different stages of disease development can be identified, it may be possible to develop pharmaceutical interventions that target the different stages separately, therefore achieving more effective treatment of the disease. Such path analysis is expected to play an important role in genetic studies.

**Visualization tools and genetic data analysis:** Complex structures and sequencing patterns of genes are most effectively presented in graphs, trees, cuboids, and chains by various kinds of visualization tools. Such visually appealing structures and patterns facilitate pattern understanding, knowledge discovery, and interactive data exploration. Visualization therefore plays an important role in biomedical data mining.

## 10.1.2 Data Mining for Financial Data Analysis

Most banks and financial institutions offer a wide variety of banking services (such as checking, savings, and business and individual customer transactions), credit (such as business, mortgage, and automobile loans), and investment services (such as mutual funds). Some also offer insurance services and stock investment services.

Financial data collected in the banking and financial industry are often relatively complete, reliable, and of high quality, which facilitates systematic data analysis and data mining. Here we present a few typical cases.

**Design and construction of data warehouses for multidimensional data analysis and data mining:** Like many other applications, data warehouses need to be constructed for banking and financial data. Multidimensional data analysis methods should be used to analyze the general properties of such data. For example, one may like to view the debt and revenue changes by month, by region, by sector, and by other factors, along with maximum, minimum, total, average, trend, and other statistical information. Data warehouses, data cubes, multifeature and discovery-driven data cubes, characteristic and comparative analyses, and outlier analysis all play important roles in financial data analysis and mining.

**Loan payment prediction and customer credit policy analysis:** Loan payment prediction and customer credit analysis are critical to the business of a bank. Many factors can strongly or weakly influence loan payment performance and customer credit rating. Data mining methods, such as feature selection and attribute relevance ranking, may help identify important factors and eliminate irrelevant ones. For example, factors related to the risk of loan payments include loan-to-value ratio, term of the loan, debt ratio (total amount of monthly debt versus the total monthly income), payment-to-income ratio, customer income level, education level, residence region, credit history, and so on. Analysis of the customer payment history may find that, say, payment-to-income ratio is a dominant factor, while education level and debt ratio are not. The bank may then decide to adjust its loan-granting policy so as to grant loans to those whose application was previously denied but whose profile shows relatively low risks according to the critical factor analysis.

**Classification and clustering of customers for targeted marketing:** Classification and clustering methods can be used for customer group identification and targeted marketing. For example, customers with similar behaviors regarding banking and loan payments may be grouped together by multidimensional clustering techniques. Effective clustering and collaborative filtering methods (i.e., the use of various techniques to filter out information, such as nearest neighbor classification, decision trees, and so on) can help identify customer groups, associate a new customer with an appropriate customer group, and facilitate targeted marketing.

**Detection of money laundering and other financial crimes:** To detect money laundering and other financial crimes, it is important to integrate information from multiple databases (like bank transaction databases, and federal or state crime history databases), as long as they are potentially related to the study. Multiple data analysis tools can then be used to detect unusual patterns, such as large amounts of cash flow at certain periods, by certain groups of people, and so on. Useful tools include data visualization tools (to display transaction activities using graphs by time and by groups of people), linkage analysis tools (to identify links among different people and activities), classification tools (to filter unrelated attributes and rank the highly related ones), clustering tools (to group different cases), outlier analysis tools (to detect unusual amounts of fund transfers or other activities), and sequential pattern analysis tools (to characterize unusual access sequences). These tools may identify important relationships and patterns of activities and help investigators focus on suspicious cases for further detailed examination.

## 10.1.3  Data Mining for the Retail Industry

The retail industry is a major application area for data mining since it collects huge amounts of data on sales, customer shopping history, goods transportation, consumption and service records, and so on. The quantity of data collected continues to expand rapidly, especially due to the increasing ease, availability, and popularity of business conducted on the Web, or **e-commerce**. Today, many stores also have Web sites where customers can make purchases on-line. Some businesses, such as Amazon.com, exist solely on-line, without any bricks-and-mortar (i.e., physical) store locations. Retail data provide a rich source for data mining.

Retail data mining can help identify customer buying behaviors, discover customer shopping patterns and trends, improve the quality of customer service, achieve better customer retention and satisfaction, enhance goods consumption ratios, design more effective goods transportation and distribution policies, and reduce the cost of business.

A few examples of data mining in the retail industry are outlined as follows.

**Design and construction of data warehouses based on the benefits of data mining:**  Since retail data cover a wide spectrum (including sales, customers, employees, goods transportation, consumption and services), there can be many ways to design a data warehouse. The levels of detail to be included may also vary substantially. Since a major usage of a data warehouse is to support effective data analysis and data mining, the outcome of preliminary data mining exercises can be used to help guide the design and development of data warehouse structures. This involves deciding which dimensions and levels to include and what preprocessing to perform in order to facilitate quality and efficient data mining.

**Multidimensional analysis of sales, customers, products, time, and region:**  The retail industry requires timely information regarding customer needs, product sales, trends and fashions, as well as the quality, cost, profit, and service of commodities. It is therefore important to provide powerful multidimensional analysis and visualization tools, including the construction of sophisticated data cubes according to the needs of data analysis. The *multifeature data cube*, introduced in Chapter 2, is a useful data structure in retail data analysis since it facilitates analysis on aggregates with sophisticated conditions.

**Analysis of the effectiveness of sales campaigns:**  The retail industry conducts sales campaigns using advertisements, coupons, and various kinds of discounts and bonuses to promote products and attract customers. Careful analysis of the effectiveness of sales campaigns can help improve company profits. Multidimensional analysis can be used for this purpose by comparing the amount of sales and the number of transactions containing the sales items during the sales period versus those containing the same items before or after the sales campaign. Moreover, association analysis may disclose which items are likely to be purchased together with the items on sale, especially in comparison with the sales before or after the campaign.

**Customer retention—analysis of customer loyalty:**   With customer loyalty card information, one can register sequences of purchases of particular customers. Customer loyalty and purchase trends can be analyzed in a systematic way. Goods purchased at different periods by the same customers can be grouped into sequences. Sequential pattern mining can then be used to investigate changes in customer consumption or loyalty, and suggest adjustments on the pricing and variety of goods in order to help retain customers and attract new customers.

**Purchase recommendation and cross-reference of items:**   By mining associations from sales records, one may discover that a customer who buys a particular brand of perfume is likely to buy another set of items. Such information can be used to form purchase recommendations. Purchase recommendations can be advertised on the Web, in weekly flyers, or on sales receipts to help improve customer service, aid customers in selecting items, and increase sales. Similarly, information such as "hot items this week" or attractive deals can be displayed together with the associative information in order to promote sales.

## 10.1.4 Data Mining for the Telecommunication Industry

The telecommunication industry has quickly evolved from offering local and long-distance telephone services to providing many other comprehensive communication services including voice, fax, pager, cellular phone, images, e-mail, computer and Web data transmission, and other data traffic. The integration of telecommunication, computer network, Internet, and numerous other means of communication and computing is also underway. Moreover, with the deregulation of the telecommunication industry in many countries and the development of new computer and communication technologies, the telecommunication market is rapidly expanding and highly competitive. This creates a great demand for data mining in order to help understand the business involved, identify telecommunication patterns, catch fraudulent activities, make better use of resources, and improve the quality of service.

The following are a few scenarios where data mining may improve telecommunication services.

**Multidimensional analysis of telecommunication data:**   Telecommunication data are intrinsically multidimensional with dimensions such as calling-time, duration, location of caller, location of callee, and type of call. The multidimensional analysis of such data can be used to identify and compare the data traffic, system work load, resource usage, user group behavior, profit, and so on. For example, analysts in the industry may wish to regularly view charts regarding calling source, destination, volume, and time-of-day usage patterns. Therefore, it is often useful to consolidate telecommunication data into large data warehouses and routinely perform multidimensional analysis using OLAP and visualization tools.

**Fraudulent pattern analysis and the identification of unusual patterns:** Fraudulent activity costs the telecommunication industry millions of dollars a year. It is important to identify potentially fraudulent users and their atypical usage patterns; detect attempts to gain fraudulent entry to customer accounts; and discover unusual patterns that may need special attention, such as busy-hour frustrated call attempts, switch and route congestion patterns, and periodic calls from automatic dial-out equipment (like fax machines) that have been improperly programmed. Many of these types of patterns can be discovered by multidimensional analysis, cluster analysis, and outlier analysis.

**Multidimensional association and sequential pattern analysis:** The discovery of association and sequential patterns in multidimensional analysis can be used to promote telecommunication services. For example, suppose you would like to find usage patterns for a set of communication services by customer group, by month, and by time of day. The calling records may be grouped by customer in the following form:

⟨*customer_id, residence, office, time, date, service_1, service_2, · · ·*⟩

A sequential pattern like "*If a customer in the Los Angeles area works in a city different from her residence, she is likely to first use long-distance service between two cities around 5 pm and then use a cellular phone for at least 30 minutes in the subsequent hour every weekday*" can be further probed by drilling up and down in order to determine whether it holds for particular pairs of cities and particular groups of persons (e.g., engineers, doctors, etc.). This can help promote the sales of specific long-distance and cellular phone combinations, and improve the availability of particular services in the region.

**Use of visualization tools in telecommunication data analysis:** Tools for OLAP visualization, linkage visualization, association visualization, clustering, and outlier visualization have been shown to be very useful for telecommunication data analysis.

## 10.2 Data Mining System Products and Research Prototypes

Although data mining is a young field with many issues that still need to be researched in depth, there are already a great many off-the-shelf data mining system products and domain-specific data mining application softwares available. As a young discipline, data mining has a relatively short history and is constantly evolving—new data mining systems appear on the market every year; new functions, features, and visualization tools are added to existing systems on a constant basis; and efforts toward the standardization of data mining language have only just begun. Therefore, it is not our intention in this book to provide a detailed description of commercial data mining systems. Instead, we describe the features to consider when selecting a data mining product and offer a quick introduction to a few typical data mining systems. Reference articles, Web sites, and recent surveys of data mining systems are listed in the bibliographic notes.

### 10.2.1 How to Choose a Data Mining System

With many data mining system products available on the market, you may ask, *"What kind of system should I choose?"* Some people may be under the impression that data mining systems, like many commercial relational database systems, share the same well-defined operations and a standard query language, and behave similarly on common functionalities. If such were the case, the choice would depend more on the systems' hardware platform, compatibility, robustness, scalability, price, and service. Unfortunately, this is far from reality. Many commercial data mining systems have little in common with respect to data mining functionality or methodology and may even work with completely different kinds of data sets.

To choose a data mining system that is appropriate for your task, it is important to have a multiple dimensional view of data mining systems. In general, data mining systems should be assessed based on the following multiple dimensional features.

**Data types:** Most data mining systems that are available on the market handle formatted, record-based, relational-like data with numerical, categorical, and symbolic attributes. The data could be in the form of ASCII text, relational database data, or data warehouse data. It is important to check what exact format(s) each system you are considering can handle. Some kinds of data or applications may require specialized algorithms to search for patterns, and so their requirements may not be handled by off-the-shelf, generic data mining systems. Instead, specialized data mining systems may be used, which mine either text documents, geospatial data, multimedia data, time-series data, DNA sequences, Weblog records or other Web data, or are dedicated to specific applications (such as finance, the retail industry, or telecommunications). Moreover, many data mining companies offer customized data mining solutions that incorporate essential data mining functions or methodologies.

**System issues:** A given data mining system may run on only one operating system, or on several. The most popular operating systems that host data mining software are UNIX and Microsoft Windows (including 95, 98, 2000, and NT). There are also data mining systems that run on OS/2, Macintosh, and Linux. Large industry-oriented data mining systems should ideally adopt a client/server architecture, where the client could be a personal computer running on Microsoft Windows, and the server could be a set of powerful parallel computers running on UNIX. A recent trend has data mining systems providing Web-based interfaces and allowing XML data as input and/or output.

**Data sources:**   This refers to the specific data formats on which the data mining system will operate. Some systems work only on ASCII text files, whereas many others work on relational data, accessing multiple relational data sources. It is important that a data mining system supports ODBC connections or OLE DB for ODBC connections. These ensure open database connections, that is, the ability to access any relational data (including those in DB2, Informix, Microsoft SQL Server, Microsoft Access, Microsoft Excel, Oracle, Sybase, etc.), as well as formatted ASCII text data. A data mining system that operates with a data warehouse should follow the OLE DB for OLAP standard, since this helps ensure that the system is able to access the warehouse data provided not only by Microsoft SQL Server 7.0, but also by other data warehouse products supporting the standard.

**Data mining functions and methodologies:**   Data mining functions form the core of a data mining system. Some data mining systems provide only one data mining function, such as classification. Others may support multiple data mining functions, such as description, discovery-driven OLAP analysis, association,[1] classification, prediction, clustering, outlier analysis, similarity search, sequential pattern analysis, and visual data mining. For a given data mining function (such as classification), some systems may support only one method, while others may support a wide variety of methods (such as decision tree analysis, Bayesian networks, neural networks, genetic algorithms, case-based reasoning, etc.). Data mining systems that support multiple data mining functions and multiple methods per function provide the user with greater flexibility and analysis power. Many problems may require users to try a few different mining functions or incorporate several together, and different methods can be shown to be more effective than others for different kinds of data. In order to take advantage of the added flexibility, however, users may require further training and experience. Thus such systems should also provide novice users with convenient access to the most popular function and method, or to default settings.

**Coupling data mining with database and/or data warehouse systems:**   A data mining system should be coupled with a database and/or data warehouse system, where the coupled components are seamlessly integrated into a uniform information processing environment. In general, there are four forms of such coupling: *no coupling*, *loose coupling*, *semitight coupling*, and *tight coupling*. Some data mining systems work only with ASCII data files and are *not coupled*

---

[1] Several commercial products refer to association mining as **linkage analysis**.

with database or data warehouse systems at all. Such systems have difficulties handling large data sets and using the data stored in database systems. In data mining systems that are *loosely coupled* with database and data warehouse systems, the data are retrieved into a buffer or main memory by database or warehouse operations, and then mining functions are applied to analyze the retrieved data. These systems tend to have poor scalability and may be inefficient when executing some data mining queries. The coupling of a data mining system with a database or data warehouse system may be *semitight*, providing the efficient implementation of only a few essential data mining primitives (such as sorting, indexing, aggregation, histogram analysis, multiway join, and the precomputation of some statistical measures). Ideally, a data mining system should be *tightly coupled* with a database system in the sense that the data mining and data retrieval processes are integrated by optimizing data mining queries deep into the iterative mining and retrieval process. Tight coupling of data mining with OLAP-based data warehouse systems is also desirable so that data mining and OLAP operations can be integrated to provide OLAP-mining features.

**Scalability:** Data mining has two kinds of scalability issues: *row* (or *database size*) *scalability* and *column* (or *dimension*) *scalability*. A data mining system is considered **row scalable** if, when the number of rows is enlarged 10 times, it takes no more than 10 times to execute the same data mining queries. A data mining system is considered **column scalable** if the mining query execution time increases linearly with the number of columns (or attributes or dimensions). Due to the curse of dimensionality, it is much more challenging to make a system column scalable than row scalable.

**Visualization tools:** *"A picture is worth a thousand words"*—this is very true in data mining. Visualization in data mining can be categorized into *data visualization*, *mining result visualization*, *mining process visualization*, and *visual data mining*, as discussed below in Section 10.3.1. The variety, quality, and flexibility of visualization tools may strongly influence the usability, interpretability, and attractiveness of a data mining system.

**Data mining query language and graphical user interface:** Data mining is an exploratory process. An easy-to-use and high-quality graphical user interface is essential in order to promote user-guided, highly interactive data mining. Most data mining systems provide user-friendly interfaces for mining. However, unlike relational database systems, where most graphical user interfaces are constructed on top of SQL (which serves as a standard, well-designed database query language), most data mining systems do not share any underlying data mining query language. Lack of a standard data mining language makes it difficult to standardize data mining products and to ensure the interoperability of data mining systems. Recent efforts at defining and standardizing data mining query languages were introduced in Chapter 4. One such language, Microsoft's OLE DB for DM, is described in Appendix A.

## 10.2.2 **Examples of Commercial Data Mining Systems**

As mentioned earlier, due to the infancy and rapid evolution of the data mining market, it is not our intention in this book to describe any particular commercial data mining system in detail. Instead, we briefly outline a few typical data mining systems in order to help the reader get an idea of what can be done with current data mining products.

Many data mining systems specialize in one data mining function, such as classification, or just one approach of a data mining function, such as decision tree classification. Other systems provide a broad spectrum of data mining functions. Here we introduce a few systems that provide multiple data mining functions and explore multiple knowledge discovery techniques.

- **Intelligent Miner** is an IBM data mining product that provides a wide range of data mining algorithms including association, classification, regression, predictive modeling, deviation detection, sequential pattern analysis, and clustering. It also provides an application toolkit containing neural network algorithms, statistical methods, data preparation tools, and data visualization tools. Distinctive features of **Intelligent Miner** include the scalability of its mining algorithms and its tight integration with IBM's DB2 relational database system.

- **Enterprise Miner** was developed by SAS Institute, Inc. It provides multiple data mining algorithms including regression, classification, and statistical analysis packages. A distinctive feature of **Enterprise Miner** is its variety of statistical analysis tools, which are built based on the long history of SAS in the market of statistical analysis.

- **MineSet** was developed by Silicon Graphics Inc. (SGI). It also provides multiple data mining algorithms including association and classification, as well as advanced statistics and advanced visualization tools. A distinguishing feature of **MineSet** is its set of robust graphics tools (using powerful graphics features of SGI computers), including rule visualizer, tree visualizer, map visualizer, and (multidimensional data) scatter visualizer, for the visualization of data and data mining results.

- **Clementine** was developed by Integral Solutions Ltd. (ISL). It provides an integrated data mining development environment for end users and developers. Multiple data mining algorithms, including rule induction, neural nets, classification, and visualization tools, are incorporated in the system. A distinguishing feature of **Clementine** is its object-oriented, extended module interface, which allows users' algorithms and utilities to be added to Clementine's visual programming environment. Clementine has been acquired by SPSS Inc.

- **DBMiner** was developed by DBMiner Technology Inc. It provides multiple data mining algorithms including discovery-driven OLAP analysis, association, classification, and clustering. A distinct feature of **DBMiner** is its data-cube-based on-line analytical mining, which includes efficient frequent-pattern mining functions, and integrated visual classification methods. A more detailed introduction to the system is presented in Appendix B.

There are many other commercial data mining products, systems, and research prototypes that are also fast evolving. Interested readers may wish to consult timely surveys on data warehousing and data mining products.

# 10.3 Additional Themes on Data Mining

Due to the broad scope of data mining and the large variety of data mining methodologies, not all of the themes on data mining can be thoroughly covered in this book. In this section, we briefly discuss several interesting themes that were not fully addressed in the previous chapters of this book.

## 10.3.1 Visual and Audio Data Mining

**Visual data mining** discovers implicit and useful knowledge from large data sets using data and/or knowledge visualization techniques. The human visual system is controlled by the eyes and brain, the latter of which can be thought of as a powerful, highly parallel processing and reasoning engine containing a large knowledge base. Visual data mining essentially combines the power of these components, making it a highly attractive and effective tool for the comprehension of data distributions, patterns, clusters, and outliers in data.

Visual data mining can be viewed as an integration of two disciplines: data visualization and data mining. It is also closely related to computer graphics, multimedia systems, human computer interfaces, pattern recognition, and high-performance computing. In general, data visualization and data mining can be integrated in the following ways:

- **Data visualization:** Data in a database or data warehouse can be viewed at different levels of granularity or abstraction, or as different combinations of attributes or dimensions. Data can be presented in various visual forms, such as boxplots, 3-D cubes, data distribution charts, curves, surfaces, link graphs, and so on. Figures 10.1 and 10.2 from StatSoft shows data distributions in multidimensional space. Visual display can help give users a clear impression and overview of the data characteristics in a database.

- **Data mining result visualization:** Visualization of data mining results is the presentation of the results or knowledge obtained from data mining in visual forms. Such forms may include scatter plots and boxplots (obtained from descriptive data mining), as well as decision trees, association rules, clusters, outliers, generalized rules, and so on. For example, scatter plots are shown in

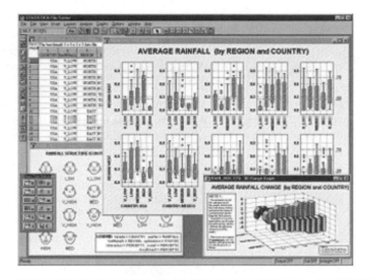

**Figure 10.1** Boxplots showing multiple variable combinations in StatSoft.

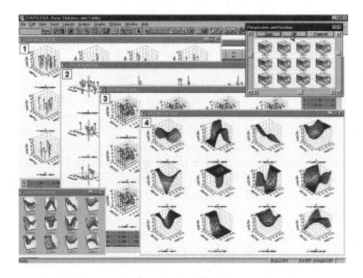

**Figure 10.2** Multidimensional data distribution analysis in StatSoft.

Figure 10.3, from SAS Enterprise Miner. Figure 10.4, from MineSet 3.0, uses a plane associated with a set of pillars to describe a set of association rules mined from a database. Figure 10.5, also from MineSet 3.0, presents a decision tree. Figure 10.6, from IBM Intelligent Miner, presents a set of clusters and the properties associated with them.

- **Data mining process visualization**: This type of visualization presents the various processes of data mining in visual forms so that users can see how the data are extracted and from which database or data warehouse they are extracted, as well as how the selected data are cleaned, integrated, preprocessed, and mined. Moreover, it may also show which method is selected for data mining, where the results are stored, and how they may be viewed. Figure 10.7 shows a visual presentation of data mining processes by the Clementine data mining system.

- **Interactive visual data mining**: In (interactive) visual data mining, visualization tools can be used in the data mining process to help users make smart data mining decisions. For example, the data distribution in a set of attributes can be displayed using colored sectors or columns (depending on whether the whole space is represented by either a circle or a set of columns). This display may help users determine which sector should first be selected for classification and where a good split point for this sector may be. An example of this is shown in Figure 10.8, which is the output of a perception-based classification system, PBC, developed at the University of Munich.

**Audio data mining** uses audio signals to indicate the patterns of data or the features of data mining results. Although visual data mining may disclose interesting patterns using graphical displays, it requires users to concentrate on watching patterns and identifying interesting or novel features within them. This can sometimes be quite tiresome. If patterns can be transformed into sound and music, then instead of watching pictures, we can listen to pitches, rhythms, tune, and melody in order to identify anything interesting or unusual. This may relieve some of the burden of visual concentration and be more relaxing than visual mining in many cases. Therefore, audio data mining can be an interesting alternative to visual mining.

## 10.3.2 Scientific and Statistical Data Mining

The data mining techniques described in this book are primarily database-oriented, that is, designed for the efficient handling of huge amounts of data that are typically multidimensional and possibly of various complex types. There are, however, many well-established statistical techniques for data analysis, particularly for numeric data. These techniques have been applied extensively to scientific data (e.g., data from experiments in psychology, medicine, electrical engineering, and manufacturing), as well as to data from economics and the social sciences.

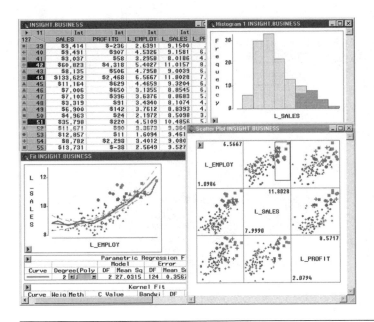

**Figure 10.3** Visualization of data mining results in SAS Enterprise Miner.

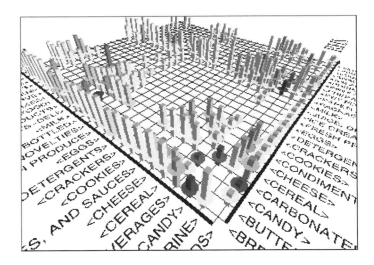

**Figure 10.4** Visualization of association rules in MineSet 3.0.

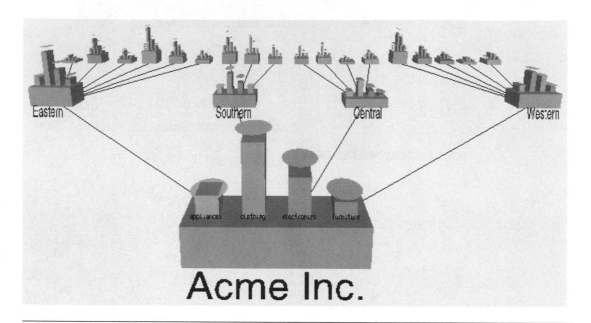

**Figure 10.5** Visualization of a decision tree in MineSet 3.0.

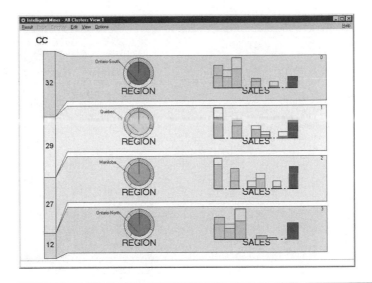

**Figure 10.6** Visualization of cluster groupings in IBM Intelligent Miner.

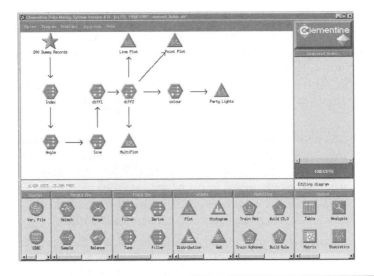

**Figure 10.7** Visualization of data mining processes by Clementine.

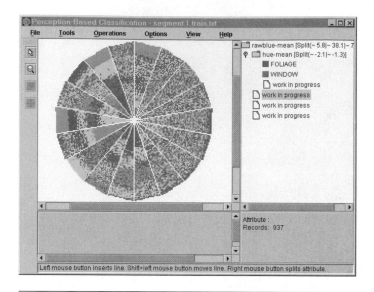

**Figure 10.8** Perception-based classification (PBC): an interactive visual mining approach.

Some of these techniques, such as principal components analysis, regression, and clustering, have already been addressed in this book. A thorough discussion of major statistical methods for data analysis is beyond the scope of this book; however, several methods are mentioned below for the sake of completeness. Pointers to these techniques are provided in the bibliographic notes.

- **Regression:** In general, these methods are used to predict the value of a *response* (dependent) variable from one or more *predictor* (independent) variables where the variables are numeric. There are various forms of regression, such as linear, multiple, weighted, polynomial, nonparametric, and robust (where robust methods are useful when errors fail to satisfy normalcy conditions or when the data contain significant outliers).

- **Generalized linear models:** These models, and their generalization (*generalized additive models*), allow a *categorical* response variable (or some transformation of it) to be related to a set of predictor variables in a manner similar to the modeling of a numeric response variable using linear regression. Generalized linear models include logistic regression and Poisson regression.

- **Regression trees:** These can be used for classification and prediction. The trees constructed are binary. A regression tree is similar to a decision tree in the sense that tests are performed at the internal nodes. A major difference is at the leaf level—while in a decision tree a majority voting is performed to assign a class label to the leaf, in a regression tree the mean of the objective attribute is computed and used as the predicted value.

- **Analysis of variance:** These techniques analyze experimental data for two or more populations described by a numeric response variable and one or more categorical variables (*factors*). In general, an ANOVA (single-factor analysis of variance) problem involves a comparison of $k$ population or treatment means to determine if at least two of the means are different. More complex ANOVA problems also exist.

- **Mixed-effect models:** These models are for analyzing grouped data—data that can be classified according to one or more grouping variables. They typically describe relationships between a response variable and some covariates in data grouped according to one or more factors. Common areas of application include multilevel data, repeated measures data, block designs, and longitudinal data.

- **Factor analysis:** This method is used to determine which variables are combined to generate a given factor. For example, for many psychiatric data it is not possible to measure a certain factor of interest directly (such as intelligence); however, it is often possible to measure other quantities (such as student test scores) that reflect the factor of interest. Here, none of the variables are designated as dependent.

- **Discriminant analysis:** This technique is used to predict a categorical response variable. Unlike generalized linear models, it assumes that the independent variables follow a multivariate normal distribution. The procedure attempts to determine several discriminant functions (linear combinations of the independent variables) that discriminate among the groups defined by the response variable. Discriminant analysis is commonly used in the social sciences.

- **Time series:** These are many statistical techniques for analyzing time-series data, such as autoregression methods, univariate ARIMA (autoregressive integrated moving average) modeling, and long-memory time-series modeling.

- **Survival analysis:** Several well-established statistical techniques exist for survival analysis, which originally were designed to predict the probability that a patient undergoing a medical treatment would survive at least to time $t$. Methods for survival analysis, however, are also commonly applied to manufacturing settings to estimate the life span of industrial equipment. Popular methods include Kaplan-Meier estimates of survival, Cox proportional hazards regression models, and their extensions.

- **Quality control:** Various statistics can be used to prepare charts for quality control, such as Shewhart charts and cusum charts (both of which display group summary statistics). These statistics include the mean, standard deviation, range, count, moving average, moving standard deviation, and moving range.

## 10.3.3 **Theoretical Foundations of Data Mining**

Research on the theoretical foundations of data mining has yet to mature. A solid and systematic theoretical foundation is important because it can help provide a coherent framework for the development, evaluation, and practice of data mining technology. There are a number of theories for the basis of data mining, such as the following:

- **Data reduction:** In this theory, the basis of data mining is to reduce the data representation. Data reduction trades accuracy for speed in response to the need to obtain quick approximate answers to queries on very large databases. Data reduction techniques include singular value decomposition (the driving element behind principal components analysis), wavelets, regression, log-linear models, histograms, clustering, sampling, and the construction of index trees.

- **Data compression:** According to this theory, the basis of data mining is to compress the given data by encoding in terms of bits, association rules, decision trees, clusters, and so on. Encoding based on the *minimum description length principle* states that the "best" theory to infer from a set of data is the one that minimizes the length of the theory and the length of the data when encoded using the theory as a predictor for the data. This encoding is typically in bits.

- **Pattern discovery:** In this theory, the basis of data mining is to discover patterns occurring in the database, such as associations, classification models, sequential patterns, and so on. Areas such as machine learning, neural network, association mining, sequential pattern mining, clustering, and several other subfields contribute to this theory.

- **Probability theory:** This is based on statistical theory. In this theory, the basis of data mining is to discover joint probability distributions of random variables, for example, Bayesian belief networks or hierarchical Bayesian models.

- **Microeconomic view:** The microeconomic view considers data mining as the task of finding patterns that are interesting only to the extent that they can be used in the decision-making process of some enterprise (e.g., regarding marketing strategies, production plans, etc.). This view is one of utility, in which patterns are considered interesting if they can be acted on. Enterprises are regarded as facing optimization problems where the object is to maximize the utility or value of a decision. In this theory, data mining becomes a nonlinear optimization problem.

- **Inductive databases:** According to this theory, a database schema consists of data and patterns that are stored in the database. Data mining is therefore the problem of performing induction on databases, where the task is to query the data and the theory (i.e., patterns) of the database. This view is popular among many researchers in database systems.

The above theories are not mutually exclusive. For example, pattern discovery can also be seen as a form of data reduction or data compression. Ideally, a theoretical framework should be able to model typical data mining tasks (such as association, classification, and clustering), have a probabilistic nature, be able to handle different forms of data, and consider the iterative and interactive essence of data mining. Further efforts are required toward the establishment of a well-defined framework for data mining, which satisfies these requirements.

## 10.3.4 Data Mining and Intelligent Query Answering

In our framework of the data mining process, the process is initiated by a data mining query that specifies the task-relevant data, the desired kinds of knowledge to be mined, the associated constraints, interestingness thresholds, and so on. However, in many cases, the user may not have a clear idea of exactly what to mine or may not even know what is contained in the database, and therefore may not be able to pose *precise* queries. Intelligent query answering may help in such cases by analyzing the user's intent and answering queries in an intelligent way.

A general framework for the integration of data mining and intelligent query answering is as follows. In a database system, there may exist two kinds of queries: *data queries* and *knowledge queries*. A **data query** finds *concrete data stored in a database* and corresponds to a basic retrieval statement in a database system. A **knowledge query** finds *rules, patterns, and other kinds of knowledge in a database* and corresponds to querying database knowledge including deduction rules, integrity constraints, generalized rules, frequent patterns, and other regularities. For example, *"Retrieve the customer ID for all customers who bought diapers in May 2000"* is a data query, whereas *"Describe the general characteristics of such customers and find what other items they are likely to buy"* is a knowledge query. Querying knowledge that is not explicitly stored in a database often involves a data mining process.

Query answering mechanisms can be classified into two categories based on their method of response: *direct query answering* and *intelligent* (or *cooperative*) *query answering*. **Direct query answering** means that a query is answered by returning *exactly what is being asked*, whereas **intelligent query answering** consists of *analyzing the intent of the query and providing generalized, neighborhood, or associated information relevant to the query*. Consider a customer's query regarding the title, author, price, and publisher of a particular book. Simply printing the values of these attributes for the book is an example of direct query answering. However, returning information that is related to the query but that was not explicitly asked for (such as book evaluation comments, sales statistics, or a list of other titles that customers who purchase the book in question are also likely to buy) provides an intelligent answer to the same query.

**Example 10.1** Suppose that a Web-based on-line shopping center maintains several databases for its business. The set of databases may include an *on-line catalog database*, an *on-line transaction history database*, and a *Weblog database*.

Data querying is a routine practice for many on-line services, with queries such as "*List all of the bicycles on sale*" or "*Find all of the items that Jack Waterman bought in April 2000*". Direct answering of such queries derives lists of items for a set of specified attributes. However, intelligent query answering provides users with additional information to help in decision making. Here are a few examples where intelligent query answering may improve on-line shopping services by incorporating data mining techniques.

- **Informative query answering by providing summary information**: When a customer requests a list of bicycles on sale, additional summary information can be provided, such as the best deal on bicycles, the volume sold for each bicycle in the last year, or attractive new features of various bicycle models. Such summary information can be obtained by using data warehousing and descriptive data mining techniques.

- **Suggestion of additional items based on association analysis**: When a customer wants to buy a particular brand of bicycle, additional association information can be provided to the customer, such as "*People who buy this kind of bike are likely to buy the following sport equipment as well*" or "*Would you consider purchasing a maintenance plan for such a bike?*" This may promote additional on-line sales for the company.

- **Product promotion by sequential pattern mining**: When a customer purchases a PC on-line, the system may suggest additional items to consider based on previously mined sequential patterns, such as "*People who buy this kind of PC are likely to buy a particular brand of printer or a particular model of CD-ROM writer within three months*", or send the customer coupons within a short period of time. ∎

From this short example, one can see that intelligent query answering by data mining methods can provide interesting services for e-commerce applications. This is likely to form an important theme in data mining applications and warrants further exploration.

# 10.4 Social Impacts of Data Mining

With the fast computerization of society, the social impacts of data mining should not be underestimated. Is data mining a hype, or is it really here to stay? What obstacles must be met in order for data mining to become accepted as a mainstream technology for business, and eventually, for everyone's personal use? What can be done toward protecting data privacy and security? This section addresses each of these questions.

## 10.4.1 Is Data Mining a Hype or a Persistent, Steadily Growing Business?

Data mining has recently become very popular, with many people jumping into data mining research, development, or business, or claiming their software systems to be data mining products. Observing this, you may wonder, *"Is data mining a hype, or is it here to stay? How well accepted is it as a technology?"*

Granted, there has been a great deal of hype regarding data mining since its emergence during the late 1980s, especially because many people expect that data mining will become an essential tool for deriving knowledge from data, to help business executives make strategic decisions, to sharpen the competitive edge of a business, and do many other wonderful things.

Data mining is a technology. Like any other technology, data mining will require time and effort to research, to develop, and to mature, and its adoption will likely go through a life cycle consisting of the following stages (Figure 10.9):

- **Innovators:** The new technology starts to take form as researchers begin to realize the need for methods to solve a particular (possibly new) problem.

- **Early adopters:** Interest increases as more and more methods for the technology are proposed.

- **Chasm:** This represents the "hurdles" or challenges that must be met before the technology can become widely accepted as mainstream.

- **Early majority:** The technology becomes mature and is generally accepted and used.

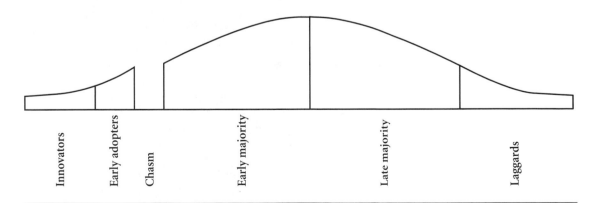

**Figure 10.9** Life cycle of technology adoption.

- **Late majority**: The technology is well accepted, but interest in it declines as the initial problem either becomes less important or is replaced by other needs.
- **Laggards**: Use of the technology starts to die out, as it becomes old and outdated.

*"So, at what stage is data mining?"* Several recent discussions have placed data mining at a chasm. In order for data mining to become fully accepted as a technology, further research and developments are needed in the many areas mentioned as *challenges* throughout this book—efficiency and scalability, increased user interaction, incorporation of background knowledge and visualization techniques, the evolution of a standardized data mining query language, effective methods for finding interesting patterns, improved handling of complex data types, Web mining, and so on.

For data mining to "climb out" of the chasm, we also need to focus on the *integration* of data mining into existing business technology. Currently, there exists a good variety of *generic* data mining systems. However, many of these tend to be designed for specifically trained experts who are familiar with data mining jargon and data analysis techniques, like association, classification, and clustering. This makes such systems difficult to use for business executives and the general public. Moreover, these systems tend to be designed to provide *horizontal solutions* that are geared to work for all kinds of businesses but are not specially designed to provide *business-specific* data mining solutions. Since effective data mining requires the smooth integration of business logic with data mining functions, one cannot expect that generic data mining systems can achieve as great a success in business intelligence as domain-independent relational database systems have done in business transaction and query processing.

Many data mining researchers and developers believe that a promising direction for data mining is to construct data mining systems that provide *vertical solutions,* that is, the integration of in-depth domain-specific business logic into data mining systems. Business conducted on the Web, or e-commerce, is an obvious venue for data mining, as more and more companies collect large amounts of data from *e-stores* set up on the Web (also called *Web stores*). We will therefore examine how to provide domain-specific data mining solutions for e-commerce applications.

Currently, more tailored systems are required that facilitate marketing campaign management (often called *e-marketing*). Ideally, such closed-loop systems bring together customer data analysis (with OLAP and mining technologies embedded under a user-friendly interface), customer profiling (or *one-to-one segments*), campaign roll-out, and campaign analysis.

These systems increasingly use data mining for **customer relationship management (CRM)**, which helps companies to provide more customized, personal service to their customers in lieu of mass marketing. By studying browsing and purchasing patterns on Web stores (e.g., by analyzing *clickstreams*, the information that consumers provide by clicks of the mouse), companies can learn more about individual customers or customer groups. This information can be applied to the benefit of both the company and the customer involved. For example, by having more accurate models of their customers, companies should gain a better understanding of customer needs. Serving these needs can result in greater success regarding cross-selling of related products, up-selling, one-to-one promotions, product affinities, larger baskets, and customer retention. By tailoring advertisements and promotions to customer profiles, customers are less likely to be annoyed with unwanted mass mailings or junk mail. These actions can result in substantial cost savings for companies. The customer further benefits in that she is more likely to be notified of offers that are actually of interest to her, resulting in less waste of personal time and greater satisfaction. Customer-tailored advertisements are not limited to company mail-outs or ads placed on Web stores. In the future, digital television and on-line books and newspapers may also provide advertisements that are designed and selected specifically for the given viewer or viewer group based on customer profiling information and demographics.

It is important to note that data mining is just one piece of the integrated solution. Other components, such as data cleaning and data integration, OLAP, user security, inventory and order management, product management, and so on, must also be in place.

### 10.4.2 Is Data Mining Merely Managers' Business or Everyone's Business?

Data mining will surely help company executives a great deal in understanding the market and their business. However, *"is data mining merely managers' business or everyone's business?"* Since more and more data are being made available on the Web or possibly on your own disks, it is likely you will need data mining to understand the data you can access to benefit your work and daily life. Moreover, in the years to come, it is expected that more and more powerful, user-friendly, diversified, and affordable data mining systems or components will be made available. Therefore, one can expect that everyone will have needs and the means for data mining. In other words, it is unlikely that data mining will remain reserved for today's traditional knowledge workers consisting of managers and business analysts. Instead, data mining will become increasingly available to everyone.

*"But, what could I do at home with data mining?"* Data mining can have multiple personal uses. For example, you might like to mine your family's medical history, identifying patterns relating to genetically related medical conditions, such as cancer or chromosome abnormalities. Such knowledge may help in making decisions about your lifestyle and health. In the future, you may be able to mine the records of the companies you deal with in order to evaluate their service to you as a customer, or to choose the best companies to deal with, based on customer service. You could apply content-based text mining to search your e-mail messages, or

automatically create a classification system to help organize your archived messages. You could mine data on stocks and company performance to assist in your financial investments. Other examples include mining Web stores to find the best deal on a particular item or type of vacation. Thus, as data mining crosses the chasm and becomes more affordable, and with the increased availability of personal computers and data on the Web, it is expected that data mining will become increasingly accessible to the general public and will eventually become a handy tool for everyone.

*"Then, do I have to understand the inside of a data mining system or the tricks of data mining algorithms in order to do data mining?"* Like using TVs, computers, or office software programs, one may expect to use a *user-friendly* data mining tool with minimal training. Moreover, there will be increasingly more "smart" softwares that may implicitly use data mining as their functional components. For example, smart Web search engines, customer-adaptive Web services, "intelligent" database systems, cooperative query answering systems, e-mail managers, calendar managers, ticket masters, and so on may take data mining modules as their built-in components, though the user may not even be aware of the existence of data mining. Such an implicit use of data mining as a built-in function is called **invisible data mining.** It is expected that invisible data mining will be an important means for the general public to perform effective data mining in the future.

## 10.4.3 Is Data Mining a Threat to Privacy and Data Security?

With more and more information accessible in electronic forms and available on the Web, and with increasingly powerful data mining tools being developed and put into use, you may wonder, *"Is data mining a threat to my privacy and information security?"* Like any other technology, data mining can be used for good or bad. Since data mining may disclose patterns and various kinds of knowledge that are difficult to find otherwise, it may pose a threat to privacy and information security if not done or used properly.

Most consumers don't mind providing companies with personal information if they think it will enable the companies to better service their needs. For example, shoppers are usually happy to sign up for loyalty cards at the local supermarket if it means they can get discounts in return.

Have you ever stopped to think about just how much information is recorded about you, and what that information says? Profiling information can be collected every time you use your credit card, debit card, supermarket loyalty card, or frequent flyer card, or apply for any of the above. It can be collected when you surf the Web, reply to an Internet newsgroup, subscribe to a magazine, rent a video, join a club, fill out a contest entry form, give information about your new baby (in order to receive coupons, free samples, or gifts), pay for prescription drugs, or present you medical care number when visiting the doctor. Clearly, the information that can easily be collected is not limited to our retail purchasing behavior, but may even reflect our hobbies as well as financial, medical, and insurance data. If you stop to think about this the next time you do any of the above actions, you may get the feeling that "Big Brother" or "Big Banker" or "Big Business" is carefully watching you.

While the collection of our personal data may prove beneficial for companies and consumers, as described in Section 10.4.1, there is also potential for its misuse. What if the data are used for other purposes such as, say, to help insurance companies determine your level of fat consumption based on the food items you purchase? One supermarket recently tried to use loyalty-card data to show that a shopper who slipped and fell was actually a heavy drinker (based on the amount of alcohol purchases). Although the case was dropped, it illustrates how data that are "invisibly" collected on consumers may be used against them.

While pondering the above, you may wonder:

- *"When I provide a company with information about myself, are these data going to be used in ways I don't expect?"*
- *"Will the data be sold to other companies?"*
- *"Can I find out what is recorded about me?"*
- *"How can I find out which companies have information about me?"*
- *"Do I have the right or the means to refuse companies to use the profiling information they have about me?"*
- *"Are there any means set up by which I can correct any errors in the profile data recorded about me? What if I want to erase, complete, amend, or update the data?"*
- *"Will the information about me be 'anonymized,' or will it be traceable to me?"*
- *"How secure are the data?"*
- *"How accountable is the company who collects or stores my data, if these data are stolen or misused?"*

There are no easy answers to these questions. International guidelines, known as **fair information practices,** were established for data privacy protection and cover aspects relating to data collection, use, quality, openness, individual participation, and accountability. They include the following principles:

- **Purpose specification and use limitation:** The purposes for which personal data are collected should be specified at the time of collection, and the data collected should not exceed the stated purpose. Data mining is typically a secondary purpose of the data collection. It has been argued that attaching a "disclaimer" that the data may also be used for mining is generally not accepted as sufficient disclosure of intent. Due to the exploratory nature of data mining, it is impossible to know what patterns may be discovered; therefore, there is no certainty over how they may be used.

- **Openness:** Individuals have the right to know what information is collected about them, who has access to the data, and how the data are being used.

*"So, what are some possible solutions that consider these principles?"* Companies should provide consumers with multiple **opt-out** choices, allowing consumers to specify limitations on the use of their personal data, such as (1) the consumer's personal data are not to be used at all for data mining; (2) the consumer's data can be used for data mining, but the identity of each consumer or any information that may lead to the disclosure of a person's identity should be removed; (3) the data may be used for in-house mining only; or (4) the data may be used in-house and externally as well. Alternatively, companies may provide consumers with positive consent, that is, by allowing consumers to *opt in* on the secondary use of their information for data mining. Ideally, consumers should be able to call a toll-free number or access a company Web site in order to opt in or out, and request access to their personal data.

*"What about data security?"* The field of database systems was initially met with some opposition as many individuals were concerned about the security risks associated with large on-line data storage. Many **data security-enhancing techniques** have since been developed so that, although some "hacker infractions" do occur, people are generally secure about the safety of their data and now accept the benefits offered by database management systems. Such data security-enhancing techniques can be used to anonymize information and securely protect privacy in data mining. These techniques include the use of *blind signatures* (which build on public key encryption), *biometric encryption* (e.g., where the image of a person's iris or fingerprint is used to encode her personal information), and *anonymous databases* (which permit the consolidation of various databases but limit access to personal information to only those who need to know; personal information is encrypted and stored at different locations).

Data mining may pose a threat to our privacy and data security. However, as we have seen, many solutions are being developed to help prevent misuse of the data collected. In addition, the field of database systems has many data security-enhancing techniques that can be used to guard the security of data collected for and resulting from data mining. Although it is possible that some of today's data mining techniques may not succeed in "crossing the chasm," data mining is bound to succeed due to the vast need for such a technology. As companies and consumers continue to take responsibility in working toward solutions to ensure data privacy protection and security, we may continue to reap the benefits of data mining in terms of time and money savings and the discovery of new knowledge.

## 10.5 Trends in Data Mining

The diversity of data, data mining tasks, and data mining approaches poses many challenging research issues in data mining. The design of data mining languages, the development of efficient and effective data mining methods and systems, the construction of interactive and integrated data mining environments, and the application of data mining techniques to solve large application problems are important tasks for data mining researchers and data mining system and application developers. This section describes some of the trends in data mining that reflect the pursuit of these challenges.

**Application exploration:** Early data mining applications focused mainly on helping businesses gain a competitive edge. As data mining becomes more popular, it is increasingly used for the exploration of applications in other areas, such as biomedicine, financial analysis, and telecommunications. In addition, the exploration of data mining for businesses continues to expand as e-commerce and e-marketing become mainstream elements of the retail industry. As generic data mining systems may have limitations in dealing with application-specific problems, we may see a trend toward the development of more application-specific data mining systems.

**Scalable data mining methods:** In contrast with traditional data analysis methods, data mining must be able to handle huge amounts of data efficiently and, if possible, interactively. Since the amount of data being collected continues to increase rapidly, scalable algorithms for individual and integrated data mining functions become essential. One important direction toward improving the overall efficiency of the mining process while increasing user interaction is **constraint-based mining.** This provides users with added control by allowing the specification and use of constraints to guide data mining systems in their search for interesting patterns.

**Integration of data mining with database systems, data warehouse systems, and Web database systems:** Database systems, data warehouse systems, and the WWW have become mainstream information processing systems. It is important to ensure that data mining serves as an essential data analysis component that can be smoothly integrated into such an information processing environment. As we discussed in Section 4.4, a desired architecture for a data mining system is the tight coupling with database and data warehouse systems. Transaction management, query processing, on-line analytical processing, and on-line analytical mining should be integrated into one unified framework. This will ensure data availability, data mining portability, scalability, high performance, and an integrated information processing environment for multidimensional data analysis and exploration.

**Standardization of data mining language:** A standard data mining language or other standardization efforts will facilitate the systematic development of data mining solutions, improve interoperability among multiple data mining systems and functions, and promote the education and use of data mining systems in industry and society. Recent efforts in this direction include Microsoft's OLE DB for Data Mining (Appendix A provides an introduction to this directive). Other efforts were described in Section 4.2.7.

**Visual data mining:** Visual data mining is an effective way to discover knowledge from huge amounts of data. The systematic study and development of visual data mining techniques will facilitate the promotion and use of data mining as a tool for data analysis.

**New methods for mining complex types of data:** As shown in Chapter 9, mining complex types of data is an important research frontier in data mining. Although progress has been made at mining geospatial, multimedia, time-series, sequence, and text data, there is still a huge gap between the needs for these applications and the available technology. More research is required, especially toward the integration of data mining methods with existing data analysis techniques for the above types of data.

**Web mining:** Issues related to Web mining were discussed in Section 9.6. Given the huge amounts of information available on the Web and the increasingly important role that the Web plays in today's society, Web content mining, Weblog mining, and data mining services on the Internet will become one of the most important and flourishing subfields in data mining.

**Privacy protection and information security in data mining:** With the increasingly popular use of data mining tools and telecommunication and computer networks, an important issue to face in data mining is privacy protection and information security. Further methods should be developed to ensure privacy protection and information security while facilitating proper information access and mining.

## 10.6 Summary

- Many customized data mining tools have been developed for **domain-specific applications**, including biomedicine and DNA analysis, finance, the retail industry, and telecommunications. Such practice integrates domain-specific knowledge with data analysis techniques and provides mission-specific data mining solutions.

- Many data mining systems and products have been developed in the last 10 years. When selecting a data mining product that is appropriate for one's task, it is important to consider various **features of data mining systems** *from a multiple dimensional point of view*. These include data types, system issues, data sources, data mining functions and methodologies, tight coupling of the data mining system with a database or data warehouse system, scalability, visualization tools, and graphical user interfaces.

- **Visual data mining** integrates data mining and data visualization in order to discover implicit and useful knowledge from large data sets. Forms of visual data mining include *data visualization, data mining result visualization, data mining process visualization,* and *interactive visual data mining*. **Audio data mining** uses audio signals to indicate data patterns or features of data mining results.

■ Several well-established **statistical methods** have been proposed for data analysis, such as regression, generalized linear models, regression trees, analysis of variance, mixed-effect models, factor analysis, discriminant analysis, time-series analysis, survival analysis, and quality control. Full coverage of statistical data analysis methods is beyond the scope of this book. Interested readers are referred to the statistical literature cited in the bibliographic notes for background on such statistical analysis tools.

■ Researchers have been striving to build **theoretical foundations** for data mining. A number of interesting proposals have appeared, including data reduction, pattern discovery, probabilistic theory, data compression, microeconomic theory, and inductive databases.

■ **Intelligent query answering** employs data mining techniques to analyze the intent of a user query, providing additional generalized or associated information relevant to the query. It extends the power and usability of query processing systems.

■ The adoption of a new technology, such as data mining, evolves through a life cycle that often consists of a **chasm** representing the challenges that must be met before the technology becomes mainstream.

■ One social concern of data mining is the issue of privacy and information security. **Opt-out policies**, which allow consumers to specify limitations on the use of their personal data, are one approach toward data privacy protection, while **data security-enhancing techniques** can anonymize information for security and privacy.

■ **Trends in data mining** include further efforts toward the exploration of new application areas and new methods for handling complex data types, algorithm scalability, constraint-based mining and visualization methods, the integration of data mining with data warehousing and database systems, the standardization of data mining languages, and data privacy protection and security.

## Exercises

10.1 Research and describe an *application of data mining* that was not presented in this chapter. Discuss how different forms of data mining can be used in the application.

10.2 Suppose that you are in the market to purchase a data mining system.

(a) Regarding the coupling of a data mining system with a database and/or data warehouse system, what are the differences between *no coupling*, *loose coupling*, *semitight coupling*, and *tight coupling*?

(b) What is the difference between *row scalability* and *column scalability*?

(c) Which feature(s) from those listed above would you look for when selecting a data mining system?

**10.3** Study an existing *commercial data mining system*. Outline the major features of such a system from a multiple dimensional point of view, including data types handled, architecture of the system, data sources, data mining functions, data mining methodologies, coupling with database or data warehouse systems, scalability, visualization tools, and graphical user interfaces. Can you propose one improvement to such a system and outline how to realize it?

**10.4** Propose a few implementation methods for *audio data mining*. Can we integrate audio and *visual data mining* to bring fun and power to data mining? Is it possible to develop some video data mining methods? State some scenarios and your solutions to make such integrated audio-visual mining effective.

**10.5** General-purpose computers and domain-independent relational database systems have become a large market in the last several decades. However, many people feel that generic data mining systems will not prevail in the data mining market. What do you think? For data mining, should we focus our efforts on developing *domain-independent* data mining tools or on developing *domain-specific* data mining solutions? Present your reasoning.

**10.6** Why is the establishment of *theoretical foundations* important for data mining? Name and describe the main theoretical foundations that have been proposed for data mining. Comment on how they each satisfy (or fail to satisfy) the requirements of an ideal theoretical framework for data mining.

**10.7** What is the difference between *direct query answering* and *intelligent query answering*? Suppose that a user requests the price, address, and rating of hotels at a particular holiday location. Give examples of how such a query could be answered using direct query answering and then using intelligent query answering.

**10.8** Suppose that your local bank has a data mining system. The bank has been studying your debit card usage patterns. Noticing that you make many transactions at home renovation stores, the bank decides to contact you, offering information regarding their special loans for home improvements.

   (a) Discuss how this may conflict with your right to *privacy*.
   (b) Describe another situation where you feel that data mining can infringe on your privacy.
   (c) What are some examples where data mining could be used to help society? Can you think of ways it could be used that may be detrimental to society?

**10.9** Based on your knowledge of current data mining systems and applications, do you think data mining will become a thriving market? What are the bottlenecks for data mining research and development? Do you believe the current approach of data mining will win a large share of the market for system applications? If not, can you propose some way out?

**10.10** Based on your study, suggest a possible *new frontier* in data mining that was not mentioned in this chapter.

## Bibliographic Notes

There are many books that discuss applications of data mining. For data mining applications in bioinformatics, including biomedical and DNA data analysis, good summaries on the methods and algorithms used can be found in Gusfield [Gus97], Waterman [Wat95], Baldi and Brunak [BB98], and Baxevanis and Ouellette [BO98]. For data mining for financial data analysis and financial modeling, see Benninga and Czaczkes [BC97] and Higgins [Hig97]. For retail data mining and customer relationship management, see reference books by Berry and Linoff [BL99] and Berson, Smith, and Thearling [BST99]. For telecommunication-related data mining, see the book by Mattison [Mat97]. Chen, Hsu, and Dayal [CHD00] report their work on scalable telecommunication tandem traffic analysis under a data warehouse/OLAP framework. Valdes-Perez [VP99] discusses the principles of human-computer collaboration for knowledge discovery in science.

Many data mining books contain introductions to various kinds of data mining systems and products. For a survey of data mining and knowledge discovery software tools, see Goebel and Gruenwald [GG99]. Detailed information regarding specific data mining systems and products can be found by consulting the Web pages of the companies offering these products, the user manuals for the products in question, or magazines and journals on data mining and data warehousing. For example, the Web page URLs for the commercial data mining systems introduced in this chapter are *http://www-4.ibm.com/software/data/iminer* for IBM IntelligentMiner, *http://www.sas.com/software/components/miner.html* for SAS Enterprise Miner, *http://www.sgi.com/software/mineset* for SGI MineSet, *http://www.isl.co.uk/clem.html* for Clementine of ISL, and *http://www.dbminer* *.com* for DBMiner of DBMiner Technology Inc. Since data mining systems and their functions evolve rapidly, it is not our intention to provide any kind of comprehensive survey on data mining systems in this book. We apologize if your data mining systems or tools were not included.

For visual data mining, popular books on the visual display of data and information include those by Tufte [Tuf83, Tuf90, Tuf97]. A summary of techniques for visualizing data is presented in Cleveland [Cle93]. The VisDB system for database exploration using multidimensional visualization methods was developed by Keim and Kriegel [KK94]. Keim summarizes data visualization and visual data mining methods in his several conference tutorials (*http://www.informatik.uni-halle.de/~keim/tutorials.html*). Ankerst, Elsen, Ester, and Kriegel [AEEK99] present a perception-based classification approach, PBC, for interactive visual classification.

Statistical techniques for data analysis are described in several books, including *Intelligent Data Analysis* edited by Berthold and Hand [BH99]; *Probability and Statistics for Engineering and the Sciences*, 4th ed., by Devore [Dev95]; *Applied Linear Statistical Models*, 4th ed., by Neter, Kutner, Nachtsheim, and Wasserman [NKNW96]; *An Introduction to Generalized Linear Models,* by Dobson [Dob90]; *Classification and Regression Trees*, by Breiman, Friedman, Olshen, and Stone

[BFOS84]; *Mixed Effects Models in S*, by Bates and Pinheiro [BP99]; *Applied Multivariate Statistical Analysis*, 3rd ed., by Johnson and Wichern [JW92]; *Applied Discriminant Analysis*, by Huberty [Hub94]; *Applied Statistical Time Series Analysis*, by Shumway [Shu88]; and *Survival Analysis*, by Miller [Mil81].

Issues on the theoretical foundations of data mining are addressed in many research papers. Mannila presents a summary of studies on the foundations of data mining in [Man97]. The data reduction point of view on data mining is summarized in *The New Jersey Data Reduction Report*, by Barbará et al. [BDF+97]. The data compression view of data mining can be found in studies on the minimum description length (MDL) principle, such as Quinlan and Rivest [QR89] and Chakrabarti, Sarawagi, and Dom [CSD98]. The pattern discovery point of view of data mining is addressed in numerous machine learning and data mining studies since methods for the discovery of patterns include decision tree induction, neural network classification, association mining, sequential pattern mining, clustering, and so on. The probability theory point of view on data mining can be seen in the statistics literature, such as in studies on Bayesian networks and hierarchical Bayesian models, as addressed in Chapter 7. Kleinberg, Papadimitriou, and Raghavan [KPR98] present a microeconomic view of data mining, treating data mining as an optimization problem. The view of data mining as the querying of inductive databases was proposed by Imielinski and Mannila [IM96].

Intelligent query answering methods have been studied by many researchers, including Imielinski [Imi87], Cuppens and Demolombe [CD88], Motro and Yuan [MY90], and Chu and Chen [CC92]. Han, Huang, Cercone, and Fu [HHCF96] studied intelligent query answering by knowledge discovery techniques.

The book *Business @ the Speed of Thought* by Gates [Gat99] discusses e-commerce and customer relationship management, and provides an interesting perspective on data mining in the future. The technology adoption life cycle, including issues on crossing the chasm, is discussed by Moore [Moo99]. Agrawal discussed data mining and the technology adoption life cycle at an invited talk given at the Fifth International Conference on Knowledge Discovery and Data Mining (KDD'99). Data mining issues regarding privacy and data security are addressed in several papers, including Laudon [Lau96] (which proposes a regulated national information market that would allow personal information to be bought and sold), Cavoukian [Cav98] (which discusses fair information practices and opt-out choices), Berry [Ber99], and Lohr [Loh99]. Agrawal and Srikant [AS00] discussed methods for privacy-preserving data mining.

# An Introduction to Microsoft's OLE DB for Data Mining

This appendix provides an informal and concise introduction to Microsoft's OLE DB for Data Mining (**OLE DB for DM**) specification.[1] The OLE DB for DM specification is a major step toward the standardization of data mining language primitives and aims to become the industry standard. It is designed to allow data mining (DM) client applications (or *data mining consumers*) to consume DM services from a wide variety of data mining software packages (or *data mining providers*).

OLE DB for DM describes an abstraction of the data mining process. As an extension of OLE DB, it introduces a new virtual object called a **Data Mining Model (DMM)** as well as commands for DMM manipulation. The manipulation of a DMM is similar to that of an SQL table. The three major operations performed by DM consumers regarding a DMM are the following:

1. **Create a data mining model object:** A DMM object is created using a **CREATE** statement, which is similar to the relational database operation **CREATE TABLE**. The **CREATE** statement specifies the columns of the DMM (e.g., corresponding to the attributes to be analyzed during mining) and the data mining algorithm to be used when the model is later trained by the data mining provider. Types of DM algorithms include decision tree, clustering (referred to as *segmentation*), and regression (for prediction). The **CREATE** statement does not define the actual content (i.e., learned graphical structure) of the DMM. The DMM is considered "empty" until the following operation is performed.

2. **Insert training data into the model and train it:** An **INSERT** command is used to "populate the model" by loading in the training data. This is similar to

---

[1] The information presented in this appendix is based on *OLE DB for Data Mining, Draft Specification*, version 0.9, Microsoft Corporation, February 2000. Please refer to this document or a more recent version of it for additional details not presented in this appendix.

**Table A.1**    A sample case that includes a nested table to describe the entity "customer".

| Customer ID | Gender | Age | Item Name | Item Quantity | Item Type |
|---|---|---|---|---|---|
| 1 | F | 40 | CD player | 1 | home entertainment |
| | | | TV | 2 | home entertainment |
| | | | car alarm | 1 | security |

the **INSERT INTO** command used to populate a table. The **INSERT** command causes the newly inserted data to be processed on the DM provider by the algorithm specified during creation of the DMM object. The resulting model (or abstraction) is stored in the DMM, instead of the training data. This result is referred to as the *DMM content*.

3. **Use of the data mining model:** A **SELECT** statement can be used to consult the DMM content in order to make predictions and browse statistics obtained by the model.

The data to be mined are represented as a collection of tables in a relational database. The data pertaining to a single entity are referred to as a **case**. The set of all relevant cases is called a **case set**. OLE DB for DM provides **nested tables** (or **table columns**), as defined by the Data Shaping Service included with Microsoft Data Access Components (MDAC) products. Nested tables allow a collection of data records to be associated with a given entity. For example, a given customer entity may be described by *Customer ID*, *Gender*, and *Age*, and a nested table describes the set of items purchased by the customer (i.e., *Item Name*, *Item Quantity*, *Item Type*), such as is shown in Table A.1. There may be more than one nested table for the case, and each table can have a variable number of rows. The main row of a case is referred to as the **case row**. Rows inside a nested table are **nested rows**.

Let's look at examples for each of the above major operations.

## A.1    Creating a DMM object

**Example A.1**    Creating a data mining model for classification: The following statement specifies the columns of (or attributes defining) a DMM object for *Age* prediction and the DM algorithm to be used later for its training.

```
CREATE MINING MODEL [Age Prediction]
(
    [Customer ID]              LONG    KEY,
    [Gender]                   TEXT    DISCRETE,
```

```
    [Age]                              DOUBLE DISCRETIZED() PREDICT,
    [Item Purchases]                   TABLE,
    (
                [Item Name]     TEXT    KEY,
                [Item Quantity] DOUBLE NORMAL CONTINUOUS,
                [Item Type]     TEXT    RELATED TO [Item Name]
    )
)
USING [Decision Trees]
```

The statement includes the following information. *Customer ID* is specified as a
**KEY**, meaning that it can uniquely identify a customer case row. The *Age* attribute
is to be predicted by the model. It is a continuous attribute but is to be discretized.
**DISCRETIZED()** indicates that a default method of discretization is to be used. Alternatively, **DISCRETIZED(***method, n***)** could have been specified, where *method* is
an alternative discretization method of the provider and *n* is the recommended
number of buckets (intervals) to be used in dividing up the value range for *Age*.
*Item Purchases* is a nested table, defined by the columns *Item Name* (a **KEY** of *Item
Purchases*), *Item Quantity*, and *Item Type*. Knowledge of the distribution of continuous attributes may be used by some DM providers. *Item Quantity* is known
to have a normal distribution. Other distribution models include **UNIFORM**, **LOG-
NORMAL**, **BINOMIAL**, **MULTINOMIAL**, **POISSON**, and so on. The specification that
*Item Type* is **RELATED TO** *Item Name* means that *Item Type* classifies *Item Name*,
for example, *"home entertainment"* classifies *"TV"*. Other attribute types not appearing above include **ORDERED**, **CYCLICAL**, **SEQUENCE_TIME**, **PROBABILITY**,
**VARIANCE**, **STDEV**, and **SUPPORT**. The **USING** clause specifies that a decision tree
algorithm is to be used by the provider to later construct the model via an **INSERT**
statement. This clause may be followed by provider-specific pairs of parameter-
value settings to be used by the algorithm.                                     ∎

**Example A.2** **Creating a data mining model for association:** The following statement creates a
DMM object for association mining:

```
CREATE MINING MODEL [Association Model]
(
    [Transaction ID]                   LONG    KEY,
    [Item Purchases]                   TABLE   PREDICT,
    (
                [Item Name]     TEXT    KEY
    )
)
USING [My Association Algorithm] (Minimum_size = 3)
```

The specification of **(Minimum_size = 3)** means that the model is only interested in association rules regarding items that are frequently sold together, where each rule contains at least three items.　　　　　■

## A.2 Inserting Training Data into the Model and Training the Model

The following statement specifies the training data to be used to populate the *Age Prediction* model. The DM algorithm (specified when creating the model object) is invoked and analyzes the data in order to generate the model.

```
INSERT INTO [Age Prediction]
(
    [Customer ID], [Gender], [Age],
    [Item Purchases] (SKIP, [Item Name], [Item Quantity], [Item Type])
)
SHAPE
{
    SELECT [Customer ID], [Gender], [Age] FROM Customers
        ORDER BY [Customer ID]
}
APPEND
(
    {SELECT [CustID], [Item Name], [Item Quantity], [Item Type]
        FROM Purchases ORDER BY [CustID]}
    RELATE [Customer ID] TO [CustID]
)
AS [Item Purchases]
```

The manner in which the DMM is populated is similar to that for populating an ordinary table. The keyword **SKIP** in the **INTO CLAUSE** is used since the source data contains a column that is not to be used by the DMM. Note that the **SHAPE** command is used to create the nested table, *Item Purchases*.

## A.3 Using the Model

A trained model is a sort of "truth table," containing a row for every possible combination of values for each column (attribute) in the DMM. For discretized attributes, all distinct values of the attribute are considered. For discreted attributes, all discretized values (or buckets) of the attribute are considered. (The midpoint of each bucket range is used.) For continuous attributes, the minimum, maximum, and mean values are considered. For each attribute type, the label "missing" is also included. This table can be browsed to make predictions or look up learned statistics. This subsection shows several examples for using a DMM to make predictions, as well as querying and browsing the general content.

The **SELECT** command is used to make predictions, as illustrated in the following OLE DB for DM statement.

```
SELECT t.[Customer ID], [Age Prediction].[Age]
FROM [Age Prediction]
PREDICTION JOIN
(
    SHAPE
    {
        SELECT [Customer ID], [Gender] FROM Customers ORDER BY [Customer ID]
    }
    APPEND
    (
        {SELECT [CustID], [Item Name], [Item Quantity] FROM Purchases
            ORDER BY [CustID]}
        RELATE [Customer ID] TO [CustID]
    )
    AS [Item Purchases]
) AS t
ON [Age Prediction].Gender = t.Gender and
    [Age Prediction].[Item Purchases].[Item Name] =
        t.[Item Purchases].[Item Name] and
    [Age Prediction].[Item Purchases].[Item Quantity] =
        t.[Item Purchases].[Item Quantity]
```

The statement employs a **PREDICTION JOIN** to join the DMM's set of all possible cases with a specified set of cases for which the attribute *Age* is not known. The **SELECT** command operates on the resulting join, returning an *Age* prediction for each *Customer ID*. Note that for a given test case, the **PREDICTION JOIN** may find a *set* of cases matching the conditions specified in the **ON** clause. If this occurs, these cases are "collapsed" into an aggregate case that contains the best prediction for *Age* (or the best predictions for all predictable columns in the model). A **SELECT** statement can also be used to retrieve the known *Age* values of test cases in order to validate the accuracy of the model.

The DMM "truth table" containing the set of all possible combinations of attribute values can be queried for various values and statistics. For example, if an attribute such as Hair Color were included in the *Age Prediction* model, then the set of distinct values for *Hair Color* could be retrieved with the statement

**SELECT DISTINCT** Hair Color **FROM** [Age Prediction]

Similarly, the list of all items that may be purchased can be obtained with the statement

**SELECT DISTINCT** [Item Purchases].[Item Name] **FROM** [Age Prediction]

Note that the dot operator (".") can be used to refer to a column from the scope of a nested table.

OLE DB for DM provides a number of functions that can used to statistically describe predictions. For example, the likelihood of a predicted value can be viewed with the **PredictProbability()** function, as shown in the following statement, which returns a table with the predicted age of each customer, along with the associated probability:

**SELECT** [Customer ID], **Predict**(Age), **PredictProbability**([Age]), . . .

The **Cluster()** and **ClusterProbability()** functions can be similarly used to view the probability associated with each cluster membership assignment, as in

**SELECT** [Customer ID], [Gender], **Cluster**() **as** C, **ClusterProbability**() **as** CP, . . .

| Customer ID | Gender | C | CP |
|---|---|---|---|
| 1 | F | 3 | 0.37 |
| 2 | M | 5 | 0.26 |
| ⋮ | ⋮ | ⋮ | ⋮ |

where C is a cluster identifier showing the most likely cluster to which a case belongs and CP is the associated probability. Additional functions that take a column name as an argument include **PredictSupport()**, which returns the count of cases in support of the predicted column value, **PredictVariance()**, **PredictStdev()**, **PredictProbabilityVariance()**, and **PredictProbabilityStdev()**. The functions **RangeMid()**, **RangeMin()**, and **RangeMax()** return the midpoint, minimum, and maximum value, respectively, of the predicted bucket for a **DISCRETIZED** column.

The **PredictHistogram()** function can be used to return a histogram of the possible values and associated statistics for a predicted or clustered column. The histogram is in the form of a nested table. For example, if predicting a discrete attribute such as *Gender*, for each case we may choose to view a histogram showing the possible *Gender* values and their associated support and probability. This information can be obtained with the following statement:

**SELECT** [Customer ID], **PredictHistogram**([Gender]) **as** GH, . . .

| Customer ID | Gender | $Support | $Probability | . . . |
|---|---|---|---|---|
| | | *GH* | | |
| 1 | F | 786 | 0.786 | |
| | M | 214 | 0.214 | |
| 2 | F | 672 | 0.672 | |
| | M | 328 | 0.328 | |
| ⋮ | ⋮ | ⋮ | ⋮ | |

Other statistics returned include **$Variance**, **$Stdev**, **$ProbabilityVariance**, and **$ProbabilityStdev**. If the argument of **PredictHistogram** is **Cluster()**, then a histogram is returned for each case showing the possible cluster identifiers and associated support, probability, and so on. In addition, OLE DB for DM provides functions for viewing the top or bottom $N$ rows in a nested table, per case. Such functions are useful when the number of nested rows per case is large.

In addition to the DMM table containing the set of all possible combinations of attribute values with corresponding predictions, a model's content may also contain a set of nodes (e.g., a decision tree), rules, formulae, or distributions. This content depends on the DM algorithm used. The content may be viewed by extracting an XML description of it in the form of a string. Interpretation of such a string, however, requires expertise on behalf of the client application. Navigational operations are provided for browsing model content represented as a directed graph (e.g., a decision tree). Discovered rules are expressed using PMML (Predictive Model Markup Language) and may be viewed by querying the model content.

# Appendix B

# An Introduction to DBMiner

**DBMiner** is a data mining system that originated from the Intelligent Database Systems Research Laboratory, Simon Fraser University, British Columbia, Canada, and has been further developed by DBMiner Technology Inc., British Columbia, Canada. It is the result of years of research into data mining and knowledge discovery in databases. This appendix provides a short introduction to the DBMiner system.[1]

**DBMiner** is an on-line analytical mining system, developed for interactive mining of multiple-level knowledge in large relational databases and data warehouses. The major distinguishing feature of the **DBMiner** system is its tight integration of on-line analytical processing (OLAP) with a wide spectrum of data mining functions, including characterization, association, classification, prediction, and clustering [Han98, HCC98, HF96]. This integration leads to a promising data mining methodology called *on-line analytical mining* (OLAM), where the system provides a multidimensional view of its data and creates an interactive data mining environment: users can dynamically select data mining and OLAP functions, perform OLAP operations (like drilling, dicing/slicing, and pivoting) on data mining results, and/or perform mining operations on OLAP results, that is, mining different portions of data at multiple levels of abstraction.

The system facilitates query-based interactive mining of multidimensional databases by implementing a set of advanced data mining techniques, including OLAP-based multidimensional statistical analysis, efficient frequent-pattern mining algorithms, progressive deepening for mining refined knowledge, visual data mining, metarule-guided mining, and data and knowledge visualization. **DBMiner** integrates smoothly with relational database and data warehouse systems to provide a user-friendly, interactive data mining environment with high performance.

---

[1] The information presented in this appendix is based on DBMiner Enterprise Version 2.0, DBMiner Technology Inc., December 1999.

# B.1 System Architecture

The system architecture of the **DBMiner** system follows the on-line analytical mining architecture we proposed in Figure 2.24, which takes data from a relational database and/or a data warehouse, integrates and transforms them into a multidimensional database (portions or all of which could be consolidated into data cubes), and then performs multidimensional on-line analytical processing and on-line analytical mining based on the user's processing requests.

The core module of the architecture is an OLAM engine, which performs online analytical mining in multidimensional databases in a manner similar to that for on-line analytical processing by an OLAP engine. The OLAM engine in the **DBMiner** system performs multiple data mining tasks, including concept description, association, classification, prediction, clustering, and time-series analysis.

More importantly, the system integrates OLAM and OLAP engines, both of which accept user on-line queries (or commands) via a graphical user interface API and work on the multidimensional database via an MDDB_API. Notice that in this architecture, OLAM and OLAP engines interact with each other since the OLAM engine can perform mining on the OLAP results and the OLAP engine can perform OLAP on the mining results. A metadata directory stores the database schema, the data warehouse schema, and concept hierarchy information. It is used to guide the access of the multidimensional database and the execution of dimension-related OLAP operations, such as drilling and slicing. The multidimensional database can be constructed by accessing databases, filtering data warehouses, and/or integrating multiple such sources via a database API (which is currently supported by Microsoft SQL Server 7.0 OLAP Manager).

A graphical user interface of the DBMiner system is presented in Figure B.1.

# B.2 Input and Output

The **DBMiner** system takes data from an SQL Server OLAP data cube, which itself is constructed from single or multiple relational tables, a data warehouse system, and/or other forms of data, such as spreadsheets.

The output of knowledge can be presented in many forms by the system, depending on the data mining task and user preference. Data summarization and characterization generate cross-tabulation tables, generalized rules, bar charts, pie charts, curves, or other forms of graphical output displayed using Microsoft Excel 2000. Association generates association rule tables, association planes, and association rule graphs. Classification generates the visual display of decision trees or decision tables. Clustering generates maps (for two-dimensional analysis) where clusters are contoured by their silhouettes and painted in different colors.

The system provides facilities to view concept hierarchies and data cube contents. Concept hierarchies are presented in a tree form similar to direc-

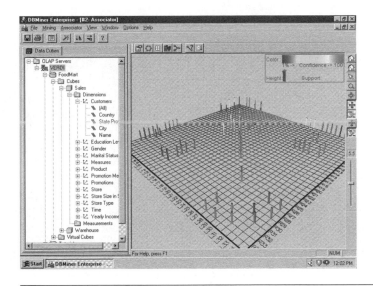

**Figure B.1**   A graphical user interface of DBMiner.

tory/subdirectory structures. Data cube contents are presented in a three-dimensional cube form, where the size and color of each cuboid in the 3-D cube represent the summarization of corresponding selected measures within a set of 3-D intervals. Moreover, a 2-D table can be viewed as a 2-D boxplot, where each boxplot represents the data dispersion view (including the median, first quartile, third quartile, whiskers, and outliers) of the corresponding intervals.

An important feature of the system is its flexible manipulation of the output knowledge via drilling, dicing, and/or other transformations. For example, after mining associations on a combination of dimensions and levels, drilling can be performed on any dimension to derive association rules over the new set of data.

# B.3  Data Mining Tasks Supported by the System

The **DBMiner** system supports the following data mining tasks:

- **OLAP analyzer.** This function presents the contents of a data cube at multiple levels of abstraction from different angles by drilling, dicing, slicing, and other OLAP operations. The output can be presented in various visual or graphical forms. Moreover, the OLAP data can be annotated to show the maximal, minimal, and standard deviation values, and other distributions by data dispersion analysis. OLAP operations can be performed on generalized data to

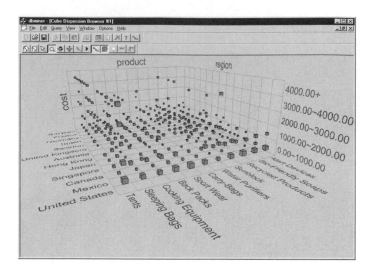

**Figure B.2** Summarized data represented by a 3-D cube.

drill or dice on regions of interest for further analysis. Figure B.2 presents a set of summarized data in the form of a 3-D cube in DBMiner.

■ **Association:** This function mines a set of association rules from a multiple dimensional database. The rules so mined can be used for cross-market analysis, correlation analysis, and so on. The search for interesting rules can be confined so as to match user-specified *metapatterns*, such as "*major*(*S:student*, *X*) ∧ *P*(*S*, *Y*) ⇒ *grade*(*S*, *Y*, *Z*)", where *major* and *grade* are predicates corresponding to attributes in a relation *student*, *S* is a variable representing a student, *P* is a predicate that can be instantiated to an attribute in *student*, and *X*, *Y* and *Z* can take on predicate values. One can also drill along any dimension to mine rules at multiple levels of abstraction. Figure B.3 presents association rules using an association ball graph, where balls represent items and arrows indicate the rule implications.

■ **Classification:** This function analyzes a set of training data (i.e., a set of objects whose class label is known), constructs a model for each class based on the features in the data, and adjusts the model based on the test data. The model so constructed is presented in the form of decision trees or classification rules, and is used to classify future data and develop a better understanding of data in the database. Figure B.4 is an example of data classification results in the form of a decision tree.

■ **Clustering:** This function groups a selected set of data objects into a set of clusters so as to ensure low intercluster similarity and high intracluster similarity. High-dimensional clustering can also be performed in multidimensional

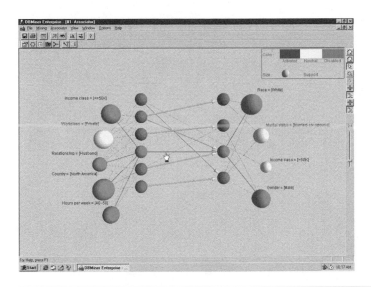

**Figure B.3**  Association rules represented by a set of balls and arrows.

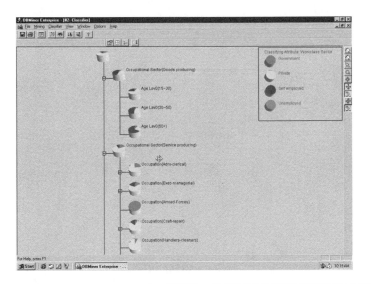

**Figure B.4**  Classification represented by a decision tree.

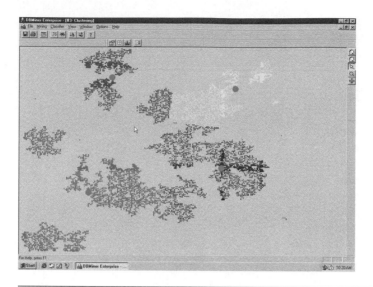

**Figure B.5**  Clustering results represented by a group of differently shaped marks.

databases. Figure B.5 is an example of data clustering results, where the two-dimensional clusters are presented in a map using a different color and a differently shaped mark per cluster.

▪ **Prediction.** This function predicts the values or value distributions for certain missing or unknown data in a selected set of objects. This involves finding the set of attributes relevant to the attribute of interest (by some statistical analysis) and predicting the value distribution based on the set of data similar to the selected object(s). For example, an employee's potential salary can be predicted based on the salary distribution of similar employees in the company.

▪ **Time-series analysis.** This module contains several time-series data analysis functions, including similarity analysis, periodicity analysis, sequential pattern analysis, and trend and deviation analysis.

The DBMiner 2.0 release consists of the following modules: OLAP analyzer, classification, association, and clustering. The prediction and time-series analysis modules are to be released in future versions.

## B.4  Support for Task and Method Selection

The **DBMiner** system supports task and method selection via a window-based graphical user interface where users can choose from various mining tasks using a mining wizard, or interact with the data mining results to mine alternative dimensions and levels. Based on the user's input, a mining query is presented to the user in the SQL-like data mining query language, DMQL, for examination. The user can modify the query, if desired, before submitting it for execution.

# B.5 Support of the KDD Process

Since the **DBMiner** system works with a data warehouse, some essential preprocessing tasks for knowledge discovery are performed, when necessary, by the (supported) underlying data warehouse system. These tasks include *data cleaning*, *data integration*, and *data consolidation* (aggregation grouped by multiple dimensions and levels). Data selection is performed in the **DBMiner** system as part of a data mining query.

In **DBMiner**, most of the postprocessing process on the discovered patterns is integrated with the data mining process. This is because a data mining query provides not only the specification of task-relevant data and the mining task, but also the interestingness measures (such as mining thresholds like support, confidence, noise, etc.) and desired rule patterns. Such an integration of mining and pattern evaluation reduces the search space and helps focus the mining process.

# B.6 Main Applications

The **DBMiner** system can be used as a general-purpose on-line analytical mining system for both OLAP and data mining in relational databases and data warehouses. The system has been used in medium to large relational databases, with fast response.

Several specialized data mining system prototypes, including GeoMiner, MultiMediaMiner, and WeblogMiner, have been developed as extensions to the DBMiner system.

# B.7 Current Status

The **DBMiner** system has evolved from a research system prototype to a system product. However, its research innovation and progress in new technology are still tightly connected with the university research laboratory.

The minimum hardware requirement for the **DBMiner** system is a Pentium-550 machine with 64 MB RAM. The system runs on Windows/NT. **DBMiner** can either be directly linked to Microsoft SQL Server 7.0 or can communicate with various relational database systems via Microsoft SQL Server OLAP Manager.

**DBMiner 2.0** can be freely downloaded at *http://db.cs.sfu.ca/DBMiner* or *http://www.dbminer.com* for 90-day trial use. User licenses for single users, group users, or educational users can be obtained via *http://www.dbminer.com*.

# Bibliography

[AAD⁺96] S. Agarwal, R. Agrawal, P. M. Deshpande, A. Gupta, J. F. Naughton, R. Ramakrishnan, and S. Sarawagi. On the computation of multidimensional aggregates. In *Proc. 1996 Int. Conf. Very Large Data Bases (VLDB'96)*, pages 506–521, Bombay, India, Sept. 1996.

[AAP00] R. Agarwal, C. Aggarwal, and V. V. V. Prasad. A tree projection algorithm for generation of frequent itemsets. In *Journal of Parallel and Distributed Computing (Special Issue on High Performance Data Mining)*, 2000.

[AAR96] A. Arning, R. Agrawal, and P. Raghavan. A linear method for deviation detection in large databases. In *Proc. 1996 Int. Conf. Data Mining and Knowledge Discovery (KDD'96)*, pages 164–169, Portland, OR, Aug. 1996.

[ABKS99] M. Ankerst, M. Breunig, H.-P. Kriegel, and J. Sander. OPTICS: Ordering points to identify the clustering structure. In *Proc. 1999 ACM-SIGMOD Int. Conf. Management of Data (SIGMOD'99)*, pages 49–60, Philadelphia, PA, June 1999.

[AD91] H. Almuallim and T. G. Dietterich. Learning with many irrelevant features. In *Proc. 9th National Conf. Artificial Intelligence (AAAI'91)*, pages 547–552, Anaheim, CA, July 1991.

[AEEK99] M. Ankerst, C. Elsen, M. Ester, and H.-P. Kriegel. Visual classification: An interactive approach to decision tree construction. In *Proc. 1999 Int. Conf. Knowledge Discovery and Data Mining (KDD'99)*, pages 392–396, San Diego, CA, Aug. 1999.

[AEMT00] K. M. Ahmed, N. M. El-Makky, and Y. Taha. A note on "Beyond market basket: Generalizing association rules to correlations." *SIGKDD Explorations*, 1:46–48, 2000.

[AFS93] R. Agrawal, C. Faloutsos, and A. Swami. Efficient similarity search in sequence databases. In *Proc. 4th Int. Conf. Foundations of Data Organization and Algorithms*, Chicago, IL, Oct. 1993.

[AGGR98] R. Agrawal, J. Gehrke, D. Gunopulos, and P. Raghavan. Automatic subspace clustering of high dimensional data for data mining applications. In *Proc. 1998*

*ACM-SIGMOD Int. Conf. Management of Data (SIGMOD'98)*, pages 94–105, Seattle, WA, June 1998.

[AGI$^+$92]  R. Agrawal, S. Ghosh, T. Imielinski, B. Iyer, and A. Swami. An interval classifier for database mining applications. In *Proc. 1992 Int. Conf. Very Large Data Bases (VLDB'92)*, pages 560–573, Vancouver, Canada, Aug. 1992.

[Agr96]  A. Agresti. *An Introduction to Categorical Data Analysis*. New York: John Wiley & Sons, 1996.

[AGS97]  R. Agrawal, A. Gupta, and S. Sarawagi. Modeling multidimensional databases. In *Proc. 1997 Int. Conf. Data Engineering (ICDE'97)*, pages 232–243, Birmingham, England, Apr. 1997.

[AIS93a]  R. Agrawal, T. Imielinski, and A. Swami. Database mining: A performance perspective. *IEEE Trans. Knowledge and Data Engineering*, 5:914–925, 1993.

[AIS93b]  R. Agrawal, T. Imielinski, and A. Swami. Mining association rules between sets of items in large databases. In *Proc. 1993 ACM-SIGMOD Int. Conf. Management of Data (SIGMOD'93)*, pages 207–216, Washington, DC, May 1993.

[AK93]  T. Anand and G. Kahn. Opportunity explorer: Navigating large databases using knowledge discovery templates. In *Proc. AAAI-93 Workshop Knowledge Discovery in Databases*, pages 45–51, Washington, DC, July 1993.

[ALSS95]  R. Agrawal, K.-I. Lin, H. S. Sawhney, and K. Shim. Fast similarity search in the presence of noise, scaling, and translation in time-series databases. In *Proc. 1995 Int. Conf. Very Large Data Bases (VLDB'95)*, pages 490–501, Zurich, Switzerland, Sept. 1995.

[AM98]  G. Arocena and A. O. Mendelzon. WebOQL: Restructuring documents, databases, and webs. In *Proc. 1998 Int. Conf. Data Engineering (ICDE'98)*, Orlando, FL, Feb. 1998.

[AMS$^+$96]  R. Agrawal, H. Mannila, R. Srikant, H. Toivonen, and A. I. Verkamo. Fast discovery of association rules. In U. M. Fayyad, G. Piatetsky-Shapiro, P. Smyth, and R. Uthurusamy, editors, *Advances in Knowledge Discovery and Data Mining*, pages 307–328. AAAI/MIT Press, 1996.

[Aok98]  P. M. Aoki. Generalizing "search" in generalized search trees. In *Proc. 1998 Int. Conf. Data Engineering (ICDE'98)*, pages 380–389, Orlando, FL, Feb. 1998.

[AP94]  A. Aamodt and E. Plazas. Case-based reasoning: Foundational issues, methodological variations, and system approaches. *AI Comm.*, 7:39–52, 1994.

[APWZ95]  R. Agrawal, G. Psaila, E. L. Wimmers, and M. Zait. Querying shapes of histories. In *Proc. 1995 Int. Conf. Very Large Data Bases (VLDB'95)*, pages 502–514, Zurich, Switzerland, Sept. 1995.

[AQM+97]  S. Abitboul, D. Quass, J. McHugh, J. Widom, and J. Wiener. The Lorel query language for semistructured data. *Int. Journal of Digital Libraries*, 1:68–88, 1997.

[AS94a]  R. Agrawal and R. Srikant. Fast algorithms for mining association rules in large databases. In Research Report RJ 9839, IBM Almaden Research Center, San Jose, CA, June 1994.

[AS94b]  R. Agrawal and R. Srikant. Fast algorithms for mining association rules. In *Proc. 1994 Int. Conf. Very Large Data Bases (VLDB'94)*, pages 487–499, Santiago, Chile, Sept. 1994.

[AS95]  R. Agrawal and R. Srikant. Mining sequential patterns. In *Proc. 1995 Int. Conf. Data Engineering (ICDE'95)*, pages 3–14, Taipei, Taiwan, Mar. 1995.

[AS96]  R. Agrawal and J. C. Shafer. Parallel mining of association rules: Design, implementation, and experience. *IEEE Trans. Knowledge and Data Engineering*, 8:962–969, 1996.

[AS00]  R. Agrawal and R. Srikant. Privacy-preserving data mining. In *Proc. 2000 ACM-SIGMOD Int. Conf. Management of Data (SIGMOD'00)*, pages 439–450, Dallas, TX, May 2000.

[Avn95]  S. Avner. Discovery of comprehensible symbolic rules in a neural network. In *Intl. Symposium on Intelligence in Neural and Biological Systems*, pages 64–67, 1995.

[AY99]  C. C. Aggarwal and P. S. Yu. A new framework for itemset generation. In *Proc. 1998 ACM Symp. Principles of Database Systems (PODS'98)*, pages 18–24, Seattle, WA, June 1999.

[BA97]  L. A. Breslow and D. W. Aha. Simplifying decision trees: A survey. *Knowledge Engineering Review*, 12:1–40, 1997.

[Bay98]  R. J. Bayardo. Efficiently mining long patterns from databases. In *Proc. 1998 ACM-SIGMOD Int. Conf. Management of Data (SIGMOD'98)*, pages 85–93, Seattle, WA, June 1998.

[BB98]  P. Baldi and S. Brunak. *Bioinformatics: The Machine Learning Approach*. Cambridge, MA: MIT Press, 1998.

[BC97]  S. Benninga and B. Czaczkes. *Financial Modeling*. Cambridge, MA: MIT Press, 1997.

[BCP93]  D. E. Brown, V. Corruble, and C. L. Pittard. A comparison of decision tree classifiers with backpropagation neural networks for multimodal classification problems. *Pattern Recognition*, 26:953–961, 1993.

[BDF+97]  D. Barbará, W. DuMouchel, C. Faloutsos, P. J. Haas, J. H. Hellerstein, Y. Ioannidis, H. V. Jagadish, T. Johnson, R. Ng, V. Poosala, K. A. Ross, and K. C. Servcik. The New Jersey data reduction report. *Bulletin of the Technical Committee on Data Engineering*, 20:3–45, Dec. 1997.

[**BDG96**]   A. Bruce, D. Donoho, and H.-Y. Gao. Wavelet analysis. In *IEEE Spectrum*, pages 26–35, Oct. 1996.

[**Ber81**]   J. Bertin. *Graphics and Graphic Information Processing*. Berlin, 1981.

[**Ber99**]   M. J. A. Berry. The privacy backlash. *Decision Support (http://www. intelligententerprise.com/992610/decision.shtml, viewed Feb. 2000)*, 2, Oct. 26, 1999.

[**BFOS84**]   L. Breiman, J. Friedman, R. Olshen, and C. Stone. *Classification and Regression Trees*. Monterey, CA: Wadsworth International Group, 1984.

[**BFR98**]   P. Bradley, U. Fayyad, and C. Reina. Scaling clustering algorithms to large databases. In *Proc. 1998 Int. Conf. Knowledge Discovery and Data Mining (KDD'98)*, pages 9–15, New York, Aug. 1998.

[**BH99**]   M. Berthold and D. J. Hand. *Intelligent Data Analysis: An Introduction*. Springer-Verlag, 1999.

[**Bis95**]   C. M. Bishop. *Neural Networks for Pattern Recognition*. Oxford, UK: Oxford University Press, 1995.

[**BL94**]   V. Barnett and T. Lewis. *Outliers in Statistical Data*. New York: John Wiley & Sons, 1994.

[**BL99**]   M. J. A. Berry and G. Linoff. *Mastering Data Mining: The Art and Science of Customer Relationship Management*. New York: John Wiley & Sons, 1999.

[**BM98**]   E. Bloedorn and R. S. Michalski. Data-driven constructive induction: A methodology and its applications. In H. Liu and H. Motoda, editors, *Feature Selection for Knowledge Discovery and Data Mining*. Boston: Kluwer Academic Publishers, 1998.

[**BMS97**]   S. Brin, R. Motwani, and C. Silverstein. Beyond market basket: Generalizing association rules to correlations. In *Proc. 1997 ACM-SIGMOD Int. Conf. Management of Data (SIGMOD'97)*, pages 265–276, Tucson, AZ, May 1997.

[**BMUT97**]   S. Brin, R. Motwani, J. D. Ullman, and S. Tsur. Dynamic itemset counting and implication rules for market basket analysis. In *Proc. 1997 ACM-SIGMOD Int. Conf. Management of Data (SIGMOD'97)*, pages 255–264, Tucson, AZ, May 1997.

[**BN92**]   W. L. Buntine and T. Niblett. A further comparison of splitting rules for decision-tree induction. *Machine Learning*, 8:75–85, 1992.

[**BO98**]   A. Baxevanis and B. F. F. Ouellette. *Bioinformatics: A Practical Guide to the Analysis of Genes and Proteins*. New York: John Wiley & Sons, 1998.

[**BP92**]   J. C. Bezdek and S. K. Pal. *Fuzzy Models for Pattern Recognition: Methods That Search for Structures in Data*. IEEE Press, 1992.

[**BP97**]   E. Baralis and G. Psaila. Designing templates for mining association rules. *Journal of Intelligent Information Systems*, 9:7–32, 1997.

[**BP98**]  S. Brin and L. Page. The anatomy of a large-scale hypertextual web search engine. In *Proc. 7th World Wide Web Conf. (WWW'98)*, Brisbane, Australia, 1998.

[**BP99**]  D. M. Bates and J. C. Pinheiro. *Mixed Effects Models in S*. New York: Springer-Verlag, 1999.

[**BR99**]  K. Beyer and R. Ramakrishnan. Bottom-up computation of sparse and iceberg cubes. In *Proc. 1999 ACM-SIGMOD Conf. on Management of Data (SIGMOD'99)*, pages 359–370, Philadelphia, PA, June 1999.

[**Bre96**]  L. Breiman. Bagging predictors. *Machine Learning*, 24:123–140, 1996.

[**BS97**]  A. Berson and S. J. Smith. *Data Warehousing, Data Mining, and OLAP*. New York: McGraw-Hill, 1997.

[**BST99**]  A. Berson, S. J. Smith, and K. Thearling. *Building Data Mining Applications for CRM*. New York: McGraw-Hill, 1999.

[**BT99**]  D. P. Ballou and G. K. Tayi. Enhancing data quality in data warehouse environments. *Communications of ACM*, 42:73–78, 1999.

[**BU95**]  C. E. Brodley and P. E. Utgoff. Multivariate decision trees. *Machine Learning*, 19:45–77, 1995.

[**Bun94**]  W. L. Buntine. Operations for learning with graphical models. *Journal of Artificial Intelligence Research*, 2:159–225, 1994.

[**BWJ98**]  C. Bettini, X. Sean Wang, and S. Jajodia. Mining temporal relationships with multiple granularities in time sequences. *Data Engineering Bulletin*, 21:32–38, 1998.

[**BYRN99**]  R. Baeza-Yates and B. Ribeiro-Neto. *Modern Information Retrieval*. Reading, MA. Addison-Wesley, 1999.

[**Cat91**]  J. Catlett. *Megainduction: Machine Learning on Very Large Databases*. Ph.D. Thesis, University of Sydney, 1991.

[**Cav98**]  A. Cavoukian. Data mining: Staking a claim on your privacy. In *Information and Privacy Commissioner/ Ontario (http://www.ipc.on.ca/Web-site.ups/Intro/Frames .html, viewed Feb. 2000)*, Jan. 1998.

[**CC92**]  W. W. Chu and Q. Chen. Neighborhood and associative query answering. *Journal of Intelligent Information Systems*, 1:355–382, 1992.

[**CCH91**]  Y. Cai, N. Cercone, and J. Han. Attribute-oriented induction in relational databases. In G. Piatetsky-Shapiro and W. J. Frawley, editors, *Knowledge Discovery in Databases*, pages 213–228. Cambridge, MA: AAAI/MIT Press, 1991.

[**CCS93**]  E. F. Codd, S. B. Codd, and C. T. Salley. Beyond decision support. *Computer World*, 27, July 1993.

[CD88]  F. Cuppens and R. Demolombe. Cooperative answering: A methodology to provide intelligent access to databases. In *Proc. 2nd Int. Conf. Expert Database Systems*, pages 621–643, Fairfax, VA, Apr. 1988.

[CD97]  S. Chaudhuri and U. Dayal. An overview of data warehousing and OLAP technology. *ACM SIGMOD Record*, 26:65–74, 1997.

[CDI98]  S. Chakrabarti, B. E. Dom, and P. Indyk. Enhanced hypertext classification using hyper-links. In *Proc. 1998 ACM-SIGMOD Int. Conf. Management of Data (SIGMOD'98)*, pages 307–318, Seattle, WA, June 1998.

[CDK$^+$99]  S. Chakrabarti, B. E. Dom, S. R. Kumar, P. Raghavan, S. Rajagopalan, A. Tomkins, D. Gibson, and J. M. Kleinberg. Mining the web's link structure. *COMPUTER*, 32:60–67, 1999.

[CDTW00]  J. Chen, D. DeWitt, F. Tian, and Y. Wang. NiagraCQ: A scalable continuous query system for internet databases. In *Proc. 2000 ACM-SIGMOD Int. Conf. Management of Data (SIGMOD'00)*, Dallas, TX, May 2000.

[CH67]  T. Cover and P. Hart. Nearest neighbor pattern classification. *IEEE Trans. Information Theory*, 13:21–27, 1967.

[CH92]  G. Cooper and E. Herskovits. A Bayesian method for the induction of probabilistic networks from data. *Machine Learning*, 9:309–347, 1992.

[CH98]  C. Carter and H. Hamilton. Efficient attribute-oriented generalization for knowledge discovery from large databases. *IEEE Trans. Knowledge and Data Engineering*, 10:193–208, 1998.

[Cha84]  C. Chatfield. *The Analysis of Time Series: An Introduction*, 3rd ed. New York: Chapman and Hall, 1984.

[Cha00]  S. Chakrabarti. Data mining for hypertex: A tutorial survey. *SIGKDD Explorations*, 1:1–11, 2000.

[CHD00]  Q. Chen, M. Hsu, and U. Dayal. A data-warehouse/OLAP framework for scalable telecommunication tandem traffic analysis. In *Proc. 2000 Int. Conf. Data Engineering (ICDE'00)*, pages 201–210, San Diego, CA, Feb. 2000.

[CHN$^+$96]  D. W. Cheung, J. Han, V. Ng, A. Fu, and Y. Fu. A fast distributed algorithm for mining association rules. In *Proc. 1996 Int. Conf. Parallel and Distributed Information Systems*, pages 31–44, Miami Beach, FL, Dec. 1996.

[CHNW96]  D. W. Cheung, J. Han, V. Ng, and C. Y. Wong. Maintenance of discovered association rules in large databases: An incremental updating technique. In *Proc. 1996 Int. Conf. Data Engineering (ICDE'96)*, pages 106–114, New Orleans, LA, Feb. 1996.

[CHY96]  M. S. Chen, J. Han, and P. S. Yu. Data mining: An overview from a database perspective. *IEEE Trans. Knowledge and Data Engineering*, 8:866–883, 1996.

[**CK98**]  M. Carey and D. Kossman. Reducing the braking distance of an SQL query engine. In *Proc. 1998 Int. Conf. Very Large Data Bases (VLDB'98)*, pages 158–169, New York, Aug. 1998.

[**Cle93**]  W. Cleveland. *Visualizing Data*. Summit, NJ: Hobart Press, 1993.

[**CM94**]  S. P. Curram and J. Mingers. Neural networks, decision tree induction and discriminant analysis: An empirical comparison. *J. Operational Research Society*, 45:440–450, 1994.

[**CN89**]  P. Clark and T. Niblett. The CN2 induction algorithm. *Machine Learning*, 3:261–283, 1989.

[**CPS98**]  K. Cios, W. Pedrycz, and R. Swiniarski. *Data Mining Methods for Knowledge Discovery*. Boston: Kluwer Academic Publishers, 1998.

[**CR95**]  Y. Chauvin and D. Rumelhart. *Backpropagation: Theory, Architectures, and Applications*. Hillsdale, NJ: Lawrence Erlbaum Assoc., 1995.

[**CS93a**]  P. K. Chan and S. J. Stolfo. Experiments on multistrategy learning by meta-learning. In *Proc. 2nd. Int. Conf. Information and Knowledge Management*, pages 314–323, 1993.

[**CS93b**]  P. K. Chan and S. J. Stolfo. Metalearning for multistrategy and parallel learning. In *Proc. 2nd. Int. Workshop on Multistrategy Learning*, pages 150–165, 1993.

[**CS96a**]  P. Cheeseman and J. Stutz. Bayesian classification (AutoClass): Theory and results. In U. M. Fayyad, G. Piatetsky-Shapiro, P. Smyth, and R. Uthurusamy, editors, *Advances in Knowledge Discovery and Data Mining*, pages 153–180. Cambridge, MA: AAAI/MIT Press, 1996.

[**CS96b**]  M. W. Craven and J. W. Shavlik. Extracting tree-structured representations of trained networks. In D. Touretzky, M. Mozer, and M. Hasselmo, editors, *Advances in Neural Information Processing Systems*. Cambridge, MA: MIT Press, 1996.

[**CS97**]  M. W. Craven and J. W. Shavlik. Using neural networks in data mining. *Future Generation Computer Systems*, 13:211–229, 1997.

[**CSD98**]  S. Chakrabarti, S. Sarawagi, and B. Dom. Mining surprising patterns using temporal description length. In *Proc. 1998 Int. Conf. Very Large Data Bases (VLDB'98)*, pages 606–617, New York, NY, Aug. 1998.

[**Dau92**]  I. Daubechies. *Ten Lectures on Wavelets*. Montpelier, VT: Capital City Press, 1992.

[**DDF$^+$90**]  S. Deerwester, S. Dumais, G. Furnas, T. Landauer, and R. Harshman. Indexing by latent semantic analysis. *J. American Society for Information Science*, 41:391–407, 1990.

[**Dev95**]  J. L. Devore. *Probability and Statistics for Engineering and the Sciences*, 4th ed. New York: Duxbury Press, 1995.

[**DH73**]  R. Duda and P. Hart. *Pattern Classification and Scene Analysis*. New York: John Wiley & Sons, 1973.

[**DL97**]  M. Dash and H. Liu. Feature selection methods for classification. *Intelligent Data Analysis: An International Journal (http://www.elsevier.com/locate/ida)*, 1, 1997.

[**DL99**]  G. Dong and J. Li. Efficient mining of emerging patterns: Discovering trends and differences. In *Proc. 1999 Int. Conf. Knowledge Discovery and Data Mining (KDD'99)*, pages 43–52, San Diego, CA, Aug. 1999.

[**DLY97**]  M. Dash, H. Liu, and J. Yao. Dimensionality reduction of unsupervised data. In *Proc. 9th IEEE Intl. Conf. on Tools with AI (ICTAI'97)*, pages 532–539. Los Alamitos, CA: IEEE Computer Society, 1997.

[**DM83**]  T. G. Dietterich and R. S. Michalski. A comparative review of selected methods for learning from examples. In Michalski et al., editors, *Machine Learning: An Artificial Intelligence Approach, Vol. 1*, pages 41–82. San Mateo, CA: Morgan Kaufmann, 1983.

[**DNR$^+$97**]  P. Deshpande, J. Naughton, K. Ramasamy, A. Shukla, K. Tufte, and Y. Zhao. Cubing algorithms, storage estimation, and storage and processing alternatives for OLAP. *Data Engineering Bulletin*, 20:3–11, 1997.

[**Dob90**]  A. J. Dobson. *An Introduction to Generalized Linear Models*. New York: Chapman and Hall, 1990.

[**DP96**]  P. Domingos and M. Pazzani. Beyond independence: Conditions for the optimality of the simple Bayesian classifier. In *Proc. 13th Intl. Conf. Machine Learning*, pages 105–112, 1996.

[**DP97**]  J. Devore and R. Peck. *Statistics: The Exploration and Analysis of Data*. New York: Duxbury Press, 1997.

[**DR99**]  D. Donjerkovic and R. Ramakrishnan. Probabilistic optimization of top $N$ queries. In *Proc. 1999 Int. Conf. Very Large Data Bases (VLDB'99)*, pages 411–422, Edinburgh, UK, Sept. 1999.

[**DT93**]  V. Dhar and A. Tuzhilin. Abstract-driven pattern discovery in databases. *IEEE Trans. Knowledge and Data Engineering*, 5:926–938, 1993.

[**EFKS98**]  M. Ester, A. Frommelt, H.-P. Kriegel, and J. Sander. Algorithms for characterization and trend detection in spatial databases. In *Proc. 1998 Int. Conf. Knowledge Discovery and Data Mining (KDD'98)*, pages 44–50, New York, Aug. 1998.

[**Ege89**]  M. J. Egenhofer. *Spatial Query Languages*. Portland, ME: UMI Research Press, University of Maine, 1989.

[**EKS97**]  M. Ester, H.-P. Kriegel, and J. Sander. Spatial data mining: A database approach. In *Proc. Int. Symp. Large Spatial Databases (SSD'97)*, pages 47–66, Berlin, Germany, July 1997.

[**EKSX96**]  M. Ester, H.-P. Kriegel, J. Sander, and X. Xu. A density-based algorithm for discovering clusters in large spatial databases. In *Proc. 1996 Int. Conf. Knowledge Discovery and Data Mining (KDD'96)*, pages 226–231, Portland, OR, Aug. 1996.

[**EKSX97**]  M. Ester, H.-P. Kriegel, J. Sander, and X. Xu. Density-connected sets and their application for trend detection in spatial databases. In *Proc. 1997 Int. Conf. Knowledge Discovery and Data Mining (KDD'97)*, pages 10–15, Newport Beach, CA, Aug. 1997.

[**EKX95**]  M. Ester, H.-P. Kriegel, and X. Xu. Knowledge discovery in large spatial databases: Focusing techniques for efficient class identification. In *Proc. 4th Int. Symp. Large Spatial Databases (SSD'95)*, pages 67–82, Portland, ME, Aug. 1995.

[**Elk97**]  C. Elkan. Boosting and naive Bayesian learning. In Technical Report CS97-557, Dept. of Computer Science and Engineering, Univ. Calif. at San Diego, Sept. 1997.

[**EN94**]  R. Elmasri and S. B. Navathe. *Fundamentals of Database Systems*, 2nd ed. Redwood City, CA: Benjamin/Cummings, 1994.

[**ET93**]  B. Efron and R. Tibshirani. *An Introduction to the Bootstrap*. New York: Chapman and Hall, 1993.

[**Fal85**]  C. Faloutsos. Access methods for text. *ACM Comput. Surv.*, 17:49–74, 1985.

[**FB74**]  R. A. Finkel and J. L. Bentley. Quad-trees: A data structure for retrieval on composite keys. *ACTA Informatica*, 4:1–9, 1974.

[**FBY92**]  W. Frakes and R. Baeza-Yates. *Information Retrieval: Data Structures and Algorithms*. Englewood Cliffs, NJ: Prentice Hall, 1992.

[**FDW96**]  U. M. Fayyad, S. G. Djorgovski, and N. Weir. Automating the analysis and cataloging of sky surveys. In U. M. Fayyad, G. Piatetsky-Shapiro, P. Smyth, and R. Uthurusamy, editors, *Advances in Knowledge Discovery and Data Mining*, pages 471–493. Cambridge, MA: AAAI/MIT Press, 1996.

[**FH87**]  K. Fukunaga and D. Hummels. Bayes error estimation using parzen and k-nn procedure. In *IEEE Trans. Pattern Analysis and Machine Learning*, pages 634–643, 1987.

[**FH95**]  Y. Fu and J. Han. Meta-rule-guided mining of association rules in relational databases. In *Proc. 1st Int. Workshop Integration of Knowledge Discovery with Deductive and Object-Oriented Databases (KDOOD'95)*, pages 39–46, Singapore, Dec. 1995.

[**FH98**]  R. Feldman and H. Hirsh. Finding associations in collections of text. In R. S. Michalski, I. Bratko, and M. Kubat, editors, *Machine Learning and Data Mining: Methods and Applications*, pages 223–240. New York: John Wiley & Sons, 1998.

[**FI93**]  U. Fayyad and K. Irani. Multi-interval discretization of continuous-values attributes for classification learning. In *Proc. 13th Intl. Joint Conf. on Artificial Intelligence (IJCAI'93)*, pages 1022–1029, Chambery, France, 1993.

[**Fis87**]  D. Fisher. Improving inference through conceptual clustering. In *Proc. 1987 AAAI Conf.*, pages 461–465, Seattle, WA, July 1987.

[**FL90**]  S. Fahlman and C. Lebiere. The cascade-correlation learning algorithm. In Technical Report CMU-CS-90-100, Computer Science Department, Carnegie Mellon University, Pittsburgh, PA, 1990.

[**FL95**]  C. Faloutsos and K.-I. Lin. FastMap: A fast algorithm for indexing, datamining and visualization of traditional and multimedia datasets. In *Proc. 1995 ACM-SIGMOD Int. Conf. Management of Data (SIGMOD'95)*, pages 163–174, San Jose, CA, May 1995.

[**FLM98**]  D. Florescu, A. Y. Levy, and A. O. Mendelzon. Database techniques for the world-wide web: A survey. *SIGMOD Record*, 27:59–74, 1998.

[**FMMT96**]  T. Fukuda, Y. Morimoto, S. Morishita, and T. Tokuyama. Data mining using two-dimensional optimized association rules: Scheme, algorithms, and visualization. In *Proc. 1996 ACM-SIGMOD Int. Conf. Management of Data (SIGMOD'96)*, pages 13–23, Montreal, Canada, June 1996.

[**FPS$^+$96**]  U. M. Fayyad, G. Piatetsky-Shapiro, P. Smyth, and R. Uthurusamy, editors. *Advances in Knowledge Discovery and Data Mining*. Cambridge, MA: AAAI/MIT Press, 1996.

[**Fri77**]  J. H. Friedman. A recursive partitioning decision rule for nonparametric classifiers. *IEEE Trans. on Comp.*, 26:404–408, 1977.

[**Fri91**]  J. H. Friedman. Multivariate adaptive regression. *Annals of Statistics*, 19:1–141, 1991.

[**FRM94**]  C. Faloutsos, M. Ranganathan, and Y. Manolopoulos. Fast subsequence matching in time-series databases. In *Proc. 1994 ACM-SIGMOD Conf. Management of Data*, pages 419–429, Minneapolis, MN, May 1994.

[**FS93**]  U. Fayyad and P. Smyth. Image database exploration: Progress and challenges. In *Proc. AAAI '93 Workshop Knowledge Discovery in Databases*, pages 14–27, Washington, DC, 1993.

[**FS97**]  Y. Freund and R. E. Schapire. A decision-theoretic generalization of on-line learning and an application to boosting. *Journal of Computer and System Sciences*, 55:119–139, 1997.

[**FSGM$^+$98**]  M. Fang, N. Shivakumar, H. Garcia-Molina, R. Motwani, and J. D. Ullman. Computing iceberg queries efficiently. In *Proc. 1998 Int. Conf. Very Large Data Bases (VLDB'98)*, pages 299–310, New York, Aug. 1998.

[FSN+95] M. Flickner, H. Sawhney, W. Niblack, J. Ashley, B. Dom, Q. Huang, M. Gorkani, J. Hafner, D. Lee, D. Petkovic, S. Steele, and P. Yanker. Query by image and video content: The QBIC system. *IEEE Computer*, 28:23–32, 1995.

[Fu94] L. Fu. *Neural Networks in Computer Intelligence*. New York: McGraw-Hill, 1994.

[FU94] U. M. Fayyad and R. Uthurusamy, editors. *Notes of AAAI'94 Workshop Knowledge Discovery in Databases (KDD'94)*. Seattle, WA, July 1994.

[FU96] U. M. Fayyad and R. Uthurusamy, editors. *Proc. 1st Int. Conf. Knowledge Discovery and Data Mining (KDD'95)*. Montreal, Canada, Aug. 1995. AAAI Press.

[FUP93] U. M. Fayyad, R. Uthurusamy, and G. Piatetsky-Shapiro, editors. *Notes of AAAI'93 Workshop Knowledge Discovery in Databases (KDD'93)*. Washington, DC, July 1993.

[Gal93] S. I. Gallant. *Neural Network Learning and Expert Systems*. Cambridge, MA: MIT Press, 1993.

[Gat99] B. Gates. *Business @ the Speed of Thought*. New York: Warner Books, 1999.

[GCB+97] J. Gray, S. Chaudhuri, A. Bosworth, A. Layman, D. Reichart, M. Venkatrao, F. Pellow, and H. Pirahesh. Data cube: A relational aggregation operator generalizing group-by, cross-tab and sub-totals. *Data Mining and Knowledge Discovery*, 1:29–54, 1997.

[GG98] V. Gaede and O. Günther. Multidimensional access methods. *ACM Comput. Surv.*, 30:170–231, 1998.

[GG99] M. Goebel and L. Gruenwald. A survey of data mining and knowledge discovery software tools. *SIGKDD Explorations*, 1:20–33, 1999.

[GGR99] V. Ganti, J. E. Gehrke, and R. Ramakrishnan. CACTUS—clustering categorical data using summaries. In *Proc. 1999 Int. Conf. Knowledge Discovery and Data Mining (KDD'99)*, San Diego, CA, 1999.

[GGRL99] J. Gehrke, V. Ganti, R. Ramakrishnan, and W.-Y. Loh. BOAT-optimistic decision tree construction. In *Proc. 1999 ACM-SIGMOD Int. Conf. Management of Data (SIGMOD '99)*, pages 169–180, Philadelphia, PA, June 1999.

[GKR98] D. Gibson, J. M. Kleinberg, and P. Raghavan. Clustering categorical data: An approach based on dynamical systems. In *Proc. 1998 Int. Conf. Very Large Data Bases (VLDB'98)*, pages 311–323, New York, Aug. 1998.

[GLF89] J. Gennari, P. Langley, and D. Fisher. Models of incremental concept formation. *Artificial Intelligence*, 40:11–61, 1989.

[GLW00] G. Grahne, L. Lakshmanan, and X. Wang. Efficient mining of constrained correlated sets. In *Proc. 2000 Int. Conf. Data Engineering (ICDE'00)*, pages 512–521, San Diego, CA, February 2000.

[**GMV96**] I. Guyon, N. Matic, and V. Vapnik. Discovering informative patterns and data cleaning. In U. M. Fayyad, G. Piatetsky-Shapiro, P. Smyth, and R. Uthurusamy, editors, *Advances in Knowledge Discovery and Data Mining*, pages 181–203. Cambridge, MA: AAAI/MIT Press, 1996.

[**Gol89**] D. Goldberg. *Genetic Algorithms in Search, Optimization, and Machine Learning*. Reading, MA: Addison-Wesley, 1989.

[**GRG98**] J. Gehrke, R. Ramakrishnan, and V. Ganti. Rainforest: A framework for fast decision tree construction of large datasets. In *Proc. 1998 Int. Conf. Very Large Data Bases (VLDB'98)*, pages 416–427, New York, Aug. 1998.

[**Gro99**] R. Groth. *Data Mining: Building Competitive Advantage*. Englewood Cliffs, NJ: Prentice Hall, 1999.

[**GRS98**] S. Guha, R. Rastogi, and K. Shim. Cure: An efficient clustering algorithm for large databases. In *Proc. 1998 ACM-SIGMOD Int. Conf. Management of Data (SIGMOD'98)*, pages 73–84, Seattle, WA, June 1998.

[**GRS99**] S. Guha, R. Rastogi, and K. Shim. Rock: A robust clustering algorithm for categorical attributes. In *Proc. 1999 Int. Conf. Data Engineering (ICDE'99)*, pages 512–521, Sydney, Australia, Mar. 1999.

[**Gus97**] D. Gusfield. *Algorithms on Strings, Trees and Sequences, Computer Science and Computation Biology*. New York: Cambridge University Press, 1997.

[**Gut84**] A. Guttman. R-tree: A dynamic index structure for spatial searching. In *Proc. 1984 ACM-SIGMOD Int. Conf. Management of Data (SIGMOD'84)*, pages 47–57, Boston, MA, June 1984.

[**Güt94**] R. H. Güting. An introduction to spatial database systems. *The VLDB Journal*, 3:357–400, 1994.

[**HAC**[+]**99**] J. M. Hellerstein, R. Avnur, A. Chou, C. Hidber, C. Olston, V. Raman, T. Roth, and P. J. Haas. Interactive data analysis: The control project. *IEEE Computer*, 32:51–59, July 1999.

[**Han98**] J. Han. Towards on-line analytical mining in large databases. *ACM SIGMOD Record*, 27:97–107, 1998.

[**Har75**] J. A. Hartigan. *Clustering Algorithms*. New York: John Wiley & Sons, 1975.

[**HB88**] S. J. Hanson and D. J. Burr. Minkowski back-propagation: Learning in connectionist models with non-euclidean error signals. In *Neural Information Processing Systems*, American Institute of Physics, 1988.

[**HC95**] R. V. Hogg and A. T. Craig. *Introduction to Mathematical Statistics*, 5th ed. Englewood Cliffs, NJ: Prentice Hall, 1995.

[**HCC93**] J. Han, Y. Cai, and N. Cercone. Data-driven discovery of quantitative rules in relational databases. *IEEE Trans. Knowledge and Data Engineering*, 5:29–40, 1993.

[**HCC98**]  J. Han, S. Chee, and J. Y. Chiang. Issues for on-line analytical mining of data warehouses. In *Proc. 1998 SIGMOD Workshop on Research Issues on Data Mining and Knowledge Discovery (DMKD'98)*, pages 2:1–2:5, Seattle, WA, June 1998.

[**HDY99**]  J. Han, G. Dong, and Y. Yin. Efficient mining of partial periodic patterns in time series database. In *Proc. 1999 Int. Conf. Data Engineering (ICDE'99)*, pages 106–115, Sydney, Australia, Apr. 1999.

[**Hec96**]  D. Heckerman. Bayesian networks for knowledge discovery. In U. M. Fayyad, G. Piatetsky-Shapiro, P. Smyth, and R. Uthurusamy, editors, *Advances in Knowledge Discovery and Data Mining*, pages 273–305. Cambridge, MA: MIT Press, 1996.

[**HF94**]  J. Han and Y. Fu. Dynamic generation and refinement of concept hierarchies for knowledge discovery in databases. In *Proc. AAAI'94 Workshop Knowledge Discovery in Databases (KDD'94)*, pages 157–168, Seattle, WA, July 1994.

[**HF95**]  J. Han and Y. Fu. Discovery of multiple-level association rules from large databases. In *Proc. 1995 Int. Conf. Very Large Data Bases (VLDB'95)*, pages 420–431, Zurich, Switzerland, Sept. 1995.

[**HF96**]  J. Han and Y. Fu. Exploration of the power of attribute-oriented induction in data mining. In U. M. Fayyad, G. Piatetsky-Shapiro, P. Smyth, and R. Uthurusamy, editors, *Advances in Knowledge Discovery and Data Mining*, pages 399–421. Cambridge, MA: AAAI/MIT Press, 1996.

[**HFW**$^+$**96a**]  J. Han, Y. Fu, W. Wang, J. Chiang, W. Gong, K. Koperski, D. Li, Y. Lu, A. Rajan, N. Stefanovic, B. Xia, and O. R. Zaïane. DBMiner: A system for mining knowledge in large relational databases. In *Proc. 1996 Int. Conf. Data Mining and Knowledge Discovery (KDD'96)*, pages 250–255, Portland, OR, Aug. 1996.

[**HFW**$^+$**96b**]  J. Han, Y. Fu, W. Wang, K. Koperski, and O. R. Zaïane. DMQL: A data mining query language for relational databases. In *Proc. 1996 SIGMOD'96 Workshop Research Issues on Data Mining and Knowledge Discovery (DMKD'96)*, pages 27–34, Montreal, Canada, June 1996.

[**HGC95**]  D. Heckerman, D. Geiger, and D. M. Chickering. Learning Bayesian networks: The combination of knowledge and statistical data. *Machine Learning*, 20:197–243, 1995.

[**HHCF96**]  J. Han, Y. Huang, N. Cercone, and Y. Fu. Intelligent query answering by knowledge discovery techniques. *IEEE Trans. Knowledge and Data Engineering*, 8:373–390, 1996.

[**HHW97**]  J. Hellerstein, P. Haas, and H. Wang. Online aggregation. In *Proc. 1997 ACM-SIGMOD Int. Conf. Management of Data (SIGMOD'97)*, pages 171–182, Tucson, AZ, May 1997.

[**Hig97**]  R. C. Higgins. *Analysis for Financial Management*. Irwin/McGraw-Hill, 1997.

[**HK91**] P. Hoschka and W. Klösgen. A support system for interpreting statistical data. In G. Piatetsky-Shapiro and W. J. Frawley, editors, *Knowledge Discovery in Databases*, pages 325–346. Cambridge, MA: AAAI/MIT Press, 1991.

[**HK98**] A. Hinneburg and D. A. Keim. An efficient approach to clustering in large multimedia databases with noise. In *Proc. 1998 Int. Conf. Knowledge Discovery and Data Mining (KDD'98)*, pages 58–65, New York, Aug. 1998.

[**HKP91**] J. Hertz, A. Krogh, and R. G. Palmer. *Introduction to the Theory of Neural Computation*. Reading, MA: Addison-Wesley, 1991.

[**HKS97**] J. Han, K. Koperski, and N. Stefanovic. GeoMiner: A system prototype for spatial data mining. In *Proc. 1997 ACM-SIGMOD Int. Conf. Management of Data (SIGMOD'97)*, pages 553–556, Tucson, AZ, May 1997.

[**HM91**] J. Hong and C. Mao. Incremental discovery of rules and structure by hierarchical and parallel clustering. In G. Piatetsky-Shapiro and W. J. Frawley, editors, *Knowledge Discovery in Databases*, pages 177–193. Cambridge, MA: AAAI/MIT Press, 1991.

[**HMM86**] J. Hong, I. Mozetic, and R. S. Michalski. AQ15: Incremental learning of attribute-based descriptions from examples, the method and user's guide. In Report ISG 85-5, UIUCDCS-F-86-949, Department of Computer Science, University of Illinois at Urbana-Champaign, 1986.

[**HN90**] R. Hecht-Nielsen. *Neurocomputing*. Reading, MA: Addison-Wesley, 1990.

[**HNFD98**] J. Han, R. T. Ng, Y. Fu, and S. Dao. Dealing with semantic heterogeneity by generalization-based data mining techniques. In M. P. Papazoglou and G. Schlageter, editors, *Cooperative Information Systems: Current Trends and Directions*, pages 207–231. San Diego, CA: Academic Press, 1998.

[**HNKW98**] J. Han, S. Nishio, H. Kawano, and W. Wang. Generalization-based data mining in object-oriented databases using an object-cube model. *Data and Knowledge Engineering*, 25:55–97, 1998.

[**HPM$^+$00**] J. Han, J. Pei, B. Mortazavi-Asl, Q. Chen, U. Dayal, and M.-C. Hsu. Freespan: Frequent pattern-projected sequential pattern mining. In *Proc. 2000 Int. Conf. Knowledge Discovery and Data Mining (KDD'00)*, Boston, MA, Aug. 2000.

[**HPS97**] J. Hosking, E. Pednault, and M. Sudan. A statistical perspective on data mining. *Future Generation Computer Systems*, 13:117–134, 1997.

[**HPY00**] J. Han, J. Pei, and Y. Yin. Mining frequent patterns without candidate generation. In *Proc. 2000 ACM-SIGMOD Int. Conf. Management of Data (SIGMOD'00)*, pages 1–12, Dallas, TX, May 2000.

[**HRU96**] V. Harinarayan, A. Rajaraman, and J. D. Ullman. Implementing data cubes efficiently. In *Proc. 1996 ACM-SIGMOD Int. Conf. Management of Data (SIGMOD'96)*, pages 205–216, Montreal, Canada, June 1996.

[**HSK98**] J. Han, N. Stefanovic, and K. Koperski. Selective materialization: An efficient method for spatial data cube construction. In *Proc. 1998 Pacific-Asia Conf. Knowledge Discovery and Data Mining (PAKDD'98) [Lecture Notes in Artificial Intelligence, 1394, Springer-Verlag, 1998]*, Melbourne, Australia, Apr. 1998.

[**Hua98**] Z. Huang. Extensions to the $k$-means algorithm for clustering large data sets with categorical values. *Data Mining and Knowledge Discovery*, 2:283–304, 1998.

[**Hub94**] C. H. Huberty. *Applied Discriminant Analysis*. New York: John Wiley & Sons, 1994.

[**Hub96**] B. B. Hubbard. *The World According to Wavelets*. Wellesley, MA: A. K. Peters, 1996.

[**HYK99**] J. Han, Q. Yang, and E. Kim. Plan mining by divide-and-conquer. In *Proc. 1999 SIGMOD Workshop on Research Issues on Data Mining and Knowledge Discovery (DMKD'99)*, pages 8:1–8:6, Philadelphia, PA, May 1999.

[**IM96**] T. Imielinski and H. Mannila. A database perspective on knowledge discovery. *Communications of ACM*, 39:58–64, 1996.

[**Imi87**] T. Imielinski. Intelligent query answering in rule based systems. *J. Logic Programming*, 4:229–257, 1987.

[**Inm96**] W. H. Inmon. *Building the Data Warehouse*. New York: John Wiley & Sons, 1996.

[**IV99**] T. Imielinski and A. Virmani. MSQL: A query language for database mining. *Data Mining and Knowledge Discovery*, 3:373–408, 1999.

[**IVA96**] T. Imielinski, A. Virmani, and A. Abdulghani. DataMine—application programming interface and query language for KDD applications. In *Proc. 1996 Int. Conf. Data Mining and Knowledge Discovery (KDD'96)*, pages 256–261, Portland, OR, Aug. 1996.

[**Jac88**] R. Jacobs. Increased rates of convergence through learning rate adaptation. *Neural Networks*, 1:295–307, 1988.

[**Jam85**] M. James. *Classification Algorithms*. New York: John Wiley & Sons, 1985.

[**JD88**] A. K. Jain and R. C. Dubes. *Algorithms for Clustering Data*. Englewood Cliffs, NJ: Prentice Hall, 1988.

[**Jen96**] F. V. Jensen. *An Introduction to Bayesian Networks*. New York: Springer-Verlag, 1996.

[**JKM99**] H. V. Jagadish, N. Koudas, and S. Muthukrishnan:. Mining deviants in a time series database. In *Proc. 1999 Int. Conf. Very Large Data Bases (VLDB'99)*, pages 102–113, Edinburgh, UK, Sept. 1999.

[JL96]   G. H. John and P. Langley. Static versus dynamic sampling for data mining. In *Proc. 1996 Int. Conf. Knowledge Discovery and Data Mining (KDD'96)*, pages 367–370, Portland, OR, Aug. 1996.

[JMF99]   A. K. Jain, M.N. Murty, and P. J. Flynn. Data clustering: A survey. *ACM Comput. Surv.*, 31:264–323, 1999.

[Joh97]   G. H. John. *Enhancements to the Data Mining Process*. Ph.D. Thesis, Computer Science Dept., Stanford University, 1997.

[JW92]   R. A. Johnson and D. A. Wichern. *Applied Multivariate Statistical Analysis*, 3rd ed. Englewood Cliffs, NJ: Prentice Hall, 1992.

[KA96]   A. J. Knobbe and P. W. Adriaans. Analysing binary associations. In *Proc. 1996 Int. Conf. Knowledge Discovery and Data Mining (KDD'96)*, pages 311–314, Portland, OR, Aug. 1996.

[Kas80]   G. V. Kass. An exploratory technique for investigating large quantities of categorical data. *Applied Statistics*, 29:119–127, 1980.

[Kei97]   D. A. Keim. Visual techniques for exploring databases. In *Tutorial Notes, 3rd Int. Conf. Knowledge Discovery and Data Mining (KDD'97)*, Newport Beach, CA, Aug. 1997.

[Ker92]   R. Kerber. Discretization of numeric attributes. In *Proc. 9th National Conf. on Artificial Intelligence (AAAI'92)*, pages 123–128. Cambridge, MA: AAAI/MIT Press, 1992.

[KH95]   K. Koperski and J. Han. Discovery of spatial association rules in geographic information databases. In *Proc. 4th Int. Symp. Large Spatial Databases (SSD'95)*, pages 47–66, Portland, ME, Aug. 1995.

[KH97]   I. Kononenko and S. J. Hong. Attribute selection for modeling. *Future Generation Computer Systems*, 13:181–195, 1997.

[KHC97]   M. Kamber, J. Han, and J. Y. Chiang. Metarule-guided mining of multi-dimensional association rules using data cubes. In *Proc. 1997 Int. Conf. Knowledge Discovery and Data Mining (KDD'97)*, pages 207–210, Newport Beach, CA, Aug. 1997.

[KHK99]   G. Karypis, E.-H. Han, and V. Kumar. CHAMELEON: A hierarchical clustering algorithm using dynamic modeling. *COMPUTER*, 32:68–75, 1999.

[KHS98]   K. Koperski, J. Han, and N. Stefanovic. An efficient two-step method for classification of spatial data. In *Proc. 8th Symp. Spatial Data Handling*, pages 45–55, Vancouver, Canada, 1998.

[Kim96]   R. Kimball. *The Data Warehouse Toolkit*. New York: John Wiley & Sons, 1996.

[KJ97]   R. Kohavi and G. H. John. Wrappers for feature subset selection. *Artificial Intelligence*, 97:273–324, 1997.

[**KK94**]  D. A. Keim and H.-P. Kriegel. VisDB: Database exploration using multidimensional visualization. In *Computer Graphics and Applications*, pages 40–49, Sept. 94.

[**Kle99**]  J. M. Kleinberg. Authoritative sources in a hyperlinked environment. *Journal of ACM*, 46:604–632, 1999.

[**KLV+98**]  R. L Kennedy, Y. Lee, B. Van Roy, C. D. Reed, and R. P. Lippman. *Solving Data Mining Problems Through Pattern Recognition*. Upper Saddle River, NJ: Prentice Hall, 1998.

[**KM90**]  Y. Kodratoff and R. S. Michalski. *Machine Learning, An Artificial Intelligence Approach*, Vol. 3. San Mateo, CA: Morgan Kaufmann, 1990.

[**KM94**]  J. Kivinen and H. Mannila. The power of sampling in knowledge discovery. In *Proc. 13th ACM Symp. Principles of Database Systems*, pages 77–85, Minneapolis, MN, May 1994.

[**KMR+94**]  M. Klemettinen, H. Mannila, P. Ronkainen, H. Toivonen, and A. I. Verkamo. Finding interesting rules from large sets of discovered association rules. In *Proc. 3rd Int. Conf. Information and Knowledge Management*, pages 401–408, Gaithersburg, MD, Nov. 1994.

[**KN96**]  E. Knorr and R. Ng. Finding aggregate proximity relationships and commonalities in spatial data mining. *IEEE Trans. Knowledge and Data Engineering*, 8:884–897, 1996.

[**KN97**]  E. Knorr and R. Ng. A unified notion of outliers: Properties and computation. In *Proc. 1997 Int. Conf. Knowledge Discovery and Data Mining (KDD'97)*, pages 219–222, Newport Beach, CA, Aug. 1997.

[**KN98**]  E. Knorr and R. Ng. Algorithms for mining distance-based outliers in large datasets. In *Proc. 1998 Int. Conf. Very Large Data Bases (VLDB'98)*, pages 392–403, New York, Aug. 1998.

[**Koh82**]  T. Kohonen. Self-organized formation of topologically correct feature maps. *Biological Cybernetics*, 43:59–69, 1982.

[**Koh95**]  R. Kohavi. A study of cross-validation and bootstrap for accuracy estimation and model selection. In *Proc. 14th Joint Int. Conf. on Artificial Intelligence (IJCAI'95)*, Vol. 2, pages 1137–1143, Montreal, Canada, Aug. 1995.

[**Kol93**]  J. L. Kolodner. *Case-Based Reasoning*. San Francisco: Morgan Kaufmann, 1993.

[**KPR98**]  J. M. Kleinberg, C. Papadimitriou, and P. Raghavan. A microeconomic view of data mining. *Data Mining and Knowledge Discovery*, 2:311–324, 1998.

[**KR90**]  L. Kaufman and P. J. Rousseeuw. *Finding Groups in Data: An Introduction to Cluster Analysis*. New York: John Wiley & Sons, 1990.

[**KS95**]  D. Konopnicki and O. Shmueli. W3QS: A query system for the world-wide-web. In *Proc. 1995 Int. Conf. Very Large Data Bases (VLDB'95)*, pages 54–65, Zurich, Switzerland, Sept. 1995.

[**KT99**]  J. M. Kleinberg and A. Tomkins. Application of linear algebra in information retrieval and hypertext analysis. In *Proc. 18th ACM Symp. Principles of Database Systems (PODS)*, pages 185–193, Philadelphia, PA, May 1999.

[**KWG$^+$97**]  M. Kamber, L. Winstone, W. Gong, S. Cheng, and J. Han. Generalization and decision tree induction: Efficient classification in data mining. In *Proc. 1997 Int. Workshop Research Issues on Data Engineering (RIDE'97)*, pages 111–120, Birmingham, England, Apr. 1997.

[**Lan96**]  P. Langley. *Elements of Machine Learning*. San Francisco: Morgan Kaufmann, 1996.

[**Lau95**]  S. L. Lauritzen. The EM algorithm for graphical association models with missing data. *Computational Statistics and Data Analysis*, 19:191–201, 1995.

[**Lau96**]  K. C. Laudon. Markets and privacy. *Communications of the ACM*, 39:92–104, Sept. 1996.

[**LDR00**]  J. Li, G. Dong, and K. Ramamohanrarao. Making use of the most expressive jumping emerging patterns for classification. In *Proc. 2000 Pacific-Asia Conf. Knowledge Discovery and Data Mining (PAKDD'00)*, pages 220–232, Kyoto, Japan, Apr. 2000.

[**LDS90**]  Y. Le Cun, J. S. Denker, and S. A. Solla. Optimal brain damage. In D. Touretzky, editor, *Advances in Neural Information Processing Systems, 2*. San Mateo, CA: Morgan Kaufmann, 1990.

[**Lea96**]  D. B. Leake. CBR in context: The present and future. In D. B. Leake, editor, *Cased-Based Reasoning: Experience, Lessons, and Future Directions*, pages 3–30. Menlo Park: AAAI Press, 1996.

[**LGT97**]  S. Lawrence, C. L Giles, and A. C. Tsoi. Symbolic conversion, grammatical inference and rule extraction for foreign exchange rate prediction. In Y. Abu-Mostafa, A. S. Weigend, and P. N Refenes, editors, *Neural Networks in the Captial Markets*. Singapore: World Scientific, 1997.

[**LHC97**]  B. Liu, W. Hsu, and S. Chen. Using general impressions to analyze discovered classification rules. In *Proc. 1997 Int. Conf. Knowledge Discovery and Data Mining (KDD'97)*, pages 31–36, Newport Beach, CA, Aug. 1997.

[**LHF98**]  H. Lu, J. Han, and L. Feng. Stock movement and $n$-dimensional intertransaction association rules. In *Proc. 1998 SIGMOD Workshop on Research Issues on Data Mining and Knowledge Discovery (DMKD'98)*, pages 12:1–12:7, Seattle, WA, June 1998.

[**LHM98**] B. Liu, W. Hsu, and Y. Ma. Integrating classification and association rule mining. In *Proc. 1998 Int. Conf. Knowledge Discovery and Data Mining (KDD'98)*, pages 80–86, New York, Aug. 1998.

[**LHO93**] W. Lu, J. Han, and B. C. Ooi. Knowledge discovery in large spatial databases. In *Proc. Far East Workshop Geographic Information Systems*, pages 275–289, Singapore, June 1993.

[**LLS00**] T.-S. Lim, W.-Y. Loh, and Y.-S. Shih. A comparison of prediction accuracy, complexity, and training time of thirty-three old and new classification algorithms. *Machine Learning*, 39, 2000.

[**LM98a**] H. Liu and H. Motoda, editors. *Feature Extraction, Construction, and Selection: A Data Mining Perspective*. Boston: Kluwer Academic Publishers, 1998.

[**LM98b**] H. Liu and H. Motoda. *Feature Selection for Knowledge Discovery and Data Mining*. Boston: Kluwer Academic Publishers, 1998.

[**LNHP99**] L. V. S. Lakshmanan, R. Ng, J. Han, and A. Pang. Optimization of constrained frequent set queries with 2-variable constraints. In *Proc. 1999 ACM-SIGMOD Int. Conf. Management of Data (SIGMOD'99)*, pages 157–168, Philadelphia, PA, June 1999.

[**Loh99**] S. Lohr. Online industry seizes the initiative on privacy. In *New York Times (http://www.nytimes.com/library/tech/99/10/biztech/articles/11priv.html)*, Oct. 11, 1999.

[**LP97**] A. Lenarcik and Z. Piasta. Probabilistic rough classifiers with mixture of discrete and continuous variables. In T. Y. Lin and N. Cercone, editors, *Rough Sets and Data Mining: Analysis for Imprecise Data*, pages 373–383. Boston: Kluwer Academic Publishers, 1997.

[**LS95**] H. Liu and R. Setiono. Chi2: Feature selection and discretization of numeric attributes. In *Proc. 7th IEEE Intl. Conf. Tools with AI (ICTAI'95)*, pages 388–391, Los Alamitos, CA: IEEE Computer Society, 1995.

[**LS97**] W. Y. Loh and Y. S. Shih. Split selection methods for classification trees. *Statistica Sinica*, 7:815–840, 1997.

[**LSBZ87**] P. Langley, H. A. Simon, G. L. Bradshaw, and J. M. Zytkow. *Scientific Discovery: Computational Explorations of the Creative Processes*. Cambridge, MA: MIT Press, 1987.

[**LSL95**] H. Lu, R. Setiono, and H. Liu. Neurorule: A connectionist approach to data mining. In *Proc. 1995 Int. Conf. Very Large Data Bases (VLDB'95)*, pages 478–489, Zurich, Switzerland, Sept. 1995.

[**LSS96**] L. V. S. Lakshmanan, F. Sadri, and S. Subramanian. A declarative query language for querying and restructuring the web. In *Proc. Int. Workshop Research Issues in Data Engineering*, Tempe, AZ, 1996.

[**LSW97**]  B. Lent, A. Swami, and J. Widom. Clustering association rules. In *Proc. 1997 Int. Conf. Data Engineering (ICDE'97)*, pages 220–231, Birmingham, England, Apr. 1997.

[**LV88**]  W. Y. Loh and N. Vanichsetakul. Tree-structured classification via generalized discriminant analysis. *Journal of the American Statistical Association*, 83:715–728, 1988.

[**Mac67**]  J. MacQueen. Some methods for classification and analysis of multivariate observations. *Proc. 5th Berkeley Symp. Math. Statist, Prob.*, 1:281–297, 1967.

[**Mag94**]  J. Magidson. The CHAID approach to segmentation modeling: CHI-squared automatic interaction detection. In R. P. Bagozzi, editor, *Advanced Methods of Marketing Research*, pages 118–159. Cambridge, MA: Blackwell Business, 1994.

[**Man97**]  H. Mannila. Methods and problems in data mining. In *Proc. 7th Int. Conf. Database Theory (ICDT'99)*, pages 41–55, Delphi, Greece, Jan. 1997.

[**MAR96**]  M. Mehta, R. Agrawal, and J. Rissanen. SLIQ: A fast scalable classifier for data mining. In *Proc. 1996 Int. Conf. Extending Database Technology (EDBT'96)*, Avignon, France, Mar. 1996.

[**Mat97**]  R. Mattison. *Data Warehousing and Data Mining for Telecommunications*. Artech House, 1997.

[**MBK98**]  R. S. Michalski, I. Brakto, and M. Kubat. *Machine Learning and Data Mining: Methods and Applications*. New York: John Wiley & Sons, 1998.

[**MCM83**]  R. S. Michalski, J. G. Carbonell, and T. M. Mitchell. *Machine Learning, An Artificial Intelligence Approach*, Vol. 1. San Mateo, CA: Morgan Kaufmann, 1983.

[**MCM86**]  R. S. Michalski, J. G. Carbonell, and T. M. Mitchell. *Machine Learning, An Artificial Intelligence Approach*, Vol. 2. San Mateo, CA: Morgan Kaufmann, 1986.

[**MD88**]  M. Muralikrishna and D. J. DeWitt. Equi-depth histograms for estimating selectivity factors for multi-dimensional queries. In *Proc. 1988 ACM-SIGMOD Int. Conf. Management of Data (SIGMOD'88)*, pages 28–36, Chicago, IL, June 1988.

[**MFS95**]  D. Malerba, E. Floriana, and G. Semeraro. A further comparison of simplification methods for decision tree induction. In D. Fisher and H. Lenz, editors, *Learning from Data: AI and Statistics*. New York: Springer-Verlag, 1995.

[**MGR92**]  D. J. Maguire, M. Goodchild, and D. W. Rhind. *Geographical Information Systems: Principles and Applications*. London: Longman, 1992.

[**MH00**]  H. Miller and J. Han. *Geographic Data Mining and Knowledge Discovery*. London, UK: Taylor and Francis, 2000.

[**Mic00**]  Microsoft Corporation. OLE DB for Data Mining Draft Specification, version 0.9. In *http://www.microsoft.com/data/oledb/dm.html*, Feb. 2000.

[**Mic83**]   R. S. Michalski. A theory and methodology of inductive learning. In Michalski et al., editors, *Machine Learning: An Artificial Intelligence Approach*, Vol. 1, pages 83–134. San Mateo, CA: Morgan Kaufmann, 1983.

[**Mic92**]   Z. Michalewicz. *Genetic Algorithms + Data Structures = Evolution Programs*. New York: Springer-Verlag, 1992.

[**Mil81**]   R. G. Miller. *Survival Analysis*. New York: John Wiley & Sons, 1981.

[**Min89**]   J. Mingers. An empirical comparison of pruning methods for decision-tree induction. *Machine Learning*, 4:227–243, 1989.

[**Mit77**]   T. M. Mitchell. Version spaces: A candidate elimination approach to rule learning. In *Proc. 5th Int. Joint Conf. Artificial Intelligence*, pages 305–310, Cambridge, MA, 1977.

[**Mit82**]   T. M. Mitchell. Generalization as search. *Artificial Intelligence*, 18:203–226, 1982.

[**Mit96**]   M. Mitchell. *An Introduction to Genetic Algorithms*. Cambridge, MA: MIT Press, 1996.

[**Mit97**]   T. M. Mitchell. *Machine Learning*. New York: McGraw-Hill, 1997.

[**MK91**]   M. Manago and Y. Kodratoff. Induction of decision trees from complex structured data. In G. Piatetsky-Shapiro and W. J. Frawley, editors, *Knowledge Discovery in Databases*, pages 289–306. Cambridge, MA: AAAI/MIT Press, 1991.

[**MM95**]   J. Major and J. Mangano. Selecting among rules induced from a hurricane database. *Journal of Intelligent Information Systems*, 4:39–52, 1995.

[**MMM97**]   A. O. Mendelzon, G. A. Mihaila, and T. Milo. Querying the world-wide web. *Int. Journal of Digital Libraries*, 1:54–67, 1997.

[**Moo99**]   G. A. Moore. *Crossing the Chasm: Marketing and Selling High-Tech Products to Mainstream Customers*. Harperbusiness, 1999.

[**MPC96**]   R. Meo, G. Psaila, and S. Ceri. A new SQL-like operator for mining association rules. In *Proc. 1996 Int. Conf. Very Large Data Bases (VLDB'96)*, pages 122–133, Bombay, India, Sept. 1996.

[**MPSM96**]   C. J. Matheus, G. Piatetsky-Shapiro, and D. McNeil. Selecting and reporting what is interesting: The KEFIR application to healthcare data. In U. M. Fayyad, G. Piatetsky-Shapiro, P. Smyth, and R. Uthurusamy, editors, *Advances in Knowledge Discovery and Data Mining*, pages 495–516. Cambridge, MA: AAAI/MIT Press, 1996.

[**MRA95**]   M. Metha, J. Rissanen, and R. Agrawal. MDL-based decision tree pruning. In *Proc. 1995 Int. Conf. Knowledge Discovery and Data Mining (KDD'95)*, pages 216–221, Montreal, Canada, Aug. 1995.

[**MS83**] R. S. Michalski and R. E. Stepp. Learning from observation: Conceptual clustering. In R. S. Michalski, J. G. Carbonell, and T. M. Mitchell, editors, *Machine Learning: An Artificial Intelligence Approach*, Vol. 1. San Mateo, CA: Morgan Kaufmann, 1983.

[**MST94**] D. Michie, D. J. Spiegelhalter, and C. C. Taylor. *Machine Learning, Neural and Statistical Classification*. New York: Ellis Horwood, 1994.

[**MT94**] R. S. Michalski and G. Tecuci. *Machine Learning, A Multistrategy Approach, Vol. 4*. San Francisco: Morgan Kaufmann, 1994.

[**MTV94**] H. Mannila, H. Toivonen, and A. I. Verkamo. Efficient algorithms for discovering association rules. In *Proc. AAAI'94 Workshop Knowledge Discovery in Databases (KDD'94)*, pages 181–192, Seattle, WA, July 1994.

[**MTV97**] H. Mannila, H Toivonen, and A. I. Verkamo. Discovery of frequent episodes in event sequences. *Data Mining and Knowledge Discovery*, 1:259–289, 1997.

[**Mur98**] S. K. Murthy. Automatic construction of decision trees from data: A multidisciplinary survey. *Data Mining and Knowledge Discovery*, 2:345–389, 1998.

[**MW99**] D. Meretakis and B. Wüthrich. Extending naive bayes classifiers using long itemsets. In *Proc. 1999 Int. Conf. Knowledge Discovery and Data Mining (KDD'99)*, pages 165–174, San Diego, Aug. 1999.

[**MY90**] A. Motro and Q. Yuan. Querying database knowledge. In *Proc. 1990 ACM-SIGMOD Int. Conf. Management of Data*, pages 173–183, Atlantic City, NJ, June 1990.

[**MY97**] R. J. Miller and Y. Yang. Association rules over interval data. In *Proc. 1997 ACM-SIGMOD Int. Conf. Management of Data (SIGMOD'97)*, pages 452–461, Tucson, AZ, May 1997.

[**NB86**] T. Niblett and I. Bratko. Learning decision rules in noisy domains. In M. A. Bramer, editor, *Expert Systems '86: Research and Development in Expert Systems III*, pages 25–34. British Computer Society Specialist Group on Expert Systems, Dec. 1986.

[**NH94**] R. Ng and J. Han. Efficient and effective clustering method for spatial data mining. In *Proc. 1994 Int. Conf. Very Large Data Bases (VLDB'94)*, pages 144–155, Santiago, Chile, Sept. 1994.

[**NKNW96**] J. Neter, M. H. Kutner, C. J. Nachtsheim, and L. Wasserman. *Applied Linear Statistical Models*, 4th ed. Chicago: Irwin, 1996.

[**NLHP98**] R. Ng, L. V. S. Lakshmanan, J. Han, and A. Pang. Exploratory mining and pruning optimizations of constrained associations rules. In *Proc. 1998 ACM-SIGMOD Int. Conf. Management of Data (SIGMOD'98)*, pages 13–24, Seattle, WA, June 1998.

[**NRS99**] A. Natsev, R. Rastogi, and K. Shim. Walrus: A similarity retrieval algorithm for image databases. In *Proc. 1999 ACM-SIGMOD Conf. on Management of Data (SIGMOD'99)*, pages 395–406, Philadelphia, PA, June 1999.

**[OG95]** P. O'Neil and G. Graefe. Multi-table joins through bitmapped join indices. *SIGMOD Record*, 24:8–11, Sept. 1995.

**[OQ97]** P. O'Neil and D. Quass. Improved query performance with variant indexes. In *Proc. 1997 ACM-SIGMOD Int. Conf. Management of Data (SIGMOD'97)*, pages 38–49, Tucson, AZ, May, 1997.

**[ORS98]** B. Özden, S. Ramaswamy, and A. Silberschatz. Cyclic association rules. In *Proc. 1998 Int. Conf. Data Engineering (ICDE'98)*, pages 412–421, Orlando, FL, Feb. 1998.

**[Pag89]** G. Pagallo. Learning DNF by decision trees. In *Proc. Intl. Joint Conf. on Artificial Intelligence (IJCAI'89)*, pages 639–644. San Mateo, CA: Morgan Kaufmann, 1989.

**[Paw91]** Z. Pawlak. *Rough Sets, Theoretical Aspects of Reasoning about Data*. Boston: Kluwer Academic Publishers, 1991.

**[PBTL99]** N. Pasquier, Y. Bastide, R. Taouil, and L. Lakhal. Discovering frequent closed itemsets for association rules. In *Proc. 7th Int. Conf. Database Theory (ICDT'99)*, pages 398–416, Jerusalem, Israel, Jan. 1999.

**[PCY95a]** J. S. Park, M. S. Chen, and P. S. Yu. An effective hash-based algorithm for mining association rules. In *Proc. 1995 ACM-SIGMOD Int. Conf. Management of Data (SIGMOD'95)*, pages 175–186, San Jose, CA, May 1995.

**[PCY95b]** J. S. Park, M. S. Chen, and P. S. Yu. Efficient parallel mining for association rules. In *Proc. 4th Int. Conf. Information and Knowledge Management*, pages 31–36, Baltimore, MD, Nov. 1995.

**[PCYH00]** S. Park, W. W. Chu, J. Yoon, and C. Hsu. Efficient searches for similar subsequences of different lengths in sequence databases. In *Proc. 2000 Int. Conf. Data Engineering (ICDE'00)*, pages 23–32, San Diego, CA, Feb. 2000.

**[PE99]** M. Perkowitz and O. Etzioni. Adaptive web sites: Conceptual cluster mining. In *Proc. 16th Joint Int. Conf. on Artificial Intelligence (IJCAI'99)*, pages 264–269, Stockholm, Sweden, 1999.

**[Pea88]** J. Pearl. *Probabilistic Reasoning in Intelligent Systems*. Palo Alto, CA: Morgan Kaufmann, 1988.

**[PH00]** J. Pei and J. Han. Can we push more constraints into frequent pattern mining? In *Proc. 2000 Int. Conf. Knowledge Discovery and Data Mining (KDD'00)*, Boston, MA, Aug. 2000.

**[PHM00]** J. Pei, J. Han, and R. Mao. CLOSET: An efficient algorithm for mining frequent closed itemsets. In *Proc. 2000 ACM-SIGMOD Int. Workshop Data Mining and Knowledge Discovery (DMKD00)*, pages 11–20, Dallas, TX, May 2000.

[**PI97**]   V. Poosala and Y. Ioannidis. Selectivity estimation without the attribute value independence assumption. In *Proc. 1997 Int. Conf. Very Large Data Bases (VLDB'97)*, pages 486–495, Athens, Greece, Aug. 1997.

[**PS89**]   G. Piatetsky-Shapiro, editor. *Notes of IJCAI'89 Workshop Knowledge Discovery in Databases (KDD'89)*. Detroit, MI, July 1989.

[**PS91a**]   G. Piatetsky-Shapiro. Discovery, analysis, and presentation of strong rules. In G. Piatetsky-Shapiro and W. J. Frawley, editors, *Knowledge Discovery in Databases*, pages 229–238. Cambridge, MA: AAAI/MIT Press, 1991.

[**PS91b**]   G. Piatetsky-Shapiro, editor. *Notes of AAAI'91 Workshop Knowledge Discovery in Databases (KDD'91)*. Anaheim, CA, July 1991.

[**PSF91**]   G. Piatetsky-Shapiro and W. J. Frawley. *Knowledge Discovery in Databases*. Cambridge, MA: AAAI/MIT Press, 1991.

[**PSM94**]   G. Piatesky-Shapiro and C. J. Matheus. The interestingness of deviations. In *Proc. AAAI'94 Workshop Knowledge Discovery in Databases (KDD'94)*, pages 25–36, Seattle, WA, July 1994.

[**PTVF96**]   W. H. Press, S. A. Teukolosky, W. T. Vetterling, and B. P. Flannery. *Numerical Recipes in C: The Art of Scientific Computing*. Cambridge, UK: Cambridge University Press, 1996.

[**PWZP00**]   C.-S. Perng, H. Wang, S. R. Zhang, and D. S. Parker. Landmarks: A new model for similarity-based pattern querying in time series databases. In *Proc. 2000 Int. Conf. Data Engineering (ICDE'00)*, pages 33–42, San Diego, CA, Feb. 2000.

[**Pyl99**]   D. Pyle. *Data Preparation for Data Mining*. San Francisco: Morgan Kaufmann, 1999.

[**QR89**]   J. R. Quinlan and R. L. Rivest. Inferring decision trees using the minimum description length principle. *Information and Computation*, 80:227–248, Mar. 1989.

[**Qui86**]   J. R. Quinlan. Induction of decision trees. *Machine Learning*, 1:81–106, 1986.

[**Qui87**]   J. R. Quinlan. Simplifying decision trees. *Internation Journal of Man-Machine Studies*, 27:221–234, 1987.

[**Qui88**]   J. R. Quinlan. An empirical comparison of genetic and decision-tree classifiers. In *Proc. 5th Intl. Conf. Machine Learning*, pages 135–141, San Mateo, CA: Morgan Kaufmann, 1988.

[**Qui89**]   J. R. Quinlan. Unknown attribute values in induction. In *Proc. 6th Int. Workshop on Machine Learning*, pages 164–168, Ithaca, NY, June 1989.

[**Qui90**]   J. R. Quinlan. Learning logic definitions from relations. *Machine Learning*, 5:139–166, 1990.

[**Qui93**]  J. R. Quinlan. *C4.5: Programs for Machine Learning*. San Mateo, CA: Morgan Kaufmann, 1993.

[**Qui96**]  J. R. Quinlan. Bagging, boosting, and C4.5. In *Proc. 13th Natl. Conf. Artificial Intelligence (AAAI'96)*, pages 725–730, Portland, OR, Aug. 1996.

[**Rag97**]  P. Raghavan. Information retrieval algorithms: A survey. In *Proc. 1997 ACM-SIAM Symp. Discrete Algorithms*, pages 11–18, New Orleans, LA, 1997.

[**RBKK95**]  S. Russell, J. Binder, D. Koller, and K. Kanazawa. Local learning in probabilistic networks with hidden variables. In *Proc. 14th Joint Int. Conf. on Artificial Intelligence (IJCAI'95)*, volume 2, pages 1146–1152, Montreal, Canada, Aug. 1995.

[**Red92**]  T. Redman. *Data Quality: Management and Technology*. New York: Bantam Books, 1992.

[**RG00**]  R. Ramakrishnan and J. Gehrke. *Database Management Systems*, 2nd ed. New York: McGraw Hill, 2000.

[**RHW86**]  D. E. Rumelhart, G. E. Hinton, and R. J. Williams. Learning internal representations by error propagation. In D. E. Rumelhart and J. L. McClelland, editors, *Parallel Distributed Processing*. Cambridge, MA: MIT Press, 1986.

[**Rip96**]  B. D. Ripley. *Pattern Recognition and Neural Networks*. Cambridge, UK: Cambridge University Press, 1996.

[**RM86**]  D. E. Rumelhart and J. L. McClelland. *Parallel Distributed Processing*. Cambridge, MA: MIT Press, 1986.

[**RM97**]  D. Rafiei and A. Mendelzon. Similarity-based queries for time series data. In *Proc. 1997 ACM-SIGMOD Int. Conf. Management of Data (SIGMOD'97)*, pages 13–25, Tucson, AZ, May 1997.

[**RMS98**]  S. Ramaswamy, S. Mahajan, and A. Silberschatz. On the discovery of interesting patterns in association rules. In *Proc. 1998 Int. Conf. Very Large Data Bases (VLDB'98)*, pages 368–379, New York, Aug. 1998.

[**RN95**]  S. Russell and P. Norvig. *Artificial Intelligence: A Modern Approach*. Englewood Cliffs, NJ: Prentice-Hall, 1995.

[**Roy00**]  A. Roy. Artificial neural networks—a science in trouble. *SIGKDD Explorations*, 1:33–38, 2000.

[**RS89**]  C. Riesbeck and R. Schank. *Inside Case-Based Reasoning*. Hillsdale, NJ: Lawrence Erlbaum, 1989.

[**RS97**]  K. Ross and D. Srivastava. Fast computation of sparse datacubes. In *Proc. 1997 Int. Conf. Very Large Data Bases (VLDB'97)*, pages 116–125, Athens, Greece, Aug. 1997.

[**RS98**]  R. Rastogi and K. Shim. Public: A decision tree classifier that integrates building and pruning. In *Proc. 1998 Int. Conf. Very Large Data Bases (VLDB'98)*, pages 404–415, New York, Aug. 1998.

[**RSC98**]  K. A. Ross, D. Srivastava, and D. Chatziantoniou. Complex aggregation at multiple granularities. In *Proc. Int. Conf. Extending Database Technology (EDBT'98)*, pages 263–277, Valencia, Spain, Mar. 1998.

[**RZ85**]  D. E. Rumelhart and D. Zipser. Feature discovery by competitive learning. *Cognitive Science*, 9:75–112, 1985.

[**SA95**]  R. Srikant and R. Agrawal. Mining generalized association rules. In *Proc. 1995 Int. Conf. Very Large Data Bases (VLDB'95)*, pages 407–419, Zurich, Switzerland, Sept. 1995.

[**SA96**]  R. Srikant and R. Agrawal. Mining quantitative association rules in large relational tables. In *Proc. 1996 ACM-SIGMOD Int. Conf. Management of Data (SIGMOD'96)*, pages 1–12, Montreal, Canada, June 1996.

[**SAD$^+$93**]  M. Stonebraker, R. Agrawal, U. Dayal, E. Neuhold, and A. Reuter. DBMS research at a crossroads: The Vienna update. In *Proc. 1993 Int. Conf. Very Large Data Bases (VLDB'93)*, pages 688–692, Dublin, Ireland, Aug. 1993.

[**Sal89**]  G. Salton. *Automatic Text Processing*. Reading, MA: Addison-Wesley, 1989.

[**SAM96**]  J. Shafer, R. Agrawal, and M. Mehta. SPRINT: A scalable parallel classifier for data mining. In *Proc. 1996 Int. Conf. Very Large Data Bases (VLDB'96)*, pages 544–555, Bombay, India, Sept. 1996.

[**SAM98**]  S. Sarawagi, R. Agrawal, and N. Megiddo. Discovery-driven exploration of OLAP data cubes. In *Proc. Int. Conf. Extending Database Technology (EDBT'98)*, pages 168–182, Valencia, Spain, Mar. 1998.

[**SBMU98**]  C. Silverstein, S. Brin, R. Motwani, and J. Ullman. Scalable techniques for mining causal structures. In *Proc. 1998 Int. Conf. Very Large Data Bases (VLDB'98)*, pages 594–605, New York, Aug. 1998.

[**SCDT00**]  J. Srivastava, R. Cooley, M. Deshpande, and P. N. Tan. Web usage mining: Discovery and applications of usage patterns from web data. *SIGKDD Explorations*, 1:12–23, 2000.

[**Schl87**]  J. C. Schlimmer. Learning and representation change. In *Proc. 5th Natl. Conf. Artificial Intelligence (AAAI'86)*, pages 511–515, Phildelphia, PA, 1986.

[**SCZ98**]  G. Sheikholeslami, S. Chatterjee, and A. Zhang. WaveCluster: A multi-resolution clustering approach for very large spatial databases. In *Proc. 1998 Int. Conf. Very Large Data Bases (VLDB'98)*, pages 428–439, New York, Aug. 1998.

[**SD90**]  J. W. Shavlik and T. G. Dietterich. *Readings in Machine Learning*. San Mateo, CA: Morgan Kaufmann, 1990.

[SD96]  P. Stolorz and C. Dean. Quakefinder: A scalable data mining system for detecting earthquakes from space. In *Proc. 1996 Int. Conf. Data Mining and Knowledge Discovery (KDD'96)*, pages 208–213, Portland, OR, Aug. 1996.

[SDJL96]  D. Sristava, S. Dar, H. V. Jagadish, and A. V. Levy. Answering queries with aggregation using views. In *Proc. 1996 Int. Conf. Very Large Data Bases (VLDB'96)*, pages 318–329, Bombay, India, Sept. 1996.

[SF86a]  J. C. Schlimmer and D. Fisher. A case study of incremental concept induction. In *Proc. 5th Natl. Conf. Artificial Intelligence (AAAI'86)*, pages 496–501. San Mateo: Morgan Kaufmann 1986.

[SF86b]  D. Subramanian and J. Feigenbaum. Factorization in experiment generation. In *Proc. 1986 AAAI Conf.*, pages 518–522, Philadelphia, PA, Aug. 1986.

[SG92]  P. Smyth and R. M. Goodman. An information theoretic approach to rule induction. *IEEE Trans. Knowledge and Data Engineering*, 4:301–316, 1992.

[SH98]  M. Stonebraker and J. M. Hellerstein. *Readings in Database Systems*, 3rd ed. San Francisco: Morgan Kaufmann, 1998.

[SHF96]  E. Simoudis, J. Han, and U. Fayyad, editors. *Proc. 1996 Int. Conf. Knowledge Discovery and Data Mining (KDD'96)*. Portland, OR, Aug. 1996, AAAI Press.

[Shi00]  Y.-S. Shih. Families of splitting criteria for classification trees. In *Statistics and Computing (to appear)*, 2000.

[Sho97]  A. Shoshani. OLAP and statistical databases: Similarities and differences. In *Proc. 16th ACM Symp. Principles of Database Systems*, pages 185–196, Tucson, AZ, May 1997.

[Shu88]  R. H. Shumway. *Applied Statistical Time Series Analysis*. Englewood Cliffs, NJ: Prentice Hall, 1988.

[SKS97]  A. Silberschatz, H. F. Korth, and S. Sudarshan. *Database System Concepts*, 3rd ed. New York: McGraw-Hill, 1997.

[SM83]  G. Salton and M. McGill. *Introduction to Modern Information Retrieval*. New York: McGraw-Hill, 1983.

[SMT91]  J. W. Shavlik, R. J. Mooney, and G. G. Towell. Symbolic and neural learning algorithms: An experimental comparison. *Machine Learning*, 6:111–144, 1991.

[SN88]  K. Saito and R. Nakano. Medical diagnostic expert system based on PDP model. In *Proc. IEEE International Conf. on Neural Networks*, volume 1, pages 225–262. San Mateo, CA: 1988.

[SOMZ96]  W. Shen, K. Ong, B. Mitbander, and C. Zaniolo. Metaqueries for data mining. In U. M. Fayyad, G. Piatetsky-Shapiro, P. Smyth, and R. Uthurusamy, editors, *Advances in Knowledge Discovery and Data Mining*, pages 375–398. Cambridge, MA: AAAI/MIT Press, 1996.

[**SON95**]  A. Savasere, E. Omiecinski, and S. Navathe. An efficient algorithm for mining association rules in large databases. In *Proc. 1995 Int. Conf. Very Large Data Bases (VLDB'95)*, pages 432–443, Zurich, Switzerland, Sept. 1995.

[**SON98**]  A. Savasere, E. Omiecinski, and S. Navathe. Mining for strong negative associations in a large database of customer transactions. In *Proc. 1998 Int. Conf. Data Engineering (ICDE'98)*, pages 494–502, Orlando, FL, Feb. 1998.

[**SR92**]  A. Skowron and C. Rauszer. The discernibility matrices and functions in information systems. In R. Slowinski, editor, *Intelligent Decision Support, Handbook of Applications and Advances of the Rough Set Theory*, pages 331–362. Boston: Kluwer Academic Publishers, 1992.

[**SS88**]  W. Siedlecki and J. Sklansky. On automatic feature selection. *Int. J. of Pattern Recognition and Artificial Intelligence*, 2:197–220, 1988.

[**SS94**]  S. Sarawagi and M. Stonebraker. Efficient organization of large multidimensional arrays. In *Proc. 1994 Int. Conf. Data Engineering (ICDE'94)*, pages 328–336, Houston, TX, Feb. 1994.

[**SSU96**]  A. Silberschatz, M. Stonebraker, and J. D. Ullman. Database research: Achievements and opportunities into the 21st century. *ACM SIGMOD Record*, 25:52–63, Mar. 1996.

[**ST96**]  A. Silberschatz and A. Tuzhilin. What makes patterns interesting in knowledge discovery systems. *IEEE Trans. Knowledge and Data Engineering*, 8:970–974, Dec. 1996.

[**STA98**]  S. Sarawagi, S. Thomas, and R. Agrawal. Integrating association rule mining with relational database systems: Alternatives and implications. In *Proc. 1998 ACM-SIGMOD Int. Conf. Management of Data (SIGMOD'98)*, pages 343–354, Seattle, WA, June 1998.

[**Sto74**]  M. Stone. Cross-validatory choice and assessment of statistical predictions. *Journal of the Royal Statistical Society*, 36:111–147, 1974.

[**Sub98**]  V. S. Subrahmanian. *Principles of Multimedia Database Systems*. San Francisco: Morgan Kaufmann, 1998.

[**SVA97**]  R. Srikant, Q. Vu, and R. Agrawal. Mining association rules with item constraints. In *Proc. 1997 Int. Conf. Knowledge Discovery and Data Mining (KDD'97)*, pages 67–73, Newport Beach, CA, Aug. 1997.

[**Swi98**]  R. Swiniarski. Rough sets and principal component analysis and their applications in feature extraction and seletion, data model building and classification. In S. Pal and A. Skowron, editors, *Fuzzy Sets, Rough Sets and Decision Making Processes*. New York: Springer-Verlag, 1998.

[**TC83**]  D. Tsichritzis and S. Christodoulakis. Message files. *ACM Trans. Office Information Systems*, 1:88–98, 1983.

[**TG97**] L. Tauscher and S. Greenberg. How people revisit web pages: Empirical findings and implications for the design of history systems. *International Journal of Human Computer Studies, Special issue on World Wide Web Usability*, 47:97–138, 1997.

[**Tho97**] E. Thomsen. *OLAP Solutions: Building Multidimensional Information Systems*. New York: John Wiley & Sons, 1997.

[**Toi96**] H. Toivonen. Sampling large databases for association rules. In *Proc. 1996 Int. Conf. Very Large Data Bases (VLDB'96)*, pages 134–145, Bombay, India, Sept. 1996.

[**TS93**] G. G. Towell and J. W. Shavlik. Extracting refined rules from knowledge-based neural networks. *Machine Learning*, 13:71–101, Oct. 1993.

[**TUA$^+$98**] D. Tsur, J. D. Ullman, S. Abitboul, C. Clifton, R. Motwani, and S. Nestorov. Query flocks: A generalization of association-rule mining. In *Proc. 1998 ACM-SIGMOD Int. Conf. Management of Data (SIGMOD'98)*, pages 1–12, Seattle, WA, June 1998.

[**Tuf83**] E. R. Tufte. *The Visual Display of Quantitative Information*. Graphics Press, 1983.

[**Tuf90**] E. R. Tufte. *Envisioning Information*. Graphics Press, 1990.

[**Tuf97**] E. R. Tufte. *Visual Explanations: Images and Quantities, Evidence and Narrative*. Graphics Press, 1997.

[**UFS91**] R. Uthurusamy, U. M. Fayyad, and S. Spangler. Learning useful rules from inconclusive data. In G. Piatetsky-Shapiro and W. J. Frawley, editors, *Knowledge Discovery in Databases*, pages 141–157. Cambridge, MA: AAAI/MIT Press, 1991.

[**Ull88**] J. D. Ullman. *Principles of Database and Knowledge-Base Systems*, Vol. 1. Rockville, MD: Computer Science Press, 1988.

[**Utg88**] P. E. Utgoff. An incremental ID3. In *Proc. Fifth Int. Conf. Machine Learning*, pages 107–120, San Mateo, CA, 1988.

[**UW97**] J. D. Ullman and J. Widom. *A First Course in Database Systems*. Englewood Cliffs, NJ: Prentice Hall, 1997.

[**Val87**] P. Valduriez. Join indices. *ACM Trans. Database System*, 12:218–246, 1987.

[**VP99**] P. Valdes-Perez. Principles of human-computer collaboration for knowledge-discovery in science. *Artificial Intellifence*, 107:335–346, 1999.

[**vR90**] C. J. van Rijsbergen. *Information Retrieval*. Butterworth, 1990.

[**Wat95**] M. S. Waterman. *Introduction to Computational Biology: Maps, Sequences, and Genomes (Interdisciplinary Statistics)*. CRC Press, 1995.

[**WB98**] C. Westphal and T. Blaxton. *Data Mining Solutions: Methods and Tools for Solving Real-World Problems*. New York: John Wiley & Sons, 1998.

[**WI98**]  S. M. Weiss and N. Indurkhya. *Predictive Data Mining*. San Francisco: Morgan Kaufmann, 1998.

[**Wid95**]  J. Widom. Research problems in data warehousing. In *Proc. 4th Int. Conf. Information and Knowledge Management*, pages 25–30, Baltimore, MD, Nov. 1995.

[**WK91**]  S. M. Weiss and C. A. Kulikowski. *Computer Systems That Learn: Classification and Prediction Methods from Statistics, Neural Nets, Machine Learning, and Expert Systems*. San Mateo, CA: Morgan Kaufmann, 1991.

[**WRL94**]  B. Widrow, D. E. Rumelhart, and M. A. Lehr. Neural networks: Applications in industry, business and science. *Communications of ACM*, 37:93–105, 1994.

[**WSF95**]  R. Wang, V. Storey, and C. Firth. A framework for analysis of data quality research. *IEEE Trans. Knowledge and Data Engineering*, 7:623–640, 1995.

[**WW96**]  Y. Wand and R. Wang. Anchoring data quality dimensions in ontological foundations. *Communications of ACM*, 39:86–95, 1996.

[**WYM97**]  W. Wang, J. Yang, and R. Muntz. STING: A statistical information grid approach to spatial data mining. In *Proc. 1997 Int. Conf. Very Large Data Bases (VLDB'97)*, pages 186–195, Athens, Greece, Aug. 1997.

[**WZL99**]  K. Wang, S. Zhou, and S. C. Liew. Building hierarchical classifiers using class proximity. In *Proc. 1999 Int. Conf. Very Large Data Bases (VLDB'99)*, pages 363–374, Edinburgh, UK, Sept. 1999.

[**YFM**+**97**]  K. Yoda, T. Fukuda, Y. Morimoto, S. Morishita, and T. Tokuyama. Computing optimized rectilinear regions for association rules. In *Proc. 1997 Int. Conf. Knowledge Discovery and Data Mining (KDD'97)*, pages 96–103, Newport Beach, CA, Aug. 1997.

[**YJF98**]  B.-K. Yi, H. V. Jagadish, and C. Faloutsos. Efficient retrieval of similar time sequences under time warping. In *Proc. 1998 Int. Conf. Data Engineering (ICDE'98)*, pages 201–208, Orlando, FL, Feb. 1998.

[**YM97**]  C. T. Yu and W. Meng. *Principles of Database Query Processing for Advanced Applications*. San Francisco: Morgan Kaufmann, 1997.

[**YSJ**+**00**]  B.-K. Yi, N. Sidiropoulos, T. Johnson, H. V. Jagadish, C. Faloutsos, and A. Biliris. Online data mining for co-evolving time sequences. In *Proc. 2000 Int. Conf. Data Engineering (ICDE'00)*, pages 13–22, San Diego, CA, Feb. 2000.

[**Zad65**]  L. A. Zadeh. Fuzzy sets. *Information and Control*, 8:338–353, 1965.

[**ZCF**+**97**]  C. Zaniolo, S. Ceri, C. Faloutsos, R. T. Snodgrass, C. S. Subrahmanian, and R. Zicari. *Advanced Database Systems*. San Francisco: Morgan Kaufmann, 1997.

[**ZDN97**]  Y. Zhao, P. M. Deshpande, and J. F. Naughton. An array-based algorithm for simultaneous multidimensional aggregates. In *Proc. 1997 ACM-SIGMOD Int. Conf. Management of Data (SIGMOD'97)*, pages 159–170, Tucson, AZ, May 1997.

[ZH95]  O. R. Zaïane and J. Han. Resource and knowledge discovery in global information systems: A preliminary design and experiment. In *Proc. 1995 Int. Conf. Knowledge Discovery and Data Mining (KDD'95)*, pages 331–336, Montreal, Canada, Aug. 1995.

[ZH98]  O. R. Zaïane and J. Han. WebML: Querying the world-wide web for resources and knowledge. In *Proc. Int. Workshop Web Information and Data Management (WIDM'98)*, pages 9–12, Bethesda, MD, Nov. 1998.

[ZHL$^+$98]  O. R. Zaïane, J. Han, Z. N. Li, J. Y. Chiang, and S. Chee. MultiMedia-Miner: A system prototype for multimedia data mining. In *Proc. 1998 ACM-SIGMOD Conf. on Management of Data (SIGMOD'98)*, pages 581–583, Seattle, WA, June 1998.

[ZHZ00]  O. R. Zaïane, J. Han, and H. Zhu. Mining recurrent items in multimedia with progressive resolution refinement. In *Proc. 2000 Int. Conf. Data Engineering (ICDE'00)*, pages 461–470, San Diego, CA, Feb. 2000.

[Zia91]  W. Ziarko. The discovery, analysis, and representation of data dependencies in databases. In G. Piatetsky-Shapiro and W. J. Frawley, editors, *Knowledge Discovery in Databases*, pages 195–209. Menlo Park: AAAI Press, 1991.

[Zia94]  W. Ziarko. *Rough Sets, Fuzzy Sets and Knowledge Discovery*. New York: Springer-Verlag, 1994.

[ZLO98]  M. J. Zaki, N. Lesh, and M. Ogihara. PLANMINE: Sequence mining for plan failures. In *Proc. 1998 Int. Conf. Knowledge Discovery and Data Mining (KDD'98)*, pages 369–373, New York, Aug. 1998.

[ZPOL97]  M. J. Zaki, S. Parthasarathy, M. Ogihara, and W. Li. Parallel algorithm for discovery of association rules. *Data Mining and Knowledge Discovery*, 1:343–374, 1997.

[ZRL96]  T. Zhang, R. Ramakrishnan, and M. Livny. BIRCH: An efficient data clustering method for very large databases. In *Proc. 1996 ACM-SIGMOD Int. Conf. Management of Data (SIGMOD'96)*, pages 103–114, Montreal, Canada, June 1996.

[ZTH99]  X. Zhou, D. Truffet, and J. Han. Efficient polygon amalgamation methods for spatial OLAP and spatial data mining. In *Proc. 6th Int. Symp. Large Spatial Databases (SSD'99)*, pages 167–187, Hong Kong, July 1999.

[ZXH98]  O. R. Zaïane, M. Xin, and J. Han. Discovering Web access patterns and trends by applying OLAP and data mining technology on Web logs. In *Proc. Advances in Digital Libraries Conf. (ADL'98)*, pages 19–29, Santa Barbara, CA, Apr. 1998.

# Index

Page numbers in *italic* are references to figures.

abstraction. *See* levels of abstraction
actionable patterns, 28
adjacency matrices, HITS, 438–439
advanced databases, 16–20
AGglomerative NESting (AGNES), 355–356
agglomerative hierarchical clustering, 355–356
aggregate functions, 54–56, 208
aggregation, 114
  of complex structured data, 397–398
  **cube by** operator, 90
  dependent, 90
  on-line aggregation, 92–93
  spatial data, 397–398
AGNES (AGglomerative NESting), 355–356
algebraic measures, 54
algorithms. *See* specific algorithms
algorithms as metadata, 84
all. *See* apex cuboids
**all**, 165–166
alternative distributions, 383
alternative hypotheses, 382–383
analysis of variance, 469
analytical characterization, 195, 198–200
analytical comparison, 195
**and**, 116
anonymous databases, 478
ANOVA, 469
antimonotone properties, 231
antimonotone rule constraints, 267

AOI (attribute-oriented induction), 22, 180–194
  algorithm for, 188
  attribute generalization, 184–185
  attribute relevance analysis, 197–198
  attribute removal, 184–185
  class-based generalization, 400–401
  conditions, 193–194
  data-cube implementation, 189–190
  data focusing, 182–183
  decision tree induction, 295
  example of, 186–187
  implementation of, efficient, 187–190
  machine learning, 219, 221
  preparing data for, 182–184
  presentation/visualization, 190–194
  prime relation (P), 188–189
  transforming queries for, 183–184
  working relation (W), 188–189
apex cuboids, 47
approximation of complex structured data, 397–398
Apriori algorithm, 230–235
  dynamic itemset counting, 238–239
  efficiency improvements, 236–239
  example of use, 232–233
  generation of candidate itemsets, *234*

  hash-based techniques, 237
  iceberg queries, 243–244
  join step, 231, 234
  partitioning, 237–238
  prune step, 231, 234
  pseudocode for, *235*
  sampling technique, 238
  transaction reduction, 237
Apriori property, 231, 426
architecture
  coupling, 172–174
  data mining, *8*, 172–174
  data warehouses, 12, *13*, 62–71
  DBMiner, 494
  of OLAM, 96–99, *97*
ARCS (Association Rule Clustering System), 255–257, 311–313
arithmetic means. *See* means
arrays, partitioning, 75–76
association analysis. *See* association rule mining; association rules
Association Rule Clustering System. *See* ARCS (Association Rule Clustering System)
association rule mining, 23–24, 225–277. *See also* association rules
  approximations of attribute values, 258
  Apriori algorithm. *See* Apriori algorithm
  ARCS (Association Rule Clustering System), 255–257
  Boolean association rules, 229–244
  classification based on, 311–314

**533**

association rule mining *(continued)*
 classification of rules, 229–230,
  269–270
 confidence, 227–228
 constraint-based mining,
  262–269
 correlation analysis, 260–262
 cross-level association rules, 250
 DBMiner, 496, *497*
 cyclic association rules, 427
 dimensional association rules,
  229
 distance-based association rules,
  257–259
 DMQL, 163–164
 DNA sequencing, 453
 extension-based rules, 230
 FP growth, 239–243
 frequent closed itemsets, 230
 frequent itemsets, 236, 239–243
 iceberg queries, 243–244
 interestingness, 259–260
 itemsets, finding, 228
 keyword-based, 433–434
 levels, abstraction, 229–230
 maxpatterns, 230
 multidimensional association
  rules, 251–259
 multilevel association rules,
  244–251
 multimedia databases, 417–418
 OLE DB for Data Mining,
  487–488
 purchase recommendations, 456
 quantitative association rules,
  229, 253–257
 rule generation, 228
 spatial databases, 410–411
 steps in process, 228
 strong rules, 228, 236, 259–260
 suggesting additional items, 472
 support, 227–228
 telecommunications industry,
  457
 thresholds, 227–228
 TID (transaction ID), 227
association rules, 23–24, 227
 classification, 229–230, 269–270
 confidence, 27
 defined, 227–228
 dimensional, 229
 distance-based, 253, 257–259

extension-based, 230
 hybrid-dimension, 252
 interdimension, 252
 intradimensional, 251
 multidimensional, 251
 multilevel. *See* multilevel
  association rules
 quantitative, 229, 253–257
 single-dimensional, 251
 single-dimensional, single-level,
  Boolean, 230–244
 single-level, 229
 strong, 228, 236, 259–260
 support, 27
attribute construction, 114, 116,
  292
attribute generalization, 184–185.
  *See also* generalization
 class comparisons, 201–203
 control, 185
 generalized relation threshold
  control, 185
 machine learning, 219
 threshold control, 185
 *vs.* machine learning, 200–201
attribute-oriented induction. *See*
  AOI (attribute- oriented
  induction)
attribute relevance analysis,
  194–200
 AOI, 197–198
 class comparisons, 201–202
 concept description generation,
  198
 data collection, 197
 information gain, 196–198
 training samples, 196
attribute removal, 184–185, 198
attributes, 10
 association rules, 23–24
 categorical data concept
  hierarchy generation,
  138–140
 class composition hierarchies,
  399–400
 class label, 280
 dimension reduction, 116,
  119–121
 fuzzy logic, 318
 highly relevant, 195–196
 lattices, 57
 list-valued, 397

normalization, 114–116
 quantitative, 252–254
 relevance analysis. *See* attribute
  relevance analysis
 relevant, 146
 sequence-valued, 397
 set-valued, 396
attribute subset selection, 119–121
audio data mining, 464
AutoClass, 379
average, 54, 209
avg(), 54, 209


back-end tools, data warehouses,
  84–85
background knowledge, 31,
  150–154
backpropagation, 303–311
 activation functions, 306
 algorithm, 306
 biases, 305, 308
 class labels, 305
 error backpropagation, 307
 example, 308–310
 fully connected networks, 304,
  *304*
 gradient descent, 308
 hidden layers, 303–305, *304*
 input layers, 303, *304*
 interpretability, 310–311
 learning rates, 308
 methodology, 305–310
 multilayer feed forward neural
  networks, 303–304
 network pruning, 311
 output layers, 303, *304*
 output units, 303–304, *304*
 rule extraction, 311, *312*
 sensitivity analysis, 311
 sigmoid function, 306
 terminating conditions, 308
 topology design, 304–305
 training samples, 305
 updating schemes, 308
 weights, 303, 305, 307–308
bagging (bootstrap aggregation),
  324–325
banking. *See* financial data analysis
bar charts, 213–214, *214*
base cuboids, 47
base fact tables, 55, 70

Bayesian belief networks, 299–302
Bayesian classification, 296–302
  Bayesian belief networks,
    299–302
  Bayes theorem, 296–297
  class conditional independence,
    296, 298
  class labels, predicting, 299
  CPTs (conditional probability
    tables), 300–301
  definition of Bayesian classifiers,
    296
  directed acyclic graphs, 300–301
  Gaussian distribution assumed,
    298
  gradient computation, 302
  learning method, 301–302
  naive Bayesian classifier,
    296–299
  posterior probability, 296–298
  prior probability, 296–299
  training, 301–302
Bayesian networks. *See* Bayesian
  belief networks
belief networks. *See* Bayesian belief
  networks
binary variables, 341–343
binning, 110
  ARCS, 255
  as discretization technique, 133
  histograms, 125–127
biomedical analysis, 451–453
BIRCH (Balanced Iterative
  Reducing and Clustering
  using Hierarchies), 357–358
bitmap indexing method, 79–80
bitmapped join indices, 81
Boolean association rules, 229–235
Boolean vectors, 227
boosting, 324–325
bottom-up design approach, 64,
  67–68
boxplots, 211
buckets, 125–126
business analysis framework,
  63–65
business metadata, 84
business processes, choosing, 65
business query view, 63

C4.5, 311–313

CAEP (classification by aggregating
  emerging patterns), 313–314
case-based reasoning (CBR),
  315–316
categorical data, concept hierarchy
  generation, 138–140
CBR (case-based reasoning),
  315–316
central tendency measures,
  209–210
certainty, 155–156
CF (clustering feature) trees,
  357–358
Chameleon, 361–363
characteristic descriptions, mining,
  168
characterization, 21, 162–163
  attribute relevance analysis,
    194–200
  presentation with comparison,
    206–208
chunking, 75–79
chunk memory, 77
CLARA. *See* CLARANS
CLARANS (Clustering LARge
  Applications based on
  RANomized Search), 353–
  354
class comparisons, 200–208
  attribute generalization, 201
  characterization, presentation
    with, 206–208
  data collection, 201
  dimension relevance analysis,
    201
  discriminant rules, 204–208
  d-weight, 204–208
  generalization, 201–203
  interestingness, 204–208
  presentation, 201, 204–208
  prime contrasting classes, 201
  prime target classes, 201
  procedure for, 201
  quantitative description rules,
    207–208
  queries, 202–203
  visualization, 204–208
class composition hierarchies,
  399–400
class/concept descriptions, 21–23
class conditional independence,
  296, 298

class description. *See* concept
  description
classes
  attribute relevance analysis,
    194–200
  class/concept descriptions,
    21–23
  clustering of. *See* cluster analysis
  comparisons. *See* class
    comparisons
  contrasting classes, 21
  generalization of hierarchies,
    399
  methods in, 396
  objects in, 396
  target classes, 21
classification, 24, 164–165,
  279–281
  accuracy of classifiers, 322–326
  ARCS, 311–313
  associative classification, 313
  backpropagation, 303–311
  bagging (bootstrap aggregation),
    324–325
  based on association rule
    mining, 311–314
  Bayesian, 296–302
  boosting, 324–325
  bootstrapping, 323
  C4.5, 311–313
  CAEP, 313–314
  CBR (case-based reasoning),
    315–316
  class label attributes, 280
  data cleaning, 282
  data transformation before, 283
  DBMiner, 496, *497*
  decision tree induction, 284–296
  defined, 279–280
  estimating accuracy, 323–324
  financial data, 454
  fuzzy logic, 317–319
  generalization before, 283
  genetic algorithms, 316
  holdout method, 281, 323
  increasing accuracy, 324–325
  instance-based, 315
  interpretability of, 283, 325
  JEP-classifier, 314
  k-fold cross-validation, 323–324
  leave-one-out, 323
  methods, criteria of, 283

classification *(continued)*
  multimedia databases, 416
  nearest-neighbor classifiers, 314–315
  normalization before, 283
  OLE DB for Data Mining, 486–487
  precision, 325–326
  predictive accuracy of, 283
  preprocessing data, 282–283
  random subsampling, 323
  relevance analysis, 282
  robustness of, 283
  rough set theory, 316–317
  scalability of, 283, 325
  second guess heuristics, 326
  sensitivity, 325–326
  spatial databases, 411–412
  specificity, 325–326
  speed of, 283
  stratified cross-validation, 323–324
  supervised learning, 280–281
  test sets, 323
  text databases, 434–435
  training samples, 280
  tree pruning, 289–290
  trees, *377*, 377–378
  *vs.* prediction, 281
  World Wide Web mining, 439–440
classifications of data mining, 28–30
CLASSIT, 379
class labels
  attribute classification, 280
  backpropagation, 305
  predicting with Bayesian classification, 299
class membership probabilities, predictors for, 296
cleaning. *See* data cleaning
Clementine, 461, 464, *467*
clickstreams, analyzing, 474–475
clients, 66–67
climbing generalization trees, 184
CLIQUE (CLustering In QUEst), 374–376
cluster analysis, 25, *26*, 335–389
  agglomerative approach, 347
  AGNES (AGglomerative ANAlysis), 355–356

applications of, 336, 388
arbitrary shapes, 358–361, 363, 369
ARCS, 256–257
attribute types, 337
AutoClass, 379
binary variables, 341–343
BIRCH, 357–358
bottom-up approach, 347
cell-based algorithm, 385
center-defined clusters, 368–369
centroid distance, 127–128
CF trees, 357–358
Chameleon, 361–363
CLARANS, 353–354
classification trees, *377*, 377–378
CLASSIT, 379
CLIQUE (CLustering In QUEst), 374–376
clusters defined, 335
COBWEB, 377–379
competitive learning, 379–380
conceptual clustering, 336, 376–379
constraint-based, 337
contingency tables, 341
CURE, 358–361, *360*
databases with mixed-type variables, 345–346
data cleaning, 111
data matrices, 338
data types, 338–346
DBMiner, 496–497, *498*
DBSCAN, 363–365
defined, 335–338
DENCLUE, 366–369
density attractors, 367–368
density-based methods, 347–348, 363–369, 374–376
density functions, 368
deviation-based outlier detection, 386–388
diameter, 127
DIANA (DIvisive ANAlysis), 355–356
differences, 338–339
dimensionality, 337
discretization techniques, 134
dissimilarity, 338–346
distance-based association rules, 257–259

distance-based outlier detection, 384–385
distance measures, 340, 342–343, 356, 365–366
divisive approach, 347
EM (Expected Maximization) algorithm, 351
Euclidean distance, 340–341
financial data, 454
grid-based methods, 348, 370–376
hierarchical methods. *See* hierarchical methods of cluster analysis
indexed-based algorithm, 384–385
influence functions, 366–367
input order, sensitivity to, 337
input parameters, 337
interpretability, 338
interval-scaled variables, 339–340
invariant similarity, 342
isothetic boundaries, 372
iterative relocation techniques, 346–347
Jaccard coefficient, 342
k-means algorithm, 347, 349–351
k-medoids algorithm, 347
k-medoids method, 351–354
Manhattan distance, 340–341
matrices, 338–339
mean absolute deviation, 339–340
measurement units, 339
methods, classification of, 346–348
Minkowski distance, 341
model-based methods, 348, 376–381
multidimensional index trees, 128–129
multiresolution algorithms, 370–376
neighborhoods, 362–363
nested-loop algorithm, 385
neural network approach, 379–381
noisy data, 337
nominal variables, 343–344
noninvariant similarity, 342

numerosity reduction, 127–129
object-by-object structure, 338–339
object-by-variable structure, 338
OLAP outlier detection, 387–388
OLE DB for Data Mining, 490
OPTICS, 365–66, *367*
ordering clusters, 365
ordinal variables, 344–345
outlier detection, 381–388
outliers, 359
PAM (Partitioning Around Medoids), 352–353
parameter setting problem, 365
partitioning methods, 346–354, 388
ratio-scaled variables, 345
relative closeness, 362–363
relative interconnectivity, 362
ROCK, 360–361
scalability, 337
sequential exception technique, 386–387
shapes, arbitrary, 337
silhouette coefficients, 354
simple matching, 343–344
simple matching coefficient, 342
SOMs (self-organized feature maps), 380–381
spatial databases, 411
standardized measurement, 340
standardizing data, 339–340
statistical approach to, 376–379
statistical-based outlier detection, 382–384
STING (STatistical Information Grid), 370–372
symmetry variables, 341–343
top-down approach, 347
unsupervised learning, 336
usability, 338
variables, 338, 341–346
WaveCluster, 372–374
wavelet transforms, 372–374
weighed Euclidean distance, 341
z-scores, 340
clustering. *See* cluster analysis
clustering feature (CF) trees, 357–358
clusters. *See also* cluster analysis
arbitrary-shaped, 369
center-defined, 368–369

defined, 258, 335, 388
ordering, 365
cluster samples, 130
COBWEB, 377–379
color histogram-based signatures, 413
combined design approach, 64
comparison. *See* class comparisons; discrimination
competitive learning, 379–380
completeness of data mining algorithms, 28
complex structured data, 396
future trends in mining, 480
generalization of, 396–397
multimedia data, 412–418
object databases, 399–401
plan databases, 401–404
spatial databases, 405–412
text data, 428–435
time-series data, 418–427
Web data, 435–442
complex types of data, mining, 395
composite join indexes, 80–81
**compute cube**, 71–73
concept description, 179–224
analytical characterization, 198–200
attribute-oriented induction, 180–194
attribute relevance analysis, 194–200
characterization, 179–180
class comparisons, 200–208
comparisons, 179–180
data generalization, 180–194
defined, 179–180
descriptive statistical measures, 208–217
incremental data mining, 220
information gain, 196–198
*vs.* machine learning, 218–220
*vs.* OLAP, 180–181
concept hierarchies, 8
3–4–5 rule, 135–138
background knowledge, 150–154
binning, 133
cluster analysis, 134
DBMiner, 494–495
with decision tree induction, 295

DMQL syntax for specifying, 165–166
drilling down, 152
entropy-based discretization, 134–135
generalizing data, 62
generation by discretization techniques, 130–138
generation from categorical data, 138–140
histograms, 133–134
keyword derivation, 414–415
multidimensional view, *403*
multilevel association rules, 245–246
OLAP, 58–61
operation-derived hierarchies, 154
rolling up, 152
rule-based hierarchies, 154
schema hierarchies, 153, 165
segmentation by natural partitioning, 135–138
set-grouping hierarchies, 153–154, 165–166
specializing data, 62
starnet query model, 56–58, 61–62
visualization of discovered patterns, 157–159
**where** clause, 183
concept tree ascension, 184
conceptual clustering, 336, 376–379
conditional databases, 239
conditional pattern bases, 240–241
conditions, AOI, 193–194
confidence, 156
association rules, 227–228, 236
deceiving, 260
in interestingness, 155
connectionist learning. *See* neural networks
constraint-based clustering, 337
constraint-based mining, 262–269
antimonotone rule constraints, 267
convertible rule constraints, 268–269
data constraints, 262
dimension/level constraints, 262
DMQL for, 265

constraint-based mining *(continued)*
  inconvertible rule constraints, 268–269
  interestingness constraints, 263
  knowledge type constraints, 262
  metarules, 263–266
  monotone rule constraints, 267–268
  rule constraints, 263–269
  succinct rule constraints, 268
  time-series databases, 426
  **where**, 266
consumers, data mining, 485
contingency tables, 261
convertible rule constraints, 268–269
correlation analysis, 113, 260–262
correlation rules, 262
cosine measure, 431
cost complexity pruning algorithm, 290
count. *See also* frequency
  for average, 209
  data cubes, 54
  d-weight, 204–208
  of itemsets, 228
  t-weight, 193
count, 54
  attribute-oriented induction, 188
  in central tendency measures, 209
  identical tuples, 186
  incremental updates, 220
  as measure, 54, 187
coupling of DM, DB, and DW architectures, 172–174
CPTs (conditional probability tables), 300–301
credit policy analysis, 454
CRISP-DM (CRoss-Industry Standard Process for Data Mining), 170
CRM (customer relationship management), 474–475
cross-level association rules, 250
cross-tabulations
  including both characterization and comparison, 206–208
  visualization with, 190, *191*, 193
**cube by**, 90

cubes. *See* data cubes
cuboids, 47. *See also* data cubes
  efficient processing of queries, 81–83
  full materialization, 74–79
  lattice of, *72*
  number per data cube, 73
  partial materialization, 73–74
  pre-computing, 72–73
CU (category utility), 377–378
CURE (Clustering Using REpresentatives), 358–361, *360*
customer relations, analysis of, 456
customer relationship management (CRM), 474–475
cyclic indexes, 421


data
  complex structured. *See* complex structured data
  image. *See* multimedia databases
  spatial, 397–398
  training. *See* training data
database queries. *See* queries
databases. *See also* data warehouses
  advanced, 16–20
  history of, 1–5
  multidimensional view, *403*
  multimedia, 412–418
  object. *See* object databases
  plan, 401–404
  raster, 412
  relational. *See* relational databases
  spatial, 405–412
  technology, evolution of, 1–2, *2*
  text, 428–435
  time-series, 418–427
  Web data, 435–442
data characterization, 21
data cleaning, 7, 106, 109–112
  binning, 110
  classification, 282
  clustering, 111
  combined computer and human inspection, 111
  inconsistent data, 112
  regression, 111–112
  tools, 84–85

data clusters, 25, *26*
data compression, 116, 121–124
  DWT (discrete wavelet transform), 121–123
  log-linear models, 125
  lossless *vs.* lossy, 121
  principal components analysis, 123–124
  theory, 470
data constraints, 262
data cube aggregation, 116–118
data cubes, 45–47, *46-47*
  abridged n-D cube searches, 264
  AOI implementation, 189–190
  apex cuboids, 47
  base cuboids, 47
  chunks, 75–79
  class comparisons, 201–202
  computation of, 71–79
  **compute cube** operator, 71–73
  **cube by** operator, 90
  cuboids. *See* cuboids
  DBMiner, input for, 494
  decision tree induction, 295
  defining with DMQL, 52–53
  dimensions. *See* dimensions
  dimension tables, 45, 48–50
  discovery-driven exploration of, 85–89
  exceptions, 86–89
  facts, 45
  generalization algorithms, 220
  generation with DMQL, 55
  **group by** operator, 72
  iceberg cubes, 79
  lattice of cuboids, 47, *48*
  measures, 54–56
  multidimensional, 12–13, *14*
  multifeature, 89–92
  multimedia, 414–416
  multiway array aggregation, 74–79
  object cubes, 400–401
  with OLAM, 96–99
  OLAP operations, 58–61, *59*
  outlier detection, 387–388
  sparse, compressing, 75
  spatial, 405–410
  task-relevant data, 148–50
data discrimination, 21–22
data extraction tools, 84
data formats, 459

data generalization. *See* attribute generalization; generalization

data integration, 7, 106–107, 112–114
 correlation analysis, 113
 detection and resolution of data value conflicts, 113

data marts, 15, 51, 67

data mining
 architecture, *8*
 choosing a system, 458–460
 commercial systems, 461–462
 components, major, 7–8
 consumers, 485
 coupling to data warehouses, 459–460
 data, functions and methodologies, 459
 defined, 5–9, 33
 engines, 8
 false, 9
 functionalities, 21–26
 functions, 146
 importance of, 1–4
 operating systems, 458–459
 primitives. *See* primitives
 providers, software, 485
 scalability, 460
 tasks. *See* tasks, defining with primitives
 tools, need for, 4
 visualization tools, 460

Data Mining Model (DMM), 485

data preprocessing, 105–108. *See also* data cleaning; data integration; data reduction; data transformations
 DBMiner, 499
 multimedia databases, 416

data queries, 471. *See also* queries

data reduction, 107, 116–130
 cluster analysis, 127–129
 data compression, 116, 121–124
 data cube aggregation, 116–118
 decision tree induction, 120–121
 dimension reduction, 116, 119–121
 DWT (discrete wavelet transform), 121–123
 histograms, 125–127
 numerosity reduction, 117, 124–130

principal components analysis, 123–124
 sampling, 129–130, *131*
 theory, 470

data selection, 7

data smoothing, 114
 log-linear models, 125
 techniques, 110–112

data source view, 63

data transformation, 7, 107, 114–116
 aggregation. *See* aggregation
 attribute construction, 114, 116
 before classification, 283
 generalization. *See* generalization
 normalization, 114–116
 smoothing, 110–112, 114, 125
 tools, 85

data warehouses, 3, 39–93
 advantages of, 63
 analytical processing, 94
 architecture, 12, *13*, 62–71
 back-end tools, 84–85
 business query view, 63
 cells, 12
 clients, 66–67
 compared to relational databases, 42–43
 as component of data mining, 7
 concept hierarchies, 56–61
 construction of, 39, 41
 coupling to data mining systems, 459–460
 data cubes. *See* data cubes
 data marts, 15, 51, 67
 data source view, 63
 data warehouse view, 63
 decision support technologies, 41
 decision tree induction, integrating with, 294–296
 defined, 12, 34, 39–42, 98
 design steps, 63–65
 development tools, 65
 dimensions, 12–13
 DMQL (data mining query language), 52–53
 enterprise warehouse model, 67
 evolution of data, 93
 fact constellations, 51
 financial data, 453–454

gateways, 65
 goals of implementations, 65
 historical perspective, 12
 incremental updates, 79
 indexing of data, 79–81
 information processing, 94
 integration of, 40
 measures, 54–56
 metadata, 83–84
 multidimensional data cubes, 12–13, *14*. *See also* data cubes
 multidimensional data model, 44–62
 multifeature cubes, 89–92
 multitier, 68–69
 non-volatility, 40
 OLAM, 95–99, 493–499
 OLAP. *See* OLAP (on-line analytic processing)
 OLAP *vs.* OLTP, 42–43
 organization around major subjects, 12
 reasons to separate from operational database, 44
 recommended development method, 68–69
 retail industry, 455–456
 schema for multidimensional databases, 48–53
 scope management, 65
 servers, 7, 66–67, 69–71
 snowflake schema, 49–50
 spatial, 405–410
 starnet model queries, 62–63
 star schema, 48–49
 subject-oriented nature of, 40
 summarization, 12, 47
 telecommunications industry, 456–457
 three-tier architecture, 65–69, *66*
 time-variance, 40
 tools for, 93
 top-down view, 63
 update-driven approach to integration, 41–42
 uses for information from, 41
 virtual warehouse model, 67–68
 *vs.* data mining, 93–95

data warehouse view, 63

DB (distance-based) outliers, 384–385

DBMiner, 461–462, 493–499
architecture, 494
association rule mining, 496,
*497*
classification, 496, *497*
cluster analysis, 496–497, *498*
concept hierarchies, 494–495
data cubes for input, 494
drilling, 495
GUI, *495*, 498–499
hardware requirements, 499
OLAP analyzer, 495–496
prediction, 498
preprocessing, 499
presentation, 494–495
queries, 498–499
time-series analysis, 498
Web site, 499
DBMS (database management
system), 10
DBSCAN (Density-Based Spatial
Clustering of Applications
with Noise), 363–365
decision tree induction, 120–121,
284–296
algorithms for, 285–286, 293
AOI, 295
attribute construction, 292
attribute selection measures, 286
classification thresholds, 295
class labels, 285–286
with concept hierarchies, 295
cost complexity pruning
algorithm, 290
data cubes, 295
DMQL, 295–296
enhancements, 291
entropy, 287
exception thresholds, 295
extracting classification rules,
290–291
fragmentation problems, 292
gain, 287–288
generalization, 295
ID3, 285
IF-THEN rules, 290–291
incremental versions, 292
information gain, 285–286, 291
integrating data warehousing
techniques, 294–296
MDL (Minimum Description
Length), 290

missing attribute values, 292
multimedia databases, 416
overfitting of data, 289–290
partitions, 286
postpruning approach, 290
prepruning approach, 290
pruning, 289–290
queries, 295–296
RainForest, 294
repetition problems, 292
replication problems, 292
scalability, 292–294
SLIQ, 293
SPRINT, 293–294
test attributes, 285–286
training samples, 292–293
decision trees, 24, *284*, 284–296.
*See also* regression trees
DBMiner, *497*
internal nodes, 284, *284*
leaf nodes, 284, *284*, 285
OLE DB for Data Mining, 487
root nodes, 284, *284*
**define cube**, 52–53
**define dimension**, 52–53
definition of data mining, 5–9
DENCLUE (DENsity-based
CLUstEring), 366–369
density-based methods of cluster
analysis, 363–369
dependent aggregates, 90
descriptive data mining, 179. *See
also* concept description
descriptive tasks, 21
deseasonalized data, 420–421
detection and resolution of data
value conflicts, 113
deviations. *See* outliers; standard
deviations
DFT (Discrete Fourier Transform),
121, 421–422
DIANA (DIvisive ANAlysis),
355–356
dicing
dice operation, 60
task-relevant data, 148–150
digital raster data, 412
dimensional association rules, 229
dimension/level constraints, 262
dimension reduction, 116, 119–121
dimension relevance analysis. *See*
attribute relevance analysis

dimensions
choosing during design process,
65
data cubes, 45–47
defining with DMQL, 52–53
group-by's, 71–72
highly relevant, 195–196
multimedia databases, 415
rules based on, 229
spatial databases, 406
star schema, 48–49
dimension tables, 45, 48–50
directed acyclic graphs, 300–301
direct query answering, 471
discernibility matrix, 317
disciplines contributing to data
mining, 28–29
discovery-driven exploration of
data cubes, 85–89, 387–388
discrete Fourier transform (DFT),
121, 421–422
discrete wavelet transform (DWT),
121–23, 421
discretization techniques, 130–
138
3-4-5 rule, 135–138
binning, 133
cluster analysis, 134
entropy-based discretization,
134–135
histograms, 133–134
OLE DB for Data Mining,
486–489
discriminant analysis, 469
discriminating weights. *See*
reliability
discrimination, 22, 163
dispersion, 210–213
**display**, 167
displaying results. *See* presentation;
visualization
dissimilarity, 342
binary variables, 342
databases with mixed-type
variables, 345–346
nominal variables, 343–344
ordinal variables, 345
ratio-scaled variables, 345
dissimilarity matrices, 338–339,
341
distance-based association rules,
253, 257–259

distance-based outlier detection, 384–385
distance measures, 340, 342–343
  association rules, 253, 257–259
  cluster analysis, 356
  core-distance, 365–366
  Manhattan, 340–341
  outlier detection, 384–385
  reachability-distance, 365–366
  similarity, 421
distributed algorithms, 32
distributive measures, 54
divide-and-conquer strategies, 401–404
divisive hierarchical clustering, 355
DMM (Data Mining Model), 485
DMQL (Data Mining Query Language), 159–170
  **and**, 162, 168
  **from**, 160, 162, 168
  **with**, 166, 168
  **add**, 167
  **all**, 165–166
  **analyze**, 162–163, 168
  characterization, 162–163, 168
  for concept hierarchy specification, 165–166
  data cube generation with, 55
  decision tree induction, 295–296
  defining multidimensional data models, 52–53
  **display**, 167–168
  **drill down on**, 167
  **drop**, 167
  **group by**, 162
  GUIs for, 170–171
  **having**, 162
  interestingness measures, 166
  keywords of, *161*
  kind of knowledge syntax, 162–165
  **matching**, 163–164
  **mine associations as**, 163–164
  **mine characteristics as**, 162–163, 168
  **mine classification as**, 163–164
  **mine comparison as**, 163, 202
  Mine_Knowledge_Specification statement, 162–164
  **order by**, 162
  presentation and visualization, 167

query example, 167–168
  **in relevance to**, 162, 167–168, 183, 189
  **roll up on**, 167
  rule constraints with, 265
  task-relevant data syntax, 160–162
  **threshold**, 166, 168
  top level syntax of, *161*
  **use database**, 160, 162, 168
  **use data warehouse**, 160
  **use hierarchy**, 165–166, 168
  **where**, 160, 162, 168, 183, 266
DNA data analysis, 451–453
document databases. *See* text databases
domain transformations, 421–422
drill-across operation, 61
drilling, DBMiner, 495
drilling down, 15, 152
  DMQL, 167
  drill-down operation, 60
  exceptions, 87–88
drill-through operation, 61
drill up, 15
dropping conditions. *See* attribute removal
d-weight class comparisons, 204–208
DWT (discrete wavelet transform), 121–123, 421
dynamic discretization of quantitative attributes, 252–257
dynamic itemset counting, 238–239

e-commerce, 455, 474–475. *See also* World Wide Web data mining
efficiency of algorithms, 32
emerging patterns (EPs), 313
EM (Expected Maximization) algorithm, 351
encapsulation, 17
Enterprise Miner, 461, 464, *465*
enterprise warehouse model, 67
entity-relationship (ER) data model, 10, 48
entropy-based discretization, 134–135

EPs (emerging patterns), 313
equidepth binning, 255
equidepth histograms, 126
equiwidth binning, 255
equiwidth histograms, 126
ER (entity relationship) data model, 10, 48
Euclidean distance, 340–341
evolution analysis, 26
exception indicators, 85–89
exceptions, 86–89
exemplars, 379–381
Expected Maximization (EM) algorithm, 351
expected patterns, 28
exploration of data, 85–89

fact constellations, 51–53
factor analysis, 469
factoring the version spaces, 219
fact tables, 45, 48
  base, 55, 70
  choosing during design process, 65
  fact constellations, 51–53
  summary, 70
fair information practice principles, 477–478
Fast Fourier Transform (FFT), 427
feature construction. *See* attribute construction
feature descriptors, 414
feature reduction, rough set theory, 316–317
feature selection. *See* relevance analysis
feature vectors, 413–414
FFT (Fast Fourier Transform), 427
filter approach, 121
financial data analysis, 453–454
five-number summaries, 211
focusing searches, 8–9
footprints, 62–63
Fourier transform, 421–422, 427. *See also* DFT; FFT
FP (frequent-pattern)
  algorithm, 242
  growth, 239–243
  trees, 239, *240*, *241*
fraud detection, 381
freehand method, 420

frequency. *See also* count
domain, 421–422
histograms. *See* histograms
itemsets, 228
matrices, 430–432
frequent itemsets, 228, 230
Apriori algorithm, 230–235
generating association rules
from, 236
level-cross filtering by k-itemset
searches, 248–249
local, 237–238
mining without candidate
generation, 239–243
multilevel association rules, 246
partitioning technique, 237–238
frequent-pattern (FP)
algorithm, 242
growth, 239–243
trees, 239, *240*, *241*
frequent predicate sets, 253–257
future trends in data mining,
473–475, 479–480
fuzzy logic, 317–319

galaxy schema, 51
gateways, 66
Gaussian distribution, 298
generalization, 114, 180–194. *See
also* attribute generalization
by AOI, example, 181–187
attributes, 184–185
class-based, 399–400
before classification, 283
cube-based, 220
decision tree induction, 295
factoring the version spaces, 219
generalized relation threshold
control, 185
of list-valued data, 396
machine learning, 218–219
multimedia data, 398
object databases, 399–401
of object identifiers, 399
operators, 184
plan databases (planbases),
401–404
removal of attributes, 184–185
of set-valued data, 396
of spatial data, 397–398
of structured data, 396–397

generalized linear models, 322,
468
generalized relations, 190–194
genetic algorithms, 316
geographic databases. *See* spatial
databases
GeoMiner, 499
Google, 439
gradient descent
backpropagation, 308
Bayesian belief networks,
301–302
greedy methods, 119
grid-based methods of cluster
analysis, 370–376
**group by**, 55, 72, 90
group-by's, 71–72
GUIs (graphical user interfaces), 9,
11, 460
components, 171
DBMiner, *495*, 498–499
for DMQL, 170–171

hash-based techniques, 237
heterogeneous databases, 19–
20. *See also* complex data
structures; data cleaning
integration, 41–42
problem, 32–33
hierarchical histograms, 129
hierarchical methods of cluster
analysis, 347, 354–363, 388
AGNES (AGglomerative
ANAlysis), 355–356
BIRCH, 357–358
Chameleon, 361–363
CURE, 358–361
DIANA (DIvisive ANAlysis),
355–356
ROCK, 360–361
**highlight exceptions** button, 87–88
hill climbing, Bayesian belief
networks, 302
histograms, 125–127, 213–214, *214*
as discretization technique,
133–134
hierarchical histograms, 129
minimum interval size, 133–134
OLE DB for Data Mining,
490–491
history of databases, 1–5

HITS (Hyperlink-Induced Topic
Search), 438
HOLAP (Hybrid OLAP), 69
holdout method, 323
holistic measures, 54
homogeneity-based binning, 255
hubs, Web, 437–438
hybrid-dimension association
rules, 252
Hyperlink-Induced Topic Search
(HITS), 438
hyperlink structures, 437–439
hypothesis-driven exploration, 85

iceberg cubes, 79
iceberg queries, 243–244
ID3, 285
identity identification problem,
112–113
image data. *See* multimedia
databases
image signatures, 413–414
incomplete data, 106
inconsistent data, 106, 112
inconvertible rule constraints,
268–269
incremental data mining, 220
indexed-based algorithm, 384–385
indexes
algorithm, 384–385
of data, 79–81
inverted, 432–433
time-series databases, 424
inductive databases theory, 470
influence functions, 366–367
information gain, 196–198
inheritance, 399
initial data relations, 148
initial working relation, 183, 198
instance-based classification, 315
Intelligent Miner, 461, 464, *467*
intelligent query answering,
471–472
interdimension association rules,
252
interestingness, 27–28, 32, 147–148
certainty, 155
class comparisons, 204–208
confidence, 155
constraints, 263
DMQL syntax for, 166

exact rules, 156
measures as primitives, 147–148, 155–157
mining association rules, 259–260
novelty, 156–157
reliability, 156
rule length, 155
simplicity, 155
strong association rules, 156
support, 156
thresholds, 9, 155
t-weight, 192–194
utility, 156
Internet mining. *See* World Wide Web mining
interpretability of classification, 283
interquartile ranges (IQRs), 210–211
intervals, 425–426
intraclass similarity, 378
invisible data mining, 476
IR (information retrieval), 428–433
itemsets, 228, 230
    Apriori algorithm, 230–235
    correlation of, 261
    frequent. *See* frequent itemsets
    independence of, 261
    level-cross filtering by k-itemset searches, 248–249
    minimal correlated, 262
itemset space, 262

Jaccard coefficient, 342
JEPs (jumping emerging patterns), 314
join indexing method, 80–81
join keys, 55
jumping emerging patterns (JEPs), 314

Karhunen-Loeve method. *See* PCA (principal components analysis)
KDD (Knowledge Discovery in Databases), 5–7, 6. *See also* knowledge discovery
keys, 10, 55

keyword-based association analysis, 433–434
keyword-based classification, Web, 440
k-fold cross-validation, 323–324
kind of knowledge
    association, 163–164
    characterization, 162–163, 168
    classification, 164–165
    discrimination, 163
    primitives, 146, 150–151
    syntax, DMQL, 162–165
*k*-itemset, 248–249
*k*-means algorithm, 349–351
*k*-medoids algorithm, 353
*k*-medoids method, 351–354
*k*-nearest neighbor graphs, 362
knowledge, patterns representing, 27, 34
knowledge bases, 8
knowledge discovery, 5–7, 6, 33
knowledge presentation, 7
knowledge queries, 471
knowledge type constraints, 262
*k*-predicate sets, 253

languages, data mining, 169–170. *See also* DMQL (data mining query language)
LAPACK, 432
latent semantic indexing, 431–432
lattice of cuboids, 47, 48, 72
lattices of attributes, 57
learning-from-examples paradigm, 218
learning (machine)
    backpropagation, 303–311
    Bayesian belief networks, 299–302
    cluster analysis, 336
    decision tree induction, 284–296
    eager learning methods, 315
    lazy learners, 315
    nearest-neighbor classifiers, 314–315
    by observation, 336
    training sets. *See* training data
    *vs.* concept description, 218–220
least squares method, 319–320, 420
legacy databases, 19–20

levels of abstraction, 31
    multilevel association rules, 244–251
    viewed with OLAP, 58–61
level-wise searches, 230
linear models, 468
linear regression, 125, 319–322
list-valued attributes, 397
loading tools, 85
loan payment prediction, 454
local frequent itemsets, 237–238
loess curves, 216–17, *217*
log-linear models, 125, 322
loose coupling, 172–173
lossless data compression, 121

machine learning. *See* learning (machine)
management tools, 85
Manhattan distance, 340–341
market basket analysis, 16, 225–227, *226*
matching coefficient, 342
materialization of cuboids, 73–74
MATLAB, 432
max(), 54, 210
MaxDiff histograms, 127
max_N(), 54
maxpatterns, 230
MBR (minimum bounding rectangle), 409–410
MDAC (Microsoft Data Access Components), 486
MDL (Minimum Description Length), 290
means, 209, 349–351
measures, 54–56
    choosing during design process, 65
    distance. *See* distance measures
median(), 54–55
medians, 209–210
medoids, 351–354
metadata, 83–84
    identity identification problem, 112–113
    repositories, 83–84
metapatterns, 150, 163–164
metaqueries. *See* metapatterns
metarules. *See* metapatterns

method of least squares, 319–320, 420
methodology issues, 31–32
methods (of classes), 396, 399
microeconomic view, 470
Microsoft Data Access Components (MDAC), 486
Microsoft OLE DB for Data Mining. *See* OLE DB for Data Mining
Microsoft SQL Server 7.0 OLAP Services, 69
midranges, 210
min(), 54, 210
minable views, 148
MINE RULE operator, 169
MineSet, 461, 464, *465-66*
minimum bounding rectangle (MBR), 409–410
Minimum Description Length (MDL), 290
mining association rules. *See* association rule mining
mining path traversal patterns, 20
min-max normalization, 115
min_N(), 54
mixed-effect models, 469
mode(), 54
model-based methods of cluster analysis, 376–381
models, 24
modes, 210
MOLAP (Multidimensional OLAP), 69–70
    chunks, 75–79
    data cubes construction, 75–79
    direct array addressing, 75
    efficient processing of queries, 81–83
    multiway array aggregation, 75–79
monotone rule constraints, 267–268
moving averages, 419–420
MSQL, 169
multidimensional analysis. *See also* multidimensional data model
    retail industry, 455–456
    telecommunications industry, 456–457

multidimensional association rules, 23, 251–259
    ARCS, 255–257
    defined, 252
    distance-based association rules, 253
    dynamic discretization of quantitative attributes, 252–257
    hybrid-dimension association rules, 252
    interdimension association rules, 252
    predicate sets, 253
    quantitative association rules, 253–257
    quantitative attributes, 252–254
    static discretization of quantitative attributes, 252–254
multidimensional data model, 44–62
    data cubes, 45–47
    defined, 98
    fact constellations, 51
    OLAP operations, 58–61, *59*
    schema for, 48–53
    snowflake schema, 49–50
    starnet model queries, 62–63
    star schema, 48–49
multidimensional histograms, 127
multidimensional index trees, 128–129
Multidimensional OLAP. *See* MOLAP (Multidimensional OLAP)
multifeature composed signatures, 413
multifeature cube graphs, 91, *91*
multifeature data cubes, 89–92, 455
multilayered Web information base construction, 440–441
multilayer feed forward neural networks, 303–304
multilevel association rules, 244–251
    concept hierarchies, 245–246
    controlled level-cross filtering by single item, 249
    cross-level association rules, 250
    frequent itemsets, 246

level-by-level independent searches, 248–249
    level-cross filtering by k-itemset searches, 248–249
    level-cross filtering by single item searches, 248–249
    reduced support method, 247–248
    redundancies, 250–251
    uniform support method, 247
multimedia databases, 19, 398, 412–418
    association rule mining, 417–418
    classification, 416
    data cubes, 414–416
    data preprocessing, 416
    decision tree induction, 416
    descriptors, 414
    dimensions, 415
    feature vectors, 413–414
    image signatures, 413–414
    keyword derivation, 414–415
    MultiMediaMiner, 414–416
    multiresolution strategy, 417
    progressive resolution refinement approach, 417
    queries, 413
    region-based granularity, 414
    retrieval systems, 412–413
    similarity searching, 412–414
    spatial relationships, 418
MultiMediaMiner, 414–416, 499
multiple regression, 125
multiresolution clustering algorithms, 370–376
multitier data warehouses, 68–69
multiway array aggregation, 74–79

naive Bayesian classifier, 296–299
nearest-neighbor classifiers, 314–315
nested-loop algorithm, 385
neural networks, 24
    backpropagation, 303–311
    cluster analysis with, 379–381
    competitive learning, 379–380
    defined, 303
    exemplars, 379–381
    hidden layers, 303–305, *304*

input layers, 303, *304*
multilayer feed forward, 303–304
network pruning, 311
neurodes, 303
output layers, 303, *304*
SOMs (self-organized feature maps), 380–381
topology design, 304–305
weights, 303, 305, 307–308
no coupling, 172–173
noise, 389. *See also* outlier detection
noisy data, 31, 106, 110–112
thresholds, 156
nominal variables, 343–344
normalization, 114–116
for backpropagation, 304
before classification, 283
by decimal scaling, 115–116
of dimension tables, 49–50
numerosity reduction, 117, 124–130
cluster analysis, 127–129
histograms, 125–127
linear regression, 125
nonparametric methods, 125
parametric methods, 124
sampling, 129–130

object cubes, 400–401
object databases, 17
aggregation, 397–398
attribute-oriented induction method, 400–401
attributes, 396
classes, 396–404
generalization of class hierarchies, 399–404
generalization of data, 396–397
list-valued attributes, 397
methods, 17, 396
multimedia data, 397–398
object cubes, 400–401
objects, 396
plan databases, 401–404
set-valued attributes, 396
object-relational databases, 17, 396. *See also* object databases
objects, 396
object variables, 151

occurrence frequency of an itemset, 228
ODBC, 459
OLAM (on-line analytical mining), 95–99
architecture of, 96–99, *97*
DBMiner, 493–499
OLAP based, 96–99
OLAP (on-line analytical processing), 3, 42–43
bitmap indexing method, 79–80
concept hierarchies, 58–61
coupling to data mining systems, 460
data mining with, 94–99
data warehouses, 15
DBMiner, 493–499
dice operation, 60
drill-across operation, 61
drill down, 15, 60
drill-through operation, 61
drill up, 15
indexing of data, 79–81
join indexing method, 80–81
multidimensional data model, 44–62
OLAM with, 95–99
operations on data, 58–61, *59*
outlier detection, 387–388
pivot operation, 60
query processing, 81–83
roll-up operation, 60
rotate operation, 60
servers, 67, 69–71
slice operation, 60
spatial databases, 406–410
*vs.* concept description, 180–181
*vs.* OLTP, 42–43
OLE DB for Data Mining, 169–170, 485–491
**APPEND** statement, 488
association mining, 487–488
attribute types, 487
case sets, 486
classification model, 486–487
cluster analysis, 490
**CONTINUOUS** statement, 487
**CREATE** statement, 485–486
discretization, 486–489
**DISCRETIZED()** statement, 487
**DISTINCT** statement, 490
distribution models, 487

DMM (Data Mining Model), 485–486
histograms, 490–491
**INSERT INTO** statement, 488
**INSERT** statement, 485–486
**KEY** statement, 486–487
nested tables, 486
**NORMAL** statement, 487
PMML, 491
**PREDICTION JOIN** statement, 489
**PredictProbability()**, 490
**PREDICT** statement, 487
queries, 489–491
**RELATED TO** statement, 487
running the model, 488–491
**SELECT** statement, 486, 489–490
**SHAPE** statement, 488
**SKIP** statement, 488
**ON** statement, 489
statistics, 490–491
support, 490
**TABLE** statement, 487
training data, 488
**USING** statement, 487
OLTP (on-line transaction processing), 3, 42–43
one-dimensional operations, 72
on-line aggregation, 92–93
on-line analytical mining. *See* OLAM (on-line analytical mining)
on-line analytical processing. *See* OLAP (on-line analytical processing)
on-line transaction processing (OLTP), 3, 42–43
operating systems, 458–459
operational metadata, 84
operation-derived hierarchies, 154
OPTICS (Ordering Points To Identify the Clustering Structure), 365–366, *367*
opt-out policies, 478
ordinal variables, 344–345
outlier detection, 25, 381–388
alternative distributions, 383
cardinality function, 387
cell-based algorithm, 385
defining outliers, 381–382
deviation-based, 386–388
discordancy tests, 382
dissimilarity function, 386

outlier detection *(continued)*
  distance-based, 384–385
  exception sets, 386
  indexed-based algorithm,
    384–385
  nested-loop algorithm, 385
  OLAP data cube technique,
    387–388
  procedures for, 383
  sequential exception technique,
    386–387
  smoothing factor, 387
  statistical-based, 382–384
outliers, 211
overfitting of data, 281, 289–290

PAM (Partitioning around
    Medoids), 352–353
parallel data mining, 220
parallel episodes, 426
parameter setting problem, 365
partitioning arrays, 75–76
partitioning methods of cluster
    analysis, 348–354, 388
  CLARANS, 353–354
  EM (Expected Maximization)
    algorithm, 351
  k-means algorithm, 349–351
  k-medoids method, 351–354
  squared-error criterion, 349
path analysis, DNA sequencing,
    453
pattern analysis in telecom-
    munications industry,
    457
pattern discovery theory, 470
pattern interestingness. *See*
    interestingness
patterns
  evaluation, 7–9
  FP (frequent-pattern) trees, 239,
    *240, 241*
  maxpatterns, 230
  representing knowledge, 27, 34
  superpatterns, 230
PCA (principal components
    analysis), 123–124
percentiles, 210
performance issues, 32
periodicity analysis, 426–427
pivot operation, 60

plan databases (planbases),
    401–404
PMML (Predictive Model Markup
    Language), 491
polysemy problem, 430
posterior probability, 296–298
precision, 325–326
predicate sets, 253–257
predicate variables, 151, 263
prediction, 24, 279, 319–322
  DBMiner, 498
  generalized linear models, 322
  linear regression, 319–320
  log-linear models, 322
  multiple regression, 320
  nonlinear regression, 321–322
  regression, 319–322
  *vs.* classification, 281
predictive accuracy of
    classification, 283
predictive tasks, 21
preprocessing. *See* data
    preprocessing
presentation. *See also* visualization
  AOI (attribute-oriented
    induction), 190–194
  class comparisons, 201, 204–208
  DBMiner, 494–495
  of discovered patterns, 157–159
  DMQL syntax for, 166
  primitives, 148
  of results, 31
primitives, 145–148
  background knowledge,
    146–147, 150–154
  data mining functions, 146
  interestingness, 147–148,
    155–157
  kinds of knowledge, 146,
    150–151
  presentation, 147–148, 157–159
  queries, 145–148
  relevant attributes, 146
  task-relevant data, 146, 148–150
principal components analysis
    (PCA), 123–124
prior probability, 296–299
privacy, 476–478
probabilistic networks. *See*
    Bayesian belief networks
probability theory, 470
**product**, 116

progressive refinement, 410
providers, data mining, 485
PRs (possible rules), 313
pyramid algorithm, 122

q-q plots, 214–215, *216*
quality control, 469
quantile plots, 214–215, *215*
quantitative association rules, 229,
    253–257
quantitative attributes, 252–254
quantitative characteristic rules,
    193
quantitative description rules,
    207–208
quantitative discriminant rules. *See*
    discriminant rules
quantitative rules, 192
quartiles, 210
queries, 11–12
  AOI (attribute-oriented
    induction), 180–194
  background knowledge,
    146–147, 150–154
  characterization, 182–183
  class comparisons, 202–203
  data, 471
  data mining, 146–148
  data mining to relational,
    183–184
  DBMiner, 498–499
  decision tree induction, 295–296
  direct query answering, 471
  efficient processing of, 81–83
  group-by's, 71–72
  GUIs with, 170–171
  iceberg, 243–244
  image, 413
  intelligent query answering,
    471–472
  interestingness, 147–148,
    155–157
  keyword-based retrieval,
    429–430
  kinds of knowledge, 146,
    150–151
  knowledge, 471
  metapatterns, 150–151
  multifeature cubes, 89–92
  OLE DB for Data Mining,
    489–491

presentation, 157–159
primitives for, 146–148
product promotion, 472
relevant attributes, 146
similarity searches, 421–424
starnet model, 62–63
strategies for quick answers, 92–93
suggesting additional items, 472
summary information, 472
task-relevant data, 146, 148–150
templates, 150–151
time-sequence query languages, 424
top N queries, 93
query language issue, 31

RainForest, 294
Random sampling, 129–130
random walk algorithms, 262
rank(), 54
raster databases, 412
raster format, 18
ratio-scaled variables, 345
reducts, 317
refresh tools, 85
regression, 319–322
analysis, 468
coefficients, 319
generalized linear models, 322
linear regression, 125, 319–320
logistic regression, 322
log-linear models, 322
method of least squares, 319–320, 420
multiple regression, 320
nonlinear regression, 321–322
Poisson regression, 322
polynomial regression, 321–322
predictor variables, 319–320
response variables, 319–320
SAS, 319
S-Plus, 319
SPSS, 319
trees, 468–469
relational databases, 10–11
compared to data warehouses, 42–43
entity-relationship data model, 48
join indexing method, 80

object-relational databases, 17, 396
query language for, 159
ROLAP (Relational OLAP), 69–70
as warehouse database servers, 66
Relational OLAP (ROLAP), 69–70, 74–75, 79
relevance analysis, 24
classification, 282
rough set theory, 316–317
text databases, 429–430
reliability, 156. *See also* confidence; support
residuals, 88–89
retail industry data mining, 455–456
robustness of classification, 283
ROCK, 360–361
ROLAP (Relational OLAP), 69–70, 74–75, 79
rolling up, 60
concept hierarchies, 152
OLAP for OLAM, 97
spatial databases, 408, *408*
rotate operation, 60
rough set theory, 316–317
rule-based hierarchies, 154
rule constraints, 263–269
rule mining. *See* association rule mining
rule quality. *See* reliability
rule strength. *See* reliability
rule templates. *See* metarules

samples, training. *See* training data
sampling, 129–130, *131*
SAS, 319, 336, 461
scalability, 32, 460
of classification, 283
clustering, 337
decision tree induction, 292–294
k-means algorithm, 349–351
scatter plots, 215–216, *216*
schema hierarchies, 57, 153, 165
schema integration, 112–113
scientific data mining, 464, 468–469
SDBs (statistical databases), 61
search engines, Web, 436

searches, 12. *See also* queries; similarity searches
seasonal indexes, 420
security of private information, 478
segmentation by natural partitioning, 135–138
selecting data mining systems, 458–460
self-organized feature maps (SOMs), 380–381
semantic integration of DNA data, 452
semi-tight coupling, 173
sensitivity, 325–326
sequence databases, 418. *See also* time-series databases
sequence matching, 421
sequence-valued attributes, 397
sequential data mining, product promotion, 472
sequential exception technique, 386–387
sequential pattern analysis, telecommunications industry, 457
sequential pattern mining, 424–426
serial episodes, 426
servers, 66, 69–71
set-grouping hierarchies, 57, 153–154, 165–166
set-valued attributes, 396
shopping services, 472
signature files, 433
similarity, 342, 421
similarity searches
DNA data, 452–453
multimedia databases, 412–414
text databases, 430–431
time-series databases, 421–424
simplicity, 155
single-dimensional association rules, 23
skewed data, measures for, 209–211
slicing, 60, 148–150
SLIQ, 293
smoothing, 114
by bin, 110
of time series, 419
snowflake schema, 49–50, 52–53
social impacts of data mining, 472–478

SOMs (self-organized feature maps), 380–381
spatial association rules, 410–411
spatial databases, 18, 405–412
  association rule mining, 410–411
  classification, 411–412
  cluster analysis, 411
  digital raster data, 412
  dimensions, 406
  heterogeneous data, 406
  merges, 408–409
  multimedia databases, 418
  nonspatial dimensions, 406
  numerical measures, 407
  object aggregation, 397–398
  OLAP, 406–410
  precomputation options, 409
  progressive refinement, 410
  spatial measures, 407
  spatial-to-nonspatial dimensions, 406
  spatial-to-spatial dimensions, 406
  star schema model, 406–408
  superset coverage property, 410
  trend analysis, 411–412
specialization, machine learning, 218
specialized SQL servers, 70
specificity, 325–326
speed of classification, 283
spiral method, 64
S-Plus, 319, 336
spread, 211–213
SPRINT, 293–294
SPSS, 319, 336
SQL Server 7.0 OLAP Services, 69
SQL servers, specialized, 70
squared-error criterion, 349
SRSWOR (simple random sample without replacement), 129
SRSWR (simple random sample with replacement), 129–130
standard deviation, 54, 211–213
standard_deviation(), 54
standardization of data mining language, 479
starnet model queries, 62–63
star schema model, 48–49
  data marts, 51
  defining with DMQL, 52

join indexing method, 80–81
  spatial databases, 406–408
static discretization of quantitative attributes, 252–254
statistical-based outlier detection, 382–384
statistical data mining, 405, 464, 468–469
statistical measures, 208–217, 490–491
  averages, 54, 209–210
  central tendency, 209–210
  dispersion of data, 210–213
  displaying, 213–217
  five-number summaries, 211
  means, 209, 349–351
  medians, 209–210
  midranges, 210
  quartiles, 210–211
  standard deviations, 54, 211–213
  variances, 211–213, 469
StatSoft, 462, *463*
stepwise backward elimination, 120
stepwise forward selection, 119–120
STING (STatistical Information Grid), 370–372
stop lists, 430
stratified cross-validation, 323–324
stratified samples, 130
strong association rules, 156, 236
subfrequent items, 249
subsequence matching, 422, *423*
succinct rule constraints, 268
**such that** operator, 90
suggesting additional items, 472
sum, 54–55
  in central tendency measures, 209
  variance from, 211–213
summarization of data cubes, 47
summary fact tables, 70
summary information, 472
superpatterns, 230
superset coverage property, 410
supervised learning, 280–281
support, 156
  association rules, 227–228
  for interestingness, 156
  of itemsets, 228
  OLE DB for Data Mining, 490

survival analysis, 469
SVD (singular value decomposition), 431–432
symbolic patterns, 425
synchronous generalization, 201–202
synonyms, 430
system performance, metadata for, 84

tables, 10–11, 15–16
task-relevant data, 146, 148–150, 160–162
tasks, defining with primitives, 146–148, *149*
taxonomy formation, 25
telecommunications industry, 456–457
temporal databases, 18, 26
text databases, 19, 428–435
  association analysis, 433–434
  classification, 434–435
  cosine measure, 431
  inverted indexes, 432–433
  IR (information retrieval), 428–433
  keyword-based association analysis, 433–434
  keyword-based retrieval, 429–430
  latent semantic indexing, 431–432
  modeling documents, 430
  phrases, detecting, 433–434
  polysemy problem, 430
  precision, 429
  recall, 429
  relevance, measuring, 429–430
  signature files, 433
  similarity-based retrieval, 430–431
  singular value decomposition, 431–432
  stop lists, 430
  synonyms, 430
  term frequency, 430–432
  term recognition, 433–434
  training sets, 434
  word stems, 430
World Wide Web. *See* World Wide Web mining

theoretical foundations of data mining, 470–471
three-tier architecture, 65–69, *66*
**threshold**, 166
thresholds, 166
  association rules, 227–228
  decision tree induction, 295
  density, 258
  frequency, 258
  reduced support method, 247–248
  uniform support method, 247
TIDs (transaction IDs), 227
tight coupling, 173
time domain to frequency domain transformations, 421–422
time-sequence query languages, 424
time series analysis, 469, 498
time-series databases, 18, 418–427
  Apriori property, 426
  atomic matching, 422
  components of, 419
  constraints, 426
  cyclic movements, 419, 421
  decomposition, 419
  DFT (discrete Fourier transforms), 421–422
  domain transformations, 421–422
  duration, 425
  event folding window, 425
  evolution analysis, 26
  FFT, 427
  freehand method, 420
  indexing methods, 424
  intervals, 425–426
  least squares method, 420
  movements, 419
  moving averages, 419–420
  offsets and amplitudes handling, 422–424
  parallel episodes, 426
  partial periodic patterns, 427
  periodicity analysis, 426–427
  query languages, 424
  random movements, 419
  seasonal movements, 419–421
  sequence matching, 421
  sequential pattern mining, 424–426
  serial episodes, 426

similarity searches, 421–424
subsequence matching, 422, *423*
symbolic patterns, 425
trend analysis, 418–421
window stitching, 422
top-down design approach, 64, 67–68
top-down view, 63
top N queries, 93
training data, 24, 280, 292–293
  backpropagation, 305
  OLE DB for Data Mining, 488
  sets, 280
  text databases, 434
transactional databases, 15–16
transaction IDs (TIDs), 227
Tree-Projection algorithms, 243
tree pruning, 289–290
trend analysis, 411–412, 418–421
tuple-by-tuple strategy, 219
tuples, 10
  classification context, 280
  clustering techniques, 127–129
  identical, 186
  machine learning generalizations, 219
  with missing values, 109–110
t-weights, 192–194
  comparison and characterization, 206–208
  count, 193

unsupervised learning, cluster analysis, 336
upward closed sets, 262
usage mining, Web, 441–442
utility, 156

variables, 341–345
variances, 211–213, 469
vector format, 18
version spaces, 219
virtual warehouse model, 67–68
visual data mining, 462–464, 480
visualization
  AOI (attribute-oriented induction), 190–194
  bar charts, 213–214, *214*
  class comparisons, 201, 204–208
  of discovered patterns, 157–159

DMQL syntax for, 167
DNA sequencing, 453
  interactive, 464
  loess curves, 216–217, *217*
  q-q plots, 214–215, *216*
  quantile plots, 214–215, *215*
  scatter plots, 215–216, *216*
  software tools for, 462–464, *465-68*
  tools, 460
V-Optimal histograms, 126–127

warehouse database servers, 66
warehouse DBMS, 41
waterfall method, 64
WaveCluster, 372–374
wavelet-based signatures, 413–414
wavelets, 372–374. *See also* DWT (discrete wavelet transform)
Web. *See* World Wide Web mining
WeblogMiner, 499
Weblogs, 404, 442, 499
Web stores. *See* e-commerce applications
weighted arithmetic mean, 209
weighted average, 209
weighted moving averages, 419–420
weights, HITS, 438–439
whiskers, 211
word stems, 430
working hypothesis, 382
World Wide Web mining, 20, 435–442
  authoritative pages, 437–439
  base set, 438
  classification, 439–440
  future of, 480
  Google, 439
  HITS (Hyperlink-Induced Topic Search), 438
  hubs, 437–438
  hyperlink structures, 437–439
  integration with data warehouses, 479
  log records, 441–442
  mining path traversal patterns, 20
  multilayered Web information base construction, 440–441
  problems with, 435–436

World Wide Web mining *(continued)*
  root set, 438
  search engines, 436
  usage mining, 441–442
  weights, 438–439
  XML, 441
  Yahoo!, 439–440
wrapper approach, 121

XML, 441

Yahoo!, 439–440

zero-dimensional operations, 72
z-score normalization, 115
z-scores, 340